Millennium 4/2007

Millennium 4/2007

Jahrbuch zu Kultur und Geschichte
des ersten Jahrtausends n. Chr.

Yearbook on the Culture and History
of the First Millennium C.E.

Herausgegeben von / Edited by

Wolfram Brandes (Frankfurt/Main), Alexander Demandt (Lindheim),
Hartmut Leppin (Frankfurt/Main), Helmut Krasser (Gießen)
und Peter von Möllendorff (Gießen)

Walter de Gruyter · Berlin · New York

∞ Gedruckt auf säurefreiem Papier, das die US-ANSI-Norm
über Haltbarkeit erfüllt.

ISBN (Print): 978-3-11-019251-3
ISBN (Online): 978-3-11-019279-7
ISBN (Print + Online): 978-3-11-019280-3

Bibliografische Information der Deutschen Nationalbibliothek

Die Deutsche Nationalbibliothek verzeichnet diese Publikation in der Deutschen
Nationalbibliografie; detaillierte bibliografische Daten sind im Internet über
<http://dnb.d-nb.de> abrufbar.

Printed in Germany

Umschlaggestaltung: Christopher Schneider, Berlin
Datenkonvertierung: Werksatz Schmidt & Schulz GmbH, Gräfenhainichen

Inhalt

Editorial VII

Thema
Constructing Identities in the Roman Empire: Three Studies
Introduction: Stephen Hinds / Thomas Schmitz 1
Introductory Generalities, mostly Roman [Stephen Hinds] 1
"Rotten Greeks?" Tales of Domination and Decadence [Thomas Schmitz] 6

Susan E. Alcock
Making sure you know whom to kill: spatial strategies and strategic
boundaries in the Eastern Roman Empire 13

Joy Connolly
Being Greek/Being Roman: Hellenism and Assimilation in the Roman
Empire 21

Helmut Krasser
Shifting Identities. Knowledge and the Construction of Social Roles
in the Roman Empire 43

Ulrike Egelhaaf-Gaiser
Kolossale Miniaturen: Der Holzfäller Hercules in Statius' „Wäldern"
(*Silve* 3,1) 63

Christian Tornau
Does Love Make Us Beautiful? A criticism of Plotinus in Augustine's
Tractates on the First Epistle of John 93

Dennis Pausch
Der Philosoph auf dem Kaiserthron, der Leser auf dem Holzweg?
Marc Aurel in der *Historia Augusta* 107

Mischa Meier
Σταυρωθεὶς δι' ἡμᾶς – Der Aufstand gegen Anastasios im Jahr 512 157

Simon MacLean
'After his death a great tribulation came to Italy ...' Dynastic Politics
and Aristocratic Factions After the Death of Louis II, c. 870 – c. 890 239

Thomas Pratsch
Mönchsorden in Byzanz? – Zur Entstehung und Entwicklung monastischer
Verbände in Byzanz (8.–10. Jh.) 261

Autoren dieses Bandes 279

Abkürzungsverzeichnis 281

Editorial

Mit den Beiträgen des vorliegenden Bandes bietet das Millennium Jahrbuch 4 (2007) eine Auswahl von Einsichten in Forschungsprobleme von der frühen Kaiserzeit bis ins ausgehende neunte Jahrhundert und beleuchtet damit unter kulturhistorischer Perspektive historische, theologische und künstlerische Entwicklungen des ersten christlichen Jahrtausends. In ihrem jeweiligen Untersuchungsgegenstand durchaus vielfältig, zeichnen sich die hier publizierten Texte dadurch aus, daß sie etablierte Forschungspositionen hinterfragen und bislang nicht hinreichend untersuchte Ereignisse und Gegenstände in den Blick nehmen. Sie gruppieren sich überdies entsprechend gemeinsamen epochalen, thematischen und methodischen Perspektiven.

So bildeten die drei Beiträge von Susan E. Alcock, Joy Connolly und Helmut Krasser das Panel 'Constructing Identities in the Roman Empire' bei der deutsch-amerikanischen Konferenz *Identities*, die im Oktober 2004 in Philadelphia unter der Schirmherrschaft der American Philosophical Association und der Alexander von Humboldt-Stiftung stattfand. In ihrer Einleitung zu dieser Gruppe von thematisch eng miteinander vernetzten Aufsätzen fokussieren Stephen Hinds und Thomas Schmitz die kaiserzeitliche Konstruktion römischer und griechischer Identität in ihrem Blick auf eine – wiederum von hier aus als identitätsstiftender Angelpunkt erst gesetzte – griechische Klassik: Hinds zeigt, wie die durchaus ambivalent empfundene römische Faszination an der alten Vorbildkultur der Griechen in zahlreichen Anekdoten kolportiert und verhandelt wird, während Schmitz die verschiedenen Facetten imperiumsgriechischer Indienstnahme der eigenen Vergangenheit darlegt.

Susan E. Alcock entwirft sodann in *Making sure you know whom to kill: spatial strategies and strategic boundaries in the Eastern Roman Empire* drei Faktoren als ausschlaggebend für den Übergang vom griechischen Genozid an den römischen Einwohnern der provincia Asia im Jahre 88 v. C. zu ihrem friedlichen Miteinander in der nachchristlichen Kaiserzeit: Elitenbildung, die über ethnische Grenzen hinweg soziale Verbindungen schafft, Kontrolle der Masse durch die auch äußerliche Differenzierung einer upper class und die Aufteilung des öffentlichen Raumes zwischen ihr und den mittleren und unteren Schichten, sowie schließlich eine vorsichtige kulturelle Abgrenzung zwischen Griechen und Römern, die im Stillen gewissermaßen eine wunde Stelle der Erinnerung an das Massaker und seine ebenso grausame Bestrafung durch Rom wachhält. Demgegenüber hebt Joy Connolly in *Being Greek/Being Roman: Hellenism and Assimilation in the Roman Empire* stärker das kulturenverbindende Moment der Konzeption einer griechischen Klassik hervor. Deren Literatur, Philosophie und Kunst waren demnach nicht im eigentlichen Sinne an Griechentum gebunden, so daß ihre Idealität ein orientierungsstiftendes Vorbild auch für Römer sein konnte; in diese Richtung operierten ebenfalls das umfassende System der Rhetorik als allgemeine Sprech- und Denkausbildung sowie ein geläufiges philosophisches, insbesondere ethisches Kosmopolitentum, die zusammen die Grundlage kaiserzeitlicher Bildung darstellten. Mit wiederum anderer Akzentuierung differenziert schließlich HELMUT KRASSER in *Shifting Identities. Knowledge and the Construction of Social Roles in the Roman Empire* zwischen drei Stufen bildungszentrierter Identität: der Identität innerhalb der jeweiligen elitären gesellschaftlichen Gruppen, der Identität innerhalb lokal-regionaler Netzwerke sowie zuletzt einer umgreifenden Reichsidentität. Im Zusammenhang mit diesem System einander wechselseitig stützender Identitäten bildet sich, so KRASSER, eine variantenreiche Literatur heraus, deren Anliegen nicht zuletzt die Demonstration jener identitätsstiftenden Bildungskompetenz ist, wodurch sie zu einem Bildungsmedium par excellence wird.

Die Beiträge von ULRIKE EGELHAAF-GAISER und CHRISTIAN TORNAU verbindet der gemeinsame methodische Ansatz einer eingehenden intertextualitätsorientierten Textanalyse. In *Kolossale Miniaturen: Der Holzfäller Hercules in Statius' „Wäldern"*, einer eindringlichen Analyse der Statianischen *Silve* 3,1, demonstriert ULRIKE EGELHAAF-GAISER das hohe metapoetische Potential dieser Okkasionsdichtung. Hier dient die zentrale Figur des Hercules als kallimacheisch gestaltete burleske Epenfigur, deren immense Kraft und Massigkeit die intellektuelle Raffinesse und subtile Form der Dichtung geradezu ins Relief setzen. Zugleich Auftraggeber und Erbauer seines Sorrentiner Tempels, kann Hercules für Patron und Klienten-Poet zugleich stehen und auf diese Weise das hierarchische Gefälle zwischen ihnen spielerisch einebnen. Dabei dient ein ganzes Bündel kaschierter Anspielungen auf aitiologische Hercules-Mythen bei Kallimachos und Vergil der Demonstration des Bildungsprofils des gefeierten Patrons Pollius. CHRISTIAN TORNAU untersucht in *Does Love Make Us Beautiful? A criticism of Plotinus in Augustine's Tractates on the First Epistle of John* die Auseinandersetzung, die Augustinus mit Plotins Darstellung der Rolle des Eros beim Aufstieg der Seele zum Einen führt, und zeigt, wie Augustinus zwar über weite Strecken bei seiner Konzeption der Liebe zu Gott implizit der Plotinischen Vorstellung folgt, ihr aber in der entscheidenden Wendung widerspricht: Der Aufstieg des Eros mündet nicht, wie bei dem Neuplatoniker, in die Rückkehr zur wahren und eigentlich menschlichen Natur, in die Schau des wahren Guten in der menschlichen Seele selbst, sondern gerade in die Abkehr vom Menschen und die Hinwendung zur göttlichen Schönheit Christi. DENNIS PAUSCH interpretiert in *Der Philosoph auf dem Kaiserthron, der Leser auf dem Holzweg? Marc Aurel in der Historia Augusta* drei miteinander verbundene Viten der *Historia Augusta*, die Biographien Marc Aurels, des Lucius Verus und seines Kontrahenten Avidius Cassius, als eine absichtsvoll konzipierte literarische Narration. Widersprüche und Unverständlichkeiten sind daher als fiktionale Strategien zu werten. Insbesondere versteht er die zweifache Erzählung des Lebens Marc Aurels mit ihren ambivalenten und sich wandelnden Wertungen als eine Technik, die den Leser zum Urteil einer

‚unreliable narration' führen soll; dem selben Zweck dient die Einführung der beiden Nebenviten, die es erlauben, einzelne biographische Akzente jeweils leicht zu verändern. Damit ist die *Historia Augusta* als eine subsidiäre Form der Historiographie zu verstehen, die einen historisch bewanderten Leser voraussetzt, wie er um die Wende vom 4. zum 5. Jh. n. Chr. angenommen werden kann.

In der abschließenden Gruppe historischer Untersuchungen legt zunächst MISCHA MEIER mit Σταυρωθεὶς δι' ἡμᾶς – *Der Aufstand gegen Anastasios im Jahr 512* eine eingehende, umfang- und materialreiche Studie des sogenannten Staurotheis-Aufstandes von 512 in Konstantinopel vor, eines in der Forschung bislang eher stiefmütterlich behandelten und kontextuell zu eingeschränkt betrachteten Ereignisses, in dem kirchen- und ‚profan'-politische Entwicklungen aufs engste miteinander verwoben sind und zuspitzend aufeinander eingewirkt haben. Er zeigt, daß der Befehl Kaiser Anastasios', das Trisagion durch den Hinweis auf den Gekreuzigten, den *staurotheis*, zu erweitern, nur der Tropfen war, der das Faß einer insgesamt heiklen innenpolitischen Gemengelage zum Überlaufen brachte. Mit durchaus vergleichbarer Fragestellung analysiert SIMON MACLEAN in *'After his death a great tribulation came to Italy ...' Dynastic Politics and Aristocratic Factions After the Death of Louis II, c. 870–c. 890* die Entwicklung des innenpolitischen Machtgefüges im Italien der Jahre 870 bis 890, vom Tod Ludwigs II. bis zum Ende der karolingischen Dynastie, und kann zeigen, daß diese Epoche nicht, wie bisher in der Forschung meist behauptet, durch ein politisches Chaos produzierendes statisches Mißverhältnis eines schwachen Königs und rivalisierender starker Adelsfamilien geprägt war, sondern vielmehr durch eine hochdynamische Interaktion zwischen königlicher Patronage und der Bildung wechselnd zusammengesetzter adeliger Interessengruppen. Zeitlich unmittelbar an MACLEAN anschließend weist schließlich THOMAS PRATSCH in *Mönchsorden in Byzanz? – Zur Entstehung und Entwicklung monastischer Verbände in Byzanz (8.–10. Jh.)* nach, daß es entgegen der in der Forschung üblichen Auffassung im byzantinischen Reich zwar keine Mönchsorden im engen Sinne des Begriffs – also Klosterbünde mit eigener Verfassung –, jedoch Klosterkongregationen gab, deren innere Organisation und Kohärenz in ihrer Dichte und Regelhaftigkeit westlichen Mönchsorden weitgehend entsprachen.

Die Mehrzahl der hier versammelten Beiträge haben ihren Schwerpunkt zwar im Bereich der Literatur- und Geschichtswissenschaften, gewinnen aber durch ihren thematischen und methodischen Zuschnitt ein entschieden transdisziplinäres Profil und öffnen sich damit auch für Interessen, die über den unmittelbaren fachspezifischen Zusammenhang hinausreichen.

Wolfram Brandes   Alexander Demandt   Helmut Krasser

Hartmut Leppin   Peter von Möllendorff

Editorial Millennium 4, 2007

The contributions presented in this volume of the Millennium Jahrbuch 4 (2007) offer a selection of insights into research problems ranging from the Early Roman Imperial period to the late-ninth century that put historical, theological and artistic developments into a culture historical perspective. In each of the quite diverse fields they cover they question the established state of research and draw attention to events and objects that have previously not received due consideration. They are grouped according to common epochal, thematic and methodic perspectives.

Thus the three contributions from SUSAN E. ALCOCK, JOY CONNOLLY and HELMUT KRASSER formed the panel 'Contructing Identities in the Roman Empire' at the German-American conference *Identities* that took place in October 2004 in Philadelphia under the auspices of the American Philosophical Association and the Alexander von Humboldt-Stiftung. In their introduction to this group of thematically closely interrelated articles STEPHEN HINDS and THOMAS SCHMITZ focus on the construction of Roman and Greek identities in the Roman Empire as a conception of classical Greece that only now became an anchor point for the creation of an identity. Hinds shows how ambivalently Rome's fascination with the culture it was inspired by was viewed, and how it was propagated and topicalised in numerous anecdotes; while Schmitz presents the various facets of how Imperial Greece drew on its own past.

In *Making sure you know whom to kill: spatial strategies and strategic boundaries in the Eastern Roman Empire* SUSAN E. ALCOCK then proposes three factors that facilitated the transition from the Greeks' genocide of the Roman inhabitants of the province of Asia in 88 B.C. to their peaceful co-existence in the first centuries A.D.: the construction of an elite that in turn led to the establishment of social connexions across ethnic borders; control of the masses through the visible differentiation of an upper class and the division of public space between the latter and the middle and lower classes; as well as a cautious cultural distinction between Greeks and Romans that was, to a certain extent, a constant reminder of a neuralgic point in the memory of the massacre and Rome's terrible punishment. In contrast, in *Being Greek/Being Roman: Hellenism and Assimilation in the Roman Empire*, JOY CONNOLLY places more emphasis on the contribution that a conception of classical Greece made towards bringing the cultures together. According to this, the literature, philosophy and art of Classical Greece were not in the real sense dependent on Greekness, so that its ideals could also be an orienting point and model for the Romans. Rhetorics, with its complex system as a general education in speaking and thinking, as well as a widespread philosophical, above all ethical, cosmopolitanism together provided the basis of education in the Imperial period and had a similar effect. A different emphasis is placed by HELMUT KRASSER in *Shifting identities. Knowledge and the Construction of*

Social Roles in the Roman Empire. He identifies three levels of identity based on education: identity within individual elite social groups; identity within local/ regional networks; as well as a wide-ranging imperial identity. It was in con-nexion with this system of mutually supporting identities that a diversified litera-ture developed, one of the prime intentions of which was to demonstrate its own competence within the role of education in creating identities, thereby establish-ing it as an educational medium par excellence.

The contributions from ULRIKE EGELHAAF-GAISER and CHRISTIAN TORNAU share a common methodical approach based on a detailed intertextual analysis of the literary sources. *Kolossale Miniaturen: Der Holzfäller Hercules in Statius' "Wäldern"* by ULRIKE EGELHAAF-GAISER, an in-depth analysis of Statius' Silva 3,1, demonstrates the enormous metaphoric potential of this occasional *verse*. Here the central character of Hercules serves as a burlesque, epic figure in the manner of Callimachus, whose immense strength and size serve to emphasize the intellectual refinements and subtle form of the poetry. As the person who not only commissioned but also built his temple at Sorrento, Hercules is able to represent both patron and client/poet, and so playfully bridges the hierarchical divide between the two. In the process a whole collection of hidden hints at aetiological Herculean myths in the works of Callimachus and Vergil provide a demonstration of how educated Pollius, the patron celebrated in the poem, was. In *Does Love Make Us Beautiful? A criticism of Plotinus in Augustine's Tractates on the First Epistle of John*, CHRISTIAN TORNAU analyses Augustine's study of how Plotinus presents the role of Eros in the soul's ascent to the One, and demonstrates that, although Augustine followed Plotinus for much of his conception of the love of God, he disagreed with him at the vital juncture: the rise of Eros does not, as the Neo-Platonist maintained, result in a return to true, real human nature, that is in the vision of the truly good in the human soul itself, but rather in the rejection of the human and in turning to the divine beauty of Christ. *Der Philosoph auf dem Kaiserthron, der Leser auf dem Holzweg? Marc Aurel in der Historia Augusta* by DENNIS PAUSCH interprets three interrelated biographies in the *Historia Augusta*, those of Marcus Aurelius, Lucius Verus and his rival Avidius Cassius, as a deliberately conceived literary narration. Contradictory and incomprehensible passages are to be seen as fictional strategies. In particular PAUSCH regards the repetition of the story of the life of Marcus Aurelius, with its ambivalent, chang-ing evaluations, as a technique that is intended to make the reader see them as an 'unreliable narration'. The introduction of the two parallel biographies serves the same end, and allow individual biographical emphases to be changed slightly. In this way the *Historia Augusta* is to be understood as a subsidiary form of histor-iography that pre-supposes a reader with a knowledge of history such as can be assumed to have existed at the turn of the fourth to the fifth centuries AD.

The first contribution in the final group of historical studies, Σταυϱωθεὶς δι' ἡμᾶς – *Der Aufstand gegen Anastasios im Jahr 512* by MISCHA MEIER, is a detailed and extensive study of the Staurotheis revolt in 512, incorporating a wide range of material. This is an event that, on the whole, has in the past been treated with kid gloves, and not been looked at in a broader context in spite of the fact that ecclesiastic and 'profane' political factors interacted and worked together to bring things to a head. MEIER demonstrates that Emperor Anastasios' order to extend the Trisagion with the phrase "who was crucified for us", the *staurotheis*, was merely the straw that broke the camel's back at a time of enormous internal tension. SIMON MACLEAN looks at similar questions in '*After his death a great tribulation came to Italy ...' Dynastic Politics and Aristocratic Factions After the Death of Louis II c. 870–890*, that is the development of the structures of internal power in Italy in 870–890, from the death of Louis to the end of the Carolingian dynasty. He manages to show that the period was not, as is generally claimed by scholars, characterised by a static imbalance of a week king and competing, powerful aristocratic families leading to political chaos, but rather by a highly dynamic interaction between royal patronage and the establishment of aristocratic interest groups which were constantly changing. Chronologically, THOMAS PRATSCH's contribution *Mönchsorden in Byzanz? – Zur Entstehung und Entwicklung monastischer Verbände in Byzanz (8.–10. Jh.)* follows closely on MACLEAN's, and shows that contrary to the normally accepted view that in the Byzantine Empire there were no orders of monks in the close sense – monastic groups with their own constitution – there were indeed monastic congregations with an internal organisation and coherence that matched western orders in their density and regularity.

Although most of the contributions presented here concentrate on topics from historical and literary studies, their thematic and methodical approach imbues them with transdisciplinary relevance, and so opens them to interests that go beyond the direct, special context of their discipline.

Constructing Identities in the Roman Empire:
Three Studies

STEPHEN HINDS & THOMAS SCHMITZ

The three papers which follow, together with the present two-part introduction, were conceived as a set for an interdisciplinary conference on the theme of *Identities*, held at Philadelphia in October 2004 under the joint auspices of the American Philosophical Society and the Alexander von Humboldt-Stiftung. The theme of the conference was in fact secondary to its main business, which was to inaugurate a regular series of encounters between early- to mid-career scholars of the Humanities based in Germany and in the United States, for the purposes of intellectual and collegial exchange across national and disciplinary boundaries: the program thus begun, "German-American Frontiers of Humanities", is one which gives greater emphasis to real-time discussion than to collective publication.[1]

In the event, however, the papers devised for the inaugural meeting by the academic representatives of ancient Greece and Rome did seem to us (as panel organizers) to be worth keeping together as an exploration of issues of identity in a particular (and particularly rich) ancient world context, and also, more obliquely, as a modest attempt on our part to represent some traits of turn-of-the-millennium Classics both to ourselves and to colleagues in neighbouring and cognate disciplines. We are most grateful to the editors of *Millennium* for publishing these papers as a linked set.

1. Introductory Generalities, mostly Roman [Stephen Hinds][2]

When classicists are invited to participate in interdisciplinary symposia, their job is usually to plot some point of chronological or conceptual origin for the matter under discussion. Thus, for the symposium on *Identities* described above, a clas-

---

1 "Identities – Four Dialogs": Symposium at the American Philosophical Society, 427 Chestnut Street, Philadelphia, 7–10 October 2004. 'German-American Frontiers of Humanities': http://www.humboldt-foundation.de/en/netzwerk/frontiers/gafoh/index.htm. We should like to express our gratitude to the two sponsoring organizations, the American Philosophical Society and the Alexander von Humboldt-Stiftung, and to all who contributed to a memorable weekend of international exchange (under the benign gaze of Benjamin Franklin) across the fields of Cultural and Media Studies, Classics, Social History and Modern Literature; especial thanks to the local hosts, APS Co-Executive Officers Richard and Mary Maples Dunn.
2 My brief remarks have been sharpened by the readings of my colleagues Catherine

sical panel might have been expected either to demonstrate that all modern ideas about identity were invented in the ancient Greco-Roman world, or to propose (in a more wary version of the same) that identity, as now understood, is a concept specific to modernity – so that the classical contribution would be to describe what the world looked like, as it were, Before Identity.[3]

However, the fact is that quests for origin are a little out of style among new-generation classicists. Thus, in helping to frame the program for the Philadelphia symposium, Thomas Schmitz and I took two early measures to subvert any expectation that our ancient-world delegation would explain How It All Began. First, a matter of timetabling: we stipulated from the outset that the Classics panel should not open the symposium. Modern Literature or Media Studies first, *then* Classics.

Second, within the classical field itself, we deliberately chose a time and a place – the Greek Roman Empire – in which the origins of classical thought are *already* a matter of ancient history. With only one chance to make an impression in a comparativist context, the more obvious choice would have been the archaic and classical period of Greece: that is after all the "Hellenic moment," primary, originary and authentic, hovering somewhere between the world of Homer and the acme of the Athenian *polis*.

But *why* is that the canonical Greek moment? In no small measure because of some very time-specific cultural work done during the age of Romanticism, in which primacy and authenticity become newly prestigious terms; much of this reinvention of Hellenism takes place in Germany, some of it in America too.[4] The winners here were the early Greeks; and the obvious losers were the Romans, now branded as secondary and inauthentic – a public relations disaster from which Roman studies have never fully recovered. But there were other losers too, who lost so badly that few outside Classics now give them even a second's

---

Connors and Alain Gowing, as also by discussion at the Philadelphia symposium itself (including a particular confluence of interest with a paper on Herder by Franz-Josef Deiters).

3   Cf. actual book titles in modern Classics: *Before Sexuality* (1990), *Before Color Prejudice* (1983). Relevant remarks on the history of "the self" in the introduction to the former book: D. Halperin, J. Winkler and F. Zeitlin, eds., *Before Sexuality: The Construction of Erotic Experience in the Ancient World* (Princeton: Princeton U.P., 1990), 5–7.

4   See M. Landfester, *Humanismus und Gesellschaft im 19. Jahrhundert* (Darmstadt: Wissenschaftliche Buchgesellschaft 1988); S. L. Marchand, *Down from Olympus. Archaeology and Philhellenism in Germany 1750–1970* (Princeton: Princeton UP, 2003); on America, and on consequences for Roman studies, see T. Habinek, "Grecian Wonders and Roman Woe: the Romantic Rejection of Rome and its Consequences for the Study of Roman Literature," in *The Interpretation of Roman Poetry: Empiricism or Hermeneutics?*, ed. K. Galinsky (Frankfurt: Peter Lang, 1992), 227–42.

thought: I mean the post-classical Greeks of antiquity, the Greeks who lived *after* the age of the independent city-states, *under* the Roman Empire. It is these Greeks, along with their contemporaries, the inherently late-coming Romans, who own the "moment" to be privileged in the pages which follow.

Hence the title of this suite of papers, "Constructing identities in the Roman Empire", a dialog about a particular zone of antiquity – embracing, as we shall see, a particular culture of belatedness – in which "Greek" no longer means what "Greek" once meant (or was thought to mean); and also, just as importantly, as Helmut Krasser's paper will show, "Roman" no longer means what "Roman" once meant.

But in fact the classicist's traditional role is not so easily escaped. In proclaiming that our focus on a hybridized post-classical world rather than on a "pure" classical world takes us away from the matter of origins, we are being more than a little disingenuous. The fact is that this later Greek world, taken over by Rome, was itself a zone in which quests for origin and myths of origin prospered as rarely before or since. Indeed, Joy Connolly will argue that this is in some ways the time and place in which the idea of Classical Greece itself was first *invented*, both as a willed construction of origins by later Greeks nostalgic for a lost – or imagined – identity, and (more unexpectedly) as a cross-cultural reference point for Greek *and* Roman elites interested in creating a shared high culture under one empire, and in differentiating themselves from non-elite contemporaries.

As a Latinist, and as one accustomed to inhabit a period slightly earlier than that under especial study here, let me fill out my half of this introduction by offering some particular glimpses of stories told about Roman identity-formation under pressure from the Greek (rather than *vice versa*); and let me pick my vignettes, not from the period of the Empire itself, but from earlier centuries in which the Greek world was not yet fully within the Roman ambit. An important asymmetry should be registered here. Whereas there was once a world, clearly and objectively, in which Greeks were innocent of any contact with Rome, any corresponding idea of early Romans unaffected by contact with Greece will always contain an element of tendentious fiction: Rome emerged into an already-Greek Mediterranean, and in many senses never had a pre-Greek period.

Every classicist learns and internalizes some version of the story of "Greece meets Rome"; and there is no version in which the facts are not heavily cloaked in ideology. As many of us first encountered it in school, it was a story featuring the rival claims of the "groovy Greeks," representing truth, beauty and democracy, and the "rotten Romans," representing plumbing, road-building and imperial coercion.[5] As the Romans themselves preferred to hear it told, it *was* a story

---

5   *The Groovy Greeks* (1996) and *The Rotten Romans* (1997) are now the titles of two mid-1990s children's books by Terry Deary, in a series called "Horrible Histories."

about empire – something to which Sue Alcock will bring an especially startling emphasis – but a story whose telling tended in some way to involve the masking or mystification of imperial power. In military terms (on this narrative), Rome gradually conquers and takes control of the Greek world; in cultural terms, a kind of reverse annexation occurs, or threatens to occur. Greek culture floods into Rome; in the aphorism made famous by the poet Horace, the conqueror is conquered.[6] The most paranoid variant has it that the moral fiber of the hardy Latin yeoman is irreparably weakened by contact with the effete decadence of the Hellene. In more benign versions (involving no less "spin," of course), Greece and Rome meet in an ideal partnership: the Greeks (an older civilization) bring art, literature and culture to the still unpolished Romans; the Romans bring practical wisdom, hard-headedness and solid governance to the Greeks, here envisaged as Rumsfeldian "old Europeans" who need to be reminded how the world has changed.

Some verbal snapshots, then, from the early years of Roman empire-building and inter-cultural identity formation. In what follows, there are elements both of pattern and of irreduceability to pattern. Old classical hands will recognize both a general repertoire of anecdotal material circulating in antiquity, and also the particular emphases of one key common source, Plutarch, author some time after 96 CE of the *Parallel Lives* of great Greeks and Romans, and himself an indefatigable builder of cultural bridges in the Greek Roman Empire.

(1) As the Roman general Marcellus is about to destroy the opulent Sicilian Greek city of Syracuse in the late third century BCE (the term "Sicilian Greek" carries its own history of identity formation), he weeps at the thought of its impending fate, and at how it will no longer be the beautiful thing it was, after his army has sacked it. He is mortified when one of his soldiers kills the celebrated Greek philosopher-scientist Archimedes, who has been masterminding the city's defenses, and seeks out the dead man's relatives to pay especial respects to them. Marcellus goes on to ship an unprecedented amount of plundered Greek art back to Rome after the fall of Syracuse: this act will enter the national mythology as an inaugural moment of cultural decline, the moment when formerly frugal and practical Romans began to waste vast amounts of time (it will be said) in "idle chatter about art and artists."[7]

---

6   Horace, *Epistles* 2.1.156–7, with its own playful exaggeration: "Greece, once captured, made a captive of her brute vanquisher, and brought the arts into rough and rural Latium."

7   Plutarch, *Marcellus* 19, 21. On Marcellus' tears for Syracuse cf. also Livy 25.24, Valerius Maximus, *Memorable Doings and Sayings* 5.1.4; on Marcellus and the death of Archimedes cf. also Livy 25.31, Valerius Maximus 8.7.ext.7.

(2) Another Roman general, Aemilius Paullus, soon-to-be conqueror of Greek Macedonia (by this point in the mid second century BCE a shadow of its own imperial past under Alexander the Great), gives his sons a comprehensive Greek education from Greek tutors; his daughter's pet dog shares a Greek mythological name with the Macedonian king (Perseus). Upon taking possession of the king's seat of power, Aemilius shows his restraint by renouncing any interest in Perseus' vast stores of silver and gold; but he does allow his sons, "lovers of letters," to take their pick of the royal book-collection. Back in Rome, when Perseus' own children are led along in the triumphal procession as slaves, the Roman crowd weeps for them: "the pleasure of the spectacle was mingled with pain until the children had passed by." Two of those children die in captivity along with their father; the third, named Alexander, learns to speak and write the Latin language, and goes on to a modestly successful career as a Roman civil servant. Aemilius had attracted favorable notice on a goodwill tour of Greece, not least with a graceful and culturally appropriate compliment about Phidias' statue of Olympian Zeus; upon his death his former enemies in Macedonia and elsewhere have such regard for his humanity that they vie to be among his pall-bearers.[8]

(3) The stern Roman moralist Cato, a scourge of contemporary Hellenophiles, but ready to embroider a tour of service abroad with an extended stay in Athens, refuses to address an early second century BCE Athenian audience in Greek, a language in which he is fluent (though he did wait to acquire the language until later in life than some); an alternative tradition will state that he *did* in fact address the Athenians in Greek, and in complimentary terms. Cato's extant writings show much influence from Greek letters; but he (famously) writes the following in an epistle to his son:[9]

> I shall speak about those Greek fellows in their proper place, son Marcus, and point out the result of my enquiries at Athens, and convince you what benefit comes from dipping into their literature, but not immersing yourself in the study of it. They are a quite worthless people, and an intractable one, and you must consider my words prophetic. When that race gives us its literature it will corrupt all things, and even all the more if it sends hither its physicians …

---

8   Plutarch, *Aemilius Paullus* 6, 10, 28, 33, 37, 39. Plutarch cites the story of the pet dog from Cicero, *On Divination* 1.103 (the dog's death, on the same day that the command against the Macedonian Perseus is entrusted to Aemilius, is taken as an omen of coming victory). The *bon mot* on the statue is at *Aemilius* 28.5: "at Olympia, as they say, he made that utterance which is now in every mouth, that Phidias had given form to the Zeus of Homer." On Macedonians at Aemilius' funeral (*Aemilius* 39.8) cf. also Valerius Maximus 2.10.3.

9   Plutarch, *Cato* 2, 12, 23; Pliny, *Natural History* 29.14 for the verbatim quotation from Cato's epistle to his son.

Some 300 years later, here is the comment on those words offered by the bridge-building Plutarch (himself a Greek):

> Time has certainly shown the emptiness of this ill-boding speech of Cato's, for while the city of Rome was at the peak of her power, she made every form of Greek learning and culture her own.[10]

More significant than the content of Plutarch's intervention here is the mere fact of it. It is notable that all these mid-Republican anecdotes of originary encounters between Roman and Greek remain fully current through the period of the Greek Roman Empire. Even after three or four centuries, when the importation of Greek culture into Rome has long since ceased to be new news, even at a time when the cultural fusions of Roman Hellenism should just be a given, these early stories of problematic Roman grappling with the Greek "other" are evidently still as important to people as ever – if not more so.[11] I close, then, with a sound-bite from one indispensable current historian of Roman culture, Mary Beard, as quoted by another, Denis Feeney:

> ... The central, essential, paradox of [Roman] culture was precisely its simultaneous *incorporability* within Greek norms and its insistent *refusal* to construct itself in those terms.[12]

2. "Rotten Greeks?" Tales of Domination and Decadence [Thomas Schmitz]

As Stephen Hinds has pointed out, the fact that classics as a professional academic discipline emerged in the nineteenth century and that this emergence was intimately tied to Romanticism (and, to a lesser degree, to German nationalism)

---

10 Plutarch, *Cato* 23.3. Cato's point about physicians (of which I give only a glimpse here) prompts another acerbic retort from Plutarch at the start of *Cato* 24; contrast Pliny, *Nat.* 29.15. Excellent unpacking of Plutarch on Cato: S. Goldhill, *Who Needs Greek? Contests in the Cultural History of Hellenism* (Cambridge: Cambridge U.P., 2002), 259–61.

11 With my snapshots above cf. esp. the account in Helmut Krasser's paper of Statius, *Silvae* 4.6 – involving a glimpse of another "distinguished [Roman] general and ... lover of Greek culture," Sulla.

12 M. Beard, "Looking (Harder) for Roman Myth: Dumézil, Declamation and the Problems of Definition," in *Mythos in mythenloser Gesellschaft: Das Paradigma Roms*, ed. F. Graf (Stuttgart and Leipzig: Teubner, 1993), 44–64 at 63; cited by D. Feeney, *Literature and Religion at Rome: Cultures, Contexts and Beliefs* (Cambridge: Cambridge U.P., 1998), 67. Cf. Feeney's own description (26) of Roman dialog with Greek religion (within a discussion of Roman interaction with Greek culture at large) as "a dialogue that the Romans were careful never fully to naturalise or domesticate."

has had a decisive influence on the way we moderns see antiquity. The Romantic predilection for everything that was "original" and could be understood as emanating from the "dichtender Volksgeist," as Herder famously put it, meant that later periods of the history of Greek literature had to pay the price for this enthusiasm for early Greek culture. While Latin literature and Roman culture in general has seen a slow, yet steady rise since the beginning of the twentieth century (due in part to somewhat unsavory political reasons), Greek culture after the Roman domination of Greece has only recently begun to recover from the neglect and outright disdain that the Romantic perspective on Greek culture entailed.

In the first part of these introductory pages, we have seen that Roman attitudes toward the Greeks and their superior culture were ambivalent. Let us now switch our focus to the Eastern half of the Roman Empire: what would a member of this Greek culture think and say about the Romans? Undoubtedly, the Romans were the conquering force; they had set up what a well-known scholar in a recent publication on *Being Greek under Rome* called the "Mother of Empires."[13] Nevertheless, the situation of the Greeks in the vast system of the Roman Empire was quite special. Unlike later builders of empires, the Romans could never claim they had come to these Eastern provinces as a "civilizing power"; no educated Roman could deny the fact that Greek culture was far older than and superior to anything Rome could lay claim to. For an educated "Greek" (we will have to come back to the problems inherent in this term), the situation was a mirror image: while many Greeks admired the great success of the Roman armies and the stability of the Roman state, at the same time they also felt superior because of the great tradition of their art, their philosophy, and their literature. Moreover, the Romans sat uneasily between the terms that Greeks used to describe themselves and others: were they, like most foreigners, simply "barbarians" (a term which originally just meant "non-Greeks," without any pejorative connotation, but which acquired its derogatory sense during the confrontations between Greeks and Persians in the fifth century B.C.E.[14]) or were they some sort of Greeks *honoris causa*? The question was never fully resolved for many educated Greeks.

These questions of Greek and Roman identity became especially prominent in the period after Augustus's reign. During the first century B.C.E., Greece and the Eastern provinces had been hit particularly hard by the Roman civil wars.

---

13   S. Goldhill, "Introduction. Setting an Agenda: 'Everything is Greece to the Wise,'" in: S. Goldhill (ed.), *Being Greek under Rome. Cultural Identity, the Second Sophistic and the Development of Empire* (Cambridge: Cambridge U.P., 2001), 25.

14   See E. Hall, *Inventing the Barbarian. Greek Self-Definition through Tragedy* (Oxford: Oxford U.P. 1989).

The region had not had time to recover from the consquences of Mithradates's defeat – Athens had made the fatal mistake of supporting the rebellious king and had been conquered and looted by the victorious Roman general Sulla in 86 B.C.E. The main battles of the civil wars between Caesar and Pompeius, Caesar's heirs and his murderers, and between Octavian and Marcus Antonius took place on Greek soil (Dyrrhachium, Pharsalos, Philippi, Actium), leaving the country exhausted. It was only during the reigns of the first emperors that the Eastern Empire slowly began to recover. Emperors such as Nero or Vespasian were fond of Greek culture and gave the Greek cities tax breaks, and, even more important- ly, the feeling that Greece had a special place in the huge empire, that it was not just another province, but Rome's partner in government. This slow recuperation gained speed with the stability of the empire during the reign of the Antonine emperors (from Trajan, 98–117, to Marcus Aurelius, 161–180), a period famously described by Edward Gibbon as the happiest period in mankind's history.

For Greece, we can say that in the course of the century between Augustus and Trajan, the country recovered from the devastations of the Roman civil wars. As Sue Alcock has shown in an important book,[15] we can see the traces of this economic recovery in the archeological remains, and it had an enormous impact on the social structure. If we want to sum up these developments, we could say that the elite in the Eastern half of the Roman Empire became much wealthier and much more powerful; they rose in rank compared to their less fortunate fel- low-citizens as well as within the social system of the Empire. One of the most manifest and most impressive elements of this rise can be seen in the so-called euergetism: wealthy citizens would spend enormous amounts of money to build theaters or aqueducts, to give meals or gifts to their citizens, to sponsor free edu- cation or public festivals. In return, they received "symbolic capital" in the form of prestige and renown, and they made their political influence visible in these gestures of generosity (which implied that the recipients of these benefactions were their inferiors).

At the same time, members of the nobility in the Greek part of the Roman Empire improved their status within the system of the Empire. Most members of the regional or municipal elite held the Roman citizenship; they could join the Roman senate or hold important offices, even rising to the consulate. These ex- terior changes and improvements were accompanied by changes in outlook and mentality that were just as important (and I would caution against assuming that these changes of mentality were mere consequences or effects of the hard eco- nomic facts; both movements were contemporaneous). For self-confident, power-

---

15 S. E. Alcock, *Graecia capta. The Landscapes of Roman Greece* (Cambridge: Cam- bridge U.P. 1993).

ful members of the Greek elite who rubbed elbows with their Roman "coloni-
zers," the question of a Greek identity became pressing: how could they project
an image that would justify their rank and influence? This image was addressed
to (at least) three layers of recipients: 1. Their Roman colleagues. In the huge
empire, the Greeks were competing with other groups for political influence and
Roman favors. In discussions with the Roman authorities, references to the special status of Greek culture could serve as an important argument. 2. Their Greek
fellow-citizens. A positive, meaningful identity gave their existence within this
unimaginably huge empire sense; this was especially the case if this identity was
based on a sense of superiority in some areas such as literature, philosophy, the
arts or the sciences. 3. Perhaps most importantly, this identity was a psychologi-
cal necessity for members of the elite themselves. It allowed them to gain the self-
confidence and composure that was a hallmark of the nobility; it signified that
their power was justified and a consequence of their natural superiority.

What is so striking about Greek identity as it was shaped and debated during
the first and second centuries C.E. is the fact that it was rooted almost exclusively in what became more and more to be seen as the "classical" past of Greece, the
fifth and fourth centuries B.C.E. Now it is a well-known fact that in the construction of most national and group identities, the past, understood as a common history and heritage, plays an important role, but the manner in which
Greeks during this period rediscovered, reenacted and reinvented "their" "classical" past might strike us as being somewhat exaggerated. When we look at
inscriptions in the Greek-speaking world, we see names recalling the cultural
heroes of the past crop up everywhere. People called their children "Demosthenes" or "Isocrates"; writers were competing for titles like "the new Xenophon"
or "the new Homer." Everything referring to or emanating from this classical
past was regarded as superior, and we can even see inscriptions imitating the let-
ter-forms of archaic alphabets that had been obsolete for several centuries.

But the most obvious sign of this classicizing outlook is the so-called Atticism which can be described as an attempt at turning back the linguistic clock by
imitating as closely as possible the Attic Greek of the fifth and fourth centuries
B.C.E. When as students we read these texts in an artificial, classicist language
today, we do not immediately realize just how odd they are – this is the language
that we still teach in our Greek composition classes, so we get a false sense that
this is just the "correct" form of Greek, a return to the classical norm after centuries of linguistic (and cultural) depravation. We get a clearer view of the exceptional nature of this artificial revival if we try to think of a modern equivalent.
The classical past was about half a millennium away, so we can roughly say that
imitating classical Attic style in the second century C.E. would be equivalent to
imitating Renaissance English today. So let us just assume that the fashion police
were to decide today that every civilized person has to imitate the English of

Edmund Spenser's time: only words and syntactic structures that can be found in Spenser's texts may be used today. And this policy is valid for every public utterance, every speech or written work that intends to be taken seriously.

The constrictions in Roman Greece were equivalent. A minor cultural industry began to develop around this classicism: Atticism was taught in the schools; children began to learn about classical vocabulary at a tender age. Numerous tools were written to facilitate this difficult task: Atticist lexica explained in detail which modern words must be avoided because they have no classical pedigree and showed their classical equivalents. The public display of proficiency in this Atticism was at the core of an entire cultural movement. The so-called Second Sophistic flourished all over the Eastern half of the Roman Empire. Sophists[16] would travel around major cities, performing in theaters and concert halls. Their big act were extemporized speeches in which they impersonated the cultural heroes of the classical past, of course in impeccable Attic Greek. Typical themes for these sophistic declamations could be "What would Demosthenes say to king Philip of Macedonia?" or "How did Themistocles convince the Athenians to evacuate their city?" So if we try to adapt this to our modern counterpart, we would have to extemporize a speech on a topic such as "What would Thomas More say to Henry VIII?" We would have to imitate More's English style as closely as possible, being careful to use only words that actually occur in his works. With feats such as this, the great stars of this Second Sophistic enthralled large audiences and gathered immense reputation and wealth – and a self-confidence that went with this public success. This is how Polemo, one of the great stars of the Second Sophistic, is described by the Philostratus, who wrote an anecdotal history of the movement:[17] "[...] he was so arrogant that he conversed with cities as his inferiors, Emperors as not his superiors, and the gods as his equals."

The Second Sophistic is just one (albeit highly visible) aspect of the cultural production of a Greek identity in the Roman Empire. It should be emphasized that this Greek identity was, to a large extent, highly artificial; it was produced, not given. This identity did not just "inherit" or accept a Greek past; instead, it created this past so it could be useful for the present. This was not done by some sort of conspiracy; it was a product of the necessities of collective memory. And,

---

16 It is difficult to say why this movement chose the term "sophistic" and if there was any connection, real or perceived, to the sophists of the fifth century B.C.E. All we can see is that many members of the elite chose to call themselves "sophists," as is amply documented in the inscriptions from this period; cf. B. Puech, *Orateurs et sophistes grecs dans les inscriptions d'époque impériale* (Paris: Vrin, Textes et Traditions 4, 2002).

17 Philostratus, *Lives of the Sophists* 1.25; 535; translation Wilmer Cave Wright, Loeb Classical Library (London: Heinemann 1921).

most importantly: this process was not just a matter of some intellectuals who liked to sit in their armchairs imagining they were still living in classical Greece. As the public, performative nature of sophistic declamations makes abundantly clear, producing Greek identity was a public process performed by highly visible public figures. Many of the sophists came from extremely rich, powerful families; some of them rose to the highest ranks of the Roman Empire. Sophistic declamations, like other enactments of classical culture, were not some sort of disinterested play in an ivory tower, far from the madding crowd; on the contrary, they were part of the political and social landscape; they were one way of "negotiating social energy," to borrow Stephen Greenblatt's terminology. Sophists embodied everything that Greeks could be proud of, thus demonstrating the superiority of the economic and intellectual elite, emphasizing their right to rule.

What about the *Roman* side of this Greek identity? One of the most fascinating aspects of Greek culture in this period is the fact that members of the Greek elite seem to have been able to function in two quite distinct modes. When they were moving in their hometowns, within the circles of their Greek peers, the "Greek mode" was switched on: they would use their grandiose classicizing names and emphasize their Greek cultural heritage. If they were in contact with Roman interlocutors, however, they could equally well switch to the "Roman mode," displaying their pride in being members and partners of such a huge and powerful empire; they might even condescendingly grant that the Romans had managed to imitate some aspects of their superior Greek culture. A manifest sign of these two modes is the use of names: as I pointed out above, most members of the Greek elite held the Roman citizenship and had, as a consequence, the Roman *tria nomina*, the three names of a free Roman citizen. Elite members would carefully choose when to call themselves, e.g., "Perikles" and when "Publius Plancius Magnianus." Good examples for these two modes can also be found in the works of the orator Publius Aelius Aristides: he has written an elaborate, powerful eulogy on the Roman Empire that historians love to quote. But he is also the author of sophistic declamations and of speeches about classical Athens, and in these speeches we could get the impression that Rome never existed, that Aristides knows absolutely nothing about any empire of which he was a part.

One could wonder, in the end, whether constructions of identity follow certain transhistorical patterns. At least, it is apt, in a suite of papers conceived within an institutional framework of German-American dialog, to observe that certain aspects of the perception of self and other in the Roman Empire sound eerily familiar at the beginning of the twenty-first century: on the one hand, we see a feeling of cultural superiority, condescension, a grudging acknowledgement of a superior political and military power; on the other hand, a feeling of intimidation by an older and superior culture, an irritation at this strange mixture of snobbery and effeminacy. In a word: Romans were from Mars, Greeks were from Venus. It may help to remember that these were constructed identities, not natural and unchangeable traits.

Abstract

Greek culture and Roman culture have often been lumped together as some "classical past" of what we like to call "Western civilization." In a discussion of "identities," this classical past might seem to offer a stable point of origin for our modern notions about social, political, cultural, and ethnic identities. Our paper attempts to demonstrate that such identites were already a contested ground in antiquity. By way of example, it looks at the cultural encounter between Greece and Rome. Hinds shows that Roman reactions to Greek culture were varied in nature and that for Romans of all periods, looking upon Greece was always an important means of defining their own self. Schmitz analyzes the various ways in which Greeks during the Roman Empire defined themselves in relation to a "classical" past which was seen as a form of origin. Again, we can observe that questions of power and representation, of self and other were highly problematic and that the image of these classical origins was shaped by the demands of contemporary society.

Making sure you know whom to kill: spatial strategies and strategic boundaries in the Eastern Roman Empire

SUSAN E. ALCOCK

In 88 B.C., a killing was ordered in the eastern half of the Roman empire. Mithradates VI Eupator Dionysos, king of Pontos and enemy of Rome, declared that all Romans and Italians in the imperial province of Asia (roughly western modern Turkey) were to die. The order was carefully synchronized to simultaneously reach the province's cities, and it was carried out in various fashions from place to place. At Ephesus, for example, terrified Romans were torn from the temple of Artemis, where they had clutched the cult image of the goddess for protection. At Pergamon, arrows were shot at those seeking sanctuary in the healing shrine of the god Asclepius. At Adramyttium, those who tried to escape by sea were followed, slain, their children drowned. At Tralles, the citizens commissioned a third party to do the dirty work. How many people died? Our sources are imprecise, and massacres are notoriously difficult to gauge, but estimates of the death toll have ranged from 80,000 to 150,000 carefully targeted individuals. In the verdict of Appian, one ancient commentator: "such was the awful fate that befell the Romans and Italians of Asia, men, women and children, their freedmen and slaves, all who were of Italian origin."[1]

The back-story here, not surprisingly, is one of war. King Mithradates of Pontos was battling the expansion of Rome in the eastern Mediterranean. A major obstacle to his success was a growing Italian diaspora population, many of whom had woven themselves into the fabric of these Asian cities, achieving economic power or political position. His ruthless command, therefore, has a terrible logic – as does Rome's ultimate harsh (if largely financial) punishment. More disturbing is the behavior of the agents in the middle, the apparent ferocity with which the province's indigenous inhabitants slaughtered their neighbors.

---

1   Appian, *Roman History* 12.4.22–23, quote at 12.4.23 (translation Horace White, Loeb Classical Library). For the estimate of 80,00 dead, see Valerius Maximus, *Memorable Deeds and Sayings* 9.2; for 150,000, Plutarch, *Sulla* 24. For some accounts of the fallout of the massacre, see Appian, *Roman History* 12.9.61–63; W. Dittenberger, *Sylloge Inscriptionum Graecarum³*, nos. 741–742; Joyce M. Reynolds, *Aphrodisias and Rome* (London: Journal of Roman Studies, 1982), no. 2. These latter texts are collected and translated in Naphtali Lewis and Meyer Reinhold, eds., *Roman Civilization Volume I. Selected Readings: The Republic and the Augustan Age*, 3rd ed. (New York: Columbia University Press, 1990), 212–214.

They knew who the Romans were. They knew where they lived. And they display every sign of hating their guts.

Roman historians tend not to dwell long on this disquieting episode. In part, this reflects a gentling, scholarly amnesia that has smoothed over the frequent violence of Rome's annexation of the east. The dialogue of Greek and Roman, Hellenism and Romanitas, has traditionally been cast – as other contributions to this volume indicate – in largely "high cultural" terms.[2] Also occluding unhappy memories is the observation, from hindsight, that things did settle down in the east. Little more than a century after Mithradates, communities such as Ephesus and Pergamon, those murderous cities, were accepted as a valued part of the imperial constellation. The Roman diaspora, far from withdrawing from the eastern Mediterranean, became ever more pervasive in its presence and power. Conversely, leading members of the Greek community would sing the praises of Rome – in fine Attic Greek. All in all, good behavior, and happy consensus, appear to emerge as the soothing order of the day.

By contrast, the premises behind this article are two-fold. First, instead of cheerfully eliding the massacre of 88 B.C., we should consider it an unforgettable backdrop to the imperial society that evolved in the decades following the Mithradatic debacle. And second, instead of readily taking this shift from violence to acceptance as inevitable (a combination of "time heals all wounds" and "if you can't beat them, join them"), we should probe into just how such a transformation was achieved, and just how uncomplicated it actually was.

Given those premises, here are my arguments. First, significant reconfigurations of group identity and social alliance took place in the cities of the Greek east following the massacre: let us say from roughly 88 B.C. to A.D. 100. Second, these developments can at least in part be traced back to the aftershocks of the killing. And third, while several lines of testimonia speak to these trends, material evidence is of key importance here. Such reconfigurations can, I argue, be witnessed in, and – more importantly – were guided and fostered by, the twin media of space and setting, the physical and material environment that shapes human interaction.

This article attempts only a brief exploration of a manifestly complex process. Three dimensions can be highlighted and traced, dimensions I will term elite

---

2   See, for example, Simon Swain, *Hellenism and Empire: Language, Classicism, and Power in the Greek World, AD 50–250* (Oxford: Clarendon Press, 1996); Simon Goldhill, ed., *Being Greek under Rome: Cultural Identity, the Second Sophistic and the Development of Empire* (Cambridge: Cambridge University Press, 2001). For one study of Greek remembrance of the Roman Republic, see Christopher Jones, "Memories of the Roman Republic in the Greek East," in *The Greek East in the Roman Context*, ed. O. Salomies (Helsinki: Foundation of the Finnish Institute at Athens, 2001), 11–18.

bonding, crowd control, and cultural caution. Each of these will be illustrated by a brief examination of representative spaces, spaces which – albeit in different ways – worked to make it unlikely, if not impossible, that such a massacre could ever happen again.

To begin with elite bonding: in a nutshell, multiple environments evolved within the cityscape where influential and wealthy Greeks and Romans moved and acted side-by-side in the decades following the massacre. The killings did not lead to a diasporan retreat to the antique equivalents of gated communities or into an enclave mentality. Nor did prominent Greeks recoil or segregate themselves from the associates and descendants of the people they had slain. Instead, leading families publicly met together, did business together, worshipped together. Most ironically, they worshipped together in the very sanctuaries where sacrilege had previously taken place. Members of the Greek and Roman elite, for example, met before Artemis of Ephesus.[3] They also visibly shared duties as priests in the new imperial cult of the Roman emperor.[4] Such unity of public action, with cooperative performances of religious and civic duties, promoted mutual self-identification and endorsed affiliations among these families.

This elite bonding could and did take the form of pageantry enacted. Less than 200 years after the massacre, in A.D. 106, a ritual procession was founded in Ephesus. In it, gold and silver images of Artemis and of Ephesian civic founders were carried side-by-side with images of the Roman emperor and the Roman people. Two hundred or so well-born male participants marched where today tourists amble, clogging up civic traffic – at least for some years – about every two weeks or so. They wound their way through the main arteries of the city, passing major monuments such as the Great Theater, beginning and ending at the temple of Artemis herself. Such a parade repeatedly performed the dominant elite vision of a harmonious past and present, and a mutually fulfilling future.[5]

---

3   From a large literature on Roman Ephesus, see Helmut Koester, ed., *Ephesos, Metropolis of Asia: An Interdisciplinary Approach to its Archaeology, Religion and Culture* (Valley Forge, PA: Trinity, 1995); R. E. Oster, "Ephesus as a Religious Centre under the Principate," *Aufstieg und Niedergang der römischen Welt* II.18.3 (1990): 1662–1728. On Roman patronage of Ephesus and the Temple of Artemis, Claude Eilers, *Roman Patrons of Greek Cities* (Oxford: Oxford University Press, 2002), 231–35.

4   On imperial shrines and temples at Ephesus, see Simon R.F. Price, *Rituals and Power: The Roman Imperial Cult in Asia Minor* (Cambridge: Cambridge University Press, 1984), 254–57.

5   Guy Rogers, *The Sacred Identity of Ephesus: Foundation Myths of a Roman City* (London and New York: Routledge, 1991); Susan E. Alcock, *Archaeologies of the Greek Past: Landscape, Monuments, and Memories* (Cambridge: Cambridge University Press, 2002), 94–96.

Crowd control is the second dimension to explore. This particular alignment of elements – and the true freedom of these shared stages – was largely restricted to the wealthy and influential. In fact, as bonds formed and tightened across that elite social horizon, they clearly marked off a new, and increasingly sharp, division from the rest of the populace – hoi polloi, the many. This was, perhaps, most blatantly demonstrated in theaters, many eastern examples of which underwent ostentatious remodeling in the early Roman period. Class segregation by seating was not new at this time, but the practice became more rigidly stratified, and more visible, with the best seats in the house inscribed for all to see.[6] A single glance across a theater audience thus communicated and inculcated the social geography of the city, with increasingly unambiguous divisions between high and low.

Concerns about crowd control – civic order and the potential rowdiness of the many – became something of a mantra in the Greek cities of the Roman world. Popular unrest could invite Roman military intervention, which no one wanted and everyone feared.[7] When outbreaks did occur, they were shut down as fast as possible. One such tumult subversively occurred in the theater of Ephesus itself. As described in the *Acts of the Apostles*, in the mid-first century A.D., people loudly demonstrated against the teachings of St. Paul. For hours, they stood and shouted: "Great is Diana (Artemis) of the Ephesians!" In the end, a civic official had both to pacify and to threaten the crowd, assuring it of Artemis' greatness, and warning that it might be charged with unlawful riot. And everyone went home.[8] Since such a peaceful resolution could not always be guaranteed, the next best thing was to distance oneself from the unruly mob. Such physical and social separation not only reinforced elite integration (elite bonding), but rejected any possibility of rekindling the murderous popular coalitions of the Mithradatic massacre.

So far, of course, this is a not unfamiliar imperial story: we see the spatial organization of life promoting the alliance of central and local elites, at the expense of ties to the broader indigenous population, and we could trace similar processes all over the Roman empire. Yet in the cities of the Greek east, there are defined limits to these trends: what can be termed – and this is my third dimension – a sense of cultural caution. However strong the sense of elite alliance and mutual identification, a subtle but enduring current continued to separate Greek

---

6   David Small, "Social Correlations to the Greek Cavea in the Roman Period," in *Roman Architecture in the Greek World*, eds. S. Macready and F. H. Thompson (London: The Society of Antiquaries, London, 1987), 85–93.

7   See, for example, the comments of Plutarch in *Praecepta Gerendae Reipublicae* 814A–C, 814F–815B, 824A.

8   *Acts* 19:23–41, quote at 19:28–29 New English Bible.

from Roman – at least in some contexts. This is generally attributed to a Hellenic desire, rooted in pride in their past, to demarcate a distinct and dynamic sphere of cultural identity, and surely this is a correct assessment.[9] But the memory of other incidents in the past, such as the massacre and its harsh punishment, must also have played a part in this ongoing tension, or caution, not least for a Roman diaspora fearful of any repetition and disinclined totally to relinquish an upper hand.

One space where such caution was acted out is the battlefield that is the dining room. Greeks and Romans both (famously) reclined at table; but otherwise, significant differences marked their dining practice. Early contact saw consequent misunderstandings: about the presence of family women at table, about correct seating plans.[10] Despite the fact that, at least in some cases, blood was shed over such matters, dining quarrels have tended to be treated, rather contemptuously, as tempests in teapots. That is, however, to undercut not only the significance of correct dining in antiquity, but also the Roman investment in status recognition and the vulnerability of Greeks in a post-massacre world.

What steps were taken to alleviate this tension? The Roman mode of dining was quickly adopted in the east, as indeed it was across the rest of the empire. This mode is characterized by the triclinium (three couches), and by a very strict and hierarchical seating plan. Each place at table possessed a certain status with, most importantly, the guest of honor next to the host. This "power corner" commanded the best views, with other places at table increasingly below the salt. Triclinia such as these, found in the homes of the wealthy, catered to small gatherings, bonding peers together through commensality. Yet such spaces also, always, required the display of status distinctions – a competition in which Roman citizens would comfortably shine.[11] On the other hand, although our evidence is limited, it would appear that dining rooms were decorated with frescoes

---

9   In addition to the references in n. 2, see Greg Woolf, "Becoming Roman, Staying Greek: Culture, Identity and the Civilizing Process in the Roman East," *Proceedings of the Cambridge Philological Society* 40 (1994): 116–43; Erik N. Ostenfeld, *Greek Romans and Roman Greeks: Studies in Cultural Interaction* (Aarhus: Aarhus University Press, 2002); Alcock (cf. fn. 5) 36–98.

10   Katherine M. D. Dunbabin, "*Ut Graeco More Biberetur*: Greeks and Romans on the Dining Couch," in *Meals in a Social Context: Aspects of the Communal Meal in the Hellenistic and Roman World*, eds. I. Nielsen and H. S. Nielsen (Aarhus: Aarhus University Press, 2001), 81–101, esp. 81–82.

11   For the most recent comprehensive treatment of Roman dining, see Katherine Dunbabin, *The Roman Banquet: Images of Conviviality* (Cambridge: Cambridge University Press, 2003); on the significance of such meals, Michael Dietler and Brian Hayden, eds., *Feasts: Archaeological and Ethnographic Perspectives on Food, Politics, and Power* (Washington, D.C. and London: Smithsonian Institution Press, 2001).

and mosaics celebrating Greek myths and legends, often with a very local significance. This is visible at the site of Antioch in northwest Turkey where, for example, the so-called Atrium House possesses a mosaic panel depicting the Judgment of Paris, an event thought to have occurred on a mountain very close by.[12] Such classical themes (which, it should be stressed, are quite different from the parallel decoration of triclinia in the western empire) invited conversation and interaction in which only those educated in Hellenic culture could excel. Side-by-side with commensal bonding, the dining room thus created room for controlled competition, and cultural differentiation.

In time, Roman citizens would become entirely versed in Hellenic culture; Greek magnates would become Roman citizens. The bonding of Greek and Roman elites would accelerate, taking the form of shared citizenship, intermarriage, and ultimately the creation of a new and hybrid culture. The notion of one side slaughtering the other would become increasingly ridiculous, defining who would kill whom an ever more impossible task. In fact, this article works somewhat against the grain of most recent discussions of identity in the Greek east, discussions that seek to downplay any sharp polarity of "Greek" and "Roman" as cultural categories. My defense is this: that in order to understand how such polarities were indeed eventually overcome, we have to consider the early stages of contact, assessment, misunderstanding – and, in this case, murder.

That returns us, in conclusion, to one of the two premises with which we began: that we must account for and explain, and not just accept, the transition from violence to consensus in the Greek east. How did we get from a willingness to slaughter someone in 88 B.C. to an eagerness to marry their daughter in A.D. 88? Part of the answer, to my mind, lies in how people with authority chose to live in that intervening period: the spaces they chose to share, the spatial divisions they chose to maintain, the arenas they chose in which quietly to compete. Rather than reifying hatred in marble or in concrete, eastern elites – together – moved away from the mob, but toward each other. Though nothing was forgotten, a new choreography of life took hold – one that would substantially recast personal identities and social relationships in the Roman east.

What of the other initial premise: that the massacre of Mithradates mattered, that it had a governing part to play in such transformations? Given the global hesitation to apply the term genocide to much better documented cases of mass slaughter, it seems inappropriate to use it of the events of 88 B.C. Yet slipping the massacre into that frame of reference is remarkably clarifying. In his book on the

---

12   Christine Kondoleon, "58: Mosaic of the Judgment of Paris," in *Antioch: The Lost Ancient City*, ed. C. Kondoleon (Princeton: Princeton University Press, 2000), 172–174. See also John J. Dobbins, "The Houses at Antioch," in Kondoleon 2000, 51–61; Christine Kondoleon, "Mosaics of Antioch," in Kondoleon 2000, 63–77.

Rwanda crisis, *We Wish to Inform You that Tomorrow We Will Be Killed With Our Families*, Philip Gourevitch says at one point, quite simply: "Genocide, after all, is an exercise in community building."[13] The killing order of Mithradates can be taken as an attempt to terminate blossoming relationships, to create new, anti-Roman identities and alliances. The tactic did not work – at least not as Mithradates had intended. Yet, as we have seen, new communities, their borders inflected by the carnage, did emerge in the Roman east, as the unintended but inescapable corollaries of violence.

How do these thoughts contribute to consideration of the frontiers of the humanities? This article's promotion of the material and the spatial in analyzing social transformation and identity formation is not particularly radical in some quarters, but remains so in others. The ability for the classical past to enter into dialogue with the most modern and terrifying of concerns is similarly uncontroversial to some, but requires explanation to others. The same is more generally true of the humanities' insistence on reflection, on the precarious guarding of memory, on the necessary connection of dots between actions and consequences. Otherwise, the Asian cities of the Roman east, in the fallout of crisis, seem hardly the place to turn for current prescriptive measures: but it is always instructive – at the very least – to observe how people can live through, live with, get by, such a shared catastrophe.

Abstract

In 88 BC, Mithradates VI Eupator Dionysos, king of Pontus and enemy of Rome, ordered the killing of resident Romans and Italians in the province of Asia. Motivated by their own hatred as well as by fear of the king, his orders were effectively carried out by the indigenous populations of numerous Asian cities. 80,000 people (we are told) were killed, in some cases torn from sanctuary and butchered: 'such was the awful fate that befell the Romans and Italians of Asia, men, women and children, their freedmen and slaves, all who were of Italian origin' (Appian, *Roman History* 12.4.23). Presumably something identified the victims as Roman or Italian, and marked them out as appropriate targets of vengeance. But just how did the killers know whom to kill? And would such a slaughter have been possible two or three centuries later – possible that is, in terms of distinguishing easily between Roman and non-Roman in the eastern Roman empire?

---

13 Philip Gourevitch, *We Wish to Inform You that Tomorrow We Will be Killed with Our Families* (New York: Picador, 1998), 95.

This brief study uses the massacre as a springboard for considering the trans-formations and pluralities of identity in this imperial context. In particular, it emphasizes the role of space in articulating cultural and political distinctions. Where people lived, where they sat in the theater, where they honored their gods and their dead, where they lay at table: the choreography of such physical rela-tionships marked allegiance and difference. Changing spatial dynamics in the east allowed the deployment of multiple and mixed identities, in which borders be-tween 'Greek' and 'Roman' could be both celebrated and ignored. A massacre on the order of that 88 B.C. 'Asian Vespers' was not impossible in the more stable conditions of the second century A.D., but the spatial strategies of life in the Roman east militated against it.

Being Greek/Being Roman:
Hellenism and Assimilation in the Roman Empire

Joy Connolly

Sites that treat knowledge as a mode of identity formation – especially schools and universities, but also libraries and museums – have always been embedded in webs of economic exchange and social capital. Beginning in the middle of the twentieth century, the traditional notion of the academy as sanctuary, an emancipatory field of cultural production that suspends or reverses dominant economies of material and capital production, began perceptibly to alter. The new university, which Clark Kerr named the multiversity, redefined itself as the servant of the globalized corporate economy and its values.[1] While this movement has usefully lifted the status of research into (for example) the practices of everyday life, from organizational theory to media studies, it has also contributed to the rise of presentism in humanistic study and a corresponding devaluation of knowledge about the past. In its response to the demands of post-industrial capitalism, the university has gradually replaced at the forefront of its pedagogy learning in literature, philosophy, religion, foreign languages, and history with studies in new technologies and a range of disciplines that intellectualize and justify the practices of the economy (finance, marketing, psychology).

It is tempting, in counter-response, to romanticize the study of the past, to advertise it as the study of human identity in the frame of difference, and to insist on the essential value of a protected space and period of time where students may withdraw from the demands of the present in order to develop habits of critical thought and self-questioning before they enter their lifetime terms of service in the market. It is in order to strengthen this defense of higher education that this essay calls for a richer understanding of the ethical and political ambiguities in the early history of the liberal arts' privileging of the past. I will discuss an historical period during which Greeks looked to the remote past as the proper and exclusive domain of high culture in which elite Hellenic identity was molded and refined. Beginning in the third century BCE, Greek intellectuals identified a particular temporal moment and geographical point – Athens in the fifth and fourth

---

1   Kerr, Clark (ex-President of the University of California, Berkeley). *The Uses of the University*. 5th ed. Cambridge, MA, 2001, especially 1–34. Pierre Bourdieu defines the espousal of values reversed from those of the dominant economy as a mark of the "most perfectly autonomous section" of the field of cultural production (*Field of Cultural Production*, 39).

century BCE – called it "Hellenism," and attached to it a set of cultural attitudes that western modernity came to call "the classical." By the second century CE, all educated Hellenes had become in an important sense "classicists," adopting patterns of thought and habits of reading that continue to influence the disciplinary practices of classical philology today.[2]

What is at stake in understanding the integral place of the classical in the ancient notion of Hellenism? In an influential study of the processes through which texts accrue value – how they become "classical" – Barbara Herrnstein Smith argues that "great works" tend to reinforce establishment ideologies. If they appear to question values such as wealth and status by reminding their readers of "more elevated" notions, she argues, this ostensibly critical stance simply strengthens the plausibility of the texts' claim to universalist appeal and authority. If they were interpreted as radically undermining the ideological and material structures that support them, they would lose their status.[3] Classic and classical texts are by definition better than the culture that produced them.[4]

Herrnstein Smith's discussion underscores the importance of sheer repetition and reproduction in the construction of value – a central issue in the Greek imperial construction of the past through pedagogy, where practices of repetitive imitation played a central part. As her choice of title suggests, however, she more or less abandons the historical processes through which great works are actually selected at the doorstep of contingency. In her account, Homer's endurance as a classic turns out to be an effect of precisely the same mechanism as that which made Dante and Shakespeare classics. What enables all these texts to reflect the values of the master classes, granting them a sense of cultural unity that transcends time, is their lucky fall into the net of intertextuality "that continuously constitutes the high culture of the orthodoxly educated population of the West."[5]

As James Porter has powerfully shown, classicism is a phenomenon every age invents for itself, each stage in its history responding to its predecessors and shaping its descendants.[6] By considering an early stage in the history of classical

---

2 They are not the first "classicists"; see my discussion of the Hellenistic scholar-librarians below.

3 Smith, Barbara Herrnstein. *Contingencies of Value*. Harvard, 1988, 51.

4 I would add that "classical" texts lend high epistemic privilege to particular ethical dilemmas arising from, for instance, the notion of private property or the unequal division of power between men and women (as opposed to dilemmas that arise, say, from the equal distribution of communal resources), thus reinforcing the dominant *doxa* by transforming its weak points into the objectified stuff of art. See further Bourdieu, *The Logic of Practice*, 110–11.

5 Smith (cf. fn. 3) 53.

6 Porter, James. "What is 'classical' about classical antiquity?" In *Classical Pasts: The Classical Traditions of Greece and Rome*, ed. James Porter, Princeton, 2006. In a private

Hellenism as it relates to Roman imperial ideology, I want to explain why its makers privileged the particular past that they did, represented by carefully chosen literary texts. Supplementing Smith's work on the significance of continuity – the repetitive valorization, over a series of present moments in time, of texts already privileged by past repetitions in the service of the dominant order – I want to explore the historical conditions under which the turn to the past becomes a definitive aspect of the classical, which emerges at once as an aesthetic, an ethic, an ideology, and an identity: Hellenism. Though treatment of modernity lies beyond the practical scope of this work, my historicization of the formation of classical Hellenism is intended to suggest why it remained useful and accessible as an ideal for eras post-dating antiquity.

Like most postmodern historicizing interventions, mine seeks to destabilize grand narrative – in this case, the traditionally sanguine account of the values notionally anchored in classicism, particularly "classical" education. The destabilizing force of my argument lies in what it reveals about the master narrative of western pedagogy: that from the very moment of its original emergence in the imperial Roman era, the promise that classical education makes us free, expressed in the Latinate label "liberal arts," is entangled with a radical redefinition of freedom and a deliberate identification of universalist education with imperial power. Education's historical formation thus encumbers the promise proffered in liberal education's name. My aim is to prompt interdisciplinary reflection on the relationship between identity and education and the truly liberatory potential of the liberal arts, all of which are bound up in the ideological pressures that shape constructions and uses of the past, and I will bring the essay full circle with a few observations on these issues at the end.

I

Today the relationship between cultural identity and the literary canon is hotly contested. Americans have invested immense energy in the so-called canon wars, some arguing on behalf of retaining tradition for its own sake, others that the cultural health of our representative democracy hangs on attaining proportional representation in our curriculum. John Guillory, questioning the motives and rationale of both attitudes, has pointed to the ideological and practical quandaries

---

communication, he cites Schegel: "everyone has found in the classics what he needed or wished to find: chiefly, himself" (*Athenaeum* fr. 151). Other essays in Porter's collection persuasively posit the existence of many different versions of the "classical past."

that have emerged out of the approach to canon revision adopted by American universities over the past generation.[7]

Amid this conflict, drawn by the rich material it offers for study of the relations of education and identity in the context of empire, scholars have turned with growing interest to the period often called the "Second Sophistic" or the "Greek imperial" era, normally understood as beginning at the end of the first century CE and lasting roughly a century and a half under the peaceful conditions maintained by a relatively stable autocratic dynasty based in Rome.[8] This period witnessed no large-scale debate over the Greek canon's consistent focus on the past, no "querelle des anciens et des modernes" at the level of intensity familiar to the modern West. The educated Greek-speaking, Greek-identified subjects of the Roman empire fixed their sights on an era over half a millennium distant, on an era that was to to them, as it is to us, "ancient" Greece.[9] His late antique compilator quotes Athenaeus, a third century CE writer, on the large number of "ancient Greek books" he owned (βιβλίων ἀρχαίων Ἑλληνικῶν, 1.3a).

The antiquity of the literary texts that dominated Greek education in the Roman empire helped justify their inclusion in the program. The habit of privileging old texts – specifically, the notion that a chosen list of texts produced in past generations formed the proper basis of education – was, by the fourth century BCE, already settled. In "classical" Athens, familiarity with ancestral achievement was viewed as a central aspect of wisdom and good character.[10] The ur-texts of Greek literature stand at the head of this tradition: Homer as the source of knowledge about heroic ancestors, and Hesiod as the repository of ancestral wis-

---

7 Take William Bennett's bitter complaint in the *New York Times* (17 Feb. 1985) that "many people in our colleges and universities aren't comfortable with the ideals of Western civilization," insightfully analyzed alongside "identity politics" critiques from the left by Guillory, John. *Cultural Capital*. Chicago, 1993, 20–25.

8 The best introduction to the current state of scholarship, including an excellent bibliography, is Goldhill (ed.), *Being Greek Under Rome*; see also Elsner (ed.), *Pausanias*. Another (indirect) reason behind scholarly interest in the Greek empire is the impact of postmodern critiques of literary values on classical scholarship, which has encouraged reconsideration of terms like "baroque" and "derivative" traditionally applied to the period (see esp. van Groningen, B. A. "General literary tendencies in the second century AD." *Mnemosyne*, 4th series 18 (1965), 47). On the role of "the classical" in literary evaluation, see Gadamer, Hans. *Truth and Method*. New York, 1982, 257–58.

9 It is from Philostratus' third century *Lives* that modern scholars have taken the phrase "Second Sophistic." Brunt, P. A. "The bubble of the second sophistic." *BICS* 43 (1994): 25–52, questions its historical accuracy. Goldhill, "Introduction," (cf. fn. 8) offers six helpful textual snapshots of the period (1–12).

10 Most, Glenn. "Canon fathers: literacy, morality, power." *Arion* n.s. 1 (1990) 35–60.

dom, the ancients' hallowed views of agriculture, astronomy, family structure, and morals. Antimachus of Colophon, a contemporary of Plato who worked in Athens early in the fourth century BCE, composed commentaries on Homer. A possible early sign of canon institutionalization is Lycurgus' legislation of the 330s BCE, which established statues of Aeschylus, Sophocles, and Euripides and punished actors who deviated from official scripts – though this evidence surfaces in a Greek imperial text whose authorship is uncertain (Pseudo-Plutarch, *Mor.* 841F). A more solidly attested key step was the activity of scholars patronized by Hellenistic emperors: Ptolemy I founded the royal library and museum in Alexandria in the late fourth century BCE, and the Attalid dynasty funded lavish collections of books and artworks in Pergamon a hundred years later.[11] In the Roman republic, aristocratic families first bought (as slaves) and later offered salaries to Greek teachers, artists, and intellectuals: Cicero and his contemporaries studied literature and rhetoric with expert Greek tutors at home and abroad.[12] In Athens, Antioch, Pella, and other urban centers around the Mediterranean, but on the largest scale in Alexandria and Pergamon, scholars collected, evaluated, sorted, copied, interpreted, and catalogued Greek literature. From collection to catalogue, the range of their activities created what we think of as the classical Greek canon, the core texts of Hellenic identity.[13]

The contrast between the political conditions of this scholarly activity and its chosen objects of study is crucially significant. Within just a century after the final fall of Athenian democracy at the hands of Alexander and his father Philip in 323 BCE, scholars working in and for the Hellenistic kingdoms of Egypt, Greece, and Asia Minor had canonized a reading list dominated by texts read or written by those fifth and fourth-century Athenian democrats: Hesiod and Homer, selected lyric poets, Herodotus and Thucydides, Aeschylus, Sophocles, and Euripides, Old Comedy (especially Aristophanes), Menander, Plato, and Xenophon. These were the ἐγκριθέντες, the "chosen ones," also called οἱ πρατ-

---

11 "Drawn by the great pleasures of book-loving, the royal Attalids set up an outstanding library at Pergamon for common delectation" (*regis Attalici magnis philologicae dulcedinibus inducti cum egregiam bybliothecam Pergami ad communem delectationem instituissent*): so Vitruvius, *De Architectura* 7.4.

12 Rawson, Elizabeth. *Intellectual Life in the Late Roman Republic.* Baltimore, 1985, surveys the roles of Greeks in Rome (3–18).

13 The word "canon" first appears in the fourth century CE Greek historian Eusebius, who refers to biblical books approved as authentic by the church (*Eccl. Hist.* 6.25). Pfeiffer, *History of Classical Scholarship* (207) quotes its first use in a non-scriptural context by David Rühnken, "Historia critica oratorum Graecorum" (1768): "out of an abundance of orators [the Alexandrian librarians] made a list of just ten, in a kind of canon" (*ex magna oratorum copia tamquam in canonem decem dumtaxat rettulerunt*).

τόμενοι, the "treated" authors, whose work the Alexandrians and Pergamenes edited and analyzed in extensive commentaries – a list imagined to frame subjective identity in the pedagogical encounter between student and text whose contours remained consistent through the imperial period and which, indeed, persists in idealizing form in doctoral reading lists today.

From its beginnings, classicizing scholarship shows a pronounced tendency to bracket Greek history by carving out a temporal empty space between itself and its most highly privileged objects of study, using analytic periodization to create a sharpened sense of self-conscious differentiation. In a now lost work entitled *Geographia*, the Alexandrian librarian Eratosthenes declared that Homer had lived a century after the Trojan war, a decision that firmly yoked the known span of historical events, starting from the watershed of Troy, to the known span of Greek creative culture, beginning with Homeric epic. The beginnings of Greek history and literature were interwoven and enshrined in calendrical time. In another lost work, *Chronographiai*, Eratosthenes calculated the fall of Troy to have occurred in 1184 BCE.[14] He proceeded to divide time from the Trojan war onward into ten epochs. The list ended not with Eratosthenes' "present," the late third century (he died in 194 BCE), but the death of Alexander the Great in 323.

Did Greek literature die with Alexander the Great? Of course it did not. Callimachus and Apollonius of Rhodes, heads of the Ptolemaic library at Alexandria, were poets whose work exerted immense influence on later literature, especially late republican and early imperial Latin poetry. The number and variety of papyrus fragments discovered in Egypt suggest that their writings, along with those of Theocritus, who composed hexameter poetry on the city and countryside that Vergil used as the jumping-off point for his bucolic *Eclogues*, were copied in their own region. In the late first century BCE, Dionysius of Halicarnassus, a prolific Greek critic active in Rome, celebrated his lifetime as an era of cultural recovery after a long period of debilitating sickness. Greek-speaking cities had been virtually terrorized, he claims, like a free-born matron who suffers abuse at the hands of unruly prostitutes: so the "ancient, native-born Athenian Muse" found herself supplanted by a whorish invader from the "pits" of Asia Minor, as "an illiterate style drove out the philosophical one; madness reigned over wisdom" (*On the Orators*, preface 1). Now the old, sober style has returned, Dionsyius declares, and civic eloquence flourishes once again.

If we ask, however, whether the scholarly construct "Greek literature" died with Alexander, the answer of ancient authors in the Greek imperial period was a

---

14   He relied mainly on inscriptions listing Olympic victors, which allowed him to calculate the date of the first games, along with similar lists of Spartan kings, and earlier research by Hippias, Aristotle, and Timaeus: see Pfeiffer, *History of Classical Scholarship*, 163–4; and for this period generally, 87–233.

qualified yes. Dionysius' own praise of the rebirth of Greek civic oratory appears in his preface to a series of essays that examine six Athenian orators whose *floruit* was four centuries earlier: he makes no reference in this work to contemporary practitioners.[15] Over time, though critics and scholars suggested supplements to the traditional list of "nine lyric poets" developed in the Hellenistic period, it was never altered. Preferences changed, in some cases providing grounds for intense disagreements over taste and the terminology of critical evaluation, but the backward-turning vector of interest never wavered.[16] Philostratus, a biographer who completed his *Lives of the Sophists* in the third century CE, records only three names (out of a total of forty-two lives) in the period from the fall of Athens to Macedon to the reign of Nero over three centuries later. "We pass over Ariobarzanes of Cilicia, Xenophron of Sicily, and Peithagoras of Cyrene," he remarks, since it was only due to the general scarcity of fine rhetoricians that their audiences admired them, "just as those who lack grain love pulses" (*Lives* 511).

The sophists whose activities Philostratus chronicles were rhetoricians who travelled the Greek-speaking eastern empire, teaching and giving performances in cities like Smyrna and Ephesus, Alexandria and Antioch.[17] As many scholars have recently noted, the content and style of their speeches are emblematic of the period's preoccupation with the pre-Alexandrian "classical" past. The well-known sophist Aelius Aristides recorded a dream in which the god commanded him to speak "in the fashion of Socrates, Demosthenes, and Thucydides" (*Sacred Tales* 4.31). Herodes Atticus imitated Kritias, an Athenian oligarch killed in the late fifth century; Marcus of Byzantium reviewed the Spartan surrender at Sphacteria in 425 BCE. Scopelian exhorted his audiences to resist the Persians, who attacked Greece in the 490s BCE; Dionysius of Miletus, imitating Demosthenes, spoke of Chaeronea, where the Athenians battled Philip of Macedon. Lollianus of Ephesus revised another famous Demosthenic speech, *Against Leptines*, while

---

15 His choice of the number six possibly rests on criticism of the larger group of ten referred to in the second century onward (the "ten Attic Orators"), which may have been fixed in Dionysius' lifetime by Caecilius of Calacte if not earlier: Worthington, Ian. "The canon of the ten Attic orators." in: *Persuasion: Greek Rhetoric in Action*, ed. Ian Worthington. London and New York, 1994, 244–263 surveys the arguments in "Ten Attic orators."

16 Porter stresses the "fierce polemics" that are unified only in the "most general outlines of a vague reverence for things vaguely classical, albeit within a fairly fixed framework of (high) genres and periods (archaic to fourth century)" (56). His (excellent) point gives me the opportunity to clarify what I am trying to explain here: the "fairly fixed framework" of texts and times.

17 On sophistic activities, see Schmitz, Thomas. *Bildung und Macht: zur sozialen und politischen Funktion der zweiten Sophistik in der griechischen Welt der Kaiserzeit.* Munich, 1997, esp. 97–112, 160–68; Brunt (cf. fn. 9) 26–37.

Polemon delivered orations in the voices of the defeated Persian kings Darius and Xerxes, and of Xenophon pondering suicide after Socrates' death.[18]

The sophists' embrace of Greek language and literature is a strategy best described as a specialist "Attic" version of Hellenism (Έλληνιμός), a word that originally referred to the correct pronunciation of the literary Greek of the canonical authors. As is widely acknowledged in studies of the period, Atticism is not limited to oratory. Historiography of the period included world histories with a fondness for the Eratosthenean ending of Greek history, the defeat of the Athenian-led resistance to Macedon in 338 BCE and the death of Alexander five years later. Along with intense interest in Athenian history and language emerged a trend in naming: in his *Lives*, Philostratus refers to the sophists by their Greek names, despite the fact that most, as Roman citizens, possessed names that combined Greek and Latin elements. A number of Greek towns reverted to their pre-Hellenistic names, and parents named their children after Homeric heroes.[19]

Why? Over the past thirty-five years, classicists have argued that Greeks living under the rule of Rome laid claim to the cultural heritage of Greece in its fifth and fourth century heyday in order to serve their political interests – declaring themselves heirs to past greatness in a defensive response, even in resistance, to the imperial domination of Rome. Locally powerful but globally weak, elite Greeks sought a visible way to lay claim to cultural authority, while conveniently reinforcing the local authority and social standing of those who could afford access to advanced education. As Ewan Bowie argued in his ground-breaking essay on the sophists, their "absorption in the Greek past complemented acquiescence in the political defective Roman present."[20] Tim Whitmarsh sensitively underscores the necessity of approaching the Greek imperial period with the understanding that "Greek identity" is a multi-ethnic, heterogeneous cultural modality, no longer identical with any blood-based definition of Greek ethnicity, and that the relations of past and present represent cultural continuity and fracture that writers both established and called into question. He shows that the imperial Greeks' claims of continuity and sameness with the past are rarely made without acknowledging the need to negotiate difference – between *polis* and principate, democratic citizen and imperial subject, autochthonous Athenian and Gaulish, Syrian, Egyptian, Asian, or Italian "Hellene."[21]

---

18   All examples drawn from Philostratus, *Lives of the Sophists*. For a detailed discussion of the dissonance between scholarly revival and contemporary politics, see Connolly, Joy. "Problems of the past in imperial Greek education." In *Education in Greek and Roman Antiquity*, ed. Yun Lee Too. Leiden, 2001. Pp. 339–372.

19   Bowie, Ewan. "Greeks and their past in the Second Sophistic." *Past and Present* 46 (1970), 185.

20   Bowie (cf. fn. 19) 209; see also Swain, 65–79, 409–422; Schmitz (cf. fn. 17) 193–96.

21   Whitmarsh, Tim. "'Greece is the world': exile and identity in the Second Sophistic."

These observations also apply to pre-Roman Greek culture. After Alexander, Hellenistic scholars and poets at Alexandria and Pergamon sought self-validation by representing themselves as the heirs to Athens, seeking "authorization in the contentious present from an idealized (but in fact hardly less contentious) past," Glenn Most observes; their limited-text version of Hellenism had the virtue of being one on which they could lay exclusive claim as master, preserver, and trans-mitter.[22] By excluding contemporaries from their copy-lists, they made the past as the exclusive target of cultural veneration, conveniently unified by temporal and geographical distance. Yun Lee Too suggests that the Hellenistic scholars' attention to matters of authenticity and accuracy play an important role in their self-affirmation as properly Greek, as though scrupulously correct grammar helps deny that Hellenistic culture is an "etiolated copy" of prior Greek great-ness.[23] Of course, Athenian culture performed its own acts of memorialization. Thucydides describes his history as a possession for all time (1.22.4), and his Pericles describes Athens as an education for all of Greece (2.41.4–5). In his *Antidosis*, Isocrates describes Athens as the source of great deeds that make it a great "teacher" (15.294). If the Athenian habit of delivering funeral orations reflects the city's impulse to commemorate the past, later imperial writers continue to imagine reading as an active practice of commemoration, one that shapes ethical and political self-consciousness in the present notwithstanding the distance be-tween exemplar and imitator. Dionysius of Halicarnassus asks his readers in an imperial city where Caesar Augustus has just consolidated autocratic power: "Who would not become a patriot (φιλόπολις) or a democrat (φιλόδημος) after reading [the fourth century BCE rhetorician Isocrates'] *Panegyricus?*" (*Isocrates* 5).

The unacknowledged dissonances of time and politics in Dionysius' question suggest there is good reason to wonder just how this canon is supposed to shape individual or collective identity. In its name, originally applied to biblical books whose authenticity received the imprimatur of the Christian church, and in the symbolic capital that shields it, aura-like, from criticism and reform, the literary canon bears a certain resemblance to scripture.[24] But we have just seen that the same canonical texts serve a wide variety of political and social conditions, and

In *Being Greek Under Rome*, ed. Simon Goldhill. Cambridge, 2001, 269–305, 273; see also 300–304.

22   Most, Glenn. "Disiecti membra poetae: the rhetoric of dismemberment in Neronian poetry." In *Innovations of Antiquity*, ed. Ralph Hexter and Daniel Selden. London, 1992. Pp. 391–419. See also Selden, Daniel. "Alibis." *Classical Antiquity* 17.2 (1998): 290–351.

23   Too, Yun Lee. *The Idea of Ancient Literary Criticism*. Oxford, 1998, 134.

24   Its first attested use is by Eusebius, an ecclesiastical historian.

that they promote ideologies, beliefs, and values that are incompatible, by any reasonable standard, with those dominant at the moment of original composition. The Roman empire was unprecedented in geographical scale, filled with many ethnicities and languages, dominated by large cities and webbed by a well-worn network of trade and military activity, and governed from the city of Rome. That Greeks living in it adopted a canon rooted in the distant past, the product of an archaic, relatively small-scale, and (in the case of the all-important Athenian literature) democratic culture, reveals an important insight: the extent to which the literary list that becomes the emergent site of "the classical" emerges in a constitutive state of *ideological flexibility*.

To be a cultured Greek in the Roman empire supremely embodies the tensions of this ideological flexibility, demanding as it does an active identification with the past that is both profound and paradoxical. Profound, because it involved not just reading and thinking, but the adoption of an archaic dialect and a highly formalized rule of manners – a demanding, artificial *habitus*. Paradoxical, because the Greek subject of the imperial Roman present is asked to make himself in the image of a dead, democratic past – to relive democracy, as Dionysius exclaims in his praise of Isocrates' *Panegyricus*. This self-fashioning was achieved through deep familiarity with and re-enactment of a literary canon that was itself, we recall, the product of an earlier age of empires, the Hellenistic Greek kingdoms that arose in the third century BCE after the death of Alexander.

To ask the question once more: is the turn to a carefully bracketed past best interpreted as an act of cultural self-definition and self-assertion in the face of Roman political domination? Thomas Schmitz reminds us that another issue is relevant here: the reinforcement, through public oratorical performance, of elite dominance over the uneducated and the poor.[25] Educated Greeks had much more in common with educated Romans than with the masses who shared their cities and public spaces. Focusing on two areas, rhetorical education and Stoic cosmopolitanism, I will argue that the turn to the Greek past, to what is being formed as "classical" Greece, did not so much provide imperial Greeks with the material of resistance as it accommodated long-established Roman tastes and Roman values. Rhetoric (public persuasion, we recall, being a central practice of contentious, democratic Athens) emerges as a tool with which to discipline obedient imperial subjects. Second, I will examine the philosophical coeval of literary Hellenism, Stoicism, and specifically, the widespread appeal of a weak but distinctive form of Stoic universalism.

"Greeks remained Greeks, at least in part, because Romans allowed them to." In an important essay on Greek cultural identity under the Roman empire,

---

25   Schmitz (cf. fn. 17) 163–196 provides context and acute analysis.

Greg Woolf admits that Romans "do seem to have bestowed benefits on Greeks for the sake of Hellenism," and that "the Hellenisms they promoted were selected and defined in relation to a range of Roman, rather than Greek, cultural preoccupations."[26] The truth, I think, cuts deeper, for imperial Hellenism brought a particular payoff to the Romans. It functioned primarily *not* as a mode of Greek self-differentiation but as an instrument of imperial assimilation. Universal, globally appealing Hellenism mapped itself as the intellectual and ideological system for universal and globalizing (if not globally appealing) Roman empire.

The invention "ancient Greece" becomes "classical Greece" through a double fold: the discursive veneration of the cultural production of ancient Athens (Hellenism and its more narrowly defined cousin, Atticism), and the globalization of that discourse as "classicism" – a globalization that translates the political freedoms of Athenian democracy into the purely social authority of a dominant Greco-Roman class. The classicizing sophists of the Roman empire transformed Athenian Kultur (by the German definition, the possession of a Volk) into the French ideal of civilisation, a universal ideal that bound the inhabitants of empire into a collective linked by common investment in the past.[27]

II

Rhetoric was the heart of education in imperial culture. Few pedagogies more effectively compel mental and physical habits to conform with the ideology of mastery over self and others that was an integral part of elite self-conception. In Greek imperial society, the rhetorical student's pronunciation, diction, and grammar had to meet the exacting standards of ἀττικισμός, "Attic" style now over half a millennium old. Scraps of papyrus preserve the endless grammatical exercises students wrote in order to perfect grammar and idiom that met the "pure" standard of their ancient literary models.[28]

The Atticizing imperative extends beyond the simple privileging of Athenian literature. Training in rhetoric, which formed men according to the demands of speaking outdoors, meant that the Atticizing imperative dug deep into the nerves

---

26   Woolf, Greg. "Becoming Roman, Staying Greek: Culture, Identity, and the Civilizing Process in the Roman east", *Proceedings of the Cambridge Philological Society* 40 (1994), 116–43, 131.

27   See further Appiah, Anthony. *The Ethics of Identity*, 119–20.

28   The best discussion of the papyrological evidence is Cribiore, Raffaella. *Gymnastics of the Mind: Greek Education in Hellenistic and Roman Egypt*. Princeton, 2001; for a fine-grained discussion of rhetorical exercises in this period, see Webb, Ruth. "The progymnasmata as practice." In *Education in Greco-Roman Antiquity*, ed. Yun Lee Too. Leiden, 2001. Pp. 289–305.

of the voice box and the sinews of the body. Attic Hellenism meant bringing the reading list to life in daily speech, adopting outdated grammatical forms and antique accent and diction. In the case of the sophists who earned a living or maintained their social status through speech-making, it was not unusual to imitate the gestures and habits of dress and deportment of famous figures of the fifth and fourth centuries BCE. Philostratus describes how one man "Hippiasizes" (<ἱππιάζειν), that is, "acts like [the fifth century sophist] Hippias," while another "Kritiasizes" (<κριτιάζειν), "acts like Kritias." The moderate Plutarch, always alert to the danger of ridicule and cliché, criticizes men who imitate Aristotle's lisp, Plato's stoop, and Alexander's up-twisted neck, instantly recognizable from the myriad busts and statues erected throughout the Greek east (*Mor.* 26b, 53c–d). This was not simply the "use" of the Athenian past, but a visual and auditory *enactment* of it before a formidably knowledgeable and demanding audience of peers.

But this educated imperial man is not simply a walking resuscitation of the Greek past: his carefully scrutinized body may be seen as a map of the body politic, the repository of the displaced anxieties of empire. Readers as far back as Gibbon have noted in the literature of this period deep preoccupation with individual health and illness, with the orifices and fissures of the body, and with individual habits of consumption, reproduction, and digestion.[29] In his biographies of notable Greeks and Romans, Plutarch carefully describes the appearance, bodily habits, and illnesses of his subjects. The physician Galen describes the dissections and vivisections he carried out in public before an awestruck audience. Describing how he was able to render the thorax motionless by tying slipknots around the muscles, he reminds his addressee that "you have often seen me display [this], not only in private but in public (δημοσία)."[30] Popular sophistic themes – war, natural disasters, and civil strife past and present – share these writers' concern with the fragility of the body of the citizen and the body politic. They speak the anxious fantasy of a larger political order, and its concerns about borders, civic integrity, and the empire's capacity to police and feed itself.

The educated man is also the walking embodiment of Roman empire in its ideal, well-ordered civil aspect. Praising a certain degree of "amplitude in a man's stride" as a sign of trustworthiness, sincerity, and other virtues, the sophist Polemon observes that men with a confident walk will "come off successful in their

---

29   Perkins, Judith. *The Suffering Self.* London and New York, 1995. discusses the phenomenon of the "sick self" as "ideology, not pathology," *The Suffering Self*, 132–199. See also the synthesis of Foucault, *The Care of the Self*, esp. 97ff.

30   Staden, Heinrich van. "Anatomy as rhetoric: Galen on dissection and persuasion." *Journal of the History of Medicine* 50 (1995): 47–66; Van Staden's translation of Galen, *Anat. Adm.* 8.8 (2.690K), "Anatomy as rhetoric," 52, accompanied by several similar texts.

encounters with emperors."[31] But a freestyle gait also signifies a disordered and uncontrolled character (Dio Chrysostom, *Or.* 32.54). "If my arguments prevail," Aelius Aristides says in a speech attacking improprieties in the oratorical performances of his rival sophists, "law and order prevail, by which not only the cities, but also the whole earth and heaven itself is held together and preserved" (*Or.* 34.63). The self-scrutiny of the Greek elite body is an implicit promise to the Roman empire that order is being maintained, that the Hellenic past provides models of educational discipline rather than democratic disputation and disorder. In Polemon's case, chaotic violence and masterful control together inscribed a visible dialectic of control and submission on his body: Philostratus speaks of the "hot, combative" quality of his speeches, which "rang like trumpets at the Olympia," whose effect was all the greater because Polemon maintained a grave expression and steady gaze (*Lives* 542, 528). Attic purism and bodily self-mastery may have played a key role in establishing coherent and mutually recognizable standards of performed identity for Greek elites, but they also formed a literal rein on the Greek tongue and body. The Atticizing imperial body turns out to be a model examples of imperial obedience; the fifth and fourth century past, and its epic struggle between Athens and Sparta, turns out to offer an education in subjecthood.[32]

Nor was the intent focus on that particular past limited to those identifying, culturally and linguistically speaking, as "Greeks." An idealizing vision of ancient Greece, and a carefully chosen list of texts with which to study and transmit that vision, were signs of membership in an elite culture that educated Romans shared. As early as the early second century BCE, the elder Cato knows Greek literature and culture well enough to warn Romans against the effects of its influence.[33] Cicero's preferred readings in Greek literature, described in his personal letters as well as his treatises on ethic and rhetoric, are drawn from the lists constructed by Hellenistic scholars. What appears to have been a central debate over oratorical styles, the flowery ornateness of the "Asianist" style versus the stripped-down purity of "Atticism," appear first in Cicero's writing on rhetoric. By adopting the terms of that debate in his essays, Dionysius of Halicarnassus is transposing the history of Greek rhetoric into a new, Romanized key. By the late first century, the assumption that Greece of the fifth and fourth century BCE had been a Golden Age of political freedom and civic culture was beyond question. As one Roman senator, the younger Pliny, wrote to a friend heading to a job in provincial adminstration:

31 Polemon, *Phys.* 2, 1.192–94F, translated and quoted by Maud Gleason, *Making Men*, 60.
32 I have made this argument at greater length in Connolly (cf. fn. 18).
33 Erich Gruen reads Cato's statement in terms of intra-elite competition, in: *Culture and National Identity in Republican Reme*, Berkeley, 1992. Pp. 52–83.

Know that you have been sent to the province of Achaia, that real and genuine Greece (*illam veram et meram Graeciam*), in which men believe humane civility, literature, even agriculture were first discovered; you have been sent to govern the affairs of free states (*liberarum civitatum*), that is, to men who are in the fullest sense men, and free men who are in the fullest sense free, who hold the right given them by their virtue, their achievements, by friendship, and further by civil compact and religious bond…Keep before your eyes that it is Athens you approach, and that it is Sparta you govern: to rip away from these men the lingering shadow, the name of freedom that remains to them (*reliquam umbram et residuum libertatis nomen*), is harsh, uncivilized, barbarous (*Ep.* 8.24).

If Pliny's letter draws a careful distinction between the realities of the present and the memory of past freedoms – a time when men were truly free (a strategic flattening of the inequalities of Athenian democracy), it also indicates the depth of Roman investment in that memory, and the extent to which Hellenism was a legitimate – and fully accessible – mode of identity formation for Roman elites.

By the second century CE, Roman Hellenism was sufficiently familiar to be an object of satire to Greeks. Dionysius, celebrator of the rebirth of civic oratory, grants Rome the prize for bringing about the Greek cultural "revolution" (μετα-βολή). By conquering the world and establishing order "according to virtue," in Dionysius' account, Rome created a renaissance for Greek culture (ἡ πάντων κρατοῦσα ῾Ρώμη, *On Orators* 3). In a sharper tone, the satirist Lucian advises a friend considering a job as a teacher in a Roman house: "The Romans are quite wasted away with longing for the wisdom of Homer, the awesome power of Demosthenes, or the great mind of Plato" (*On Service for Hire in a Rich Household* 25). These "longings" are satisfied by hiring a Greek speaker with a long beard and a Greek-style tunic, an economic exchange that permits the Roman vicariously to experience Greek culture firsthand, plausibly granting him (at least in some circles) symbolic capital by confirming his identity as "a lover of Greek learning and a refined lover of beauty in the area of education" while the Greek is relegated to a condition of "slavery" (17, 23). The stuff of Greek identity formation is subject to commodification and exchange not only within Greek social and economic networks, but outside the system, among the very dominant political order in opposition to which imperial Greek culture is often characterized in contemporary scholarship as seeking to define itself.

Educated Greeks' compartmentalization of their cultural heritage into a handily learnable set of texts and attitudes, and the long-standing Roman sense of Greek culture's accessibility and vulnerability, meet and dovetail in the second century CE, making the imperial era the moment when Greek Hellenism merges with imperial classicism. Now "classicism" is a Latin word embedded in the economic and political order of the Roman state. The *classicus*, as defined by the Roman Aulus Gellius around 160 CE, is a highly cultured man, one educated in ancient Roman literature from Plautus to Cicero and Caesar (*classicus adsiduus-que aliquis scriptor, non proletarius, Attic Nights* 9.8.15). The usage derives from the Latin word *classis*, the top rank of the economic census that counted and categorized all Roman citizens.[34] By Roman and Greek accounts, by the second century CE, Hellenism is and has been available for generations to Romans seeking the imprimatur of elite education: it has intermingled with and helped to shape the Roman notion of the *classicus*. Hellenism is a discourse that rewrites the values proclaimed by its texts in order to provide a crosscultural imperial elite with a valuable sense of continuity, a literary tradition that in turn makes available a common temporal and geographical locus of cultural valorization, the fifth and fourth century past.

This is a high culture created under empire, to be shared via empire. Possession of it is certainly a matter of contestation, with Greeks and Romans arguing for special rights – Cicero claims that Rome now bears responsibility for Greek culture, since the Greeks themselves are too weak to uphold their own tradition (*De Oratore* 3.43) – but these contests, while they uphold hierarchies of political authority and sensibilities of social superiority, powerfully underscore the commonality between elite Greek and Roman that knowledge of "the classical" brings. Not only do Romans appropriate the Greek past, but Greek elites rescript it. There is suggestive evidence of cultural cross-fertilization that demands further study: the fascination shown in Polemon's Marathon orations with the fragmentation of the body into bloody parts, for instance, resonates with Roman literary taste of the Neronian and Flavian eras, and specifically, with what one scholar has called the "rhetoric of dismemberment."[35]

Another way Hellenism embedded itself in the discourse of empire was through the language of cosmopolitan universalism. Although a wealth of different philosophical systems flourished during this period, the educated and the powerful subscribed overwhelmingly to what one scholar calls a single "secular ideology": Stoicism.[36] A central tenet of Stoicism was that all men are, in some sense, universal brothers; the corollary to this was that the traditional identity framework of city-state or kingdom cannot hold. According to Plutarch, the Stoic Zeno's *Republic* "is directed to this one main point, namely that our life should not be based on cities (πόλεις) or peoples (δῆμοι), each with its own

---

34 Curtius: "What a tidbit for a Marxist sociology of literature," *European Literature and the Latin Middle Ages*, 250.

35 Most (cf. fn. 22) speculates on the reasons that might lie behind the "fascination" with representations of cutting, flaying, beheading, and other forms of bodily disintegration that he traces in Roman literature of the first century CE.

36 I rely heavily in these paragraphs on Shaw, Brent. "The divine economy: Stoicism as ideology." *Latomus* 44 (1985): 16–54.

peculiar idea of right and wrong, but we should regard all men (πάντας ἀνθρώ-
πους) as our fellow countrymen (δημόται) and fellow citizens (πολῖται) and
that there should be one life (εἷς βίος) and one order (εἷς κόσμος), like that of
a single flock in a common pasture feeding together under a common law"
(*Mor.* 329).

Adherents of Stoicism were supposed to be *kosmios*, cosmic, as the philosopher Epictetus put it: "Never say "I am Athenian" or "I am Corinthian" but
rather I am of the whole world (κόσμιος)," or as we might say, "globalized"
(1.9.3–6). One of the appeals of Stoic ideology, as Shaw observes, was that strong
elements of social definition and role-playing were built into it. In the Stoic view,
each person had a definite place in the social order and had "a role to play,
whether as slave, father, husband, king, or councillor, and also had specific duties
attached to that role." Epictetus, the slave turned Stoic philosopher, and Marcus
Aurelius, the famous Stoic emperor, stress a conception of individuals as fixed in
the world order, in a "station or military post. And to a great extent, one's post of
station in life was considered as given" from birth.[37]

For modern champions of Stoic cosmopolitanism, like the philosopher
Martha Nussbaum, cosmopolitanism would seem to offer moral roots in a world
in which the older roots of home, family, and nation either no longer possess
much meaning or have become threats in their own right.[38] The true cosmopolitan, Nussbaum argues, is a person who seeks a politics that is "based upon
reason rather than patriotism or group sentiment, a politics that is truly universal." Yet cosmopolitan universalism, as an ideology, sits remarkably well with an
imperial rule that liked to conceive of itself as universal. Certainly the Greek
sophist could and did praise Rome in just these terms. Here is Aelius Aristides:

> Once some chronicler, speaking of Asia, asserted that the ruler of Asia ruled as much
> land as the sun passed over; but his statement was not true, because he placed all Afri-
> ca and Europe outside the limits where the sun goes. Now it has turned out to be true.
> Your possession is equal to what the sun can pass over…nor do you rule within fixed
> boundaries, but the sea like a girdle lies extended, at once in the middle of the civilized
> world and of your hegemony (*On Rome* 10).

Aristides' panegyric of Rome pushes the coincidence of the ethical and the juridi-
cal to the extreme: in the Empire there is peace, there is the guarantee of justice
for all peoples; there is the promise of universalist knowledge; empire is presented as a unitary power that both maintains the social peace and produces and
anchors its ethical truths. Two fundamental justifications of empire emerge from

---

37   Shaw (cf. fn. 36) 34–5.
38   Nussbaum, M. "Kant and Stoic cosmopolitanism." *Journal of Political Philosophy* 5
     (1997): 1–25.

it, both resting on universalism: first, the notion of power affirmed in the construction of a new order that envelops the entire space of what it considers civilization, a boundless, universal space; and second, a notion of law that encompasses all of time within its ethical foundations. In the words of recent scholars of empire, "Empire exhausts historical time, suspends history, and summons the past and the future within its own ethical order."[39] In a sense, Hellenic Stoicism becomes the enabler and justifier of the Roman empire – for Greek and Roman alike. As Athenaeus comments in suggestively literary terms, the Roman empire is "the epitome of the civilized world" (τὴν ἐπιτομὴν τῆς οἰκουμένης, 1.20b).

Through rhetorical education and the Stoic discourse of universalism, imperial Hellenism suited itself to Roman needs and purposes. If they offer a certain capacity for cultural self-definition in terms of resistance, Hellenism also functions discursively as a unifying sign of collaboration and mutual support.[40] In his work on the structures of power and authority in the Roman empire, Clifford Ando develops Jürgen Habermas' notion of communicative rationality, that communication, as a process for reaching consensus, demands that both ruler and ruled must arrive at a mutual or intersubjective language. Ando argues that the discourse of Roman imperial administrators reveals their belief that imperial legitimacy derived directly from the consensus of its participants.[41] The Roman empire achieved its unique status among world empires through its gradual extension of government by consensus formation to all its subjects, by creating, adopting or extending the institutions of communicative practice throughout its territory. Greek elites, in Ando's analysis, cooperated enthusiastically.[42]

III

The Greek imperial period has suffered at the hands of critics like Edward Gibbon, who complained in his history of Rome's decline and fall about the derivative and baroque nature of its literature, and more recently by scholars commenting critically on contemporary preoccupations with illness, dream analysis, and so forth. In scholarship in this mode, imperial Greeks are made to pay

---

39   Hardt, Michael and Antonio Negri. *Empire.* Cambridge, MA, 2001, 11.
40   A historical comparison may usefully be made with 18th century European classicism, which both reviles the empire of state and Church in its decisive turn away from Rome to Greece, and accommodates selected central values of Christianity: see Porter (cf. fn. 6).
41   Ando, Clifford. *Imperial Ideology and Provincial Loyalty in the Roman Empire.* Berkeley, 2000, 77.
42   Ando (cf. fn. 41) 127.

a price for seeming "modern." In this limited analysis, there is a gleam of insight. Imperial Greek culture shares with modernity a visible desire for periodicity, the official fixing of a period of past time as definitively representative of the past that permits its mining for models of moral and literary vice and virtue. So fixed, the unit of time becomes, just like a literary classic, a source of almost infinite significations, floating virtually free of the constraints under which it originally came into existence.

For Greeks under Rome, the pastness of "ancient Greece" (what we now might begin to call "classical Greece," since Latin speakers were at this moment beginning to use the term *classicus* in this sense) confirmed and established certain aspects of "being Greek" – literary greatness, scientific and historical knowledge, and political freedom (recall Pliny's emphasis, *maxime*, on the unique *libertas* of Greek men). In the process of the their reinscription in the imperial context, these things are not and cannot be untangled from the fact of their temporal distance, their "pastness" in historical time. The centuries that separated Roman Greece from its classical forebears mean that their claim to Greek heritage is always made "at a distance." That is, the greatness, the wisdom, and the unique freedom that "ancient Greek culture" comes to signify – what we might take to be the essence of the classical – is inseparable from the fact that in the imperial Greek context it is always the *memory* of greatness, the *memory* of wisdom, the *memory* of freedom. It no longer exists, except in the rereading of literary texts – and this is not quite the same thing.

In a passage quoted by Stephen Hinds in his contribution to this volume, Mary Beard argues that the essential paradox of Roman cultural identity "was precisely its simultaneous incorporability within Greek norms and its insistent refusal to construct itself in those terms."[43] I have tried to show that the pronouns in her claim may easily be inverted: imperial Greek culture incorporated itself within Roman norms while insistently refusing to identify with them. However, their refusal must be understood in a broader context. It rested on the special status given to the Greek past and the small number of literary works that were chosen to represent it. As we have seen, the very terms in which the Greeks defined Hellenism – the reverence and commitment to a certain version of the Greek past, centered on the culture of democratic Athens – were terms shared by Roman culture as well. Latin and Greek speakers share a vision of the Greek past: for both groups, it was an object of intense desire. The enshrining turn to the long distant past of archaic and Athenian history, "the classical age," is an act of shared deracination that, paradoxically, works its objects of concentration and

---

43 Beard, Mary. "Looking (harder) for Roman myth: Dumézil, declamation and the problems of definition.", in *Mythos in mythenloser Gesellschaft: Das Paradigma Roms*. Stuttgart and Leipzig, 1993, 63.

value loose from their original history. The imperial Greek commitment to the literature and culture of "ancient Greece" thus is as much an act of assimilation as it is an act of self-definition through difference.

In rhetoric's disciplinary ordering of the body, in the adoption of a set of texts that had for generations overlapped with the reading preferences of educated Romans, and in the globalizing discourse of cosmopolitanism, I have argued that we see the reorientation of Hellenism, a reorientation I view as a founding moment in its gradual translation into "classicism." While emphasizing attachments to a sharply delimited geographical and temporal space – the democratic Athenian past and its culture of epic and lyric song – imperial classicism erases the political specificity of its past in favor of a transcendent domestication, Hellenism as a discourse of universal culture and the underpinning of empire. Classicism emerges as an instrument simultaneously of cultural difference and accommodation to the dominant order. The freedom promised by a classical education in the liberal arts is stamped by the knowledge of freedom lost – a past loss that in turn justifies present patterns and practices of domination. The imperial travel writer Pausanias recalls that after a brief period of exemption under Nero, the emperor Vespasian re-established taxes and a Roman governor in Achaia, remarking that the Greeks "have forgotten to be free" (7.17.2). Imperial memories of the independence of the ancient city-state (especially democratic Athens) are always accompanied by reminders that that independence was the cause of Greece's fall. The insistent bracketing of time that is usually interpreted as imperial nostalgia or appropriation of past greatness – the Eratosthenean identification of the death of Alexander as the "end of history" – is also a symptom of the imperial fetishization of the end. A new definition of "Hellenism" emerges: a love affair with the memory of failure.

The Greek literary canon was seen as promoting a set of values related to social identity, especially individual freedom. The process of deracination that accompanies the formation of Hellenism as classicism underway in imperial Greece reveals a fault line in the emergent notion of "the classical." When texts that emerged from a democratic culture of political equality and freedom under the law are used as the touchstones of identity formation under monarchy, what it means to be free, to exercise free speech, and to express dissent must be violently depoliticized. Thus Aelius Aristides can plausibly call Rome "the democracy of the whole world" (κοινὴ τῆς γῆς δημοκρατία, *On Rome* 60), the "only empire to rule over men who are truly free" (μόνοι γὰρ τῶν πώποτε ἐλευθέρων ἄρχετε, 36–38), while Athenaeus describes it in suggestively literary terms "the epitome of the civilized world" (τὴν ἐπιτομὴν τῆς οἰκουμένης, 1.20b). Through memory preserved by a shared, selected list of literary works, the social imaginary of classical Athens posits a shared culture of amity in the face of real social, linguistic, and cultural division, an imperial cultural identity for both Greek and Roman elites. This in turn enables another kind of imagination that serves dominant interests: seeing themselves as consumers and preservers of ancient Greece, Greeks and Romans can, as Dionysius and Aristides put it, think themselves "lovers of the people" and members of a peaceful, secure worldwide "democracy."

Hans Gadamer speaks of a "historical process of preservation that through the constant proving of itself sets before us something that is true."[44] If "classical Greece" becomes "true" through the intensive process of rereading I have described, it also loses contact with the lived truth of Athenian democracy, with irremediable consequences for the meaning of "freedom" that is, literally, the way we and the ancient Romans alike speak of education: the *liberales artes* or "liberal arts."[45] This view of "ancient Greece" lies at the heart of "the classical." The font of culture, Athenian democracy in the fifth and fourth centuries BCE, is emptied of its political specificity in the act of enshrining it as the font of culture; and over time, as it is read, preserved, copied, memorized, studied, cited, and so on, the text becomes, not a sign of freedom remembered, but a sign of freedom that enshrines wthin itself the memory of freedom destroyed.

What does it mean to say that "classical Greece" is largely a creation of antiquity? In a thoughtful essay, Barry Strauss has explored Thucydides' decision to write the "history of the Peloponnesian war" as just that – a single conflict lasting from 431 to 404 BCE – in the face of contemporaries or near-contemporaries (including Aristophanes, Plato, and the orators Andocides and Lysias) who viewed the period as embracing two or three different wars. At stake here, Strauss argues, is the construction of historical memory, which in turn shapes future practice: many a war has been justified on past models.[46]

Certain central aspects of "the classical," and in particular, "classical education" – the practices of identity formation that inculcate and advertise classical values – exist in modernity in the idealizing form of liberal education. My historicization of Greek Hellenism under the Roman empire is intended to prompt critique of the conception of freedom implied by the label "liberal education." In short, I am asking: in what sense may we call education "liberal," when both its

---

44 Gadamer (cf. fn. 8) 255.
45 By speaking of the "lived truth" of Athenian democracy, I am not denying the real inequalities and injustices deeply rooted in Athenian society, from slavery to imperialistic militarism to the denial of civic rights to women and foreigners. But I think it is a mistake to say that those inequalities make it impossible to speak of Athens as a free state, especially when the context is clearly the way in which Athens *was remembered* in later (more or less unjust) ages.
46 Strauss, Barry S. "The problem of periodization: the case of the Peloponnesian war." In Inventing *Ancient Culture: Historicism, Periodization, and the Ancient World.* Mark Golden and Peter Toohey, eds. London and New York, 1997, 165–7.

historical roots and much of contemporary educational practice so deeply embedded in structures of illiberal governance? Is there an essential connection between the pedagogical and the political, or may the two be disentangled in such a way that the pedagogical is preserved and its liberal aims reconstituted?

Early in this essay, I asked whether it was possible to work from an analysis of Greek and Roman identity politics in the imperial period toward an answer to the question "why the past, and why this particular past," is chosen as the privileged site of identity formation in the empire and beyond? Athens of the fifth and fourth century BCE (bundled together with its own literary culture, Homer and the lyric poets) is chosen as the privileged source of the classical, I suggest, because politically speaking, democratic Athens was free. This makes freedom (or rather, the memory of freedom) a central aspect of "the classical." In the historical conditions under which that notion is invented and elaborated, however, the political values of democratic freedom are reduced to proof of membership in classicizing Hellenic "high culture" – and its "proper" claims to political power and social authority. I am not saying, in a mode of glib self-abjection, that freedom is an illusion, but rather that we should understand the ways in which the human good of freedom is vulnerable to appropriation by discourses and practices – like education – which do not always serve its ends. This, as I understand it, is the value of understanding the evolution of ancient notions of identity, where rhetorical education and philosophical cosmopolitanism helped transform Hellenism into a discourse of political subservience and deracination, in a strategy that helped conceal the contradictions and brutalities of Roman imperial rule – a concealment that classicism and its ideology of freedom-reinscribed-as-dominance is called upon to play over and over again in western history.

These points offer, I believe, a useful critique of contemporary practice in the humanities. The intermittent but intense pressure to transform the teaching of literature into entertainment (asking students whether they "like" the texts they read) or corporate indoctrination (teaching writing styles that suit the company cubicle) – even the universalist defense of liberal arts education – are issues to which the ancient experience directly relates. Not literally, of course, antiquity and modernity being too distant from each other for that claim to be plausible, but conceptually, the way in which ancient classicism is implicated in the discourse and interests of empire sheds light on the implication of our professional discourse in the humanities in globalized capitalism and the corporatization of the academy. It is easy to forget the geopolitics of education, the interests it sustains and the identities it suppresses. Understanding the constitutive ideological flexibility of "the classical" should prompt left and right alike to reconsider the moralizing assumptions we make about the link between education, identity, and freedom. In short, by historicizing the ancient invention of the classical past, and in particular by asking the Roman jurist's question *cui bono?*, "for whose profit" was it invented in the first place?, we may free ourselves to view the classical past in new ways, and we may better understand why western pedagogy has so insistently and for so long reclaimed classical Greece, or rather, "classical Greece," as its special domain.[47]

Abstract

In the second century CE, Greeks living throughout the Roman empire consolidated the Hellenistic Greek invention of the great "classical" past, centred on the history and literature of Athens in the fifth and fourth centuries BCE, by writing travel guides, building library collections, studying a small list of carefully selected texts, even reviving outdated dialects of spoken Greek. This reconstructed Athens was the primary point of reference in practices of identity formation, especially education, for Greek elites under Rome. Recent scholarship has argued that the pursuit of a "classical," "Attic" ideal served to separate Greek from Roman, cementing exclusive Greek ownership of a tradition whose cultural glories compensated for the political subordination of the Roman-dominated present. This essay defends a different interpretation of imperial Hellenism. First, it argues, precisely because the Greeks constructed Athens as a universal model of human greatness, classical Hellenism turned out to be a habit available to all, including the Romans who had conquered Greece. If Athens could be claimed as the model for refined human culture on a global scale, it was Roman military might that made its memory and continued cultural circulation possible. Second, the habits of thought and practice advocated by classical Hellenism, especially training in rhetoric and Stoic-style cosmopolitanism, promoted a worldview peculiarly favorable to imperial, unified government. Classical Hellenism thus not only accommodated itself to the demands of empire; it provided imperial elites with a common cultural heritage that justifies and celebrates empire.

Like most disciplines, classical philology tends to avoid critical investigations of its own history. The paper concludes with the reminder that some Greek imperial attitudes continue to shape our professional self-image and our own disciplinary uses of the past. It calls for a close look at the way classical Hellenism's ideological flexibility anticipates the modern academy's tendency to accommodate current structures of inequality and injustice.

---

47   I am very grateful to Stephen Hinds and Thomas Schmitz for their invitation to the German-American Frontiers of the Humanities conference for which this paper originated, and for their editorial interventions at a later stage. I would like to thank Michael Peachin for his helpful comments on a draft, and to Jim Porter and Michèle Lowrie for their insights into classicism and Roman Hellenism.

Shifting Identities.
Knowledge and the Construction of Social Roles in the Roman Empire

HELMUT KRASSER

Ernst A. Schmidt zum 70. Geburtstag

1. The multiple identities of king Philopappos

In the years 114–116 c. e. Athens saw a remarkable monument being erected for a remarkable man. The location chosen for this tomb was nothing else but the hill of the muses right in the centre of Athens, and it even surpassed the acropolis in height.[1] The man in whose memory this monument was built was C. Iulius Antiochus Epiphanes Philopappus, the son of the king of Commagene, archon of Athens, member of the Roman fraternity of arval priests and consul suffectus two years after Pliny the younger. Both words and images commemorate his noble birth, his accomplishments and the honours he had been granted. On the upper frieze we encounter Philopappus surrounded by his ancestors, nude just like the gods; this representation recalls the traditional image of hellenistic rulers. The zone below shows him as a roman consul, wearing a toga and driving a four-hourse carriage. The inscription reflects this double aspect: it is bilingual, Latin and Greek.[2]

What strikes us most is the combination of rather different and, at first sight, even contradictory modes of self-representation within one and the same monu-

---

1   I wish to thank Vera Binder, Katharina Lorenz and Ulrike Egelhaaf-Gaiser for their great assistance in translating and discussing my paper. For the monument see Travlos, John 1971, *Bildlexikon zur Topographie des antiken Athen*, Tübingen, 462–465 (with fig. 585–587); on the kind of self-fashioning Miles, Richard, "Communicating culture, identity and power", in: Huskinson, Janet (ed.) 2000, *Experiencing Rome. culture, Identity and Power in the Roman Empire*, London; New York, 29–36.

2   *Orientis Graeci Inscriptiones selectae* (OGIS) 409–413. The statues are furnished with inscribed identifications: in Greek language Βασιλεὺς Ἀντίοχος Φιλόπαππος βασιλέως Ἐπιφανοῦς τοῦ Ἀντίοχου. Βασιλεὺς Σέλευκος Ἀντίοχου Νικάτωρ. Βασιλεὺς Ἀντίοχος βασιλέως Ἀντίοχου. The Latin inscription puts forward the Roman credentials of Philopappus: *C. Iulius C. f. Fab. Antiochus Philopappus cos., frater arvalis, allectus inter praetorios ab imp(eratore) Caesare Nerva Traiano Optumo Augusto Germanico Dacico.* Other inscriptions for Philopappus exist in Lycosura (OGIS 407) and Egypt (OGIS 408). On the dynasty of Commagene see Sullivan, Richard D. 1977, "The Dynasty of Commagene", in: Hildegard Temporini; Wolfgang Haase (edd.), *Aufstieg und Niedergang der römischen Welt* II 8, Berlin; New York, esp. 796–797 (Philopappus and Balbilla).

ment: different local traditions and different social roles coalesce to create the image of one and the same individual. We see a Greek Basileus and a Roman Consul in direct confrontation and yet, both images, in their respective separate frames, contribute to form a whole and integral impression in the eyes of the beholder. We can be confident that in contemporary Athens there existed a public capable to decipher the complex message this monument conveys. Philopappus, being of royal descent and highly elevated social status is, of course, an exceptional case. But nonetheless, we are entitled to regard his way of self-fashioning as typical of his time and his class. It is the normal way the élite wished to be represented. In this monument, the plurality of the Roman Empire manifests itself in an exemplary way; we see how the leading class had multiple constructions of their own identity at their disposal to be employed, either partially in single aspects or in its whole range, in accordance to the intended public and the respective situation.[3] References to local traditions – for example, the Polis and its specific cults or the region[4] – and imperial structures and mentalities accompany and complement each other.[5] This observation is valid not only for the East; we find an interest for local knowledge in the West as well. What provides a coherent framework for this diversity of traditions is the shared ideal of paideia. It is not only the emperor, the army and the law who build up a common

3   The problem of Greek identity in the Roman empire is actually much discussed, e.g.: Swain, Simon C.R. 1996, *Hellenism and Empire. Language, classicism, and power in the Greek World AD 50–250*, Oxford; Schmitz, Thomas 1997, "Bildung und Macht. Zur sozialen und politischen Funktion der zweiten Sophistik in der griechischen Welt der Kaiserzeit", *Zetemata* 97, München, 175–181; Huskinson (cf. fn. 1); Whitmarsh, Tim 2001, *Greek Literature and the Roman Empire. The Politics of Imitation*, Oxford; New York; Goldhill, Simon (ed.) 2001, *Being Greek under Rome. The second sophistic, cultural conflict and the development of the roman empire*, Cambridge; Malkin, Irad (ed.) 2001, *Ancient Perceptions of Greek Ethnicity, Center for Hellenic Studies Colloquia 5*, Cambridge; Stephan, Eckhard 2002, *Honoratioren, Griechen, Polisbürger. Kollektive Identitäten innerhalb der Oberschicht des kaiserzeitlichen Kleinasien*, Hypomnemata 143, Göttingen; Jones, Christopher P. 2004, "Multiple identities in the age of the second sophistic", in: Borg, Barbara E. 2004, *Paideia. The world of the second sophistic*, Millennium-Studien 2, Berlin; New York, 13–21.
4   On the city-festivals in the empire Stephan (cf. fn. 3) 122–140; 229–235; the significance of local traditions becomes obvious in the epideictic *encomia* of the cities (Dion of Prusa, Aelius Aristides, Menander Rhetor) as well as in learned *aitia* and local histories (e.g. Pausanias). See further Touloumakos, Johannes 1971, *Zum Geschichtsbewußtsein der Griechen in der Zeit der römischen Herrschaft*, Göttingen, 55–79; Bowie, Ewen L. 1974. "The Greeks and their past in the second sophistic", in: M.I. Finley (ed.), *Studies in ancient society*, London, 166–209; Swain (cf. fn. 3) 65–100; Schmitz (cf. fn. 3) 181–196; Stephan (cf. fn. 3) 22–24; 208–222.
5   Against the hypothesis of 'cultural resistance' by the Greeks Touloumakos (cf. fn. 4) 75; Schmitz (cf. fn. 3) 178–179; Stephan (cf. fn. 3) 246–260.

horizon in the context of an Empire; it is *paideia* who allows identification and permits orientation.[6] Philopappus, by the way, is an excellent example of the phenomenon I have just described. His noble descent and his conspicuous position in society and politics have already been mentioned. But this remarkable man could boast of further qualities which guaranteed his prestige among his contemporaries: namely, his erudition together with the ability to show it off in an elegant fashion. In Plutarch's table-talks, a highly interesting document of Greco-Roman discourse, he figures among the participants, and Plutarch does not fail to mention that he qualifies as philanthropos and philomathes to a high degree.[7] These are the basic and, I may add, scarcely contested assumptions for my following considerations. In which way, I would like to ask, and with which intentions are social roles combined and employed? I am going to concentrate on the significance of cultural knowledge, intellectual practice, literary performance, the combining of Greek and Latin stock knowledge and ways of life: in short, I would like to elucidate the importance of paideia in imperial constructions of identity and the variety of ways in which paideia is employed to serve this purpose. Furthermore, I would like sketch the relevant factors for this development and the ways in which the manipulation of cultural knowledge undergoes changes in the first and second centuries c. e.

Let us start with a glimpse of the times of Augustus which should be considered as the formative phase of these phenomena. Let me just name two observations:

It was during Augustus' reign that the Roman empire began to be established as a common horizon of self-perception. It is being referred to on different levels and in different media.[8] During these times emphasis is being put on representa-

---

6   The relevance and the media of *paideia* in the construction of identity is discussed by Schmitz (cf. fn. 3); Borg (cf. fn. 3).

7   Plut. *quaest. conv.* 1,10 (*mor.* 628A): ἔσχε γὰρ ὁ ἀγὼν ἐντονωτάτην ἅμιλλαν, ἀγωνοθετοῦντος ἐνδόξως καὶ μεγαλοπρεπῶς Φιλοπάππου τοῦ βασιλέως ταῖς φυλαῖς ὁμοῦ πάσαις χορηγοῦντος. ἐτύγχανε δὲ συνεστιώμενος ἡμῖν καὶ τῶν παλαιῶν τὰ μὲν λέγων τὰ δ' ἀκούων διὰ φιλανθρωπίαν οὐχ ἧττον ἢ φιλομάθειαν.

8   E.g. Agrippa's monumental map of the Augustan empire, exposed in the *Porticus Vipsania* in Rome (Dilke, Oswald A. W. 1985, *Greek and Roman Maps*, London, 41–53); the *milliarium aureum*, the virtual crosspoint of all Roman roads in the centre of the Forum Romanum (erected 20b. c.); the spatial administration of Rome and Italy by newly organized regions (Nicolet, Claude 1996, *L'inventaire du monde. Géographie et politiique aux origines del'Empire romain*, Paris, esp. 265–290); the monumental *horologium* on the campus Martius; the reformation and spreading of the roman calendar (Rüpke, Jörg 1995, „Kalender und Öffentlichkeit. Die Geschichte der Repräsentation und religiösen Qualifikation von Zeit in Rom", *Religionsgeschichtliche Versuche und Vorarbeiten* 40, Berlin; New York, 165–188); the increasing number of uni-

tion of dominance, of abundance of ressources and disponibility of both material and immaterial goods. As an example we may cite Pliny the Elder: the geographical books not only supply detailed information on the nature and customs of the respective territories, but view the oikoumene under the aspect of Roman dominance.[9] Secondly, with the establishment of the principate, the princeps begins to monopolize the fields of competition of the former ruling class. It is the princeps who celebrates a triumph, and nobody else.[10] Thus, the elite found the normal republican career-track and the usual access to fame and renown at least partly barred. Of course, political engagement did not lose its attraction, and high-ranking personalities did not cease to proudly commemorate their involvement in high politics and list the ranks and offices attained on tomb monuments, honorary statues and inscriptions, but nevertheless, the all-embracing importance of the princeps, the far-reaching administrative reforms, most notably the professionalization of civil servants, entailed a diminishing relevance of formerly undisputed honours. The nobility had to look for other goals, for other accomplishments to boast of and other achievements to strive for. The traditional forms of self-representation were, to be sure, far from being abandoned, but still, they were no longer regarded as sufficient and came to be supplemented by new aspects. Political power and influence still conferred marks of distinction, but

---

versal histories and geographic works (Diodorus Siculus, Strabo, Pomponius Trogus: Clarke, Katherine 1999, "Universal Perspectives in Historiography", in: Christina Shuttleworth Kraus (ed.), *The Limits of Historiography. Genre and Narrative in Ancient Historical Texts*, Mnemosyne Suppl. 191, Leiden; Boston; Köln, 249–279) as well as the archivistic studies of the Antiquarians (Varro); the founding of public libraries (Balensiefen, Lilian 2002, "Die Macht der Literatur. Über die Büchersammlungen des Augustus auf dem Palatin", in: Wolfram Hoepfner (ed.), *Antike Bibliotheken*, Mainz, 97–116). For the processes of universalizing in the Augustan principate Krasser, Helmut 2005, "Universalisierung und Identitätskonstruktion. Formen und Funktionen der Wissenskodifikation im kaiserzeitlichen Rom", in: Günter Oesterle (ed.), *Erinnerung, Gedächtnis, Wissen.Studien zur kulturwissenschaftlichen Gedächtnisforschung*, Formen der Erinnerung 26, Göttingen 2005, 357–375 .

9   Conte, Gian Biagio 1991, "L' inventario del mondo. Forma della natura e progetto enciclopedico nell'opera di Plinio il Vecchio", in: Gian Biagio Conte, *Genere e lettori*, Mailand 1991, 95–144; Naas, Valérie 2002, "Le projet encyclopédique de Pline l'ancien", *Collection de l'école française de Rome* 303, Rom; Carey, Sorcha 2003, *Pliny's Catalogue of culture. Art and Empire in the Natural History*, Oxford; Murphy, Trevor 2004, *Pliny the Elder's Natural History. The empire in the encyclopedia*, Oxford; Krasser, Helmut 2006, "Plinius der Ältere. Imperium und Enzyklopädie", in: Helmut Krasser/Friedrich Vollhardt (edd.), *Schatzkammern des Wissens. Wissensspeicher und Medien der Bildungskultur*, Formen der Erinnerung, Göttingen (forthcoming).

10 Künzl, Ernst 1988, *Der römische Triumph. Siegesfeiern im antiken Rom*, München, 119–133.

now, there were other roads to gain high reputation as well, one of the most important being commitment to culture. Demonstration of cultural superiority was one of the most favoured means to distinguish oneself and to display excellence. These structural changes within Roman society bestowed a new dignity on erudition and knowledge. To be aware of local traditions, of facts and, equally often, fictions from all parts of the Empire, particularly, as is to be expected, from the Greek-speaking East, in short, to command a treasury of knowledge played a major part in acquiring and affirming social status and in constructing one's own identity as a member of the leading class. Occasions and opportunities to put this superiority on display were numerous. You could be a collector or launch a donation, you could fund a poet or be a poet yourself. You might excel in the art of elegant conversation or become an acknowledged master of erudite discussion. You could be a brillant essayist or a thrilling orator.

At this point, I would like to discuss the Roman senator Pliny the Younger, the 'professional' poet Statius and the Latin sophist Apuleius as three examples to illustrate these possibilities of cultural practice and their relevance for the construction and demonstration of one's own identity. At the same time, these examples are intended to show in which ways Roman and Greek features and attitudes are amalgamated.

2. *paideia* in the network of cultural communication: Pliny and Statius

One of the most obvious examples is a member of the Roman upper class, namely Pliny the Younger. As he has been treated exhaustively in recent research,[11] I will restrict myself to some general remarks. His activities are notoriously numerous and variegated. Thus, he combines different ways of self-fashioning and can be seen as a Roman equivalent to Philopappus. Manifold are his businesses. He pursues an extensive career,[12] serves several official duties, acts as orator and

---

11 Ludolph, Matthias 1997, "Epistolographie und Selbstdarstellung. Untersuchung zu den 'Paradebriefen' 'Plinius' des Jüngeren", *Classica Monacensia* 17, Tübingen; Hoffer, Stanley E. 1999, *The Anxieties of Pliny the Younger*, Atlanta; Beutel, Frank 2000, *Vergangenheit als Politik. Neue Aspekte im Werk des jüngeren Plinius*, Frankfurt; Luigi Castagna/Eckard Lefèvre (edd.) 2003, *Plinius der Jüngere und seine Zeit*, Beiträge zur Altertumskunde 187, München; Leipzig; various articles in *Arethusa* 36 (2003); Pausch, Dennis 2004, *Biographie und Bildungskultur. Personendarstellungen bei Plinius dem Jüngeren, Gellius und Sueton*, Millennium-Studien Berling; New York, 51–146.

12 See *Corpus Inscriptionum Latinarum* (CIL) V 5262 and Strobel, Karl 1983, "Laufbahn und Vermächtnis des jüngeren Plinius. Zu CIL V 5262", in: Werner Huß/Karl

advocate[13] and shows himself a generous Euergetes in his home-town Como where he builds a public library.[14] Poets from all over the Empire have him to thank for lavish grants.[15] Even more, he is an amateur poet himself.[16] His most important work are, of course, his letters, a collection he compiled and published himself. Here, we see him diligently constructing a complex image of himself where all these different facets are adroitly combined, culture and education being associated mainly with Pliny's leisure life.[17] His cultural commitment permits him even to place himself on the same footing as Cicero: at least in this respect he can, so are we supposed to understand, match his great role-model.[18] But there is another aspect that research has tended to slightly underestimate: it is not only his private life that is constitutive of his self-representation, but his public life as well. Culture, education and erudition do not belong exclusively to Pliny's private life, but play an important part in his official life. Commitment to culture

Strobel (edd.), *Beiträge zur Geschichte*, Bamberger Hochschulschriften 9, Bamberg, 37–56; Eck, Werner 2001, „Die große Pliniusinschrift aus Comum. Funktion und Monument", in: Gabriella Angeli Bertinelli/Angela Donati (edd.), *Varia Epigraphica. Atti del Colloquio Internazionale di Epigrafia, Bertinoro, 8–10 giugno 2000*, Faenza, 225–235.

13 Nicols, John 1980, "Pliny and the Patronage of Communities", *Hermes* 108, 365–385; Riggsby, Andrew M. 1998., "Self and Community in the Younger Pliny", *Arethusa* 31, 75–98; Mayer, Roland 2003, "Pliny and *gloria dicendi*", *Arethusa* 36, 227–234.

14 Krasser, Helmut 1996, *"Sine fine lecturias"*. *Zu Leseszenen und literarischen Wahrnehmungsgewohnheiten zwischen Cicero und Gellius*, unpubl. Habilitation Tübingen, 135–141; Manuwald, Gesine 2003, "Eine 'Schule' für novum Comum (*epist.* 4,13). Aspekte der *liberalitas* des Plinius", in: Castagna/ Lefèvre (cf. fn. 11), 203–217.

15 E.g. Martial (*epist.* 3,21), Sueton (*epist.* 24); Vergilius Romanus (*epist.* 6,21); Arrius Antoninus (*epist.* 4,3; 4,18). On Pliny as patron of literature Rühl, Meike 2004, *Zwischen Okkasionalität und Professionalität. Die Silven des Statius im Kontext sozialer und literarischer Bedingungen von Dichtung im ausgehenden 1. Jh. n. Chr.*, unpubl. Diss. Gießen, chapter 2.

16 E.g. *epist.* 4,14; 4,27; 5,10; 7,4. See further Krasser, Helmut 1997, *Poesie und Freundschaft. Zur Catull-Rezeption im 1. Jahrhundert n. Chr.*, unpubl. lecture Tübingen; Roller, M. 1998, "Pliny's Catullus. The Politics of Literary Appropriation", *Transactions and Proceedings of the American Philological Association* 128, 265–304.

17 See Leach, Eleanor W. 1990, "The Politics of Self-Presentation. Pliny's Letters and Roman Portrait Sculpture", *Classical Antiquity* 9, 14–40; Radicke, Jan 1997, "Die Selbstdarstellung des Plinius in seinen Briefen", *Hermes* 125, 447–469; Radicke Jan 2003, "Der öffentliche Privatbrief als ‚Kommunizierte Kommunikation' (Plin. *epist.* 4,28)", in: Castagna/Lefèvre (cf. fn. 11), 23–34.

18 On Pliny's imitation of Cicero Riggsby (cf. fn. 13); Lefèvre, Eckard 1996, "Pliniusstudien VII. Cicero, das unerreichbare Vorbild", *Gymnasium* 103, 333–353; Wenskus, O. 1999, "‚Gespräche' unter Freunden. Rhetorik als Briefthema bei Cicero und Plinius", in: Siegmar Döpp (ed.), *Antike Rhetorik und ihre Rezeption. Symposion zu Ehren von Professor Carl Joachim Classen*, Stuttgart, 29–40.

is also a crucial feature of Pliny the public person. At least, this is the reading I would propose for the 10th book of collection, dedicated to the exchange of letters between the princeps Trajan and Pliny in his position as provincial governor of Bithynia. It should not be seen as an accidental appendix, come down to us through historical coincidence, but as an integral part of Pliny's self-fashioning by means of publishing a selection of his letters. Here, Pliny puts his social and political role on the literary stage.[19] Pliny shifts social roles in a most elegant and efficient manner; in the end, Pliny emerges as a person endowed with multiple identities, but always as as incarnation of relevant collective values. Pliny, in this manner, both reaffirms and propagates these values as collective values, reached at by a consensus of relevant people. The fact that he generally names his addressees and that he inserts several letters containing portraits and characterizations of his fellow nobles underlines the consensual and collective character of these values: these values are, above all, values shared by valuable persons. So we can interpret his collection of letters as an idealizing portrait of a group Pliny belongs to and a means of creating, confirming and reinforcing a group identity.[20]

Another example of how cultural activities represent a decisive element in the formation of a collective identity is provided by the poet Statius, roughly a contemporary of Pliny. Statius was born and raised in Greek-speaking Naples; he grew up in a society where Greek language and culture dominated. But he started his literary career as a poet on demand in Latin, his patrons belonging to the Roman upper class. The *Silvae* – this is the title of his collection of occasional poetry – reflect equally well as do Pliny's letters social standards and collective identity-creating values of Roman nobles. Originally, these poems were ordered and therefore written for private recitations and for circulation within a very restricted public, namely the closer friends and relations of the addressee.[21] It was his self-representation they were intended to promote. A splendid banquet, a country house or a garden landscape, magnificent baths, decorated with choice marble form the vital elements of these poems, together with specific events such as marriages or even deaths.[22] But the overarching aspect under which all these different subjects are subsumed is a gentleman's adequate behaviour and impeccable conduct; Statius accentuates the addressee's cultural competences and

---

19   See e.g. *epist.* 10,41 and 10,61; 10,70 (building projects of an aqueduct and a public bath); *epist.* 10,8 (statues for an imperial sanctuary); 10,81 (statue in honor of the princeps Trajan in a library).

20   On the network of the provincial élite in the Transpadana Mratschek-Halfmann, Sigrid 2003, "*Illa nostra Italia.* Plinius und die Wiedergeburt der Literatur in der Transpadana", in: Castagna/Lefèvre (cf. fn. 11), 219–241.

21   See Rühl (cf. fn. 15) chapter 3.6.

22   E.g. *silv.* 4,6 (banquet); 1,3 (villa); 1,5 (bath); 1,2 (marriage); 2,6 (death).

achievements. Connoisseurship, taste and education are the most salient features.[23] Let us consider one of the most convincing examples: Silva 4.6. The poem is dedicated to Novius Vindex who obviously had gained a certain prominence as an art collector, preferably of small objects. In this poem, Statius imagines an invitation to join a banquet at Vindex's place; central theme of the poem is a Herakles Epitrapezios, a small statue of Herakles used to adorn a table at the symposium.[24] Statius first gives an introduction into the situation, quoting Horace's satires (I will return to that), then continues to give a characterization of Vindex as a brillant connoisseur of art and a collector of no mean significance.

mille ibi tunc species aerisque eborisque vetusti
atque locuturas mentito corpore ceras
edidici. quis namque oculis certaverit usquam
Vindicis, artificum veteres agnoscere ductus
et non inscriptis auctorem reddere signis?
hic tibi quae docto multum vigilata Myroni
aera, laboriferi vivant quae marmora caelo
Praxitelis, quod ebur Pisaeo pollice rasum,
quid Polycleteis iussum spirare caminis,
linea quae veterem longe fateatur Apellen,
monstrabit: namque haec, quotiens chelyn exuit, illi
desidia est, hic Aoniis amor avocat antris.

There and then did I learn of a thousand beauties of bronze and ancient ivory, and deceiving shapes of wax on the verge of speech. For who ever rivalled the keen glance of Vindex in recognizing the hand of an old master and telling the author of an untitled work? 'Tis he who will show you on what bronzes cunning Myron spent anxious vigils, what marbles the chisel of untiring Praxiteles has made to live, what ivories the thumb of the Pisaean has smoothed, what statues have been bidden breathe in Polyclitus' furnaces, what lines confess from afar the old Apelles; for this, whensoe'er he puts his lyre from him, is his leisure, this passion calls him from Aonian dells. (vv 20–31)

23　See Krasser, Helmut 2003, "Poeten, Papageien und Patrone. Statius Silve 2,4 als Beispiel einer kulturwissenschaftlichen Textinterpretation", in: Jürgen-Paul Schwindt (ed.), *Klassische Philologie inter disciplinas. Aktuelle Konzepte zu Gegenwart und Methode eines Grundlagenfaches,* Heidelberg, 151–168. on *silv.* 2,3.

24　On the poem in general Cancik-Lindemaier, Hildegard 1971, "Ein Mahl vor Hercules. Ein Versuch zu Statius, Silve IV 6: Hercules Epitrapezios", *Der Altsprachliche Unterricht* 14.3, 43–65; Coleman, K.M. 1988, *Statius* Silvae *IV. Ed. with an translation and commentary*, Oxford, 173–194; Henriksén, Christer 1998, "Martial and Statius", in: Farouk Grewing (ed.), Toto notus in orbe. *Perspektiven der Martial-interpretation,* Palingenesia 65, Stuttgart, 108–111; Newlands, Carole E. 2002, *Statius' Silvae and the poetics of empire,* Cambridge, 73–87; Rühl (cf. fn. 15) chapter 5.5.

After these introductory remarks Statius turns his attention to the statuette, sculpted, as Statius observes – a connoisseur himself – by Lysippus' own hand, and gives a detailed ekphrasis of this delicate work of art. In his typical manner, Statius evokes overwhelming feelings of astonishment and admiration thereby signalling the adequate manner in which one should react when given the opportunity to marvel at Vindex's treasures. But the small statue, lively and charming as it is to behold, has even more attractions to offer: there is a highly interesting story behind it, full of historical depth.

> *Digna operi fortuna sacro. Pellaeus habebat*
> *regnator laetis numen venerabile mensis*
> *et comitem occasus secum portabat et ortus,*
> *praestabatque libens modo qua diademata dextra*
> *abstulerat dederatque et magnas verterat urbes.*
> *semper ab hoc animos in crastina bella petebat,*
> *huic acies semper victor narrabat opimas,*
> *sive catenatos Bromio detraxerat Indos,*
> *seu clusam magna Babylona refregerat hasta,*
> *seu Pelopis terras libertatemque Pelasgam*
> *obruerat bello; magnoque ex agmine laudum*
> *fertur Thebanos tantum excusasse triumphos.*
> *ille etiam, magnos fatis rumpentibus actus,*
> *cum traheret letale merum, iam mortis opaca*
> *nube gravis vultus alios in numine caro*
> *aeraque supremis timuit sudantia mensis.*
>   *Mox Nasamoniaco decus admirabile regi*
> *possessum; fortique deo libavit honores*
> *semper atrox dextra periuroque ense superbus*
> *Hannibal. Italicae perfusum sanguine gentis*
> *diraque Romuleis portantem incendia tectis*
> *oderat, et cum epulas, et cum Lenaea dicaret*
> *dona, deus castris maerens comes ire nefandis,*
> *praecipue cum sacrilega face miscuit arces*
> *ipsius immeritaeque domos ac templa Sagunti*
> *polluit et populis Furias immisit honestas.*
>   *Nec post Sidonii letum ducis aere potita*
> *egregio plebeia domus. convivia Syllae*
> *ornabat semper claros intrare penates*
> *assuetum et felix dominorum stemmate signum.*

So divine a work had a worthy fate.
It was a deity revered at the merry banquets of the Pellaean monarch, and alike in East and West it bore him company; gladly did he set it before him, with that same hand that had given crowns and taken them away, and had ruined mighty cities. From it he sought courage for to-morrow's battle, to it he related, triumphant, the glorious fight,

whether he bad despoiled Bromius of fettered Indians, or with his strong spear bad burst the enclosing walls of Babylon, or overwhelmed in war the lands of Pelops and Pelasgian freedom; and of all that tale of mighty deeds he is said to have asked pardon only for his Theban triumph. He too, when the Fates cut short his prowess, and he drank the deadly draught, in the very gloom and heaviness of death, was afraid at the altered face of his favourite deity, and at the bronzes that dripped sweat at that last banquet.

Next its marvellous beauty was possessed by the Nasamonian chief; and Hannibal, that ruthless warrior, haughty and treacherous in fight, paid honours to the valiant god. Yet the god hated him, drenched in Italian blood and threatening Roman homes with terrible flame, ay, even when he set feasting and gifts of wine before him; in sorrow did the god go forth with that cursed troop, especially when his own shrines were impiously fired, when the homes and temples of innocent Saguntum were outraged, and its people filled with righteous frenzy.

And after the death of the Sidonian leader 'twas no plebeian house obtained the peerless bronze. Ever wont to enter famous houses and blest in the lineage of its lords it adorned the feasts of Sulla. (vv. 59–88)

Among the alleged former possessors count, lo and behold!, no lesser persons than Alexander the Great, Hannibal and Sulla. Statius treats himself to a parade of these illustrious ancestors in a series of small emblematic portraits, employing all his extensive historical knowledge to imagine situations of the past in which these great men might have made use of this Herakles Epitrapezios – situations of course which are suitable to illustrate the, to say the least, not always undisputed character of the respective owner. These figures of the past, now, form the background against which the actual owner Novius Vindex can be portrayed most favourably: he is the one in whose abode the god will dwell permanently.

> *Nunc quoque, si mores humanaque pectora curae*
> *nosse deis, non aula quidem, Tirynthie, nec te*
> *regius ambit honos, sed casta ignaraque culpae*
> *mens domini, cui prisca fides coeptaeque perenne*
> *foedus amicitiae.*

Now too, if deities care to know the hearts and souls of men, no palace, no royal Pomp surrounds thee, O Tirynthian, but thy master's soul is pure and innocent of error; old-world loyalty is his, and the unfailing bond of a friendship once begun. (vv. 89–93)

In my opinion, this poem gives us two important items of information concerning our initial question.

Let us first consider the message of the text.

We have seen how this poem confirms the decisive role of cultural competence for affirming social status and creating collective identity. To reach his aim, Statius employs different textual strategies. First, he explicitly names desirable features and abilities of a nobleman – connoisseurship, historical knowledge, a gift for poetry – and attributes them to his addressee. At the same time he pictures the environment where such a style of living finds its natural home. Secondly, there is also an implicit level in his poetic presentation. The bare fact that his patron obviously considers a poetic text as a suitable medium of self-representation – otherwise he would not have ordered the poem in the first place – qualifies him as a cultured and educated man. On the textual level, this message is further intensified: Statius inserts into his text a panoply of intertextual allusions, quotations and hints that nobody but a very well-read reader will be able to decipher. Thus, by naming Vindex as addressee, Statius explicitly attributes to Vindex himself and all the readers who have attained the same level of education, the qualities mentioned above; implicitly he attributes to them the ability to appreciate this complex text with all the literary tradition behind it, and thus portrays both Vindex and the expert reader as men with a highly refined literary taste.

Let us now consider the message of the statuette. The symbolic potential of the statuette, a Greek god who makes his home in a Roman household, is enormous. Just by naming the god Hercules Epitrapezios, a Greek name in its latinized form combined with a purely Greek epithet, Statius emphasizes the merging of Roman and Greek culture. This is reinforced by telling the story behind the statue and by mentioning Alexander, Hannibal and Sulla. In this way, the statue is made to symbolize the Roman success story. It functions as a monument of Roman triumph. Had Rome not conquered Greece and Carthage – events hinted at by the naming of Alexander and Hannibal – the statue would never have been owned by a Roman. If this interpretation explains Statius' intentions, the next question has to be: why, then, Sulla? It does not really matter if Statius got his facts right or not. In this context, Sulla is an obvious choice. More than anybody else he is both a distinguished general and a lover of Greek culture, a hard-boiled politician and an admirer of Greek life-style, possessing both the will to exercise power and a refined taste. He can be understood as a role-model for the upper class and its ideals as we have sketched them before.[25] But the most important point Statius has to make is the following: Statius evokes, to be sure, Roman success, Roman victory and Roman power, but then replaces these concepts with a completely different one. Within the poem, the statue does *not* function as a symbol of power or as a monument of battles won. This is what the former possessors saw in the statue, so Statius implicitly suggests, but they were at fault. They

---

25 See Sall. *BJ* 95,3; Nep. *Att.* 4,1–2; on Sulla as example of the cultivated republican élite La Penna, Antonio 1976, "Il ritratto 'paradossale' da Silla a Petronio", *Rivista di Filologia e d'Istruzione Classica* 14, 283–285; Griffin, Jasper 1985, *Latin Poets and Roman Life*, London, 9; 12–13; 38–40.

were incapable of doing justice to the real qualities of the statue. Now, finally, the god has found his real home in the house of Vindex. It is the object of subtle connoisseurship and equally subtle poetry, namely the poetry of Novius Vindex who adequately takes into account above all the god himself and his glorious deeds. Thus, Statius shows Novius Vindex as member of a world which is saturated in culture and as an incarnation of its values.

> hic tibi sollemni memorabit carmine quantus
> Iliacas Geticasque domos quantusque nivalem
> Stymphalon quantusque iugis Erymanthon aquosis
> terrueris, quem te pecoris possessor Hiberi,
> quem tulerit saevae Mareoticus arbiter arae;
> hic penetrata tibi spoliataque limina mortis
> concinet et flentes Libyae Scythiaeque puellas.
> nec te regnator Macetum nec barbarus umquam
> Hannibal aut saevi posset vox horrida Syllae
> his celebrare modis. certe tu, muneris auctor,
> non aliis malles oculis, Lysippe, probari.

Here then hast thou a welcome resting-place, Alcides, most valiant of gods, nor beholdest battles or savage fights, but the lyre and chaplets and music-loving bays. Here in solemn chant will he recount to thee in what might thou didst terrify Getic and Ilian homes and snowy Stymphalus and Erymanthus with its streaming ridges; how the owner of the Iberian herd, how the Mareotic guardian of the cruel shrine endured thy power; he will sing of the gates of Death penetrated and spoiled by thee, of the weeping maids of Libya and of Scythia. Neither the ruler of the Macetae nor barbarous Hannibal nor the uncouth accents of fierce Sulla could e'er have celebrated thee in such strains. And of a surety thou, Lysippus, the author of the gift, wouldst not have chosen to be approved by other eyes than these. (vv. 96–109)

This is a remarkable construction: a Greek god, a Greek work of art need a Roman – who, incidentally, is a better Greek than any living Greek – to find a suitable place and become part of a cultural practice as the sculptor originally had intended. It takes a Roman to do justice to a Greek artist. This attitude is not only a demonstration of cultural competence and even superiority so typical of the higher classes in this epoch, and it is not only a monument of élite self-fashioning. It is also an indicator of a transformed perception of the cultural environment. It is not Roman power that is on display nor the command of cultural resources as resources of a conquered empire. What is on stage is the connoisseur, the expert, the intellectual, equally well-versed in Greek and Latin culture.

3. *paideia* instrumentalized on the stage of rhetoric: Apuleius and the second sophistic

Statius' Silvae are the first instance of a culture of taste and refinement, a culture of knowledge and erudition that is rapidly expanding during the 2nd century c. e. This culture is the roof under which an imperial intellectual élite can thrive and prosper, an elite whose social status and self-image is based on cultural traditions and inventories of knowledge which the empire makes available. The most impressive figures of this élite are, of course, the orators who came to be classed as the sophists of the second sophistic, travelling artists of the word, famous lecturers, whom we encounter in towns and cities all over the empire, champions of self-fashioning, successfully aspiring to power and status.[26] This is not only a professional show-off designed to delude the uneducated; instead, it is an indispensable element of self-understanding.

I would like to illustrate this by discussing Apuleius' defence speech de Magia, held in the year 158 in Sabratha when the orator, philosopher and writer found himself accused of witchraft before the proconsul of Africa, a certain Claudius Maximus.[27] Apuleius was born in Madaurus, a Roman colony; there he belonged to the local upper class. His father served as a duumvir – the highest office a provincial town could pride itself on. If Apuleius tells us the truth, his father's inheritance amounted to 2 billion sesterces, a sum that would have been sufficient to gain him the rank of a Roman knight no less than five times. Apuleius was given the best education that money could buy, both in Carthage and Athens, where he came in close contact with members of the imperial élite such as Aemilianus Strabo, consul suffect in 156. This Aemilianus, incidentally, granted Apuleius a honorary statue. Until this very day he is famous for his novel, the

---

26 On the *habitus* of the sophists in the 2nd century Hahn, Johannes 1989, *Der Philosoph und die Gesellschaft. Selbstverständnis, öffentliches Auftreten und populäre Erwartungen in der hohen Kaiserzeit*, Heidelberger Althistorische Beiträge und Epigraphische Studien 7, Stuttgart, 33–45; Zanker, Paul 1995, *Die Maske des Sokrates. Das Bild des Intellektuellen in der antiken Kunst*, München, 190–251; Schmitz (cf. fn. 3) 26–38; Korenjak, Martin 2000, *Publikum und Redner. Ihre Interaktion in der sophistischen Rhetorik der Kaiserzeit*, München; Borg, Barbara E. 2004a, "Glamorous intellectuals. Portraits of *pepaideumenoi* in the second and third centuries AD", in: Borg (cf. fn. 3), 157–178.

27 On the life and the writings of Apuleius in the context of the second sophistic Sandy, Gerald 1997, The *greek world of Apuleius. Apuleius and the second sophistic*, Mnemosyne Suppl. 174, Leiden; New York; Köln, 1–41; Harrison, Stephen J. 2000, *Apuleius. A Latin Sophist*, Oxford, 1–38; Hammerstaedt, Jürgen 2002, "Apuleius. Leben und Werk", in: Jürgen Hammaestaedt et al., *Apuleius. De magia*, Sapere 5, Darmstadt, 9–22.

Metamorphoses or the *Golden Ass*. But he was a far more versatile writer than is usually known. He wrote philosophical and scientific essays and even occasional poetry. He made his appearance as travelling lecturer and orator. Unfortunately, only some extracts of his speeches have come down to us. We have good reasons to assume that he was at certain times a resident of Rome and Samos, and that he spent some time in Phrygia and Alexandria. His stay in Alexandria is connected with the chain of events that brought him to the court of justice: one of the stations on his way to Alexandria was the town of Oea, today's Tripolis, where, for reasons of health, he had to remain longer than he had anticipated. During his stay he married the widow Pudentilla, the mother of his friend and fellow student Pontianus. Now, Pudentilla's family saw the property jeopardized and took measures to prevent losses: Apuleius was accused of witchcraft.[28] It was by magic, so they claimed, that the young sophist had tricked the elder widow into marriage. It was a serious charge. Apuleius was threatened with capital punishment. Now, things are getting intricate: Pudentianus having died, Sicinius Aemilianus, member of a respectable and well-to-do family, appeared on the scene as the plaintiff in the name of his nephew Pudens, who was Pudentianus' brother. Of course, we cannot read the speech of the accusation, held by a certain Tannonius Pudens, of whom we know nothing but the name, but we can draw some conclusions regarding its content, because we do read Apuleius' answers. Apparently, Tannonius found fault with Apuleius' outer appearance – namely, his beauty –, his personal habits (Apuleius went so far as to treat himself to regular tooth-brushing) and pecuniary circumstances. He interpreted several predilections and preferences – such as Apuleius' interest in fishes (*apol.* 29–41) and his worship of statues (*apol.* 61–65) – as indications of magic practices. To confirm this view, he cited even Apuleius' literary works and poetry. Now, Apuleius tackles these reproaches in a highly surprising manner. Of course, he argues against all accusations brought forward by his opponents on a factual level. But at the same time, he transforms a criminal procedure into a dispute concerning social status and social roles. He turnes a virtually life-threatening conflict into a class argument. His defence strategy is based mainly on the staging of cultural and social difference. Apuleius answers accusations by representing himself as intellectual and philosopher, flattering himself by not altogether discreetly evoking parallels with Socrates, the role-model of the unjustly accused and condemned philosopher-saint.[29] His speech and its performance is his medium to transmit a construction

---

28 On the background and the argumentation of the speech in general Hunink, Vincent 1997, *Apuleius of Madauros* Pro se de magia. *Ed. with a Commentary*, Amsterdam, 11–22 and Schenk, Peter 2002, "Die Schrift", in: Jürgen Hammerstaedt et. al., Apuleius. De magia, Sapere 5, Darmstadt, 23–57.

29 On the parallels between the Apuleian and the Platonic apology see Schenk (cf. fn. 28) 54–56.

of his own identity – and this construction is meant to serve as an argument. Instead of rational discussion, he plays the trump card of personality. Demonstration of cultural superiority replaces explanations and arguments. Display of erudition can and does work as a substitute for reasoning. Thus, education serves as efficient authentication even in the court-room. Just to illustrate this observation, I will cite an example. On his arrival in Oea Apuleius, Tannonius informs us, was accompanied by just a small number of slaves – actually it might even have been only one. This points to relative poverty: consequently, Apuleius, right at his arrival, must have speculated on concluding a favourable marriage. Apuleius' refutation takes two directions. First, he proves the inherent implausibility of this point by mentioning his emancipation of three slaves during his sojourn in Oea (*apol.* 17–23). But he does not stop here. On the contrary: he gives an entire history lecture. He presents a whole catalogue of historical examples, a parade of most famous figures from the Greek and Roman past, intellectual heroes and elder statesmen, poets and politicians, military leaders and profound thinkers, all of whom have one thing in common: they had but few slaves. Apuleius sings the praise of poverty and modesty. Starting with Aristides and Epaminondas Apuleius cites Socrates and Gaius Fabricius, Atilius Regulus and Marcus Cato – and this is only a small sample. He concludes this catalogue of exempla with the following words:

> *M. autem Cato nihil oppertus, ut alii de se praedicarent, ipse in o[pe]ratione sua scriptum reliquit, cum in Hispania<m> consul proficisceretur, tris seruos solos ex urbe duxisse; quoniam ad uillam publicam uenerat, parum uisum qui uteretur, iussisse duos pueros in foro de mensa emi, eos quinque in Hispaniam duxisse. haec Pudens si legisset, ut mea opinio est, aut omnino huic maledicto supersedisset aut in tribus seruis multitudinem comitum philosophi quam paucitatem reprehendere maluisset.*

> Marcus Cato did not wait for others to tell it of him, but himself records the fact in one of his speeches that when he set out as consul for Spain he took but three slaves from the city with him. When, however, he came to stay at a state residence, the number seemed insufficient, and he ordered two slaves to be bought in the market to wait on him at table, so that he took five in all to Spain. Had Pudens come across these facts in his reading, he would, I think, either have omitted this particular slander or would have preferred to reproach me on the ground that three slaves were too large rather than too small an establishment for a philosopher. (chapter 17)

Apuleius elegantly puts his own knowledge on display, thereby representing himself as a member of an, one feels tempted to say, international, but at least boundary-transgressing res publica litterarum, if I may use an expression originally coined for early modern times. Thus, he makes his opponent appear a hopeless ignoramus not worth listening to. Even worse: Apuleius' Roman exempla are characters-in-stock, treated ad nauseam in elementary school. Even the most basic knowledge should be sufficient to know those! Apuleius' whole speech is characterized by this double strategy to represent himself as a full member of the cultured class and to ridicule the low level of his rival's education. But Apuleius is not content to walk the well-trodden paths of commonplace knowledge. He combines in a witty and highly spirited manner even the most disparate subjects. When Tannonius reproaches him for exaggerated body care by quoting one of Apuleius' poems in which he recommends the use of tooth-powder, Apuleius counters by alluding to a poem of Catullus scoffing at a certain Spaniard's practice of polishing his teeth with urine and by indulging in speculations about Tannonius' hygienic habits, only to conclude his refutation with a digression on natural history and the tooth-cleaning method of crocodiles on the banks of the Nile (*apol.* 6–7). Both Catullus and Egyptian crocodiles are called to testify as respectable authorities on the indispensability of body care. Here, Apuleius not only aims at provoking amazement and laughter among his public; he also draws the first lines of a self-portrait as a philosopher and scientist of Aristotelian stamp – a self-characterization that comes in extremely handy at a later point of his discourse, namely when he has to counter another attack: Apuleius' habit of dissecting fish, Tannonius wants to make us believe, is only explainable as a method to extract fishy substances needed for the preparation of magic potions. But once the audience has swallowed the bait – namely to see Apuleius as a serious researcher in the venerable Stagirite's footsteps – Apuleius is out of danger, and we find it perfectly natural for a man like him to amuse himself with the cutting open of animals. Additionally, he mentions – slightly tongue-in-cheek – his preference for savoury meals. As was to be expected, he tops up his discourse by filling it up to the brim with literary quotations and allusions which he employs in order to prove that no literary source at all ever lists fish as ingredient of love potions: again, we find the double strategy of representing himself as a man of erudition and of exposing his opponent's ignorance. And this is how Apuleius apologizes for avoiding Greek quotations:

> *memorassem tibi etiam Theocriti paria et alia Homeri et Orphei plurima, et ex comoe-diis et tragoediis Graecis et ex historiis multa repetissem, ni te dudum animaduertissem Graecam Pudentillae epistulam legere nequiuisse. igitur unum etiam poetam Latinum attingam, uersus ipsos, quos agnoscent qui Laeuium legere:*

> I would also have quoted for your benefit similar passages from Theocritus with many others from Homer and Orpheus, from the comic and tragic poets and from the historians, had I not noticed ere now that you were unable to read Pudentilla's letter which was written in Greek. I will, therefore, do no more than cite one Latin poet. Those who have read Laevius will recognize the lines. (chapter 30)

This type of defamation of his rival is one of the main motifs of the whole speech. He criticizes not only the plaintiff's lack of knowledge of Greek language and literature, but presents him as a man who is not even capable of pronouncing a Latin poem correctly.

eundem me aio facundissimum esse, nam omne peccatum semper nefas habui; eundem disertissimum, quod nullum meum factum uel dictum extet, de quo di<s>serere publice non possim ita, ut iam de uorsibus di<s>sertabo quos a me factos quasi pudendos protulerunt, cum quidem me animaduertisti cum risu illis suscensentem, quod eos absone et indocte pronuntiarent.

Nay, my eloquence is consummate, for I have ever held all sin in abomination; I have the highest oratory at my command, for I have uttered no word, I have done no deed, of which I need fear to discourse in public. I will begin therefore to discourse of those verses of mine, which they have produced as though they were something of which I ought to be ashamed. You must have noticed the laughter with which I showed my annoyance at the absurd and illiterate manner in which they recited them. (chapter 5)

But the climax is a direct attack on Aemilianus, who started the whole affair:

quem tu librum, Aemiliane, si nosses ac non modo campo et glebis, uerum etiam abaco et puluisculo te dedisses, mihi istud crede, quanquam teterrimum os tuum minimum a Thyesta tragico demutet, tamen profecto discendi cupidine speculum inuiseres et aliquando relicto aratro mirarere tot in facie tua sulcos rugarum. At ego non mirer, si boni consulis me de isto distor-tissimo uultu tuo dicere, de moribus tuis multo truculentioribus reticere. ea res est: praeter quod non sum iurgiosus, etiam libenter te nuper usque albus an ater esses ignoraui et adhuc <h>ercle non satis noui. id adeo factum, quod et tu rusticando obscurus es et ego discendo occupatus. ita et tibi umbra ignobilitatis a probatore obstitit, et ego numquam studui male facta cuiusquam cognoscere, sed semper potius duxi mea peccata tegere quam aliena indagare. igitur hoc mihi aduersum te usu uenit, quod qui forte constitit in loco lumine conlustrato atque eum alter e tenebris prospectat. nam ad eundem modum tu quidem, quid ego in propatulo et celebri agam, facile e tenebris tuis arbitraris, cum ipse humilitate abdita et lucifuga non sis mihi mutuo conspicuus.

If you had only read this book, Aemilianus, and, instead of devoting yourself to the study of your fields and their dull clods, had studied the mathematician's slate and blackboard, believe me, although your face is hideous enough for a tragic mask of Thyestes, you would assuredly, in your desire for the acquisition of knowledge, look into the glass and sometimes leave your plough to marvel at the numberless furrows with which wrinkles have scored your face.

But I should not be surprised if you prefer me to speak of your ugly deformity of a face and to be silent about your morals, which are infinitely more repulsive than your features. I will say nothing of them. In the first place I am not naturally of a quarrelsome disposition, and secondly I am glad to say that until quite recently you might have been white or black for all I knew. Even now my knowledge of you is inadequate. The reason for this is that your rustic occupations have kept you in obscurity, while I have been occupied by my studies, and so the shadow cast about you by your insignificance has shielded your character from scrutiny, while I for my part take no interest in others' ill deeds, but have always thought it more important to conceal my own faults than to track out those of others. As a result you have the advantage of one who, while he is himself shrouded in darkness, surveys another who chances to have taken his stand in the full light of day. You from your darkness can with ease form an opinion as to what I am doing in my not undistinguished position before all the world; but your position is so abject, so obscure, and so withdrawn from the light of publicity that you are by no means so conspicuous. (chapter 16)

The most obvious aim of this strategy is, of course, to contrast the plaintiff with the accused to the latter's benefit and to render evident the social and cultural gap that separates the parties. But this is not the end of Apuleius' refinement. He even makes audience and judge collude in his game. At a certain point, Apuleius has to find a justification for his erotic poems. What he does in fact is to stage a quiz show making his public guess of whom he's talking. He cites quite a number of Latin poets who wrote the same kind of poetry, mentioning them by their full names. It's the usual strategy of justifying his activities by naming predecessors of universally acknowledged glory. But when it comes to Greek poets, presumably totally unknown to his accusers, he passes their names in silence and only mentions their home towns (*apol.* 9,6). Only auditors with a high degree of education can have been capable of supplying the respective names. Thus, by introducing a funny little riddle, Apuleius plays his own game of exclusion and inclusion and defines subtly who belongs and who does not. He thereby reaffirms the general superiority of those who catch his point and draws them on his side employing an indirect strategy of insuring the public's sympathy – at least of those who count. This is a way of establishing a consensus with his judge, and Apuleius does not hesitate to apply this tactic openly.

> *bene quod apud te, Maxime, causa agitur, qui pro tua eruditione legisti profecto Aristotelis* περὶ ζῴων γενέσεως, περὶ ζῴων ἀνατομῆς, περὶ ζῴων ἱστορίας *multi-iuga uolumina, praeterea problemata innumera eiusdem, tum ex eadem secta ceterorum, in quibus id genus uaria tractantur. quae tanta cura conquisita si honestum et gloriosum illis fuit scribere, cur turpe sit nobis experiri, praesertim cum ordinatius et cohibilius eadem Graece et Latine adnitar conscribere et in omnibus aut omissa adquirere aut defecta supplere?*
>
> *permittite, si operaest, quaedam legi de magicis meis, ut sciat me Aemilianus plura quam putat quaerere et sedulo explorare. prome tu librum e Graecis meis, quos forte hic amici habuere sedulique, naturalium quaestionum, atque eum maxime, in quo plura de piscium genere tractata sunt. interea, dum hic quaerit, ego exemplum rei competens dixero.*

It is a good thing, Maximus, that this case is being tried before a scholar like yourself, who have read Aristotle's numerous volumes 'on the generation, the anatomy, the history of animals', together with his numberless 'Problems' and works by others of his school treating of various subjects of this kind. If it is an honour and glory to them that they should have put on record the results of their careful researches, why should it be disgraceful to me to attempt the like task, especially since I shall attempt to write on those subjects both in Greek and Latin and in a more concise and systematic manner, and shall strive either to make good omissions or remedy mistakes in all these authors?

I beg of you, if you think it worth while, to permit the reading of extracts from my 'magic' works, that Aemilianus may learn that my sedulous researches and inquiries have a wider range than he thinks. Bring a volume of my Greek works – some of my friends who are interested in questions of natural history may perhaps have them with them in court – take by preference one of those dealing with problems of natural philosophy, and from among those that volume in particular which treats of the race of fish. While he is looking for the book, I will tell you a story which has some relevance to this case. (chapter 36)

At this point the trial transforms itself to an erudite discussion between two intellectuals of equal rank who share a common horizon of knowledge and attitudes and who respect the same values. They constitute a social group which evidently does not embrace the plaintiff. Apuleius anticipates an agreement with his judge. The man who is accused of wilfully and intentionally having secured himself a fortune by illegal means models his trial as a confrontation of life styles. He was supposed to fight for survival and staged a competition of identities and social roles instead. Where we expected an argument between plaintiff and accused we see a provincial African ignoramus at the mercy of an elegant philosopher and cosmopolitan. The accusation appears to be founded in sheer stupidity, launched by persons of too limited an intellectual horizon to understand the motives and actions of a man like Apuleius. No judge, so Apuleius insinuates, could condemn such a man without degrading himself into being a companion of boorish provincials. Apuleius's efforts were crowned with success. Without further ado, he was acquitted.

4. Summary

Finally I would like to summarize my observations.

First: education, knowledge and activities, customs and habits connected with this field are pivotal elements of élite status demonstration; they are of undisputed relevance to groups of very different provenance and profession, for instance the Roman nobility, the provincial leading classes and professional declaimers.

Second: One of the most salient features of this culture is the fact that paideia and its representatives are integrated in local networks – cities or regions – where they continue local traditions. They may keep local history alive, maintain local cults, interest themselves in local mythology or carry on local literary traditions, in short, they keep up a locally defined identity. But at the same time they form an empire-wide network of cultural communication in which they integrate their specific and more often than not disparate local knowledge into an overarching translocal context. Roman and Greek traditions are brought into interaction and tend to be amalgamated.

Third: The result of this process is an empire-wide group identity, a common way of élite self-fashioning which can be profitably instrumentalized in a whole variety of situations, from banquets to criminal trials, and which usually win the competition with other constructions of identity.

Fourth: This is the greenhouse in which proliferate numerous literary genres: occasional poetry, collections of letters and speeches and declamations, to name but a few. These genres are the vehicles of imparting and staging this knowledge so indispensable for the self-understanding of an imperial elite.

Abstract

In Augustan times, the ways of perceiving and imagining the Roman Empire changed significantly; I take this observation as my point of departure for discussing the relevance of knowledge and education in the construction of social roles. It is my aim to demonstrate that we have to assume multiple identities – that is, coexistence and interaction of diverse local and translocal frames of self-perception – for the representants of the imperial élites. This can be shown for example for Pliny the Younger, Statius and Apuleius – three representative authors who share the feature of being part of the culture of paideia in the 1st and 2nd centure c.e. Taking Statius, Silva 4.6 and Apuleius' Apology as my basic texts, the following aspects of paideia in imperial society can be singled out: 1. The importance of paideia for the self-construction of the élites (viz. the élites of urban Rome, the provincial élites and the professional rhetors) and for the establishment and preservation of their group identity; 2. the relevance of local networks and local traditions within this process of identy-formation; 3. the significance of a perspective which transcends the purely local level and the construction of a specifically imperial identity by means of having knowledge of the most diverse provenience at one's disposal; 4. the importance of this cultural situation for the development of a variety of literary genres, which in their turn serve as vehicle and means of demonstration of the competences which have been mentioned before.

Kolossale Miniaturen:
Der Holzfäller Hercules in Statius' „Wäldern" (*Silve* 3,1)

ULRIKE EGELHAAF-GAISER

1. Die *Silven* als Gelegenheitsdichtung[1]

Gelegenheit macht Dichter: Niemand könnte dies besser bezeugen als der Stegreifdichter Statius, der am Ende des 1. Jahrhunderts n. Chr. aktuelle gesellschaftliche Ereignisse verarbeitet hat.[2] Anlaß seiner Gedichte mit dem Namen „Wälder" – lateinisch: *Silvae* – sind die klassischen Casualien wie Geburtstag, Hochzeit und Tod; Einweihungen von Gebäuden und offizielle wie private Festlichkeiten. Der „Sitz im Leben" äußert sich in der Gelegenheit und im Personenbezug: Jede *Silve* hat einen Adressaten, der an den Ereignissen prominent beteiligt ist. Die genannten Personen sind dem Ritterstand, der senatorischen Oberschicht und dem Kaiserhof zuzuordnen.[3] Mit seinen kleinen, aber feinen Ehrengaben verfolgt Statius sehr konkrete Ziele: Indem die *Silven* aus gegebenem Anlaß den Adressaten ehren, empfehlen bzw. bestätigen sie zugleich die Fähigkeiten des förderungswürdigen Dichters.[4]

Aufgrund der Situationsgebundenheit der *Silven* ist mit deren zweifacher Veröffentlichung zu rechnen:[5] Auf den mündlichen Vortrag bzw. die zeitnahe Übergabe des Einzelgedichts folgt die Zusammenstellung zum Buch. Einleitende

---

1 Gedankt sei an dieser Stelle Helmut Krasser, Peter von Möllendorff, Dennis Pausch (Gießen), Ivana Petrovic (Durham) und Meike Rühl (Göttingen) für engagierte Diskussionen, Literaturhinweise und die kritische Lektüre des Manuskripts.

2 Zum Begriff der Gelegenheitsdichtung und zur Charakteristik der *Silven* als okkasionelle Dichtung Rühl, M. 2006, *Literatur gewordener Augenblick. Die Silven des Statius im Kontext literarischer und sozialer Bedingungen von Dichtung*, UaLG 81, Berlin; New York, 83–113.

3 Zu den Adressaten Nauta, R. R. 2002, *Poetry for Patrons. Literary Communication in the Age of Domitian*, Mnemosyne Supplements 236, Leiden; Boston; Köln, 204–248; Johannsen, N. 2006, *Dichter über ihre Gedichte. Die Prosavorreden in den „Epigrammaton libri" Martials und in den „Silvae" des Statius*, Hypomnemata 166, Göttingen, 341–355.

4 Zur Personenpanegyrik Newlands, C. E. 2002, *Statius' Silvae and the Poetics of Empire*, Camdridge, 18–27. Zu den *Silven* als Ehrengaben Rühl (s. Anm. 2) 27–29; Johannsen (s. Anm. 3) 355.

5 Zu den Modalitäten der Rezeption Nauta (s. Anm. 3) 249–290; Rühl (s. Anm. 2) 128–140; Gauly, B. M 2006, „Das Glück des Pollius Felix. Römische Macht und privater Luxus in Statius' Villengedicht *Silv.* 2,2", *Hermes* 134, 455.

Widmungsbriefe begründen jeweils die Zueignung und informieren über Inhalt, Anlaß und Begleitumstände der Gedichte. Im ersten Vorwort erklärt der Dichter das Programm seiner „Wälder".[6] Eigentlich ist nämlich das Epos die klassische Form, um hochrangige Personen zu preisen: Verheißt doch ein großes Werk auch großes Ansehen. Vor diesem Hintergrund[7] definiert Statius, der ja dem Publikum als Epiker bereits bekannt ist, seine Gelegenheitsdichtung als leichte Poesie, deren Reiz in der spontanen Schnelligkeit liegt.[8] Ganz bewußt verzichten die *Silven* auf Volumen und Gewicht.[9] Sie wollen statt dessen mit ihrer eleganten Raffinesse und ihrem literarischen Anspielungsreichtum bestechen. Nach Statius' Selbstanspruch sind die *Silven* kleine Kunstwerke mit großer Wirkung, anders gesagt: kolossale Miniaturen.[10]

2. Der Holzfäller Hercules in Statius' „Wäldern"

Die poetische Selbstreferentialität der kolossalen Miniatur möchte ich an einem wenig behandelten Einzelgedicht präzisieren, nämlich an der *Silve* 3,1, die der Dichter im Buchvorwort als „Hercules von Surrent" bezeichnet.[11] Daß der *Her-*

---

6 Zur ersten Praefatio Rühl (s. Anm. 2) 119–121, Johannsen (s. Anm. 3) 241–261.
7 Zur Relation von Epos und *Silven* Hardie, A. 1983, *Statius and the Silvae. Poets, Patrons and Epideixis in the Graeco-Roman World*, Classical and Medieval Texts, Papers and Monographs 9, Liverpool, 85–91; Gibson, B. 2006, „The *Silvae* and epic", in: R.R. Nauta; H.-J. van Dam; J.J.L. Smolenaars (Hrsg.), *Flavian poetry*, Mnemosyne Supplements 270, 163–183; Dam, H.-J. van 2006, „Multiple Imitation of Epic Models in the *Silvae*", in: Nauta; van Dam; Smolenaars (Hrsg.), 185–205; Johannsen (s. Anm. 3) 307–316; 331–335.
8 *Silv.* 1, *praef.* 1–16. Zur Technik der Improvisation Rühl (s. Anm. 2) 128–134. Allgemein zu Spielarten des Improvisierens und raschen Dichtens (u.a. im Rahmen von Wettkämpfen) Döpp, S. 1996, „Das Stegreifgedicht des Q. Sulpicius Maximus", *ZPE* 114, 99–104.
9 Vgl. *Silv.* 2, *praef.* 16: *scis a me leves libellos quasi epigrammatis loco scriptos.*
10 Ausgeführt wird das ästhetische Konzept der „kolossalen Miniatur" in *Silve* 4,6, in deren Zentrum eine Tischstatuette des Hercules steht. Dort ist das kallimacheische Kunstprinzip der *Silven* in der Überlegenheit des ingeniösen Lysipp gegenüber den mythischen Schmieden des Großepos (Vulcanus und den „tumben" Kyklopen) anschaulich gemacht (*silv.* 4,6,35–49). Ob der anerkannt metapoetischen Qualität der Ekphrasis hat der *Hercules epitrapezios* in der Forschung mehr Beachtung gefunden als der hier diskutierte *Hercules Surrentinus*, siehe Newlands (s. Anm.4) 73–87; Rühl (s. Anm. 2) 241–248 mit älterer Literatur. Zur ästhetischen Kategorie der Kolossalität am Beispiel der *Silve* 1,1 Cancik, H. 1990, „Größe und Kolossalität als religiöse und ästhetische Kategorien. Versuch einer Begriffsbestimmung am Beispiel von Statius, Silve I 1. Ecus Domitiani Imperatoris", *Visible Religion* 7, 51–68.
11 *Silv.* 3, *praef.* 9f.: *nam primum limen eius Hercules Surrentinus aperit.*

cules Surrentinus ähnlich wie sein Pendant (der *Hercules epitrapezios* in *Silve* 4,6) als ein poetologisches Programmgedicht zu lesen ist, lassen bereits seine herausragende Stellung am Buchanfang und auch der Adressat vermuten. Denn dem reichen Villenbesitzer und Kulturpatron Pollius Felix ist das ganze dritte Buch gewidmet; er gehört zu den ausgezeichneten, lang und eng bekannten Förderern, die Statius mit mehreren Gedichten ehrt.[12]

Bevor ich meine Thesen formuliere, sei zunächst die *Silve* kurz paraphrasiert: Statius führt sich als Festteilnehmer ein, der vom Patron zur Neuweihung eines restaurierten Herculestempels geladen ist. Dieser steht auf Pollius' privatem Villenbesitz bei Surrent. Der Dichter, der zuletzt im vergangenen Sommer auf der Villa zu Gast war, erkennt die Örtlichkeiten kaum wieder: Die bescheidene Hütte des Hercules hat sich nämlich mittlerweile zu einem strahlenden Tempel gewandelt (1–22). Nachdem Statius sein Staunen über das Bauwunder geäußert hat, ruft er Hercules in einem Hymnus auf, in sein neues Heim einzutreten. Anders als damals vor seinem Löwenkampf bei Nemea, als er beim Bauern Molorchus eine notdürftige Unterkunft fand, erwarte ihn jetzt in Surrent ein wirklich komfortabler Wohnsitz. Dort könne er die ihm zu Ehren eingerichteten Spiele unbeschwert genießen (23–48).

Da nun dem Festpublikum auch der Anlaß der Restauration erklärt werden soll, ruft der Dichter die Muse Calliope an, die vom Sänger Hercules begleitet werden soll. Dann wird in einer eingelegten Erzählung das Aition des Tempelneubaus präsentiert: Heute vor einem Jahr, am 13. August, hatten die Villenbesitzer ein Freiluftpicknick am Meeresstrand veranstaltet (49–67). Als plötzlich ein Gewitter aufzieht, sucht die Festgesellschaft beim benachbarten Hercules Zuflucht. Dessen beengte Hütte kann freilich die Zahl der Gäste nicht fassen (68–88). Leicht pikiert über seine unbefriedigende Gastlichkeit tritt Hercules an seinen Nachbarn heran – und zwar in Form einer intimen Gotteserscheinung unter vier Augen. Im Verweis auf Pollius' luxuriöse Villa bittet Hercules um einen würdigen Wohnsitz. Am angetragenen Bauprojekt werde er sich auch selbst beteiligen, indem er die schwierige Planierung des Geländes übernehme (89–116).

Ein Heros steht zu seinem Wort: Nachdem Pollius' Bautrupp die Vorarbeiten geleistet hat, wird Hercules zu nächtlicher Stunde tätig. Mit einer mächtigen Holzfälleraxt durchgräbt er schweißgebadet die Erde, trägt die Felsklippen ab und befestigt den sandigen Boden. Staunend stehen die Arbeiter am nächsten Morgen vor dem kolossalen Werk (117–138). Der Vollendung des dekorativen Rundtempelchens steht nun nichts mehr im Wege, und so kann Pollius schon nach einem Jahr die ersten Wettkämpfe ausrichten (139–164).

---

12 *Silv.* 2,2; 3,1; 4,8. Zu Pollius Felix als Mehrfachadressat Rühl (s. Anm. 2) 297–307; vgl. Laguna, M. 1992, *Estacio, Silvas III*, Madrid; Sevilla, 121f.; Nauta (s. Anm. 3) 222f.; 238f.

Der inspirierte Sänger hat seine aitiologische Erzählung kaum beendet, da sieht er den herbeigerufenen Heros mit eigenen Augen an der Tempelschwelle erscheinen: Vollmundig dankt Hercules dem Restaurator seines Tempels. Das vom Dichter bezeugte Wunder der Epiphanie wird am Schluß der *Silve* durch religiöse Vorzeichen bestätigt (164–186).

Um nun die postulierte Selbstreferentialität der *Silve* plausibel zu machen, gilt es vor allem die Frage zu klären: In welcher Weise proklamiert der *Hercules Surrentinus* das Konzept der ehrenden Gelegenheitsdichtung? Das Problem einer poetologischen Programmatik erhält dadurch noch größere Brisanz, daß der *Hercules von Surrent* ein echtes Stiefkind der Forschung ist. Sofern die *Silve* nicht als eine bloße Reprise des (aufgrund seiner ausführlichen Ekphrasis häufiger behandelten) Villengedichts 2,2 gelesen wurde,[13] konzentrierte man sich auf die Analyse der literarischen Prätexte und Genera[14] und auf die Darstellung des Patrons.[15] Obwohl die komischen Züge des Hercules außer Frage standen,[16] hat man über die Funktion eines betont burlesk gezeichneten Heros in einem panegyrischen Preisgedicht nicht ernsthaft nachgedacht, sondern sich mit dem allgemeinen Verweis auf Hercules' Prominenz in der Komödie begnügt.[17]

Eine solche Erklärung bleibt unbefriedigend. Denn sie berücksichtigt nicht, daß die Aussagen über den Heros auf mehreren Ebenen – nämlich im Buchvorwort, in der okkasionellen Gedichtrahmung und in der aitiologischen Binnenerzählung – getroffen werden und die jeweilige Sprecherinstanz eine durchaus unterschiedliche Autorität und Glaubhaftigkeit besitzt.[18] Zudem unterschätzt sie die Bedeutung des Hercules, der für den Auftragsdichter nicht nur ob seiner Kolossalität ein *unbequemer*, sondern auch aus gegebenem Anlaß ein *unver-*

---

13   So Newlands (Anm. 4) 154–198. Zu 2,2 Gauly (s. Anm. 5) mit älterer Literatur.

14   Zu den Prätexten Thomas, R. F. 1983, „Callimachus, the 'Victoria Berenices' and Roman Poetry", *CQ* 33, 92–113; Newlands, C. E. 1991, „Silvae 3.1 and Statius' Poetic Temple", *CQ* 41, 438–452; zur Formen- und Gattungsmischung Hardie (s. Anm. 7) 125–128; Laguna (s. Anm. 12) 122–127; van Dam (s. Anm. 7) 203–205. Auf eine reine Strukturanalyse beschränkt sich Newmyer, S. T. 1979, *The Silvae of Statius. Structure and theme*, Mnemosyne Suppl., 100–105.

15   Damon, C. 2002, „The Emperor's New Clothes, or, on the Flattery and Encomium in the *Silvae*", in: John F. Miller, Cynthia Damon, K. Sara Myers (Hrsg.), *Vertis in usum. Studies in Honor of Edward Courtney*, München; Leipzig, 174–188 (zur Stilfigur der rhetorischen Überbietung, in diesem Fall des konkurrierenden Vergleichs zwischen dem Heros und dem Patron); Rühl (s. Anm. 2) 302–306 (die *Silve* 3,1 im Kontext der drei an Pollius Felix adressierten *Silven*).

16   Exemplarisch Newlands (s. Anm. 14) 444: „the mythical guise which Statius invokes for Hercules for his entry to the temple is a comic one." Vgl. ebenda 447 und Vollmer, F. 1898, *P. Papinii Statii Silvarum libri*, Leipzig, 385; Laguna (s. Anm. 12) 159.

17   Vollmer (s. Anm. 16) 387 f.; Newlands (s. Anm. 14) 444.

18   Zum Begriff der „Rahmung" und zur Sprecherinstanz Johannsen (s. Anm. 3) 45–51.

meidlicher Gelegenheitsgeber[19] ist: In einer *Silve*, die zur Tempelweihung als Trankspende am neu entstandenen Altar dargebracht wird,[20] *muß* der göttliche Hausherr noch vor dem menschlichen Baustifter zum Erstadressaten und zum primären Erzählgegenstand werden.

In Abgrenzung von den bisherigen Gedichtanalysen möchte ich daher die Figur des Hercules ins Zentrum meiner Interpretation stellen. In der Tat ist die *Silve* 3,1 unter den 32 Gelegenheitsgedichten singulär, insofern sie offiziell einem Heros als poetische Ehrengabe zugeeignet ist.[21] Darüber hinaus ist die Weihung des restaurierten Herculestempels die einzige in den *Silven* verarbeitete Gelegenheit, in der eine Mythenfigur gleich zweimal das Wort an dieselbe Person, nämlich an den Villenbesitzer Pollius, richtet und damit ihre besondere Nähe zu dem generösen Baustifter bestätigt.[22]

Nun ist aber – und damit beginnen die Probleme – der Heros erklärtermaßen ein Mann fürs Grobe: Mit seinen mächtigen Pranken bezwingt Hercules jedes Ungeheuer, und als Kulturstifter hat er sich durch die Anlage monumentaler Wassergräben und Gebirgsstraßen verdient gemacht.[23] Um so weniger sind freilich seine plumpen Hände für jede Art der Feinarbeit geeignet. Das mythische Profil reflektieren die Textarten, in denen der Heros als literarische Figur eine große Rolle spielt:[24] Hercules ist der ideale Mann für epische Großtaten. Als großer Esser und Frauenheld ist er zudem wie geschaffen für die Komödie, Travestie und Burleske.[25] Für Statius' miniaturhafte „Wäldchen" ist Hercules da-

---

19 Zu Göttern als Gelegenheitsgebern im Rahmen von Opfern und *lectisternia* Rüpke, J. 2005, „Gäste der Götter – Götter als Gäste. Zur Konstruktion des römischen Opferbanketts", in: S. Georgoudi; R. Koch Piettre; F. Schmidt (Hrsg.), *La cuisine et l'autel. Les sacrifices en questions dans les sociétés de la méditerranée ancienne*, Bibliothèque de l'École des Hautes Études, Sciences Religieuses 124, Turnhout, 233 f.

20 *Silv.* 3,1,163 f.: *haec ego nascentes laetus bacchatus ad aras / libamenta tuli*.

21 Zu Hercules als Adressat der *Silve* siehe 3,1,1 f.: *intermissa tibi renovat, Tirynthie, sacra / Pollius.*

22 Zur ehrenden Anrede renommierter Adressaten durch mythische Figuren Coleman, K. M. 1999, „Mythological figures as spokespersons in Statius' Silvae", in: F. de Angelis; S. Muth (Hrsg.), *Im Spiegel des Mythos. Bilderwelt und Lebenswelt*, Palilia 6, Wiesbaden, 67–80, zur *Silve* 3,1 ebenda 73–76.

23 Vgl. die Säuberung der Ställe des Augias und die Kanal- und Straßenbauten anläßlich der Entführung der Rinder des Geryoneus (Diod. 4,18,47; 4,19,3; 4,22,2).

24 Galinsky, G. K. 1972, *The Heracles theme*, Oxford; Effe, B. 1980, „Held und Literatur. Der Funktionswandel des Herakles-Mythos in der griechischen Literatur", *Poetica* 12, 145–166; Köhnken, A. 2003, „Herakles und Orpheus als mythische Referenzfiguren (‚Identifikations-' bzw. ‚Integrationsfiguren') im hellenistischen Epos", in: B. Aland; J. Hahn; C. Ronning (Hrsg.), *Literarische Identifikationsfiguren in der Antike*, Studien zu Antike und Christentum 16, Tübingen, 19–27.

25 Exemplarisch der als Herakles verkleidete Dionysos in Aristoph. *ran.* 108–115. Zu Herakles in der Komödie Galinsky (s. Anm. 24) 81–100.

gegen ein recht grob geschnitzter Akteur. Auch als situationsbedingter Inspirationsgott scheint der ungetüme Heros kaum tauglich. Nicht nur, daß er nicht in den Kanon der klassischen Musengötter gehört; ein Koloß wie Hercules hat auch kaum das Fingerspitzengefühl, um den grazilen Griffel des Silvendichters zu führen.[26] Um das Maß der erschwerenden Vorgaben voll zu machen, ist der Baustifter Pollius Felix als ein Mann von breiter Belesenheit und musischen Fähigkeiten gezeichnet. Da er Statius' produktives Schaffen stets mit wohlwollender Kritik begleitet hat,[27] wird er den ihm zugeeigneten Festbeitrag um so aufmerksamer rezipieren.

Wie kann der Auftragsdichter einen so feinsinnigen Literaturkenner mit dem unhandlichen Hercules angemessen ehren? Nach meiner Ansicht trägt Statius der Bildung seines Patrons und der literarischen Prominenz des Heros Rechnung, indem er sich in besonderer Intensität der Intertextualität bedient. Da der exemplarische Held in Mythos, Kult und Literatur viele Rollen spielt, stellt er ein ganzes Sortiment an Herculesbildern und -taten bereit. Wohlgemerkt arbeitet nun der Dichter ausschließlich mit Formen der indirekten Textüberlagerung, die seinen Leser gerade nicht durch wörtliche Zitate oder die Autoren- und Werknennung auf die gemeinten Prätexte festlegen. Vielmehr sind die Motivanleihen nur angedeutet und die Vorlagen umgeformt.[28] Dem Gedichtempfänger werden somit ein waches Auge und eine umfassende Literaturkenntnis unterstellt.

Als literarisches Vorbild ist in erster Instanz an die hellenistische Dichtung zu denken, die sich durch einen hohen Allusionsreichtum auszeichnet und die Technik der literarischen Aussparung, der epischen Alternativerzählung in kunstvoll ausgefeilter Miniatur und der ironisch-parodistischen Brechung tradi-

---

26 Kontrastiv vergleichbar ist die *Silve* 1,5, in der Statius zur Einweihung eines Privatbads explizit die klassischen Inspirationsgeber – die Musen, Apollo, Bacchus und Mercur – entläßt und statt dessen den feuermächtigen Vulcanus und die Najaden für seine kunstreiche Ekphrasis in den Dienst nimmt (1–8). Obwohl auch hier unkonventionelle, rein situationsbedingte Musengötter engagiert werden, sind der ausgewiesene Künstler Vulcanus und die zierlich verspielten Wassernymphen mit der eleganten Form der *Silve* ganz unproblematisch vereinbar. Ähnlich plausibel werden im Saturnaliengedicht *silv.* 1,6,4–7 die etablierten Musengötter durch die festlichen Inspirationsgeber Saturnus, December, Iocus et Sales ersetzt und in *silv.* 2,3,6–7 entsprechend dem landschaftlichen Ambiente Faun und die Naiaden angerufen. Meines Erachtens läßt sich aus dieser situationsbedingten Wahl der Inspirationsgottheiten nicht auf einen niedrigeren Wirkungsanspruch der Silven schließen, pace Johannsen (s. Anm. 3) 308–310.

27 *Silv.* 3, *praef.*, dazu unten Kapitel 2.5.

28 Zu den Optionen der schwach markierten Intertextualität Helbig, J. 1996, *Intertextualität und Markierung. Untersuchungen zur Systematik und Funktion der Signalisierung von Intertextualität*, Heidelberg, 91–111.

tioneller Mythenstoffe perfektioniert hat.[29] Wie Statius' *Silven*, so sind etwa die kallimacheischen *Aitien* und Theokrits *Idyllien* exklusiv an ein belesenes Publikum adressiert, das die verdeckten Zitate und poetischen Umformungen erkennt und die erzählerischen Leerstellen zu füllen vermag.[30] Kallimachos wie Theokrit haben sich bekanntlich auch schon das komische Wirkungspotential des kolossalen Heros in poetischer Miniatur zu Nutzen gemacht und lassen Herakles vorzugsweise in unkonventionellen und burlesken Rollen auftreten – etwa als Liebhaber des zarten Hylas, als Schlangentöter in der Wiege und als unerfahrenen Jungheros, der sich seine Sporen erst noch verdienen muß.[31] Als einschlägig für den *Hercules Surrentinus* wird sich namentlich die kallimacheische (und in *Silve* 3,1 explizit zitierte) Molorchus-Episode erweisen,[32] in der, wie Ambühl überzeugend gezeigt hat, Kallimachos „gerade *den* Helden als ‚Werbeträger' für sein Dichtungsprogramm verpflichtet, der sich dafür am wenigsten zu eignen scheint."[33]

Im vorliegenden Beitrag soll gezeigt werden, was Statius durch den gesuchten Rekurs auf kallimacheische Kunstformen für die Figurenzeichnung des Hercules im Dienste der panegyrischen Gelegenheitsdichtung gewinnt: Einschlägig ist dafür vor allem die aitiologische Binnenerzählung, in der die literarische Gestalt des großen Heros in unausgesprochener Anerkennung der beidseitigen Bildungskompetenzen zur gemeinsamen Denkfigur für Poet und Patron geformt wird. Der menschennahe und erreichbare Held vereint in einer Person den bereitwilligen Wohltäter und den beauftragten Akkordarbeiter. Hercules kann demnach als Projektionsfläche für die komplementären Interessen des Auftraggebers und des Gelegenheitsdichters dienen. Da Hercules' Taten zwischen gött-

---

29 Asper, M. 2004, *Kallimachos. Werke. Griechisch und deutsch*, Darmstadt, 51–53.

30 Zum Zielpublikum der kallimacheischen Dichtung Asper (s. Anm. 29) 6–22.

31 Theokrit *Id.* 13; 24; Call. *Ait.* 3, frg. 59–66 Asper; vgl. Prop. 4,9. Zu Herakles in der hellenistischen Dichtung Gutzwiller, K. J. 1981, *Studies in the Hellenistic Epyllion*, Beiträge zur Klassischen Philologie 114, Königstein, 10–38; Merriam, C. U. 2001, *The Development of the Epyllion Genre Through the Hellenistic and Roman Periods*, Studies in Classics 14, Lewiston; Queenston; Lampeter, 25–49 (Herakles bei Theokrit); Effe, B. 2003, „Der Held als Gott. Die Apotheose des Herakles in der alexandrinischen Dichtung", in: G. Binder; B. Effe; R. Glei (Hrsg.), *Gottmenschen. Konzepte existentieller Grenzüberschreitung im Altertum*, Bochumer Altertumswissenschaftliche Colloquia 55, Trier, 27–43. Zur paradigmatischen Funktion des kallimacheischen Herakles Fuhrer, T. 1992, *Die Auseinandersetzung mit den Chorlyrikern in den Epinikien des Kallimachos*, Basel; Kassel, 104–112.

32 Siehe unten Kapitel 2.1. Unverkennbar ist der kallimacheische Einfluß auf die Ekphrasis des *Hercules epitrapezios* in *Silve* 4,6, siehe Newlands (s. Anm. 4) 73–79.

33 Ambühl, A. 2005, *Kinder und junge Helden. Innovative Aspekte des Umgangs mit der literarischen Tradition bei Kallimachos*, Hellenistica Groningana 9, Leuven; Paris; Dudley, MA, 92–96, Zitat 95.

lichem Auftrag und Eigeninitiative stehen, können sie zudem das Spannungsverhältnis zwischen der hierarchischen Patronage und der inszenierten Freundschaft abbilden, in der sich beide Beteiligten unaufgefordert mit ehrenden Gaben überbieten. Daß der Adressat und der Dichter ungeachtet aller Standesunterschiede miteinander und mit dem großen Hercules um die freiwillige Bestleistung konkurrieren können, verdankt sich ganz prominent den ironischen Brechungen, durch die der vorbildhafte Heros in kallimacheischer Manier von seinem hohen Sockel geholt und zur burlesken Figur gestaltet wird. Denn gerade in komischen Situationen läßt sich der Abstand zwischen Heroen und Menschen ungezwungen überspielen.

Das junge Alter des neu restaurierten Tempels gleicht der Preisdichter literarisch aus, indem er seine Erzählung der letztjährigen Ereignisse mit Motivanleihen aus Kallimachos und Vergil anreichert, die von uralten Kult- und Feststiftungen des Hercules an der stadtrömischen *Ara maxima* und in Nemea erzählen. Meine These ist, daß die transparenten Prätexte dem renovierten Heiligtum vor Surrent eine archaische Aura und kultgeschichtliche Dignität verleihen, die weit über den realen Wirkungsbereich des Privatkultes hinausstrahlt. Damit konkurriert der professionelle Festdichter als gedichtimmanenter Sprecher ebenso selbstbewußt wie kokett mit Hercules' rustikalen Preissängern – dem Salierchor der *Aeneis* – und mit der Person des opfernden Siegesdichters in Kallimachos' Epinikion auf Berenike.

Die Literarizität der *Silve* gibt demnach in vielfacher Weise Anlaß, über das Verhältnis der kleinformatigen Silvendichtung zum großen Epos sowie der konkreten, in Literatur gefaßten Okkasion und des rein literarisch erzeugten Festraums nachzudenken. Dieser poetologische Diskurs ist zunächst in der festlichen Rahmenhandlung verortet und wird dann nachträglich im Zuge der Buchpublikation auf den programmatischen Widmungsbrief ausgedehnt. Die zweifache Erscheinung des Hercules in der aitiologischen Binnen- und der festlichen Rahmenerzählung der *Silve* 3,1 wird dabei durch eine literarische Epiphanie des Hercules eingeleitet, die den kolossalen Heros zum unorthodoxen, aber situationsangemessenen Inspirationsgott des ganzen Silvenbuchs erhebt.

Ich möchte nun meine Thesen in einem Textdurchgang erläutern, bei dem jeweils auch verschiedene Formen und Funktionen der intertextuellen Markierung[34] diskutiert werden: so das Leitmotiv der Gastlichkeit im Namensverweis auf Molorchus (Kapitel 2.1.; Rahmenhandlung), die Inszenierung von Initiative und Auftrag in burlesker Transformation vergilischer Götterszenen (Kapitel 2.2.; Binnenerzählung), die literarische Konstruktion einer „modernen Kulttradition"

---

34 Zum Begriff der intertextuellen Markierung bzw. Markiertheit Helbig (s. Anm. 22)
    64–81.

durch Kombination kallimacheischer und vergilischer Aitien (Kapitel 2.3.; Binnenerzählung) und Hercules' Epiphanie an der Tempelschwelle auf dem Hintergrund von Kallimachos, Vergil und Horaz (Kapitel 2.4.; Rahmenhandlung). Am
nachträglich verfaßten Buchvorwort soll abschließend gezeigt werden, wie der
Hercules Surrentinus als okkasioneller Inspirationsgott dem Leser den Zugang
zum dritten Silvenbuch erschließt (Kapitel 2.5.).

2.1 Hercules in Molorchus' gastlicher Hütte

Daß Statius' Publikum gehalten ist, sich im Vollzug der Tempelweihung nicht
nur den Herculesmythos allgemein, sondern ganz bestimmte Textvorlagen zu
vergegenwärtigen, wird erstmals in der festlichen Epiklese des Hercules (konkret: in der namentlichen Erwähnung des Molorchus) angezeigt. Diese Figur ist
nämlich in der römischen Literatur ganz selten erwähnt,[35] und alle Belege verweisen auf ein und dieselbe Quelle:[36] Der Dichter Kallimachos eröffnet das dritte
Buch seiner *Aitien* mit einem Preis auf die Königin Berenike, die bei den Nemeischen Spielen gesiegt hat. In einer aitiologischen Einlage wird dann erzählt, wie
Hercules, der mythische Stifter bzw. Erneuerer[37] der Nemeischen Spiele, am
Vorabend des Löwenkampfs in der Hütte des armen Molorchos einkehrt.[38] Eben
diese Gastgeschichte greift Statius auf, um sie mit seinem *Hercules Surrentinus* zu
überbieten.[39]

Die literarische Konkurrenz zielt allerdings nur mittelbar auf Kallimachos;
als Zwischenglied dient nämlich Statius' eigenes Großepos, die *Thebais*.[40] Dort
tritt in einem Truppenkatalog die Streitmacht von Nemea auf. Als besondere
Ortsattraktion wird die „hochgerühmte Hütte des Molorchus" hervorgehoben.
An ihrer Weidenholztür sind die Waffen des großen Helden abgebildet; und im
Acker kann der Tourist noch heute die Abdrücke besichtigen, die Hercules'

---

35 Verg. *Georg.* 3,19; Paneg. in Mess. 12 f.; Mart. 4,64,30; Stat. *Theb.* 4,159–164; Stat. *silv.*
    4,6,51 f.
36 So bereits Parsons, P.J. 1977, „Callimachus. Victoria Berenices", *ZPE* 25, 43; Thomas
    (s. Anm. 14) 103. Die besondere Bedeutung des Georgica-Prooms für die *Silve* betont
    Newlands (s. Anm. 14) 441–446. Vgl. unten Anm. 124.
37 Aus den überlieferten Fragmenten läst sich nicht sicher erschließen, welcher Mythen-
    version Kallimachos gefolgt ist bzw. inwiefern er Mythentraditionen transformiert
    hat. Zu einer ausführlichen Diskussion der denkbaren Optionen Fuhrer (s. Anm. 31)
    78–85.
38 Call. *Ait.* 3, frg. 59–66 Asper.
39 Stat. *silv.* 3,1,29–38. Zu Statius' Rezeption der kallimacheischen Molorchus-Episode
    Thomas (s. Anm. 14) 103–105; Newlands (s. Anm. 14) 445 f.
40 Das Selbstzitat notiert bereits Thomas (s. Anm. 14) 104.

Keule, Bogen und Ellbogen hinterlassen haben.[41] Der epische Prätext wird in der
Silve 3,1 gleich durch mehrere Referenzen aufgerufen: Wenn der Sprecher in seiner Hymnenepiklese den Heros auffordert, neben seinen anderen Waffen die
„von königlichem Blut befleckte" Keule abzulegen (35), so erinnert dies an den
Kontext des thebanischen Feldzugs und an die Keulenspuren im nemeischen
Ackerboden. Anders als zu Zeiten des Löwenkampfs muß der kaiserzeitliche
Hercules in seiner Luxuswohnung von Surrent nicht mehr im Baumschatten auf
der harten Erde lagern, sondern kann es sich im schicken Rundtempel auf einem
weichen Polstersitz bequem machen, der zum Zweck des *lectisternium* aufgestellt
ist (37–38);[42] und die einstigen Weidenholztüren von Nemea sind nun in das
glänzende Portal des neuen „Palastheiligtums" (*aula recens*) überführt (5–11).
    Was leistet die markierte Intertextualität zwischen Kallimachos' *Aitien*, Sta-
tius' *Thebais* und der *Silve*? Inhaltlich ist das Leitmotiv der Gastlichkeit von zen-
traler Bedeutung, da in diesem Rahmen traditionell die Standesunterschiede
überspielt werden.[43] Das kleine Dach des Molorchus faßt daher die Freund-
schaftsbesuche des Silvendichters bei seinem Patron[44] und die mythische Theoxenie, die Einkehr von Göttern bei den Menschen.[45] Pollius empfängt den großen
Hercules ebenso herzlich wie einstmals der Bauer Molorchus. Zu seinem Verständnis der Gastlichkeit gehört aber auch der moderne Komfort, der seinen
eigenen Villengästen und demzufolge auch dem Heros als „Service des Hauses"
geboten wird. Die ehrwürdige Hütte von Nemea wird durch Pollius' modernen
Prunkbau überstrahlt, der sich nun seinerseits als Ausflugsziel für Menschen und
Götter empfiehlt.[46]
    Die hellenistische Originalerzählung bringt ihrerseits – und dieser Aspekt
der Intertextualität wurde in der bisherigen Forschung ignoriert – eine komische
Note ein:[47] Nicht nur, daß bei Kallimachos der arme Molorchus den gewaltigen

---

41 Stat. *Theb.* 4,159–164.
42 Zur Scheidung des Anbietens eines Tempels als Wohnort und des *lectisternium*
    respektive Kultmahls Rüpke (s. Anm. 19) 233f. Die Trennung der menschlichen und
    göttlichen Mahlgemeinschaft spiegelt sich in der *Silve* 3,1,106–109: Hercules bittet
    Pollius um einen würdigen Tempel, in dem er die olympischen Götter angemessen
    bewirten kann.
43 Vössing, K. 2004, *Mensa Regia. Das Bankett beim hellenistischen König und beim
    römischen Kaiser*, Beiträge zur Altertumskunde 193, München; Leipzig, 253–264.
44 Zum *convivium* als Ort der Patronage Vössing (s. Anm. 43) 240–244; Stein-Hölkes-
    kamp, E. 2005, *Das römische Gastmahl. Eine Kulturgeschichte*, München, 92–101.
45 Zur Theoxenie des Hercules in Mythos und Kult Flückiger-Guggenheim, D. 1984,
    *Göttliche Gäste. Die Einkehr von Göttern und Heroen in der griechischen Mytholo-
    gie*, Bern; Frankfurt; New York, 70–78.
46 *Silv.* 3,1,106–109; 144–150.
47 Zur Molorchus-Erzählung bei Kallimachos Fuhrer (s. Anm. 31) 66–85; Ambühl
    (s. Anm. 33) 58–97 mit älterer Literatur.

Hunger seines Ehrengasts nicht stillen kann; er leidet zudem unter einer Mäuse-
plage. Die zerstörerischen Nager besiegt er durch die trickreiche Erfindung einer
Mäusefalle.[48] Der Jungheld Hercules wird mit dieser pseudoheroischen Lektion
auf seinen Löwenkampf vorbereitet. Das Herbergsmotiv erschöpft sich – dies die
Folgerung für Statius' *Silve* – nicht im Luxusvergleich, der dem Surrentiner Tempel gegenüber der Hütte von Nemea einen höheren Standard bescheinigt. Vielmehr bietet Kallimachos ein lehrreiches Beispiel des ironisierenden Kontrasts
von Groß und Klein, da der Mäusekrieg des Molorchus den nicht auserzählten
Löwenkampf *en miniature* vorwegnimmt. Die implizite Referenz auf den kallimacheischen Mäusekrieg unterstreicht zugleich programmatisch den alexandrinischen Kunstanspruch der *Silven*: So hatte Statius bereits im ersten Buchproöm
die Publikation seiner leichtgewichtigen Gelegenheitsdichtung im Verweis auf
zwei parodistische Kleinepen, nämlich die homerische *Batrachomachie* und den
vergilischen *Culex*, gerechtfertigt, die als unterhaltendes „Präludium der epischen Großdichtung" beim kompetenten Publikum Anerkennung fänden.[49]

Wenn also unter dem Herculestempel von Surrent mit der Hütte des Molorchus eine bescheidenere Unterkunft des Heros transparent wird, die vor allem
literarische Berühmtheit erlangt hat, so ist dieser intertextuelle Durchblick als
Statius' erlesenes Gastgeschenk an den Patron zu verstehen. Als erklärter Musenfreund ist der Gastgeber Pollius der ideale Adressat für ein Festgedicht, dessen
Reiz im Anspielungsreichtum liegt. Im Rekurs auf die gastliche Hütte des Molorchus hat Statius seine *Silve* zudem mit den beiden Textarten unterlegt, auf die
er sich anschließend in der eingelegten Ursprungserzählung bezieht: das aitiologische, burlesk gefärbte Epyllion[50] und das myth-historische Großepos.

2.2 Hercules als burlesker Inspirationsgott

Wenden wir uns nun dem Anlaß der Tempelrestauration und damit dem narrativen Mittelteil der *Silve* zu. Ich möchte in einem Doppelschritt (Kapitel 2.2. und
2.3.) zeigen, daß der Surrentiner Hercules den Festdichter nicht nur zu einer
charmanten Erzählung der Baugeschichte und der Stiftung athletischer Spiele,
sondern auch zu einer ingeniösen Aitienkonstruktion inspiriert. Anstatt im Ha-

---

48 Zum Passus Rosenmeyer, P. A. 1991, „The Unexpected Guests. Patterns of Xenia in
    Callimachus' ‚Victoria Berenices' and ‚Petronius' ‚Satyricon'", *CQ* 41, 408–413; Fuh-
    rer (s. Anm. 31) 69 f.; Ambühl (s. Anm. 33) 82–87.
49 *Silv.* 1, *praef.* 7–10.
50 Zu den Spezifika des hellenistischen Epyllions Gutzwiller (s. Anm. 31) 2–9; Merriam
    (s. Anm. 31) 1–24. Zur Erzählstruktur und Erzähltechnik speziell der *Victoria Bereni-
    ces* mit eingelegtem Aition Fuhrer (s. Anm. 31) 112–127.

bitus des gelehrten Antiquars „längst vergessene" Kultwurzeln des neu geweihten Herculestempel zu eruieren, überrascht Statius sein gebildetes Publikum mit
einem ganz modernen Aition, das nur ein Jahr zurückdatiert. Das geringe Alter
des Herculestempels kompensiert der Festdichter dann literarisch, indem er seine
eigene Erzählung auf die aitiologischen Herculesgeschichten renommierter Prätexte bezieht. Für das kleine, aber feine Villenheiligtum vor Surrent nimmt das
festliche Herculesgedicht zugleich die ehrwürdige Aura der *Aeneis* und den
Esprit der kallimacheischen *Aitien* in Anspruch. Dabei mimt Hercules in einer
burlesken Doppelrolle sowohl den inspirierenden Auftraggeber als auch den lei-
stungsstarken Werkarbeiter.

Gleich im Auftakt kündigt das aparte Sängerduett von Calliope und Hercules
indirekt die literarische Doppelbödigkeit und die ironisierende Verarbeitung
großepischer Traditionen an.[51] Der Dichter bittet zunächst Calliope als Muse des
Epos um Inspiration. Allerdings wird die kundige Sängerin von der laut schallen-
den Stimme des Hercules übertönt, der die epische Melodie auf seinem gespannten Bogen nachahmt.[52] In der formellen Eröffnung des aitiologischen Kleinepos
wird also Hercules in der Funktion des Musenführers zugleich herbeizitiert und
parodiert. Als *Hercules Musagetes* und Gott der Musik spielt Hercules nämlich
die mehrsaitige Leier, wie Text- und Bildzeugnisse bestätigen.[53] Dagegen kann er
auf dem zweckentfremdeten Bogen gerade mal *einen* Klangton produzieren. Der
kolossale Heros gibt demzufolge bestenfalls einen burlesken Inspirationsgott ab.
Der Musenanruf dient der poetischen Abgrenzung und Leserlenkung: Vom professionellen Gelegenheitsdichter kann das Publikum anläßlich der Tempelweihung ein anspruchsvolles und amüsantes Aition mit vielfachen Assonanzen erwarten. Seine Kunstfertigkeit will Statius in kallimacheischer Manier auf der
Folie großformatiger, d.h. epischer Heldentaten beweisen.[54]

------

51 So auch schon Newlands (s. Anm. 14) 446–449, die allerdings nicht auf die Komposition der Binnenerzählung, sondern auf Hercules' zivilisatorische Leistung als Flur-
   bereiniger fokussiert.
52 *Silv.* 3,1,49–51: *sed quaenam subit, veneranda, exordia templi / dic age, Calliope; so-
   cius tibi grande sonabit / Alcides tensoque modos imitabitur arcu.* Den unkonventionellen Musenanruf könnte Ov. *fast.* 6,811 f. (zum stadtrömischen Heiligtum des Hercules Musarum) angeregt haben. Zur Relevanz der ovidischen *Fasten* für die *Silve* 3,1
   siehe unten die Kapitel 2.3. und 2.5.
53 Boardman, J. 1988, „Herakles in various non-narrative roles", in: *LIMC* 4.1, Zürich;
   München, 810–817.
54 Auf die hellenistisch-kallimacheische Programmatik des statianischen Hercules verweist bereits Newlands 1991, 443: „Statius' Hercules is likewise a programmatic figure, but for a different kind of poetry, a kind that has deliberately moved away from
   epic's typical concern with destructive violence and has adopted Hellenistic principles
   of playfullness, allusiveness, and wit. Here Statius departs significantly from his Ver-

Nur wenig später gibt dann ein Vergleich als intertextuelles Wegzeichen den vergilischen Prätext an:[55] Das aufziehende Gewitter wird dem Sturmregen gleichgesetzt, mit dem Iuno die Königin Dido und deren Gast Aeneas auf der Jagd überraschte und in einer Höhle Zuflucht suchen ließ. Ein geübter Leser wie Pollius Felix, der diese Fährte aufgenommen hat, wird nun aber alsbald feststellen, daß sich der epische Sturmvergleich nicht in dem evidenten Verweis auf das Didobuch erschöpft, sondern ihn auf eine andere Textspur der *Aeneis* führt, auf die das Aition nicht mehr explizit, sondern motivisch abgestimmt ist. Dieser Textuntergrund erhellt sich an zwei Götterszenen, die ich näher vorführen möchte.

Vom Gewitter aufgescheucht, hat die Festgesellschaft bei Hercules eine Notunterkunft gefunden. Gegenüber der einleitenden Molorchusgeschichte sind die Rollen nun witzig getauscht. Unvermutet sieht sich der vormalige Einkehrer zum Gastgeber in seiner eigenen Hütte bestellt. Deren Dürftigkeit läßt ihn verlegen erröten. Denn jetzt kann Hercules selbst seine Gäste nicht angemessen beherbergen. Kurz entschlossen nimmt sich der Hüttenbewohner daher den „hoch geschätzten Pollius" unter vier Augen zur Brust. In schmeichelnder Umarmung sucht er seinen Ehrengast zu veranlassen, ihm einen feinen Tempel zu errichten, der sich mit Pollius' großartigen Bauten in Neapel, Puteoli und Surrent messen könne.

Die auffällige Intimität der Begegnung hat zu Recht die Editoren und Kommentatoren der *Silve* irritiert.[56] Denn die körperliche Nähe widerspricht allen Regeln einer Epiphanie:[57] Eine warme Umarmung paßt so gar nicht zum großen Moment einer Gottesschau – um so weniger, als der enge Körperkontakt unter zwei Männern der Erzählung eine pikant-erotische Note gibt. Der Vorschlag, die schmeichelnde Annäherung als Metapher für Hercules' Gedankenübertragung

---

gilian model." Wenig plausibel scheint mir vor diesem Hintergrund Newlands' forcierte Abgrenzung des *Hercules Surrentinus* von Kallimachos' *Aitien*, 450: „the playfullness has a serious side, however. Statius avoids the eccentricities of Callimachean aetia, the sometimes grim obscurity, the interest in poverty and humble life, features that do not suit the life of the cultivated, philosophical leisure and detachment from public life which he wishes to exalt."

55 *Silv.* 3,1,73–75. Vgl. Verg. *Aen.* 4,160–168.

56 Laguna (s. Anm. 12) 159: „para virum, Markland propuso su conjetura animum, con el argumento de que Hércules no puede abrazar físicamente a Félix si su epifanía es exclusivamente espiritual."

57 Zur Topik der Epiphanie Gladigow, B. 1990, „Epiphanie, Statuette, Kultbild. Griechische Gottesvorstellungen im Wechsel von Kontext und Medium", *Visible Religion* 7, 98–121.

an Pollius aufzufassen,[58] überzeugt nicht, weil er das störende Moment weg-radiert und nicht erklärt.[59]

Das Problem löst sich jedoch in verblüffender Weise, wenn man die *Aeneis* zu Rate zieht. Denn Hercules orientiert sich offenkundig an einer motivver-wandten Werbungsmaßnahme der vergilischen Venus: Im achten Buch erbittet sich Venus beim Ehemann Vulcanus neue Waffen für ihren Sohn.[60] Gleich zu Beginn haucht sie ihren Worten göttliche Liebe ein (*Aen.* 8,373: *incipit et dictis divinum aspirat amorem*); und ihrer schmeichelnden Rede hilft sie mit einer zärt-lichen Umarmung nochmals nach.[61] Der Schmiedegott Vulcanus steht denn auch sofort in wohlvertrauten Flammen und sagt im Vorblick auf eine „heiße" Liebes-nacht seine Hilfe zu.[62]

Auf diesem Hintergrund lassen sich die Statiuskommentare korrigieren: Hercules' Tête-à-tête mit Pollius ist keine Metapher, sondern eine witzige Ver-formung der vergilischen Inspirationsszene. Deren erotisches Potential hat Sta-tius genutzt, um sein Aition pikant zu würzen. Da in der *Silve* just der Frauen-held Hercules[63] die Rolle der Liebesgöttin mimt, wird die epische Szene zur Burleske: Statt von Venus' Armen sanft umfangen zu werden, sieht sich Pollius von den Pranken des Löwentöters halb erdrückt.[64]

Daß die Motivparallelen zwischen den Inspirationsszenen der *Silve* und der *Aeneis* beabsichtigt sind und erkannt werden sollen, beweist die weitere Erzäh-lung. Wenn nämlich Hercules des Nachts in Aktion tritt, vergleicht Statius die laut hallenden Axthiebe des Helden mit der dröhnenden Kyklopenschmiede am Aetna.[65] Dort hatte ja einstmals Vulcanus, durch die Liebesnacht mit Venus hochmotiviert, den Schild des Aeneas gefertigt.[66] Hercules schlüpft also nun in

---

58 Laguna (s. Anm. 12) 159: „sin embargo *virum complectitur* es una metáfora concreta que caracteriza una acción abstracta."
59 Zur Irritation des Lesers als Instrument der Signalisierung von Intertextualität Helbig (s. Anm. 28) 162.
60 Verg. *Aen.* 8,370–406.
61 Verg. *Aen.* 8,387–394.
62 Zur vergilischen Szene Schmidt, V. 1973, „Dans la chambre d'or de Vulcan (à propos de Virg. *Aen.* 8,370 sqq.)", *Mnemosyne* 26, 350–375; Maselli, G. 1989, „Venere e Vul-cano (*Aen.* VIII, 369–406). Stratigrafia e diffrazione semica", *Aufidus* 7, 31–50; Holz-berg, N. 2006, *Vergil. Der Dichter und sein Werk*, München, 184–186.
63 Siehe Loraux, N. 1990, „Herakles. The Super-Male and the Feminine", in: D. M. Hal-perin; J. J. Winkler; F. I. Zeitlin (Hrsg.), *Before Sexuality. The Construction of Erotic Experience in the Ancient Greek World*, Princeton, 21–52.
64 Laguna (s. Anm. 12) 159: „con todo, la imagen resultante es irónica, pues los brazos de Hércules, con los que rodéo el cuello del león de Nemea para ahogarlo o con los que ahogó a anteo, no so precisamente un modelo de delicadeza."
65 *Silv.* 3,1,128–133.
66 Verg. *Aen.* 8,407–453. Zur Stelle Egelhaaf-Gaiser, U. 2008, „Werkstattbesuch bei Vul-

die Rolle des epischen Handwerkers. Doch auch in diesem Gewand wirkt der
Held komisch. Namentlich dem Kunstanspruch des göttlichen Schmieds wird
der ungetüme Holzfäller in keiner Weise gerecht. Wohl wissend um dieses Defi-
zit hatte er ja selbst seinem Villennachbarn den Neubau als Gemeinschaftspro-
jekt angetragen,[67] in dem Leistung und Gewinn angemessen verteilt sind: Während Hercules im freien Gelände seine Muskeln spielen läßt, zeichnet Pollius für
die Tempelarchitektur und den eleganten Dekor verantwortlich.[68] Der Heros
erhält dadurch einen schicken Wohnsitz, Pollius aber Ruhm und Ehre.

Spätestens wenn Hercules seine grobe Axt in Statius' gepflegtem „Wäldchen"
schwingt, tritt die hohe Selbstreferentialität des Festbeitrags zutage.[69] Die *Silve*
qualifiziert sich zum Programmgedicht dadurch, daß sie das System von Auftrag
und Initiative aus verschiedenen Blickwinkeln und auf mehreren Textebenen
beleuchtet: Zum einen bestätigt sie implizit die feinsinnige Literaturkenner- und
-könnerschaft von Patron und Poet. Denn für Pollius gewinnt der ehrende Festbeitrag des Dichters ganz beträchtlich an Charme, sobald er die Ebene der
episch-burlesken Götterhandlung im hauseigenen Aition erkennt. Zum anderen
hat der Silvendichter sein eigenes Leistungsverständnis nicht nur auf den „Bau-
vertrag" von Pollius und Hercules, sondern auch auf die Übereinkunft zwischen
Venus und Vulcanus übertragen. Hercules ist in einer Person inspirierender Auftraggeber (wie Venus und Pollius) und leistungsstarker Akkordarbeiter (wie Vulcanus und Statius); beide Rollen übernimmt er aus eigenem Wunsch und in eigenem Interesse. In kokettem Vergleich mit Vulcans historischem Meisterwerk
verweist Statius mit der dreizehnten Herculestat vor Surrent[70] auf die Originali-
tät seiner *Silve*, die zu gegebenem Anlaß das passende Aition für den kleinen,
aber feinen Tempel präsentiert. Im Verhältnis von Auftrag und Initiative ist die

canus. Triumphale Geschichtsbilder aus Vergils intertextueller Waffenschmiede (*Aen.*
8,407–453)", in: H. Krasser; D. Pausch; I. Petrovic (Hrsg.), „*Triplici invectus trium-
pho*". *Der römische Triumph in augusteischer Zeit*, Stuttgart (29 Ms.-Seiten, im
Druck).

67   *Silv.* 3,1,106–114.
68   Deutlich angezeigt wird die Verteilung der Kompetenzen nach Hercules' nächtlichem
      Werken (*silv.* 3,1,135): *artifices* (scil. die Bauarbeiter des Pollius) *mirantur opus* (scil.
      die Planierung des Landes durch Hercules).
69   *Silv.* 3,1,125–128. Verstärkt wird die Selbstreferentialität noch durch die metapoeti-
      sche Qualität des Holzfällens, das einerseits auf die epische Motivtradition und ande-
      rerseits auf den Werktitel *Silvae* referiert. Zur Diskussion des Werktitels Bright, D.
      1980, *Elaborate disarray. The nature of Statius' Silvae*, BzA 108, Meisenheim, 20–49;
      Nauta (s. Anm. 3) 252–255; Newlands (s. Anm. 4) 36–38; zum intertextuellen An-
      spielungsreichtum und zur poetischen Selbstreferentialität des Begriffs *Silva* Hinds,
      S. 1998, *Allusion and intertext. Dynamics of appropriation in Roman poetry*, Cam-
      bridge, 10–16, Johannsen (s. Anm. 3) 305–307.
70   *Silv.* 3,1,123 f.; 3,1,19–22.

spontane Festgabe sogar dem Epos überlegen. Denn unter idealen Freunden wie Statius und Pollius bedarf es keiner Weisungen und Werkaufträge; sie erbringen freiwillige Leistungen, die beide Seiten ehren.

2.3 Aitiologisches Sommerpicknick mit Hercules

Nachdem sich die Götterszenen der *Aeneis* als inspirierender Ideengeber für den *Hercules Surrentinus* erwiesen haben, erhebt sich rückblickend die Frage, ob in der eingelegten Erzählung womöglich schon vor dem unübersehbaren Wegweiser des epischen Sturmvergleichs der vergilische Prätext – namentlich das extensiv zitierte Rombuch – anklingt. Allein aufgrund des aitiologischen Charakters und des Leitmotivs der peinlichen Gastlichkeit liegt ein Bezug auf Vergils Geschichte von Hercules und Cacus nahe,[71] die in der *Aeneis* den in der *Silve* persiflierten Götterszenen unmittelbar vorangeht: Bei seinem Besuch im vorrömischen Pallanteum trifft Aeneas den König Euander und die Stadteinwohner beim Festbankett an der *Ara maxima* an, die einst Hercules persönlich nach seinem Sieg über den Unhold Cacus errichtet hatte. Nachdem Euander den ortsfremden Aeneas über das lokale Kultaition aufgeklärt hat und der Salierchor zum Abschluß des Opferfests Hercules' Heldentaten nochmals hymnisch gepriesen hat, geleitet der König seinen Gast Aeneas zum Palatin, wo er ihm seine ärmliche Hütte als nächtliche Herberge anbietet.[72] In ebendieser Nacht motiviert Venus ihren Ehemann zur Fertigung der Heldenwaffen.

Was gewänne der Silvendichter im impliziten Bezug auf die Geschichte von Hercules und Cacus? Primär eröffnet sich hier eine Möglichkeit, mit rein literarischen Mitteln für die nur ein Jahr zurückdatierende Bauinitiative eine kultgeschichtliche Tiefe zu konstruieren. Der Surrentiner Tempelbau und zugehörige Herculeskult könnten damit elegant ihr Altersdefizit kompensieren; sie erhielten ein archaisches Kolorit und eine neue Dignität, ohne dabei auf ihren Modernitätsanspruch verzichten zu müssen. Bei dieser Gelegenheit ließen sich nicht nur die unterstellten Literaturkompetenzen des Erstlesers Pollius bestätigen, sondern auch um eine besondere Versiertheit in Kult, Kalender und aitiologischen Fragen ergänzen.

Falls das Aition zum Herculestempel vor Surrent tatsächlich gezielt auf Vergils Herculesgeschichte rekurriert, sollte der Silvendichter dies zumindest schwach signalisiert haben. Ein erstes Indiz dafür scheint mir das Festdatum zu sein, das sorgfältig exponiert ist: Den 13. August hat Statius im Gestus aitiologischer Gelehrsamkeit mit dem Jahresfest der Diana Nemorensis verklausuliert

---

71 So bereits Laguna (s. Anm. 12) 125 f.
72 *Aen.* 8,102–369.

(55–60). Ein Blick auf den stadtrömischen Kalender lehrt nun aber, daß am selben Tag auch Hercules Invictus an der Porta Trigemina sein Jahresopfer erhielt; und am 12. August wurde Hercules Victor beim Circus Maximus geehrt.[73] Das kundige Zielpublikum der *Silven* – allen voran der Baustifter Pollius – wird zweifellos den mit stadtrömischen Festterminen umschriebenen *dies natalis* des Surrentiner Privatheiligtums entschlüsselt und die Verbindung zu den nicht explizit genannten, aber populären Herculesfesten in der Hauptstadt hergestellt haben.[74]

Meines Erachtens lädt die scheinbar zufällige Koinzidenz der Festtage in Rom und Surrent nicht nur zum konkurrierenden Ortsvergleich, sondern auch zur intertextuellen Lektüre ein – um so mehr, als die motivverwandten Bankettszenen des Herculesfests am Tiberufer und des spontanen Sommerpicknicks am Villenstrand durch eine sprachliche Assonanz als Parallelszenen markiert sind.[75]

Nehmen wir einmal, basierend auf den bisher festgestellten Vergilallusionen, an, daß Statius seine Erzählung nicht nur punktuell, sondern konsequent auf die epische Handlung der *Aeneis* abgestimmt hat, so müßte die gewitterbedingte Notunterkunft von Pollius' Festgesellschaft im unrestaurierten Heiligtum analog zu Aeneas' abendlicher Einkehr bei Euander gestaltet sein. Tatsächlich zeigt sich der unfreiwillig zum Gastgeber bestellte Hercules vor der exklusiven Festgesellschaft ob der Dürftigkeit seiner rustikalen Herberge[76] ähnlich peinlich berührt wie der König Euander. Der bittet nämlich den Ehrengast Aeneas mit einem entschuldigenden Wort in seine palatinische Hütte: Da einst Hercules die ärmliche Herberge nicht geringgeschätzt habe, solle jetzt auch der große Aeneas „es wagen, die luxuriöse Pracht zu verachten" (*Aen.* 8,364: *aude, hospes, contemnere opes*) und sich dadurch dem heroischen Vorbild als würdig erweisen.[77] Das Motiv der peinlichen Gastlichkeit gewinnt nochmals an Evidenz dadurch, daß bereits Vergil die Hütte des Euander auf der Folie der kallimacheischen Molorchus-Episode inszeniert hatte.[78]

---

73 Scullard, H.H. 1981, *Festivals and Ceremonies of the Roman Republic*, London, 171–174.

74 Pace Newlands (s. Anm. 14) 443 und 446.

75 *Silv.* 3,1,68–70: *forte diem Triviae dum litore ducimus udo / angustasque fores adsuetaque tecta gravati / frondibus et patula defendimus arbore soles; Aen.* 8,102–104: *forte die sollemnem illo rex Arcas honorem / Amphitryoniadae magno divisque ferebat / ante urbem in luco.* Auch Hercules' Versprechen an Pollius, er werde selbst den „böswilligen Berg" (110f.) bezwingen und „das raue Innere der widerspenstigen Erde sprengen" (113), läßt erneut an Hercules' Kampf mit Cacus denken, in dem der Held unter vollem Krafteinsatz einen über der Höhe aufragenden Fels aus dem Steilhang gebrochen hatte, siehe Verg. *Aen.* 8,233–238.

76 *Silv.* 3,1,82–89.

77 *Aen.* 8,359–369.

78 Dazu George, E.V. 1974, *Aeneid VIII and the Aitia of Callimachus*, Mnemosyne

Was leistet nun aber die Vergegenwärtigung der vergilischen Herculeserzählung für die Gastgeschichte der *Silve*? Die asymmetrische Nahbeziehung zwischen Heros, Dichter und Patron läßt sich erneut in der umgekehrten Theoxenie literarisch überhöhen. Demzufolge werden der Gegensatz des „großen Gastgebers" (83: *magnum Alciden*) und seines unerwarteten Ehrengasts und die demonstrative Nivellierung der Rangunterschiede unter „geistesverwandten Freunden" (89 f.: *dilecta Polli corda*) anschaulich ausgemalt.

Dabei gibt sich einerseits der *Hercules Surrentinus* im Vergleich zu seinem epischen Vorgänger betont fortschrittlich und urban: Rhetorisch versiert spielt er die peinliche Gastsituation aus, um seinen begüterten Nachbarn (91: *largitor opum*[79]) zur Finanzierung eines schicken Tempels zu verpflichten.[80] Da Pollius, so das Argument, sein Land unlängst mit einer prangenden Villa geziert habe, werde er sich jetzt doch nicht gegenüber seinem bedürftigen Nachbarn als kleinlich erweisen, der lange Jahre ganz uneigennützig das Villenland geschützt habe.[81] Pollius bestätigt prompt alle Erwartungen, indem er die mythischen Gastgeber Molorchus und Euander dank seiner Geldmittel weit überbietet: Großzügig errichtet er Hercules einen schmucken Tempel, der mit seiner eleganten Villa mithalten kann, und ehrt den ortsnahen Gott mit einem jährlichen Festtag und neu gestifteten Spielen.[82]

Andererseits verleiht das vergilische Herculesfest dem jungen Kultableger vor Surrent ein archaisches Kolorit: Unversehens wird Euanders rustikales Freiluftbankett am Tiberufer zum mythischen Prototyp nicht nur des letztjährigen Strandpicknicks, sondern auch des aktuellen und aller künftigen Herculesfeste auf der Surrentiner Villa gekürt. Denn entsprechend der stadtrömischen Kultpraxis dürfte auch Pollius den Weihetag seines Privatheiligtums alljährlich mit einem *lectisternium* für Hercules und einer festlichen Bewirtung seiner Gäste begangen haben.[83] Folgerichtig knüpft Statius' aktueller Festbeitrag an die Tradition des

---

Supplements 27, Leiden, 25–42; Tueller, M. A. 2000, „Well-Read Heroes. Quoting the *Aetia* in *Aeneid* 8", *HSPh* 100, 371–377.

79 Vgl. die Beschreibung der luxuriösen Gerätschaften (86 f.); auch in seiner Schlußansprache würdigt Hercules die Reichtümer des Baustifters Pollius (166). Zum Reichtum als „Glück" des Villenbesitzers, der diese Eigenschaft bereits in seinem Beinamen trägt und dabei sein Glück nicht vom materiellen Reichtum abhängig macht, jetzt Gauly (s. Anm. 5).

80 Naheliegend ist die Vermutung, daß Hercules' Erröten auf die eigentliche Motivation der Tempelrestauration deutet, da dem Villenbesitzer Pollius der baufällige Zustand des Heiligtums vor den Gästen womöglich peinlich war: siehe Rühl (s. Anm. 2) 304.

81 *Silv.* 3,1,96–104. Zu Hercules als Schützer des Villenlands siehe bereits *silv.* 2,2,23 f.

82 *Silv.* 3,1,45.

83 Zum jährlichen Herculesfest an der *Ara maxima* siehe *Aen.* 8,268–305.

ehrwürdigen Salierchors an, der im achten Buch der *Aeneis* vor der *Ara maxima* an Hercules' Heldentaten erinnert.[84]

Pollius' neu eingerichtete Wettkämpfe mit Kranzverleihung an den Sieger[85] profitieren ihrerseits von der aitiologischen Motivanleihe bei Kallimachos, laut dessen Aussage der erfolgreich zurückgekehrte Löwentöter Hercules die Spiele von Nemea gestiftet und den Selleriekranz zum Siegespreis bestimmt hat.[86] Im koketten Vergleich mit dem berühmten Vorbild gibt Statius den lokalen Agonen vor Surrent (selbstverständlich!) den Vorzug.

Der intertextuelle Bezug auf Hercules' Kultgründungen in Nemea und Rom ehrt nicht nur den großzügigen Tempelstifter und gebildeten Leser Pollius, sondern verweist auch auf die Leistung des professionellen Dichters: Er darf es sich als Verdienst anrechnen, die spontane Bauinitiative seines Patrons in ein literarisch wie kultgeschichtlich ambitioniertes Aition gekleidet zu haben. Dank seiner poetischen Kunst sind die Herculesgeschichten des Kallimachos und Vergil im Surrentinischen Festgedicht subsumiert; das moderne Herculesheiligtum auf privatem Grund hat dabei seinerseits historischen Glanz und erlesene Dignität gewonnen.

2.4 Panegyrische Opferdienste für Hercules

Nachdem Hercules in der aitiologischen Einlage als rhetorischer Charmeur, als imposanter Holzfäller und Kultstifter zum Einsatz kam, soll nun am Schlußteil der *Silve* die Rollenkonstruktion des Dichters als panegyrischer Opferdiener auf dem Untergrund von Kallimachos, Vergil und Horaz beleuchtet werden.

Der Festsänger hat seine inspirierte Rückblende kaum beendet, da sieht er schon, wie Hercules an der Schwelle des Heiligtums steht und selbst zu einer Lobeshymne auf den Restaurator anhebt. Die Forschung hat sich an der Motivdoppelung nie gestört.[87] Dabei stellt die zweite Epiphanie Pollius' erste Privatbegegnung mit dem Heros zumindest in Frage – um so mehr, als diesmal Hercules nicht in burlesker Epenverkleidung, sondern mit göttlicher Aura und Würde auftritt. Formal ist die Schlußrede höher gestuft, da sie nicht in der eingelegten Erzählung, sondern in der szenischen Rahmenhandlung steht. Zudem könnte ein

---

84 Verg. *Aen.* 8,285–305.
85 *Silv.* 3,1,43–45; 139–153.
86 Call. *Ait.* 64–66 Asper.
87 Coleman (s. Anm. 22) 73 f. behandelt beide Reden unterschiedslos als Instrument der panegyrischen Überhöhung und die Selbsterniedrigung des mythologischen Sprechers, der sich in „Augenhöhe" zu seinem menschlichen Gegenüber begibt, als Zeichen der vorbehaltlosen Anerkennung.

Leser begründet vermuten, daß Hercules bei der ersten, intimen Epiphanie aus strategischen Werbungsgründen die wunderbaren Bauleistungen des Pollius[88] rhetorisch überhöht habe. Dagegen scheint Hercules' emphatischer Dank durch das Augenzeugnis des Dichters und durch religiöse *omina* (184–186) „wasserdicht" beglaubigt zu sein.

In der Tat nimmt Hercules in der zweiten Epiphanie seine vormalige Aussage zurück. Entgegen dem Angebot einer gleichberechtigten Arbeitsteilung macht er jetzt erneut die Hierarchie zwischen Menschen und Heroen geltend: Indem er den Tempelstifter zum großen Nachahmer seiner Taten kürt, ehrt er Pollius' wohltätige Leistungen mit einem exzellenten Gütesiegel, nämlich mit dem Titel des „kleinen Hercules".[89] Für sich selbst beansprucht er freilich im Gegenzug den alleinigen Ruhm des wegbereitenden Ideengebers.

Der Dichter nutzt die Gelegenheit, um sein eigenes Lob des Tempelstifters mit Hercules' Stentorstimme zusammenzuführen. Im aitiologischen Musenanruf hatte Statius Calliope als epische Vorsängerin engagiert und sich vom burlesken Bogenmusikant Hercules distanziert. Jetzt spendet der Dichter die *Silve* als sein eigenes Trankopfer auf Hercules' Altar. Der professionelle Gelegenheitsdichter nimmt sich in diesem selbstbewußten Opfergestus ein letztes Mal an Kallimachos ein Beispiel. Der hellenistische Preisdichter bezeichnet nämlich im Eingang des dritten Aitienbuchs das rahmende Siegeslied auf Berenike als ein geschuldetes Dankesgeschenk an Zeus und die Nymphe Nemea.[90] Kallimachos ehrt also seine Adressatin auf Umwegen, d.h. über Zeus, der als Gelegenheitsgeber zum Sieg im Wagenrennen die poetische Weihegabe empfängt.

Statius arbeitet in seiner Selbstinszenierung als Kultdiener des Hercules die kallimacheische Rollenkonstruktion konsequent aus: Als engagierter Festdichter tritt er nicht etwa bescheiden ab, sobald Hercules selbst erscheint. Vielmehr schreibt er seiner eigenen Stimme die Autorität des kolossalen Heros zu.[91] Ein geschultes Ohr kann in Hercules' vollmundigem Lob die feine Stimme des Dichters heraushören. Der göttliche Festredner sagt dem Heiligtum von Surrent nämlich eine Kultkontinuität voraus, für die „keine Zeitgrenze gesetzt sei".[92] In

---

88 *Silv*. 3,1,91–103; zu Pollius als Wundertäter Coleman (s. Anm. 22) 74f.
89 *Silv*. 3,1,166–170.
90 Call. *Ait*. frg. 56, 1–2 Asper. Zum okkasionellen Einleitungsteil der *Victoria Berenices* Fuhrer (s. Anm. 31) 64–66; 86–103.
91 Dieser poetische Selbstanspruch wird im Vergleich mit der *Silve* 4,3 evident: Während dort der Preisdichter im Schlußpassus (124–163) der göttlichen Autorität der Sibylle von Cumae das ultimative Lob der *via Domitiana* überträgt, endet die *Silve* 3,1 nicht mit Hercules' Rede, sondern schließt vielmehr die hymnische Ansprache in den inszenierten Rahmen der Festhandlung ein.
92 *Silv*. 3,1,180f.: *nam templis numquam statuetur terminus aevi / dum me flammigeri portabit machina caeli.*

diesen Schlußworten ist ein letztes Mal die Autorität der *Aeneis* für die Festgelegenheit der *Silve* in Anspruch genommen. Und da der Koloß Hercules auch als Panegyriker aufs Ganze geht, bezieht er sich auf die epochale Rede, in der Iuppiter Roms unbegrenzte Weltherrschaft verkündet hatte mit dem geflügelten Wort *imperium sine fine dedi* – „ein Reich ohne Grenzen habe ich gegeben".[93] In diesem Eposzitat hat der Silvendichter das intertextuelle i-Tüpfelchen auf seiner ehrenden Festgabe plaziert. Als Bauherr und Literaturpatron kann sich Pollius vom zweistimmigen Lob des großen Kulturstifters Hercules und des professionellen Gelegenheitsdichters wahrhaft festlich gewürdigt fühlen.

Die aus der finalen Opferszene abgeleiteten Folgerungen für die poetologische Qualität der *Silve* lassen sich im Rückblick auf die Eröffnungsverse bestätigen.[94] Da nämlich Statius den Baustifter Pollius beim feierlichen Vollzug der Opferhandlung einführt, gestaltet er seine eigene Libation für Hercules[95] zum poetischen Pendant des realen Weiheakts. Der lyrische Sprecher profiliert sich also nicht nur als Opferdiener des Hercules, sondern auch als Kulthelfer seines Patrons, auf dessen rituelle Weihung er in kallimacheischer Manier mit einer aitiologischen Opfergabe respondiert.[96] Dementsprechend wird Pollius als Erstrezipient der *Silve* gleich anfangs zum Beweis seiner Bildungskompetenzen aufgerufen, da er dem Tempelbesitzer Hercules die Ursachen der einjährigen Kultunterbrechung (2: *causas designat desidis anni*) erläutern soll; und wenig später verbürgt das verstrichene Kalenderjahr die staunenswerte Geschwindigkeit der Tempelrestauration in Anspielung auf die Zahl der Herculestaten, die den Monaten exakt entspricht.[97] Die Gemeinschaft zwischen Tempelbesitzer, Poet und Patron wird also bereits eingangs mit den aitiologischen Interessen begründet.

Ein weiteres intertextuelles Indiz für ein gesteigertes Leistungsbewußtsein des Auftragsdichters ist das erste Wort der *Silve* (*intermissa*), das, wie die Statiuskommentare längst vermerkt haben, auf die Einleitung zum vierten Odenbuch des Horaz verweist.[98] Poetologisch relevant wird dieser Rückbezug bereits dadurch, daß das zitierte *carmen* 4,1 den Leser in die panegyrische Dichtkunst des vierten Odenbuchs einführt.

---

93 Verg. *Aen.* 1,279. Die Vergilallusion notiert bereits Laguna (s. Anm. 12) 188.

94 *Silv.* 3,1,1–2: *intermissa tibi renovat, Tirynthie, sacra / Pollius et causas designat desidis anni.*

95 *Silv.* 3,1,163 f.: *haec ego nascentes laetus bacchatus ad aras / libamenta tuli.*

96 Einen gesuchten Bezug auf die *Aitien* des Kallimachos postuliert für die Eröffnungsverse auch Newlands (s. Anm. 14) 439f. Vgl. Parsons (s. Anm. 36) 39: „epinicion embraced aetion." Thomas (s. Anm. 14) 97 vermutet darüber hinaus, daß Berenike ihren Rennsieg mit einer Statuen- oder Tempelweihung verewigt hat.

97 *Silv.* 3,1,17–19.

98 Vollmer (s. Anm. 16) 386; Laguna (s. Anm. 12) 128.

Nun ist sich die aktuelle Forschung weitgehend einig, daß die Oden des
Horaz im Unterschied zu Statius' ortsgebundenen *Silven* im Medium des Texts
fiktive Gelegenheiten und Festräume erzeugen, innerhalb derer der lyrische
Sprecher seine jeweilige Rolle und Position bestimmt.[99] So definiert denn Horaz
im *carmen* 4,1 die neue Sprechhaltung eines mittlerweile fünfzigjährigen Lyrikers, der die Wiederaufnahme der Odendichtung nach einer mehrjährigen Pause
(*intermissa*) begründet.[100] Nachdem er sich von den Liebes- und Festfreuden der
Jugend und von der lyrischen Dichtung bereits verabschiedet hat, entbrennt er
nun ganz unerwartet durch die grausame Venus in später Liebe. Die Liebesgöttin
verweist dabei nicht nur auf die biographische Situation, sondern figuriert darüber hinaus als Chiffre der horazischen Liebesdichtung und der horazischen
Lyrik insgesamt.[101]

Das Spannungsverhältnis von Liebe (d. h. Lyrik im Stil der ersten Odenedi-
tion) und Alter markiert der Sprecher in einem abwehrenden Verweisgestus: Pas-
sender sei es, wenn Venus in das Haus des jungen Paulus Maximus einziehe.
Denn dessen glänzende Begabung und Stellung machten ihn zu einem idealen
Krieger der Venus: Nach den Liebestriumphen werde Maximus „seiner" Sieges-
göttin auf der eigenen Villa am Albaner See ein Marmorbild in einem eleganten,
mit Zitrusholz überdachten Heiligtum stiften. Dort werde Venus in einem fort-
dauernden Liebesfest von Mädchen- und Jungenchören, Musikanten und Rei-
gentänzern geehrt.[102]

Die Parallelen zwischen dem lyrisch imaginierten Venusheiligtum und dem
realen Herculestempel vor Surrent liegen auf der Hand. Die eigentliche Pointe
des in die *Silve* integrierten Zitats ist aber meines Erachtens darin zu sehen, daß
der flavische Gelegenheitsdichter im gesuchten Bezug auf den augusteischen
Lyriker sein eigenes Leistungsprofil definiert:[103] In der Horazode ist der Ort der

---

99 Exemplarisch Schmidt, E. A. 2001, „Fiktionale Okkasionalität. Zur Funktion fiktiver
    Gelegenheiten in der horazischen Ode", in: ders., *Zeit und Form. Dichtungen des
    Horaz*, Heidelberg, 297–315; Rühl (s. Anm. 2) 90 f.; Krasser, H. 2007, „Poeta triumph-
    hans. Die Inszenierung von Sieghaftigkeit im vierten Odenbuch des Horaz", in:
    A. Arweiler; B. M. Gauly (Hrsg.), *Machtfragen. Festschrift für Konrad Heldmann*,
    Stuttgart (im Druck).
100 Hor. *c.* 4,1,1–2: *intermissa, Venus, diu / rursus bella moves? parce, precor, precor.*
101 Kerkhecker, A. 1988, „Zur Komposition des vierten Horazischen Odenbuches",
    Antike und Abendland 34, 130–132.
102 Hor. *c.* 4,1,9–28.
103 Schief ist m. E. der von Newlands (s. Anm. 14) 440 f. konstatierte Kontrast zwischen
    Horazens Zuwendung zur politischen Panegyrik und einem Programm des politi-
    schen Rückzugs, das Statius im dritten Silvenbuch proklamiere. Denn zum einen
    werden im dritten Silvenbuch durchaus auch Persönlichkeiten aus dem engeren
    Umfeld des Kaiserhofs geehrt (*silv.* 3,2: Maecius Celer; 3,4: Flavius Earinus), zum
    anderen finden sich die meisten Domitiangedichte in Buch 4 (*silv.* 4,1–3). Grundsätz-

Götterbegegnung unbestimmt, so wie die angesprochene Venus für den Leser in keinem konkreten Erscheinungsbild greifbar wird. Auch die „lange Dauer" (c. 4,1,1: *diu*) der lyrischen Pause ist ausschließlich an der gewandelten Selbstwahrnehmung des Dichters gemessen (c. 4,1,3: *non sum qualis eram*). Statius betritt die Bühne dagegen als Augenzeuge vor Ort. Sowohl die Dauer der Kultpause als auch das Datum der Neuweihung sind kalendarisch vermerkt; und der Heros wird eigens in einem literarisierten Kulthymnus herbeigerufen, um pünktlich zum rituell angesetzten Termin seinen Wohnsitz zu übernehmen.[104]

Auf dem Hintergrund der Horazode wird also der okkasionelle Charakter als Leistungsprofil der *Silven* gestärkt. Die Professionalität des Stegreifdichters beweist sich in der Fähigkeit, als Festteilnehmer sein spontanes Staunen über die gewandelte Ortssituation adäquat zur Sprache zu bringen.[105] Im Unterschied zum „Durchschnittspublikum" weiß er das geschaute Wunder in einen mythologischen und literarischen Kontext einzuordnen und im Interesse des Bauherrn und des Tempelbesitzers für das neu geweihte Heiligtum eine Kulttradition literarisch zu konstruieren. Der Silvendichter hat sich, so könnte man sagen, die krönende Schlußbegegnung mit Hercules ehrlich verdient, da er mit seinem aitiologischen Festgedicht gegenüber dem Heros bereits in Leistungsvorlage getreten ist.

Hier wird aber auch erkennbar, in welcher Weise sich Statius den Selbstanspruch des augusteischen Lyrikers zu eigen gemacht hat. Denn das horazische Eröffnungsgedicht deutet im Verweis auf den „besser geeigneten" Paulus Maximus[106] bereits als neue Option des lyrischen Sprechens das Lobpreis anderer im Festkontext an. Der Blick des Lesers wird vorausdeutend auf die hochrangigen Adressaten des vierten Odenbuchs gelenkt: Deren historische Leistungen wird Horaz in seinen kunstvollen, und das heißt: kostbaren Festgaben zur Geltung bringen. Im Akt des ostentativen Beiseitetretens und des panegyrischen Kompliments, das sich mit einem hohen ästhetischen Selbstanspruch verbindet, bietet Horaz ein *exemplum*, das dem professionellen Stegreifdichter zugleich Anschluß an die große Festlyrik und die Möglichkeit zur Abgrenzung gibt.[107]

Zusammenfassend begründet Statius selbstbewußt die literarische Leistung seiner *Silve* auf der Folie des hellenistischen Epinikiendichters Kallimachos und

---

lich fungiert das literarische, oftmals epikureisch geprägte *otium* in den *Silven* als alternative Repräsentationsform zur politischen Karriere, siehe Nauta (s. Anm. 3) 308–323; Rühl (s. Anm. 2) 33–39.

104 *Silv.* 3,1,28: *huc ades et genium templis nascentibus infer.* Zur „Einladung" im Sinne des Anbietens eines Tempels zum Wohnen Rüpke (s. Anm. 19) 230.

105 *Silv.* 3,1,8–22.

106 *C.* 4,1,9 f.: *tempestivius in domum / Pauli.*

107 Zum unterschiedlichen gesellschaftlichen Status und den dadurch bedingten Patronagebeziehungen des Statius und Horaz allgemein Newlands (s. Anm. 4) 27–36.

zweier augusteischer Preisdichter *par excellence*: Er eröffnet sein Gedicht situa-
tionsgemäß mit dem vorbildhaften Festlyriker Horaz. Seine Aitienkonstruktion
bringt er in kallimacheischem Gestus dar als poetische Libation, die auf Hercules' Altar gespendet wird;[108] und als auserwähltes Sprachrohr des an der Schwelle
erscheinenden Tempelbesitzers signiert er dessen Festansprache mit einem geflügelten Wort aus der vergilischen Iuppiterrede, das Pollius' neu geweihtem Privatheiligtum zeitlose Dauer verheißt.

2.5 Der Bucheintritt durch den Herculestempel

Im letzten Schritt der Interpretation soll der Diskurs um das poetische Konzept
der Gelegenheit im Blick auf das ganze Silvenbuch auf einer anderen Ebene fort-
geführt werden: Wie ändert sich die Gedichtrezeption, wenn die Einzelsilve in
den Kontext eines Gedichtbuchs gestellt wird und sich nun einer Leserschaft präsentiert, die weder bei der Tempelweihung anwesend war noch den Adressaten
persönlich kennt?[109] Was qualifiziert unter diesen neuen Bedingungen den *Hercules Surrentinus* zum Programmgedicht, das Anspruch auf die exponierte Kopf-
stellung erheben kann? Da die *Silven* auch in der Zweitpublikation ihren okkasionellen Charakter wahren, scheint es geraten, beim nachträglich verfaßten und
der *Silve* unmittelbar vorangestellten Widmungsbrief erneut von den äußeren
Vorgaben – der Gelegenheit und dem Personenbezug – auszugehen.

   In der Tat läßt sich im Vergleich mit den beiden ersten *praefationes* für die
Eröffnung des dritten Buchs ein neues Selbstbewußtsein des Dichters konstatieren, das auf die wohlwollende Förderung des Pollius Felix zurückgeführt wird:[110]
Seien doch viele *Silven* unter dem direkten, positiven Einfluß des jetzigen Buch-
empfängers entstanden. Da Pollius Felix nicht nur der Kronzeuge (*testis*), sondern der Erzeuger des Buchs (*auctor*) ist, kann Statius ihm seine Werke unbesorgt
übersenden. Der musische Patron, der selbst in verschiedenen Literaturgattungen
dilettiert, der sich durch große Beredsamkeit auszeichnet und den professionellen Gelegenheitsdichter intensiv gefördert hat, wird als ein kompetenter und
wohlwollend-kritischer Modell-Leser der *Silven* gezeichnet.[111] Im epikureischen

---

108 *Silv.* 3,1,162 f. Vgl. das gleichfalls poetologisch konnotierte Opfer des Preislyrikers
    Horaz, der in *c.* 4,2,14–60 ein zartes Kälbchen (*tener vitulus*) als Siegesopfer darbrin-
    gen will.
109 Zu den Konsequenzen der schriftlichen Zweitpublikation der *Silven* allgemein Rühl
    (s. Anm. 2) 135–140.
110 *Silv.* 3, *praef.* 1–9. Zur Praefatio des dritten Buchs Rühl (s. Anm. 2) 121 f.; Johannsen
    (s. Anm. 3) 272–283.
111 So bereits Rühl (s. Anm. 2) 122. Dagegen Johannsen (s. Anm. 3) 276: „tatsächlich
    spielt der Widmungsadressat im folgenden aber nur eine auffallend geringe Rolle."

refugium der Surrentiner Villa hat Pollius seinen gelehrigen Schützling Statius immer tiefer in die Welt seiner literarischen Studien und Wissenschaften einge-führt.[112] Produkt dieses vertrauten Umgangs sind die kleinen Gelegenheitswerke, die dem Silvendichter wie von selbst, in spontaner Eingebung entspringen. Damit ist der umfassend gebildete Patron in den Rang einer Inspirationsgottheit er-hoben.[113]

Unter den von Pollius motivierten *Silven* steht nun der *Hercules Surrentinus* seinem geistigen Vater besonders nahe[114] – im realen und übertragenen Sinne. Aus der lokalen und geistigen Affinität des großen und kleinen Hercules begrün-det sich auch die Sonderstellung des zugehörigen Festgedichts im Silvenbuch. Die Nähe des *Hercules Surrentinus* zum Buchadressaten wird im Vorwort eigens betont: „Seine (d. h. des Buchs) Anfangsschwelle öffnet der Surrentinische Her-cules, der an deinem Strand eine Weihestätte hat und dem ich, sofort als ich ihn gesehen hatte, mit diesen Versen meine Verehrung erwiesen habe."[115]

Wie in der anschließenden *Silve*, so wird nun also auch im Proöm die freund-schaftliche Patronagebeziehung zwischen Pollius Felix und Statius über den ge-meinsam verehrten Hercules geführt. Die in der *Silve* inszenierte Nähe zwischen dem Heros, dessen Gegenwart dem Land reichen Segen bringt, und dem Grund-besitzer, der das Glück bereits im Beinamen „Felix" mit sich trägt,[116] wird im Vorwort präzisiert und zur Dreieckskonstellation erweitert: Es sind die musi-schen Interessen, die den Heros, den Villenbesitzer und den Silvendichter verbin-

---

112 Vgl. die Konstruktion eines exklusiven Nahverhältnisses zum Literaturpatron in *silv.* 3,1,64–67.

113 Vorbild könnte das Proöm im dritten Buch von Vergils *Georgica* sein, in dem Mae-cenas als Inspirationsgottheit für ein Augustusepos figuriert (3,42–48). In der frühkai-serzeitlichen Panegyrik wird dann der *princeps* zur erstrangigen Inspirationsquelle, vgl. etwa das Neropreis in Lucan. 1,66; das Domitianpreis in Mart. 8, *praef.* Eine Imi-tation kaiserlicher Euergesie sieht Newlands (s. Anm. 4) 176–178 auch durch Pollius' Tempelweihung gegeben. Diese Annahme ist jedoch insofern problematisch, als be-reits in der späten Republik die Sakralisierung des eigenen Villengartens durch die Einrichtung eines Privatheiligtums eine durchaus gängige Praxis in den nobilitären Kreisen war, siehe Coarelli, F. 1983, „Architettura sacra e architettura privata nella tarda Repubblica", in: *Architecture et société. De l'archisme grec à le fin de la républi-que Romaine. Actes du Colloque international organisé par le Centre national de la recherche scientifique et l'École française de Rome* (Rome 2–4 décembre 1980), Paris; Rom, 191–271.

114 Zur thematischen Ordnung und Struktur des dritten Silvenbuchs Bright (s. Anm. 69) 62–66.

115 *Silv.* 3, *praef.* 9–11: *nam primum limen eius Hercules Surrentinus aperit, quem in litore tuo consecratum, statim ut videram, his versibus adoravi.*

116 *Silv.* 3,1,32 f.; vgl. *silv.* 2,2,23 f.; *silv.* 2,2,107. Dazu Gauly (s. Anm. 5).

den.[117] Letzterer hatte bereits im poetischen Festbeitrag zur Tempelweihung dem Heros und dem Baustifter „spontane Ehren" erwiesen; nun wertet er nochmals im nachträglich verfaßten Prooöm den in neuem Glanz erstrahlenden Herculestempel zum privaten Musenheiligtum seines Förderers Pollius auf.[118]

Die römische Leserschaft, die bei der Tempelweihung nicht anwesend war, erhält an dieser Stelle die Vorinformation, daß das Gedicht tatsächlich im Rahmen der Tempelweihung vorgetragen (und nicht etwa, wie andere *Silven*, nachträglich übersandt) wurde. Der geladene Auftragsdichter, der mit Sicherheit Vorkehrungen für den großen Festtag getroffen hatte, kokettiert hier erneut mit der Rolle des frommen Festteilnehmers. Dieser äußert nämlich, vom unmittelbaren Anblick des im Kultbild gegenwärtig gedachten Gottes[119] überwältigt, seine Verehrung in einem spontanen Lobgesang.[120] Implizit ist freilich der Leser durch diese Regieanweisung im Prooöm gehalten, auf die letzte Epiphanieszene besonders zu achten und gerade ihre Literarisierung zu würdigen.

Durch die Erstplazierung des *Hercules Surrentinus* hat sich Statius zudem die Möglichkeit eröffnet, den kolossalen Heros als situationsbedingten Inspirationsgott seines ganzen Silvenbuchs einzuführen. Vermittels des poetischen Konzepts der Gelegenheit läßt sich nämlich bei der schriftlichen Zweitpublikation der *Silven* eine Analogie zwischen der festlichen Tempeleröffnung und der ehrenden Bucheröffnung konstruieren: Der literarischen Förderung, ja Autorschaft des Pollius entspricht seine Initiative zur Restauration des Heiligtums, die ähnlich spontan wie die Produktion der improvisierten *Silven* erfolgt. Das zur Einweihung verfaßte Festgedicht exponiert sich durch den Akt der realen und literarischen Dedikation nicht nur als „ausgeschriebenes Weihepigramm mit okkasionellem Material"[121], sondern darüber hinaus als programmatisches Eröffnungsgedicht der nachträglich zum Buch zusammengestellten *Silven*: Wie das dritte Buch Pollius' Namen in der ehrenden Widmung trägt, so ist dem neuen Tempel in einer prominent plazierten Inschrift „zur Freude des Großvaters der Name

---

117 Zur Villa als epikureischer „Musensitz" des Pollius Gauly (s. Anm. 5) 466–469.
118 Als Vorbild ist an den Tempel des *Hercules Musarum* zu denken, den M. Fulvius Nobilior nach seiner Einnahme von Ambrakia gestiftet hat. Wichtiger noch als die enge Verbindung des Hercules mit Sieg und Triumph ist das symbolisch konstituierte Nahverhältnis zwischen den Musen/ Hercules, dem Feldherrn und dem panegyrischen Preisdichter Ennius, der als professioneller *poeta cliens* den Ruhm seines Patrons verkündet: siehe Rüpke, J. 1995, *Kalender und Öffentlichkeit. Die Geschichte der Repräsentation und religiösen Qualifikation von Zeit in Rom*, RGVV 40, Berlin; New York, 332–339.
119 Zur Präsenz der Gottheit im Kultbild Gladigow (s. Anm. 57) 104–106.
120 Burnett, A. P. 1998, „Spontaneity, savaging, and praise in Pindar's sixth Paean", *AJPh* 119, 496 f. zur „natürlichen Spontantität" als Ideal des „aufrichtigen" Gotteslobs.
121 So Hardie (s. Anm. 7) 126, der die *Silve* 3,1 unter dem Primäraspekt der Gattungsmischung interpretiert.

des Priesters angeschrieben".[122] Gemeint ist Pollius' junger Enkel, der selbst – so der Dichter – dem kindlichen Schlangenwürger vergleichbar sei. Das Weihedatum des restaurierten Tempels und Altars wird, wie üblich, mit einem Geburtstagsfest (*dies natalis*) begangen;[123] und Statius' „plötzlicher" Silvengeburt infolge der inspirierenden Nähe zum „Musenfreund" Pollius entspricht sein extemporiertes Gotteslob vor Ort.

Bis der Leser dann am krönenden Schluß der ersten *Silve* kraft seiner Imagination den kolossalen Heros durch die Augen des Erzählers an der Tempelschwelle (*silv.* 3,1,164: *nunc ipse in limine*) sehen und Hercules' Stimme in poetischer Vermittlung hören kann, hat er seine eigene Gottesbegegnung bereits erlebt: Hat ihm doch *Hercules Surrentinus* im vorgeschalteten Widmungsbrief den Eingang ins Silvenbuch (*limen libri*) durch seinen neu geweihten Tempel eröffnet.[124] Damit nimmt Statius den imposanten Heros als Pförtner in den Dienst, der dem Leser die Tür zu den von Pollius inspirierten *Silven* aufschließt.

Anders als die beiden folgenden Epiphanieszenen bleibt diese allererste Gottesbegegnung allein dem Leser vorbehalten. Als Vorbild für den musischen Hercules, der mit dem Leser und Dichter in einen Dialog tritt, ist an Ovids *Fasten* zu denken, in denen gleichfalls sehr unkonventionelle Inspirationsgötter auftreten: prominent etwa die Epiphanie des aitiologisch versierten Ianus (*fast.* 1,89–102) oder des kriegerischen Mars (*fast.* 3,1–8), der zwar eigentlich, wie der Sprecher selbst anmerkt, mit der Dichtkunst nichts zu tun hat, sich aber im Rahmen „seines" Monats für die aitiologische Namensgebung interessiert. Motiviert ist das Engagement neuer Musengötter in Ovids Kalenderdichtung und in Statius' *Silven* durch die äußeren Zwänge, denen die poetischen Werke jeweils unterliegen. In beiden Fällen muß der elegische bzw. lyrische Dichter seine Kreativität beweisen, indem er sich durch Transposition, Umformung und ingeniöse Neudeutung von dem engen Korsett der Vorgaben befreit und seinen Stoff in der selbst gewählten Ordnung und Form präsentiert.

---

122 *Silv.* 3,1,46–48.

123 *Silv.* 3,1,28; 3,1,163 f.

124 Als ideengebendes Vorbild für den imaginierten Herculestempel hat Newlands (s. Anm. 14) zu Recht auf das Proöm des dritten Georgica-Buchs verwiesen (*Georg.* 3,1–48), in dem Vergil die Errichtung eines epischen Siegestempel für den Triumphator Octavian ankündigt. Allerdings gerät in Newlands' poetologischer Interpretation über der Selbstinszenierung des Silvendichters dessen Patron gänzlich aus dem Blick (452): „thus the tempel to Hercules reflects the complex features of Statius' own poetry in these first three books: speedily composed, joyful and playful of mood, peaceful of theme, Hellenistic in various topoi, grand in style, and innovative." Von diesem Ansatz setzt sich meine Deutung insofern ab, als m. E. der Silvendichter als professioneller *poeta cliens* größten Wert darauf legt, daß seine Leserschaft den poetisch evozierten Herculestempel vor Surrent als ein vom geehrten Patron und Buchadresssat Pollius initiiertes Bauprojekt begreift.

Abgesehen vom allgemeinen Bezug auf die gleichfalls okkasionsbedingten Inspirationsgottheiten in Ovids Kalendergedicht ist der Surrentiner Hercules am Eingang des dritten Silvenbuchs offenbar ganz konkret als Pendant zum stadtrömischen Hercules Musarum konstruiert, der mit seiner Lyra das sechste Buch der *Fasten* zustimmend beschließt.[125] Die Analogien beschränken sich dabei keineswegs auf die exponierte Stellung des musischen Hercules an der jeweiligen Buchgrenze:[126] Sind doch beide Texte auch darin vergleichbar, daß sie ein (genealogisches bzw. geistiges) Nahverhältnis zwischen dem geehrten Dichterpatron (Fabius Maximus[127] bzw. Pollius) und dem musischen Heros lancieren und gerade nicht – wie eigentlich in aitiologischem Kontext zu erwarten – dem Tempel eine lange Kulttradition zuschreiben, sondern ganz im Gegenteil die Tempelrestauration in jüngster Vergangenheit anpreisen.[128]

Des weiteren ist auf Parallelen zwischen Statius und Martial zu verweisen, der ebenfalls seinen Epigrammbüchern briefliche Prosaeinleitungen voranstellt. So wendet sich der Epigrammatiker in der *praefatio* des achten Buchs an den zum Idealleser stilisierten Kaiser Domitian, um „gleich an der Eingangsschwelle des Buchs" (*praef.* 17f.: *in ipso libelli huius limine*) den richtigen Erwartungshorizont betreffs der Thematik, Gattung und des Unterhaltungswerts seiner Epigramme zu konstituieren. Wie Martial, so reagiert auch Statius auf die literarischen Produktions- und Rezeptionsbedingungen und den florierenden Buchhandel der fla-

---

125 Ov. *fast* 6,811f.: *sic cecinit Clio, doctae adsensere sorores; adnuit Alcides increpuitque lyra.* Zu den komplexen historischen und literarischen Anspielungen des finalen Kalendereintrags Newlands, C. E. 1995, *Playing with Time. Ovid and the Fasti*, Ithaca; London, 209–236; Barchiesi, A. 1997, *The Poet and the Prince. Ovid and augustan Discorse*, Berkeley; Los Angeles; London, 259–272.

126 Überdeutlich markiert Ovid mit der uneingelösten Ankündigung des „morgigen Geburtstag der Iulischen Kalenden" die Vor- und Rückbezogenheit des liminalen Hercules, der im letzten, resümierenden Bucheintrag zugleich die Fortsetzung des Kalendergedichts als Zukunftsoption lanciert (*fast.* 6,797f.): *tempus Iuleis cras est natale Kalendis :/ Pierides, coeptis addite summa meis.*

127 Der auch von Horaz (*c.* 4,1) gepriesene Literaturpatron Paullus Fabius Maximus war der Ehemann der Marcia, deren Vater L. Marcius Philippus den Herculestempel restauriert hatte und zugleich mit Augustus verwandtschaftlich verbunden war. Die Fabier führten ihrerseits laut Ovid (*fast.* 2,237) ihre *gens* auf Hercules zurück.

128 Dies ist zumal für Ovids *Fasten* bemerkenswert, da dort just die für Geschichte zuständige Muse Clio Auskunft gibt. Ungeachtet ihrer aitiologisch-antiquarischen Gelehrsamkeit blendet aber Clio in ihrer gelehrten Erklärung die ursprüngliche Tempelstiftung durch M. Fulvius Nobilior gänzlich aus: Die ehrwürdige Vergangenheit der Siegesweihung, die nicht nur mit Fulvius' Beutestiftung der ambrakischen Musen, sondern auch mit den Fulvischen Fasten und den Annalen des Ennius untrennbar verbunden war, wird damit vom aktuellen Tempel als Werbeträger der augusteischen Familienpolitik, der Kultur- wie Kultförderung komplett überblendet.

vischen Zeit:[129] Durch seine Epiphanie im Widmungsbrief würdigt der Türöffner Hercules implizit das Buch als sekundären Publikationsort mehrerer inhaltsverwandter *Silven*. Die nachträgliche Gedichtlektüre im Werkzusammenhang ist demnach durch göttliche Autorität zur gleichberechtigten, ja unverzichtbaren Ergänzung des einmaligen Stegreifvortrags erklärt.

3. Zusammenfassung

Mein Ausgangspunkt war der Selbstanspruch des Silvendichters Statius, zu gegebenem Anlaß hochrangige Patrone in kunstvoller Kleinform wirkungsvoll zu loben. Das Konzept der „kolossalen Miniatur" wurde am *Hercules Surrentinus* überprüft, dessen vermutete Sonderstellung als Programmgedicht sich in der Textanalyse bestätigen ließ:

Der Dichter spielt das literarische Potential des göttlichen Gelegenheitsgebers aus, indem er den gewaltigen Heros in kallimacheischer Manier als burleske Epenfigur in Szene setzt. Je größer und massiger er dabei seinen Akteur gestaltet, desto mehr treten die subtile Form und intertextuelle Komplexität der *Silve* hervor, die in Rücksicht auf die literarischen Bildungskompetenzen des adressierten Patrons überwiegend mit implizit und motivisch markierten Textreferenzen arbeitet.

Dabei nutzt Statius das erreichbare Vorbild des großen und zugleich menschennahen Heros, um die Standesunterschiede zwischen Poet und Patron zu überspielen. In Hercules' inspirierender und aktiver Beteiligung am Tempelbau wird das für die *Silven* grundlegende Spannungsverhältnis von Initiative und Auftrag reflektiert. Das charmante Aition gereicht Poet und Patron zur Ehre, da es einerseits Pollius eine formelle Preisrede und ein erotisches Tête-à-tête mit seinem göttlichen Nachbarn zuerkennt und andererseits eine natürliche Nähe zwischen dem Improvisationsdichter und seinen vorrangigen „Inspirationsquellen", sprich: Pollius und Hercules, glaubhaft macht.

Darüber hinaus verleiht Statius im Motivbezug auf Kallimachos' und Vergils aitiologische Herculeserzählungen dem Tempel vor Surrent eine neue geschichtliche Größe, aufgrund derer das kleine Privatheiligtum sogar den kokettierenden Vergleich mit der ehrwürdigen *Ara maxima* in der Hauptstadt und der panhellenischen Wettkampfstätte von Nemea wagen darf. Der aitiologisch versierte Fest-

---

129 Zur Verbreitung brieflicher Prosavorworte in neuen, namentlich poetischen Gattungen als Charakteristikum flavischer Zeit Janson, T. 1964, *Latin Prose Prefaces. Studies in Literary Conventions*, Stockhom; Göteborg; Uppsala, 106–112; Johannsen (s. Anm. 3) 33–35. Speziell zur Praefatio des achten Martialbuchs Johannsen (s. Anm. 3) 87–97 mit älterer Literatur.

sänger kann durchaus erfolgreich mit dem rustikalen Salierchor in Vergils *Aeneis* in Wettbewerb treten und zugleich von der vergilischen Stentorstimme des Festredners Hercules profitieren; sein kunstreiches Gedicht spendet er in kallimacheischem Gestus auf dem neu geweihten Herculesaltar.

Nicht zuletzt macht der Silvendichter dem zeitgenössischen Leser durch die im Proöm exponierte Analogie der Buch- und Tempeleröffnung die spezifische Leistung seiner *Silven* anschaulich: Diese müssen sich angesichts der engen – und bisweilen höchst unbequemen! – Vorgaben, nämlich dem Adressaten und der konkreten Gelegenheit, ihre Gestaltungsräume erst erschließen. Unter diesen Konditionen kann sogar der kolossale Holzfäller Hercules zur unorthodoxen Inspirationsgottheit und zum symbolischen Türöffner des Silvenbuchs werden.

Abstract

This article takes as a starting point the self-declared – and seemingly paradoxical – ambition of the Flavian occasional poet Statius to express elaborate and sophisticated praise for high-ranking patrons in the form of miniature poems (the so-called *Silvae*). The poetic concept of the "colossal miniature" is explored in a discussion of poem 3.1, whose introductory position at the opening of the book may be read as a programmatic statement of intention. The textual interpretation focuses on the literary figure of Hercules, whose newly restored temple motivates the festive poem.

The "colossal hero" is presented by the poet as a burlesque epic figure in the manner of Callimachus: the larger and bulkier his protagonist appears, the greater the contrast with the intricate form and intertextual complexity of the poem itself. In the implicit and carefully muted references to individual motifs from the etiological Herculean myths narrated by Callimachus and Virgil, Statius pays homage to his patron's cultural refinement, while also lending an air of historical greatness to the thoroughly modern private sanctuary outside Surrentum.

At the same time, Statius invokes the attainable ideal of the powerful yet very human hero in order to graciously downplay the class differences between poet and patron. Hercules' inspiring and active participation in the construction of the temple is thus an illustration of the inherent tension within the *Silvae* between initiative and assignment.

By introducing a deliberate analogy between the opening of his book and the opening of the temple, Statius advertises, in a complementary fashion, the singular nature and accomplishment of his *Silvae*: since their external parameters are specified (by the addressee and the occasion), the poet's creativity must find other outlets. To this purpose even Hercules, the colossal hero, can become an unorthodox god of inspiration and "door opener" for Statius' book of *Silvae*.

Does Love Make Us Beautiful?

A criticism of Plotinus in Augustine's
Tractates on the First Epistle of John[1]

CHRISTIAN TORNAU

At first sight, Platonic love (in Greek, ἔρως) and Christian love (in Greek, ἀγάπη, in Latin, *caritas*), have little in common. In Plato's *Symposium*, love is conceived of as man's natural desire for the beautiful; and although this desire can ultimately only be satisfied through a kind of mystical union with the incorporeal Form of Beauty itself, it has also strong erotic and even sexual aspects. The essence of Christian love is expressed in the Gospel's double commandment of love: "You shall love the Lord your God with all your heart, with all your soul, and with all your mind; [and] you shall love your neighbour as yourself" (Matthew 22,37 and 39). Here love primarily seems to mean man's faithful devotion to God and altruistic care for others, the latter culminating in the willingness to follow the example of Christ and sacrifice oneself for one's friends. Any erotic overtone is absent.[2] Augustine, however, from the first writings that date from the time of his conversion till the end of his life never gave up introducing erotic elements into his descriptions of Christian love and, in particular, viewing the Christian's love for God as a kind of Platonic ascent to Absolute Beauty or the Supreme Good.[3] In the Neoplatonic tradition these two are largely the same, so one of Augustine's reasons was certainly that he considered erotic mysticism as part and parcel of the eudaemonism that, as he had learned long ago from Cicero's *Hortensius*, was the natural foundation of any philosophical ethics. In 1930, he was therefore accused by Anders Nygren for having distorted the bi-

---

1 This paper was first read at the conference "L'univers de saint Augustin. 1650ᵉ anniversaire de sa naissance", Vilnius (Lithuania), 15–16 October 2004. A Lithuanian translation has appeared in the proceedings of the conference (C. Tornau, Ar meile daro mus gražius? Plotino kritika Augustino *Traktatuose pagal pirmąjį Jono laišką*, in: D. Alekna (ed.), Šv. Augustinas. Tradicijos, kontekstai, interpretacijos, Vilnius 2006 (*Christiana Tempora* 2), 101–116). I am grateful to the editor, Darius Alekna, for his kind permission to publish the English original here.

2 This is generally true for the New Testament texts on love, but not for the Old Testament: Augustine finds texts from the prophetic books and, of course, from the Song of Songs that seem to justify the introduction of erotic elements into the biblical concept of love.

3 This has been justly emphasized by J. M. Rist, Augustine. Ancient Thought Baptized, Cambridge 1994, 156f.

blical message of love by contaminating it with the self-centered Platonic ethics
of self-perfection.[4] Nygren's book triggered a debate that lasted for decades and
from which it emerged quite clearly that the focus of Augustine's thinking about
love is, first and foremost, the biblical commandment, of which he is concerned
to provide an exegesis that avoids degrading the love of the neighbour to an
instrumental or preliminary role as compared with the love of God. In general
the elements taken from the Platonic tradition, which are certainly present, are
subordinate to this overall aim. But although this general picture seems relatively
clear, considerable room remains for discussion about the details, which is precisely what I intend to do in this paper.

In one of Augustine's most important texts on *caritas*, the *Tractates on the
Epistle of John* – a series of ten sermons probably preached in 407 – there is, in the
9th chapter of the 9th sermon, a text that discusses the question whether love of
God, the supreme beauty, makes the lover himself beautiful. Not only is this a
Neoplatonic theme but moreover, what Augustine has to say is both strikingly
similar to and markedly deviating from some passages in Plotinus, especially
from *Ennead* VI 7, which is one of Plotinus' most impressive treatises on the crucial importance of Eros for the soul's ascent to the One or the Good. It can of
course not be proved that Augustine had these particular passages in mind when
he composed his sermon, much less that he expected his audience, the members
of his congregation at Hippo, to recognize the allusion. Nevertheless, I think that
the similarity is not just superficial and that a reading of Augustine's text as a criticism of Plotinus can contribute to clarify to what extent Augustine follows
Neoplatonic teaching about love and where and for what reasons he departs from
it. I will proceed as follows. First, I will give a brief outline of Plotinus' discussion of love and beauty in *Ennead* VI 7. Second, I will sketch what I think is the
Neoplatonic heritage in Augustine's theology of love in the *Tractates on the
Epistle of John*. Third and last, I will return to *Tractates* 9,9 and undertake a more
detailed comparison with the Plotinian passages.

---

4   A. Nygren, Eros und Agape. Gestaltwandlungen der christlichen Liebe (2 vols.,
     Gütersloh 1930, 1937; first published in Swedish 1930, 1936). For an overview of the
     subsequent debate and a pertinent criticism of both Nygren and his adversaries, see
     R. Holte, Béatitude et sagesse. Saint Augustin et le problème de la fin de l'homme
     dans la philosophie antique, Paris 1962.

I

The main bulk of Plotinus' *Ennead* VI 7 deals with the question, "What is the Good?"[5] The background of this is the debate about the *telos* or supreme goal that is specific for Greek ethics from Aristotle onwards: What is the supreme good that every human being instinctively desires and whose possession guarantees happiness? At the same time, for a Platonist, to ask, "What is the Good?" is to ask for the correct exegesis of the notoriously enigmatic phrase from Plato's Sun Simile in Book 6 of the *Republic*: "The Good is not Being, but even beyond Being (ἐπέκεινα τῆς οὐσίας), surpassing it in rank and power" (Pl. *R.* 509b). The question of the Good thus concerns both the structure of reality and the good life, and *Ennead* VI 7 is a treatise about both ethics and metaphysics. The conclusion Plotinus eventually reaches is that the soul attains happiness and the good only when, ascending beyond the totality of being and even beyond her own self, she becomes one with Plato's absolute, all-transcending Good itself. As Plotinus takes Plato's statement that the Good is not Being very seriously and consequently denies that the Good is anything like an object, the union with it is of such a kind that any distinction between soul and Good, perceiver and perceived, lover and beloved, me and you becomes impossible. Where there is no object, there is no subject either; all that remains is absolute unity. It is characteristical for Plotinus that he describes this union in strongly erotic terms.[6]

Plotinus begins his discussion of the Good by asking what the three basic aspects of true being, viz. Being, Life and Intellect, have in common so that we think that each of them is good – precisely the method that, in Plato's dialogues, leads to the theory of Forms. A first answer is attempted by means of one of Plotinus' famous speculations about how it is possible that being, which is a one-many and whose diverse elements are, e.g., Being, Life and Intellect, proceeds from the absolute unity which is the Good or the One.[7] It is, however, peculiar to the discussion in VI 7 that this speculation, impressive though it is, does not pro-

---

5   For *Ennead* VI 7, its structure and its content, see P. Hadot, Plotin: Traité 38 (VI,7), introduction, traduction, commentaire et notes, Paris 1988, 15–30, and C. Tornau, Der Eros und das Gute bei Plotin und Proklos, in: M. Perkams/R.-M. Piccione (edd.), Proklos. Methode, Seelenlehre, Metaphysik. Akten der Konferenz in Jena am 18.– 20. September 2003, Leiden 2006, 201–229, esp. 204–206. See also, in general, my article: Eros versus Agape? Von Plotins Eros zum Liebesbegriff Augustins, Philosophisches Jahrbuch 112 (2005) 271–291, esp. 273–281.

6   It seems that Plotinus' eroticism was abandoned in later Neoplatonism. Cf. esp. Procl. *Th. Pl.* 1,25, and Tornau (cf. fn. 5) 216–228.

7   VI 7,16–17. See J. Bussanich, The One and Its Relation to Intellect in Plotinus, Leiden 1988, 148–171.

vide a solution to the initial question: Even if we accept the causal reduction of Being, Life and Intellect to the Good, we still do not understand what is that "something" about each of them that makes it good.[8] What has gone wrong? It would seem that the problem is due to an error of perspective. The Good has eluded us because, by opening a metaphysical inquiry into its nature as the First Cause of Being, we have inadvertently viewed it as if it were just an object among others, in spite of all our assertions of its transcendence. So in what follows, Plotinus, changing from an external to an internal point of view, now focuses on the soul herself and asks: What does it mean for the soul to desire the Good, and what does she experience when that desire is fulfilled? From the outset, this experience is conceived of as an experience of love.[9] This is not just a metaphor or a poetic colouring of a philosophical exposition; for, as Plotinus is now able to show, what is distinctive about love is that we never love anybody or anything just for what it is, but for something else that is not contained in its substance but by which it is illuminated and coloured, a kind of transcendent light that is irreducible to the being of the beloved and unattainable by a definition. This is true even for everyday physical love. Nobody falls in love with a statue; what kindles our erotic desire is a living person whose attraction is not a matter of his or her purely corporeal properties (e.g., good proportions) but of his grace and charme, which are the causes of a body's beauty but are incorporeal themselves. The same rule, Plotinus contends, applies to our love for Intellect itself, which is the totality of intelligible being and, from a Platonist's point of view, the totality of being as a whole. What happens when we love the beauty of intelligible reality? Once again, Plotinus emphasizes the transcendence of the desired. We may admire Intellect for its perfect rationality and completeness, but these alone would never cause the soul to fall in love with it. What makes intelligible being desirable can never be contained within being as one of its elements nor captured by its definition; it is – to use Plotinus' own metaphors – the light of the Good that plays on the surface of intelligible being and illuminates it but is not a part of intelligible being itself. This is why only love, but not intellect can attain the Good that is beyond Being: Intellectual cognition, by its very definition, has intelligible Being as its object and is therefore confined to its limits. By contrast, love, even when it desires an object, actually desires not that object but something that transcends it, even if the object transcended is intelligible Being as a whole.[10]

---

8 VI 7,18.

9 Cf. e.g. Plot. VI 7,21,11–17, where Plotinus gives a summary of the Sun simile in erotic terms.

10 Cf. esp. VI 7,22. For this curious chapter, see A. H. Armstrong, Elements in the Thought of Plotinus at Variance with Classical Intellectualism, The Journal of Hellenic Studies 93 (1973) 13–22 (= Id., Plotinian and Christian Studies, London 1979, Study XVI), esp. 20–22.

Let us now – still following Plotinus – imagine the moment when this kind of love attains its satisfaction. The possibilities of any form of cognition, be it discursive thinking or intellectual intuition, end here, since cognition, however unified, always distinguishes its object from itself. Now, as it were, only desire is left, and it has finally become one with what it really desires, not any *thing* but the transcendent Good itself. In order to give an idea of what this must be like, Plotinus, once again using the analogy of physical and transcendent love, mentions the union of lovers in sexual intercourse.[11]

Let me close this paragraph by quoting a curious text from *Ennead* VI 8. There Plotinus, pursuing his attempt to make positive statements about the One or the Good *per viam analogiae*, says that "he, that same self, is lovable and love and love of himself" (αὐτοῦ ἔρως; Plot. VI 8,15,1).[12]

If we take into account what we have learnt from *Ennead* VI 7, this can hardly mean that the Good loves itself. Rather, αὐτοῦ ἔρως is an alternative phrasing for the paradoxical notion that in the "mystical union" there is nothing present but desire itself and the Good itself and that both are identical. Love, that always longs for the beyond, is our only clue to the Good; so the Good can only be "known" if love is isolated from anything external and becomes self-referential – as Plotinus puts in in VI 8, αὐτοῦ ἔρως.[13]

II

Let us now turn to Augustine's *Tractates on the Epistle of John*. This series of ten sermons is best described as an exhortation to practise *caritas*, cast in the form of a line-by-line commentary on a biblical text that – as Augustine puts it in the preface – is almost entirely devoted to love and recommends it passionately.[14] Augus-

---

11 VI 7,33,22–27; 34,14–16.

12 καὶ ἐράσμιον καὶ ἔρως ὁ αὐτὸς καὶ αὐτοῦ ἔρως. Plotinus is quoted from the *editio minor* of P. Henry/H.-R. Schwyzer, Plotini Opera, 3 vols., Oxford 1964–1982. Translations are based on A. H. Armstrong, Plotinus, with an English translation, 7 vols., London/Cambridge (Mass.) 1966–1988.

13 There is an excellent discussion of this passage in F. M. Schroeder, Form and Transformation. A study in the philosophy of Plotinus, Montreal 1992, 105–107. For a different interpretation, see J. M. Rist, Eros and Psyche. Studies in Plato, Plotinus, and Origen, Toronto 1964, 76–86. See also A. Pigler, Plotin – une métaphysique de l'amour. L'amour comme structure du monde intelligible, Paris 2002, 27–36.

14 *praesertim quia in ipsa epistula […] maxime caritas commendatur. locutus est multa et prope omnia de caritate.* The *Tractates* are quoted from P. Agaësse, Saint Augustin: Commentaire de la première épître de saint Jean, texte latin, introduction, traduction et notes, Paris 1961 (Sources chrétiennes 75) who follows the text of the *PL*; a modern

tine discusses such topics as Christ's death on the cross as a token of God's love for us, self-sacrifice as the greatest achievement of fraternal love, and the relationship of fraternal love and love of one's enemy. But first of all, he puts forward a remarkable interpretation of the double commandment of love designed to give both its parts their full right and to avoid any marginalization of the commandment to love one's neighbour. Quoting 1 John 4,20, he says that whoever claims to love God and hates his neighbour is a lier, and adds that conversely, anyone who truly loves his neighbour and says that he does not love God is in error, since the two parts of the commandment are connected by strict mutual implication. The foundation for Augustine's exegesis is provided by 1 John 4,8 and 16 "God is love", which, he explains, means that our love for our neighbour is nothing less than the presence of God himself in our souls; and since all love is self-reflexive, it is necessary that when we love our neighbour we love God, who *is* that love, too.

It would seem that the framework of all this is entirely biblical and that Augustine's concerns are primarily pastoral. The world of Neoplatonic love, as sketched in the previous paragraph, seems far away. Yet an accurate reading of the *Tractates* shows that even here, where we would least expect it, some of Augustine's arguments clearly have a Neoplatonic background. As is well-known, for Augustine *caritas* does not consist of a set of good actions but is essentially a disposition of the will. To form a moral judgment of someone's behaviour, it is necessary to pay attention, not to his or her actions themselves, but to the underlying intentions or motives by which these actions are governed. An action is good if – and only if – it is performed out of love for God; it is bad if – and only if – it is governed by excessive self-love and contempt of God.[15] The Latin terms for these inner dispositions (*amores* or *voluntates*) are *caritas* and *superbia*. Thus *caritas*, for Augustine, is nothing external but a purely and exclusively internal phenomenon. Since this intentionalism, as we may call it, had no real biblical antecedents,[16] it was natural for Augustine to resort to other, mainly philosophical traditions in order to explain and defend it. At this point Neopla-

---

critical edition is lacking. Translations are my own. For the date of the sermons cf. D. Dideberg, *Epistulam Iohannis ad Parthos tractatus decem (In –)*, Augustinus-Lexikon 2 (1996–2002), 1064–1070; for their theology cf. Id., Saint Augustin et la première épître de saint Jean. Une théologie de l'agape, Paris 1975. Cf. also Tornau (cf. fn. 5) 281–289.

15 Cf. Aug. *civ.* 14,28. The best recent treatment of this aspect of Augustine's thought and of his thinking about love in general is O. O'Donovan, The Problem of Self-Love in Augustine, New Haven 1980. For the eudaemonistic background, see Holte (cf. fn. 4).

16 Though Augustine, of course, finds biblical texts to corroborate his view.

tonic internalism is put to service in the *Tractates*, and even Neoplatonic love is
allowed to re-enter the picture.

In the *Tractates*, Augustine is extraordinarily drastic about the fact that there
is no external criterion by which we can determine *caritas*. Even actions that are
explicitly prescribed in the New Testament, such as "clothing the naked", "feeding the hungry", are, he says, performed by *superbia* as well as by *caritas*. The
same is true of asceticism, and a little later he extends this verdict even to martyr-
dom which he, and ancient Christianity in general, usually accepts as a sufficient
proof that the martyr is in possession of God's grace.[17] But if this is true, then the
only criterion of *caritas* must be an invisible, internal one. What does it mean for
a human soul to possess *caritas*? Augustine, taking up his exegesis of 1 John 4,8
and 16 "God is love" (*deus dilectio est* or *deus caritas est*),[18] answers: Having *caritas* in one's soul is exactly the same as having God himself in one's soul. Nothing
less is required if we are to act truly virtuously. For God is love, and love is God,
so by the very same act by which fraternal love turns to itself and loves itself, we
love God who is nowhere but within ourselves. Augustine goes on to illustrate
what he means by means of a simile: Just as a single general (*imperator*) commands an entire army and disposes each part of it according to his needs and
makes it operate properly, so our Lord Jesus Christ is an *imperator* whose seat is
in our soul, from where he commands the single virtues (which are inner dispositions too and, as it were, the diverse branches of *caritas*) and makes them result in
appropriate external actions.[19] This inner *imperator* Christ is explicitly equated
with *caritas*: "That *imperator* has no beginning, nor must he ever have an end. Let
your inner *caritas* not be interrupted – but let the works of *caritas* be done
according to the circumstances" (Aug. *ep. Io. tr.* 8,3).[20] Thus Augustine grounds
his ethical intentionalism in a metaphysical theory according to which God or
Christ is in us.[21] It is fairly obvious that the background of this is the Neoplato-

---

17   Aug. *ep. Io. tr.* 8,9.
18   The Latin text varies in Augustine, though in the *Tractates* the version *deus dilectio est*
     is predominant.
19   Aug. *ep. Io. tr.* 8,1.
20   *ille autem imperator nec inchoatur, nec cessare debet. caritas intus non intermittatur:
     officia caritatis pro tempore exhibeantur* (*PL* 35,2037; SC 75,344).
21   It might of course be disputed how the case of wicked people who lack *caritas* is to be
     explained. Does this mean that Christ is not present in them? The problem is analo-
     gous to the one about the pagans' knowledge of theological truths and ethical values,
     which is difficult to explain if Christ is truth. The solution is probably to be found in
     the *imago Dei*-discussion from *De trinitate* 14–15. On the one hand, man never stops
     being the image of God, however stupid or wicked he is; on the other, he is an image
     of God in the full sense only if he repairs the distortions that image has undergone
     through sin. Only men who are an image of God in the latter sense are saved; to be-
     come (again) such an image, we need divine grace.

nic idea, often adduced by Augustine, that what is most transcendent to us is at the same time the most internal and most intimate, so that the journey to God, the supreme Good, is, first, an inward return to our own true self. But it seems that we can be even more specific. In his early dialogue *De magistro*, Augustine develops his famous epistemological theory that we have access to non-empirical truth because our souls are inhabited by Jesus Christ who, according to the Gospel, is truth itself (John 14,6: *ego sum veritas*). Notwithstanding its biblical foundation, this theory is clearly based on some Neoplatonic version of Plato's Theory of Ideas. What we have in the *Tractates*, I suggest, is a transposition of the earlier epistemological theory of *Christus veritas*, the inner teacher, into a new ethical theory of *Christus caritas*, the inner *imperator*. Just as true knowledge is only within our reach because Truth is in us, so true love or, to put it more traditionally, true virtue is only possible because Love itself is in us. And Truth and Love are ultimately one and the same thing, viz. God.

III

It might be objected that in order to explain Augustine's metaphor of the inner *imperator* there is no need to appeal to Neoplatonism and that the background might as well be Stoic intentionalism, although, as far as I know, an exact Stoic parallel cannot be found. Now I am quite convinced that the presence of Stoicism in Augustine's inner-life ethics, as it has aptly been called,[22] is considerable and far too little studied.[23] However, the present case does not allow for a full explanation along these lines, as we shall now see when we return to the text of *Tractates* 9,9 and to the theme of Neoplatonic love. The relevant part of the chapter is an exegesis of 1 John 4,19 "Let us love Him, because He first loved us";[24] it reads as follows:

> By loving him (= God), we become beautiful. What can an ugly man with a deformed face do if he loves a fair woman? Or what can an ugly, deformed, dark woman do if

---

22 W. E. Mann, Inner-Life Ethics, in: G. B. Matthews (ed.), The Augustinian Tradition, Berkeley 1999, 140–165.

23 An obstacle for any research on Stoicism in Augustine is of course the vexed problem of the sources. M. L. Colish, The Stoic Tradition from Antiquity to the Early Middle Ages II: Stoicism in Christian Latin Thought through the Sixth Century, Leiden ²1990, is a good start, but too general and far from exhaustive.

24 *nos diligamus, quia ipse prior nos dilexit.* Augustine consistently quotes the verse in this form. The Vetus Latina is divided between *diligimus* and *diligamus*; the latter is also the Vulgate's version. Most modern translators and commentators take the ambiguous Greek ἀγαπῶμεν as an indicative.

she loves a beautiful man? Will she be able to become beautiful by loving? Or will he, the man I just mentioned, be able to become handsome by loving? He loves a fair woman; and when he looks at himself in the mirror, he feels ashamed to lift his face to his beloved, the fair one. What shall he do in order to become beautiful? Wait for beauty to come? Certainly not – while he is waiting, old age supervenes and makes him even uglier. So there is nothing he can do, no advice you may properly give him except to control himself [...].
But our soul, my brothers, is ugly because of her iniquity – and she becomes beautiful by loving God. What kind of love is this, which makes the lover beautiful? Look: God is always beautiful, he is never deformed, he never changes. He loved us first, he who is always beautiful; and what were we, whom he loved, other than ugly and deformed? But he did not love us to leave us ugly as we were, but to change our ugliness into beauty. How will we become beautiful? By loving him who is always beautiful. The more love (*amor*) increases within you, the more your beauty increases; for love (*caritas*) itself is soul's beauty.[25]

In this text Augustine explains the first part of the biblical commandment of love, the love of God, not in terms of faith but of desire. When he urges his audience to fall in love with God because God is the supreme beauty, he obviously presupposes the traditional Greek understanding of love as erotic desire for a beautiful object as well as the sublime explanation it received in the Platonic tradition according to which the only truly desirable object is the transcendent God or Good. He even goes as far as to compare God's love for man (which is of course an un-Platonic, entirely Christian theme) with corporeal love in order to point out that God's love, paradoxically, is not love for the beautiful. But at the centre of the text is the idea that the soul by loving God's beauty leaves behind the ugliness she contracted in her sinful life and becomes beautiful herself. In this respect, Christian love contrasts favourably with bodily love, as Augustine shows by means of an elaborate comparison of the two. It is noteworthy that in

---

25　*diligendo pulchri efficimur. quid facit homo deformis et distorta facie, si amet pulchram? aut quid facit femina deformis et distorta et nigra, si amet pulchrum? numquid amando poterit esse pulchra? numquid et ille amando poterit esse formosus? amat pulchram; et quando se in speculo videt, erubescit faciem suam levare ad illam formosam suam quam amat. quid faciet ut pulcher sit? exspectat ut veniat pulchritudo? immo exspectando senectus additur, et turpiorem facit. non est ergo quid agere, non est quomodo illi des consilium, nisi ut compescat se [...]. anima vero nostra, fratres mei, foeda est per iniquitatem: amando deum pulchra efficitur. qualis amor est qui reddit pulchram amantem? deus autem semper pulcher est, nunquam deformis, nunquam commutabilis. amavit nos prior qui semper est pulcher; et quales amavit, nisi foedos et deformes? non ideo tamen ut foedos dimitteret; sed ut mutaret, et ex deformibus pulchros faceret. quomodo erimus pulchri? amando eum qui semper est pulcher. quantum in te crescit amor, tantum crescit pulchritudo; quia ipsa caritas est animae pulchritudo* (PL 35,2051; SC 75,396–398).

the last sentence quoted Latin *amor* and *caritas* are successively used for the concept of "love": It is our erotic desire (*amor*) for God that causes our soul's beauty; and our soul's beauty is precisely that *caritas* which we learned earlier was an inner disposition of love that enables us to become truly virtuous. Thus the concept of *caritas*, which hitherto seemed to be almost exclusively biblical and moral, can now be seen to have also an erotic, and Platonic, aspect.

Now the governing ideas of *Tractates* 9,9, the parallelism of bodily and transcendent love and the beautifying effect of love, are also expressed in a passage from Plotinus' *Ennead* VI 7:

> It [= the soul] saw, as if in utter amazement, and, since it held something of it [= the Good] in itself, it had an intimate awareness of it and came into a state of longing, like those who are moved by an image of the loved one to wish to see that same beloved. And just as here below those who are in love shape themselves to the likeness of the beloved, and make their bodies handsomer and bring their souls into likeness, since as far as they can they do not want to fall short of the integrity and all the other excellence of the loved one – if they did they would be rejected by loved ones like these – and these are the lovers who are able to have intercourse; in this way the soul also loves that Good, moved by it to love from the beginning. (Plot. VI 7,31,8–19; tr. Armstrong)[26]

Plotinus even connects love and morality, as does Augustine. But there is a marked difference between the two texts. In Plotinus, a fully intact analogy of bodily love and love for the Good is drawn and fleshed out with motives from Plato's *Phaedrus*: When a man falls in love with someone physically and mentally beautiful, his love, by stirring him into action and inducing him to improve his own physical and mental shape in order to appear attractive and acceptable to his beloved, has a beautifying effect on the lover himself; and the same is true for the soul that, driven by her innate desire for the highest Good, endeavours to prepare herself for the union with it and by so doing becomes beautiful herself. In Augustine, this analogy is present too, but it is significantly disturbed. His vivid description of the helpless ugly lover whom shame overwhelms when he sees his own image in the mirror, whom old age quietly and inexorably approaches and whose only reasonable choice is resignation, is reminiscent of baroque vanity

---

26 Εἶδε δὲ οἷον πληγεῖσα καὶ ἐν αὐτῇ ἔχουσά τι αὐτοῦ συνήσθετο καὶ διατεθεῖσα ἐγένετο ἐν πόθῳ, ὥσπερ οἱ ἐν τῷ εἰδώλῳ τοῦ ἐρασμίου κινούμενοι εἰς τὸ αὐτὸ ἰδεῖν ἐθέλειν τὸ ἐρώμενον. Ὥσπερ δὲ ἐνταῦθα σχηματίζονται εἰς ὁμοιότητα τῷ ἐραστῷ οἳ ἂν ἐρῶσι, καὶ τὰ σώματα εὐπρεπέστερα καὶ τὰς ψυχὰς ἄγοντες εἰς ὁμοιότητα, ὡς μὴ λείπεσθαι κατὰ δύναμιν θέλειν τῇ τοῦ ἐρωμένου σωφροσύνῃ τε καὶ ἀρετῇ τῇ ἄλλῃ – ἢ ἀπόβλητοι ἂν εἶεν τοῖς ἐρωμένοις τοῖς τοιούτοις – καὶ οὗτοί εἰσιν οἱ συνεῖναι δυνάμενοι, τοῦτον τὸν τρόπον καὶ ψυχὴ ἐρᾷ μὲν ἐκείνου ὑπ' αὐτοῦ ἐξ ἀρχῆς εἰς τὸ ἐρᾶν κινηθεῖσα.

scenes rather than of Plato's *Phaedrus*. Why this change? Rather than blaming Augustine's notoriously peculiar theory of sexuality,[27] we should seek the reason in a systematic difference between Augustine and Plotinus that is neatly express-ed in the texts. In Plotinus, the soul is capable of undertaking her beautifying efforts because "she has something of the Good in herself". Since her supreme goal is in some way already present to her, her ascent to it is more or less a return to her natural state. There is nothing comparable to this in Augustine. According to him, the natural features of the human soul in her postlapsarian state are ugliness and wickedness. All the soul can do is to wait for God's love to turn to her; and what will make her beautiful is not a divine element within herself, but her positive response to God's love.

This statement however needs a qualification. In *Tractates* 9,9, there has so far not been any connection between Augustine's discussion of love and beauty and his earlier explanation of *caritas* as Christ the inner *imperator*. But this aspect is added at the end of the chapter:

> 'He had not form nor beauty' (Isaiah 53,2): yes, so that he might give form and beau-ty to you.[28] What form? What beauty? The love of love (*dilectionem caritatis*), that you may run while you love and love while you run.[29] You are beautiful now; but do not look at yourself, that you may not lose what you have received; look at him, by whom you were made beautiful.[30]

As we saw above, *caritas* is the beauty of the soul who loves God; moreover Augustine's exegesis of 1 John 4,8 and 16 "God is love" entailed that the presence of *caritas* in the soul is equivalent to the presence of Christ himself. Hence the memorable phrase *dilectio caritatis*, "love of love",[31] is ambiguous: On the one hand it can be referred to our own *caritas* which results from our desire for God and which is identical with our soul's beauty; on the other hand it refers to Christ who, as *Christus caritas*, is present in us. Thus *dilectio caritatis* at one and the

---

27 Of course, Plotinus too warns us not to fall in love with bodily images, that we may not be drowned like Narcissus (Plot. I 6,8).

28 Augustine means that the incarnation, in which Christ took on the form of a slave, is a prerequisite for man's becoming beautiful, i.e. for man's salvation. Philippians 2,6–7 is quoted immediately before.

29 *currere*; this seems to be a biblical metaphor (cf. Romans 9,16) for the lover's desire.

30 '*non habebat speciem neque decorem*', *ut tibi daret speciem et decorem. quam spe-ciem? quem decorem? dilectionem caritatis; ut amans curras, currens ames. pulcher es iam: sed noli te attendere, ne perdas quod accepisti; illum attende, a quo factus es pul-cher* (PL 35,2052; SC 75,400).

31 We should refrain from the temptation to connect this with Plotinus' αὐτοῦ ἔρως, which, with its paradoxical and mystical associations, belongs to a quite different con-text.

same time refers both to self-love and love of God. Again, there is a text from Plotinus that is strikingly similar: "How then can you see the sort of beauty a good soul has? Go back into yourself and look!" (Plot. I 6,9,6f.; tr. Armstrong)[32]

Here too a soul that has acquired beauty through moral virtue becomes the object of her own love, a love that, ultimately, leads up to the beauty of the Good itself. Augustine, however, is careful to dissolve the ambiguity of the phrase and to draw a clear distinction between *Christus caritas* and the soul inhabited and beautified by him. His warning: "Do not look at yourself!", sounds like a direct reply to Plotinus; and the following amplification, "Look at him by whom you were made beautiful", points out the boundary between God and soul which in Plotinus' philosophy of ascent is deliberately blurred. The reason Augustine gives for his deviation from Plotinus is most characteristical: "that you may not lose what you have received (*accepisti*)". This is a clear allusion to the biblical verse that, on Augustine's reading, embraced his complete theology of humility and grace, 1 Corinthians 4,7: "And what do you have that you did not receive?" (*quid enim habes quod non accepisti?*).[33] From this it becomes quite obvious what Augustine objects to Plotinus. For Augustine, falling in love with oneself after the Plotinian model, even with one's own perfect *caritas*, would be just another example of human self-love of the kind that almost inevitably outgrows the love for God and results in the deadly sin of *superbia*. A soul that is conscious of her own *caritas* must be especially careful not to succumb to this temptation; in order to avoid *superbia* she must constantly remember that she is not God and that her beauty by which she might feel seduced is not her own but Christ's. Augustine may have adapted certain Neoplatonic ideas about beauty and love to his own thinking and even to his preaching; but the Plotinian vision of a complete fusion of lover and beloved, man and god, is precluded by the basic assumptions of Augustine's anthropology.

Abstract

This contribution explores the Neoplatonic background of some of Augustine's ideas on Christian love. In Plotinus, love is indispensable for the soul's ascent to the Good or the One "beyond Being". The satisfaction of love in the mystical union, which Plotinus analyzes philosophically by means of an exegesis of the

---

32 Πῶς ἂν οὖν ἴδοις ψυχὴν ἀγαθὴν οἷον τὸ κάλλος ἔχει; Ἄναγε ἐπὶ σαυτὸν καὶ ἴδε. It is generally agreed that *Ennead* I 6 was known to Augustine.

33 A thorough study of Augustine's use of this verse is provided by P.-M. Hombert, *Gloria Gratiae. Se glorifier en Dieu, principe et fin de la théologie augustinienne de la grâce*, Paris 1996.

Sun Simile from Plato's *Republic*, is a deeply paradoxical experience, like "love loving itself". Although Augustine's biblically-influenced philosophy of love is principally different, it can be shown that his ethical intentionalism is, at least partly, indebted to Neoplatonic internalism. The notion that love of God makes the lover himself beautiful, as expressed in the 9th *Tractate on the First Epistle of John*, is strikingly similar to a passage from Plotinus' *Ennead* VI 7 on the fusion of the soul and the One in the mystical ascent. But whereas in Plotinus (*Ennead* I 6) a truly beautiful soul may reach the beauty of the supreme Good by lovingly turning to herself, Augustine, in a passage that reads like a direct criticism of Plotinus, warns his hearers not to look to themselves but to Christ in order to avoid misguided self-love and *superbia*.

Der Philosoph auf dem Kaiserthron, der Leser auf dem Holzweg?

Marc Aurel in der *Historia Augusta*[*]

DENNIS PAUSCH

1. ‚Wer einmal lügt, dem glaubt man nicht?‘

1.1 Die *Historia Augusta* als Forschungsproblem

Wenn man das letzte Kapitel von Friedrich Leos epochaler, 1901 erschienener Studie ‚Die griechisch-römische Biographie nach ihrer litterarischen Form‘ aufschlägt, stößt man auf folgende, nicht gerade der üblichen Proömialtopik gehorchende Einleitung: „… und was sich an Sueton … ferner angeschlossen hat, trägt so sehr die Zeichen des Ephemeren und Nichtigen, der Rest dieser Production ist so abschmeckend und auch stofflich unbrauchbar, dass man sich hier einmal gerne der Philologenpflicht entzöge, Kehrichthaufen umzuwühlen."[1] Eine solche, mit Widerwillen gepaarte Geringschätzung stellt eine der beiden in der Forschungsliteratur häufig anzutreffenden Reaktionen auf die *Historia Augusta* dar. In der zweiten, ebenso charakteristischen Einschätzung mischen sich hingegen eher Schrecken und Ratlosigkeit, wie vielleicht am eindrucksvollsten der von Ronald Syme angestellte Vergleich mit dem vergilischen Kyklopen zeigen kann: „From an inspection of the Historia Augusta, the first reaction can only be bewilderment or alarm. The thing is portentous, unexampled, unexplained: a *monstrum horrendum informe ingens, cui lumen ademptum.*"[2]

Und tatsächlich dürfte es keinen anderen antiken Text geben, der weitgehend vollständig erhalten ist und mit dem dennoch soviele offene Fragen verbunden

[*] Mein Dank gilt dem Seminar für Alte Geschichte und Epigraphik der Universität Heidelberg, in dessen Forschungskolloquium ich im Mai 2006 eine erste Fassung dieses Beitrages zur Diskussion stellen durfte, sowie Vera Binder, Ulrike Egelhaaf-Gaiser, Daniela Franz, Helmut Krasser und Peter von Möllendorff für kritische Lektüre und zahlreiche hilfreiche Hinweise.

[1] Vgl. Friedrich Leo, Die griechisch-römische Biographie nach ihrer litterarischen Form, Leipzig 1901, 269.
[2] Vgl. Vergil, Aeneis 3,658 u. Ronald Syme, The History Augusta. A call of clarity, Bonn 1971, 9.

sind.[3] Die ungelösten Rätsel beginnen bereits bei elementaren Kategorien wie der Entstehungszeit, die mit letzter Sicherheit nur sehr vage auf die Jahre zwischen 360/61 und 526 eingegrenzt werden kann,[4] und der Bestimmung des Autors, der wohl auch trotz neuerer Versuche einer Identifikation in der von ihm selbst gewählten Anonymität verbleiben wird.[5] Als weitere Schwierigkeit erweist sich der Titel, da die heute gebräuchliche – und der Einfachheit halber auch hier verwendete – Bezeichnung als *Historia Augusta* sicher nicht auf den Autor zurückgeht,[6] sondern erst im Laufe der Überlieferungsgeschichte aufgekommen ist.[7]

Als problematisch muß diese Bezeichnung vor allem deswegen gelten, weil mit ihr von vorneherein eine falsche, nämlich primär historiographische Erwartungshaltung geweckt wird. Diese stimmt bereits mit der vom Autor selbst vor-

---

3 Vgl. Syme (s. Anm. 2) 1: „The Historia Augusta is without question or rival the most enigmatic work that Antiquity has transmitted."

4 Den *terminus post quem* liefert das in der *Historia Augusta* offenkundig verwendete Werk des Aurelius Victor, während sich der *terminus ante quem* aus der Verwendung der *Historia Augusta* durch Q. Aurelius Memmius Symmachus ergibt (vgl. Holger Sonnabend, Geschichte der antiken Biographie. Von Isokrates bis zur Historia Augusta, Stuttgart 2002, 216 f.). Aus den hier vorgestellten Überlegungen ergibt sich eine Datierung, die mit dem von der Mehrheit der Forschung verfolgten Ansatz um die Wende zum 5. Jh. n. Chr. übereinstimmt.

5 Vgl. z. B. François Paschoud, L'auteur de l'Histoire Auguste est-il un apostat?, in: François Chausson u. Étienne Wolff, Consuetudinis amor. Fragments d'histoire romaine (IIe–VIe siècles), Mélanges Jean-Pierre, Rom 2003, 357–369, sowie den Bericht von Ralf Behrwald über das *Historiae Augustae Colloquium* des Jahres 2005: „In Bamberg schlug nun S. Ratti (Dijon) vor, den Verfasser mit Virius Nicomachus Flavianus senior zu identifizieren. Dagegen schlug M. Festy (Rennes) eine Identifikation mit dem jüngeren Nicomachus Flavianus vor, so daß die Historia Augusta zwar im senatorischen Milieu Roms, aber in den 420er Jahren entstanden wäre – nicht mehr als Dokument der christlich-heidnischen Kontroversen theodosianischer Zeit, sondern als ferner Reflex aus dem Abstand einer Generation. Eine erste Fassung des Werkes sei sogar dem christlichen Kaiser Theodosius gewidmet gewesen, und erst eine Überarbeitung habe der Historia Augusta ihre antichristliche Tendenz gegeben." (http://hsozkult.geschichte.hu-berlin.de/tagungsberichte/id=774).

6 Der Originaltitel ist nicht bekannt, lautete aber vielleicht *de vita principum* (vgl. HA trig. tyr. 33,8; Aurelian. 1,2; Prob. 2,7 mit Mark Thomson, The Original Title of the *Historia Augusta*, Historia 56,1 (2007), 121–125); eine Vermutung, die auch die Diskussion um die Aufnahme der Prinzen, Gegenkaiser und Usurpatoren verständlicher machen würde (vgl. v. a. HA quadr. tyr. 1–2).

7 Der Name *Historia Augusta* geht auf die Bezeichnung des Tacitus als *scriptor historiae Augustae* (HA Tac. 10,3) und die überlieferungsgeschichtliche Praxis zurück, aus der Addition mehrerer antiker ‚Kaiserhistoriker' eine Gesamtdarstellung der römischen Kaiserzeit zu gewinnen; der für diese Sammelwerke gebräuchliche Titel *scriptores historiae Augustae* wurde dann schließlich von Casaubonus in seiner Pariser Edition von 1603 auf die heute noch so genannte Biographiensammlung eingeengt.

genommenen Zuordnung zur Gattung der Biographie nicht überein,[8] bereitet den Rezipienten aber vor allem nur unzureichend auf die zahlreichen fiktionalen und eher an den antiken Roman erinnernden Elemente vor.[9] Die durch den Titel zunächst geschürte und im Laufe der Lektüre dann enttäuschte Hoffnung, in der *Historia Augusta* die schmerzlich vermißte historische Quelle für die Jahre zwischen 117 und 284 n. Chr. vor sich zu haben, dürfte nicht unwesentlich zu der lange Zeit allgemein geteilten Geringschätzung des Werkes[10] wie seines Verfassers[11] beigetragen haben.

An diesem rätselhaften Befund, der den philologischen wie den historischen Scharfsinn immer wieder herausgefordert hat, sind zum einen die Launen der Überlieferung schuld: Geht doch die Forschung mehrheitlich davon aus, daß der Anfang des Werkes verloren gegangen ist[12] und die *Historia Augusta* ursprünglich mit den Biographien Nervas und Trajans einen direkten Anschluß an die Darstellung Suetons hergestellt hat,[13] der immer wieder als Vorbild und wichtiger

---

8   Vgl. Andrea Scheithauer, Kaiserbild und literarisches Programm: Untersuchungen zur Tendenz der Historia Augusta, Frankfurt 1987, 129 ff.

9   Vgl. z. B. Klaus-Peter Johne, Art.: Historia Augusta, Der Neue Pauly 5 (2001), 637–640, h. 639: „Durch eingestreute Wundergeschichten, Novellen und Anekdoten nähern sich Teile der *Historia Augusta* der Romanliteratur."

10 So bezeichnete etwa der um klare Worte selten verlegene Theodor Mommsen die *Historia Augustua* als „eine der elendsten Sudeleien, die wir aus dem Altertum haben" (vgl. Mommsen (s. Anm. 23) 229).

11 Am deutlichsten kommt die Verzweiflung des nach zuverlässigen Quellen suchenden Historikers bei der Lektüre der *Historia Augusta* wohl in der Charakterisierung ihres Autors als „erbärmlicher Stümper" zum Ausdruck (vgl. Ernst Hohl, Das Ende Caracallas, in: Miscellanea Academica Berolinensia, Berlin 1950, Bd. 2,1, 276–293, h. 291).

12 Für die Lücke in der Darstellung zwischen den Jahren 244 und 253 geht die *communis opinio* ebenfalls von einem Verlust im Laufe der Überlieferungsgeschichte aus; doch wurde bereits von Casaubonus auch die These einer bewußten Aussparung vertreten (vgl. v. a. Anthony R. Birley, The Lacuna in the Historia Augusta, Bonner Historia-Augusta-Colloquium 1972/74 (1976), 55–62, u. ferner z. B. Daniel den Hengst, The Prefaces in the Historia Augusta, Amsterdam 1981, 70 ff., sowie dag. z. B. Ronald Syme, Emperors from Illyricum, in: ders., Emperors and Biography, Oxford 1971, 194–207, h. 200 f., u. Karl-Heinz Stubenrauch, Kompositionsprobleme der Historia Augusta (Einleitungen – Der verlorene Anfang), Diss. Göttingen 1982, 100 ff.).

13 Vgl. z. B. Stubenrauch (s. Anm. 12) 59 ff., u. den Hengst (s. Anm. 12) 14 ff., sowie dag. v. a. Werner Hartke, Römische Kinderkaiser. Eine Strukturanalyse römischen Denkens und Daseins, Berlin 1951, 326 ff., u. Michael Louis Meckler, The beginning of the Historia Augusta, Historia 45 (1996), 364–375, der zunächst darauf hinweist, daß diese Annahme nicht zuletzt auf unserer Wahrnehmung der Adoptivkaiserzeit als abgeschlossener Epoche beruht, und im folgenden Gründe nennt, warum der Verfasser der *Historia Augusta* (der selbst sogar behauptet, sein Werk mit Caesar begonnen

Vorgänger genannt wird.[14] Diesen Viten wäre dann wohl – wie für die suetonischen *Caesares* bezeugt[15] – eine *praefatio* vorangegangen, deren Verlust deswegen als besonders ärgerlich empfunden wird, weil sie vielleicht die entscheidenden Hinweise zur Entschlüsselung des ganzen Werkes enthalten hat. Angesichts der in dieser Hinsicht wenig erhellenden Bemerkungen am Ende der *vita Carini*, der letzten der Sammlung, sollte man von allzu großen Erwartungen allerdings wohl besser Abstand nehmen.[16]

Die Hauptlast der Schuld an unserer Ratlosigkeit hat jedoch der Verfasser selbst zu tragen, zumindest dann, wenn man nicht hinter den von Hermann Dessau 1889 erreichten Stand der Diskussion zurückfallen und die Angaben des Textes für bare Münze nehmen will, der in diokletianisch-konstantinischer Zeit von sechs unterschiedlichen Autoren geschrieben worden sein will.[17] Deren klangvolle Namen[18] sind ebenso fiktiv wie die durch die häufigen Anreden an Diokletian und Konstantin vorgegebene Datierung falsch ist. Doch damit nicht genug: Auch die Lebensbeschreibungen selbst strotzen vor ungenauen, veränderten

---

zu haben: vgl. Ael. 7,5) bewußt Hadrian als Ausgangspunkt gewählt haben könnte (vgl. z. B. Hadr. 16,1: Publikation einer Autobiographie unter Pseudonymen als Hinweis auf das Spiel mit Autorennamen in der *Historia Augusta*).

14 Vgl. z. B. HA Max. Balb. 4,5; HA Prob. 2,7 u. quadr. tyr. 1,1–2 sowie ferner André Chastagnol, L'Histoire Auguste et les ‚Douze Césars' de Suétone, BHAC 1970 (1972), 109–123.

15 Vgl. Lyd. mag. 2,6.

16 Vgl. HA Car. 21,2–3: *habe, mi amice, meum munus, quod ego, ut s<a>ep[a]e dixi, non eloquentiae causa sed curiositatis in lumen edidi, id praecipu[a]e agens, ut, si quis eloque<n>s vellet facta principum reserare, materiam non requireret, habiturus meos libellos ministros eloquii. (3) te quaeso, sis contentus nosque sic voluisse scribere melius quam potuisse contendas.* („So nimm denn, lieber Freund, diese meine Gabe; wie ich des öfteren gesagt, habe ich sie nicht ans Licht gebracht, um mit Stilkünsten zu prunken, sondern um die Wißbegier zu befriedigen. Dabei war es mein Hauptanliegen, einem kommenden beredten Darsteller der Kaisergeschichte den erforderlichen Stoff zu bieten; er mag meine kleinen Bücher als Hilfsmittel seiner Kunstprosa verwenden. (3) An Dich richte ich die Bitte, Dich mit dem Gebotenen abzufinden und anzuerkennen, daß unser guter Wille bei der Abfassung stärker war als unser Vollbringen." Diese und alle folgenden Übersetzungen sind übernommen aus: Ernst Hohl, Johannes Straub et al., Historia Augusta, 2 Bde., Zürich-München 1976/85).

17 Vgl. Hermann Dessau, Über Zeit und Persönlichkeit der Scriptores historiae Augustae, Hermes 24 (1889), 337–392, u. ders., Über die Scriptores historiae Augustae, Hermes 27 (1892), 561–605. Im technischen Sinne handelt es sich bei der *Historia Augusta* also um ein Pseudepigraphon (vgl. Wolfgang Speyer, Die literarische Fälschung im heidnischen und christlichen Altertum. Ein Versuch ihrer Deutung, Handbuch der Altertumswissenschaft I 2, München 1971, 13f.).

18 Es handelt sich um Aelius Spartianus, Iulius Capitolinus, Vulcacius Gallicanus, *vir clarissimus*, Aelius Lampridius, Trebellius Pollio und Flavius Vopiscus aus Syrakus.

oder frei hinzugefügten Angaben,[19] und sogar bei einigen der Protagonisten handelt es sich um reine Erfindungen der *Historia Augusta*.[20] Die hierdurch ausgelösten Irritationen werden auch dadurch nicht geringer, daß der Verfasser in zahlreichen Kommentaren die *fides historica* des eigenen Werkes beschwört und die mangelnde historische Sorgfalt anderer Autoren kritisiert.[21] Solche Widersprüche lassen sich auf ganz unterschiedlichen Ebenen beobachten und stören den Rezipienten immer wieder bei dem Versuch, sich ein einheitliches Bild von diesem *monstrum horrendum informe ingens* zu machen.[22]

Obwohl diese Punkte in den Jahren seit 1889 schon vielfach behandelt wurden und nach zum Teil kontroverser Debatte heute weitgehend anerkannt sind,[23] hat sich die daran anschließende philologische Diskussion im wesentlichen auf die Ebene des Gesamtwerkes konzentriert,[24] das seither vielen als die raffinierteste literarische ‚Fälschung' der Antike gilt,[25] während bei der Beschäftigung mit einzelnen Viten oder Stellen nach wie vor Fragestellungen im Vordergrund stehen, die sich aus den Erkenntnisinteressen der Geschichtswissenschaft ergeben. Bei der Interpretation kleinerer Abschnitte wird daher in der Regel eine Perspektive eingenommen, die von der jeweiligen Stelle in der *Historia Augusta* ausge-

---

19 Für eine repräsentative Auswahl vgl. Ronald Syme, Fiction and Credulity, in: ders., Emperors and Biography. Studies in the Historia Augusta, Oxford 1971, 263–280.

20 Wieviele vor allem der *triginta tyranni* fiktiv sind, läßt sich aufgrund der lückenhaften Parallelüberlieferung nicht abschließend sagen, mit relativ großer Sicherheit können aber Saturninus (trig. tyr. 23), Trebellianus (trig. tyr. 26) und Censorinus (trig. tyr. 33) als Erfindungen gelten.

21 Vgl. z. B. HA trig. tyr. 11,6; 33,8 u. Aurel. 17,1; 35,1 sowie ferner Jan Burian, Fides Historica als methodologischer Grundsatz der Historia Augusta, Klio 59 (1977), 285–298.

22 Speziell zu diesem Widerspruch s. u. S. 131 f.

23 Die wichtigste Gegenposition besteht in der Annahme einer redakionellen Überarbeitung am Ende des 4. Jh. vgl. zuerst Theodor Mommsen, Die Scriptores Historiae Augustae, Hermes 25 (1890), 228–292 (= ders., Gesammelte Schriften, Bd. 7, Berlin 1909, 302–362), sowie ferner v.a. Arnaldo Momigliano, An Unsolved Problem of Historical Forgery: The Scriptores Historiae Augustae, Secondo contributo alla storia degli studi classici, Rom 1960, 105–143 [= Studies in Historiography, London 1966, 143–180]; Burckhard Meißner, Computergestützte Untersuchungen zur stilistischen Einheitlichkeit der *Historia Augusta*, in: Historia Augusta Colloquium Bonnense, Bari 1997, 175–215; Adolf Lippold (hg. v. Gerhard H. Waldherr), Die Historia Augusta: eine Sammlung römischer Kaiserbiographien aus der Zeit Konstantins, Stuttgart 1998, u. Daniel den Hengst, The discussion of authorship, Historiae Augustae Colloquium Perusinum, Bari 2002, 187–195.

24 Vgl. v.a. den Hengst (s. Anm. 12) u. Scheithauer (s. Anm. 8).

25 Zu den unterschiedlichen Definitionen einer Fälschung in der Geschichts- und in der Literaturwissenschaft vgl. Timothy D. Barnes, Was heißt Fälschung?, Archiv für Kulturgeschichte 79,2 (1997), 259–267.

hend die literarische, numismatische oder archäologische Parallelüberlieferung in den Blick nimmt und damit letztlich auf eine Rekonstruktion der historischen Realität zielt.[26]

Diese Vorgehensweise läßt sich jedoch gewinnbringend durch eine stärker philologisch geprägte Perspektive ergänzen, die zur Erklärung eines bestimmten Abschnittes seinen Kontext in der *Historia Augusta* selbst heranzieht. Das scheint auch deswegen sinnvoll zu sein, weil es sich bei diesem Werk um einen Text handelt, der heute nur noch selten in Form einer kontinuierlichen Lektüre von Anfang bis Ende rezipiert wird. Weitaus häufiger ist eine partielle Form des Zugriffs, die in der Regel über das Inhaltsverzeichnis oder den Index erfolgt und sich auf die im jeweils aktuellen Zusammenhang relevanten Stellen konzentriert.[27]

1.2 Die *Historia Augusta* als narrativer Text

Im folgenden soll daher der Versuch unternommen werden, das heute unter der Bezeichnung *Historia Augusta* bekannte Werk nicht primär als historische Quelle zu betrachten, sondern als einen literarischen Text dadurch ernst zu nehmen, daß ein kleineres, aber doch mehrere Viten umfassendes Segment als erzählerisches Kontinuum aufgefaßt und unter narratologischen Kategorien untersucht wird.[28]

---

26 Für einen aktuellen Überblick hierzu vgl. Hartwin Brandt, Facts and Fictions – Die Historia Augusta und das 3. Jahrhundert, in: Klaus-Peter Johne et al., *Deleto paene imperio Romano*. Transformationsprozesse des Römischen Reiches im 3. Jahrhundert und ihre Rezeption in der Neuzeit, Stuttgart 2006, 11–23.

27 Eine solche partielle Form der Lektüre war zwar auch in der biographischen Literatur der Antike durchaus üblich, hat aber dennoch immer nur eine Möglichkeit neben der kontinuierlichen Rezeption dargestellt. Wenn man die Vielzahl von textimmanenten und paratextuellen Strategien, die Sueton verwendet, um seinem Leser einen selektiven Zugriff zu ermöglichen, als Vergleich heranzieht, zeigt sich zudem deutlich, daß der Verfasser der *Historia Augusta* sein Werk nicht in gleichem Maße zum gezielten Nachschlagen einzelner Informationen konzipiert hat. Die einzigen Stellen, an denen sich der Autor Gedanken über den Komfort für den Leser macht, beschäftigen sich mit der Frage der Bucheinteilung (vgl. z. B. Max. 1,1–3; trig. tyr. 31,5). Dementsprechend sind wahrscheinlich auch die in der handschriftlichen Überlieferung dem Text in unterschiedlichen Versionen nachgestellten Inhaltsverzeichnisse als sekundär zu betrachten (vgl. Ernst Hohl, Beiträge zur Textkritik der Historia Augusta, Klio 13 (1913), 258–288.387–423, h. 395), obwohl Indizes und Inhaltsverzeichnisse in der lateinischen Literatur seit dem 1. Jh. n. Chr. häufig nachgewiesen sind.

28 Zur generellen Anwendbarkeit der Erkenntnisse der Erzählforschung auch auf die ihrem Anspruch nach nicht fiktionalen der antiken Geschichtsschreibung vgl. z. B.

Für ein solches Vorgehen bietet sich aus verschiedenen Gründen die Dreiergruppe an, die von den eng mit einander verzahnten Biographien Marc Aurels, seines Mitregenten Lucius Verus und seines Gegenspielers Avidius Cassius gebildet wird. Während die Schwierigkeiten und Dissonanzen, mit denen der Rezipient bei der Lektüre dieser Vitengruppe konfrontiert wird, bislang vornehmlich unter Perspektive der Quellenkritik untersucht wurden, sollen die drei Lebensbeschreibungen im folgenden als ein aus drei aufeinander bezogenen Versionen bewußt konzipiertes narratives Ganzes verstanden werden. Dieser methodische Ansatz hat zur Folge, daß zur Erklärung der widersprüchlichen oder in anderer Weise schwer verständlichen Stellen in dem ausgewählten Textausschnitt nicht das mangelnde Verständnis der Quellen oder andere Defizite des Verfassers herangezogen werden, sondern daß diese Elemente der Darstellung als gezielt eingesetzte literarische Strategeme aufgefaßt werden.

Über diesen ‚Umweg‘ kann sich die Auseinandersetzung mit der *Historia Augusta* auch wieder als gewinnbringend für die Beschäftigung mit der historiographischen Literatur der römischen Kaiserzeit erweisen. Daß die in dieser Zeit entstandenen Geschichtswerke bei der Wiedergabe historischen Geschehens nicht nur eine zunehmend biographische Perspektive bevorzugen,[29] sondern hierfür auch über das in der Antike ohnehin übliche Maß hinaus auf Darstellungsmuster und Präsentationsformen der fiktionalen Literatur zurückgreifen, ist in den letzten Jahren verstärkt in das Blickfeld der Forschung gerückt.[30]

Die Erkenntnis, daß es sich bei der gesteigerten Bedeutung der narrativen Technik und der damit verbundenen stärkeren Berücksichtung des Unterhaltungsinteresses des Lesers um allgemeine Entwicklungen in der kaiserzeitlichen Historiographie handelt, hat unter anderem zur Neubewertung eines lange Zeit wenig geschätzten Autors wie Herodian geführt.[31] Der bei ihm zu beobachtende

---

Manfred Fuhrmann, Narrative Techniken im Dienste der Geschichtsschreibung (Livius, Buch 21–22). Eine Skizze, in: Eckart Lefèvre u. Eckart Olshausen, Livius. Werk und Rezeption, FS Erich Burck, München 1983, 19–29, u. Tim Rood, Thucydides. Narrative and Explanation, Oxford 1998 (²2004), v. a. 9–14.

29 Vgl. v. a. Albrecht Dihle, Die Entstehung der historischen Biographie, Sitzungsbericht der Heidelberger Akademie der Wissenschaften 1986/3, Heidelberg 1987, 69.

30 Vgl. allg. den Überblick bei Martin Zimmermann, Enkomion und Historiographie: Entwicklungslinien der kaiserzeitlichen Geschichtsschreibung vom 1. bis zum frühen 3. Jh. n. Chr., in: ders., Geschichtsschreibung und politischer Wandel im 3. Jh. n. Chr., Historia Einzelschriften 127, Stuttgart 1999, 17–56, h. 41ff., sowie inbesondere zur wechselseitigen Beeinflussung von Historiographie und Roman ders., Kaiser und Ereignis. Studien zum Geschichtswerk Herodians, Vestigia 52, München 1999, 8 ff., u. Niklas Holzberg, Der antike Roman. Eine Einführung, Düsseldorf-Zürich ²2001, 45ff.

31 Vgl. Zimmermann (s. Anm. 30) v. a. 325 f.: „Zumindest ein Teil der potentiellen Adressaten hat vermutlich keinen Anstoß daran genommen, daß eine überzeugende

Einsatz verschiedener, jeweils unterschiedlich fokalisierter Erzählperspektiven[32] bietet darüber hinaus eine enge und bislang wenig beachtete Parallele zur *Historia Augusta*. Das gleiche gilt für die Ergebnisse, die sich aus der Untersuchung der von Ammianus Marcellinus angewandten literarischen Technik ergeben. Hier sind es vor allem die Überlegungen zur Funktion der Widersprüche, die sich bei der Charaktersierung seiner Protagonisten feststellen lassen, die für unsere Fragestellung aufschlußreich sind.[33]

Gesamtbewertung einzelner Zeitabschnitte und historischer Figuren mangelnde Präzision, ja selbst Verfälschung von Fakten bedingen konnte. Daraus darf vielleicht der Schluß gezogen werden, daß die Gestaltung des Geschichtswerkes auch etwas darüber verrät, wie ein Teil der Leser glaubte, sich dem Verständnis zeitgeschichtlicher Ereignisse nähern zu können. Es hat den Anschein, daß beide Seiten, nämlich Autor und ein Teil des Publikums, historische Wahrheit nicht in erster Linie im zuverlässig rekonstruierten Detail, sondern in den inneren Gesetzmäßigkeiten des Geschilderten gesucht haben. Dies wirft die grundsätzliche Frage auf, ob diese Haltung möglicherweise ein Hinweis darauf ist, mit welcher Skepsis die Zeitgenossen jenen Informationen gegenüberstanden, die gewissermaßen offiziell zur Verfügung gestellt wurden. Ist der Grad der Umgestaltung durch den Historiker Herodian vielleicht sogar Maßstab für das geringe Vertrauen, das seine Leser dem zugänglichen Material und den unterschiedlichen, bereits existierenden Berichten entgegenbrachten?" u. Thomas Hidber, Herodians Darstellung der Kaisergeschichte nach Marc Aurel, Basel 2006. Zur Bedeutung von Herodian als Quelle für die *Historia Augusta* vgl. Frank Kolb, Literarische Beziehungen zwischen Cassius Dio, Herodian und der Historia Augusta, Bonn 1972, u. ders., Herodian in der Historia Augusta, BHAC 1972–74, Bonn 1976, 143–152.

32 Vgl. Thomas Hidber, Zeit und Erzählperspektive in Herodians Geschichtswerk, in: Martin Zimmermann, Geschichtsschreibung und politischer Wandel im 3. Jh. n. Chr., Historia Einzelschriften 127, Stuttgart 1999, 145–167, h. 160ff., v. a. 164 „Charakteristisch an Herodians Erzählperspektive ist, dass er oft dieselben Personen und Entwicklungen aus verschiedenen Blickwinkeln schildert: So werden die Hauptcharaktereigenschaften der einzelnen Kaiser bald aus der Sicht ihrer Vorgänger, bald aus jener der Soldaten und bald aus jener des Volkes geschildert, zeigen sich in ihren eigenen Aussagen und Taten und werden schließlich immer auch vom auktorialen Erzähler noch explizit gemacht." Vgl. Zimmermann (s. Anm. 30).

33 Vgl. v. a. Petra Riedel, Faktoren des historischen Prozesses: Eine vergleichende Studie zu Tacitus und Ammianus Marcellinus, Classica Monacensia 25, Tübingen 2002, 282ff. u. 397: „Das Werk Ammians weist vereinzelt Unstimmigkeiten auf, die in dieser Form in den Historien so gut wie nicht zu beobachten sind. Zwar zeigen die Akteure auch in den Res gestae einen insgesamt konstanten Charakter, doch stößt man zuweilen auf bemerkenswerte Widersprüche, die sich nicht mit der Vielschichtigkeit ihres Wesens erklären lassen. Sie hängen vielmehr davon ab, wer die augenblickliche Kontrastfolie darstellt, ob beispielsweise Gallus für sich oder gegenüber Constantius betrachtet wird bzw. ob Constantius als Vertreter Roms nach außen oder als Gegner Julians auftritt. Auch Unstimmigkeiten zwischen Nekrolog und narrativem Geschehensbericht, wie sie bei Ammian gelegentlich vorkommen, sind in dieser

Vor diesem Hintergrund kann im Anschluß an die im folgenden vorgestellten Überlegungen auch der Versuch unternommen werden, den Ort genauer zu bestimmen, den die *Historia Augusta* in dem breiten Spektrum der unterschiedlichen Literaturformen, die in der Kaiserzeit zur Darstellung von Vergangenheit dienten, ursprünglich einmal eingenommen hat, sowie aus dieser Einordnung Rückschlüsse auf potentielle Adressaten und die Entstehungszeit zu ziehen (Kapitel IV). Bevor der Blick jedoch auf diese Weise erweitert werden kann, ist zunächst eine Engführung auf die eigentliche Fragestellung notwendig, die in zwei Schritten erfolgen soll: Ein allgemeinerer Teil, der sich mit der Bewertung von Protagonisten in der *Historia Augusta* und den hierzu verwendeten Formen beschäftigt und dabei zugleich die Auswahl der um die Figur Marc Aurels zentrierten Biographiengruppe erläutert (Kapitel II), wird die ausführliche Besprechung dieses konkreten Textabschnittes vorbereiten, die in ihrem Aufbau den Verlauf einer kontinuierlichen ‚Erstlektüre‘ simuliert (Kapitel III).

2. Strategien der indirekten Bewertung und die Funktion der Nebenviten

In der antiken Literatur stellt die Bewertung von in unterschiedlicher Hinsicht bedeutsamen Personen ein geradezu ubiquitäres Phänomen dar, das in der rhetorischen Ausbildung mit der Anweisung *laudare claros viros et vituperare improbos*[34] beginnt und in der Geschichtsschreibung ebenso einen festen Platz hat wie in der Biographie. Auch der Autor der *Historia Augusta* möchte seine Protagonisten nicht nur darstellen, sondern auch beurteilen. Diese Absicht tritt in den programmatischen Äußerungen, mit denen er sich vorgeblich an Diokletian oder Konstantin wendet, deutlich hervor,[35] zeigt sich aber auch im Text selbst, vor allem in der starken Betonung von Tugenden und Lastern[36] oder in der Verwendung einer festen Terminologie, nach der sich die römischen Kaiser in *principes boni*, *mali* und *medii* unterteilen lassen.[37]

Die Bewertung des Herrschers durch den Dichter wird in der *Historia Augusta* zudem noch auf einer weiteren Ebene thematisiert: An mehreren Stellen werden die Kaiser selbst als Rezipienten von Literatur gezeigt, die sich der Macht

---

Form in den Historien nicht zu finden.“ Sowie zu seiner Erzähltechnik ferner Frank Wittchow, Exemplarisches Erzählen bei Ammianus Marcellinus. Episode, Exemplum, Anekdote, Beiträge zur Altertumskunde 144, München–Leipzig 2001.

34 Vgl. z. B. Quint. inst. 2,40,20.

35 Vgl. zu diesen Stellen zusammenfassend den Hengst (s. Anm. 12).

36 Vgl. Scheithauer (s. Anm. 8) 19 ff.

37 Vgl. v. a. HA Aurel. 42,3–6 u. Car. 3,8 sowie ferner Scheithauer (s. Anm. 8) 36 ff.

des Autors bei der Gestaltung ihres Bildes bei der Nachwelt durchaus bewußt sind. So erfährt man von dem als ‚Musterkaiser' präsentierten Alexander Severus, daß er die Schriftsteller deswegen immer in Ehren hielt, weil er eine unfreundliche Darstellung seiner eigenen Regierung fürchtete,[38] während Commodus aus dem gleichen Grund die Lektüre der Caligula-Vita Suetons, dessen kritisches Urteil er offenbar auf sich bezogen hat, drakonisch bestraft haben soll.[39]

Angesichts der großen Bedeutung, die der Beurteilung von Protagonisten in der *Historia Augusta* zukommt, muß es um so mehr überraschen, daß es bislang nicht gelungen ist, in diesen Bewertungen eine gemeinsame Tendenz zu erkennen oder aus ihnen Rückschlüsse auf eine Intention des Gesamtwerks zu ziehen, die über die in der historiographischen Literatur der Kaiserzeit fast schon einen Allgemeinplatz darstellende prosenatorische Perspektive[40] und die immer noch umstrittene Frage einer heidnisch-antichristlichen Geschichtsauffassung hinausgeht.[41] Ihre Ursache haben diese Schwierigkeiten darin, daß die Mehrzahl der

---

38 Vgl. HA Alex. 3,4–5: *nec valde amavit Latinam facundiam, sed amavit litteratos homines vehementer, eos etiam reformidans, ne quid de se asperum scriberent.* (5) *denique eos, <quos> dignos [ad discendum] videbat, singula quaeque, quae publice privatim agebat, se ipso docente volebat addiscere, si forte ipsi non adfuissent, esque petebat ut, si vera essent, in litteras mitterent.* Seine Rolle als ideale Verkörperung eines ‚kaiserlichen Rezipienten' wird dadurch noch deutlicher, daß er sich auf der anderen Seite Panegyrik verbittet, zumindest wenn sie allzu plumb daherkommt (vgl. HA Alex. 35,1: *oratores et poetas non sibi panegyricos dicentes, quod exemplo Nigri Pescenni stultum ducebat, sed aut orationes recitantes aut facta veterum ca[m]ne<n>tes liben[i]ter audivit, libentius tamen, si quis et recitavit Alexandri Magni laudes aut [h]i<t>e<m> bo<no>rum retro principum aut magnorum urbis Romae virorum*). Darüber hinaus hat er angeblich auch selbst diejenigen seiner Vorgänger, die als Vorbilder taugten, in Form von Gedichten (vgl. HA Alex. 27,8), mit der Aufstellung von Statuen (vgl. HA Alex. 28,6) und durch die Aufnahme unter seine ‚Hausgötter' (vgl. HA Alex. 29,2) geehrt.

39 Vgl. HA Comm. 10,2: *eum etiam, qui Tranquilli librum vitam Caligulae continentem legerat, feris obici iussit, quia eundem diem natalis habuerat, quem et Caligula.* („Sogar einen Mann, der ein Buch des Tranquillus mit der Caligulabiographie gelesen hatte, ließ er den wilden Tieren vorwerfen, dieweil er am selben Tage Geburtstag hatte wie Caligula."). Zu einer ähnlichen Stelle im Zusammenhang mit Marc Aurel s. u. S. 143 f.

40 Vgl. v. a. Klaus-Peter Johne, Kaiserbiographie und Senatsaristokratie, Berlin 1976, u. Scheithauer (s. Anm. 8) 126 f., sowie speziell zur Biographie Marc Aurels: Alain Dubreuil, Le message idéologique de la Vita Marci dans le recueil de l'Histoire Auguste, Cahiers des études anciennes 1995, 171–178, u. ders., La biographie de l'empereur Marc-Aurèle dans le recueil de l'*Histoire Auguste*, Ann Arbor 1996, 270ff.

41 Vgl. zuerst Norman H. Baynes, The Historia Augusta. Its date and purpose, Oxford 1926, der die *Historia Augusta* als Propagandaschrift für Iulianus Apostata deutet, u. ferner v. a. Johannes Straub, Heidnische Geschichtsapologetik in der christlichen Spätantike, Bonn 1963, sowie ferner den Bericht von Ralf Behrwald über das *Historiae Augustae Colloquium* 2005: „Der Frage der Tendenz dieses Werkes ging K. Rosen

Viten in ihrer Tendenz weder eindeutig als Enkomion noch als Invektive angelegt sind. Zwar gibt es Ausnahmen wie die vorwiegend positive Darstellung des Alexander Severus oder die Biographie des Commodus, die ein eindrucksvolles Beispiel für die literarische Strategie einer *damnatio* durch *memoria* darstellt.[42] Doch offenbar war es die Absicht des Autors, solche eindeutigen Charakterisierungen abwechseln zu lassen mit Beurteilungen, die auf eine indirekte, vom Rezipienten erst zu entschlüsselnde Weise erfolgen und sich dabei häufig sogar als ambivalent erweisen. Die damit verbundene stärkere Involvierung des Lesers in den Prozeß der Urteilsbildung stellt zugleich einen literarischen Reiz dar, der über die Unterhaltung durch drastische Schilderungen oder skurrile Details deutlich hinausgeht.[43]

Dem Ziel einer stärker indirekten Charakterisierung dient in der *Historia Augusta* eine ganze Reihe literarischer Strategien. Zunächst spielt hier die Ironie in ihren verschiedenen Facetten eine wichtige Rolle, was schon deswegen naheliegt, weil ironisches Sprechen einen wichtigen Bestandteil der rhetorischen Ausbildung bildete.[44] Eng damit verwandt sind unterschiedliche Formen des Humors, die in der *Historia Augusta* auch im Vergleich mit anderen antiken Biographien auffallend viel Platz einnehmen.[45] Eine Besonderheit stellen hier unter

---

(Bonn) nach, der zahlreiche Bezüge auf den Kaiser Julian aufdeckte, auf den vor allem die Vita Marc Aurels in der Historia Augusta anspiele." (http://hsozkult. geschichte.hu-berlin.de/tagungsberichte/id=774).

42 Zur Darstellung des Commodus vgl. Scheithauer (s. Anm. 8) 48ff.; zum Begriff einer *damnatio* durch *memoria* vgl. Wittchow (s. Anm. 33) 348f., 358: „Für Sueton ist eine Anekdote wie um den Fliegenfänger Domitian eine Weise, wie Senatoren statt einer *damnatio memoriae* eine *damnatio* durch *memoria* an einem Kaiser vornehmen können. Das ist eine andere Strategie, mit dem allgegenwärtigen Kaiser umzugehen, als sie Tacitus verfolgt hat, aber sie gehört in die gleichen Kommunikationsbedingungen."

43 Zu einer solchen aktiveren Form der Rezeption vgl. z.B. Umberto Eco, Lector in fabula. Die Mitarbeit der Interpretation in erzählenden Texten, München 1987 (ital. Mailand 1979).

44 Vgl. z.B. Quint. inst. 8,6,54–56.

45 Vgl. Tony Reekmans, Notes on verbal humour in the Historia Augusta, Ancient Society 28 (1997), 175–207, v.a. 175f.: „Biographers such as Plutarch and Suetonius appear to have considered the production of humour as an activity which they were to cover, but without having to practice it themselves. The authour of the *Historia Augusta*, on the contrary, seems to have taken pleasure in producing humour himself, not only by attributing to his protagonists and his supernumeraries verbal and practical jokes of his own invention, but also by ridiculing rulers whom he disliked, by playing various tricks on his readers, by ironising *toto genere orationis* traditional historiography and by practising aretalogy." u. allg. zur charakterisierenden Funktion der Komik in der *Historia Augusta* Antonio Cascón, El humor en la Historia Augusta: características literarias y función crítica, Historiae Augustae Colloquium Barcinonense, Bari 1996, 147–163.

anderem die Wortspiele dar, die sich der Autor besonders gerne mit den Namen seiner Protagonisten erlaubt und die häufig unmittelbar wertende Funktion haben.[46]

Diese erstaunlich distanzierte Haltung den eigenen Inhalten gegenüber findet sich erneut im Text selbst abgebildet. An zwei prominenten Stellen, die sich durchaus als allgemeine Rezeptionshinweise verstehen lassen, wird dem Leser empfohlen, die historischen Angaben in der *Historia Augusta* nicht für bare Münze zu nehmen: Dabei handelt es sich zum einen um die Szene zu Beginn der *quadriga tyrannorum*, die Ernst Hohl treffend als Darstellung eines literarischen ‚Kränzchens‘ bezeichnet hat.[47] Dort zeigt sich der Autor im Gespräch mit Marcus Fonteius, der als *amator historiarum* bezeichnet wird, und drei weiteren fiktiven Personen, mit denen er sehr freimütig über die Widersprüche und Fälschungen in seinem eigenen Werk debattiert.[48] Zum anderen gilt dies für die

---

46 Vgl. allg. Reekmans (s. Anm. 45) 187 ff. u. 192 ff. Ein gutes Beispiel hierfür bietet Erzählung, auf welche Weise der in der *Historia Augusta* konsequent Regilianus genannte Usurpator Regalianus (vgl. Aur. Vict. Caes. 33,2 u. RIC V 2 p. 586 f.) angeblich an die Macht gelangt ist (HA trig. tyr. 10,4–7): *nam cum milites cum eo quidam c[a]enarent, extitit vicarius tribuni qui diceret: ‚Regiliani nomen unde credimus dictum?‘. alius continuo: ‚credimus quod a regno‘. (5) tum is qui aderat scolasticus, coepit quasi grammaticaliter declinare et dicere: ‚rex regis regi Regilianus‘. (6) milites, ut est hominum genus pronum ad ea, quae cogitant: ‚ergo potest rex esse‘ item alius: ‚deus tibi regis nomen inposuit‘. (7) quid multa? his dictis cum alia die mane processisset, a principiis imperator est salutatus. ita quod aliis vel audacia vel iudicium, huic detulit ioculais astutia.* („Als nämlich etliche Soldaten mit ihm speisten, traf es sich, daß ein Vizetribun die Frage aufwarf: ‚Woher mag bloß der Name Regilianus kommen?‘ Darauf alsbald ein anderer: ‚Meiner Ansicht nach von regnum.‘ (5) Da begann ein gerade anwesender Schulfuchs gleichsam nach den Regeln der Grammatik zu deklinieren mit den Worten: ‚rex, regis, regi, Regilianus‘. (6) Darauf die Soldaten, ein Menschenschlag, der aus seinem Herzen keine Mördergrube macht: ‚Demnach kann er Herrscher sein?‘ Ein anderer meinte: ‚Demnach kann er über uns herrschen?‘ Wieder ein anderer: ‚Gott hat dir den Herrschernamen verliehen.‘ (7) Kurz und gut, infolge dieser Äußerungen wurde Regilian, als er sich am anderen Morgen blicken ließ, von den vorderen Reihen der Truppen als Kaiser begrüßt. So gewann Regilian durch einen guten Witz, was anderen durch ihre Kühnheit oder durch die Meinung, die man von ihnen hat, zuteil wird.").

47 Vgl. Ernst Hohl, Über den Ursprung der Historia Augusta, Hermes 55 (1920), 296–310, h. 302 f.: „In der historisch wertlosen Vita des ‚Tyrannen‘ Firmus lernen wir eine Art von ‚Kränzchen‘ kenne, in dem vornehme Dilettanten im Verein mit dem Biographen, Vopiscus, die Streitfrage diskutieren, ob der Rebell den Augustustitel geführt habe oder bloß ein *latrunculus* gewesen sei. Wer denkt da nicht an Saturnalien des Marcobius, in denen der gelehrte Servius mit römischen Aristokraten um die Wette die verschiedensten Fragen erörtert?"

48 Vgl. HA quadr. tyr. 2,1–3 u. ferner den Hengst (s. Anm. 12) 140 f.

ebenso programmatische Szene, die in der Kutsche des Stadtpräfekten Iunius Tiberianus[49] spielt und sich ausgerechnet an den Hilarien zugetragen haben soll. Hier läßt sich der Autor von diesem Würdenträger ausdrücklich Erlaubnis zum lockeren Umgang mit der historischen Wahrheit geben: ‚*scribe*‘, *inquit*, ‚*ut libet. securus, quod velis, dices, habiturus mendaciorum comites, quos historicae eloquentiae miramur auctores*‘.[50]

Neben diesen bereits weitgehend bekannten Techniken lassen sich in der *Historia Augusta* jedoch auch noch andere literarische Strategien beobachten, die einer stärker indirekten und gelegentlich ambivalenten Charakterisierung der Protagonisten dienen. Hier spielen vor allem unterschiedliche Formen intertextueller Bezüge eine zentrale Rolle, die vom Erzähler, aber auch von den Personen auf der Ebene der Handlung vorgenommen werden können. Den Referenzpunkt dieser Anspielungen bilden einerseits andere Werke, bei denen es sich zwar häufig um die Kaiserviten des ja auch sonst als Vorbild präsenten Sueton handelt,[51]

---

49 Iunius Tiberianus ist keine fiktive Person, sondern als *praefectus urbi* für 291–292 bezeugt; allerdings könnte auch sein gleichnamiger Sohn gemeint sein, der das Amt 303–304 innehatte (vgl. André Chastagnol, Le problème de l'Histoire Auguste, BAHC 1963 (1964), 43–71, h. 60).

50 Vgl. HA Aurel. 2,1–2: *et quoniam sermo nobis de Treb<ell>io Pollione, qui a duobus Philippis usque ad divum Claudium et eius fratrem Quintillium imperatores tam claros quam obscuros memoriae prodidit, in eodem vehiculo fuit adserente Tiberiano, quod Pollio multa incuriose, multa breviter prodidisset, me contra dicente neminem scriptorum, quantum ad historiam pertinet, non aliquid esse mentium, prodente quin etiam, in quo Livius, in quo Trogus manifestis testibus convincerentur, pedibus in sententiam transitum faciens ac manum porrigens iocando[m] praeterea: (2) ‚scribe‘, inquit, ‚ut libet. securus, quod velis, dices, habiturus mendaciorum comites, quos historicae eloquentiae miramur auctores‘.* („Unser Gespräch während besagter Wagenfahrt kam auch auf Trebellius Pollio, der von den beiden Philippern bis auf den vergöttlichten Claudius und dessen Bruder Quintillus die Geschichte der Kaiser, sowohl der berühmten wie der unberühmten, geschrieben hat; da behauptete nun Tiberianus, Pollio habe vieles mit mangelnder Sorgfalt, vieles allzu kurz dargestellt; demgegenüber machte ich geltend, es gäbe in dem Bereich der Geschichtsschreibung keinen Autor, der nicht ein bißchen geflunkert habe; ich wies auch auf Fälle hin, in denen Livius, Sallust, Cornelius Tacitus und schließlich auch (Pompeius) Trogus durch einwandfreie Zeugen überführt werden; da pflichtete er mir lebhaft bei, reichte mir die Hand und sagte überdies im Scherz: (2) ‚Schreib, wie es dir beliebt. Du magst unbesorgt erzählen, was du willst, wirst du dich doch mit deinen Lügen in der Gesellschaft von Männern befinden, denen wir als Meistern historischer Kunstprosa Bewunderung entgegenbringen.‘") und ferner Timothy P. Wiseman, Lying Historians. Seven Types of Mendacity, in: ders. u. Christopher Gill, Lies and Fiction in the Ancient World, Austin 1993, 122–146, v. a. 124 f.

51 Vgl. Chastagnol (s. Anm. 14). Von den Biographen werden neben Sueton vor allem Marius Maximus und der wahrscheinlich fiktive Cordus häufiger angeführt. Aber auch Plutarch ist verschiedentlich präsent: vgl. z. B. HA Marc. 27,11.

deren breites Spektrum aber zugleich auf eine vergleichsweise profunde Bildung des Autors schließen läßt.[52] Andererseits ergeben sich jedoch auch zahlreiche intertextuelle Bezüge zwischen den einzelnen Viten der *Historia Augusta*, die in der Forschung bislang auschließlich unter Fragestellung, ob sich aus den möglichen Widersprüchen Rückschlüsse auf die Zahl der Verfasser ziehen lassen, berücksichtigt wurden.[53]

Das fehlende Interesse an der narrativen Funktion dieser ‚intratextuellen‘ Bezüge ist umso erstaunlicher, wenn man sich vor Augen hält, daß sie durch eine Besonderheit der *Historia Augusta* in diesem Werk in besonderer Häufigkeit vorkommen. Zwar sind inhaltliche Überschneidungen und damit die Möglichkeit, zwei Darstellungen des gleichen Ereignisses aufeinander zu beziehen, in einer chronologisch fortlaufenden Sammlung von Herrscherbiographien gar nicht zu vermeiden, doch wird dieser Effekt durch die sogenannten Nebenviten, in denen das Leben ‚sekundärer‘ Herrscher wie Gegenkaiser, Mitregenten oder nicht zum Zuge gekommener Thronanwärter beschrieben wird,[54] noch einmal erheblich verstärkt.[55] Daß deren Darstellung nicht im Rahmen der Vita des jewei-

---

52 Vgl. z. B. Scheithauer (s. Anm. 8) 147 ff. u. Daniel Den Hengst, The author's literary culture, Historiae Augustae colloquium Parisinum, Macerata 1991, 161–169.

53 Zu den Widersprüchen zwischen den programmatischen Äußerungen in den unterschiedlichen Viten vgl. Daniel Den Hengst, Selbstkommentar in der Historia Augusta, Historiae Augustae Colloquium Maceratense, Bari 1995, 151–167.

54 Zur inhaltlichen Differenzierung und sprachlichen Unterscheidung dieser Kategorien in der *Historia Augusta* vgl. Alfons Rösger, Zur Herrscherterminologie der Historia Augusta: Princeps und Purpuratus, in: ders., Studien zum Herrscherbegriff der Historia Augusta und zum antiken Erziehungswesen, Frankfurt 2001, 65–92 (zuerst: BHAC 1977/78 (1980), 179–201). Zu den stilistischen Besonderheiten der Nebenviten vgl. allg. Syme (s. Anm. 55) 292 f.

55 Die Unterscheidung zwischen Primär- und Sekundärviten geht inhaltlich auf entsprechende Bemerkungen des Autors zurück (vgl. v.a. HA Ael. 1,1: *in animo mihi est, Diocletiane Auguste, tot principum maxime, non solum eos, qui principum locum in hac statione, quam temperas, retentarunt, ut usque ad divum Hadrianum feci, sed illos etiam, qui vel Caesarum nomine appellati sunt nec principes aut Augusti fuerunt vel quolibet alio genere aut in famam aut in spem principatus venerunt, cognitioni[s] numinis tui sternere*; u. ferner z. B. Ael. 7,4–5; Avid. 3,1–3; Pesc. 1,1–2; 9,1–2; Opil. 1,1; quadr. tyr. 1,1–4) und wurde erstmals (allerdings nur im Hinblick auf die Biographien von Hadrian bis Opilius Macrinus) von Theodor Mommsen in die Diskussion um die Entstehungsgeschichte der *Historia Augusta* eingebracht: vgl. Mommsen (s. Anm. 23) 243 ff., sowie ferner Ronald Syme, The Secondary Vitae, BHAC 1968/1969 (1970), 285–307 (= ders., Emperors and Biography. Studies in the Historia Augusta, Oxford 1971, 54–77), h. 286 f., u. Alfons Rösger, Usurpatorenviten in der Historia Augusta, in: ders., Studien zum Herrscherbegriff der Historia Augusta und zum antiken Erziehungswesen, Frankfurt 2001, 11–64 (zuerst in: Adolf Lippold u.

ligen ,primären' Kaisers, sondern in einer eigenen Lebensbeschreibung erfolgt, wird vom Autor mehrfach als wesentliche Neuerung seines Werkes gegenüber der biographischen Tradition betont.[56]

In den auktorialen Bemerkungen, die sich häufig am Anfang oder am Ende einer Nebenvita finden und in der Regel an einen der beiden vermeintlichen kaiserlichen Widmungsträger gerichtet sind, wird der historische Wert dieser Biographien und die durch sie erreichte Vollständigkeit betont.[57] Deswegen und aufgrund der Häufung von theoretischen Aussagen in den Nebenviten wurde verschiedentlich die Vermutung geäußert, daß der Autor der *Historia Augusta* gerade hier, in der Bearbeitung biographischen ,Neulands',[58] seine primäre Leistung erblickte, während die Behandlung der regulären Kaiser in den Spuren seiner Vorgänger für ihn eine gleichsam sekundäre Aufgabe dargestellt habe.[59] Eine solche Annahme ist vor dem Hintergrund literarischer Usancen in der Antike nicht unplausibel. Doch muß bereits der Umstand, daß dem Leser die Bedeutung des hier präsentierten Materials mehrfach in Erinnerung gerufen wird, Zweifel daran aufkommen lassen, daß historische Vollständigkeit wirklich das primäre Interesse des Autors bei der Abfassung der Nebenviten gewesen ist.[60] Diese Zweifel wachsen, wenn man sich neben der tatsächlichen Irrelevanz vieler An-

---

Nikolaus Himmelmann, Bonner Festgabe Johannes Straub zum 65. Geburtstag, Bonn 1977, 359–393), h. 12 ff.

56 Vgl. v. a. HA quadr. tyr. 1,1–2 u. Opil. 1,1–5 sowie ferner Syme (s. Anm. 55) 286 f.; den Hengst (s. Anm. 12) 44 ff., 68 ff.; Rösger (s. Anm. 55) 20 ff.; u. Scheithauer (s. Anm. 8) 137 f.

57 Vgl. z. B. HA Ael. 1,1–3; Avid. 3,3; Max. 1,1–3 u. Gord. 1,1–5 mit den Hengst (s. Anm. 12) 10 ff., u. Scheithauer (s. Anm. 8) 138.

58 Vgl. Rösger (s. Anm. 55) 22 ff., v. a. 27: „Wir halten also fest, daß sich in der mit Sicherheit der Historia Augusta zeitlich voraufliegenden biographischen Überlieferung keinerlei greifbare Spuren für das Vorhandensein von selbständigen ,Nebenviten' nachweisen lassen." Zur Frage, ob die Nebenviten von Anfang an Bestandteil des Werkes waren oder erst im Laufe bzw. nach Abschluß der Arbeit an den anderen Biographien hinzukamen vgl. Syme (s. Anm. 55) 298 ff., der die zweite Variante favorisiert.

59 Vgl. z. B. Syme (s. Anm. 55), v. a. 300 f.; Scheithauer (s. Anm. 8) 138, u. den Hengst (s. Anm. 53) 166.

60 Eine besondere Pointe liegt möglicherweise darin, daß er sich zur Begründung der Behandlung auch der auf illegitime Weise an die Macht gekommenen Herrscher ausgerechnet auf das angebliche Interesse Diokletians und Konstantins beruft, alle ihre Vorgänger kennenzulernen (vgl. Meckler (s. Anm. 13) 371: „In a sense, the author is legitimizing usurpers – and questioning the legitimacy of canonical emperors – by writing usurpers' biographies. The Author will do this with the purported justification of correcting history.").

gaben den weitgehend fiktiven Charakter dieser häufig zu großen Teilen aus gefälschten Dokumenten[61] bestehenden Biographien vor Augen hält.[62]

Es ist daher davon auszugehen, daß der Informationswert einer Nebenvita als solcher bereits für den Leser in der Antike ähnlich niedrig war wie für den Historiker heutzutage. Erst wenn man diese Biographien nicht isoliert zur Kenntnis nimmt, sondern sie als eng auf die jeweilige Hauptvita bezogene Kompositionen versteht, werden die mit ihrer Einführung verbundenen Vorteile deutlich: Der Autor erhält durch die Verteilung des Materials auf verschiedene Viten die Möglichkeit, ein Ereignis oder eine Figur aus mehreren Perspektiven zu schildern. Die Verwendung von Nebenviten, die gegenüber der biographischen Gattungstradition eine wesentliche Innovation der *Historia Augusta* darstellt, läßt sich also als eine Form des multiperspektivischen Erzählens begreifen und bildet daher ein wichtiges Element der unterschiedlichen narrativen Strategien, die auf eine indirekte und vom Leser erst zu entschlüsselnde Charakterisierung der Protagonisten abzielen.

Die große Bedeutung, die in diesem Zusammenhang den Nebenviten zukommt, liefert zugleich die Erklärung für die Wahl der um Marc Aurel zentrierten Biographiengruppe als konkretes Beispiel für die weiteren Überlegungen. Denn obwohl der ‚Philosoph auf dem Kaiserthron‘ in der *Historia Augusta* gemeinhin und mit einem gewissen Recht als ‚Musterkaiser‘ gilt,[63] unterliegt das zunächst eindeutig positive Bild bei genauerem Hinsehen doch signifikanten

---

61 Zu der in diesen Dokumenten angewandten literarischen Technik vgl. v. a. Daniel den Hengst, Verba, non res. Über die Inventio in den Reden und Schriftstücken in der Historia Augusta, BHAC 1984/1985 (1987), 157–174, u. ferner Hanna Szelest, Rollen und Aufgabe der Reden und Brief in der Historia Augusta, Eos 65 (1971), 325–338, sowie zur Unterscheidung zwischen historischer und literarischer Fälschung Barnes (s. Anm. 25).

62 Vgl. Syme (s. Anm. 55) 300: „Another question now obtrudes, not wholly idle. Why were those products written at all? Introducing his Geta the author confesses that the emperor Constantine and other readers may well ask *cur etiam Geta Antonianus a me tradatur*. The reasons, as has been shown, are fraudulent. In epilogue on the biography of Aelius Caesar he had proffered the justification for all ‚Nebenviten‘ – *meae satisfaciens conscientiae, etiamsi multis nulla sit necessitas talia exquirendi* (7,5). That is to say, he does it from a sense of duty, which recalls a biographer's noble professions elsewhere. Further, there was no necessity to write those Vitae. The author himself makes the admission.".

63 Zur insgesamt positiven Darstellung Marc Aurels in seiner Biographie vgl. z.B. Scheithauer (s. Anm. 8) v. a. 28 ff., u. Giuseppe Solaro, *Historia Augusta* e qualità *speculari* in Marco Aurelio, Annali Facolta Lettere Bari 46 (2003), 159–169; aber auch sonst findet er verschiedentlich als vorbildlicher Herrscher Erwähnung, häufig im Zusammenhang mit dem *nomen Antinorum* (vgl. z.B. HA Elag. 2,4 sowie ferner den Hengst (s. Anm. 12) 28ff. u. Scheithauer (s. Anm. 8) 65 ff.).

Schwankungen. Dies gilt vor allem, wenn man die beiden ihm zugeordneten Nebenviten mit in den Blick nimmt, in denen die Schilderung seines Lebens mit den Biographien des Mitregenten Lucius Verus und des Gegenkaisers Avidius Cassius konfrontiert wird. Um diesen Prozeß einer sich nach und nach änderenden Wahrnehmung Marc Aurels besser nachzeichnen zu können, wird auch die folgende Besprechung die normale Leserichtung einer ,Erstlektüre' weitgehend beibehalten.

3. ,Man lebt nur einmal?' – die Metamorphosen Marc Aurels im Laufe der Lektüre

3.1 Marc Aurel und die Philosophie

Bei der Bewertung Marc Aurels spielt vor allem seine Affinität zur Philosophie eine zentrale Rolle. Diese wird bereits in der singulären Erweiterung des Titels seiner Biographie um den Zusatz *philosophus* angesprochen und wird auch im folgenden immer wieder, jedoch aus sehr unterschiedlichen Perspektiven beleuchtet, so daß eine Konzentration auf diesen Aspekt auch für die folgenden Überlegungen sinnvoll erscheint.

Gleich in den ersten Worten der dem Iulius Capitolinus zugeschriebenen *vita Marci Antonini philosophi* wird eine positive Beurteilung des Protagonisten vorgenommen und diese mit dem Verweis auf seine philosophische Lebenshaltung und seine *sanctitas* [64] begründet: *Marco Antonino, in omni vita philosophanti viro et qui sanctitate vitae omnibus principibus antecellit, pater Annius Verus, ...* [65] Daß erst danach – wenn auch in enger syntaktischer Verknüpfung – der Abschnitt beginnt, der sich mit der Familie und den Vorfahren des Protagonisten beschäftigt,[66] stellt zwar eine markante Abweichung von der biographischen

---

64 Zur positiven Konnotation dieses Begriffes in der *Historia Augusta* vgl. z. B. Scheithauer (s. Anm. 8) 30: „Als *sancti* bezeichnet der Autor der Historia Augusta diejenigen, die streng nach den Gesetzen der Götter leben und den nicht kodifizierten *mos maiorum* beachten." u. zu einer möglichen antichristlichen Tendenz ferner Jan Burian, *Sanctus* als Wertbegriff in der Historia Augusta, Klio 63 (1981), 623–638.

65 Vgl. HA Marc. 1,1. („Marcus Antoninus, in allen Lebenslagen als Philosoph bewährt und durch unsträflichen Wandel allen Kaisern überlegen, hatte zum Vater den Annius Verus, ...").

66 Vgl. HA Marc. 1,1–1,10 u. für eine Interpretation des genealogischen Abschnittes ferner François Chausson, Variétés généalogiques I: Numa Pompilius ancêtre de Marc Aurèle, Historiae Augustae Colloquium Perusinum, Bari 2002, 109–149.

Technik des immer wieder als Vorbild angeführten Sueton dar,[67] ist aber in der *Historia Augusta* nicht ohne Parallele, da ihr Verfasser dieser Rubrik[68] häufiger eine explizite Wertung des jeweiligen Protagonisten voranstellt.[69]

Während der Gedanke der *sanctitas* danach in den Hintergrund tritt und erst später wieder aufgegriffen wird,[70] wird Marc Aurels besondere Affinität zur Philosophie auch in dem nun folgenden ersten Hauptteil seiner Biographie immer wieder thematisiert.[71] Dieser besteht aus den Kapiteln 1–19 und enthält einen kompletten Durchgang durch das Leben des Kaisers, dessen Schwerpunkt allerdings auf den Jahren zwischen 121 bis 169 n. Chr. liegt, also der Zeit vor dem Tod seines Mitregenten Lucius Verus.[72] Eine gute Gelegenheit, auf die philosophi-

---

67 Die *Historia Augusta* orientiert sich ohnehin nicht allzu eng an dem Aufbau der suetonischen Biographien; vgl. allg. Leo (s. Anm. 1) 272 ff. u. Scheithauer (s. Anm. 8) 141. Für einen Vergleich speziell der *vita Marci* mit dem üblichen Aufbau einer Biographie vgl. Alain Dubreuil, Le modèle suétonien dans la Vita Marci du recueil de l'Histoire Auguste, Cahiers des études anciennes 1993, 123–128, u. Dubreuil (s. Anm. 40) 241 ff. Dies kann um so weniger überraschen, als auch Sueton seine Biographien relativ flexibel gliedert und erst nach und nach ein festeres Schema entwickelt; vgl. Dennis Pausch, Biographie und Bildungskultur. Personendarstellungen bei Plinius dem Jüngeren, Gellius und Sueton, Millennium Studien 4, Berlin 2004, 252 ff. (mit weiterer Literatur).

68 Die Behandlung der Geneaologie ist natürlich auch in der *Historia Augusta* obligatorisch, wie vor allem bei der Rechtfertigung seines Fehlens deutlich wird: vgl. z. B. HA Comm. 1,1 u. Carac. 1,2.

69 Vgl. z. B. HA Comm. 1,1–1,9 u. Elag. 1,1–1,3 sowie ferner Stubenrauch (s. Anm. 12) 19 ff., der unterschiedliche ,Eröffnungstypen' der Biographien in der *Historia Augusta* vorstellt.

70 Vgl. HA Marc. 15,3 u. 19,6.10. Eine quellenkritische Erklärung hierfür bietet Klaus Rosen, Sanctus Marcus Aurelius, Historiae Augustae Colloquium Argentoratense, Bari 1998, 285–296, h. 287f. (s. u. Anm. 72).

71 Für eine Gliederung der Biographie s. Anhang 1.

72 Vgl. HA Marc. 1–14. Aus der Perspektive einer quellenkritische Analyse gelten die Kapitel 1–14 und 20–29 als aus einer zuverlässigen Quelle übernommen, die man entweder mit Marius Maximus oder mit Symes ,Ignotus' identifiziert (vgl. allg. Ronald Syme, *Ignotus*, the Good Biographer, in: ders., Emperors and Biography. Studies in the Historia Augusta, Oxford 1971, 30–53; Timothy D. Barnes, The Sources of the Historia Augusta, Brüssel 1978, 99 ff.; Anthony R. Birley, Marius Maximus: the Consular Biographer, in: ANRW 2,34.3, Berlin–New York 1997, 2678–757; Herbert W. Benario, ,Ignotus', the ,good biographer', in: ANRW 2,34.3, Berlin–New York 1997, 2759–2772, u. Dubreuil (s. Anm. 40) 251 ff., 313 ff., der sich entschieden für den ,Ignotus' als Vorlage der *vita Marci* ausspricht). Demgegenüber gelten die Kapitel 15–19 als ein Einschub, dessen Material der Verfasser der *Historia Augusta* aus anderen Quellen (v. a. Eutrop und Aurelius Victor) geschöpft oder völlig frei erfunden hat (vgl. Scheithauer (s. Anm. 8) 102 ff. u. Dubreuil (s. Anm. 40) 258). Für eine inhaltliche Begründung des Einschubes vgl. Rosen (s. Anm. 70) 287: „Mit dem Einschub will er den

schen Vorlieben des späteren Kaisers einzugehen, bot naturgemäß die in seinem
Fall ziemlich ausführliche Behandlung der intellektuellen Ausbildung, deren spezifische Darstellungsabsicht bereits in den ersten Worten angedeutet wird: *fuit a
prima infantia gravis.*[73] Dieser nicht recht altersgemäße Ernst wird unter anderem mit Hilfe von Anekdoten wie der folgenden illustriert:

> *philosophi<a>e operam vehementer dedit et quidem adhuc puer. nam duodecimum
> annum ingressus habitum philosophi sumpsit et deinceps tolerantiam, cum studeret in
> pallio et humi cubaret, vix autem matre agente instrato pellibus lectulo accubaret.*[74]

Auch wenn der Biograph am Ende des Abschnittes, der dem Leben vor der
Adoption durch Antoninus Pius gewidmet ist, eine Art Fazit zieht, spielt die Philosophie eine zentrale Rolle. Denn sie ist es, die alle anderen Interessen verdrängt
und Marc Aurel *serius et gravis* gemacht hat.[75] Eine explizite Kritik an solchen,
weit über das in Rom übliche Maß der Beschäftigung mit der Philosophie hin-
ausgehenden, Verhaltensweisen findet jedoch hier, wenn man von einem knappen

---

Erwartungen gerecht werden, die er im programmatischen Eingangssatz geweckt hat.
Er muß sich dazu jedoch nach anderen Quellen umsehen. Denn die Autoren, die er
bisher benutzte, haben der *sanctitas* des Kaisers nicht genügend Aufmerksamkeit
geschenkt und ihm im Grunde den Rang eines *optimus* versagt."

73 Vgl. HA Marc. 2–3.
74 Vgl. HA Marc. 2,6 („Der Philosophie ergab er sich leidenschaftlich, und zwar schon
    als er noch ein Knabe war. Trug er sich doch nach dem Eintritt in sein zwölftes Jahr
    wie ein Philosoph und übte in der Folge auch die entsprechende Askese, indem er im
    Mantel studierte und auf dem Fußboden nächtigte und nur schwer von seiner Mutter
    dazu zu bewegen war, auf einem mit Fellen belegten Lager zu schlafen.") u. ferner
    Dubreuil (s. Anm. 40) 120: „Ce passage à caractère anecdotique pourrait fort bien
    avoir été tiré de Marius Maximus."
75 Vgl. HA Marc. 4,8–4,10: *fuit autem vitae indulgentia, ut cogeretur nonnumquam vel
    in venationes pergere vel in theatrum descendere vel spectaculis interesse. (9) operam
    praeterea pingendo sub magistro Diogeneto dedit. amavit pugilatum <et> luctamina
    et cursum et aucupatus et pila lusit adprime et venatus est. (10) sed ab omnibus his
    intentioni<bu>s studium eum philosophiae abduxit seriumque et gravem reddidit, non
    tamen prorsus abolita in eo comitate, quam praecipue suis, mox amicis atque etiam
    minus notis exhibebat, cum frugi esset sine contumacia, verecundus sine ignavia, sine
    tristitia gravis.* („Gegen die Dinge des täglichen Lebens verhielt er sich so gleichgültig,
    daß er genötigt werden mußte, mitunter zu einer Tierhetze zu gehen oder im Theater
    zu erscheinen oder einer Vorstellung beizuwohnen. (9) Im Übrigen beschäftigte er
    sich mit Malkunst unter Anleitung des Diogenetus. Er liebte Faust- und Ringkämpfe,
    Rennen und Vogelstellen, war ein hervorragender Ballspieler und ging auch zur Jagd.
    (10) Doch von allen diesen [Hohl: sportlichen] Beschäftigungen zog ihn der Drang
    zur Philosophie ab und machte ihn ernst und gesetzt, ohne jedoch in ihm die Heiter-
    keit ganz zu ersticken, die er vor allem gegen Angehörige, sodann gegen Freunde und
    auch gegen Fernstehende an den Tag legte, war er doch ordnungsliebend, aber kein
    Pendant, zurückhaltend, aber nicht schlapp, ernsthaft, aber kein Griesgram.").

Hinweis auf eine generelle Überbeanspruchung durch die *studia* in seiner Jugend absieht,[76] nicht statt. Dies gilt auch für die Bewertung der Philosophie im Zusammenhang mit seiner weitgehend positiv dargestellten Regierungstätigkeit.[77]

Nachdem zunächst die gemeinsame Herrschaft mit Lucius Verus und im unmittelbaren Anschluß daran seine Alleinregierung behandelt wurde,[78] folgt nun die Schilderung seines Todes und seiner Divinisierung[79] sowie die Diskussion des Verhältnisses zu seinem Nachfolger Commodus, die sogar mit einer Anrede an Diokletian, wie sie sich häufig am Ende einer Vita findet, abgeschlossen wird.[80] Zur großen Überraschung des unvorbereiteten Lesers ist die Biographie danach jedoch nicht zu Ende, sondern es folgt ein zweiter Durchgang durch das Leben Marc Aurels, in dessen Verlauf sich auch die Wahrnehmung seiner philosophischen Studien signifikant zu wandeln beginnt.

Die Schilderung seiner Regierungstätigkeit nach dem Tod des Verus läßt zwar eine chronologische Gliederung erkennen, die vor allem an der Zäsur des Aufstandes des Avidius Cassius im Jahre 175 n. Chr. sichtbar wird, orientiert sich aber zugleich auch an thematischen Gesichtspunkten.[81] Im ersten, den Jahren vor 175 n. Chr. gewidmeten Abschnitt wird an zwei Stellen anonymen Zeitgenossen Kritik an Marc Aurels philosophischer Lebenshaltung in den Mund gelegt. Diese

---

76 Vgl. HA Marc. 3,7: *tantumque operis et laboris studiis inpendit, ut corpus adficeret, atque in hoc solo pueritia eius reprehenderetur.* („Mit solchem Arbeitseifer warf er sich auf seine Studien, daß er seine Gesundheit beeinträchtigte; dies ist aber auch der einzige Vorwurf, den man seiner Jugend machen konnte.").

77 Vgl. HA Marc. 6,5 (*per eadem tempora, cum tantis honoribus occuparetur et cum formandus ad regendum statum rei publicae patris actibus interesset, studia cupidissime frequentavit*); 8,3 (*dabat se Marcus totum et philosophiae, amorem civium adfectans*) u. 16,5 (*erat enim ipse tantae tranquillitatis, ut vultum numquam mutaverit maerore vel gaudio, philosophiae deditus stoicae, quam et per optimos quosque magistros acceperat et undique ipse collegerat*).

78 Vgl. HA Marc. 7,5–14 u. 15–17.

79 Vgl. HA Marc. 18. Eine Interpretation dieses Abschnittes und seiner Plazierung bietet Rosen (s. Anm. 70) 289ff., v. a. 296: „Der Einschub in der Marcusvita ist ein Stück ‚heidnische Geschichtsapologetik' (J. Straub). Die hintergründige historische Argumentation hatte den Vorteil, daß sie ihren Verfasser nicht gefährden konnte, aber den Nachteil, daß sie leicht übersehen wurde. Die auffällige, scheinbar ungelenke Komposition war ein Mittel, um den Nachteil abzuhelfen. Der Biograph hätte, wie bemerkt, den Marcuskult mit seinen historischen und erfundenen Angaben an den Schluß der Hauptvita stellen können. Damit hätte er der Erwartung des Lesers entsprochen, der das Thema bereits aus dem Schluß der Vita Hadriani und der Vita Pii kannte. Der Biograph verstieß gegen diese Erwartung. Er machte so den Leser stutzig und gab ihm den Anstoß, seine Botschaft zu entziffern.".

80 Vgl. HA Marc. 19.

81 Vgl. HA Marc. 21–24,5 (~ 169–175 n. Chr.) u. 24,5–27 (~175–180 n. Chr.). Für eine Gliederung s. Anhang 1.

bezieht sich einmal explizit auf den militärischen,[82] zum anderen ebenso eindeutig auf den zivilen Bereich;[83] beide Male aber darf der Kaiser das letzte Wort behalten und die Vorwürfe zurückweisen.

Dagegen sind die beiden einschlägigen Passagen im zweiten Abschnitt zwar nicht als Kritik formuliert, erweisen sich bei einer genaueren Lektüre durch ihren jeweiligen Kontext aber als zumindest ambivalent: Daß sich von seiner philosophischen Milde ausgerechnet die Syrer und Ägypter beeindruckt zeigen,[84] die doch zuvor, wie der Leser später erfahren wird, aus genau den entgegengesetzten Gründen die treuesten Anhänger des Avidius Cassius waren,[85] kann ebenso Anlaß zu Bedenken geben wie die Plazierung des von jedem halbwegs gebildeten antiken Rezipienten sicherlich schon geraume Zeit erwarteten Zitates aus Platons

---

82 Vgl. HA Marc. 22,5–6: *sane quia durus videbatur ex philosophiae institutione Marcus ad militiae labores atque ad omnem vitam, graviter carpebatur, (6) sed male loquentum vel sermoni vel litteris respondebat.* („Da aber Marcus die Härte gegenüber den Strapazen des Lagerlebens wie überhaupt in seinem ganzen Wandel aus seiner philosophischen Unterweisung zu beziehen schien, (6) sah er sich herber Kritik ausgesetzt, blieb aber den Nörglern in Wort und Schrift seinerseits die gebührende Antwort nicht schuldig").

83 Vgl. HA Marc. 23,9: *fama fuit sane, quod sub philosophorum specie quidam rem publicam vexarent et privatos. quod ille purgavit* („Übrigens ging das Gerücht um, daß gewisse Leute unter der Philosophenmaske Staat und Privatpersonen drangsalierten. Dagegen verwahrte er sich") u. ferner M. Aur. 10,36,2 (σπουδαῖος καὶ σοφὸς ἦν· μὴ τὸ πανύστατον ἔσται τις ὁ καθ' αὑτὸν λέγων· ἀναπνεύσομέν ποτε ἀπὸ τούτου τοῦ παιδαγωγοῦ; χαλεπὸς μὲν οὐδενὶ ἡμῶν ἦν, ἀλλὰ ᾐσθανόμην ὅτι ἡσυχῇ καταγινώσκει ἡμῶν.).

84 Vgl. HA Marc. 26,2–3: *omnibus orientalibus provinciis carissimus fuit. apud multas etiam philosophiae vestigia reliquit. (3) apud Aegyptios civem se egit et philosophum in omnibus studiis, templis, locis.* („Alle Provinzen des Ostens schätzten ihn aufs höchste. In vielen hinterließ er auch Spuren seiner philosophischen Gesinnung. (3) Bei den Ägyptern gab er sich in allen Bildungsstätten, Tempeln und allerwärts als Bürger und Philosoph.").

85 Vgl. HA Avid. 6,5–7: *ergo correcta disciplina et in Armenia et in Arabia et in Aegyptores optime gessit amatusque est ab omnibus orientalibus et speciatim ab Antiochenibus, (6) qui etiam imperio eius consenserunt, ut docet Marius Maximus in vita divi Marci. (7) nam cum et Bucolici milites per Aegyptum gravia multa facerent, ab hoc retunsi sunt, ut idem Marius Maximus refert in eo libro, quem secundum de vita Marci [et] Antonini edidit.* („Nachdem er also die Mannszucht gehoben hatte, verrichtete er in Armenien und in Arabien und in Ägypten große Taten und wurd der Liebling des ganzen Orients und insbesondere der Antiochener, (6) die auch seine Thronbesteigung mit Genugtuung begrüßten, wie Marius Maximus in der Biographie des vergöttlichten Marcus hervorhebt. (7) Denn als auch die kriegerischen Bukolen in Ägypten viele Ausschreitungen begingen, wurden sie von ihm an die Kandare genommen, wie wiederum Marius Maximus in dem Buch berichtet, das er als zweites über das Leben des Marcus Antoninus veröffentlicht hatte.").

Politeia.[86] Denn die von Marc Aurel angeblich immer im Munde geführte Glücksverheißung für ein Gemeinwesen, dessen Philosophen Könige oder Könige Philosophen sind, taucht nicht nur erst gegen Ende der Biographie auf, sondern folgt auch noch fast unmittelbar auf die offizielle Ernennung des Commodus zum Mitregenten:

> Commodum deinde sibi collegam in tribuniciam potestatem iunxit, coniarium populo dedit et spectacula mirifica; dein civilia multa correxit. (6) gladiatorii muneris sumptus modum fecit. (7) sententia[m] Platonis semper in ore illius fuit florere civitates, si aut philosophi imperarent aut imperantes philosopharentur.[87]

Daß auf diese Weise die für das Bild des ‚Philosophen auf dem Kaiserthron' zentrale Maxime ausgerechnet in einen Kontext mit der Wahl seines leiblichen Sohnes zum Nachfolger gestellt wird, muß die mit ihr verbundene Selbstwahrnehmung Marc Aurels in ein bedenkliches Licht rücken. Denn die Bestimmung des – zuvor bereits mit einer längeren Invektive bedachten[88] – Commodus zum Thronerben und die damit verbundene Abkehr vom Prinzip des Adoptivkaisertums bildet sowohl hier[89] als auch rückblickend in den späteren Viten den zentralen Kritikpunkt an der Person Marc Aurels.[90]

---

86 Vgl. Plat. rep. 5,473c–d u. ferner Cic. ad Q. fr. 1,1,29.

87 Vgl. HA Marc. 27,5–7 („Sodann nahm er sich den Commodus zum Mitinhaber der tribunizischen Gewalt und gab dem Volk eine Spende und staunenerregende Schauspiele; in der Folge traf er viele innenpolitische Reformen. (6) Er normierte den Aufwand beim Gladiatorenspiel. (7) Ständig führte er Platos Wort im Munde, wonach die Staaten blühen, wenn entweder die Philosophen herrschen oder die Herrscher Philosophen seien.") u. dag. für eine positive Lesart z. B. Scheithauer (s. Anm. 8) 88.

88 Vgl. v. a. HA Marc. 19 u. ferner 16,1.

89 Vgl. v. a. HA Marc. 18,4: hic sane vir tantus et talis ac diis vita et morte coniunctus filium Commodum dereliquit: qui si felix fuisset, filium non reliquisset („Dieser so große und einzigartige Mann, der den Göttern im Leben wie im Sterben nahe stand, hinterließ nun als seinen Sohn Commodus: wie glücklich wäre er gewesen, hätte er keinen Sohn hinterlassen.") u. ferner 27,11–12: ante biduum quam exspiraret, admissis amicis dicitur ostendisse sententiam de filio eandem quam Philippus de Alexandro, cum de male sentiret, addens minime se aegre ferre <quod moreretur, sed quod moreretur talem> filium superstitem relinquens; (12) nam iam Commodus tupem se et cruentum ostentabat.

90 Vgl. v. a. HA Sept. 21,4–5. Im analogen Fall des Carus wird die positive Bewertung des Kaisers aus diesem Grund sogar explizit relativiert (vgl. HA Car. 3,8: veniamus ad Carum, medium, ut ita dixerim, virum et inter bonos magis quam inter malos principes conlocandum et longe meliorem, si Carinum non reli[n]quisset heredem). Zur Propagierung der Adoption als beste Form der Nachfolgeregelung in der Historia Augusta vgl. François Béranger, Julien l'Apostat et l'hérédité du pouvoir impérial, BHAC 1970 (1972), 75–93, u. Françoise Delande, La fonction des ‚Vies secondaires' dans les biographies antonines de l'Histoire Auguste, Cahiers des études anciennes 28 (1993), 135–144.

Im Anschluß an diese Stelle beschäftigt sich nun auch der zweite Durchgang der *vita Marci* mit dem Lebensende ihres Protagonisten, das diesmal vor allem in Form einer ausführlichen *narratio* der Sterbeszene, wie sie in antiken Biographien häufig zu finden ist, behandelt wird.[91] Auf diese folgt sodann noch ein weiteres Kapitel, dessen heterogener Inhalt sich kaum überzeugend erklären läßt, wenn man nur diese Vita alleine in den Blick nimmt,[92] der sich jedoch recht gut in das Bild fügt, das die Biographiengruppe in ihrer Gesamtheit von ihrer Hauptfigur zeichnet.[93]

Zunächst ist jedoch die Frage zu klären, wie es überhaupt zu dem nicht nur auf den ersten Blick verblüffenden Umstand kommt, daß Marc Aurel in seiner Biographie nicht nur zweimal leben, sondern sogar zweimal sterben muß.[94] Wenn man sich nicht damit zufrieden geben will, den gleichsam helixartigen Aufbau dieser Vita entweder mit quellenkritischen Argumenten[95] oder mit unterschiedlichen Bearbeitungsphasen durch einen oder mehrere Autoren[96] oder auch einfach nur mit der Inkompetenz eines ,erbärmlichen Stümpers' zu begründen,[97]

---

91 Vgl. HA Marc 28.

92 Vgl. HA Marc. 29 u. ferner z. B. Scheithauer (s. Anm. 8) 48: „Weil diese crimina ohne Stellungnahme des Autors lose aneinandergereiht sind, hinterlassen sie nicht viel Eindruck beim Leser."

93 Zum Zusammenhang mit *vita Avidii* vgl. Klaus Rosen, Das Schlußkapitel der Marc Aurel-Vita und der Konflikt zwischen Gesinnung und Verantwortung, Historiae Augustae Colloquium Genevense, Bari 1994, 189–196, h. 193 ff., u. s. u. S. 136–145.

94 Vgl. z. B. Rosen (s. Anm. 70) 285: „Wie kaum ein anderer Autor erlaubt sich der Biograph Brüche und Sprünge in der Darstellung. In den Nebenviten sind sie häufiger als in den Hauptviten. Unter diesen ist es vor allem die Vita Marc Aurels, die in ihrem zweiten Teil einer ordentlichen Komposition spottet. Sie behandelt nämlich nach Verus' plötzlichem Tod die nachfolgende Alleinherrschaft des Marcus in zwei Durchgängen, einem kürzeren (15,3–19,12) und einem längeren (20,1–29). Der Verfasser macht keine Anstalten, die unterschiedlichen Angaben in beiden Abschnitten ineinander zu arbeiten oder Wiederholungen zu vermeiden."

95 Wenn man davon ausgeht, daß Marius Maximus die Hauptquelle für diese Vita darstellt, bietet sich der Verweis auf dessen Unterteilung der Biographie Marc Aurels in zwei Bücher als Erklärung an: vgl. HA Avid. 9,5 (*si quis autem omnem hanc historiam scire desiderat, legat Mari Maximi secundum librum de vita Marci, in quo ille ea dicit, quae solus Marcus mortuo iam Vero egit*) mit z. B. Leo (s. Anm. 1) 289, u. Jacques Schwartz, Avidius Cassius et les Sources de l'Histoire Auguste, BHAC 1963 (1964), 123–133, sowie dag. Dubreuil (s. Anm. 40) 285.

96 Für die Frage nach der Zahl der Autoren ist die zweite Hälfte der Biographie u. a. von Eduard Wölfflin, Die Scriptores Historiae Augustae, Sitzungsberichte der Bayerischen Akadamie der Wissenschaften, München 1891, 465–538, u. Joseph Schwendemann, Der historische Wert der vita Marci bei den Scriptores Historiae Augustae, Heidelberg 1923 v. a. 197 ff., herangezogen worden.

97 Vgl. z. B. Ronald Syme, Literary Talent, in: ders., Emperors and Biography. Studies in the Historia Augusta, Oxford 1971, 248–262, h. 255: „Several of the earlier *Vitae* in

so bietet es sich an, die vorwiegend produktionsästhetische Herangehensweise
um eine rezeptionsästhetische Dimension zu ergänzen und zu fragen, was es für
einen Leser, der nicht professionell auf der Suche nach verwendeten Vorlagen ist,
bedeutet, wenn er eine Geschichte oder Teile von ihr zweimal erzählt bekommt.
Aus der Perspektive der Narratologie ergibt sich als Antwort, daß er versuchen
wird, beide Versionen mit einander zu harmonisieren, und daß er, wenn er dabei
auf Schwierigkeiten stößt, an der Glaubwürdigkeit der Erzählinstanz zu zweifeln
beginnt.[98]

Auch für die weitergehende Vermutung, daß die narratologische Kategorie
des unzuverlässigen Erzählens nicht erst bei einer modernen Lektüre der *Historia Augusta* relevant ist,[99] sondern bereits von ihrem Verfasser als bewußte litera-

---

the main series are defaced by abridgement, distorted by insertions or appendages.
And the author, when he has a free hand, prolongs a biography which seemed to have
reached ist due termination. The same sort of incompetence is on show in later sec-
tions." Im Mittelalter hat der sogenannte Redaktor der Σ-Klasse übrigens versucht,
diesen Befund zu korrigieren: vgl. Hermann Peter, Scriptores Historiae Augustae,
Leipzig ²1884, xxv: „velut vitam Marci, opus Capitolini ex duobus auctoribus sine
arte excerptum (...), in partes suas dissolvit plurimisque enuntiatis aut transpositis aut
omissis opus quasi novum fecit, quod multo melius est quam Capitolini." u. Hohl
(s. Anm. 27) 400: „Daß der ‚Herausgeber' die *Historia Augusta* nicht ohne Verständnis und mit hingebendem Eifer las und bei der Umarbeitung der *v. MA.*, mochte sie
gleich literarhistorisch ein Verbrechen sein, mit auffallendem Geschick zu Werke
ging, muß anerkannt werden. ... Die Zeit dieses Anonymus vermag ich freilich nicht
näher zu bestimmen. Man wird sich – statt eines verwegenen Ratens auf ein bestimm-
tes Jahrhundert – mit dem weiten Spielraum, der die Karolinger Zeit vom Anfang des
14. Jahrhunderts trennt, zu begnügen haben."

98 Das im folgenden verwendete Konzept eines ‚unreliable narrator' geht auf Wayne
Booth zurück, dessen Definition allerdings eng auf Differenzen in der moralischen
Bewertung des erzählten Geschehens fokussiert ist und vor allem den Fall eines
homodiegetischen Ich-Erzählers im Blick hat (vgl. Wayne Booth, The Rhetoric of
Fiction, Chicago 1961, v. a. 158 f.: „I have callded a narrator *reliable* when he speaks
for or acts in accordance with the norms of the work (which is to say, the implied author's norms), *unreliable* when he does not."); demgegenüber wurde von Ansgar
Nünning eine erweiterte und auch auf andere Erzählformen anwendbare Bestimmung
des Begriffes vorgeschlagen, die auch Widersprüche auf der Ebene der Fakten und der
Selbststilisierung des Erzählers bzw. Autors umfaßt (vgl. Ansgar Nünnning, *Unreliable Narration* zur Einführung: Grundzüge einer kognitiv-narratologischen Theorie
und Analyse unglaubwürdigen Erzählens, in: ders., Unreliable Narration: Studien zur
Theorie und Praxis unglaubwürdigen Erzählens in der englischsprachigen Erzähllite-
ratur, Trier 1998, 3–40).

99 Zur rezeptionsästhetischen Konzeptualisierung vgl. Nünning (s. Anm. 98) 25 „Das
bedeutet, daß ein Erzähler nicht an sich unglaubwürdig ‚ist', sondern daß es sich dabei
um eine Festellung des Betrachters handelt, die historisch, kulturell und letztlich
sogar individuell stark variieren kann."

rische Strategie angewendet wurde, lassen sich eine Reihe von Gründen anführen. Zum einen ist das Konzept der *unreliable narration* keineswegs auf fiktionale Texte beschränkt,[100] und der allgemeine Trend zu einer stärkeren literarischen Durchformung, der sich in der Geschichtsschreibung der Kaiserzeit
beobachten läßt, lädt dazu ein, nach einer solchen Technik auch in der *Historia
Augusta* Ausschau zu halten, zumal es sich bei ihr trotz des heute gebräuchlichen
Titels ja nur mit großen Einschränkungen um einen ‚faktualen' Text handelt.[101]

Zum anderen wird die Verwendung eines solchen Verfahrens durch die zahlreichen Stellen nahegelegt, an denen der Autor sich selbst mit seiner spezifischen
Art zu schreiben auseinandersetzt. Ein besonders markantes Beispiel bietet die
vita Taciti, in der er freimütig eingesteht, daß die sich zuvor über immerhin 105
Teubnerzeilen erstreckende Schilderung der Senatssitzung, in welcher der nichts-
ahnende und sich zunächst sträubende Tacitus spontan zum Kaiser ausgerufen
worden sein soll, nur in seiner Fiktion stattgefunden hat.[102] In diesen Kontext
gehört auch die Einführung des aller Wahrscheinlichkeit nach erfundenen Biographen Cordus, der mal als wichtige Quelle genannt, mal zur weitergehenden
Lektüre empfohlen, in der Regel aber für die Art und Weise, wie seine Biographien geschrieben sind, scharf getadelt wird.[103] Die Figur des Cordus ist hier
nicht nur wegen der inkonsistenten Beschreibung seines Werkes einschlägig,[104]

---

100 Vgl. Nünning (s. Anm. 98) 35 f. „Die Frage nach der Glaubwürdigkeit des Sprechers
    ist keineswegs nur für fiktionale Erzähltexte relevant, sondern auch für Sprecher in
    anderen literarischen Gattungen … sowie für nichtfiktionale Textsorten."
101 Zum Begriff des ‚faktualen' Textes vgl. Gérard Genette, Fiktion und Diktion, Mün-
    chen 1992 [frz.: Fiction et diction, Paris 1991], 65 ff.
102 Vgl. HA Tac. 3,1–7,4 u. 7,5: *hoc loco tacendum non est plerosque <in> litteras rettulisse
    Tacitum absentem et in Campania positum principem nuncupatum: verum est nec dis-
    simulare possum.* („In diesem Zusammenhang darf nicht verschwiegen werden, daß
    viele Autoren berichtet haben, Tacitus sei in seiner Abwesenheit, während er in Kam-
    panien weilte, zum Kaiser ernannt worden: dies ist wahr, ich kann es nicht verheim-
    lichen.") Eine ähnliche Relativierung der eigenen Schilderung hat möglicherweise in
    der *vita Elagabali* mit Blick die Darstellung des Diadumenus stattgefunden, doch ist
    die entscheidende Stelle der Überlieferung zum Opfer gefallen: vgl. HA Elag. 8,4–5
    (*insecutus es<t> famam Macrini crudeliter, sed multo magis Diadumeni, quod Antoni-
    nus dictus est, Pseudoantoninum ut Pseodophilippum eum appellans, simul quod ex
    luxuriosissimo extitisse vir fortissimus, optimus, gravissimus, severissimus diceretur.* (5)
    *coegit denique scriptores nonnullos nefanda, immo potius imp<i>a[ce] de eiusdem
    victu et luxuria disputare, ut in vita eius …* [*dictum* P; *dictu* Σ *Diadumeni* Pet.; *dictum
    post in vita eius* ubi Pet. significavit lacunam, transposuit Jord. *victu et* Ho.]).
103 Vgl. v. a. Clod. 11,2; Opil. 1,1–5; Max. 29,10; Gord. 21,3–4 u. Max. Balb. 4,5 sowie fer-
    ner den Hengst (s. Anm. 12) 46 ff. u. Scheithauer (s. Anm. 8) 133 ff.
104 Selbst sein Gentilnomen schwankt zwischen Iunius und Aelius; vgl. Syme (s. Anm. 55)
    305, u. Scheithauer (s. Anm. 8) 133 mit Anm. 5.

sondern weil an seinen Biographien gerade diejenigen Aspekte kritisiert werden, die – wie der Verstoß gegen die *fides historica* oder die mangelnde Konzentration auf die *digna memoratu*[105] – für die *Historia Augusta* selbst in hohem Maße charakteristisch sind.[106] Denn gerade solche Diskrepanzen zwischen expliziten Aussagen und impliziter Stilisierung gelten als wichtige Indizien bei der Identifizierung eines ‚unreliable narrator'.[107]

3.2 Marc Aurel und Lucius Verus

Die Bedeutung des Konzepts des unzuverlässigen Erzählens läßt sich aber auch gut an dem Verhältnis Marc Aurels zu seinem Mitregenten Lucius Verus zeigen,[108] das ein weiteres zentrales Thema der Biographiengruppe darstellt. Die Behandlung dieses Punktes ist in der *Historia Augusta* mit seiner Darstellung als Philosoph gleich auf doppelte Weise verbunden, da einerseits der Umgang Marc Aurels mit seinen Mitmenschen stets als Prüfstein für seine philosophischen Gesinnung verwendet[109] und andererseits Verus in seinem gesamten Wesen als

---

105 Vgl. den Hengst (s. Anm. 12) 44 ff. u. Scheithauer (s. Anm. 8) 139 ff.

106 Dies gilt in gleicher Weise für die Auseinandersetzung mit den anderen fiktiven und auch den realen Vorgängern in der *Historia Augusta*; vgl. Scheithauer (s. Anm. 8) v. a. 130: „Aber trotz theoretischer Fundierung besteht eine große Diskrepanz zwischen der Konzeption der idealen Biographie und der tatsächlichen Ausführung im Werk; denn der Verfasser der Historia Augusta verfällt in alle Fehler, die er bei anderen scharf verurteilt hat. Zweck dieser theoretischen Erörterungen ist wohl, den Leser von den Fiktion der Historia abzulenken oder sie ihm glaubhaft zu machen.".

107 Vgl. die Zusammenstellung textueller Anzeichen für das Vorliegen einer *unreliable narration* bei Nünning (wie Anm. 98) 27 f.: z. B. „explizite Widersprüche des Erzählers und andere interne Unstimmigkeiten innerhalb des narrativen Diskurses"; „Unstimmigkeiten zwischen den expliziten Fremdkommentaren des Erzählers über andere und seiner impliziten Charakterisierung bzw. unfreiwilligen Selbstentlarvung"; „Diskrepanzen zwischen der Wiedergabe der Ereignisse durch den Erzähler und seinen Erklärungen und Interpretationen des Geschehens sowie weitere Unstimmigkeiten zwischen *story* und *discourse*"; „multiperspektivische Auffächerung des Geschehens und Kontrastierung unterschiedlicher Versionen desselben Geschehens"; „Häufung von Leseranreden und bewußten Versuchen der Rezeptionslenkung durch den Erzähler" u. „explizite, autoreferentielle, metanarrative Thematisierung der eigenen Glaubwürdigkeit (...)".

108 Zur staatsrechtlichen Form dieser Doppelherrschaft vgl. Klaus Rosen, Die angebliche Samtherrschaft von Marc Aurel und Lucius Verus: ein Beitrag der Historia Augusta zum Staatsrecht der römischen Kaiserzeit, Historiae Augustae colloquium Parisinum, Macerata 1991, 271–285.

109 Dies gilt in auch für seinen Umgang mit dem Usurpator Avidius Cassius, dem angesichts der hohen Zahl von mehr oder weniger erfolgreichen Gegenkaiser in diesen

das genaue Gegenbild eines Philosophen präsentiert wird. Die Annahme, daß die Figur des Lucius Verus in der *Historia Augusta* vor allem dazu dient, Marc Aurels Persönlichkeit aus einer zusätzlichen Perspektive zu beleuchten,[110] wird dadurch gestützt, daß sich auch das Bild des Verus im Laufe der Lektüre wandelt und dabei vor allem seine Stilisierung zum ,Anti-Philosophen' sukzessive stärker hervortritt.

Denn im ersten Durchgang der *vita Marci* wird das Verhältnis Marc Aurels zu seinem Mitregenten als weitgehend unproblematisch geschildert.[111] Die Harmonie der beiden *Augusti* wird lediglich durch ihre unterschiedliche Beurteilung der Lage im Vorfeld des Markomannenkrieges[112] und durch die Nachricht kurzfristig getrübt, daß sich Verus während des Partherfeldzuges in Antiochia dem Lotterleben hingegeben haben soll,[113] wobei der prekärste Aspekt von Verus' Affäre mit einer gewissen Pantheia,[114] nämlich seine geplante Hochzeit mit einer Tochter Marc Aurels, hier unerwähnt bleibt.[115] Ansonsten betont die *Historia Augusta* in Übereinstimmung mit Marc Aurels eigener Sichtweise, wie dieser sie in den ,Selbstbetrachtungen' festgehalten hat,[116] seine philosophisch motivierte Nachsicht gegenüber den Fehlern seines Mitregenten und stellt in einem ersten Fazit fest:

Jahrhunderten der römischen Geschichte vielleicht noch ein höherer Grad an Repräsentativität zukommt.

110 Vgl. z.B. Baynes (s. Anm. 41) 83: „The interest of this Vita lies, in my judgement, in the contrast drawn between Marcus and Verus."

111 Vgl. HA Marc. 7,5–9,7 u. 12,7–14,8.

112 Vgl. HA Marc. 14,4–7.

113 Die *Historia Augusta* zeichnet insgesamt ein negatives Bild von Lucius' Rolle in diesem Feldzug (162–166 n.Chr.), die Fronto immerhin in einer historiographischen Monographie darstellen wollte (vgl. Fronto, princip. hist. p. 202–214 van den Hout sowie ferner Karl Strobel, Zeitgeschichte unter den Antoninen: Die Historiker des Partherkrieges des Lucius Verus, in: ANRW 2,34,2, Berlin–New York 1993, 1315–60, u. Shamus Sillar, The eastern expedition of Lucius Verus (AD 162–166), Journal of Ancient Civilization 17 (2002),13–38).

114 Pantheia ist der Gegenstand von Lukians Dialogen *Imagines* und *Pro imaginibus* (vgl. Peter von Möllendorff, Puzzling Beauty. Zur ästhetischen Konstruktion von *Paideia* in Lukians ,Bilder'-Dialogen, Millennium 1 (2004), 1–24).

115 Vgl. HA Marc. 8,12–14: *et Verus quidem, posteaquam in Syriam venit, in deliciis apud Antiochiam et Daphnen vixit armisque se gladiatoriis et venatibus exercuit, cum per legatos bellum Parthicum gerens imperator appellatus esset, (13) cum Marcus horis om<n>ibus rei publicae actibus incubaret patienterque delicias fratris et prope <non> invitus ac volens ferret. (14) denique omnia, quae ad bellum erant necessaria, Romae positus et disposuit Marcus et ordinavit.* u. ferner HA Marc. 9,1–6.

116 Vgl. M. Aur. 1,17,6 u. ferner Scheithauer (s. Anm. 8) 64.

> *tantae autem sanctitatis fuit Marcus, ut Veri vitia et celaverit et defenderit, cum ei vehementissime displicerent, mortuumque eum divum appellaverit amitasque eius et sorores honoribus et salariis decretis sublevaverit atque provexerit sacrisque eum plurimis honoraverit.*[117]

Dementsprechend wird auch das Gerücht, Marc Aurel habe ihn mit einer vergifteten Sautasche ermordet, an dieser Stelle mit aller Entschiedenheit zurückgewiesen.[118]

Mit umso größerer Verwunderung muß der Leser zu Beginn des zweiten Durchgangs die deutliche Distanzierung Marc Aurels von dem verstorbenen Mitregenten zur Kenntnis nehmen:

> *dein cum gratias ageret senatui, quod fratrem consecrasset, occulte ostendit omnia bellica consilia sua fuisse, quibus superati sunt Parthi. (3) addidit praeterea quaedam, quibus ostendit nunc demum se quasi a principio acturum esse rem publicam amoto eo, qui remissior videbatur.*[119]

Daß die *Historia Augusta* dem Leser erst in dem Moment Marc Aurels wahre Meinung über Verus mitteilt, in dem auch die Akteure auf der Ebene der wiedergegebenen Geschichte erfahren, daß es mit der *concordia Augustorum* offenbar doch nicht so weit her war, wie ihnen etwa die zeitgenössischen Münzbilder versichert hatten,[120] muß im Nachhinein nicht nur das Vertrauen in die philosophi-

---

117 Vgl. HA Marc. 15,3 („So untadelig war die Gesinnung des Marcus, daß er Verus' Fehler, sosehr sie ihm mißfielen, teils vertuschte, teils beschönigte, den Verstorbenen unter die Götter versetzte, dessen Tanten und Schwestern durch Bewilligung von Auszeichnungen und Apanagen unterstützte und förderte und ihn durch eine Menge von Opfern ehrte.") u. ferner z. B. HA Marc. 8,13.

118 Vgl. HA Marc. 15,5–6.

119 Vgl. HA Marc. 20,2 („Als Marcus dann dem Senat für die Vergöttlichung des Bruders seinen Dank abstattete, deutete er dunkel an, sämtliche Kriegspläne, die zur Überwindung der Parther geführt hätten, seien sein Werk gewesen. Außerdem fügte er einige Bemerkungen hinzu, durch die er bekundete, jetzt erst werde er gewissermaßen von vorn mit der Staatsführung beginnen, nachdem derjenige abberufen sei, der sich allzu lästig gezeigt habe."). Daß Marc Aurel die Regierung nun leichter falle, wurde allerdings auch schon vorher thematisiert: vgl. HA Marc. 16,3–4 (*post Veri obitum Marcus Antoninus solus rem publicam tenuit, (4) multo melior et feracior ad virtutes, quippe qui nullis Veri iam impediretur aut simulatis callidae severitatis, qua ille ingenito vitio laborabat, erroribus aut his, quae praecipue displicebant Marco Antonino iam inde a primo aetatis suae tempore, vel institutis mentis pravae vel moribus*) u. zu dieser Passage ferner Paolo Soverini, Aspetti della figura di Lucio Vero nella storiografia tardoantica, BStudLat 32,1 (2002), 68–81, der die Emendation <in>simulatis vorschlägt.

120 Zu den *Concordia*-Prägungen vgl. Rosen (s. Anm. 108) 277 f. Zum möglichen Kenntnisstand der Zeigenossen vgl. HA Ver. 9,1: *et haec vitae diversitas atque alia multa inter Marcum ac Verum simultates fecisse non aperta veritas indicabat, sed occultus rumor inseverat.*

sche Milde des Kaisers, sondern auch in die Zuverlässigkeit eines sich als allwissend ausgebenden Erzählers erschüttern.

Beide Effekte werden in der ebenfalls dem Iulius Capitolinus zugeschriebenen *vita Lucii Veri*, die in gewisser Weise den dritten Durchgang der *vita Marci* darstellt, noch einmal verstärkt. Diese beginnt nach der für eine Nebenvita typischen Rechtfertigung des eigenen Tuns[121] ebenfalls mit einer expliziten und vorab erfolgenden Bewertung des Protagonisten, diesmal als *princeps medius*.[122] Doch behält diese neutrale Charaktisierung ihre Gültigkeit nur in der unmittelbar folgenden Behandlung seines Lebens vor dem Regierungsantritt,[123] wobei vor allem seine lediglich durchschnittliche literarische Begabung als Chiffre für seine Mittelmäßigkeit fungiert.[124] Wenn im Anschluß daran jedoch ihre gemeinsame Regierung ein weiteres Mal dargestellt wird, liegt der Fokus fast ausschließlich auf den verschiedenen Verfehlungen, die Verus zur Last gelegt werden.[125]

---

121 Vgl. HA Ver. 1,1–2. Daher und wegen weiterer Gemeinsamkeiten wird die *vita Veri* in der Regel als Nebenvita angesehen (vgl. Mommsen (s. Anm. 23) 246), allerdings wird sie mit Blick auf die historische Zuverlässigkeit des in ihr präsentierten Materials von anderen auch den Hauptviten zugerechnet (vgl. Timothy D. Barnes, Hadrian and Lucius Verus, Journal of Roman Studies 57 (1967), 65–79; Syme (s. Anm. 55) 287 f. u. den Hengst (s. Anm. 12) 16 f.).

122 Vgl. HA Ver. 1,3: *igitur Lucius Ceionius Aelius Commodus Verus Antoninus, qui ex Hadriani voluntate Aelius appellatus est, ex Antonini coniunctione Verus et Antoninus, neque inter bonos neque intermalos principes ponitur.* („So hat denn Lucius Ceionius Aelius Commodus Verus Antoninus, der den Namen Aelius auf Wunsch Hadrians, die Namen Verus und Antoninus aufgrund seiner Verbindung mit Antoninus erhielt, seinen Platz weder unter den guten noch unter den schlechten Fürsten."); u. zur Gestaltung dieser Eingangssequenz ferner Stubenrauch (s. Anm. 12) 44 ff.

123 Vgl. HA Ver. 2–3 u. ferner zu diesem Abschnitt Jean-Pierre Callu, Verus avant Verus, Historiae Augustae colloquium Parisinum, Macerata 1991, 101–122. Für den Aufbau der *vita Veri* s. Anhang 1.

124 Vgl. HA Ver. 2,5–2,8: *audivit Scaurinum grammaticum Latinum, Scauri filium, qui grammaticus Hadriani fuit, Graecos Telephum atque Hefaestionem, Harpocrationem, rhetores Apollonium, Celerem Caninium et Herodem Atticum, Latinum Cornelium Frontonem, philosophos Apollonium et Sextum. (6) hos omnes amavit unice, atque ab his in vicem dilectus est, nec tamen ingeniosus ad litteras. (7) amavit autem in pueritia versus facere, post orationes. et melior quidem orator fuisse dicitur quam poeta, immo, ut verius dicam, peior poeta quam rhetor. (8) nec desunt, qui dicant eum adiutum ingenio amicorum atque abaliis ei illa ipsa, qualiacumque sunt, scripta; si quidem multos disertos et eruditos semper secum habuisse dicitur. educatorem habuit Nicomedem.*

125 Vgl. HA Ver. 4,1–9,11. Der Wandel zeigt sich auch darin, daß Verus am Ende der Vita explizit mit Nero verglichen wird (vgl. HA Ver. 10,6–10,9 u. ferner Sillar (s. Anm. 113) 35 f.), der in der *Historia Augusta* ebenso zu *principes mali* zählt wie später dann auch Verus selbst (vgl. HA Opil. 7,7 u. ferner Scheithauer (s. Anm. 8) 26 f. u. 59). In der neueren Forschung wurde der Versuch unternommen, ein positiveres Bild von Verus zu zeichnen; vgl. z. B. Pierre Lambrechts, Der Kaiser Lucius Verus. Versuch einer

Indem eine Reihe von Konflikten zwischen den beiden *Augusti* erst hier erwähnt[126] oder erst jetzt in ihrer ganzen Dimension deutlich werden,[127] wird zum einen die in der *vita Marci* präsentierte Version einer harmonischen Koregentschaft konsequent konterkariert, zum anderen aber auch die Zuverlässigkeit der – zudem weiterhin Iulius Capitolinus genannten – Erzählinstanz noch mehr in Zweifel gezogen.[128] Von diesen Zweifeln muß dann aber auch die Wahrnehmung Marc Aurels durch den Rezipienten beeinflußt werden, auch wenn dessen Verhalten nicht direkt kritisiert wird. Vielmehr nimmt ihn der Autor erneut explizit gegen den Vorwurf in Schutz, Verus vergiftet zu haben,[129] hat aber, indem er das Gerücht noch einmal und in detaillierter Form erwähnt, zumindest erreicht, daß seinen Lesern die Existenz dieser Vorwürfe sicher im Gedächtnis bleiben wird.

3.3 Marc Aurel und Avidius Cassius

Wenn wir die kontinuierliche Lektüre des Marc Aurel gewidmeten Abschnittes der *Historia Augusta* fortsetzen, stoßen wir nun auf die Biographie des Avidius Cassius,[130] der sich auf die – vielleicht von ihm selbst gestreute[131] – falsche Nachricht vom Tode des Kaisers 175 n. Chr. in Syrien zum Imperator hatte ausrufen

---

Rehabilitation, in: Richard Klein, Marc Aurel, Wege der Forschung 550, Darmstadt 1979, 25–57 (zuerst: ders., L'empereur Lucius Verus. Essai de Réhabilitation, L'Antiquité Classique 3 (1934), 173–201), u. Scheithauer (s. Anm. 8), 63 f.; dag. aber auch Barnes (s. Anm. 121) 74: „If there is undue concentration on Lucius' delinquencies, that is surely because the emperor really was something of a playboy."

126 So beispielsweise die Gerüchte einer Ermordung des M. Annius Libo: vgl. HA Ver. 9,1–2.

127 So beispielsweise die Affäre mit Pantheia vgl. HA Ver. 7,1–7,8.

128 Für eine Interpretation, die stärker die Gemeinsamkeiten der Darstellung des Verus in beiden Viten betont, vgl. Scheithauer (s. Anm. 8) 63.

129 Vgl. HA Ver. 10–11. Zu den auktorialen Kommentaren in den Iulius Capitolinus zugeschriebenen Viten vgl. Vicente Picón, Los comentarios de autor/narrador en las Vitae de la HA atribuidas a Julio Capitolino, Historiae Augustae Colloquium Barcinonense, Bari 1996, 279–295.

130 Avidius war zuvor kurz als einer der drei führenden Generäle des Partherfeldzuges (162–166 n. Chr.) unter dem Oberbefehl des Lucius Verus erwähnt worden (vgl. HA Ver. 7,1 sowie ferner zu seiner Karriere vor der Erhebung Jürgen Spieß, Avidius Cassius und der Aufstand des Jahres 175, Diss. München 1975, 14 ff., u. Ronald Syme, Avidius Cassius. His rank, age and quality, BHAC 1984/1985 (1987), 207–222).

131 Vgl. HA Marc. 24,7: *alii dicunt, ementita morte Antonini Cassium imperatorem se appellasse, cum divum Marcum appellasset* u. Avid. 7,2: *alii autem dicunt hanc artem adhibuisse militibus et provincialibus Cassium contra Marci amorem, ut sibi posset consentiri, quod diceret Marcum diem suum obisse.*

lassen, um bereits drei Monate später von seinen eigenen Soldaten ermordet zu werden.[132] Gerade in dieser Vita treten sowohl die lediglich marginale historische Bedeutung des Protagonisten als auch die Schwierigkeit, zuverlässige Informationen über sein Leben zu erhalten, besonders deutlich zum Vorschein, was der Autor auch – wie in den Nebenviten häufig – selbst einräumt.[133] Dementsprechend kann es auch nicht überraschen, daß die Lebensbeschreibung überwiegend aus fiktiven Angaben, die schon mit der Zurückführung auf die republikanischen Cassii und der ausführlichen Vorstellung eines falschen Vaters beginnen,[134] und aus den üblichen gefälschten Dokumenten,[135] bei denen es sich hier vor allem Briefe handelt,[136] besteht,[137] so daß sich die Frage nach dem historischen Wert einer solchen Nebenvita in diesem Fall in besonderer Schärfe stellt.

Daß der Großteil der Informationen über Avidius Cassius frei erfunden ist und ihr fiktiver Charakter vom Leser auch ohne weiteres durchschaut werden kann, stellt die Beteuerung des Autors, daß er auch diese Biographie nur verfaßt habe, um alle Träger des *imperatorium nomen* vollständig zu behandeln,[138] nachhaltig in Frage. Vielmehr liegt die Vermutung nahe, daß die Funktion dieser Vita

---

132 Vgl. Cass. Dio 72,22–27 u. ferner allg. Spiess (s. Anm. 130).

133 Vgl. HA Avid. 3,1: *sed nos hominis naturam et mores breviter explicabimus; neque enim plura de his sciri possunt, quorum vitam et inlustrare nullus audet eorum causa, a quibus oppressi fuerint.* („Wir aber wollen in Kürze das Wesen und den Charakter dieses Mannes schildern; denn reichlichere Kunde ist von denen nicht möglich, deren Leben niemand ins Licht zu setzen wagt mit Rücksicht auf ihre Überwinder.") u. ferner den Hengst (s. Anm. 12) 19 ff.

134 Vgl. HA Avid. 1,1–3: *Avidius Cassius, ut quidam volunt, ex familia Cassiorum fuisse dicitur per ma<t>rem, homin<e> novo genitus Avidio Severo, qui ordines duxerat et post ad summas dignitates pervenerat;* (2) *cuius Quadratus in historiis meminit, et quidemgraviter, cum illum summum virum et necessarium rei p. adserit et apud ipsum Marcum praevalidum;* (3) *nam iam eo imperante perisse fatali sorte perhibetur* u. ferner Alfred von Domaszewski, Die Personennamen bei den Scriptores historiae Augustae, Sitzungsberichte der Heidelberger Akademie der Wissenschaften 9 (1918), 13. Abhandlung, Heidelberg 1918, 123, sowie zu C. Avidius Heliodorus, seinem tatsächlichen Vater, Spiess (s. Anm. 130) 16 ff., u. Syme (s. Anm. 130) 217 f.

135 Zu der in diesen Dokumenten angewandten literarischen Technik s. o. 122 Anm. 61.

136 Für die Annahme, daß den Angaben in den Briefen zumindest ein historisch verwertbarer Kern zugrundeliegt, vgl. Schwartz (s. Anm. 95).

137 Für eine quellenkritische Untersuchung vgl. Elimar Klebs, Die Vita des Avidius Cassius, Rheinisches Museum für Philologie 43 (1888), 321–346, sowie allg. zum historischen Wert Spiess (s. Anm. 130) v. a. 84 ff., u. Syme (s. Anm. 130).

138 Vgl. HA Avid. 3,3: *proposui enim, Diocletiane Auguste, omnes, qui imperatorium nomen sive <iusta causa sive> iniusta habuerunt, in litteras mittere, ut omnes purpuratos, Auguste, cognosceres* („Ist es doch, Kaiser Diokletian, mein Vorhaben, sämtliche Träger des Kaisertitels, die legitimen wie die illegitimen, literarisch zu behandeln, damit sämtliche Purpurträger zu Deiner Kenntnis, durchlauchtigster Fürst, gelangen.")

vor allem darin besteht, die Figur Marc Aurels aus einer weiteren Perspektive zu schildern. Diese Annahme findet ihre Bestätigung schon in der quantitativen Bedeutung, die Marc Aurel in der gesamten *vita Avidii* zukommt: Er ist nicht nur entweder Verfasser oder Adressat so gut wie aller der in diese Biographie eingelegten Briefe, sondern ist auch in den Passagen, die sich stärker mit dem eigentlichen Porträtierten beschäftigen, fast immer präsent.[139]

Bereits der erste fiktive Briefwechsel, in dem Lucius Verus seinen Mitregenten über einen angeblichen früheren Putschversuch des Avidius Cassius[140] informiert und ein hartes Vorgehen gegen diesen fordert, dient in erster Linie zur Charakterisierung Marc Aurels.[141] Denn in einem raffinierten Spiel mit unterschiedlichen Sprecherrollen wird dem Leser hier von Verus mitgeteilt, daß Marc Aurel von Avidius als *philosopha anicula* bezeichnet worden sei,[142] wobei angesichts des fiktiven Charakters des ganzen Briefes aber natürlich davon auszugehen ist, daß diese Formulierung auf das Konto des Verfassers der *Historia Augusta* geht.[143]

In seinem mit literarischen Anspielungen gespickten Antwortschreiben[144] sieht Marc Aurel zwar zunächst wie der sichere Sieger aus, weil es ihm gelingt,

---

139 Vgl. die Gliederung in Anhang 1. Wenn man die Zeilen zählt, die sich in dieser Vita primär mit Avidius Cassius einerseits und Marc Aurel andererseits beschäftigen, ergibt sich in der Teubnerausgabe ungefähr die gleiche Zahl für den nominellen Protagonisten der Vita (ca. 175) wie für den ‚primären' Kaiser Marc Aurel (ca. 190).

140 Die Neigung des Avidius Cassius zur Usurpation wird dabei nicht nur durch seine angebliche Verwandtschaft mit dem gleichnamigen Caesarmörder (vgl. HA Avid. 1,4 u. ferner Spiess (s. Anm. 130) 86 f.), sondern auch durch eines der für die *Historia Augusta* charakteristischen Wortspiele erklärt: *Avidius Cassius avidus est … imperii* (HA Avid. 1,7 sowie ferner Syme (s. Anm. 55) 294, u. Barry Baldwin, The Vita Avidii, Klio 58 (1976), 101–119, h. 106 f.).

141 Vgl. HA Avid. 1,6–2,8.

142 Vgl. HA Avid. 1,8: *omnia ei nostra displicent, opes non mediocres parat, litteras nostras ridet. te philosopham aniculam, me luxuriosum morionem vocat. vide quid agendum sit* („Alles an uns erregt sein Mißfallen, er häuft nicht unbeträchtliche Reichtümer an, unsere Verfügungen verlacht er. Dich nennt er eine Vettel von einem Philosophen, mich einen ausschweifenden Schwachkopf. Sieh zu, was da zu tun ist.").

143 Vgl. z. B. Syme (s. Anm. 8) 294: „But *philosopha anicula* and *luxuriosus morio* for Marcus and Verus (Avid. 1,8) might be his own invention." Wenn man davon ausgeht, daß diese Negativurteile vom Autor selbst stammen, ist auch nicht davon auszugehen, daß das Spiel mit den unterschiedlichen Sprecherrollen ihrer Relativierung dient (vgl. aber dag. Scheithauer (s. Anm. 8) 47: „In der Absicht, Marcus in jeder Beziehung als vorbildlich hinzustellen, schreibt der Autor alles, was seinem Idealkaiser schaden könnte, fremden Gewährsleuten oder irgendwelchen Gerüchten zu, die er ohne eigene Wertung in den Text übernimmt.").

144 Vgl. HA Avid. 2,1–2,8 u. ferner Elke W. Merten, Zu den Quellen des Marcusbriefes im zweiten Kapitel der Vita Avidii Cassii, Historiae Augustae Colloquium Genevense, Bari 1994, 181–188.

Verus' Drängen auf eine Eliminierung des Avidius souverän zurückzuweisen. Zu diesem Zweck führt er unter anderem zwei Zitate an, mit denen er belegen will, daß es auch für einen guten Herrscher nicht möglich ist, sich vor einem Anschlag auf sein Leben zu schützen, und die er deswegen Trajan – *scis enim proavi tui dictum: ,successorem suum nullus occidit'*[145] – und Hadrian zuschreibt: *scis enim ipse, quid avus tuus Hadrianus dixerit: ,misera conditio imperatorum, quibus de affecta<ta> tyrannide nisi occisis non potest credi.'*[146] Diese Argumentation büßt allerdings erheblich an Überzeugungskraft ein, wenn der Autor Marc Aurel selbst unmittelbar nach der Hadrian zugeschriebenen Sentenz folgende Bemerkung anfügen läßt:

> *eius autem exemplum ponere <malui> quam Domitiani, qui hoc primus dixisse fertur; tyrannorum enim etiam bona dicta non habent tantum auctoritatis, quantum debent.*[147]

Das Eingeständnis, daß es sich bei diesem Zitat in Wirklichkeit um einen Ausspruch Domitians handelt, stellt deswegen eine besonders gravierende Erschütterung der Glaubwürdigkeit des Sprechers dar, weil mit der Ersetzung des positiv bewerteten Kaisers Hadrian durch den als Tyrannen stigmatisierten letzten Flavier Marc Aurels gesamte Argumentation in diesem Antwortschreiben konterkariert wird. Eine analoge Funktion läßt sich auch für das erste, hier Trajan zugeschriebene Dictum vermuten, auch wenn seine Provenienz aus neronischem Kontext nicht mit letzter Sicherheit bewiesen werden kann.[148] Jedenfalls wird mit

---

145 Vgl. HA Avid. 2,2 („Du kennst doch das Wort Deines Urgroßvaters: ,Seinen Nachfolger hat noch niemand umgebracht.'"). Die ersten Worten des Briefs (vgl. HA Avid 2,1: *epistulam tuam legi, sollicitam potius <quam> imperatoriam et non nostri temporis*) erinnern zwar an die prominente Formulierung Trajans in seinem Antwortbrief zur Frage der Christenverfolgung (vgl. Plin. ep. 10,97,2: *sine auctore vero propositi libelli <in> nullo crimine locum habere debent. nam et pessimi exempli nec nostri saeculi est*), doch handelt es sich um eine in juristischen Rescripten häufiger anzutreffende Wendung (vgl. Merten (s. Anm. 144) 182).

146 Vgl. HA Avid. 2,5 („Du weißt doch selbst, was Dein Großvater Hadrian gesagt hat: ,Beklagenswert ist das Los der Kaiser: ihnen pflegt man Umtriebe von Thronräubern nicht eher zu glauben, als bis sie selbst erschlagen sind.'").

147 Vgl. HA Avid. 2,6 („Ich wollte mich lieber auf Hadrian berufen als auf Domitian, der sich als erster in diesem Sinne geäußert haben soll; denn Worte aus Tyrannenmund haben, auch wenn sie treffend sind, nicht das Vollgewicht, das ihnen an sich zukommt.") u. Suet. Dom. 20: *condicionem principum miserrimam aiebat, quibus de coniuratione comperta non crederetur nisi occisis.*

148 Vgl. Cass. Dio 61,18,3 mit Merten (s. Anm. 144) 182 ff.; sowie ferner zum Ende des Schreibens Baldwin (s. Anm. 140) 108: „It is contrived as a tissue of quotations and fatalistic clichés. The latter might be intended as parody of the *Meditations*." u. Klaus Rosen, Herrschaftstheorie und Herrschaftspraxis bei Marc Aurel, in: Peter Neukam,

der hier noch in der wörtlichen Rede ein und desselben Sprechers stattfindenden Widerlegung einer zuvor aufgestellten Behauptung ganz bewußt weiter auch an der Zuverlässsigkeit der allgemeinen Erzählinstanz gerüttelt.

Die wenig freundliche Sicht auf Marc Aurels philosophische Interessen, die im Rahmen des fiktiven Brief zunächst nur als Wiedergabe einer Äußerung des Avidius formuliert war, macht sich im folgenden Abschnitt aber auch der Biograph selbst zu eigen. Nachdem er den Charakter des Protagonisten in fünf Gegensatzpaaren ebenso knapp wie nichtssagend umrissen hat,[149] erwähnt er einen angeblich zeitgenössischen Vergleich mit Catilina, den Avidius freudig aufgegriffen habe: *futurum se Sergium, si dialogistam occidisset.*[150] Die folgende Erklärung, daß mit der abschätzigen Bezeichnung *dialogista* hier nicht Cicero, sondern Marc Aurel gemeint ist, weil dieser seinen Aufbruch in den Krieg gegen die Markomannen einer philosophischen Disputation zuliebe um drei Tage verschoben hatte,[151] steht aber bereits nicht mehr in indirekter Rede[152] und muß daher als

---

Motiv und Motivation, München 1993, 94–105, h. 104: „Auf Verus' Vorhaltungen, er solle, wenn nicht für sich, so doch für seine Kinder die Herrschaft bewahren, entgegnet er mit einer Selbstverleugnung, die der gesamten Geschichte der römischen Kaiserzeit ins Gesicht schlägt: *plane liberi mei pereant, si magis amari merebitur Avidius quam illi et si rei p. expediet Cassium vivere quam liberos Marci* (2,8). Das hieß die Ethik der Selbstbetrachtungen auf die Spitze treiben. Krasser als mit diesem historisch fiktiven, philosophisch aber folgerichtigem Satz hätte man die Realitätsferne des Werkes nicht entlarven können."

149 Vgl. HA Avid. 3,4: *fuit his moribus, ut nonnumquam trux et asper videretur aliquando mitis et lenis, saepe religiosus, alias contemptor sacrorum, avidus vini item abstinens, cibi adpetens et inediae patiens, Veneris cupidus et castitatis amator* („Es lag in seinem Wesen, daß er mitunter trutzig und barsch erschien, manchmal milde und sanft, nicht selten religiös gestimmt, dann wieder als ein Verächter des Heiligen, als ein Weinschwelg, aber auch wieder enthaltsam, als Freßsack und als Hungerkünstler, als Schürzenjäger und als Keuscheitsapostel.") u. ferner Syme (s. Anm. 55), 295 „To render character, the author invents contrary traits that add up to precisely nothing."

150 Vgl. HA Avid. 3,5: *nec defuerunt qui illum Catilinam vocarent, cum et ipse se ita gauderet appellari, addens futurum se Sergium, si dialogistam occidisset* („Auch fehlt es nicht an Leuten, die ihn Catilina nannten; er selbst hörte diese Bezeichnung gern und bemerkte dazu, er werde ein Sergius sein, wenn er den Klugschwätzer umgebracht habe.") sowie ferner Spiess (s. Anm. 130) 88 f., u. Baldwin (s. Anm. 140) 112 f.

151 Vgl. HA Avid. 3,6–7: *Antoninum hoc nomine significans, qui tantum enituit in philosophia, ut iturus ad bellum Marcomannicum timentibus cunctis, ne quid fatale proveniret, rogatus sit non adulatione sed serio, ut praecepta philosophiae ederet. (7) nec ille timuit, sed per ordinem par<a>eneseos – hoc est praeceptionum – per triduum disputavit.* („Damit meinte er den Antonius, der eine solche Leuchte der Philosophie war, daß man ihn noch kurz vor seinem Aufbruch in den Markomannenkrieg, als alles vor einem Schicksalsschlag bangte, nicht aus Liebdienerei, sondern allen Ernstes bat, seine philosophischen Lehren bekannt zu geben. (7) Er aber zierte sich nicht, sondern hielt drei Tage lang in Form einer regelrechten Paränese – das heißt von Unterweisungen –

Äußerung der übergeordneten Erzählinstanz verstanden werden. Diese trägt im übrigen hier nicht mehr – wie in den Viten Marc Aurels und des Lucius Verus – den Namen Iulius Capitolinus, sondern wird jetzt – und nur in dieser einzigen Biographie – als Vulcacius Gallicanus, *vir clarissimus*, bezeichnet.[153]

Der Wandel in der Wahrnehmung des Philosophen auf dem Kaiserthron aber kann mit diesem ‚Sprecherwechsel' natürlich nicht hinreichend erklärt werden,[154] wie sich auch daran zeigt, daß der in der gesamten *vita Avidii* zentrale Konflikt zwischen dem von einem Herrscher erwarteten resoluten Handeln und der philosophisch motivierten Milde Marc Aurels bereits in den am Ende der *vita Marci* zusammengestellten Vorwürfen angeklungen war.[155] Vielmehr soll Avidius Cassius als ein bewußt konzipiertes Gegenbild zu Marc Aurel verstanden werden – ein Umstand, der zwar schon verschiedentlich bemerkt wurde,[156] aus dem aber noch keine Rückschlüsse auf weitergehende Darstellungsabsichten der *Historia Augusta* gezogen wurden.

Allerdings ist auch die auf den Kontrast zu Marc Aurel berechnete Stilisierung des Avidius zum ‚Soldatenkaiser' ihrerseits wieder mit einer in hohem Maße ambivalenten Wertung verbunden. Denn in der nun folgenden Schilderung seines

---

Lehrvorträge.") u. ferner Aur. Vict. Caes. 16,9, der das gleiche Ereignis ohne kritischen Unterton schildert.

152 Eine ähnliche Argumentation legt der Autor dann auch wieder Avidius in einem fiktiven Brief am Ende der Biographie in den Mund: vgl. v. a. HA Avid. 14,5 u. s. u. S. 145.

153 Zu diesem Pseudonym vgl. Mommsen (s. Anm. 23) 245; von Domaszewski (s. Anm. 134) 13: „Daß er ihn als *vir clarissimus* bezeichnet hat gar nichts zu bedeuten; diesen Titel wie auch *praefectus praetorio, praefectus urbi* gebrauchte er ganz beliebig."; Syme (s. Anm. 55) 305: „He enjoys a double distinction. The only one to bear a title of rank and be allocated a single biography (the *Avidius Cassius*)." u. Baldwin (s. Anm. 140) 101 ff.

154 Es ist bislang nicht gelungen, den sechs fiktiven Autoren der Historia Augusta ein individuelles inhaltliches oder stilistisches Profil zuzuordnen; vgl. z. B. Syme (s. Anm. 55) 305: „The conclusion is clear. The labels are an afterthouht, and were casually attached."

155 Vgl. HA Marc. 29. Zum engen Zusammenhang der dort nicht weiter kommentierten Vorwürfe mit der *vita Avidii* vgl. Rosen (s. Anm. 93) 193 ff., sowie allg. zur Kritik an Marc Aurels übertriebener *clementia* Ronald F. Newbold, Pardon and revenge in Suetonius and the Historia Augusta, Prudentia 33 (2001), 41–58, h. 48 f.

156 Vgl. schon Klebs (s. Anm. 137) 334: „Wir haben es hier mit der freien Phantasie eines Rhetors zu thun, der statt der abgedroschenen Schulthemen sich als Vorwurf nahm: Avidius Cassius als der strenge, republikanische Staatsmann, und Marcus der milde Philosoph auf dem Thron." sowie ferner z. B. Delande (s. Anm. 90) 143; Rosen (s. Anm. 148) 101 ff., u. Rosen (s. Anm. 93) 194 f.: „Avidius soll nicht nur Rebell, sondern politisches Gegenbild zu Marcus sei. Der Realpolitiker tritt gegen den Philosophen an."

Charakters und seiner Maßnahmen als Legionskommandant in Syrien[157] werden abwechselnd seine an republikanische Vorbilder gemahnende und positiv verstandene[158] *severitas* und seine geradezu beispiellose *crudelitas* betont.[159] Dieser Gegensatz wird bis zum Ende der Biographie nicht aufgehoben, wo ein fiktiver Brief des Avidius mit den Worten eingeleitet wird, daß er sich, wäre er zur Herrschaft gelangt, als *non modo clemens sed bonus, sed utilis et optimus imperator* erwiesen hätte,[160] während das Fazit am Ende des Schreibens lautet: *haec epistola eius indicat, quam severus et quam tristis futurus fuerit imperator.*[161]

---

157 Zwar hat die Disziplinlosigkeit der syrischen Legionen schon fast topischen Charakter (vgl. Syme (s. Anm. 130) 219 f.), doch werden seine Erfolge bei der Führung dieser Truppen auch in einem Brief Frontos erwähnt (vgl. Fronto, ad amicos 1,6 u. ferner Spiess (s. Anm. 130) 90 f.).

158 Vgl. aber auch Raban von Haehling, Zur Struktur und Funktion der Zeitbezüge in der Historia Augusta, in: Martin Flashar, Retrospektive. Konzepte von Vergangenheit in der griechisch-römischen Antike, München 1996, 227–240, v. a. 235: „Die Erzähleingriffe in Form von Zeitbezügen vermitteln ein merkwürdig blasses, ja konturloses Bild von Roms Vergangenheit, insbesondere der glanzvollen Frühzeit der *libera res publica*. Der Biograph mißt ihr hierbei keinerlei exemplarische oder gar eine für die Zeitgenossen verpflichtende Bedeutung bei. Eine Ausrichtung auf die Postulate des *mos maiorum* fehlt gänzlich."

159 Vgl. HA Avid. 4–6 u. ferner zu dem fiktiven Aemilius Parthenianus als vermeintlicher Quelle Baldwin (s. Anm. 140) 104 f. Wichtige Elemente der positiven Sicht auf den Charakters des Avidius legt der Autor in einem erneuten fiktiven Briefwechsel ausgerechnet Marc Aurel in den Mund; vgl. HA Avid 5,4–5,7: *extat de hoc epistula divi Marci ad praefectum suum talis:* (5) *„Avidio Cassio legiones Syriacas dedi diffluentes luxuria et Dafnidis moribus agentes, quas totas excaldantes se repperisse Caesonius Vectilianus scripsit.* (6) *et puto me non errasse, si quidem et tu notum habeas Cassium, hominem Cassian<a>e severitatis et disciplinae.* (7) *neque enim milites regi possunt nisi vetere disciplina. scis enim versum a bono poeta dictum et omnibus frequentatum: ,moribus antiquis res stat Romana virisque.'*".

160 Vgl. HA Avid. 13,10: *qui si optinuisset imperium, fuisset non modo clemens sed bonus, sed utilis et optimus imperator* („Hätte er den Thron erobert, so wäre er nicht nur ein milder, sondern auch ein guter, brauchbarer und ganz vortrefflicher Regent geworden.") u. ferner Cass. Dio 72,22,2. Ein ebenso positives Fazit zieht die *Historia Augusta* von einer möglichen Herrschaft des Pescennius Niger (vgl. HA Pesc. 12,3).

161 Vgl. HA Avid. 14,8 („Dieser sein Brief bekundet, wie streng und hart er sich als Kaiser gezeigt hätte.") u. ferner Rosen (s. Anm. 93) 196: „Trotzdem entscheidet sich der Verfasser nicht eindeutig für den Rebellen, dem die Geschichte versagt hat, das Dilemma von Gesinnung und Verantwortung zu lösen. Es aufgezeigt zu haben, bleibe sein Verdienst, das ist das unausgesprochene Fazit der Vita. Für den rückblickenden Betrachter ergeben erst die Lebensbeschreibungen des Kaisers und des Empörers zusammen das politische Ideal. Der Bewunderer beider Männer kann nur bedauern, daß das Ideal selbst dem besten aller Kaiser unerreichbar geblieben ist. *Miser Marcus, homo sane optimus*, urteilt Avidius Cassius Schlußdokument (14,3). Es ist das Urteil, das der Biograph im Stillen bereits über das Schlußkapitel der Marcusvita gesetzt hatte."

Schon der Verzicht auf eine kohärente Charakterisierung zeigt, daß Avidius Cassius in seiner eigenen Vita nur eine Nebenrolle spielt. Dieser Eindruck wird noch einmal erheblich verstärkt, wenn der Autor im Anschluß die Ereignisse zwischen seiner Ausrufung zum Kaiser und seiner Ermordung in extremer Kürze abhandelt,[162] um sich sodann in der ganzen zweiten Hälfte der Biographie so gut wie ausschließlich mit Marc Aurels Nachsicht gegenüber den Aufständischen zu beschäftigen.[163] Dabei stehen hier weniger die bereits in der *vita Marci* erwähnten konkreten Fakten im Vordergrund,[164] sondern die Diskussion der politischen Angemessenheit der philosophischen Milde des Kaisers.

Marc Aurels Verhalten wird zunächst von einem anonymen *quidam* getadelt,[165] dem der Kaiser mit einem Überblick über die Todesarten seiner Vorgänger antwortet, mit dem er nachweisen will, daß gute Herrscher ohnehin nicht ermordet werden:

> *enumeravit deinde omnes principes, qui occisi essent, habuisse causas, quibus mererentur occidi, ne<c> quemquam facile bonum vel victum a tyranno vel occisum, (4) dicens meruisse Neronem, debuisse Caligulam, Othonem et Vitellium nec imperare voluisse. (5) nam de [Pertinace et] Galba paria sentiebat, cum diceret {in} imperatore avaritiam esse acerbissimum malum. (6) denique non Augustum, non Traianum, non Hadrianum, non patrem suum a rebellibus potuisse superari, cum et multi fuerint et ipsis vel invitis vel insciis extincti.[166]*

Zwar findet an dieser Stelle keine explizite Relativierung des Gesagten statt, doch kann man sich des Eindrucks nicht erwehren, daß die spezifische Konstellation von Inhalt und Sprecher – ein amtierender Herrscher, der sein Verhalten damit

---

162 Vgl. HA Avid. 7. Auch die Schilderung in der *vita Marci* fällt ähnlich knapp aus: vgl. HA Marc. 24,5–26,3 u. ferner Vicente Picón García, Los comentarios de autor/narrador y la composición de la Vita Cassii, Historiae Augustae Colloquium Bonnense, Bari 1997, 217–228, h. 221 ff. Zur historischen Rekonstruktion des Geschehens vgl. Spiess (s. Anm. 130) 31 ff.

163 Vgl. HA Avid. 8,1–14,8.

164 Vgl. HA Marc. 25,3–26,4 u. ferner Spiess (s. Anm. 130) 59 ff.

165 Vgl. HA Avid. 8,2.

166 Vgl. HA Avid. 8,3–6 („Und dann zählte er alle ermordeten Kaiser her unter Angabe der Gründe, aus denen sie ein gewaltsames Ende verdient hätten, und wies nach, daß kaum je ein guter Herrscher von einem Gegenkaiser besiegt oder getötet worden sei; (4) Nero habe sein Los verdient, Caligulas Beseitigung sei eine Notwendigkeit gewesen, während Otho und Vitellius überhaupt keinen Herrscherwillen besessen hätten. (5) Entsprechend urteilte er über [Pertinax und] Galba mit der Bemerkung, Geiz sei an seinem Kaiser das aufreizendste Laster. Schließlich hätten weder Augustus noch Trajan noch Hadrian noch sein Vater von Empörern überwunden werden können, obwohl es ihrer viele gegeben habe, die ohne Willen oder Wissen der Genannten vernichtet worden seien.").

rechtfertigt, wie seine Vorgänger zu Tode gekommen sind – auch hier auf eine Ironisierung abzielt. Zumindest kann dieser Exkurs aber als augenzwinkernder Hinweis sowohl auf den Nutzen biographischer Literatur im allgemeinen als auch auf das Darstellungsprinzip einer zum Leben passenden Sterbeszene im besonderen verstanden werden.[167]

Im Anschluß daran darf Faustina in zwei fiktiven Schreiben, die den Briefwechsel mit Verus wieder aufgreifen, der das richtige Verhalten gegenüber Empörern bereits zu Beginn der Vita gleichsam avant la lettre thematisiert hatte,[168] nun ihrerseits Kritik an der Schonung der Aufständischen vortragen[169] und auf diese Weise zugleich dem Gerücht ihrer eigenen Verwicklung in den Putsch des Avidius entgegentreten.[170] Darauf folgt ein weiterer fiktiver Brief, in dem Marc Aurel den Senat um Zustimmung zu seiner Amnestie bittet,[171] und die Reaktion dieses Gremiums, zu deren Schilderung die Akklamationen der Senatoren während der betreffenden Sitzung in vermeintlich wörtlicher Form wiedergegeben werden.[172] Mit dieser – auch in anderen Viten angewandten[173] – Technik gewinnt

---

167 Vgl. Tobias Arand, Das unverdiente Ende – Suizid- und Todesdarstellungen in der *Historia Augusta* als Elemente literarischer Bewertung im Kontext paganer Selbstbehauptung, Berlin 1999, u. Hartwin Brandt, *De mortibus principum et tyrannorum*: Tod und Leichenschändung in der Historia Augusta, Historiae Augustae Colloquium Perusinum, Bari 2002, 65–72.

168 Vgl. HA Avid. 1,6–2,8 u. s. o. S. 138–140.

169 Vgl. HA Avid. 9,6–11,8.

170 Vgl. HA Marc. 24,6; Avid. 7,1 u. Cass. Dio 71,22,3 sowie ferner vgl. Scheithauer (s. Anm. 8) 90 f. Die Möglichkeit, daß Faustina tatsächlich auf diese Weise Vorsorge für eine sichere Thronfolge ihres damals noch minderjährigen Sohnes Commodus hatte treffen wollen, wurde verschiedentlich erwogen (vgl. z. B. Spiess (s. Anm. 130) 33 f. u. Syme (s. Anm. 130) 221 f.).

171 Vgl. HA Avid. 12.

172 Vgl. HA Avid. 13,2–5: ,*Antonine pie, di te servent. Antonine clemens, di te servent. tu voluisti quod licebat, nos fecimus quod decebat.* (3) *Commodo imperium iustum rogamus. progeniem tua robora. fac securi sint liberi nostri.* (4) *bonum imperium nulla vis laedit. Commodo Antonino tribuniciam potestatem rogamus, praesentiam tuam rogamus.* (5) *philosophiae tuae, patientiae tuae, doctrinae tuae, nobilitati tuae, innocentiae tuae. vincis inimicos, hostes exuperas, di te tuentur.' et reliqua.* („Frommer Antonius, die Götter mögen dich erhalten. Gütiger Antonius, die Götter mögen dich erhalten. Du hast gewollt, was erlaubt war, wir haben getan, was sich ziemte. (3) Wir erbitten für Commodus die rechtmäßige Herrschaft. Mach stark dein eigen Fleisch und Blut. Mach, daß unsere Kinder in Sicherheit wohnen. (4) Einem guten Regiment kann keine Gewalt etwas anhaben. Für Commodus Antonius bitten wir um die tribunizische Gewalt, wir bitten um deine Gegenwart. (5) Heil deiner Lebensweisheit, Heil deiner Nachsicht, deiner Gelehrsamkeit, deinem Edelmut, deiner unsträflichen Gesinnung. Du besiegst die inneren, du überwindest die äußeren Feinde, die Götter beschirmen dich' usw.").

173 Vgl. z. B. HA Ant. 3,1; Max. 16,3–7.26,2–4; Gord. 5,7; Alex. 6,3–12,1; Claud. 4,3–

der Autor eine neue, vielstimmige Sprecherinstanz. Diese äußert zwar vordergründig Zustimmung, doch der senatorische Lobpreis der kaiserlichen *philosophia*, *patientia*, *doctrina*, *nobilitas* und *innocentia* wird mit zahlreichen Hinweise auf Commodus verbunden und damit erneut nachhaltig in Frage gestellt.[174] Denn daß es denn auch ausgerechnet Commodus war, der die durch die Milde Marc Aurels und diesen Senatsbeschlusses verschonten Angehörigen des Avidius schließlich doch umgebracht hat, erfährt der Leser bereits kurz darauf.[175]

Darauf folgt in der Biographie nur noch ein weiteres fiktives Schreiben,[176] in dem Avidius Cassius selbst den letzten Beitrag zu dieser Diskussion liefern und der nachsichtigen Art der Herrschaftsausübung durch Marc Aurel die klassischen *exempla* tatkräftiger *virtus* aus der Republik gegenüberstellen darf.[177] Wenn er ihn dann in seinem Schlußwort noch einmal als weltfremden Philosophen charakterisiert – *Marcus Antoninus philosophatur et quaerit de elementis et de animis et de honesto et iusto nec sentit pro re publica*[178] –, dann ergibt sich für den Leser, der am Ende der *vita Avidii* und damit der Behandlung der Zeit Marc Aurels in der *Historia Augusta* angekommen ist, doch eine deutliche Relativierung der weitgehend positiven Sicht auf philosophische Interessen dieses Kaisers, die er in dessen eigener Biographie kennengelernt hatte.[179]

4.182–3; Tac. 4,2–4.5,1–3.7,1.4.; Prob. 11,6–9. Als authentisch gelten allein die Akklamationen nach dem Tod des Commodus, für die sich der Autor auf Marius Maximus beruft, der an der entsprechenden Sitzung wahrscheinlich teilgenommen hat: vgl. HA Comm. 18–19 mit Scheithauer (s. Anm. 8) 96 ff.

174 Vgl. dag. z. B. Scheithauer (s. Anm. 8) 46.

175 Vgl. HA Avid. 13,6–7: *vixerunt igitur posteri Avidii Cassii securi et ad honores admissi sunt.* (7) *sed eos Commodus Antoninus post excessum divi patris sui omnes vivos incendi iussit, quasi in factione depr[a]ehensos.* („So lebten denn die Nachkommen des Avidius Cassius ungekränkt und erhielten Zutritt zur Ämterlaufbahn. (7) Doch Commodus Antoninus ließ sie nach dem Hingang seines vergötlichten Vaters sämtlich lebendig verbrennen, als wären es ertappte Verschwörer.").

176 Zum Abschluß der Biographie mit einem Brief vgl. Leo (s. Anm. 1) 296 ff., der unter anderem auf die Briefanhänge in den Viten des Diogenes Laertius verweist.

177 Vgl. HA Avid. 14,3–4: *miser[a] Marcus, homo sane optimus, qui, dum clemens dici cupit, eos patitur vivere, quorum ipse non probat vitam.* (4) *ubi Lucius Cassius, cuius nos frustra tenet nomen? ubi Marcus ille Cato Censorius? ubi omnis disciplina maiorum? quae olim quidem intercidit, nunc vero nec quaeritur.* („Bedauernswert [ist] Marcus, gewiß ein vortrefflicher Mensch, der in dem Wunsch im Ruf der Milde zu stehen, diejenigen am Leben läßt, deren Lebenswandel er mißbilligt. (4) Wo ist Lucius Cassius geblieben, dessen Name für uns Schall und Rauch ist? Wo der berühmte Marcus Cato Censorius? Wo die ganze straffe Zucht der Altvordern? Sie ist zwar schon längst entschunden, doch heutzutage vermißt man sie nicht einmal mehr.").

178 Vgl. HA Avid. 14,5 („Marcus Antoninus spielt den Weltweisen und spintisiert über die Elemente und über das Wesen der Seele und über Sittlichkeit und Gerechtigkeit und hat kein Herz für den Staat.").

179 Vgl. Delande (s. Anm. 90) 144: „La biographie de Marc-Aurèle a fait de son empereur

4. Fazit und Ausblick

Wenn man abschließend noch einmal die Wandlungen in der Wahrnehmung des ‚Philosophen auf dem Kaiserthron' in diesen drei Biographien Revue passieren läßt, so zeigt sich deutlich, daß die in der *vita Marci* präsentierte freundliche Version, die im übrigen Marc Aurels eigenen Äußerungen zu diesem Thema in seinen ‚Selbstbetrachtungen' sehr nahekommt,[180] im Laufe der Lektüre mehrfach in Frage gestellt wird, ohne dadurch jedoch vollständig aufgehoben zu werden. Vielmehr ergibt sich auf diese Weise eine differenziertere und durch den Leser erst nach und nach zu erschließende Form der Darstellung und Bewertung.

Zu diesem Zweck greift der Autor der *Historia Augusta* neben einer ganzen Reihe anderer Darstellungstechniken vor allem auf zwei narrative Strategien zurück: Zum einen kommt in diesem Zusammenhang bereits der grundsätzlichen Entscheidung, den Mitregenten Lucius Verus und den Gegenkaiser Avidius Cassius in eigenen Biographien zu behandeln, große Bedeutung zu, weil es durch die Einführung dieser Nebenviten – ebenso wie durch die Aufteilung der *vita Marci* in zwei inhaltlich zum Teil redundante Durchgänge – möglich wird, dieselben Ereignisse in mehreren Versionen und damit zugleich aus unterschiedlichen Perspektiven zu schildern. Zum anderen führen die zahlreichen impliziten und vor allem die bewußt inszenierten expliziten Widersprüche dazu, daß der Leser das Vertrauen in die Glaubwürdigkeit des Erzählers verliert und daher nach und nach auch an der auf den ersten Blick zustimmenden Version der *vita Marci* zu zweifeln beginnt.

---

philosophe, le meilleur des candiats à l'Empire. La *Vita Veri* dresse aussi un portrait élogieux de Marcus. Mais la vie politique de Marc-Aurèle ne fur dénuée d'épreuves et il est possible de se demander d'après la *Vita Marci* si les vertus stoïciennes de l'empereur qui se reflètent dans le gouvernement de l'Empire, ont donné satisfaction à tous. Avec la *Vita Cassii*, le biographe pose clairement la question, et il devient facile de déceler dans ce texte le portrait selon lui de l'empereur idéal.", u. dag. z.B. Baynes (s Anm. 41) 84; Syme (s. Anm. 55) 297: "Setting Avidius against Marcus, he is not proposing to depreciate that lay-saint. Indeed, the Vita (it has been claimed) is not so much a panegyric of Avidius as an illustration of the clemency of Marcus.", u. Scheithauer (s. Anm. 8) 90 ff.

180 Vgl. v. a. M. Aur. 6,47,6 (τοῖς μηδ' ὀνομαζομένοις ὅλως; ἓν ὧδε πολλοῦ ἄξιον, τὸ μετ' ἀληθείας καὶ δικαιοσύνης εὐμενῆ τοῖς ψεύσταις καὶ ἀδίκοις διαβλοῦν) u. 6,50,1 sowie ferner Peter Brunt, Marcus Aurelius in his Meditations, Journal of Roman Studien 64 (1974), 1–20, h. 11 f., u. Rosen (s. Anm. 148) 94 ff. Eine direkte Verwendung der ‚Selbstbetrachtungen', die von ihrem Autor nicht zur Publikation bestimmt waren und auch sonst kaum Rezeptionsspuren hinterlassen haben, ist aber eher unwahrscheinlich; vgl. Klaus Rosen, Marc Aurels Selbstbetrachtungen und die Historia Augusta, Historiae Augustae Colloquium Perusinum, Bari 2002, 421–425.

Aus der Relativierung der positiven Sicht auf den ‚Philosophen auf den Kaiserthron' sollte aber auch nicht auf die Propagierung des in der *vita Avidii* entworfenen Gegenbildes als Intention geschlossen werden. Zwar lassen sich in der *Historia Augusta* nicht nur weitere Beispiele für eine positive Präsentation skrupelloser Soldatenkaiser,[181] sondern auch für eine negative Bewertung der intellektuellen Interessen eines Herrschers finden. Denn trotz einiger programmatischer Aussagen zur ihrer Relevanz[182] spielt der Aspekt der Bildung in der *Historia Augusta* – im Gegensatz etwa zu Sueton[183] – bei der eigentlichen Darstellung der Protagonisten mit wenigen Ausnahmen[184] nur eine geringe[185] und häufig nicht sehr vorteilhafte Rolle: So wird bei Hadrian vor allem seine Arroganz im Umgang mit Intellektuellen hervorgehoben[186] und bei Aelius dient die Nennung von Apicius, Ovid und Martial als Lieblingslektüre in erster Linie der Illustration seines Hanges zur *luxuria*.[187] Letztlich jedoch ergibt sich aus der Interpretation der Einzelstellen weder ein kohärentes Bild für die Bewertung von Bildung im allgemeinen[188] noch von Marc Aurels philosophischen Interessen im besonderen.

Die Beobachtung, daß die Beurteilung von Personen oder Sachverhalten in der *Historia Augusta* häufig in der Schwebe gelassen wird, kann jedoch nur denjenigen überraschen, der dieses Werk primär in historiographischen Kategorien

---

181 Vgl. z.B. Pesc. 3,3–4,8; Clod. 10,4–11,6 u. Opil. 12 sowie ferner Syme (s. Anm. 55) 295 ff., u. allg. zur positiven Bewertung auch einer rigiden Form der *disciplina* in der *Historia Augusta* allg. Bohumila Mouchova, *Crudelitas principis optimi*, BHAC 1970 (1972), 167–194.

182 Vgl. z.B. HA Tac. 4,4: *ecquis melius quam litteratus imperat*? sowie ferner Alfons Rösger, Herrschererziehung in der Historia Augustua, Bonn 1978, 9 ff., u. Wolfgang Kirsch, *Cura vatum*. Staat und Literatur in der lateinischen Spätantike, Philologus 124 (1980), 274–89.

183 Vgl. Andrew Wallace-Hadrill, Suetonius. The Scholar and his Caesars, London 1983 (= ²1995), 83 ff. u. ferner allg. zur Rolle der *studia* bei der Darstellung von Personen im Kontext der Bildungskultur des 2. Jh. n. Chr. Pausch (s. Anm. 67) 9 ff.

184 Die wichtigste Ausnahme stellt die ausführliche Behandlung der positiv bewerteten, wahrscheinlich aber fiktiven literarischen Aktivitäten des ‚Musterkaisers' Severus Alexander dar (vgl. HA Alex. 27,5–8; 30,1–3 u. 31,4–5 sowie ferner z.B. Gord. 3,2–3 u. 4,7).

185 Dies gilt selbst dann, wenn es wegen der allgemein günstigen Beurteilung des Kaisers (vgl. z.B. HA Ant. 11,2–3) oder aufgrund besonderer Umstände nahegelegen hätte (vgl. die Tätigkeit des Pertinax als *grammaticus*: HA Pert. 1,4 sowie ferner 11,3 u. 12,7).

186 Vgl. HA Hadr. 14,8–9 u. 15,10–16,11 sowie ferner Rösger (s. Anm.182) 24.

187 Vgl. HA Ael. 5,9. Zu Verus' geistigen Talenten als Chiffre der Mittelmäßigkeit; vgl. HA Ver. 2,5–2,8 u. s. o. S. 135.

188 Vgl. aber den Versuch von Rösger (s. Anm. 182) 21 ff., der eine Unterscheidung zwischen positiv bewerteter ‚praktischer' Schulbildung und negativ bewerteter ‚zweckfreier' Beschäftigung mit Kunst und Wissenschaft in der *Historia Augusta* vorschlägt.

wahrnimmt. Die von seinem Autor angewandten literarischen Techniken zielen hingegen gerade darauf, den Leser an einer zu schnellen und zu einfachen Urteilsbildung zu hindern und auf diese Weise für ihn den Reiz der Lektüre zu erhöhen. Der literarische Charakter des Textes wird auch noch durch einen anderen Effekt gesteigert, der sich einstellt, wenn sich eine Erzählinstanz als unzuverlässig erweist, und der darin besteht, daß die Aufmerksamkeit des Lesers auf die Art und Weise der Präsentation gelenkt wird.[189]

Diese starke Betonung der artifiziellen Seite und der ästhetischen Aspekte des eigenen Werkes scheint nur schlecht zu der vom Autor der *Historia Augusta* mehrfach aufgestellten Behauptung zu passen, daß ihm die Zuverlässigkeit des Inhalt weitaus wichtiger sei als die Gefälligkeit der Form und daß er sein Werk als bloße Materialsammlung für einen begabteren Schriftsteller verstanden wissen will.[190] Hält man sich jedoch vor Augen, daß dieser ohnehin topische Ge-

---

189 Vgl. Nünning (wie Anm. 98) 19 „Das allgemeine Resultat des als *unreliable narration* bezeichneten Phänomens besteht somit darin, die Aufmerksamkeit des Rezipienten von der Ebene des Geschehens auf den Sprecher zu verlagern und dessen Idiosynkrasien hervorzuheben (…). Nicht die Handlung steht im Zentrum, sondern die Perspektive und die Normabweichung des Erzählers."

190 Vgl. Prob. 2,6–7: *illud tantum contestatum volo me et rem scripsisse, quam, si quis voluerit, honestius eloquio celsiore demonstret, et mihi quidem id animi fuit, (7) <ut> non Sallustios, Livios, Tacito<s>, Trogos atque omnes disertissimos imitarer viros in vita principum et temporibus disserendis, sed Marium Maximum, Suetonium Tranquillum, Fabium Marcellinum, Gargilium Martialem, Iulium Capitolinum, Aelium Lampridium ceterosque, qui haec et talia non tam diserte quam vere memoriae tradiderunt* („Nur das wünsche ich ausdrücklich festgestellt zu haben, daß ich den Stoff geliefert habe, den, wer will, in höherem Stil glänzender aufputzen mag, (7) sowie daß es meine Absicht war, in der Behandlung von Leben und Zeit der Kaiser nicht Männer wie Sallust, Livius, Tacitus und Trogus und alle Meister der Kunstprosa nachzuahmen, sondern den Marius Maximus, den Suetonius Tranquillus, den Fabius Marcellinus, den Gargilius Martialis, den Iulius Capitolinus, den Aelius Lampridius und die übrigen, die bei der Behandlung dieser und ähnlicher Themen nicht so sehr auf einen glatten, gefälligen Stil als vielmehr auf Wahrhaftigkeit gehalten haben.") u. Car. 21,2–3: *habe, mi amice, meum munus, quod ego, ut s<a>ep[a]e dixi, non eloquentiae causa sed curiositatis in lumen edidi, id praecipu[a]e agens, ut, si quis eloque<n>s vellet facta principum reserare, materiam non requireret, habiturus meos libellos ministros eloquii. (3) te quaeso, sis contentus nosque sic voluisse scribere melius quam potuisse contendas* („So nimm denn, lieber Freund, diese meine Gabe; wie ich des öfteren gesagt, habe ich sie nicht ans Licht gebracht, um mit Stilkünsten zu prunken, sondern um die Wißbegier zu befriedigen. Dabei war es mein Hauptanliegen, einem kommenden beredten Darsteller der Kaisergeschichte den erforderlichen Stoff zu bieten; er mag meine kleinen Bücher als Hilfsmittel seiner Kunstprosa verwenden. (3) An Dich richte ich die Bitte, Dich mit dem Gebotenen abzufinden und anzuerkennen, daß unser guter Wille bei der Abfassung stärker war als unser Vollbringen.") sowie ferner den Hengst (s. Anm. 12) 119ff.

danke[191] zum ersten Mal ausgerechnet in der *vita* des fiktiven Kaisers Censorinus formuliert wird,[192] und zieht man ferner den wenig glaubwürdigen Charakter der übrigen programmatischen Aussagen in der *Historia Augusta* zum Vergleich heran, so zeigt sich schnell, daß das genaue Gegenteil richtig sein dürfte:[193] Trotz seiner anderslautenden Beteuerungen steht für den Autor weder die Vermittlung historischen Wissens noch die Propagierung eines bestimmten Geschichtsbildes im Vordergrund.[194]

---

191 Die Strategie, sein eigenes Werk als bloßen *commentarius* auszugeben, wurde bekanntermaßen bereits von Caesar angewandt und auch schon von seinen Zeitgenossen durchschaut (vgl. Cic. Brut. 262).

192 Vgl. HA tyr. trig. 33,8: *da nunc cuivis libellum non tam diserte quam fideliter scriptum. neque ego eloquentiam mihi videor pollicitus esse, sed rem, qui hos libellos, quos de vita principum edidi, non scribo sed dicto, et dicto cum ea festinatione, quam, si quid vel ipse promisero vel tu petieris, sic perurgueo, ut respirandi non habeam facultatem* („Gib nun, wem Du willst, dieses Büchlein, das weniger auf gepflegten Stil als auf Zuverlässigkeit bedacht ist. Denn ich bin mir bewußt, nicht eine elegante Darstellung, sondern den Stoff selbst in Aussicht gestellt zu haben; denn diese kleinen Bücher, die ich über das Leben der Kaiser verfaßt habe, schreibe ich nicht, sondern diktiere sie, und zwar diktiere ich in solcher Hast, die ich, wenn ich ein Versprechen gegeben habe oder Du einen Wunsch geäußert hast, so forciere, daß ich nicht mehr zu Atem komme.").

193 Vgl. z. B. den Hengst (s. Anm. 12) 174: „Der Autor verspricht seinen Lesern wiederholt *res, non verba*. Er macht genau das Gegenteil von dem, was er verspricht. Die Leser können sich aber damit trösten, daß es zwischen dem historischen Wert des Werkes und seinem literarischen eine ratio inversa gibt." u. Andreas Mehl, Römische Geschichtsschreibung. Grundlagen und Entwicklungen, Stuttgart 2001, 152: „Indem er dabei für sein eigenes Vorhaben höhere stilistische Ansprüche zurückweist und die von ihm abgelehnten Autoren als ‚überaus beredt‘, die von ihm als vorbildlich vorgestellten jedoch als ‚nicht so beredt wie wahrheitsliebend‘ bezeichnet, nimmt er zwar eine Haltung ein, mit der antike Historiker immer wieder die Ernsthaftigkeit ihrer Sache herausgestellt und verteidigt haben, doch zugleich diskreditiert er das als bloße Attitüde: …"

194 Vgl. z. B. den Hengst (s. Anm. 12) 161: „I do not believe that the author intended to teach his readers any lesson, moral or otherwise." u. dag. z. B. Scheithauer (s. Anm. 8) 142 mit Anm. 37: „… der Biograph ist trotz des lockeren Spiels, das er mit seinem Publikum treibt, darauf bedacht, auf die Leser mit seinem Werk im Sinn der prosenatorischen Tendenz einzuwirken." Insbesondere läßt sich die Vermittlung eines bestimmten Geschichtsbildes nur schwer mit der Unzuverlässigkeit der historischen Erzählung vereinbaren: vgl. Jörn Rüsen, Historischer Vernunft. Grundzüge einer Historik I: Die Grundlagen der Geschichtswissenschaft, Göttingen 1983, 78: „Identität, die im Erzählen von Geschichten zur Sprache kommt, ist kein fixer Tatbestand. … Weil das so ist … pflegen Geschichten nicht blind geglaubt zu werden. Sie müssen so erzählt werden, daß der an ihnen im Kampf um Anerkennung geäußerte Zweifel nicht aufkommen kann oder durch sie selbst, in der Art, wie sie erzählt werden, ausgeräumt wird. Geschichten begegnen solch einem Zweifel dadurch, daß sie ihre

Zugleich wollte er aber wohl auch kein mit mehr oder weniger glaubwürdigen historischen Mirabilien gefülltes ‚Volksbuch‘[195] schreiben, obwohl eine solche Rezeption natürlich nicht ausgeschlossen werden kann.[196] Vielmehr erweist sich die *Historia Augusta* als ein Werk, in dem der historische Inhalt in literarisch anspruchsvoller Form mit der Unterhaltung des Lesers verbunden ist. Seine volle Wirkung kann es jedoch nur dann entfalten, wenn es auf einen Rezipienten trifft, der über Kenntnisse der römischen Geschichte bereits in einem hinreichendem Maße verfügt,[197] um die besondere Version, die ihm die *Historia Augusta* bietet, adäquat goutieren zu können.[198] Vor dem Hintergrund dieser Überlegungen wird es bei dem Zielpublikum des Werkes wahrscheinlich um den nicht allzu großen Kreis der Bildungselite innerhalb der senatorischen Oberschicht gehandelt haben.[199] Auch der Autor selbst wird in diesem Milieu zu suchen sein, entweder

---

Glaubwürdigkeit begründen. Sie geben Gründe dafür, warum man ihnen trauen und sich mit ihnen in der Zeit orientieren kann. Es geht ihnen dabei um das, was man ihre ‚Wahrheit‘ (umgangssprachlich) nennt. ‚Wahr‘ pflegt man diejenigen Geschichten zu nennen, denen man zustimmen kann, …“

195 Vgl. z.B. Hohl (s. Anm. 47) 298: „Wenn man die Historia Augusta gelegentlich ein ‚Volksbuch‘ bezeichnet hat, so trifft dieser Begriff, cum grano salis genommen, ihr Wesen nicht übel. Daß aber auch ein vornehmer Mann wie Symmachus es nicht verschmäht, ein so vulgäres Machwerk nicht nur zu lesen, sondern als fast wörtlich reproduzierte Quelle der eigenen ‚historia‘ zugrunde zu legen, das ist immerhin auffallend.“ u. ferner die ablehnende Diskussion der These bei Scheithauer (s. Anm. 8) 151 f. (mit weiterer Lit.).

196 Vgl. z.B. Scheithauer (s. Anm. 8) 150: „Personen mit geringerer Bildung dagegen sind nicht in der Lage, diese Anspielungen zu verstehen, sondern halten sie für das geistige Eigentum des Autors und freuen sich an den Kuriositäten, die ihnen das Werk vermittelt.“

197 Erinnert sei erneut an die Spiegelung der intendierten Rezeptionsformen im Text, vor allem in Form des sogenannten literarischen ‚Kränzchen‘ mit dem *amator historiarum Marcus Fonteius* (vgl. HA quadr. tyr. 2,1–3 u. s. o. S. 118 f.).

198 Daß der Autor mit dem Begriff *mythistoriae*, den er zur Bezeichnung der Schriften des Cordus (vgl. HA Opil. 1,5) und des Marius Maximus (vgl. HA Quadr. 1,2) verwendet, auch die spezifische Form der Präsentation von historischem Wissen in seinem eigenen Werk charakterisieren wollte, ist denkbar (vgl. z.B. Syme (s. Anm. 55) 307, u. Scheithauer (s. Anm. 8) 143), aber nicht zwingend anzunehmen.

199 Wenn man davon ausgeht, daß die *Historia Augusta* in ihrem Geschichtsbild keine klare Tendenz verfolgt, ist eine darüber hinausgehende Eingrenzung auf den heidnischen Teil der Senatsaristokratie nicht notwendig (vgl. aber z.B. Scheithauer (s. Anm. 8) 150: „Um zur vom Autor intendierten Leserschaft zu zählen, ist neben höherer Bildung noch ein weiteres Kriterium wichtig, nämlich die Identifikation mit senatorischen Idealen und Wertmaßstäben, die bei den meisten Mitgliedern des Senates eine einheitliche Denk- und Verhaltensweise hervorruft. Die Anforderungen, die der Biograph mit seinem Werk an die Leser stellt, erfüllen am besten die Nachkommen der senatorischer Familien, die mit ihrem geerbten Vermögen, den Verhaltens-

als Mitglied der Aristokratie[200] oder als professioneller ‚Intellektueller‘, wenn auch vielleicht nicht unbedingt als *grammaticus*.[201]

Jedenfalls läßt sich annehmen, daß beide Seiten, der für uns anonym bleibende Autor und seine ursprünglichen Adressaten, Elemente wie eine indirekte und häufig ambivalente Charakterisierung der Protagonisten oder die mehrfache Wiedergabe eines Ereignisses aus unterschiedlichen Perspektiven als reizvolle literarische Techniken zu schätzen wußten. Vergleichbare Strategien zur stärkeren Narrativierung der Wiedergabe historischen Geschehens sind zwar in der Geschichtsschreibung der römischen Kaiserzeit durchaus nicht unüblich. Mit der Häufung und der Konsequenz ihrer Verwendung geht die *Historia Augusta* jedoch deutlich über das etwa bei Herodian oder Ammianus Marcellinus zu beobachtende Maß hinaus.[202] Eine solche Verlagerung des Akzentes von der reinen Informationsvermittlung hin zur stärkeren Literalisierung der Darstellung sowie zur intensiveren Beteiligung und Unterhaltung des Lesers ist vor allem dann unproblematisch, wenn den zeitgenössischen Rezipienten zugleich Geschichtswerke im engeren Sinne zur Verfügung standen, die sie mit den zum vollen Verständnis der *Historia Augusta* notwendigen geschichtlichen Grundkenntnissen versorgen konnten.

Eine solche Situation läßt sich für die Jahre um die Wende vom 4. zum 5. Jh. n. Chr. plausibel rekonstruieren: Der zu dieser Zeit an historischen Informationen interessierte Leser konnte neben verschiedenen älteren Darstellungen zum einen auf die von Aurelius Victor (360/61) und Eutrop (um 370) vor rund einer Generation verfassten Überblicksdarstellungen zurückgreifen, zum anderen lag ihm aber vor allem das gegen Ende des 4. Jh. n. Chr. beendete Werk des Ammianus Marcellinus vor, das im Anschluß an die Annalen und Historien des Tacitus den Zeitraum von Nerva bis Valens (96–378) behandelte und auf diese Weise eine ausführliche und seriöse Darstellung der gesamten römischen Kaiserzeit bot.[203] Der Umstand, daß zu Beginn des 5. Jh. n. Chr. gleich mehrere im engeren Sinne historiographische Werke vorhanden waren, macht das Entstehen eines Werkes wie der *Historia Augusta* in diesem Zeitraum besonders wahrscheinlich.[204] Ordnet man

---

weisen einer vornehmen Person, einer guten Ausbildung in Recht, Redekunst, Literatur und Geschichte den traditionsbewußten, angesehenen Adel bilden, dessen typischer Vertreter Symmachus ist.“

200 Vgl. z. B. Scheithauer (s. Anm. 8) 152 f. Zur Identifizierung mit Nicomachos Flavianus *senior* bzw. *iunior* s. o. Anm. S. 108 Anm. 5.

201 Vgl. aber Hohl (s. Anm. 47) 306 ff. u. Syme (s. Anm. 212) 183 ff., 197 f.

202 Zu den narrativen Parallelen in diesen beiden Werken s. o. S. 113 f.

203 Daneben ist auch an die in diesem Zeitraum entstandene christliche Historiographie zu denken (z. B. die zwei Bücher umfassene *Chronica* des Sulpicius Severus aus dem Jahre 403 n. Chr.).

204 Zum Verständnis der Jahre zwischen 350 und 430 n. Chr. als einer besonders produk-

nämlich die *Historia Augusta* in das breite Spektrum der Literatur, die sich in der römischen Kaiserzeit mit der Vermittlung historischen Wissens beschäftigt, ein, so läßt sie sich am ehesten als eine subsidiäre oder komplementäre Form begreifen, die die Verfügbarkeit regulärer Geschichtswerke voraussetzt.

Aus diesen Überlegungen läßt sich in zugespitzter Form die Folgerung ableiten, daß die Existenz der *res gestae* des Ammianus Marcellinus aus literaturgeschichtlicher Sicht den *terminus post quem* für die Abfassung der *Historia Augusta* darstellen. Eine solche Konstellation würde im übrigen diejenige wiederholen, die sich an der Wende vom 1. zum 2. Jh. n. Chr. ergeben hatte: Auch nach der Fertigstellung der taciteischen Historien und Annalen läßt sich im Umgang mit historischen Inhalten ein stärkeres Interesse für die literarische Form und eine stärkere Betonung der Unterhaltung des Lesers beobachten.[205]

Weniger exakt läßt sich aus literaturgeschichtlicher Sicht ein *terminus ante quem* bestimmen. Allerdings ändert sich vor dem Hintergrund der politischen und militärischen Wirren des 5. Jh. n. Chr. auch bald das kulturelle Klima. An die Stelle der souveränen und selbstverständlichen Beherrschung der Bildungsinhalte, die den lockeren und spielerischen Umgang mit ihnen erst ermöglicht hatte, tritt angesichts des drohenden Verlustes dieser Tradition eine ernstere und konzentriertere Art des Rekurses, in der gerade den Bezügen auf die eigene Geschichte eine in hohem Maße identitätsstiftende Funktion zukommen.[206] Daher bieten gerade die Jahre unmittelbar um die Wende vom 4. zum 5. Jh. und noch vor der in ihrer symbolischen Wirkung nicht zu unterschätzenden Einnahme Roms durch den Gotenkönig Alarich im Jahre 410 n. Chr., in denen auch die in ihrem Umgang mit literarischer Bildung vergleichbaren *Saturnalia* des Macrobius entstanden sein dürften,[207] sicherlich das plausibelste Umfeld für die Enstehung der *Historia Augusta*.[208]

---

tiven ‚Blütezeit der lateinischen Literatur in der Spätantike' vgl. Siegmar Döpp, Die Blütezeit latinischer Literatur in der Spätantike (350–430 n. Chr.). Charakteristika einer Epoche, Philologus 132 (1988), 19–52, u. Manfred Fuhrmann, Rom in der Spätantike. Porträt einer Epoche, München 1994, 51 ff.

205 Diese Entwicklung setzt bereits in den Briefen des jüngeren Plinius ein, läßt sich aber auch bei Sueton und Gellius beobachten; vgl. Pausch (s. Anm. 67) v. a. 30 ff.

206 Vgl. Ulrich Eigler, *lectiones vetustatis*. Römische Literatur und Geschichte in der lateinischen Literatur der Spätantike, Zetemata 115, München 2003.

207 Die Abfassungszeit dieses Dialoges, der an den an den Saturnalien wahrscheinlich des Jahres 384 n. Chr. spielt, ist jedoch umstritten. Der aus den obengenannten Gründen sehr plausiblen These einer Entstehung vor 410 n. Chr. (vgl. v. a. Siegmar Döpp, Zur Datierung von Macrobius ‚Saturnalia', Hermes 106 (1978), 619–632) steht eine Spätdatierung in die 430er Jahre gegenüber (vgl. v. a. Alan Cameron, The Date and Identity of Macrobius, Journal of Roman Studies 56 (1966), 25–38).

208 Diese Datierung der *Historia Augusta* entwickelt sich auch aus anderen Gründen mehr und mehr zur *communis opinio*: vgl. Johne (s. Anm. 9) 637 f.

Hält man sich die Vielzahl historiographischer Werke unterschiedlichen Zuschnitts vor Augen, die dem zeitgenössischen Rezipienten zu Beginn des 5. Jh. n. Chr. zur Verfügung standen, wird deutlich, daß erst der Zufall der Überlieferungsgeschichte, der auch für die heute gebräuchlichen Bezeichnung verantwortlich ist,[209] aus einem Werk, das sich als eine komplementäre Form verstanden hat und historische Inhalte in bewußt literarisierter Form bieten wollte,[210] faute de mieux eine historische Quelle gemacht hat. Befreit man sich bei der Lektüre von dieser falschen Erwartungshaltung, wird man es auch nicht mehr in erster Linie als ‚erbärmliches Machwerk' und ‚Lügenbuch'[211] empfinden, sondern als den schon von Sir Ronald Syme angekündigten „garden of delights, with abundant refreshment."[212]

Abstract

Whereas research activities on the Corpus known as "Historia Augusta" usually tend to focus on comparing the content with the informations procured by parallel traditions, it will be attempted here to confront a substantial passage of the work – which comprises the lives of Marcus Aurelius, his co-ruler Lucius Verus and the rival princeps Avidius Cassius – with other passages within the corpus of the Historia Augusta itself.

Thus, certain contradictions jump to the eye, especially with regard to the assessment of Marcus Aurelius' philosophical preferences; in the course of the work, these tend to find less and less favour with the author. I take these contra-

---

209 Zur Genese des heute gebräuchlichen Titels s. o. S. 108.

210 Damit muß nicht zwingend die Intention einer Persiflage der Historiographie im engeren Sinne einhergehen; vgl. aber Mehl (s. Anm. 193) 152: „Wenn … die *Historia Augusta* in raffinierter, oft erst auf den zweiten Blick erkennbarer Weise zwischen Wirklichkeit und Fiktion hin- und herpendelt und gerade dies als Charakteristikum der Geschichtsschreibung ausgibt (…), dann kann man den Verfasser oder Überarbeiter der Kaiserbiographien über die Zunft der Historiker und ihre hehren Prinzipien schallend lachen hören. Was ist also die *Historia Augusta*? Am Ende einer langen Reihe historiographischer und historisch-biographischer Werke, die stets ernstgenommen werden wollen, ist sie eine Persiflage auf die antike Geschichtsschreibung, genauer auf das, was diese laut eigenem Bekunden sein will. Das dürfte die zentrale Tendenz der *Historia Augusta* sein."

211 Vgl. Hohl (s. Anm. 47) 310: „Ein erbärmliches Machwerk ist und bleibt das Lügenbuch der sogenannten Scriptores, und wenn die Sache des Heidentums zu solchen Waffen greifen mußte, dann hatte sie den Untergang verdient."

212 Vgl. Ronald Syme, Ammianus and the Historia Augusta, Oxford 1968, 4: „However, the Historia Augusta is a garden of delights, with abundant refreshment."

dictions as my starting point , going on to interpret several other internal discrepancies to be found in a number of passages of the historia Augusta as elements of a consciously chosen literary strategy that could profitably be described within the conceptual framework of "unreliable narration".

This strategy is aimed at increasingly involving the reader during the course of his reading in a process of forming his own judgment on the respective historical personalities; consequently, the Historia Augusta tends to become a more stimulating work once one commits oneself to perceiving it primarily as a literary work. Today – due to the contingencies of textual transmission – the Historia Augusta is being read predominantly as a historical source; but to refrain from specifically literary interpretation does not do justice to the functionality of this work in the context of the times when it presumably has been composed, viz. around the turning point from the 4th to the 6th century A. D.

Anhang 1: Aufbau der besprochenen Biographien

vita Marci Antonini philosophi (Iulius Capitolinus)

Erster Durchgang (1–19):

– Familie und Geburt (1)
– Leben vor der Adoption (2–4)
– Adoption und Leben als Thronfolger (5–7,4)
– Gemeinsame Regierung mit Lucius Verus (7,5–14)
– Alleinregierung (15–17)
– Tod und Divinisierung (18)
– Verhältnis zu Commodus und Fazit (19)

Zweiter Durchgang (20–29):

– Distanzierung von Verus (20)
– Regierung bis zum Aufstand des Avidius Cassius (21–24,5)
– Regierung nach dem Aufstand des Avidius Cassius (24,5–27)
– Ausführliche *narratio* seines Todes (28)
– Vorwürfe wegen verschiedener negativer Charakterzüge (29)

vita Lucii Veri (Iulius Capitolinus)

– Bewertung als *princeps medius* (1,1–1,5)
– Familie und Geburt (1,6–1,9)
– Adoption, Erziehung und Leben als Thronfolger (2–3)
– Gemeinsame Regierung mit Marc Aurel (4,1–9,11)
– Diskussion der Gerüchte um eine Ermordung und Fazit (10–11)

vita Avidii Cassii (Vulcacius Gallicanus)

- Vorfahren und Jugend (1,1–2,8)
  - Briefwechsel zwischen Verus und Marc Aurel (1,6–2,8)
- Rechtfertigung der Behandlung von Gegenkaisern (3,1–3,3)
- Schilderung seines strengen Charakters (3,4–5,12)
  - Briefwechsel Marc Aurels mit einem Präfekten (5,4–5,12)
- Avidius als Legionskommandant in Syrien (6)
- Ausrufung zum Kaiser und Ermordung (7)
- Marc Aurels Milde gegenüber den Aufständischen (8,1–13,7)
  - Briefwechsel Marc Aurels mit Faustina (9,6–11,8)
  - Brief Marc Aurels an den Senat und dessen Reaktion (12,1–13,5)
- Fazit (13,8–14,8)
  - Brief des Avidius Cassius (14,1–14,8)

Σταυρωθεὶς δι' ἡμᾶς – Der Aufstand gegen Anastasios im Jahr 512

Mischa Meier

Im 5. und 6. Jahrhundert wurde Konstantinopel wiederholt von schweren Aufständen und Ausschreitungen erschüttert – Unruhen, die innerhalb kürzester Zeit mitunter derart gefährliche Dimensionen annehmen konnten, daß selbst die Kaiser um Thron und Leben fürchten mußten. Als Höhepunkt innerhalb einer Kette blutiger Tumulte in der Hauptstadt des Oströmischen Reiches gilt der sog. Nika-Aufstand gegen Justinian im Jahr 532; allein seine Niederschlagung soll etwa 30.000–35.000 Menschen das Leben gekostet haben, und ungezählt sind die Opfer, die diese Erhebung bereits bis zu diesem Zeitpunkt gefordert hatte.[1] Häufig verbanden sich mit den Unruhen schwere Plünderungen, Brandstiftungen und Verwüstungen in Konstantinopel; so gingen etwa im Nika-Aufstand große Teile des Stadtzentrums – darunter die Hagia Sophia – in Flammen auf.

Obwohl das Phänomen der *wiederholten* Aufstände in der östlichen Kaiserstadt während der ausgehenden Spätantike seit langem bekannt ist – Alexandra Čekalova zählt allein für die Regierungszeit der Kaiser Anastasios, Justin I. und Justinian (d. h. für die Jahre 491–565) mehr als 30 Erhebungen –,[2] wird der Nika-Aufstand weiterhin zumeist als herausragendes, geradezu singuläres Ereignis behandelt. Die Forschung erliegt dabei mehr oder weniger unreflektiert der Selbstdarstellung Justinians, der zur Stabilisierung seiner eigenen Herrschaft ganz gezielt darauf hingewirkt hat, daß die enorme Opferzahl des Jahres 532, die bis heute ihre furchtbare Ausdruckskraft nicht verloren hat, dauerhaft und überall bekannt wurde.[3] Demgegenüber tritt leicht in den Hintergrund, daß der Nika-Aufstand im Kontext des frühen 6. Jahrhunderts keineswegs einmalig war. Nur 20 Jahre zuvor, im November 512, war es unter Anastasios zu einem Aufruhr gekommen, dessen politische Sprengkraft durchaus erheblich war (mehr noch als

---

1 Zum Nika-Aufstand s. die noch immer grundlegende Arbeit von J. B. Bury, The Nika Riot, JHS 17 (1897), 92–119; daneben vgl. auch Chr. Gizewski, Zur Normativität und Struktur der Verfassungsverhältnisse in der späteren römischen Kaiserzeit, München 1988, 148 ff.; G. Greatrex, The Nika Riot: A Reappraisal, JHS 117 (1997), 60–86 (mit kurzem Forschungsüberblick: 60, Anm. 1); M. Meier, Die Inszenierung einer Katastrophe: Justinian und der Nika-Aufstand, ZPE 142 (2003), 273–300.

2 A. A. Čekalova, Der Nika-Aufstand, in: F. Winkelmann (Hg.), Volk und Herrschaft im frühen Byzanz. Methodische und quellenkritische Probleme, Berlin 1991, 11–17, hier 16.

3 Vgl. Meier (s. Anm. 1) 275 f.

beim Nika-Aufstand, bei dem vieles von höchster Ebene aus inszeniert war und
Justinian zu keinem Zeitpunkt die Handlungshoheit verlor)[4] und der lediglich
durch eine demonstrative Demutsgeste des Kaisers beendet werden konnte;[5] nur
aufgrund dieses brillanten Schachzugs des Anastasios erfahren die Ereignisse des
Jahres 512 in der althistorischen Forschung überhaupt eine gewisse Beachtung,
während in kirchengeschichtlichen Arbeiten vor allem die religions- und kirchenpolitischen Rahmenbedingungen erörtert werden. Eine umfassende Detail-
studie zu den Ausschreitungen des Jahres 512, dem sog. *Staurotheis*-Aufstand,
existiert m. W. jedenfalls nicht. Daß selbst Ernst Stein ihn lediglich als einen Ein-
leitungsakt zur Rebellion Vitalians (513–515) betrachtet, ist in dieser Hinsicht ein
mehr als deutliches Signal.[6]

---

4   Dazu im einzelnen Meier (s. Anm. 1) *passim*.
5   Vgl. G. Wirth, Anastasius, Christen und Perser. Zu den Problemen des Verhältnisses
    zwischen Staat und Kirche um die Wende zum 6. Jh., JbAC 32 (1990), 81–139, hier
    123: „[…] den schwersten Aufstand […], den die Stadt bisher gesehen hatte".
6   E. Stein, Histoire du bas-empire, tome II, publié par J.-R. Palanque, Paris/Bruges
    1949, ND Amsterdam 1968, 177f. Eine kurze Ereignisskizze bieten J. B. Bury, His-
    tory of the Later Roman Empire from the Death of Theodosius I to the Death of
    Justinian I, Bd. I, London 1923, ND 1958, 438f.; E. Schwartz, Publizistische Samm-
    lungen zum Acacianischen Schisma, in: Abhandlungen der Bayerischen Akademie der
    Wissenschaften, Phil.-hist. Abt., N.F. 10, Jg. 1934, München 1934, 247f.; C. Capizzi,
    L'imperatore Anastasio I (491–518), Rom 1969, 119–121; F. Tinnefeld, Die früh-
    byzantinische Gesellschaft. Struktur – Gegensätze – Spannungen, München 1977,
    188f.; C. Heucke, Circus und Hippodrom als politischer Raum. Untersuchungen
    zum großen Hippodrom von Konstantinopel und zu entsprechenden Anlagen in
    spätantiken Kaiserresidenzen, Hildesheim u. a. 1994, 282–285; L.-M. Günther, Ana-
    stasius 491–518, in: M. Clauss (Hg.), Die römischen Kaiser. 55 historische Portraits
    von Caesar bis Iustinian, München 1997, 418–424, hier 421f.; B. Croke, Count Mar-
    cellinus and His Chronicle, Oxford 2001, 111f. Kaum mehr als eine Erwähnung des
    Aufstandes findet sich bei A. H. M. Jones, The Later Roman Empire 284–602. A So-
    cial, Economic, and Administrative Survey, Vol. I, Oxford 1964, ND Baltimore 1986,
    234; A. Demandt, Die Spätantike. Römische Geschichte von Diocletian bis Justinian
    284–565 n. Chr., München 1989, 194; W. Treadgold, A History of the Byzantine State
    and Society, Stanford 1997, 171; A. D. Lee, The Eastern Empire: Theodosius to
    Anastasius, in: Av. Cameron/B. Ward-Perkins/M. Whitby (Hgg.), The Cambridge
    Ancient History, Vol. 14: Late Antiquity: Empire and Successors, A. D. 425–600,
    Cambridge 2000, 33–62, hier 56; P. Allen, The Definition and Enforcement of Ortho-
    doxy, ebd., 811–834, hier 819; B. Flusin, Triomphe du christianisme et définition de
    l'orthodoxie, in: C. Morrisson (Hg.), Le monde byzant. Tome I: L'Empire romain
    d'Orient 330–641, Paris 2004, 49–75, hier 72. Aus kirchenhistorischer Perspektive
    finden sich kurze Skizzen bei L. Duchesne, L'Église au VIe siècle, Paris 1925, 35f.;
    R. Haacke, Die kaiserliche Politik in den Auseinandersetzungen um Chalkedon (451–
    553), in: A. Grillmeier/H. Bacht (Hgg.), Das Konzil von Chalkedon. Geschichte und
    Gegenwart. Bd. 2: Entscheidung um Chalkedon, Würzburg ²1962, 95–177, hier 134;

Auf den ersten Blick erscheint der *Staurotheis*-Aufstand in einem ausschließ-lich kirchenpolitischen Kontext: Die Quellen berichten übereinstimmend, daß der Versuch, dem *Trisagion* die umstrittene theopaschitische *Staurotheis*-Formel hinzuzufügen, die Ausschreitungen ausgelöst habe.[7] Insofern gelten die Unruhen

---

P. Charanis, Church and State in the Later Roman Empire. The Religious Policy of Anastasius the First, 491–518, Thessaloniki ²1974, 78 f.; P. T. R. Gray, The Defense of Chalcedon in the East (451–553), Leiden 1979, 40 f., sowie ganz kurz bei H.-G. Beck, Die frühbyzantinische Kirche, in: K. Baus/H.-G. Beck/E. Ewig/H. J. Vogt (Hgg.), Die Reichskirche nach Konstantin dem Großen, Zweiter Halbband: Die Kirche in Ost und West von Chalkedon bis zum Frühmittelalter (451–700) (= Handbuch der Kir-chengeschichte, hg. v. H. Jedin, Bd. 2), Freiburg 1975/1985, ND 1999, 1–92, hier 13 f. Sehr knapp ist W. H. C. Frend, The Rise of the Monophysite Movement. Chapters in the History of the Church in the Fifth and Sixth Centuries, Cambridge 1972, 220. – Die soeben erschienene Arbeit von F. Haarer, Anastasius I: Politics and Empire in the Late Roman World, Leeds 2006, war mir noch nicht zugänglich.

7   Zu Ursprung und Geschichte des *Trisagions* (d. h. der liturgischen Hymnos-Formel ῎Αγιος ὁ θεός, ἅγιος ἰσχυρός, ἅγιος ἀθάνατος, ἐλέησον ἡμᾶς) s. etwa S. Brock, The Thrice-Holy Hymn in the Liturgy, Sobornost [Incorporating Eastern Churches Review] 7 (1985), 24–34, bes. 28 ff.; A. Louth, Trishagion, TRE 34 (2002), 121–124. – Die Offenbarung und Einführung des *Trisagions*, das erstmals von Nestorios erwähnt wird (Nestorius. Le livre d'Héraclide de Damas. Traduit en français par F. Nau, Paris 1910, 319) und auf dem Konzil von Chalkedon 451 bereits bekannt war (E. Schwartz [Ed.], Concilium Universale Chalcedonense, Vol. I, Pars 1 [= ACO II.1.1], Berlin/ Leipzig 1933, p. 195,30), erscheint in der Überlieferung in legendenhafter Verzerrung (vgl. etwa C. de Boor [Ed.], Theophanis Chronographia, Vol. I, Leipzig 1883, ND Hildesheim 1963, p. 93,5–20 [a. m. 5930]; H. Delehaye [Ed.], Synaxarium Ecclesiae Constantinopolitanae, Brüssel 1902, p. 79,18–80,21 Nr. 5 [zum 25. September]; M. Pinder [Ed.], Ioannis Zonarae Epitome Historiarum Libri XVIII, Tomus III, Ber-lin 1897, p. 112,13–18 [= Zon. 13,23,45–46]). Demzufolge soll der Hymnos im Jahr 438 in Konstantinopel während einer Bittprozession infolge mehrerer Erdbeben der bußfertigen Menge in einer Wundererscheinung verkündet worden sein (zur Datierung s. B. Croke, Two Early Byzantine Earthquakes and Their Liturgical Com-memoration, Byz 51 [1981], 122–147, bes. 126–131). In Konstantinopel, Jerusalem und im Westen wurde die Formel auf die Trinität bezogen, während sie in Syrien christologisch, d. h. auf Christus den Sohn bezogen, ausgelegt wurde. Als Petros der Walker (Petros Knapheus, Petrus Fullo; zu ihm s. P. Bruns, Petrus der Walker [Fullo], in: S. Döpp/W. Geerlings [Hgg.], Lexikon der antiken christlichen Literatur, Frei-burg/ Basel/Wien ³2002, 572 f.), seit 471 mit Unterbrechungen Patriarch von Antiocheia, zur Verdeutlichung der christologischen Interpretation dem *Trisagion* die *Staurotheis*-Formel ὁ σταυρωθεὶς δι' ἡμᾶς hinzufügen ließ, stieß er damit auf mas-siven Widerstand der Chalkedon-Anhänger, die – ausgehend von einer trinitarischen Deutung des Hymnos – in dem Zusatz eine miaphysitische Verzerrung im Sinne eines Postulats der Leidensfähigkeit der göttlichen Natur (Theopaschismus) erblickten. Im frühen 6. Jh. hatte sich die Frage um den *Trisagion*-Zusatz – zumindest in Konstanti-nopel – bereits zu einem brisanten Politikum mit erheblichem Symbolwert entwickelt.

des Jahres 512 mitunter als ein religiös motiviertes Pendant zum späteren Nika-Aufstand, der als vorwiegend politischer Akt gesehen wird.[8] Bereits die Tatsache, daß die umstrittene Weisung, das *Trisagion* zu ergänzen, vom Kaiser ausging und daß dieser selbst schließlich den Aufstand ausgerechnet im Hippodrom, dem Zentrum der politischen Kommunikation zwischen Herrscher und städtischer Bevölkerung, beenden konnte, verweist jedoch auf die unmittelbar politischen Implikationen der Ereignisse. Kirchen- und ‚profan‘-politische Aspekte lassen sich somit – dies wird insbesondere die Analyse der Vorgeschichte des *Stauro-theis*-Aufstandes erweisen – überhaupt nicht voneinander trennen.[9] Auffällig ist zudem, daß die Frequenz der bezeugten Unruhen in Konstantinopel – insbesondere diejenigen unter Beteiligung der Zirkusgruppen – seit Mitte des 5. Jahrhunderts zunimmt und unter Anastasios ihren Höhepunkt erreicht (s. u.);[10] daß es sich hierbei um eine vornehmlich politische Entwicklung handelt, in deren Kontext man daher zwangsläufig auch den Aufstand des Jahres 512 als prominentestes Ereignis dieser Art zu sehen hat, wird wohl niemand bezweifeln wollen. Die Frage, wie sich in diesem Aufstand politische und religiöse Entwicklungen miteinander vermengt und zugespitzt haben und in welchen größeren Zusammenhängen er insofern zu interpretieren ist, wurde bisher allerdings noch nicht ausführlich behandelt. Die folgenden Überlegungen sollen in dieser Hinsicht einen ersten Aufriß bieten. Dabei bietet es sich an, in drei Schritten vorzugehen:

Zunächst sollen die Quellen zum *Staurotheis*-Aufstand insbesondere im Hinblick auf den konkreten Ereignisablauf analysiert werden. In der Folge wird nach der Rolle der namentlich genannten Akteure zu fragen sein, bevor dann der kirchenpolitische sowie der – davon kaum zu trennende – allgemeine politische Kontext zu rekonstruieren ist.

---

8 Vgl. etwa Greatrex (s. Anm. 1) 64; s. auch Al. Cameron, Porphyrius the Charioteer, Oxford 1973, 235; Gizewski (s. Anm. 1) 205 f.; W. Liebeschuetz, The Circus Factions, in: Convegno per Santo Mazzarino: Roma 9–11 maggio 1991 (= Saggi di storia antica 13), Rom 1998, 163–185, hier 178: „the great religious riot at Constantinople".

9 Die enge Vernetzung der kirchen- und der ‚profan‘-politischen Sphäre gerade auch unter Anastasios wurde zuletzt vor allem von Wirth (s. Anm. 5) 81–139, noch einmal eindrucksvoll demonstriert. Vgl. aber auch bereits Charanis (s. Anm. 6) 31: „The religious history of the later Roman Empire is inextricably interwoven with its political and social history".

10 Cameron (s. Anm. 8) 232–239; Al. Cameron, Circus Factions. Blues and Greens at Rome and Byzantium, Oxford 1976, ND 1999, 130 ff.

I

Die wichtigste Quelle zum *Staurotheis*-Aufstand wird in der Schilderung des Augenzeugen[11] Marcellinus Comes gesehen, auf dessen Grundlage auch das chronologische Gerüst aller modernen Rekonstruktionen beruht. Dieser Bericht wird ergänzt durch einige bedeutsame Einzelheiten, die sich ursprünglich bei Theodoros Anagnostes (1. Hälfte 6. Jh.) und in der *Chronik* des Johannes Malalas (6. Jh.) fanden; da aber der nur in einer einzigen Handschrift (*Codex Barocci-anus Graecus* 182) erhaltene Malalas-Text im Verlauf des Überlieferungsprozesses mehrfachen Kürzungen ausgesetzt war, bietet er nicht mehr die originale, vollständige Darstellung. Allerdings läßt sich diese zumindest annähernd rekonstruieren: auf der Basis einiger späterer Chronisten, die noch Einblick in den sog. Ur-Malalas hatten, die dessen Bericht andererseits aber auch durch Sondermaterial unterschiedlicher Herkunft ergänzt haben.

1. Marcellinus Comes

Marcellinus verfaßte den in unserem Zusammenhang wichtigen Teil seiner *Chronik* wohl unmittelbar nach dem Tod des Anastasios im Jahr 518.[12] Als kompromißloser Chalkedonier stand er Anastasios ausgesprochen ablehnend gegenüber,[13] was sich u. a. auch im Bericht über den Aufstand des Jahres 512 niederschlägt.

Im einzelnen läßt sich aus Marcellinus folgender Ereignishergang rekonstruieren:

Am Sonntag, den 4. November 512, verkünden Marinos der Syrer[14] (damals wohl noch *numerarius* des *scrinium Orientis* und noch nicht *praefectus praetorio*

---

11 Vgl. B. Croke, The Chronicle of Marcellinus. A Translation and Commentary, Sydney 1995, 115 („quite likely an eyewitness account"); Croke (s. Anm. 6) 111 („eyewitness"); vgl. auch 24.

12 Vgl. Croke (s. Anm. 6) 17 ff., bes. 20; 26. In einer zweiten Auflage erweiterte Marcellinus seine *Chronik* später um die Darstellung der Jahre 519–534; ein unbekannter Fortsetzer hat den Text schließlich bis zum Jahr 548 weitergeführt. Edition: Th. Mommsen (Ed.), Chronica Minora Saec. IV. V. VI. VII, Vol. II, Berlin 1894 (= MGH AA XI), 37–109. Den Text (Reproduktion der Edition Mommsens) mit englischer Übersetzung und kurzem Kommentar bietet auch Croke, Chronicle of Marcellinus (s. Anm. 11).

13 Vgl. Croke (s. Anm. 6) 130 f., bes. 131: „All in all, Marcellinus' treatment of Anastasius is consistently hostile but oversimplified".

14 PLRE II 726–728 (Marinus 7).

Orientis, dazu s. u.) und der Stadtpräfekt Platon[15] auf Anweisung des Anastasios in der Hagia Sophia die Formel ὁ σταυρωθεὶς δι' ἡμᾶς, ἐλέησον ἡμᾶς als Zusatz zum *Trisagion*. Als zahlreiche anwesende Chalkedonier (*multi orthodoxorum*) das *Trisagion* dennoch in der ursprünglichen Version singen, kommt es zu Tumulten. Einige Anhänger des *Chalcedonense* sollen bereits an Ort und Stelle niedergemacht worden sein, andere verenden später im Kerker.[16]

Am Montag, den 5. November, kommt es wegen derselben Angelegenheit in der Kirche Hagios Theodoros[17] zu einem recht großen Blutbad unter Chalkedoniern (*maiore caede catholici pro fide unica perculsi sunt*). Aus diesem Grund formieren sich am Dienstag, den 6. November, überall in der Stadt Chalkedonier zu Prozessionen und kommen am Konstantin-Forum zusammen.[18]

Marcellinus merkt an, daß es sich damals ohnehin um einen Gedenktag gehandelt habe, der an einen schweren Ascheregen in ganz Europa habe erinnern sollen.[19] Aus späteren liturgischen Kalendern geht hervor, daß an diesem Tag stets eine feierliche Gedenkprozession von der Hagia Sophia zum Forum stattfand.[20] Dies dürfte die Prozession gewesen sein, an der auch Anastasios im Jahr 512 teilnahm.[21]

Einige Chalkedonier verbringen den Tag und die anschließende Nacht mit Hymnengesang; andere jedoch durchstreifen die Stadt und machen dabei Mönche, die auf der Seite des Anastasios stehen (*Anastasii Caesaris monastico habitu adsentatores*), nieder. Wiederum andere haben die Schlüssel der Stadttore und die Standarten der Truppen (wohl derjenigen, die in der Stadt stationiert sind) zum Forum gebracht, wo ein ‚religiöses Camp' (*religionis castra*) entsteht. Als Anastasios im Rahmen der (oben erwähnten) Gedenkprozession das Forum passiert, fordern die dort lagernden Chalkedonier Areobindos als neuen Kaiser.[22]

15　PLRE II 891 f. (Plato 3).

16　Marc. Com. ad ann. 512,2 p. 97 Mommsen.

17　Zu Geschichte und Lage dieser Kirche s. R. Janin, La géographie ecclésiastique de l'empire byzantin. Première partie: Le siège de Constantinople et le patriarcat œcuménique. Tome III: Les églises et les monastères, Paris ²1969, 152 f.

18　Marc. Com. ad ann. 512,3 p. 97 Mommsen.

19　Marc. Com. ad ann. 512,3 p. 97 Mommsen: *[...] in quo die memoria cineris dudum totam Europam tegentis apud Byzantios celebratur [...]*. Dieser Ascheregen war Folge eines Vesuv-Ausbruchs im Jahr 472, vgl. Croke (s. Anm. 11) 115.

20　J. Mateos (Ed.), Le Typicon de la Grande Église, Tome I, Rom 1962, p. 90: Ἕωθεν συντρέχουσιν ἐν τῇ ἁγιωτάτῃ Μεγάλῃ Ἐκκλησίᾳ, καὶ λιτανεύοντες ἀπέρχονται ἐν τῷ Φόρῳ [...]. Vgl. auch *Synax. Eccl. Const.* Nr. 2 (zum 6. November) p. 198,7–199,12 Delehaye.

21　Marc. Com. ad ann. 512,4 p. 98 Mommsen.

22　Marc. Com. ad ann. 512,4 p. 98 Mommsen.

Nun kommt es zum offenen Aufstand gegen den Herrscher: Kaiserbilder und Kaiserstatuen werden zerstört; Anastasios versucht (am Mittwoch, den 7. November?) auf friedlichem Weg, die Situation unter Kontrolle zu bringen, und entsendet die Senatoren Keler[23] und Patrikios[24] *supplicandi sibi vel satisfaciendi gratia*. Die beiden müssen sich jedoch in einem Steinhagel zurückziehen. Die Häuser des Marinos und des – Chalkedoniers – Pompeios[25] gehen in Flammen auf.[26]

Vom Forum aus strömen die Massen in den Hippodrom, wo sie sich vor dem dort anwesenden Kaiser versammeln, demonstrativ das *Trisagion* ohne *Staurotheis*-Zusatz singen, ein Evangeliar und ein Kreuz präsentieren. In Sprechchören werden Marinos und Platon für die Ergänzung des *Trisagion*s verantwortlich gemacht; die Forderung, die beiden Beamten den wilden Tieren vorzuwerfen, wird laut.[27]

Anastasios geht auf die (theologischen) Postulate des Volkes ein – wie Marcellinus behauptet, jedoch nur zum Schein (*solitis periuriis simulatisque vocibus*). Es gelingt ihm, die Menge zu beruhigen und sie ohne irgendein Ergebnis (*sine ullo rerum effectu*) am dritten Tag, seitdem sie sich auf dem Forum versammelt hatte (also am Donnerstag, den 8. November), wieder in ihre Wohnungen zu zerstreuen.[28]

In der Folge beruft Anastasios eine Synode nach Sidon ein, die vom Chalkedonier Marcellinus allerdings als Versammlung von Häretikern beurteilt wird.[29]

Die wichtigsten Punkte, die sich damit aus dem Bericht des Marcellinus ergeben, seien noch einmal kurz zusammengefaßt:

Ausgangspunkt der Ereignisse ist der Befehl des Anastasios, das *Trisagion* um die *Staurotheis*-Formel zu erweitern; bei der Verkündigung dieses Befehls durch Marinos und Platon in der Hagia Sophia, kommt es zu ersten Gewaltakten seitens der Chalkedon-Gegner. Nach weiteren Ausschreitungen am nächsten Tag besetzen die Chalkedonier das Konstantin-Forum; ein wesentlicher Grund könnte – neben der symbolischen Bedeutung dieses Ortes mit seinem Bezug auf

---

23 PLRE II 275–277 (Celer 2).
24 PLRE II 840–842 (Fl. Patricius 14).
25 PLRE II 898 f. (Pompeius 2).
26 Marc. Com. ad ann. 512,5 p. 98 Mommsen.
27 Marc. Com. ad ann. 512,6 p. 98 Mommsen.
28 Marc. Com. ad ann. 512,7 p. 98 Mommsen.
29 Marc. Com. ad ann. 512,8 p. 98 Mommsen. Diese Synode wird allerdings in der Forschung vielfach in das Jahr 511, d. h. *vor* den *Staurotheis*-Aufstand, datiert, vgl. A. Grillmeier, Jesus der Christus im Glauben der Kirche, Bd. II.1: Das Konzil von Chalkedon (451). Rezeption und Widerspruch (451–518), Freiburg/Basel/Wien ²1991, ND 2004, 316, Anm. 159; zur Synode vgl. ebd., 316 f.

den ersten christlichen und natürlich ‚orthodoxen' Kaiser Konstantin – die Tatsache gewesen sein, daß Anastasios hier während der Gedenkprozession am 6. November Station machen mußte, man ihn dort also ‚abfangen' konnte, um die eigenen Forderungen zu artikulieren. Unterdessen kommt es auch zu Ermordungen von Anhängern des Anastasios durch Chalkedonier. Als der Kaiser schließlich auf dem Forum erscheint, eskaliert die Situation: Ein neuer Herrscher wird gefordert, die Bilder des Anastasios werden geschändet. Nach dem Scheitern eines ersten Beschwichtigungsversuchs durch Mittelsmänner gelingt es Anastasios erst im Hippodrom, die Menge wieder unter Kontrolle zu bringen.

2. Johannes Malalas und die (griechische[n]) Malalas-Tradition(en) (inkl. Johannes von Nikiu)

In der griechischen Malalas-Tradition (die in zwei unterschiedliche Stränge zerfällt, s. u.) erscheinen die Ereignisse in etwas anderem Licht:[30] Der Aufruhr im Volk wegen des christlichen Dogmas (δημοτικὴ ἐπανάστασις περὶ τοῦ χρι-

---

30 Folgende Autoren und Texte gehören der griechischen Malalas-Tradition an: Johannes Malalas selbst (6. Jh., Edition: I. Thurn [Ed.], Ioannis Malalae Chronographia, Berlin/New York 2000 [CPG 7511]); Euagrios (spätes 6. Jh., Edition: J. Bidez/L. Parmentier [Edd.], The Ecclesiastical History of Evagrius with the Scholia, London 1898, ND Amsterdam 1964 [CPG 7500]); das *Chronicon Paschale* (um 629, Edition: L. Dindorf [Ed.], Chronicon Paschale, Vol. I, Bonn 1832 [CPG 7960]); Johannes von Nikiu (spätes 7. Jh., englische Übersetzung des nur äthiopisch überlieferten Textes: The Chronicle of John [c. 690 A.D.], Coptic Bishop of Nikiu. Translated by R. H. Charles, London 1916 [CPG 7967]); Georgios Monachos (9. Jh., Edition: C. de Boor [Ed.], Georgii Monachi Chronicon, ed. corr. cur. P. Wirth, Vol. II, Stuttgart 1978); das Konstantinische Malalas-Exzerpt (10. Jh., Edition: Excerpta Historica iussu Imp. Constantini Porphyrogeniti confecta, edd. U. Ph. Boissevain, C. de Boor, Th. Büttner-Wobst. Vol. III: Excerpta de Insidiis, ed. C. de Boor, Berlin 1905); die unter dem Namen Leon Grammatikos bekannte Kompilation (frühes 11. Jh., Edition: I. Bekker [Ed.], Leonis Grammatici Chronographia, Bonn 1842); Georgios Kedrenos (frühes 12. Jh., Edition: J.-P. Migne [Ed.], Georgii Cedreni Compendium Historiarum, PG 121, Turnhout 1857); Johannes Zonaras (12. Jh., Edition: M. Pinder [Ed.], Ioannis Zonarae Epitome Historiarum Libri XVIII, Tomus III, Berlin 1897).
Zu Johannes Malalas vgl. bes. die Arbeiten von E. Jeffreys/B. Croke/R. Scott (Hgg.), Studies in John Malalas, Sydney 1990; Thurn, Ioannis Malalae Chronographia (s. o.), 1*–15*; E. Jeffreys, The Beginning of Byzantine Chronography: John Malalas, in: G. Marasco (Hg.), Greek and Roman Historiography in Late Antiquity. Fourth to Sixth Century A. D., Leiden/Boston 2003, 497–527; J. Beaucamp (Hg.), Recherches sur la chronique de Jean Malalas I, Paris 2004. – Zu Euagrios vgl. P. Allen, Evagrius Scholasticus the Church Historian, Leuven 1981; M. Whitby, The Church Historians and Chalcedon, in: Marasco, a. a. O., 449–495, bes. 477ff. – Zum *Chronicon Paschale*

στιανικοῦ δόγματος) habe, wie auch Marcellinus schon betont hatte, seinen Ausgang genommen in einem Befehl des Kaisers, das *Trisagion* um die *Staurotheis*-Formel zu ergänzen, „so wie sie es in den Städten des Ostens singen" (καθὼς ἐν ταῖς ἀνατολικαῖς πόλεσιν λέγουσιν [Malalas]).[31] Marinos der Syrer (für ihn steht die Bezeichnung λογοθέτης bei Georgios Monachos, Leon Grammatikos, Kedrenos und bei Zonaras als Umschreibung seiner Stellung als *numerarius* des *scrinium Orientis*)[32] und der Stadtpräfekt (ἔπαρχος, ὕπαρχος) beginnen in der Hagia Sophia mit der Verkündigung des Befehls.[33] Daraufhin gerät die versammelte Menge in erheblichen Aufruhr (ἐστασίασαν δυνατῶς).[34] Der Stadtpräfekt Platon muß sich vor dem Volkszorn (ἡ τοῦ δήμου ὀργή/ἡ ὀργὴ τοῦ λαοῦ) in Sicherheit bringen.[35] Gemäß der Chronologie des Marcellinus dürfte es sich dabei um die Ereignisse des 4.–6. November handeln.

Die Aufständischen, unter denen sich auch Soldaten befunden haben dürften,[36] fordern in Sprechchören einen neuen Kaiser (ἄλλον βασιλέα τῇ ῾Ρωμα-

---

vgl. H. Hunger, Die hochsprachliche profane Literatur der Byzantiner, Bd. 1, München 1978, 328 f.; Chronicon Paschale 284–628 AD. Translated with Notes and Introduction by Mi. Whitby/Ma. Whitby, Liverpool 1989, IX ff.; K. Fittschen, Chronicon Paschale, in: Döpp/Geerlings (s. Anm. 6) 147 f. – Zu Johannes von Nikiu, der seine *Chronik* ursprünglich auf Griechisch (eventuell mit einigen koptischen Passagen) verfaßt hat, vgl. A. Carile, Giovanni di Nikius, Cronista Bizantino-Copto del VII secolo, FR 121/122 (1981), 103–155, sowie (sehr knapp) P. Bruns, Johannes von Nikiu, in: Döpp/Geerlings (s. Anm. 6) 397. Der griechisch/koptische Originaltext ist nicht erhalten; er wurde zu einem unbekannten Zeitpunkt ins Arabische übertragen; diese ebenfalls nicht überlieferte Version bildete die Grundlage für die heute einzig vorliegende äthiopische Übersetzung. – Zu Georgios Monachos vgl. Hunger, a. a. O., 347–350. Zu Leon Grammatikos vgl. Hunger, a. a. O., 354–357. – Zu Kedrenos vgl. Hunger, a. a. O., 393f. – Zu Zonaras vgl. Hunger, a.a.O., 416–419.

31 Malal. p. 333,12–16 Thurn. Vgl. Euagr. *HE* 3,44 p. 146,3–6 Bidez/Parmentier; Georg. Mon. p. 620,3–6 de Boor; *Exc. de insid.* 42 p. 170,4–6 de Boor [Auszug aus Johannes Malalas]; Leon Gramm. p. 119,4–6 Bekker; Kedren. PG 121 p. 688 [631] B (Leon Grammatikos und Kedrenos fügen hinzu, daß Severos den Kaiser zu diesem Schritt bewogen habe); Zon. 14,3,31 p. 138,12–14 Pinder.

32 Vgl. W. Brandes, Finanzverwaltung in Krisenzeiten. Untersuchungen zur byzantinischen Administration im 6.–9. Jahrhundert, Frankfurt a. M. 2002, 66; 87; 88, Anm. 165.

33 Georg. Mon. p. II 620,6–8 de Boor; Leon Gramm. p. 119,6–8 Bekker; Kedren. PG 121 p. 688 [631] B; Zon. 14,3,32 p. 138,14–16 Pinder.

34 Malal. p. 333,16 Thurn; Georg. Mon. p. II 620,8–9 de Boor; Leon Gramm. p. 119,8 Bekker; Kedren. PG 121 p. 688 [631] B; Zon. 14,3,33 p. 138,17–18 Pinder.

35 Malal. p. 333,17–19 Thurn; vgl. Joh. Nik. 89,60 p. 128 Charles; Georg. Mon. p. II 620,9–10; 11–13 de Boor; Zon. 14,3,34 p. 138,18–19 Pinder.

36 So jedenfalls Joh. Nik. 89,60 p. 128 Charles; dies deckt sich mit Marcellinus' Bemerkung, wonach die Aufständischen sich auch der Standarten der Truppen bemächtigt

νία) – dies dürfte ebenfalls noch am 6. November, während der oben erwähnten Prozession, geschehen sein.[37] Teile der Hauptstadt gehen in Flammen auf.[38] Die Aufrührer plündern (wohl am 7. November, s. o.) das Haus des Marinos und brennen es nieder – Marinos selbst, dem man unterstellte, den Kaiser zu dem verhängnisvollen *Trisagion*-Zusatz bewogen zu haben, kann jedoch kurz zuvor entkommen. Die in seinem Haus vorgefundenen Silberschätze werden verteilt.[39] Davon, daß auch das Haus des Pompeios ein Opfer der Flammen geworden sein soll, weiß die Malalas-Tradition nichts; statt dessen findet sich bei Georgios Monachos und bei Zonaras die Nachricht, daß neben dem Haus des Marinos auch dasjenige des Stadtpräfekten Platon niedergebrannt worden sei.[40]

Im Haus des Marinos wird ein Mönch aus dem Osten aufgegriffen und gelyncht (Johannes von Nikiu zufolge hielt man ihn irrtümlich für Severos, eine zentrale Identifikationsfigur der Miaphysiten;[41] Euagrios berichtet immerhin, man habe in dem Mönch denjenigen gesehen, der Anastasios zur Ergänzung des *Trisagion*s geraten habe).[42] Die Menge spießt seinen Kopf auf und schmäht ihn in Sprechchören: „Das ist der Feind der Trinität" (οὗτός ἐστιν ὁ ἐπίβουλος τῆς τριάδος).[43] Daraufhin erscheinen die Aufrührer vor dem Haus der Anicia Iuliana und fordern, ihr Mann, Areobindos, solle die Herrschaft übernehmen – dieser aber ist zuvor ebenfalls geflohen.[44] Die Lage spitzt sich weiter zu: Es kommt zu großen Tumulten (γενομένης ταραχῆς μεγάλης καὶ στάσεως), vielfachen

---

hätten (Marc. Com. ad ann. 512,4 p. 98 Mommsen, s. o.); die Truppen dürften diese jedenfalls kaum gegen ihren Willen herausgegeben haben.

37 Malal. p. 333,19–20 Thurn; Georg. Mon. p. II 620,11 de Boor; Leon Gramm. p. 119,8–9 Bekker; Kedren. PG 121 p. 688 [631] B.

38 Euagr. *HE* 3,44 p. 146,15 Bidez/Parmentier. Vgl. Georg. Mon. p. II 620,10 de Boor.

39 Malal. p. 333,20–334,26 Thurn; Georg. Mon. p. II 620,13–16 de Boor; Joh. Nik. 89,61–63 p. 128 Charles. Johannes von Nikiu, der als Miaphysit mit Marinos sympathisiert, stellt den *praefectus praetorio* naturgemäß positiv dar („[…] an illustrious man […]; he […] was saved through the strong aid of our Lord Jesus Christ"), s. dazu auch u. Vgl. Zon. 14,3,34–35 p. 138,19–139,2 Pinder.

40 Georg. Mon. p. II 620,13–16 de Boor; Zon. 14,3,34 p. 139,1 Pinder.

41 Diese Einzelnachricht wird von Allen (s. Anm. 30) 165, Anm. 109, mit Skepsis betrachtet; Allen kann allerdings für ihr Mißtrauen keine Argumente außer einem allgemeinen Unbehagen gegenüber dem Wert der Darstellung des Johannes von Nikiu vorbringen, das sie insbesondere an Joh. Nik. 89,60 p. 128 und 89,66 p. 129 Charles festmacht.

42 Malal. p. 334,26–27 Thurn; Euagr. *HE* 3,44 p. 146,17–18 Bidez/Parmentier; Joh. Nik. 89,64 p. 129 Charles.

43 Malal. p. 334,27–28 Thurn; Joh. Nik. 89,64 p. 129 Charles. Vgl. Euagr. *HE* 3,44 p. 146,15–20 Bidez/Parmentier.

44 Malal. p. 334,28–31 Thurn; Joh. Nik. 89,65 p. 129 Charles. An dieser Stelle setzt der nur fragmentarisch erhaltene Bericht des *Chronicon Paschale* ein: *Chron. Pasch.* p. I 610,1–6 Dindorf.

Brandlegungen (ἐμπρησμοὺς οἴκων πολλῶν ἐποιήσαντο) und zahllosen Mordtaten (φόνους μυρίους εἰργάσαντο).[45] Die Menge beschimpft Anastasios und ruft nun den bekennenden Chalkedonier Vitalian zum Kaiser aus.[46]

Mit der Ausrufung Vitalians zum Kaiser berühren wir erstmals eine Tradition, die den Ereignishergang in etwas anderer Weise berichtet als Malalas (in der im *Codex Baroccianus Graecus* 182 erhaltenen Form), das *Chronicon Paschale*, Johannes von Nikiu und das Konstantinische Malalas-Exzerpt (diese Autoren und Texte seien im folgenden als Malalas I-Tradition zusammengefaßt). Es handelt sich bei den abweichenden Darstellungen um Chroniken, die zwar in jedem Fall *auch* von Malalas abhängen, daneben aber – unter Verzicht auf Episoden aus dem Ur-Malalas – auch Sondermaterial verarbeiten (Kaiserproklamation Vitalians statt des Areobindos; Ermordung des Vorstehers des Klosters Hagios Philippos und einer Asketin anstelle der Ermordung des Mönchs im Haus des Marinos, dazu s. u.). Frühester *in toto* erhaltener Zeuge für diese abweichende, im folgenden als Malalas II bezeichnete Tradition ist Georgios Monachos. Auf ihm bzw. seiner Quelle (vielleicht Theodoros Anagnostes bzw. – wahrscheinlicher – eine u. a. von diesem abhängige Chronik, dazu s. u.) beruhen offenbar auch die Berichte des Leon Grammatikos (als Vertreter der Symeon-Magistros/Logothetes-Gruppe), des Georgios Kedrenos und des Johannes Zonaras.

Die Proklamation Vitalians findet sich *als Einzelelement* hingegen schon in der Theophanes-*Chronik*, auf deren Basis auch der Bericht des Theodoros Anagnostes – über die sog. *Kirchengeschichtliche Epitome* (frühes 7. Jh.) als Vermittlerin – rekonstruiert wird.[47] In der Forschung hat man allerdings sowohl die entsprechende Passage bei Theodoros als auch diejenige bei Theophanes für unglaubwürdig gehalten: „Theophanes has presumably substituted Vitalian as his champion of orthodoxy" (sc. anstelle des Areobindos, über dessen Proklamation

---

45 Georg. Mon. p. II 620,16–19 de Boor; Leon Gramm. p. 119,9–10 Bekker; Kedren. PG 121 p. 688 [631] B; Zon. 14,3,35 p. 139,4–5 Pinder.

46 Georg. Mon. p. II 620,19–20 de Boor; Leon Gramm. p. 119,9–10 Bekker; Kedren. PG 121 p. 688 [631] B (Leon und Kedrenos jeweils ohne die Ausrufung Vitalians zum Kaiser); Zon. 14,3,35 p. 139,3–4 Pinder.

47 Theoph. a. m. 6005 p. 159,16–17 de Boor; G. Chr. Hansen [Ed.], Theodoros Anagnostes. Kirchengeschichte, Berlin 1971, p. 145,16–17 (*fr.* 508) [CPG 7503]. Zur *Kirchengeschichtlichen Epitome* als Vermittlerin des Theodoros-Textes an Theophanes s. Hansen, ebd., XXIX f.; XXXVII–XXXIX. Unklar sind die Ausführungen zum Verhältnis von Theodoros Anagnostes, der *Kirchengeschichtlichen Epitome* und Theophanes zueinander in: The Chronicle of Theophanes Confessor. Byzantine and Near Eastern History AD 284–813. Translated with Introduction and Commentary by C. Mango and R. Scott, with the Assistance of G. Greatrex, Oxford 1997, LXXV f., vgl. dazu die Anmerkungen von W. Brandes, in: BZ 91 (1998), 549–561, hier 553.

Theodoros Anagnostes bzw. Theophanes nichts sagt).[48] Dabei ist jedoch zu bedenken, daß nicht nur Theophanes (bzw. die *Kirchengeschichtliche Epitome*) und der daraus rekonstruierte Theodoros, sondern auch die gesamte oben erwähnte Malalas II-Tradition von einer Ausrufung Vitalians zu berichten weiß.

Eine weitere, hieran wohl anschließende Episode findet sich nur in der Malalas II-Tradition (frühester mir bekannter Beleg ist Georgios Monachos, 9. Jh.). Demzufolge zieht die Menge nun zur Mokios-Zisterne[49] und trifft dort auf den vom Kaiser geliebten (τὸν ὑπὸ τοῦ βασιλέως ἀγαπώμενον), namentlich nicht bekannten Vorsteher des Klosters Hagios Philippos;[50] nachdem auch er getötet worden ist, wird sein Kopf auf einer Lanze angebracht, und die Aufrührer ziehen weiter mit dem Sprechchor: „Das ist der Freund des Feindes der heiligen Trinität" (οὗτός ἐστιν ὁ φίλος τοῦ ἐχϑροῦ τῆς ἁγίας τριάδος).[51] Kurz darauf wird auch eine Asketin getötet, die der Menge beim Xerokerkos (= Xylokerkos)-Tor[52] in die Hände fällt und zu der Anastasios ebenfalls ein vertrauensvolles Verhältnis gepflegt haben soll. Die Leichen der beiden werden zum Studios-Kloster[53] geschleift und verbrannt.[54]

Auf den ersten Blick wirkt diese Episode wie eine Dublette zur Ermordung des Mönches im Haus des Marinos (Malalas I), ähnlich wie ja auch die Ausrufung Vitalians zum Kaiser (Theodoros/Theophanes [*Kirchengeschichtliche Epitome*] + Malalas II) angesichts der Proklamation des Areobindos am Haus der Anicia Iuliana (Malalas I) in der Forschung Mißtrauen hervorgerufen hat (s. o.). Es sei aber vor voreiligen Schlüssen gewarnt. Denn die Sprechchöre weisen in beiden

---

48 Mango/Scott/Greatrex (s. Anm. 47) 242, Anm. 17. Vgl. auch Hansen (s. Anm. 47) 145, App.: „Vitalian sicher irrtümlich genannt statt Areobindos (Malal.)"; daneben PLRE II 144 (Areobindus 1): „[…] the name of Vitalian appears in error for Areobindus".

49 Sie wurde unter Anastasios angelegt, vgl. A. Berger, Untersuchungen zu den Patria Konstantinupoleos, Bonn 1988, 615 f.

50 Die Gründung der Philippos-Kirche wird Anastasios zugeschrieben, vgl. Janin (s. Anm. 17) 493 f.

51 Georg. Mon. p. II 620,20–621,4 de Boor; Leon Gramm. p. 119,10–15 Bekker; Kedren. PG 121 p. 688 [631] B; Zon. 14,3,36 p. 139,5–7 Pinder.

52 ,Xerokerkos' ist eine jüngere, irrtümliche Bezeichnung für ,Xylokerkos', die sich aus der Nähe des Xerolophos-Hügels ergab.

53 Zum Studios-Kloster s. W. Müller-Wiener, Bildlexikon zur Topographie Istanbuls. Byzantion – Konstantinopulis – Istanbul bis zum Beginn des 17. Jahrhunderts, Tübingen 1977, 147 ff. Das bei seiner Gründung Mitte des 5. Jh. mit Akoimeten-Mönchen bevölkerte Kloster war eine Hochburg der Chalkedonier; vgl. Janin (s. Anm. 17) 430–440.

54 Georg. Mon. p. II 621,4–8 de Boor; Leon Gramm. p. 119,15–18 Bekker; Kedren. PG 121 p. 688 [631] B; Zon. 14,3,37 p. 139,7–11 Pinder.

Fällen einen signifikanten Unterschied auf: Während der Mönch im Haus des Marinos, den man Johannes von Nikiu zufolge ja sogar für Severos selbst gehalten hatte (s. o.), als „Feind der Trinität" inkriminiert wird, heißt es über den Vorsteher des Philippos-Klosters, er sei „der *Freund* des Feindes der heiligen Trinität"; die Anklage ist also nicht ganz so scharf, die Sprechchöre sind jedenfalls keineswegs identisch. Muß man daher also sowohl mit einer doppelten Kaiserproklamation als auch mit zwei verschiedenen demonstrativen Akten der Hinrichtung und Schändung von Mönchen rechnen? Die Frage läßt sich wohl nicht eindeutig klären:

In jedem Fall muß man wohl die Existenz einer weiteren, heute verlorenen Chronik einkalkulieren, auf die sich Georgios Monachos – und damit die u. a. von ihm abhängigen Autoren (= Malalas II) – gestützt haben könnten. Diese Chronik müßte die Kaiserproklamation Vitalians (nicht aber die des Areobindos) sowie die Ermordung des Klostervorstehers und der Asketin (nicht aber den Lynchmord an dem Mönch im Haus des Marinos) berichtet haben. Sie müßte damit unabhängig von Malalas (aber wohl in Kenntnis von dessen Text) neue Episoden zum *Staurotheis*-Aufstand eingeführt bzw. solche stärker akzentuiert haben, die bei den zeitnahen Zeugen nicht sonderlich prominent hervorgetreten waren.

Im folgenden wird sich zeigen, daß diese Chronik zumindest teilweise auf Theodoros Anagnostes basiert haben muß. Denn Theodoros (in der Rekonstruktion auf Basis der Theophanes-*Chronik*) weiß nicht nur ebenfalls von der Ausrufung Vitalians (s. o.), sondern bietet in der Schilderung von Aufruhr, Brandlegungen, zahllosen Morden und den Schmähungen gegenüber Anastasios Formulierungen, die denjenigen in der Malalas II-Tradition fast wörtlich gleichen (s. u.). Allerdings fehlt bei Theodoros (zumindest in den vorliegenden Fragmenten) die Beschreibung der Ermordung des Vorstehers des Philippos-Klosters und der Asketin. Andererseits berichtet das Konstantinische Malalas-Exzerpt – nur in diesem Punkt abweichend von der Malalas I-Tradition, aber darin auf die Malalas II-Tradition verweisend – von der Ermordung eines Mönches und einer Asketin, weiß also ebenfalls von dem Doppelmord, der somit kaum eine Erfindung aus der mittelbyzantinischen Zeit gewesen sein dürfte.[55]

Auf der Basis dieses Befundes läßt sich erschließen, daß ein heute unbekannter Chronist sowohl Material aus Theodoros Anagnostes als auch aus Johannes Malalas verarbeitet hat und etwa in der Weise selektiert und gegliedert hat, wie es sich aus dem erhaltenen Bestand der Malalas II-Tradition erschließen läßt. Die Erwähnung einer Kaiserproklamation Vitalians bei Theophanes – sofern man

---

55 *Exc. de insid.* 42 p. 170,6–7 de Boor [aus Malal.]: καὶ ἐφόνευσαν καὶ ἔγκλειστον καὶ ἐγκλείστην ὁ δῆμος.

diese nicht für einen gezielten Eingriff des Theophanes oder des Verfassers der *Kirchengeschichtlichen Epitome* hält (s. o.) – deutet darauf hin, daß diese Chronik bereits vor dem frühen 9. Jh. bekannt gewesen sein muß. Selbst aber, wenn man sie aus Skepsis gegenüber der Authentizität der Vitalian-Stelle bei Theophanes erst nach dessen Werk ansetzen möchte, muß man sie dennoch *vor* Georgios Monachos datieren, der selbst nicht der Archeget der Malalas II-Tradition gewesen sein kann, da er seine Quellen in der Regel nur abgeschrieben hat. Zudem fehlt bei Georgios der lakonische Schlußsatz über die Beendigung des Aufstandes, den die anderen Autoren der Malalas II-Tradition (außer Zonaras) hingegen anführen (ὁ δὲ βασιλεὺς φοβηθεὶς πρὸς μικρὸν ἐπαύσατο τῆς αἱρέσεως).[56]

Darüber, welche Chronisten als Begründer der Malalas II-Tradition infragekommen, kann freilich nur spekuliert werden: Unwahrscheinlich dürfte aufgrund Phot. *cod.* 67 der schattenhafte Sergios Homologetes sein, der seit einiger Zeit als wichtiger Historiker des 9. Jh. gehandelt wird; hingegen wäre durchaus an eine Chronik des 8. bzw. sehr frühen 9. Jh. (*Megas Chronographos*? Traianos Patrikios?), eventuell aus dem Umfeld des Sergios, zu denken.[57] Möglicherweise –

---

56 Leon Gramm. p. 119,18–19. Bekker; Kedren. PG 121 p. 688 [631] B (ἐπὶ τούτοις ὁ βασιλεὺς φοβηθεὶς ἐπαύσατο πρὸς βραχὺ τῆς αἱρέσεως).

57 In der Forschung wird seit längerer Zeit über Inhalt, Umfang und Charakter einer heute nicht mehr erhaltenen Chronik spekuliert (möglicherweise handelt es sich auch um mehrere Werke), die indes existiert haben *muß*, weil die Chronisten seit dem 9. Jh. vielfach auf Material zurückgegriffen haben, das in der Historiographie der frühbyzantinischen Zeit offenbar noch keine besondere Prominenz besessen hat. Diese Chronik (oder Gruppe von Chroniken) dürfte im 8., spätestens im frühen 9. Jh. entstanden sein. Vgl. etwa G. Moravcsik, Byzantinoturcica I: Die byzantinischen Quellen der Geschichte der Turkvölker, Berlin ²1958, 277: „[...] eine unbekannte Quelle [...], deren Spuren auch bei anderen Chronisten nachgewiesen werden können" (zu Georgios Monachos); das Problem wird auch von F. Winkelmann, Quellenstudien zur herrschenden Klasse von Byzanz im 8. und 9. Jahrhundert, Berlin 1987, behandelt. Möglicherweise werden die Überlieferungswege und Abhängigkeiten klarer, wenn grundlegende Quellenprobleme im Zusammenhang der unterschiedlichen Redaktionen der *Chronik* des Symeon Magistros bzw. Logothetes (10. Jh.) geklärt und alle zugehörigen Varianten ediert sind (eine davon stellt der unter dem Namen des Leon Grammatikos überlieferte Text dar). Vielleicht treten dann auch Autoren der mittelbyzantinischen Zeit wie der *Megas Chronographos* oder Traianos Patrikios schärfer hervor); insbesondere letzterer könnte entscheidendes Material weitervermittelt haben. Zur Symeon-Gruppe s. Hunger (s. Anm. 30) 354–357. Zum *Megas Chronographos* s. C. Mango, The *Breviarium* of the Patriarch Nicephorus, in: Byzance. Hommage à André N. Stratos, Vol. II, Athen 1986, 539–552, bes. 545 ff., mit der These, daß der *Megas Chronographos* u. a. auf Theophanes basiere; ein umgekehrtes Abhängigkeitsverhältnis erschließt M. Meier, Die Erdbeben der Jahre 542 und 554 in der byzantinischen Überlieferung. Quellenkritische Überlegungen zur Geschichte des 6. Jahrhunderts n. Chr., ZPE 130 (2000), 287–295.

wenngleich unwahrscheinlich – handelt es sich aber auch um den Fortsetzer des Johannes Antiochenus (7. Jh.).[58] Die Frage muß – wie gesagt – letztlich offen bleiben (zumindest aus quellenkritischer Sicht), und damit bleibt zunächst einmal auch unklar, ob man wirklich mit zwei Kaiserproklamationen und zwei besonders barbarischen Akten der Hinrichtung von Mönchen/Asketen während des *Staurotheis*-Aufstandes rechnen muß.

Um die Lage unter Kontrolle zu bringen, erscheint Anastasios in Begleitung aller Senatoren ohne Diadem (δίχα διαδήματος) im Hippodrom.[59] Auch das Volk

---

Sergios Homologetes (PmbZ 6665) wurde von C. Mango, The Liquidation of Iconoclasm and the Patriarch Photios, in: A. Bryer/J. Herrin (Hgg.), Iconoclasm. Papers Given at the Ninth Spring Symposium of Byzantine Studies. University of Birmingham March 1975, Birmingham 1977, 133–140, als Vater des Patriarchen Photios identifiziert und mit dem von Photios *cod.* 67 genannten Historiker gleichgesetzt (R. Henry [Ed.], Photius. Bibliothèque, Tome I, Paris 1959, p. 99; gegen die Identifikation des Sergios mit dem Vater des Photios s. allerdings A. Nogara, Sergio il Confessore e il Cod. 67 della *Biblioteca* di Fozio patriarca di Costantinopoli, Aevum 52 [1978], 261–266). Den Ausführungen des Photios zufolge reichte Sergios' Geschichtswerk allerdings nicht bis in die spätrömische Zeit zurück.

58 Zu Johannes Antiochenus vgl. Hunger (s. Anm. 30) 326–328. Hunger und mit ihm die gesamte ältere Forschung datieren Johannes in die Zeit nach Phokas, d. h. in das frühe 7. Jh. Demgegenüber hat P. Sotiroudis, Untersuchungen zum Geschichtswerk des Johannes von Antiocheia, Thessaloniki 1989, 39 ff., zeigen können, daß die als authentisch anzusehenden Johannes-Fragmente mit Berichten über die Zeit des Anastasios enden; alle dem Johannes Antiochenus zugeschriebenen Fragmente, die sich auf die spätere Zeit bis Phokas beziehen, weisen demgegenüber signifikante Eigenheiten auf, die Sotiroudis zu der (bisher nicht widerlegten) These geführt haben, daß Johannes von Antiocheia sein Werk um 520/530 verfaßt haben müsse und mit dem von Euagrios erwähnten Johannes Rhetor identisch sei (ebd., 148–153). Das für die spätere Zeit einschlägige Textmaterial wäre dementsprechend einem anonymen Johannes-Continuator zuzuschreiben. Eine neue Edition der Fragmente mit umfangreicher Einleitung und italienischer Übersetzung liegt jetzt vor: Ioannis Antiocheni Fragmenta ex Historia chronica. Introduzione, edizione critica e traduzione a cura di U. Roberto, Berlin/New York 2005 (eine weitere Edition befindet sich in Vorbereitung).

59 Malal. p. 334,31–32 Thurn; Euagr. *HE* 3,44 p. 146,20–23 Bidez/Parmentier; *Chron. Pasch.* p. I 610,3–4 Dindorf; Joh. Nik. 89,66 p. 129 Charles; *Exc. de insid.* 42 p. 170,7–8 de Boor [aus Malal.]. Die Anwesenheit der Senatoren erwähnt nur Johannes von Nikiu, der auch als einziger Autor ausdrücklich anmerkt, Anastasios sei im Kaiserornat erschienen – was freilich überhaupt nicht zum Verzicht des Diadems paßt. Hier dürfte jedoch im Verlauf des komplizierten Überlieferungs- und Übersetzungsprozesses der *Chronik* des Johannes von Nikiu der aus Malalas stammende Hinweis auf das *Fehlen* des Diadems/Kaiserornats in eine *Betonung* des Kaiserornats verschrieben und damit ins Gegenteil verkehrt worden sein. Es wäre jedenfalls grundsätzlich gar nicht erforderlich gewesen, den Auftritt im Kaiserornat eigens zu betonen, da dieser ja ein ganz übliches Element der kaiserlichen Repräsentation darstellte. Zudem ver-

strömt nun dort zusammen und läßt sich vom Kaiser beschwichtigen, fordert ihn sogar auf, das Diadem wieder aufzusetzen.[60] Sogleich geht Anastasios hart gegen die Aufrührer vor: Durch den Stadtpräfekt Platon erfolgen viele Tage lang (ἐπὶ πολλὰς ἡμέρας) zahlreiche Verhaftungen und Hinrichtungen. Nachdem das Strafgericht zahllose Opfer gefordert hat (καὶ πλήθους ἀπείρου φονευθέντος), herrschen Ordnung und Angst in Konstantinopel und in jeder anderen Stadt des Reiches.[61]

Eine interessante Variante hinsichtlich des Ausbruchs und Verlaufs des Aufstandes findet sich in der *Chronik* des antichalkedonisch-miaphysitisch orientierten Johannes von Nikiu aus dem späten 7. Jahrhundert, der Malalas ausgiebig exzerpiert hat. Seinem – allerdings nur in mehrfacher Brechung (Übersetzungen) noch vorliegenden – Bericht zufolge soll der Chalkedonier Makedonios nach seiner Kaltstellung dem Kaiser zur Einführung des umstrittenen *Trisagion*-Zusatzes geraten haben, um so gezielt eine Revolte der Chalkedonier zu provozieren.[62]

---

merkt der Autor der *Chronik von Zuqnîn* ausdrücklich, Anastasios sei nicht nur ohne Diadem, sondern auch ohne sonstigen Ornat erschienen, vgl. Pseudo-Dionysios of Tel-Mahre. Chronicle, Part III, transl. by W. Witakowski, Liverpool 1996, 9 („in ordinary dress") = The Chronicle of Zuqnîn. Parts III and IV A. D. 488–775. Translated by A. Harrak, Toronto 1999, 43 („clothed in a simple manner").

60 Malal. p. 334,32–36 Thurn; Euagr. *HE* 3,44 p. 146,27–30 Bidez/Parmentier; *Chron. Pasch.* p. I 610,4–6 Dindorf; Joh. Nik. 89,66 p. 129 Charles; *Exc. de insid.* 42 p. 170,8–12 de Boor [aus Malal.] (die Forderung, das Diadem wieder aufzusetzen, findet sich nur bei Malalas, Euagrios und im Konstantinischen Malalas-Exzerpt, daneben allerdings auch in der syrischen Malalas-Tradition [dazu s. u.]: *Chronik von Zuqnîn* [Joh. Eph.?] p. 9 Witakowski = p. 43 Harrak; J.-B. Chabot, Chronique de Michel le Syrien, Patriarche Jacobite d'Antioche [1166–1199], Tome II, Paris 1901, ND Brüssel 1963, p. 162 [= Mich. Syr. 9,9]). Euagrios zufolge habe Anastasios in seiner Ansprache darauf hingewiesen, daß – selbst wenn der Aufstand Erfolg habe – das Reich auch weiterhin von einem Alleinherrscher und nicht von den Massen regiert werde (Euagr. *HE* 3,44 p. 146,23–27 Bidez/Parmentier) – ein bemerkenswerter Hinweis darauf, daß das Kaiser*tum* als spezifische Form politischer Organisation auch in der Spätantike möglicherweise doch nicht so unangefochten war, wie zumeist angenommen wird, ganz unabhängig davon, ob derartige Spekulationen tatsächlich im Jahr 512 artikuliert wurden oder eher auf persönliche Überlegungen des Euagrios zurückgehen. Die folgende Anmerkung des Euagrios, daß nach der Rede des Kaisers, das Volk „wie auf einen göttlichen Wink hin" nachgegeben habe (Euagr. *HE* 3,44 p. 146,28 Bidez/Parmentier: ὁ λεὼς ὥσπερ ἔκ τινος θείας <ῥοπῆς>; ῥοπῆς ist allerdings Konjektur), nimmt den vorangehenden Überlegungen dann allerdings ihre politische Sprengkraft und führt den Exkurs mit einer Bestätigung der von Gott eingesetzten Ordnung wieder zurück in den üblichen Rahmen.

61 Malal. p. 334,36–41 Thurn; Joh. Nik. 89,67–68 p. 129 Charles; *Exc. de insid.* 42 p. 170,12–17 de Boor [aus Malal.].

62 Joh. Nik. 89,58–59 p. 128 Charles.

Nachdem es dann zu den erhofften Ausschreitungen gekommen ist, soll Makedonios nachträglich den integren Marinos für die Entscheidung des Kaisers verantwortlich gemacht haben: „It is Marinus who turns the heart of the emperor from the faith".[63] Anastasios selbst soll nach der Beendigung des Aufstandes im Hippodrom sogar ausdrücklich eine allgemeine Amnestie verkündet haben.[64] Zu den harten Strafmaßnahmen im Anschluß an die Revolte sei er hingegen gezwungen worden, als erneut Unruhen unter den Chalkedoniern ausgebrochen seien (diese Sondervariante findet sich auch in der *Chronik von Zuqnîn*, s. u.).[65] Erst danach sei Makedonios als Urheber all dieser Ereignisse abgesetzt und verbannt worden.[66] – Es ist offensichtlich, daß Johannes von Nikiu als Gegner des Konzils von Chalkedon und Sympathisant der von Anastasios betriebenen Politik den Kaiser und seinen Getreuen Marinos möglichst integer und unschuldig erscheinen lassen will, während die Ursache des Aufstandes in einer stark personalisierenden Reduktion der Komplexität der Zusammenhänge allein auf den Chalkedon-Anhänger Makedonios projiziert wird.

Der Versuch, Makedonios für die Unruhen verantwortlich zu machen, könnte indes seinen Ursprung im Umfeld des Severos gehabt haben. Bezeichnenderweise kennt nämlich auch der pro-chalkedonisch orientierte Kirchenhistoriker Euagrios (Ende 6. Jh.) das Gerücht über die vermeintliche Urheberschaft des Makedonios und bezieht sich dabei ausdrücklich auf einen Brief des Antichalkedoniers Severos an Soterichos.[67] Ein Schreiben des Severos an diesen Bischof von Kaisareia in Kappadokien ist in der Tat fragmentarisch in einer koptischen Version erhalten,[68] wird in der Forschung allerdings um das Jahr 510, d. h. *vor* den

---

63　Joh. Nik. 89,62 p. 128 Charles.
64　Joh. Nik. 89,67 p. 129 Charles.
65　Joh. Nik. 89,67 p. 129 Charles.
66　Joh. Nik. 89,68 p. 129 Charles.
67　Euagr. *HE* 3,44 p. 146,6–11 Bidez/Parmentier. Den bemerkenswerten Umstand, daß Euagrios als Chalkedonier auch Quellen aus dem antichalkedonischen Umfeld herangezogen hat – was für den Wert und die Zuverlässigkeit seiner Darstellung spricht –, hebt auch Allen (s. Anm. 30) 166, hervor. – Zu Soterichos und seiner Karriere s. E. Honigmann, Évêques et évêchés monophysites d'Asie antérieure au VIe siècle, Louvain 1951, 109–113; ders., Heraclianus of Chalcedon (537 A. D.?), Soterichus of Caesarea in Cappadocia and Achillius, in: ders., Patristic Studies, Città del Vaticano 1953, 205–216.
68　G. Garitte, Fragments coptes d'une lettre de Sévère d'Antioche a Sotérichos de Césarée, Le Muséon 65 (1952), 185–198 [CPG 7070 (13)]. Der Brief schildert zunächst, wie eine Gruppe von Miaphysiten in der Hagia Sophia das *Trisagion* mit dem *Staurotheis*-Zusatz gesungen hat (p. 191–192); daraufhin habe Makedonios einige Aufrührer in die Kirche entsandt, die gewaltsam auf die anwesenden Severianer losgegangen seien (p. 192–194). Gleichzeitig habe man versucht, auch die Bevölkerung gegen sie aufzuhetzen (p. 193). Nach einem Hinweis darauf, daß sich unter den drangsalierten

Aufstand datiert.[69] Aus ihm geht aber immerhin klar hervor – und dies wird im folgenden noch von Bedeutung sein –, daß es auch zuvor schon Konflikte zwischen Severos und Makedonios um das *Trisagion* gegeben haben muß (dazu s. u.). Möglicherweise bezog sich Euagrios auf einen anderen Brief des Severos an Soterichos aus der Phase nach der Revolte.[70] Daß der *Staurotheis*-Aufstand der Grund für die Verbannung des Makedonios gewesen sei, wie Euagrios und Johannes von Nikiu trotz widerstreitender christologischer Orientierungen übereinstimmend behaupten,[71] ist jedenfalls auszuschließen; zum Zeitpunkt der Revolte befand sich Makedonios bereits im Exil. Daß er dabei trotz allem noch über gute Kontakte in die Hauptstadt verfügte und möglicherweise Aggressionen schüren konnte (insbesondere über die radikal-chalkedonischen Akoimeten, deren Verbindung mit Makedonios in der *Kirchengeschichte* des Ps.-Zacharias ausdrücklich bezeugt ist),[72] ist freilich nicht auszuschließen.[73]

3. Die syrische Malalas-Tradition

Im späten 8. Jahrhundert entstand im nordmesopotamischen Raum eine syrische Universalchronik, die in der Forschung unter den Bezeichnungen *Chronik von Zuqnîn* bzw. *Chronik* des Ps.-Dionysios bekannt ist. Dieses Werk basiert in seinem dritten Teil (der u. a. auch Nachrichten über die Zeit des Anastasios enthält) über weite Strecken auf dem verlorenen zweiten Teil der *Kirchengeschichte* des Johannes von Ephesos aus dem späteren 6. Jahrhundert.[74] Letzterer wiederum

---

Severianern durchaus auch angesehene, reiche Personen befunden hätten, bricht der Text zunächst ab (p. 195). Nach der Lücke, deren Umfang unklar ist, wird von einer Diskussion berichtet, an der u. a. Anastasios' Schwager Secundinus (PLRE II 986 [Secundinus 5]) teilnahm und in deren Verlauf Makedonios gezwungen wurde, auf die miaphysitische Position zuzugehen.

69   Vgl. J. Lebon, Le monophysisme sévèrien, Louvain 1909, 46, Anm. 1; Honigmann (s. Anm. 67) 109; Allen (s. Anm. 30) 165; M. Whitby, The Ecclesiastical History of Evagrius Scholasticus. Translated with an Introduction, Liverpool 2000, 195, Anm. 175. – Möglich wäre aber auch noch eine Datierung in die 1. Hälfte des Jahres 511, jedenfalls vor die Disputation zwischen Severos und Makedonios am 20. Juli 511, mit welcher die Intrige gegen Makedonios einsetzt (s.u.).

70   Allen (s. Anm. 30) 165, hingegen rechnet schlichtweg mit einem Versehen des Euagrios.

71   Euagr. *HE* 3,44 p. 146,11–12 Bidez/Parmentier; Joh. Nik. 89,68 p. 129 Charles.

72   Die sogenannte Kirchengeschichte des Zacharias Rhetor. In deutscher Übersetzung herausgegeben von K. Ahrens/G. Krüger, Leipzig 1899, p. 120 (cap. 7,7).

73   Vgl. so auch Whitby (s. Anm. 69) 195, Anm. 175.

74   Zur *Chronik von Zuqnîn* (Ps.-Dionysios) und ihrem Rückgriff auf Johannes von Ephesos vgl. Pseudo-Dionysius of Tel-Mahre: Chronicle, Part III. Translated with

hat sich für die Ereignisgeschichte des *frühen* 6. Jahrhunderts vielfach auf Johannes Malalas bezogen,[75] so daß mit guten Gründen in dem Bericht des Ps.-Dionysios über den *Staurotheis*-Aufstand ein Reflex der Malalas-Tradition, vermittelt wohl vor allem (aber wohl nicht nur) durch Johannes von Ephesos, vermutet werden kann.[76] Diese Hypothese wird zusätzlich dadurch gestützt, daß der spätere Chronist Michael Syrus (s. u.), der sich nachweislich auf Johannes von Ephesos gestützt hat,[77] eine Darstellung des *Staurotheis*-Aufstandes bietet, die sich mit dem Bericht in der *Chronik von Zuqnîn* sehr eng berührt, was auf eine gemeinsame Vorlage – wohl Johannes von Ephesos – schließen läßt.

Daß die Darstellung in der *Chronik von Zuqnîn* jedenfalls in der Tat ganz wesentlich auf Johannes Malalas als ,Urquelle' zurückzuführen ist, geht aus einem Vergleich der griechischen Malalas-Tradition mit Ps.-Dionysios klar hervor: Der syrische Text berichtet ebenfalls vom Wunsch des Anastasios, dem *Trisagion* die umstrittene *Staurotheis*-Formel hinzuzufügen, und auch Malalas' Hinweis, daß dies im Osten bereits Praxis gewesen sei, wurde vom syrischen Chronisten übernommen.[78] Wohl mit Blick auf ein spezifisch miaphysitisches und mit den Zuständen im Konstantinopel des frühen 6. Jahrhunderts nicht vertrautes Publikum scheint die darauf folgende Passage eingefügt worden zu sein, die erläutert, daß damals die Familie der Anicia Iuliana (zu ihr s. u.), ja sogar ganz Konstantinopel dem Nestorianismus angehangen habe (d. h. in diesem Kontext pro-chalkedonisch gesinnt war), weshalb es unter Führung der Akoimeten zu Unruhen und Tumulten gegen das veränderte *Trisagion* gekommen sei, weil es – dies greift nun wieder auf Malalas zurück – „something new and alien" sei.[79] Ebenfalls keine Entsprechung in der griechischen Malalas-Tradition finden die

---

Notes and Introduction by W. Witakowski, Liverpool 1996, XV ff.; daneben s. auch J. J. van Ginkel, John of Ephesus. A Monophysite Historian in Sixth-Century Byzantium, Diss. Groningen 1995, 48. Grundlegend ist darüber hinaus weiterhin die Arbeit von F. Haase, Untersuchungen zur Chronik des Pseudo-Dionysios von Tell-Mahrê, OC 65–90; 240–270 (zur Benutzung des Johannes von Ephesos durch Ps.-Dionysios s. ebd., 70 ff., bes. 79; 90). Zu Johannes von Ephesos selbst s. vor allem S. Ashbrook Harvey, Johannes von Ephesus, RAC 18 (1998), 553–564.

75 Vgl. van Ginkel (s. Anm. 74) 61 f.
76 Vgl. W. Witakowski, Sources of Pseudo-Dionysius for the Third Part of His Chronicle, Orientalia Suecana 40 (1991), 252–275, hier 257; Witakowski (s. Anm. 74) 9, Anm. 68; van Ginkel (s. Anm. 74) 105 f.; 230.
77 Vgl. Haase (s. Anm. 74) 90; Witakowski (s. Anm. 74) XXVII; van Ginkel (s. Anm. 74) 47 f.; 230; D. Weltecke, Die „Beschreibung der Zeiten" von Mōr Michael dem Grossen (1126–1199). Eine Studie zu ihrem historischen und historiographiegeschichtlichen Kontext, Louvain 2003, 12; 148.
78 *Chronik von Zuqnîn* [Joh. Eph.?] p. 7–8 Witakowski = p. 42 Harrak.
79 *Chronik von Zuqnîn* [Joh. Eph.?] p. 8 Witakowski = p. 42 Harrak.

vermeintlichen Spottgesänge der empörten Chalkedonier, von denen Ps.-Diony-
sios unmittelbar danach berichtet.[80]

Im Folgenden orientiert sich der syrische Text der Chronik wieder enger an
der griechischen Malalas (I)-Tradition: Die Menge fordert vor dem Palastviertel
einen neuen Kaiser, der Stadtpräfekt Platon muß fliehen. Die Aufrührer ziehen
zum Haus des Marinos, um ihn zu töten. Nachdem sich herausgestellt hat, daß er
bereits geflohen ist, werden seine Besitztümer geplündert und das Haus geht in
Flammen auf.[81] Ganz eng an Malalas angelehnt ist der Hinweis, daß man Marinos, weil er Syrer gewesen sei, unterstellt habe, den Kaiser zu seinem Entschluß
verleitet zu haben; auch die Erwähnung der Verteilung der in seinem Haus vorgefundenen Silberschätze verweist auf Malalas.[82]

Das Folgende bietet nur wenige Überraschungen: Der Lynchmord an dem
syrischen Mönch, der im Haus des Marinos aufgegriffen wird, und die Verspottung seines aufgespießten Hauptes durch Sprechchöre; der Zug zum Haus der
Anicia Iuliana und die Kaiserproklamation ihres Mannes Areobindos, der allerdings geflohen ist.[83]

Anastasios habe daraufhin Wagenrennen angesetzt und sei selbst ohne Kaiserornat und Diadem erschienen. Als die Bevölkerung ihn so gesehen und seine
beschwichtigenden Worte gehört habe, sei Ruhe eingekehrt und man habe den
Kaiser aufgefordert, sein Diadem wieder anzulegen. Dieser habe seinerseits um
allgemeine Beruhigung der Lage nachgesucht, und sein Wunsch sei erfüllt worden.[84] Allerdings – und hier ähnelt der Bericht des Ps.-Dionysios dem des ebenfalls miaphysitischen und mit Anastasios sympathisierenden Johannes von Nikiu
(so daß man wohl auf eine spezifisch miaphysitische ‚Umgestaltung‘ des aus
Malalas gewonnenen Ereignishergangs wird schließen können) – seien kurz darauf aus anderen Gründen erneut Unruhen ausgebrochen. Erst jetzt habe Anastasios hart durchgegriffen, und das nun folgende Strafgericht habe zahlreiche
Opfer gefordert. Danach habe in der Hauptstadt und im gesamten Reich Ruhe
geherrscht.[85] Auch Ps.-Dionysios (bzw. seine miaphysitische Quelle, wohl Johannes von Ephesos) versucht also, Anastasios von der Schuld an einem unmittelbar an den Aufstand anschließenden Blutbad freizusprechen.

Kaum zusätzliche Informationen bietet schließlich die Darstellung des ‚jako-
bitischen‘ Patriarchen und Chronisten Michael Syrus aus dem späten 12. Jahr-

---

80 *Chronik von Zuqnîn* [Joh. Eph.?] p. 8 Witakowski = p. 42–43 Harrak. Vgl. dazu auch
     ebd., Anm. 60.
81 *Chronik von Zuqnîn* [Joh. Eph.?] p. 8 Witakowski = p. 43 Harrak.
82 *Chronik von Zuqnîn* [Joh. Eph.?] p. 9 Witakowski = p. 43 Harrak.
83 *Chronik von Zuqnîn* [Joh. Eph.?] p. 9 Witakowski = p. 43 Harrak.
84 *Chronik von Zuqnîn* [Joh. Eph.?] p. 9 Witakowski = p. 43 Harrak.
85 *Chronik von Zuqnîn* [Joh. Eph.?] p. 9 Witakowski = p. 43 Harrak.

hundert († 1199). Seine Schilderung berührt sich – wie angedeutet – über weite Strecken eng mit dem Bericht des Ps.-Dionysios (allerdings ohne explizite Erwähnung der Anicia Iuliana) und dürfte ebenfalls auf Johannes von Ephesos zurückgehen,[86] enthält daneben aber auch Material aus der sog. *Kirchengeschichte* des Ps.-Zacharias Rhetor (zu dieser s. u.);[87] möglicherweise kannte Michael sogar auch die *Chronik von Zuqnîn*: Die prominente Rolle des Marinos in der gesamten Affäre wird hervorgehoben, ebenso wie der auf die Initiative des Syrers zurückgeführte Befehl des Anastasios, das *Trisagion* künftig mit dem Zusatz zu singen.[88] Die „Nestorianer" (also die Chalkedonier) hätten daraufhin Unruhen entfacht und einen neuen Kaiser gefordert (Michael Syrus nennt allerdings keine Namen).[89] Es folgt der Bericht vom Zug der Menge zum Haus des Marinos, von der Brandlegung und der Plünderung der Silberschätze sowie schließlich vom Lynchmord an dem dort vorgefundenen Mönch und der Verspottung seines aufgespießten Hauptes.[90] Bemerkenswert ist freilich der Hinweis, daß Anastasios trotz der Turbulenzen nicht vom *Trisagion*-Zusatz abgelassen habe.[91]

An dieser Stelle bricht Michaels Bericht zunächst ab. Wenige Seiten später findet sich jedoch eine Fortsetzung, die sich wiederum eng mit dem Material berührt, das auch die *Chronik von Zuqnîn bietet*: Anastasios habe Wagenrennen im Hippodrom veranstaltet und sei dazu ohne Diadem erschienen; das Volk habe ihn aufgefordert, das Diadem wieder aufzusetzen. Wenige Tage später habe die Menge dann erneut revoltiert, was Anastasios zu den erwähnten Strafmaßnahmen veranlaßt habe.[92]

4. Theodoros Anagnostes (Victor von Tunnuna, Theophanes-*Chronik*)[93]

Näher an Marcellinus Comes steht wiederum der Bericht des Theophanes, der aller Wahrscheinlichkeit nach über die sog. *Kirchengeschichtliche Epitome* (frü-

---

86 Haase (s. Anm. 74) 85–87; 259, der annimmt, daß Michael „indirekt, durch eine gemeinsame Mittelquelle, mit Ps.-Dion. übereinstimmt" (87); van Ginkel (s. Anm. 74) 230.

87 Haase (s. Anm. 74) 85; 89; Witakowski (s. Anm. 76) 257.

88 Mich. Syr. 9,7 p. 155–156 Chabot.

89 Mich. Syr. 9,7 p. 156 Chabot.

90 Mich. Syr. 9,7 p. 156–157 Chabot.

91 Mich. Syr. 9,7 p. 157 Chabot: „L'empereur ne cessa pas d'obliger à proclamer le: ὁ σταυρωθεὶς δι' ἡμᾶς".

92 Mich. Syr. 9,9 p. 162–163 Chabot.

93 Zu Theodoros Anagnostes vgl. Hansen (s. Anm. 47) IX ff.; Whitby (s. Anm. 30) 467–472. – Zur Theophanes-*Chronik* vgl. Mango/Scott/Greatrex (s. Anm. 47) XLIII ff. (mit den ergänzenden und korrigierenden Bemerkungen von W. Brandes, in: BZ 91

hes 7. Jh.) aus Theodoros Anagnostes geschöpft hat (s. o.).[94] Letzterer war Zeit-
genosse der Ereignisse, die er – wie schon Marcellinus – aus einer strikt chalkedonischen und damit Anastasios gegenüber ausgesprochen ablehnenden Haltung
dargestellt hat. Aus Theodoros Anagnostes scheint zudem auch Victor von Tunnuna (Mitte/2. Hälfte 6. Jh.) große Teile seines Materials bezogen zu haben, so
daß der ursprüngliche Bericht des Theodoros sich in den wichtigsten Punkten
recht gut rekonstruieren läßt. Theodoros/Theophanes bzw. Theodoros/Victor
beginnen mit den Unruhen während der Verkündigung des *Trisagion*-Zusatzes in
der Theodoros-Kirche (gemäß der Chronologie bei Marcellinus am 5. November) durch die kaiserlichen Beamten Platon und Marinos.[95] Aus diesem Grund
habe sich die erregte Menge am Tag der Gedenkprozession (6. November) versammelt.[96] Patriarch Timotheos habe trotz allem in einer schriftlichen Anweisung allen Kirchen der Stadt befohlen, das *Trisagion* mit dem Zusatz zu singen,
und die meisten hätten aus Furcht gehorcht.[97] Aber „die Mönche" hätten etwas
anderes gesungen (Victor von Tunnuna hebt wie Marcellinus die prominente
Rolle des Konstantin-Forums als Versammlungsort hervor)[98] und seien daraufhin vom Volk als „orthodox" gefeiert worden.[99] Nun sei es zu offenem Aufruhr
gekommen, wobei Victor von Tunnuna sogar von einem Zusammenschluß der
sonst verfeindeten Zirkusgruppen der Grünen und Blauen gegen Anastasios
spricht[100] (an dieser Stelle setzt bei Theodoros/Theophanes eine Passage ein, die

---

[1998], 553) – Zu Victor von Tunnuna vgl. W. Geerlings, Victor von Tunnuna, in:
Döpp/Geerlings (s. Anm. 6) 717; ferner Vittore da Tunnuna. Chronica. Chiesa e
impero nell'età di Giustiniano, a cura di A. Placanica, Florenz 1997 (mit der Kritik
von W. Brandes, BZ 92 [1999], 278 f.).

94 Vgl. Hansen (s. Anm. 47) XXIX.
95 Theod. Anagn. *fr.* 508 p. 144,24–25 Hansen; Theoph. a. m. 6005 p. 159,5–8 de Boor;
Vict. Tunn. ad ann. 513 (= Th. Mommsen [Ed.], Chronica Minora Saec. IV. V. VI. VII,
Vol. II, Berlin 1894 [= MGH AA XI], p. 195,13–15 = A. Placanica [Ed.], Vittore da
Tunnuna. Chronica. Chiesa e impero nell'età di Giustiniano, Florenz 1997, p. 30 = C.
Cardelle de Hartmann [Ed.], Victoris Tunnunensis Chronicon cum Reliquiis ex Con-
sularibus Caesaraugustanis et Iohannis Biclarensis Chronicon, Turnhout 2001, p. 31).
96 Theod. Anagn. *fr.* 508 p. 144,25–27 Hansen; Theoph. a. m. 6005 p. 159,8–9 de Boor.
97 Theod. Anagn. *fr.* 508 p. 144,27–145,14 Hansen; Theoph. a. m. 6005 p. 159,9–12 de
Boor; V. Grumel, Les regestes des actes du patriarcat de Constantinople, Vol. I.1,
Paris 1972, p. 145 f., Nr. 200.
98 Vict. Tunn. ad ann. 513 p. 195,15 Mommsen = p. 30 Placanica = p. 31 Cardelle de
Hartmann.
99 Theod. Anagn. *fr.* 508 p. 145,14–15 Hansen; Theoph. a. m. 6005 p. 159,12–14 de Boor.
100 Vict. Tunn. ad ann. 513 p. 195,18–19 Mommsen = p. 30 Placanica = p. 31 Cardelle de
Hartmann. Allerdings gingen die Unruhen nicht, wie sonst häufig, von den Zirkusgruppen aus; vielmehr schlossen sich diese dem allgemeinen Widerstand gegen Anastasios und seine Religionspolitik erst an, als die Tumulte schon ausgebrochen waren,
vgl. Cameron (s. Anm. 10) 292 f.

z. T. wörtlich der Malalas II-Tradition entspricht): Erhebliche Unruhen (στάσις [...] πολλὴ γέγονε), Brandlegungen (ἐμπρησμὸς οἴκων πολλῶν) und zahllose Morde (φόνοι μυρίοι).[101] Die Menge habe Anastasios beschimpft und Vitalian als neuen Kaiser gefordert.[102] Anastasios sei in das Blachernenviertel geflohen, und selbst seine Gattin Ariadne habe ihm erhebliche Vorhaltungen gemacht, weil er großes Unheil über die Christen gebracht habe (ὡς πολλῶν κακῶν αἴτιον Χριστιανοῖς).[103]

Wie schon an der kurzen Inhaltswiedergabe deutlich geworden sein dürfte, ist die Darstellung des Theodoros/Theophanes Kaiser und Patriarch gegenüber extrem feindlich gesinnt. Anastasios muß sich sogar von seiner Frau noch zurechtweisen lassen; Timotheos hingegen gerät wegen seines Befehls an alle Kirchen Konstantinopels ins Zwielicht – ganz so, wie in der miaphysitischen Tradition (Johannes von Nikiu) Makedonios für das Unheil verantwortlich gemacht wird.

5. Ps.-Zacharias

In der Kompilation kirchengeschichtlicher Nachrichten, die nach 568/69 von einem wohl in Amida anzusiedelnden Miaphysiten verfaßt wurde und gemeinhin unter dem Titel ‚*Kirchengeschichte* des (Ps.-)Zacharias Rhetor' gehandelt wird,[104] findet sich im Kontext einer ausführlichen Beschreibung der Auseinandersetzungen zwischen Anastasios und dem Patriarchen Makedonios auch eine sehr knappe Darstellung der Ereignisse im Zusammenhang des *Staurotheis*-Aufstandes.[105] Der Bericht ist deshalb von besonderem Wert, weil hier ein miaphysitischer Antichalkedonier offen verkündet, daß Anastasios mit dem Befehl zur Erweiterung des *Trisagions* einem Ratschlag des Marinos gefolgt sei. Dieser, „ein wachsamer, kluger, in Geschäften gewandter, weiser und unterrichteter Mann [...], fest im Glauben und ein vertrauter Freund des Kaisers, [...] riet ihm, was er thun solle".[106] Daraufhin habe Anastasios den verhängnisvollen Befehl erteilt, das *Trisagion* auch in Konstantinopel so zu singen, wie es bereits in Antiocheia üblich

---

101 Theod. Anagn. *fr.* 508 p. 145,15–16 Hansen; Theoph. a.m. 6005 p. 159,14–15 de Boor; vgl. Vict. Tunn. ad ann. 513 p. 195,19–22 Mommsen = p. 30–32 Placanica = p. 31 Cardelle de Hartmann.

102 Theod. Anagn. *fr.* 508 p. 145,16–17 Hansen; Theoph. a.m. 6005 p. 159,15–17 de Boor.

103 Theod. Anagn. *fr.* 508 p. 145,17–19 Hansen; Theoph. a.m. 6005 p. 159,17–19 de Boor.

104 Vgl. Ahrens/Krüger (s. Anm. 72) XII ff.; P. Allen, Zachariah Scholasticus and the *Historia Ecclesiastica* of Evagrius Scholasticus, JThS 31 (1980), 471–488, sowie kurz A. Baumstark, Geschichte der syrischen Literatur mit Ausschluß der christlich-palästinensischen Texte, Bonn 1922, ND Berlin 1968, 183 f.

105 Ps.-Zach. *HE* 7,9 p. 128,36–130,10 Ahrens/Krüger.

106 Ps.-Zach. *HE* 7,9 p. 129,8–17 Ahrens/Krüger.

gewesen sei.[107] Bemerkenswert ist allerdings, daß der Autor über den darauf folgenden Aufstand schweigt.

Zwischen dem Bericht des Ps.-Zacharias und demjenigen des Johannes von Nikiu – beide der antichalkedonisch-miaphysitischen Seite zugehörig – muß eine Verbindung existiert haben, denn Johannes von Nikiu überliefert im Kontext einen Ausspruch des Severos, den Ps.-Zacharias dem Marinos in den Mund legt[108] und den auch Michael Syrus kennt,[109] der damit offenbar noch eine zusätzliche Quelle neben der *Chronik von Zuqnîn* (oder ihrer Quelle) für seine Darstellung herangezogen hat.

Das folgende Schaubild soll die Überlieferungszusammenhänge zum Staurotheis-Aufstand – soweit sie sich rekonstruieren lassen – noch einmal graphisch verdeutlichen:

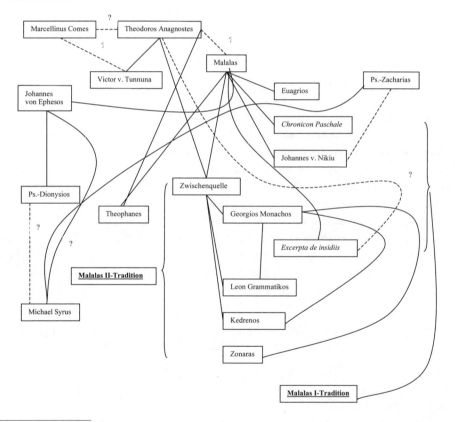

---

107 Ps.-Zach. *HE* 7,9 p. 130,3–5 Ahrens/Krüger.
108 Ps.-Zach. *HE* 7,9 p. 129,22–130,3 Ahrens/Krüger; Joh. Nik. 89,54–57 p. 127–128 Charles.
109 Mich. Syr. 9,7 p. 155–156 Chabot.

Die – teilweise erheblich voneinander abweichenden – Berichte in den Quellen lassen sich vorläufig zum nachstehenden tabellarischen Ereignisablauf zusammenfassen. Dabei ist freilich zu berücksichtigen, daß sich die in den einzelnen Schilderungen referierten Vorgänge nicht einfach summarisch zu einem möglichen Gesamtgeschehen zusammenfassen lassen. Vielmehr soll die Übersicht lediglich den aus den Quellen erschließbaren Materialbestand darlegen. Die Historizität einzelner Elemente aus diesem Reservoir ist – soweit sie sich quellenkritisch nicht abklären läßt – im Zusammenhang der historischen Analyse weiterzudiskutieren. In jedem Fall sollte aber schon jetzt deutlich geworden sein, daß keineswegs „lediglich die Notiz des Marcellinus Comes über den Bericht des Malalas hinaus für die Fragestellung wertvolle Informationen" bietet,[110] sondern daß der Ereignishergang aus einem komplexen Quellenmaterial, das sich nicht nur auf Malalas und Marcellinus Comes beschränkt, heraus rekonstruiert werden muß.

4. Nov. 512	Verkündigung des *Trisagion*-Zusatzes durch Marinos und Platon in der Hagia Sophia; erste Tumulte, die Marcellinus zufolge vor allem unter den Chalkedoniern zahlreiche Opfer fordern.
5. Nov. 512	Weitere Übergriffe gegen Chalkedonier in der Kirche des Hagios Theodoros
6. Nov. 512	Chalkedonier formieren sich zu Prozessionen und sammeln sich auf dem Konstantin-Forum, wo sie ein Lager errichten. Anweisung des Timotheos an alle Kirchen Konstantinopels, das *Trisagion* in der erweiterten Form zu singen. Übergriffe gegen Mönche, die auf der Seite des Anastasios stehen. Als der Kaiser im Rahmen einer Gedenkprozession den Ort passiert, fordern die Aufständischen Areobindos als neuen Kaiser. Kaiserstatuen werden niedergerissen; evtl. Zusammenschluß der Zirkusgruppen.
7. Nov. 512 (?)	Ein Beschwichtigungsversuch, den die Senatoren Keler und Patrikios im Auftrag des Anastasios unternehmen sollen, scheitert. Das Haus des Marinos wird von der tobenden Menge geplündert und in Brand gesetzt (auch die Häuser Platons und des Pompeios könnten niedergebrannt worden sein –

110 So aber Heucke (s. Anm. 6) 283.

7. Nov. 512 (?)	die Berichte differieren in diesem Punkt). Bei der Erstürmung des Hauses des Marinos wird ein Mönch aufgegriffen und gelyncht. Die Menge zieht zum Haus der Anicia Iuliana und proklamiert deren Mann Areobindos zum Kaiser; Areobindos aber ist bereits geflohen. Weitere schwere Ausschreitungen; Brandstiftungen, Straßenschlachten. Vitalian wird zum Kaiser ausgerufen (nur Theophanes [Theodoros Anagnostes] + Malalas II). Ermordung des Vorstehers des Philippos-Klosters und einer weiteren Asketin – beide galten als Vertraute des Kaisers (nur Malalas II).
8. Nov. 512	Konfrontation von Kaiser Anastasios und aufständischem Volk im Hippodrom. Durch eine demonstrative Demutsgeste und eine offenbar wirkungsvolle Ansprache beruhigt Anastasios die Massen. Der Aufstand kollabiert.
Die folgenden Tage	Das anschließende kaiserliche Strafgericht und die Säuberungsmaßnahmen fordern zahllose Opfer.

II

Mehrere der in die Ereignisse um den *Staurotheis*-Aufstand verwickelten Personen werden in den Quellen namentlich genannt. Um zu einer angemessenen Beurteilung des Gesamtgeschehens zu gelangen, erscheint es angebracht, zunächst die dazu erforderlichen Informationen über diese Akteure zusammenzutragen (soweit sie vorhanden sind) und ihre jeweiligen Hintergründe zu beleuchten.

1. Marinos von Apameia (Marinos der Syrer):[111]

Marinos scheint ein begnadeter Finanzfachmann gewesen zu sein; er hat die Finanzpolitik des Anastasios, unter dessen Herrschaft er schrittweise bis zum *praefectus praetorio Orientis* aufgestiegen ist, maßgeblich beeinflußt.[112] Gebürtig im syrischen Apameia, soll er Johannes Lydos zufolge zunächst ἐν τῶν λεγομέν-

---

111 W. Enßlin, RE 14.2 (1930), 1798–1800, s. v. Marinus 13; PLRE II 726–728 (Marinus 7).
112 Brandes (s. Anm. 32) 65; 86.

ων σκρινιαρίων τῆς ἑῴας διοικήσεως tätig gewesen sein, bevor er dann zum Prätorianerpräfekten befördert wurde.[113] Auf den ersten Blick steht dies allerdings im Gegensatz zu einer anderen Nachricht desselben Autors, wonach Marinos εἷς τῶν τῆς Συρίας σκρινιαρίων gewesen sei.[114] Wenn man aber davon ausgeht, daß Marinos zunächst als *tractator* für die Provinz Syria im *scrinium Orientis* tätig gewesen und danach zu dessen *numerarius* aufgestiegen ist, löst sich der vermeintliche Widerspruch plausibel auf.[115] Als *numerarius* des *scrinium Orientis* war der Syrer u. a. für die Einführung der *vindices* verantwortlich, die – dem Prätorianerpräfekten unterstehend – die Steuererhebung verschiedener (wohl kaum sämtlicher) Kurien unter ihre Kontrolle brachten – ein Eingriff, der in der Überlieferung vielfach als Unterdrückungsmaßnahme gewertet wird.[116]

Marinos scheint schon als *numerarius* in einem besonderen Nahverhältnis zu Anastasios gestanden zu haben. In der *Kirchengeschichte* des Ps.-Zacharias wird berichtet, daß er dem Kaiser als „vertrauter Freund" und *chartularius*[117] vielfach mit seinem Rat zur Seite gestanden habe.[118] Dabei werden sich seine Ratschläge aber wohl kaum nur auf Fragen der Finanzpolitik und der Administration beschränkt haben. Schon während des *Staurotheis*-Aufstandes Anfang November 512 wurde Marinos von den Anhängern des *Chalcedonense* für die Einführung des *Trisagion*-Zusatzes verantwortlich gemacht, und Autoren aus dem antichalkedonischen Lager bekennen dies sogar ganz offen;[119] insofern wird man in

---

113 Ioannes Lydus, On Powers or: The Magistracies of the Roman State. Introduction, Critical Text, Translation, Commentary, and Indices by A. C. Bandy, Philadelphia 1983, p. 204,7 (cap. 3,46).

114 Joh. Lyd. *mag.* 3,36 p. 188,20–21 Bandy.

115 So der Vorschlag von Brandes (s. Anm. 32) 66. Malal. p. 327,71–79 Thurn zufolge soll Anastasios Marinos anstelle Johannes' des Paphlagoniers (der *comes sacrarum largitionum* wurde) zum τρακτευτὴς καὶ λογοθέτης befördert haben. Auch damit könnte eine Karriere als *tractator* und *numerarius* umschrieben sein. Vgl. dazu auch Stein (s. Anm. 6) 204 f., mit Anm. 2.

116 Vgl. Joh. Lyd. *mag.* 1,28 p. 44,20–23; 3,46 p. 204,3–10 Bandy; 3,49 p. 208,16–28 Bandy; Euagr. *HE* 3,42 p. 144,24–32 Bidez/Parmentier; Malal. p. 327,74–76 Thurn. S. dazu Stein (s. Anm. 6) 210–215; E. Chrysos, Die angebliche Abschaffung der städtischen Kurien durch Kaiser Anastasios, Byzantina 3 (1971), 94–102; A. Chauvot, Curiales et paysans en Orient à la fin du Ve et au début du VIe siècle: note sur l'institution du *Vindex*, in: E. Frézouls (Hg.), Sociétés urbaines, sociétés rurales dans l'Asie Mineure et la Syrie hellénistiques et romaines, Strasbourg 1987, 271–281; Brandes (s. Anm. 32) 87, Anm. 159; 408.

117 Die Bedeutung der Bezeichnung *chartularius* für Marinos ist unklar, vgl. Enßlin (s. Anm. 111) 1798; Stein (s. Anm. 6) 204 f., Anm. 2.

118 Ps.-Zach. *HE* 7,9 p. 129,8–22 Ahrens/Krüger.

119 Vgl. etwa Marc. Com. ad ann. 512,6 p. 98 Mommsen; Malal. p. 333,23–24 Thurn (zur Haltung der Anhänger des *Chalcedonense*); daneben aus antichalkedonischer Sicht vor allem Ps.-Zach. *HE* 7,9 p. 129,17–22 Ahrens/Krüger.

der Tat dem Einfluß des Marinos einen erheblichen Anteil an dieser religionspolitischen Grundsatzentscheidung des Anastasios zumessen müssen. Welch große
Bedeutung der Rat des Syrers für die Haltung des Kaisers besaß, geht im übrigen
auch aus einem Vorfall hervor, den Kyrill von Skythopolis überliefert: Im Jahr
511 bat der Hl. Sabas den Kaiser um einen Steuernachlaß für Jerusalem und Palästina, den dieser auch gewährte und mit dessen Umsetzung er den damaligen
praefectus praetorio Orientis Zotikos betraute.[120] Marinos jedoch intervenierte
erfolgreich, indem er die Einwohner der Heiligen Stadt Nestorianer und Juden
nannte.[121] Sabas rief daraufhin Marinos dazu auf, seinen religionspolitischen
„Kriegszug" (πόλεμος) aufzugeben und auch von seiner Habsucht abzulassen;[122]
wenn er dem nicht Folge leiste, dann drohten ihm selbst und dem Kaiser erhebliche Schwierigkeiten.[123] Die Tatsache, daß dann tatsächlich wenige Monate später das Haus des Marinos im Rahmen des *Staurotheis*-Aufstandes (δήμου στάσις) in Flammen aufgegangen sei, führt Kyrill als Beweis dafür an, daß die
Warnung des Mönchsvaters sich bewahrheitet habe.[124]

Diese Begebenheit ist nicht nur zur Illustration des erheblichen Einflusses,
den Marinos noch vor seiner Prätorianerpräfektur auf den Kaiser ausübte, von
Bedeutung. Sie zeigt überdies, daß der *Staurotheis*-Aufstand trotz seiner auf den
ersten Blick rein religiösen Motivation durchaus auch genuin politische Implikationen besaß: Sabas (bzw. Kyrill von Skythopolis) rügt an der Person des Marinos dessen religiöse Haltung *zusammen mit* seiner Habsucht (und ihren Auswir-
kungen auf die Finanzpolitik des Kaisers).

Marinos stieg – wohl Ende des Jahres 512 oder später (s. u.) – als Nachfolger
des Zotikos zum *praefectus praetorio Orientis* auf, wird aber bereits für das Jahr
515 als Ex-Präfekt bezeichnet.[125] Trotzdem erwies er sich weiterhin als treuer
Gefolgsmann des Anastasios und leistete dem Kaiser wichtige Dienste bei der
Niederwerfung Vitalians.[126] Im übrigen korrespondierte er mit Severos von

---

120 E. Schwartz (Ed.), Kyrillos von Skythopolis, Leipzig 1939, p. 145,14–146,4 (*Vita
    Sabae*, cap. 54) [CPG 7536]. Zu Zotikos vgl. PLRE II 1206.
121 Kyrill. Skythop. *V. Sabae* 54 p. 146,4–11 Schwartz: [...] Νεστοριανοὺς τοὺς κατὰ
    τὴν ἁγίαν πόλιν ἀποκαλῶν καὶ ᾿Ιουδαίους καὶ τῶν βασιλικῶν δωρεῶν ἀναξίους.
122 Kyrill. Skythop. *V. Sabae* 54 p. 146,13–15 Schwartz: [...] παῦσαι τοῦ κατὰ τῶν
    ἁγίων τοῦ θεοῦ ἐκκλησιῶν πολέμου· παῦσαι τῆς τοσαύτης φιλοχρηματίας καὶ
    πονηρίας καὶ ἀσφάλισαι σεαυτόν.
123 Kyrill. Skythop. *V. Sabae* 54 p. 146,15–18 Schwartz.
124 Kyrill. Skythop. *V. Sabae* 54 p. 147,2–6 Schwartz.
125 Malal. p. 330,38; 332,79 Thurn. Die Prätorianerpräfektur des Marinos ist mehrfach
    bezeugt: Joh. Lyd. *mag.* 3,36 p. 188,22; 3,46 p. 204,6–10 Bandy; Euagr. *HE* 3,42
    p. 144,26–28 Bidez/Parmentier; Just. *Ed.* 13,15.
126 Vgl. Malal. p. 329,11–332,94 Thurn; Euagr. *HE* 3,43 p. p. 145,1–29 Bidez/Parmentier;
    Joh. Nik. 89,71–88 p. 130–132 Charles; *Exc. de insid.* 41 p. 169,8–170,3 de Boor [aus
    Malal.].

Sozopolis/Antiocheia,[127] und dieser wiederum empfahl dem Bischof Stephanos von Apameia einen Verwandten des Marinos für die Priesterwürde.[128]

Nach dem Tod des Anastasios geriet Marinos offenbar rasch in Konflikt mit dem Regime Justins I. und Justinians – möglicherweise aufgrund der mit diesen Namen verbundenen religionspolitischen Neuorientierung. Zwar ist er für das Jahr 519 kurzfristig noch einmal als *praefectus praetorio Orientis* bezeugt,[129] aber er scheint konspirative Kontakte zu Amantios[130] gepflegt zu haben[131] und zog sich den Zorn Justins zu, als er dessen Aufstieg aus niedrigsten Verhältnissen in Form eines Bilderzyklus auf einem öffentlichen Gebäude darstellen ließ.[132] Justin I. entließ ihn.[133]

Für die Analyse des *Staurotheis*-Aufstandes ist die Frage, wann Marinos zum *praefectus praetorio Orientis* befördert wurde, von nicht geringer Bedeutung. Wie bereits angedeutet, findet man in den Handbüchern zumeist die Jahreszahl 512,[134] die in der PLRE mit einem Fragezeichen versehen ist. Aus der skizzierten Episode bei Kyrill von Skythopolis ergibt sich, daß Zotikos in der Tat wohl noch bis zur Abreise des Sabas aus Konstantinopel im Mai 512 als Prätorianerpräfekt amtiert hat.[135] In der Malalas-Tradition (Georgios Monachos, Leon Grammatikos, Kedrenos, Zonaras, s. o.)[136] wird Marinos für die Zeit des Aufstandes selbst als λογοθέτης bezeichnet, was dafür spricht, daß er zu diesem Zeitpunkt ebenfalls noch als *numerarius* des *scrinium Orientis* amtierte. Unterstellt man einmal, daß diese Angabe korrekt ist, dann müßte der Zeitpunkt seiner Beförderung – entgegen der traditionellen Sichtweise[137] – *nach* dem Aufstand anzusetzen sein, und dies erscheint auch aus einer anderen Perspektive heraus plausibel: Nach dem Ende des Aufstandes folgte ein hartes Strafgericht, das selbst ein Johannes

---

127 The Sixth Book of the Select Letters of Severus Patriarch of Antioch in the Syriac Version of Athanasius of Nisibis. Edited and Translated by E. W. Brooks, Vol. II.1, London/Oxford 1903, ND 1969, p. 381 (= *epist.* 7,6) [CPG 7070].

128 Sev. Ant. *epist.* 7,6 p. 381 Brooks.

129 *Cod. Iust.* 5,27,7 (9. Nov. 519); 2,7,25 (1. Dez. 519).

130 PLRE II 67 f. (Amantius 4).

131 *Exc. de insid.* 43 p. 170,18–171,5 de Boor [aus Malal.].

132 Ps.-Zach. *HE* 8,1 p. 140,4–24 Ahrens/Krüger.

133 Joh. Lyd. *mag.* 3,51 p. 212,1–2 Bandy.

134 Vgl. etwa Bury (s. Anm. 6) I 470; Stein Histoire (s. Anm. 6) 783; Capizzi (s. Anm. 6) 141.

135 Kyrill. Skythop. *V. Sabae* 54 p. 146,22–23 Schwartz. Nach Joh. Lyd. *mag.* 3,27 p. 174,6 Bandy bekleidete Zotikos die Prätorianerpräfektur etwas länger als ein Jahr; seine Amtszeit ist somit auf die Jahre 511/12 anzusetzen.

136 Georg. Mon. p. II 620,6 de Boor; Leon Gramm. p. 119,6 Bekker; Kedren. PG 121 p. 688 [631] B; Zon. 14,3,32 p. 138,14–15 Pinder.

137 Vgl. etwa Enßlin (s. Anm. 111) 1798; Stein (s. Anm. 6) 177; 204 f., Anm. 2; 783.

von Nikiu, der Anastasios ansonsten in jeder Hinsicht zu exkulpieren versucht, nicht leugnen konnte (s. o.). Dem Kaiser war es somit zwar gelungen, die Unruhen durch eine demonstrative Demutsgeste bzw. ein regelrechtes Abdankungsangebot zu beschwichtigen, aber in der Folge übte er ein umso strengeres Regiment aus. Der Stadtpräfekt Platon, während des Aufstandes von der Menge massiv attackiert, leitete die Säuberungsaktionen. Es ist gut denkbar, daß Anastasios, um seine Kompromißlosigkeit zusätzlich zu unterstreichen, nun auch den wegen seiner Finanz- und Religionspolitik weithin verhaßten Marinos in besonderer Weise ausgezeichnet haben könnte, indem er ihn zum Prätorianerpräfekten beförderte. Auch das Festhalten an Severos, der am 16. November 512 – nur wenige Tage nach dem Ende des Aufstandes – zum Bischof von Antiocheia geweiht wurde, fügt sich in dieses Bild.[138]

---

138 Das Datum der Konsekration ist allerdings nur schwer rekonstruierbar und deshalb lange Gegenstand einer Forschungskontroverse gewesen: Malal. p. 327,68–70 Thurn gibt den 6. November als Zeitpunkt der Übernahme der Patriarchenwürde an (ihm folgen etwa Duchesne, Église [s. Anm. 6], 30; R. Devreesse, Le Patriarcat d'Antioche depuis la paix de l'église jusqu'a la conquête arabe, Paris 1945, 69; Charanis, Church and State [wie Anm. 6], 76; vgl. Frend, Rise [s. Anm. 6], 219f.; 223: Wahl am 6., Weihe am 8. November). Andere Dokumente – vor allem ein koptisches Manuskript über die in diesem Kontext gehaltene Ansprache des Severos (inzwischen als Teil seiner 1. *Homilie* identifiziert, s. u.) sowie die *Chronik* des Elias von Nisibis (s. u.) – bezeugen jedoch, daß die Bischofsweihe am 16. November – also knapp eine Woche nach dem Ende des *Staurotheis*-Aufstandes – durch 12 anwesende Bischöfe (die Namen nennt Honigmann, Évêques et évêchés monophysites [s. Anm. 67], 15, auf Basis der Edition der entsprechenden Dokumente durch Kugener [s. u.], 273ff.) erfolgt sein muß. Die Zeremonie fand in der Hauptkirche zu Antiocheia statt. Direkt nach seiner Konsekration hielt Severos eine Ansprache (προσφώνησις), in der er das Konzil von Chalkedon und den *Tomus Leonis* verurteilte – entgegen seiner Zusage dem Kaiser gegenüber, sich nicht zu einer derart scharfen Sprachregelung hinreißen zu lassen, vgl. Theod. Anagn. *fr.* 499 p. 142,23–27 Hansen (eine syrische Übersetzung des Textes wurde ediert von M.-A. Kugener, Allocution prononcée par Sévère après son élévation sur le trône patriarcal d'Antioche, OC 2 [1902], 265–282 [mit französischer Übersetzung] = M. A. Kugener [Ed.], Notices relatives a Sévère, PO 2,316–325, hier 322–325 [CPG 7036]; vgl. Sev. Ant. *hom.* 1,14, in: M. Brière/F. Graffin [Edd.], Les *Homiliae cathedrales* de Sévère d'Antioche, Turnhout 1976 [PO 38.2], p. 254–269, 260f. [CPG 7035]). Aufgrund der Unruhen, die der kontroverse Vorgang bereits während der Weihe ausgelöst hatte und die dazu geführt hatten, daß Severos' Ansprache nur teilweise zu den Zuhörern durchdringen konnte, wiederholte er seine Rede (= Sev. Ant. *hom.* 1) zwei Tage später, am Fest des Hl. Romanos (das sicher auf den 18. November datiert werden kann, vgl. P. H. Engberding, Wann wurde Severus zum Patriarchen von Antiochien geweiht, OC 37 [1953], 132–134, hier 133), in der Romanos-Kirche und dann noch einmal in der Euphemia-Kirche in Daphne. Aufgrund der klaren Bezugnahme auf das Romanos-Fest in der koptisch überlieferten Beschreibung und der dort ebenfalls enthaltenen Angabe, die Wiederholung der

Vor diesem Hintergrund erscheint es plausibel, die Prätorianerpräfektur des Marinos auf die Zeit *nach* dem 8. November 512 – und zwar explizit als *Resul-*

προσφώνησις an diesem Tag habe *zwei Tage nach der Bischofsweihe* stattgefunden, läßt sich letztere unzweifelhaft auf den 16. November datieren (koptischer Text und französische Übersetzung: E. Porcher, Sévère d'Antioche dans la littérature copte, ROC 2 [1907], 119–124, hier 120, sowie jetzt als Eingangskapitel zu Sev. Ant. *hom.* 1, edd. Brière/Graffin, PO 38.2, p. 254–269, hier 254). Auch Elias von Nisibis gibt dieses Datum an (PO 2,308). Daß der über die Geschichte Antiocheias gewöhnlich gut unterrichtete Johannes Malalas (in der uns vorliegenden Form) hingegen den 6. November nennt, kann auch auf einen Fehler im Verlauf des komplizierten Überlieferungsprozesses zurückgehen (so auch die Vermutung von E. W. Brooks, Rez. zu M.-A. Kugener [Ed.], Les *Homiliae Cathedrales* de Sévère d'Antioche. Homélie LXXVII [PO 16.5], Paris 1922, in: JThS 24 [1923], 346–348, hier 348). Für die Annahme solcher Verschreibungen spricht ohnehin auch die Tatsache, daß in zwei anonymen Notizen in syrischen Manuskripten gar der 8. November als Konsekrationsdatum erscheint (PO 2,317f.).
Schwartz (s. Anm. 6) 247, Anm. 2, verweist darauf, daß die Weihe des Severos schon deshalb nicht am 6. November habe stattfinden können, weil dies kein Sonntag gewesen sei (ähnlich Brooks, a. a. O., 348). Ein Sonntag war der 16. November allerdings auch nicht, wohl aber der 18. Allerdings „bietet das von der sog. Apostolike Paradosis zuerst formulierte Gesetz vom Sonntag als dem eigentlichen Bischofsweihetag keine unbedingt zuverlässige Gewähr für die Anwendung auf jeden einzelnen Fall" (Engberding, a. a. O., 133 f.).
Engberding, a. a. O., 132–134, nimmt – u. a. wegen des Sonntags-Arguments – den 18. November als Weihetermin an und bezieht sich dabei explizit auf Homilien, die Severos anläßlich der Jahrestage seiner Weihe am Romanos-Fest gehalten habe (*hom.* 1 [edd. M. Brière/F. Graffin, PO 38,254–269]; *hom.* 35 zum 1. Jahrestag [edd. M. Brière/ F. Graffin/C. J. A. Lash, PO 36,438–457]; *hom.* 80 zum 3. Jahrestag [ed. M. Brière, PO 20,324–343]; *hom.* 99 zum 4. Jahrestag [ed. I. Guidi, PO 22,207–229]). Ähnlich argumentiert Brooks, a. a. O., 348, mit Hinweis auf *hom.* 1 und 35. Beide übersehen dabei aber die erwähnte Notiz in der koptischen Handschrift (= *hom.* 1,1 p. 254 Brière/Graffin), die das Fest des Hl. Romanos ausdrücklich zwei Tage *nach* der Konsekration des Severos ansetzt. Möglicherweise hat aber Severos selbst später versucht, den Tag seiner Weihe nachträglich mit dem Romanos-Fest zu synchronisieren (so auch M. Brière, Introduction générale aux homélies de Sévère d'Antioche, Paris 1960 [PO 29.1], 7–72, hier 13), um ihr so ein stärkeres und für Antiocheia bedeutsameres Gewicht zu verleihen. Dies erscheint mir angesichts der vorliegenden Nachrichten wahrscheinlicher als die Annahme Brooks', a. a. O., 348, daß Severos am 16. November gewählt und am 18. November geweiht worden sei (vgl. allerdings auch P. Allen/ C. T. R. Hayward, Severus of Antioch, London/New York 2004, 12: Wahl am 6., Weihe am 16. November [mit Bezug auf Brière, a. a. O., 14, der aber den Tag der Weihe – den 16. November – als eigentlich entscheidend ansieht]).
Zur Rekonstruktion des Ereignishergangs und zur Datierungsfrage s. auch G. Downey, A History of Antioch in Syria from Seleucus to the Arab Conquest, Princeton 1961, 511f., mit Anm. 36–39; Grillmeier (s. Anm. 29) 318.

tat des Staurotheis-*Aufstandes* – zu datieren.[139] Als Indiz für eine signifikant kompromißlose Haltung des Anastasios ist dieser Sachverhalt nicht ohne Bedeutung.

2. *Platon*[140]

Platon begegnet in den Quellen zunächst als Anhänger und Förderer (πάτ-ρων)[141] der Grünen, zugleich aber auch als ‚Spezialist‘ im Umgang mit den Zirkusgruppen. Seine Stunde schlug, als die Grünen im Hippodrom gegen Anastasios revoltierten, da dieser nicht auf ihre Forderung eingegangen war, einige Randalierer aus der Haft zu entlassen. Daraufhin kam es zu Zusammenstößen zwischen den Grünen und der kaiserlichen Leibwache; Anastasios selbst wäre im Kathisma beinahe durch einen Steinwurf getötet worden, dem er nur knapp ausweichen konnte. Im Verlauf des Aufstandes kam es dann zu Brandstiftungen, die den Nordteil des Hippodroms bis zum Kathisma und u. a. auch das Konstantin-Forum[142] schwer in Mitleidenschaft zogen. Erst als Platon zum Stadtpräfekten befördert worden war und hart durchgriff, kehrte wieder Ruhe ein: πολλῶν δὲ συσχεθέντων καὶ τιμωρηθέντων ἐγένετο ἡσυχία, προαχθέντος ἐπάρχου πόλεως Πλάτωνος, ὅς ὑπῆρχε πάτρων τοῦ Πρασίνου μέρος.[143]

---

139 Auch die Tatsache, daß Joh. Nik. 89,61 p. 128 Charles Marinos im Kontext des Aufstandes als „illustrious man" bezeichnet, muß dem nicht entgegenstehen.

140 PLRE II 891 f. (Plato 3); Cameron (s. Anm. 10) 131 f.

141 Malal. p. 322,61 Thurn.

142 Vgl. dazu Müller-Wiener (s. Anm. 53) 255; F. A. Bauer, Stadt, Platz und Denkmal in der Spätantike. Untersuchungen zur Ausstattung des öffentlichen Raums in den spätantiken Städten Rom, Konstantinopel und Ephesos, Mainz 1996, 182.

143 Malal. p. 321,46–322,61 Thurn; *Exc. de insid.* 38 p. 168,11–25 de Boor [aus Malal.]; *Chron. Pasch.* p. I 608,1–18 Dindorf. Das Zitat Malal. p. 322,59–61 Thurn. Auf dieselben Ereignisse bezieht sich auch Joh. Nik. 89,18–22 p. 123–124 Charles, allerdings von verschiedenen Mißverständnissen durchsetzt. – Bei dem Theoph. a.m. 5997 p. 147,17–20 de Boor, für das Jahr 504/05 bezeugten Aufstand wird es sich wohl um ein anderes Ereignis gehandelt haben: Zum einen erscheint hier klar ein Konflikt zwischen den Grünen und den Blauen als Auslöser der Unruhen, zum anderen soll in deren Verlauf ein unehelicher Sohn des Anastasios den Tod gefunden haben – ein Ereignis, das die Malalas-Tradition sicherlich in irgendeiner Weise vermerkt hätte. – Verschiedentlich wurde auch darüber spekuliert, ob sich der Bericht Victors von Tunnuna über den *Staurotheis*-Aufstand (der von ihm irrtümlich in das Jahr 513 datiert wird, vgl. Vict. Tunn. ad ann. 513 p. 195,13–22 Mommsen = p. 30–32 Placanica = p. 31 Cardelle de Hartmann) nicht vielleicht auf diese Unruhen bezieht, denn er enthält als einziges Zeugnis unter den Quellen zum *Staurotheis*-Aufstand einen Hinweis auf Beteiligung der Zirkusgruppen und berichtet von ähnlichen Zerstörungen, wie sie für den ‚Steinwurf-Aufstand‘ bezeugt sind (in diesem Sinne PLRE II 892; zu Recht aber

Allerdings ist die Datierung dieses Vorgangs nicht ganz klar: Der erhaltene griechische Malalas-Text (*Baroccianus*) läßt im Kontext keine nachvollziehbare Chronologie erkennen. In den Konstantinischen Exzerpten steht der Vorgang zwischen dem Isaurier-Krieg (492–497/98, *fr.* 37) und dem Brytai-Aufstand einige Jahre später (*fr.* 39). Weil im Text des *Chronicon Paschale* im Anschluß an den ‚Steinwurf-Aufstand' von der Befestigung Daras berichtet wird[144] (die ab ca. 505/06 erfolgte)[145] und weil die entsprechende Nachricht in der *Osterchronik* chronologisch falsch plaziert ist (zum Jahr 498), wurde gemutmaßt, daß der Bericht über den ‚Steinwurf-Aufstand' zusammen mit jenem über den Ausbau von Dara ‚verrutscht' sein, jedenfalls in zeitliche Nähe mit letzterem Ereignis gehören könnte.[146] Diese Vermutung könnte eine Bestätigung in einer Nachricht des Marcellinus Comes finden, der für das Jahr 507 eine *seditio popularis in circo* vermerkt und sich damit möglicherweise auf den beschriebenen Vorfall bezieht.[147] Freilich gibt es aber auch Stimmen, die den Aufstand entsprechend dem Lemma in der *Osterchronik* auf das Jahr 498 datieren.[148]

Daß die Ernennung Platons zum Stadtpräfekten im Kontext dieser Unruhen tatsächlich nur „a desperate attempt to pacify the Greens after [the] unnecessari-

---

ablehnend Croke, Chronicle of Marcellinus [wie Anm. 11], 113; auch Cameron, Circus Factions [s. Anm. 10], 131 f., bezieht Victors Nachricht nur auf das Jahr 512). Dem ist allerdings entgegenzuhalten, daß Victor mit der Erwähnung der *Staurotheis*-Formel und mit verschiedenen weiteren Einzelheiten (dazu s. o.) klar auf die Ereignisse des Jahres 512 verweist. Zudem erwähnt er nicht nur die Grünen, sondern auch die Blauen und berichtet überdies von einem Zusammenschluß der Gruppen – in den Berichten zum ‚Steinwurf-Aufstand' werden die Blauen hingegen nicht einmal erwähnt. Es ist daher eher davon auszugehen, daß Victor lediglich die Aufzählung der zerstörten Bauten irrtümlich vom ‚Steinwurf-Aufstand' auf den *Staurotheis*-Aufstand übertragen haben könnte (so verstehe ich auch Whitby/Whitby, Chronicon Paschale [s. Anm. 30], 100, Anm. 316); möglicherweise wurden aber auch schlichtweg bei beiden Revolten ähnliche Teile der Stadt in Mitleidenschaft gezogen.

144 Vgl. *Chron. Pasch.* p. I 608,19–609,7 Dindorf.
145 Vgl. dazu A. Luther, Die syrische Chronik des Josua Stylites, Berlin/New York 1997, 210 ff. Zu Dara s. auch M. P. Collinet, Une „Ville Neuve" byzantine en 507: la fondation de Dara (Anastasiopolis) en Mésopotamie, in: Mélanges offerts a M. Gustave Schlumberger a l'occasion du quatre-vingtième anniversaire de sa naissance (17 octobre 1924), I, Paris 1924, 55–60; B. Croke/J. Crow, Procopius and Dara, JRS 73 (1983), 143–159, bes. 148 ff., sowie jetzt auch G. Brands, Ein Baukomplex in Dara-Anastasiopolis, JbAC 47 (2004), 144–155.
146 Whitby/Whitby (s. Anm. 30) 100, Anm. 316.
147 So Whitby/Whitby (s. Anm. 30) 100, Anm. 316, und auch schon PLRE II 892; ferner Croke (s. Anm. 11) 113; Heucke (s. Anm. 6) 278. Vgl. Marc. Com. ad ann. 507,1 p. 96 Mommsen: *Seditio popularis in circo facta est: miles ei armatus obstitit.*
148 Vgl. Cameron (s. Anm. 8) 234; ders. (s. Anm. 10) 21; 131.

ly harsh suppression of their protest" gewesen ist,[149] möchte ich indes bezweifeln. Wollte der frischberufene *praefectus urbi* sich als zuverlässiger, dem Kaiser
treu ergebener Beamter profilieren, so konnte er – ja mußte es in der gegebenen
Situation sogar – dies vor allem durch ein rigoroses Vorgehen gegen die von ihm
bisher favorisierte Gruppe inszenieren. Anastasios, dessen politische Geschicklichkeit man nicht unterschätzen sollte (wie insbesondere die Ereignisse um den
Staurotheis-Aufstand verdeutlichen), könnte dies einkalkuliert und mit Platons
Beförderung insofern einen geschickten Schachzug vollzogen haben.

Jedenfalls verschaffte der nicht sicher datierbare ‚Steinwurf-Aufstand' Platon
das begehrte und einflußreiche Amt des Stadtpräfekten, und er scheint den Kaiser dabei nicht enttäuscht zu haben. Daß er vor Beginn der Unruhen im November 512 gemeinsam mit Anastasios' engem Vertrauten Marinos den Zusatz zum
Trisagion verkünden durfte, spricht dafür, daß der Kaiser auch zu diesem Zeitpunkt auf ihn setzte. Und auch die delikate Aufgabe, nach dem Ende des Aufstandes wieder einmal die Säuberungsaktionen durchführen zu ‚dürfen', deutet
mindestens auf eine funktionierende Zusammenarbeit zwischen dem Kaiser und
seinem Stadtpräfekten hin. Geht man überdies davon aus, daß Platon seit dem
‚Steinwurf-Aufstand' ununterbrochen das Amt des Stadtpräfekten bekleidet
hat,[150] dann wäre er wohl mit dem „Oberhyparchen" bzw. „Hyparchen" gleich-
zusetzen, der dem Bericht des Ps.-Zacharias zufolge eine prominente Rolle bei
der Einfädelung der Absetzung des Makedonios gespielt hat[151] – auch dies würde
einmal mehr auf das besondere Vertrauensverhältnis zwischen ihm und Anastasios verweisen.

Marinos und Platon weisen eine signifikante Gemeinsamkeit auf: Ihre Beförderung in höchste Ämter erfolgte jeweils aus gefährlichen Aufständen in der
Hauptstadt heraus. Anastasios nutzte derartige Situationen offenbar als Gelegenheiten, um den Kreis derer, auf die er zählen konnte, zu sondieren.

3. Keler und Patrikios[152]

Diesen beiden Senatoren, die der Kaiser dem Bericht des Marcellinus zufolge als
Unterhändler aussandte, nachdem der Aufstand bereits offen ausgebrochen und

---

149 So Cameron (s. Anm. 10) 131; vgl. auch Tinnefeld (s. Anm. 6) 190: „ausdrücklich eine
   Konzession".
150 Dies ist insofern wahrscheinlich, als für die Jahre vor 512 kein anderer Kandidat
   bekannt ist und die Quellen für das Jahr 512 nicht von einer Iteration der Präfektur
   sprechen, vgl. PLRE II 892.
151 Vgl. Ps.-Zach. *HE* 7,8 p. 123,21; 123,25; 125,28; 125,33; 127,12 Ahrens/Krüger.
152 PLRE II 275–277 (Celer 2); II 840–842 (Fl. Patricius 14); G. Greatrex, Flavius Hypatius, *quem vidit validum Parthus sensitque timendum.* An Investigation of His Ca-

Areobindos als neuer Kaiser proklamiert worden war, kommt für den Fortgang der Ereignisse – soweit erkennbar – nur eine marginale Bedeutung zu. Denn ihre Mission endete, noch bevor sie eigentlich begonnen hatte, im Steinhagel der empörten Menge. Ohnehin berichtet lediglich Marcellinus von ihren Bemühungen.[153] Aus dieser Tatsache aber zu folgern, daß die Episode erfunden sei, erscheint wiederum verfehlt, denn der Chronist hätte dafür überhaupt kein erkennbares Motiv besessen. Wahrscheinlich haben die anderen Zeugen diesem randständigen Detail des Aufstands schlichtweg so wenig Bedeutung zugemessen, daß sie es ihrerseits nicht für berichtenswert hielten.

Wichtiger erscheint die Mission der beiden Senatoren allerdings im Kontext einer Gesamtanalyse des *Staurotheis*-Aufstandes. Denn sie wirft einmal mehr ein interessantes Licht auf die Personalpolitik des Kaisers – zumal in Krisensituationen.

Keler und Patrikios profilierten sich im Perserkrieg des Anastasios 502–506. Der Illyrier Keler, der unter Anastasios mindestens 15 Jahre lang das hohe Amt des *magister officiorum* innehatte (spätestens seit 503, bis 518)[154] und im Jahr 508 das Konsulat bekleidete,[155] wurde Ende des Jahres 503 als „commander-in-chief"[156] zum östlichen Kriegsschauplatz entsandt, um die Kräfte der bis dahin zerstrittenen Heerführer (Hypatios und Patrikios auf der einen, Areobindos auf der anderen Seite) neu zu bündeln und gemeinsam mit Areobindos effektiv einzusetzen; zugleich sollte er dabei wohl auch als besonderer Vertrauensmann des Kaisers agieren.[157] Sein Versuch, Patrikios bei der Belagerung des von den Per-

---

reer, Byz 66 (1996), 120–142, bes. 125 f. (Patrikios) und 126 f. (Keler). Zu Keler s. überdies M. Clauss, Der magister officiorum in der Spätantike (4.–6. Jahrhundert). Das Amt und sein Einfluß auf die kaiserliche Politik, München 1980, 150 f., mit einem kurzen Überblick über seine Karriere.

153 Marc. Com. ad ann. 512,5 p. 98 Mommsen.

154 So PLRE II 275, auf Basis von Marc. Com. ad ann. 503; 504 p. 96 Mommsen; Prok. *BP* 1,8,2; Euagr. *HE* 3,32 p. 130,23–24 Bidez/Parmentier; *Cod. Iust.* 4,29,21; 12,19,12; 12,20,6.

155 PLRE II 277; Clauss (s. Anm. 152) 151.

156 So Greatrex 1996 (s. Anm. 152) 126; vgl. ders., Rome and Persia at War, 502–532, Leeds 1998, 108: „supreme commander".

157 Malal. p. 326,47–50 Thurn. Luther (s. Anm. 145) 202; Greatrex 1998 (s. Anm. 156) 108. Zur Uneinigkeit der oströmischen Heerführer bis zu diesem Zeitpunkt s. ebd., 98 ff. Aus Theoph. a. m. 5998 p. 147,31–148,2 de Boor, läßt sich erschließen, daß der Oberbefehl wohl bei Keler lag, Areobindos ihm jedoch beinahe gleichgestellt war. Prok. *BP* 1,8,1–2, vermittelt hingegen den mißverständlichen Eindruck, daß alle *magistri militum* und Keler dieselben Befugnisse gehabt hätten, vgl. auch Ps.-Zach. *HE* 7,4 p. 111,28–33 Ahrens/Krüger; beide Autoren gehen allerdings auch davon aus, daß Keler gleichzeitig mit den anderen Feldherrn in den Krieg entsandt worden sei, und zeichnen die Lage insofern ohnehin nicht korrekt nach, vgl. Greatrex, a. a. O., 108,

sern eroberten Amida zu unterstützen, führte im Jahr 504 allerdings nicht zu nennenswerten Ergebnissen.[158] Erfolgreicher gestaltete sich sein Einfall in persisches Territorium im selben Jahr, der den Perserkönig immerhin zur Aufnahme von Verhandlungen bewog.[159] Im weiteren Verlauf des Krieges erscheint Keler wiederholt als zentrale Figur in den Kampfhandlungen und diplomatischen Bemühungen. Die Aushandlung des Siebenjährigen Friedens 506 war im wesentlichen seine Leistung.[160]

Keler erwies sich nicht nur in militärischen und diplomatischen Fragen als außerordentlich wichtig für Anastasios, sondern unterstützte diesen auch im Jahr 511 geschickt in seinem Vorgehen gegen den widerspenstigen Patriarchen Makedonios,[161] obwohl er unmittelbar zuvor möglicherweise sogar noch auf dessen Seite gestanden hatte.[162] Ausdrücklich hatte er sich zudem um die sichere Rückkehr des Severos und seiner Begleiter nach Syrien zu kümmern.[163] Trotz allem scheint Keler sich auch um die Wahrung der Interessen der Chalkedonier bemüht zu haben, wie aus dem Briefwechsel des Severos hervorgeht, mit dem er im übrigen auch selbst korrespondierte.[164] Der *magister officiorum* warb in einem Schreiben an Severos für die Wiedereinsetzung chalkedonischer Bischöfe in ihre Sitze in der Provinz Syria Secunda,[165] zudem verteidigte er offen die Beschlüsse des Konzils von Chalkedon. Dies dürfte zu seiner negativen Charakterisierung bei Ps.-Zacharias geführt haben.[166]

Anm. 98. Ein besonderes Vertrauensverhältnis zwischen Anastasios und Keler konstatiert bereits Joh. Lyd. *mag.* 3,17 p. 160,9–11 Bandy.

158 A. Luther (Ed.), Die syrische Chronik des Josua Stylites, Berlin/New York 1977, p. 79–82 (cap. 69–75). Im einzelnen zum Ereignishergang s. Greatrex 1998 (s. Anm. 156) 110–112.

159 Jos. Styl. 75–80 p. 82–85 Luther; Greatrex 1998 (s. Anm. 156) 112–114.

160 Jos. Styl. 97–98 p. 93–94 Luther; Prok. *BP* 1,9,24; Malal. p. 326,50–53 Thurn; Theoph. a.m. 5998 p. 147,31–148,149,9 de Boor; Joh. Lyd. *mag.* 3,53 p. 214,14–26 Bandy; *Chronik von Zuqnîn* [wohl aus Jos. Styl.] p. 7 Witakowski = p. 42 Harrak; Greatrex 1998 (s. Anm. 156) 115–118.

161 Theod. Anagn. *fr.* 487 p. 138,21–26; *fr.* 490–491 p. 139,11–24 Hansen; Theoph. a.m. 6004 p. 154,25–156,9 de Boor; Joh. Lyd. *mag.* 3,17 p. 160,6–11 Bandy; Euagr. *HE* 3,32 p. 130,21–25 Bidez/Parmentier; Ps.-Zach. *HE* 7,7–8 p. 119,29–128,35 Ahrens/Krüger; M.-A. Kugener (Ed.), Vie de Sévère par Jean, supérieur du monastère de Beith-Aphthonia (PO 2.3), Paris 1904, p. 237 [CPG 7527]. Clauss (s. Anm. 152) 94.

162 Dies legt jedenfalls eine Bemerkung bei Ps.-Zach. *HE* 7,7 p. 120,26–28 Ahrens/Krüger, nahe: „Der Magistros aber schloß sich ihm [sc. dem Makedonios] an, da er von ihm durch Geschenke geehrt wurde".

163 M.-A. Kugener (Ed.), Vie de Sévère par Zacharie le Scholastique (PO 2.1), Paris 1904, p. 105 [CPG 6999].

164 Sev. Ant. *epist.* 1,21 p. 73–75 Brooks.

165 Sev. Ant. *epist.* 1,24 p. 84 Brooks.

166 Vgl. Ps.-Zach. *HE* 7,7–8 p. 119,29–128,35 Ahrens/Krüger.

Nach dem Tod des Anastasios bemühte sich Keler mit großem Einsatz um eine rasche und reibungslose Klärung der Nachfolgefrage.[167] Justin I. scheint den engen Vertrauten des Anastasios trotz seiner pro-chalkedonischen Bemühungen rasch abgesetzt zu haben,[168] ohne den Mann, der über weitreichende überregionale Beziehungen, u. a. zu Bischof Avitus von Vienne,[169] verfügte, aber völlig entmachten zu können. Es waren möglicherweise gerade seine diplomatischen Fähigkeiten, gepaart mit seinen prinzipiellen Bemühungen um einen Ausgleich zwischen Befürwortern und Gegnern des Konzils von Chalkedon, die ihn auch in die Verhandlungen um die Beendigung des Akakianischen Schismas involvierten.[170] Papst Hormisdas jedenfalls bat ausdrücklich ihn und Patrikios (!) um Unterstützung für die päpstlichen Gesandten in Konstantinopel.[171]

Die Karriere Kelers läßt eine gewisse ‚Flexibilität‘ im Hinblick auf die Frage nach der Akzeptanz bzw. Ablehnung des Konzils von Chalkedon erkennen.[172] Während seine Mitwirkung an den Intrigen gegen den Chalkedonier Makedonios dabei das eine Extrem markiert, weisen seine offenbar guten Kontakte zu Papst Hormisdas in die andere Richtung. Dieser großzügige, jeweils situativ justierbare Umgang mit der großen religiösen und kirchenpolitischen Streitfrage seiner Zeit mag mit zu Kelers Ansehen als herausragender Diplomat beigetragen haben. In jedem Fall sicherte seine Haltung ihm eine langjährige erfolgreiche Karriere und einen politischen Einfluß, der auch nach dem Tod des Anastasios nicht zu unterschätzen war.

Eine ähnlich indifferente, der jeweiligen aktuellen Lage ‚angemessene‘ Haltung gegenüber Chalkedon läßt sich auch für den Phryger Patrikios konstatieren, dessen politische Aktivitäten sich mehrfach mit denjenigen Kelers berührt haben, so daß Anastasios die beiden offenbar nicht ohne Grund im Kontext des *Staurotheis*-Aufstandes *gemeinsam* zu Verhandlungen mit den Aufrührern aufgeboten hat. Flavios Patrikios bekleidete im Jahr 500 gemeinsam mit dem Neffen des Kaisers, Hypatios, das Konsulat und amtierte über den langen Zeitraum 500–518 als *magister militum praesentalis*.[173] Während des Perserkrieges agierte Patrikios

---

167 I. I. Reiske (Ed.), Constantini Porphyrogeniti Imperatoris De Cerimoniis Aulae Byzantinae Libri Duo, Vol. I, Bonn 1829, p. 427,8–13 (cap. 1,93); dazu Stein (s. Anm. 6) 219; Greatrex 1996 (s. Anm. 152) 127.

168 Vgl. PLRE II 277.

169 Vgl. R. Peiper (Ed.), Alcimi Ecdicii Aviti Viennensis Episcopi Operae quae supersunt, Berlin ²1961 (MGH AA VI.2), p. 77 (*epist.* 48 [nach März 515]).

170 Vgl. O. Guenther (Ed.), Epistulae Imperatorum Pontificum Aliorum inde ab a. CCCLXVII usque ad a. DLIII datae. Avellana quae dicitur collectio. Pars II, Prag/ Wien/Leipzig 1898, p. 657 (*epist.* 197).

171 *Coll. Avell.* 152 p. 600–601 Guenther.

172 Dieser Punkt wird besonders von Greatrex 1996 (s. Anm. 152) 126 f., betont.

173 PLRE II 840 mit den Belegen.

lange gemeinsam mit Hypatios;[174] beide waren zunächst mit der Belagerung des von den Persern eroberten Amida befaßt.[175] Einen Teilerfolg erzielte Patrikios dann immerhin mit einem Einfall in die Arzanene.[176] Weniger glorreich gestalteten sich allerdings die anschließenden Aktionen der beiden Feldherren. Dem hart bedrängten Areobindos kamen sie trotz eindringlicher Aufforderung erst viel zu spät zur Hilfe – der empörte Areobindos fühlte sich verraten und wollte zunächst nach Konstantinopel zurückkehren;[177] im Sommer 503 erlitten Hypatios und Patrikios eine schwere Niederlage gegen die Perser und gerieten nun endgültig in den Geruch der Feigheit.[178] Während Hypatios nach Konstantinopel zurückbeordert wurde,[179] durfte Patrikios jedoch auf dem Kriegsschauplatz verbleiben und kümmerte sich weiter um die Belagerung von Amida – später unterstützt durch Keler (s. o.). Militärisch trat er danach aber nicht mehr sonderlich hervor.[180]

Wie sein ‚Partner‘ Keler war auch Patrikios unmittelbar in die kirchenpolitischen Kontroversen involviert: In seinem Haus in Konstantinopel fanden zwischen 508 und 511 Diskussionen zwischen Severos und Johannes von Klaudiopolis statt.[181] An der Absetzung des Makedonios war er ebenfalls nicht unbeteiligt: Eine Gruppe von Mönchen überreichte Patrikios im Jahr 511 ein Dokument zur Weitergabe an den Kaiser, das den Patriarchen des Nestorianismus beschuldigte;[182] Ende Juli 511 nahm Patrikios an einem *silentium* teil, in dem der Fall Makedonios besprochen wurde.[183] Zudem sollten Keler und er gemeinsam Makedonios über seine religiöse Haltung befragen.[184]

---

174 Vgl. Prok. *BP* 1,8,2.
175 Einzelheiten und Quellenbelege bei Greatrex 1998 (s. Anm. 156) 94 ff.; gemeinsame Belagerung Amidas: ebd., 96 f.; vgl. Luther (s. Anm. 145) 186 f.
176 Ps.-Zach. *HE* 7,5 p. 112,23–24 Ahrens/Krüger. Luther (s. Anm. 145) 188; 203; Greatrex 1998 (s. Anm. 156) 97, mit Anm. 72.
177 Jos. Styl. 55–56 p. 69–70 Luther; Theoph. a. m. 5997 p. 146,19–24 de Boor. Luther, Josua Stylites (s. Anm. 145) 187 f.; Greatrex 1996 (s. Anm. 152) 125; Greatrex 1998 (s. Anm. 156) 98.
178 Jos. Styl. 57 p. 70–71 Luther; Marc. Com. ad ann. 503 p. 96 Mommsen; Prok. *BP* 1,8,17–19. Zum Vorwurf der Feigheit: Marc. Com. ad ann. 503 p. 96 Mommsen (*sine audacia*); Joh. Lyd. *mag.* 3,53 p. 214,11–12 Bandy; Prok. *BP* 1,8,19. Vgl. Greatrex 1998 (s. Anm. 156) 99–101.
179 Jos. Styl. 88 p. 89 Luther; Malal. p. 326,47–50 Thurn; Theoph. a. m. 5998 p. 148,2–6 de Boor. Luther (s. Anm. 145) 209 f.; Greatrex 1998 (s. Anm. 156) 108 f.
180 Greatrex 1998 (s. Anm. 156) 109 ff.
181 Sev. Ant. *epist.* 1,1 p. 3–11 Brooks. Zu diesen Diskussionen, die möglicherweise im Zusammenhang des sog. *Typos* des Anastasios (dazu s.u.) erfolgten, s. Grillmeier (s. Anm. 29) 312 f.
182 Ps.-Zach. *HE* 7,8 p. 122,20–29 Ahrens/Krüger.
183 Ps.-Zach. *HE* 7,8 p. 124,28–125,24 Ahrens/Krüger.
184 Joh. *Vita Sev.* (PO 2.3) p. 237 Kugener.

Weil er ein langjähriger Freund des strengen Chalkedoniers Vitalian und seiner Familie war, wurde Patrikios 513 zu Verhandlungen mit dem Rebellen entsandt.[185] Diese Beziehung zu Vitalian war immerhin derart eng, daß Patrikios sich 515 sogar weigerte, einem Befehl des Anastasios zu gehorchen und Vitalian anzugreifen.[186]

Nach dem Tod des Anastasios wurde Patrikios kurzfristig von den *scholares* als Nachfolgekandidat präsentiert, scheiterte aber am Einspruch der *excubitores* und mußte sein Leben sogar von Justinian schützen lassen.[187]

Im November 519 befand sich Patrikios in Edessa in der heiklen Mission, Bischof Paulos zur Akzeptanz des Konzils von Chalkedon zu zwingen. Als dieser sich weigerte, setzte Patrikios ihn gewaltsam ab und verbannte ihn nach Seleukeia.[188]

Ebenso wie Keler fällt auch Patrikios durch seine religiöse ‚Flexibilität‘ auf,[189] die den Verdacht eines politischen Opportunismus zumindest stark suggeriert: Während er unter Anastasios an der Absetzung des Chalkedoniers Makedonios maßgeblich beteiligt war, exilierte er unter Justin I. den Chalkedon-Gegner Paulos. Auch Patrikios wurde im übrigen ebenso wie Keler von Papst Hormisdas um Unterstützung der römischen Legaten gebeten (s. o.).[190]

Keler und Patrikios waren offenbar geschickte politische Köpfe, ersterer zudem ein durchaus erfolgreicher Heerführer. Beiden gelang es jedenfalls, auch in turbulenten Zeiten jeweils einen Kurs zu steuern, der ihnen auch später Einfluß und hohe Ämter sicherte. Im Zuge der Absetzung des Makedonios hatten beide ihre Loyalität gegenüber dem Kaiser bewiesen, Keler konnte sich überdies noch mit seinen diplomatischen Erfolgen in den Verhandlungen mit den Persern schmücken. Diese Geschicklichkeit, gepaart mit hohem Ansehen und dem Ruf, Extrempositionen zu verabscheuen, prädestinierte sie geradezu für ihre Rolle als kaiserliche Unterhändler während des *Staurotheis*-Aufstandes. Daß sie dabei vollkommen erfolglos geblieben sind, dürfte in erster Linie auf die harsche Reaktion der Aufrührer zurückzuführen sein, die einen Beginn der Verhandlungen – in denen die beiden Senatoren dann sicherlich ihr ganzes Geschick entfaltet hätten – gar nicht erst ermöglichten.

---

185 *Exc. de insid.* 103 p. 144,4–9 de Boor [aus Joh. Ant.].
186 Malal. p. 331,48–55 Thurn. Vgl. Greatrex 1996 (s. Anm. 152) 125.
187 *De caerim.* 1,93 p. 427,19–428,5 Reiske.
188 I. Guidi (Ed.), Chronicon Edessenum, in: Chronica Minora I interpretatus est I. Guidi, Louvain 1955, p. 1–11, hier p. 9,14–29 (= *Chron. Edess.* ad ann. 831); *Chronik von Zuqnin* p. 25–27 Witakowski = p. 55–56 Harrak.
189 Vgl. Greatrex 1996 (s. Anm. 152) 126 f., bes. 126: „his doctrinal loyalties were not inflexible“.
190 *Coll. Avell.* 152 p. 600–601 Guenther.

4. Areobindos und Anicia Iuliana[191]

Anastasios hat sicherlich ganz bewußt ausgerechnet Keler und Patrikios für die Verhandlungen mit den Aufrührern ausgewählt, nachdem unmittelbar zuvor der Chalkedonier Areobindos zum Kaiser proklamiert worden war.[192] Zweifelsohne dürfte dabei – wie gezeigt – insbesondere Kelers bekanntes Verhandlungsgeschick eine wichtige Rolle gespielt haben; auffällig ist darüber hinaus aber auch, daß beide Gesandte den erhaltenen Zeugnissen zufolge ausgerechnet zu Areobindos ein gespanntes Verhältnis gehabt haben müssen und es damit sicherlich auch in ihrem persönlichen Interesse gelegen haben dürfte, einen Übergang der Kaiserwürde auf den Ehemann der Anicia Iuliana zu verhindern: Von Patrikios (und Hypatios) – fühlte sich Areobindos verraten, nachdem er im Sommer 503, von den Persern bedrängt, vergeblich auf ihre Hilfe hatte warten müssen (s. o.),[193] die Aktivitäten Kelers hingegen wird er mindestens mit Argwohn beobachtet haben, seitdem dieser ihm Ende 503 als leitender Feldherr im Perserkrieg übergeordnet worden war (s. o.).

Als Enkel Ardaburs (cos. 447)[194] und Urenkel des Flavius Ardabur Aspar (cos. 434)[195] entstammte Flavios Areobindos Dagalaiphos einer Familie des höchsten oströmischen Militäradels,[196] die vor allem um die Mitte des 5. Jahrhunderts – vor dem Aufstieg der Isaurier – beträchtlichen Einfluß besessen hatte. Durch die Heirat mit Anicia Iuliana gelang es ihm, diese namhafte Ahnenreihe noch zusätzlich zu veredeln, denn Iuliana war die Tochter des weströmischen Kaisers Olybrius (472), eine Enkelin Valentinians III. (425–455) und Urenkelin Eudokias (der Frau Theodosius' II. [408–450]), konnte ihre Abstammung also bis auf die theodosianische Dynastie zurückführen.[197]

---

191 PLRE II 143f. (Fl. Areobindus Dagalaiphus Areobindus 1); II 635 f. (Anicia Iuliana 3). Zu Anicia Iuliana s. zudem die wortreiche Studie von C. Capizzi, Anicia Giuliana (462 ca–530 ca). Ricerche sulla sua famiglia e la sua vita, RSBN 5 (1968), 191–226; ferner Ch. Pazdernik, Anicia Juliana, in: G. W. Bowersock/P. Brown/O. Grabar (Hgg.), Late Antiquity. A Guide to the Postclassical World, Cambridge (Mass.)/London 1999, 300 f.
192 S. Marc. Com. ad ann. 512,4–5 p. 98 Mommsen.
193 Vgl. Greatrex 1998 (s. Anm. 156) 98: „Areobindus, feeling himself betrayed by his colleagues [...]".
194 PLRE II 135–137 (Ardabur iunior 1).
195 PLRE II 164–169 (Fl. Ardabur Aspar).
196 Vgl. das Stemma PLRE II 1310.
197 Vgl. das Stemma PLRE II 1309, Nr. 3 (mit dem Stemma 1308); Capizzi (s. Anm. 191) 193 ff.

Areobindos agierte in den Jahren 503–504 (505?) als *magister militum per Orientem*; 506 bekleidete er das Konsulat.[198] Die erhaltenen Konsulardiptychen nennen für ihn darüber hinaus das Amt des *comes sacri stabuli*.[199]

Ebenso wie Keler und Patrikios spielte auch Areobindos eine prominente Rolle im Perserkrieg des Anastasios. Als im Jahr 503, nach dem Fall Amidas, die römische Gegenoffensive begann, übernahmen Hypatios und Patrikios die Belagerung der eroberten Stadt, während Areobindos in persisches Territorium einfiel.[200] Nach einigen kleineren Gefechten versuchte er sich sogar an einer Belagerung von Nisibis, mußte das hoffnungslose Unterfangen aber bald schon wieder aufgeben und geriet rasch in zusätzliche Bedrängnis, als Kabades ihm ein überlegenes Heer entgegensandte.[201] Areobindos mußte sich eilig zurückziehen, wartete vergeblich auf die von seinen Mitfeldherrn Hypatios und Patrikios angeforderten Entsatztruppen und konnte nach dem Desaster – wie bereits berichtet – nur mit Mühe daran gehindert werden, voller Zorn den Kriegsschauplatz ganz zu verlassen, da er sich im Stich gelassen fühlte (s. o.).[202] Im September 503 befand er sich in Edessa, eingeschlossen von Kabades. Wiederholte Verhandlungen mit dem Perserkönig über ein Lösegeld für die Stadt scheiterten; Kabades zog zunächst zwar ab, kehrte aber kurz darauf wieder zurück; in den nachfolgenden Handgemengen behielten die Römer die Oberhand – schließlich gab Kabades auf und zog sich endgültig von der Stadt zurück.[203] Kurz darauf erschien Keler als neuer Oberkommandant für den Perserkrieg; Areobindos mußte sich ihm nun unterordnen.[204]

Im folgenden Jahr führte Areobindos, dem im März von der ansässigen Bevölkerung ein frischgelegtes Gänseei mit der geheimnisvollen Aufschrift „Die Römer werden siegen" übergeben worden war,[205] erfolgreich einen Einfall in Persarmenien durch, der zahlreiche Gefangene und große Mengen an Beute einbrachte. Auf dem Rückzug nach Amida gelang es ihm sogar noch, die Besatzung von Nisibis in einen Hinterhalt zu locken und den Persern dadurch hohe Verluste zuzufügen.[206] Den Winter 504/05 verbrachte er in Antiocheia.[207]

---

198 PLRE II 143.
199 Vgl. PLRE II 143.
200 Vgl. Jos. Styl. 54 p. 69 Luther.
201 Jos. Styl. 55 p. 69–70 Luther; Ps.-Zach. *HE* 7,5 p. 112,24–34 Ahrens/Krüger; Prok. *BP* 1,8,10–11; Theoph. a. m. 5997 p. 146,9–24 de Boor. Vgl. Greatrex 1998 (s. Anm. 156) 97.
202 Greatrex 1998 (s. Anm. 156) 98.
203 Greatrex 1998 (s. Anm. 156) 103–106, mit den Belegen.
204 Greatrex 1998 (s. Anm. 156) 108.
205 Jos. Styl. 67–68 p. 78–79 Luther.
206 Jos. Styl. 75 p. 82 Luther; Theoph. a. m. 5998 p. 148,11–13 de Boor. Vgl. Greatrex 1998 (s. Anm. 156) 112 f.
207 Jos. Styl. 87 p. 88 Luther.

Die Mißerfolge der römischen Kriegführung vor der Entsendung Kelers wurden in späterer Zeit offenbar durchaus diskutiert: Während Johannes Lydos sowohl Hypatios als auch Patrikios Unerfahrenheit und Feigheit vorwirft,[208] führt er die militärische Erfolglosigkeit des Areobindos auf dessen verweichlichte und luxusgesättigte Lebensführung zurück; er sei ein Freund des Gesangs (φιλῳδός) und des Flötenspiels (φίλαυλος) gewesen, und überdies auch noch geldgierig (φιλοχρήμων).[209] In dieser Tradition wurde also in der grundsätzlichen Negativbewertung nicht zwischen Hypatios und Patrikios auf der einen sowie Areobindos auf der anderen Seite differenziert. Andere Zeugnisse zeichnen Areobindos hingegen als durchaus fähigen Heerführer (Josua Stylites, Theophanes-*Chronik*).[210]

Wann Areobindos aus dem Amt des *magister militum per Orientem* ausschied (504 oder 505?), ist unklar; zum Zeitpunkt seines Konsulats 506 – möglicherweise u. a. eine Belohnung für seinen Einsatz im Krieg[211] – hatte er es jedenfalls bereits abgegeben.[212] Über sein weiteres Schicksal ist abgesehen von seiner Proklamation zum Kaiser durch die tobenden Massen während des *Staurotheis*-Aufstandes nichts bekannt.[213]

Seine eigenen prominenten Vorfahren und die Herkunft seiner Frau Anicia Iuliana sicherten Areobindos – auch in religiösen Fragen – innerhalb der bestehenden Grenzen eine gewisse Unabhängigkeit gegenüber dem Kaiser und seiner Familie,[214] die mit dem Herrschaftsantritt des Anastasios zunehmend an Einfluß und Bedeutung zu gewinnen begann.[215] Diese Unabhängigkeit, die namentlich Anicia Iuliana demonstrierte, barg allerdings stets auch die Gefahr der Unberechenbarkeit, so daß Anastasios Areobindos und seiner Frau eine besondere Aufmerksamkeit geschenkt haben dürfte. Die rasche Eliminierung der Isaurier – erklärter Feinde der Familie des Areobindos – in den 490er Jahren, das Amt des *magister militum per Orientem* und das Konsulat 506 dürften auch unter diesem Gesichtspunkt zu bewerten sein. Hingegen scheinen die ungünstigen personellen Konstellationen, die sich im Verlauf des Perserkrieges ergaben, für erhebliche Spannungen gesorgt zu haben, die zweifelsohne auch das Verhältnis zwischen Areobindos und dem Kaiser belastet haben. Nach dem Konsulat jedenfalls sind für Areobindos keine weiteren Ämter mehr bezeugt.

---

208 Joh. Lyd. *mag.* 3,53 p. 214,11–12 Bandy.
209 Joh. Lyd. *mag.* 3,53 p. 214,9–11 Bandy.
210 Vgl. dazu Greatrex 1996 (s. Anm. 152) 127.
211 So Greatrex 1996 (s. Anm. 152) 127.
212 Vgl. PLRE II 144.
213 Vgl. Capizzi (s. Anm. 191) 221 f.
214 Greatrex 1996 (s. Anm. 152) 127.
215 Zur Familie des Anastasios s. Al. Cameron, The House of Anastasius, GRBS 19 (1978), 259–276.

Das vor allem auf der adeligen Herkunft beruhende Selbsbewußtsein und die daraus resultierende *relative* Unabhängigkeit vom Kaiser manifestierten sich aber besonders in Anicia Iuliana, die ihre strikt chalkedonische Haltung niemals verheimlicht hat. Die *patricia*[216] – der *patricius*-Titel ist für Areobindos bezeichnenderweise nicht bezeugt – pflegte enge Kontakte zum Hl. Sabas,[217] einem 511/12 in Konstantinopel weilenden prominenten Vorkämpfer für Chalkedon, der freilich auch von Anastasios mit hoher Achtung behandelt wurde.[218] Obwohl der Kaiser und auch Patriarch Timotheos erheblichen Druck auf sie ausübten, blieb sie bei ihrer theologischen Position[219] und schaltete sich unter Justin I. dann sogar eifrig in die Verhandlungen um die Beilegung des Akakianischen Schismas ein, wobei sie eine rege Korrespondenz mit Papst Hormisdas entfaltete.[220]

Besondere Berühmtheit erlangte Anicia Iuliana aufgrund ihrer zahlreichen Kirchenbau-Initiativen. Mehrere Gotteshäuser wurden von ihr finanziert, darunter der monumentale Neubau der Polyeuktos-Kirche (524–527), der ausdrücklich an den Tempel Salomons gemahnen sollte und sogar Justinian in einen aristokratischen Wettstreit trieb: ,Seine' 532–537 neu errichtete Hagia Sophia sollte u. a. die Polyeuktos-Kirche Anicia Iulianas in den Schatten stellen.[221]

Gerade die auf Anicia Iuliana zurückgehenden Kirchenbauten zeugen nicht nur von der Frömmigkeit, sondern auch vom aristokratischen Selbstbewußtsein ihrer Stifterin. Unter Anastasios blieb sie konsequent bei ihrer religiösen Linie, obwohl diese sich zur kaiserlichen Kirchenpolitik konträr verhielt; unter dem chalkedonischen Regime Justins I. und Justinians bewahrte sie sich ihre Unabhängigkeit dadurch, daß sie mit ihren Kirchen das aristokratische Standesbewußtsein der Kaiser provozierte – die adelige Konkurrenz zwischen ihr und

---

216 Zu den Belegen s. PLRE II 636.
217 Kyrill. Skythop. *V. Sabae* 53 p. 145,7–13 Schwartz.
218 Kyrill. Skythop. *V. Sabae* 51 p. 141,24–143,15; 52 p. 143,16–144,28; 54 p. 145,14–146,23 Schwartz.
219 Theod. Anagn. *fr.* 504 p. 144,5–8 Hansen; Theoph. a. m. 6005 p. 157,34–158,4 de Boor.
220 *Coll. Avell.* 164 p. 615; 179 p. 635; 198 p. 657–658 Guenther.
221 Zu Justinian, Anicia Iuliana und der Polyeuktoskirche vgl. R. M. Harrison, The Church of St. Polyeuktos in Istanbul and the Temple of Solomon, in: C. Mango/O. Pritsak (Hgg.), Okeanos. Essays Presented to Ihor Ševčenko on His Sixtieth Birthday by His Colleagues and Students, Cambridge (Mass.) 1983, 276–279; M. Harrison, Ein Tempel für Byzanz. Die Entdeckung und Ausgrabung von Anicia Julianas Palastkirche in Istanbul, Zürich/Stuttgart 1990, bes. 36; 40; 137 f.; M. Meier, Das andere Zeitalter Justinians. Kontingenzerfahrung und Kontingenzbewältigung im 6. Jahrhundert n. Chr, Göttingen ²2004, 66, Anm. 94; 188 f.; J. D. Alchermes, Art and Architecture in the Age of Justinian, in: M. Maas (Hg.), The Cambridge Companion to the Age of Justinian, Cambridge 2005, 343–375, hier 364 f.

Justinian hat im übrigen auch einen literarischen Reflex gefunden.[222] Es gab kaum etwas Gefährlicheres für eine stabile Kaiserherrschaft als eine solche Frau und ihren Ehemann sowie deren Präsenz in der Hauptstadt. Hier zeigt sich deutlich die politische Sprengkraft der Kaiserproklamation des Areobindos im Jahr 512, denn dieser hätte zweifelsohne erhebliche Ressourcen gegen Anastasios mobilisieren können. Zugleich macht die Flucht des Areobindos und seine dadurch signalisierte Ablehnung der Kaiserwürde aber auch deutlich, daß es Anastasios bis dahin gelungen zu sein scheint, Areobindos und seine Frau – u. a. durch die oben genannten Maßnahmen – hinreichend an sich zu binden und sich ihre Loyalität trotz wiederholter Verstimmungen zu erhalten.

5. Pompeios[223]

Die Nachricht, daß zusammen mit dem Haus des Marinos auch das Anwesen des Pompeios niedergebrannt worden sein soll, findet sich lediglich bei Marcellinus Comes (s. o.).[224] Es ist verlockend, daraus zunächst den Schluß zu ziehen, der Chronist habe möglicherweise Pompeios mit Platon verwechselt, dessen Haus der Malalas-Tradition zufolge gemeinsam mit dem des Marinos in Flammen aufgegangen sein soll.[225] Andererseits ist aber zum einen zu bedenken, daß Marcellinus als Augenzeuge und gewissenhafter Berichterstatter kaum einen solchen Fehler begangen hätte, zumal er insgesamt recht sorgfältig mit der Beschreibung der einzelnen Personen und der sie betreffenden Vorgänge verfahren zu sein scheint; zum anderen hat sich bereits mehrfach gezeigt, daß die Schilderungen des *Staurotheis*-Aufstandes in unseren Zeugnissen mitunter erheblich voneinander abweichen können, ohne daß in jedem Fall Irrtümer angenommen werden müßten – auch die gescheiterte Verhandlungsmission Kelers und des Patrikios ist ja nur aus Marcellinus bekannt und fügt sich dennoch durchaus in die historischen Konstellationen. Da sich insofern kein überzeugendes Argument gegen eine Brandlegung auch am Haus des Pompeios beibringen läßt, wird im folgenden von der Historizität dieses Vorgangs ausgegangen.

Der *patricius* Pompeios, Neffe des Anastasios und Bruder des Hypatios, bekleidete im Jahr 501 das Konsulat.[226] Einer Notiz des Iordanes zufolge erlitt er als Heerführer (evtl. als *magister militum*) bei Adrianopel eine Niederlage gegen

---

222 Vgl. Greg. Tur. *Glor. mart.* 102 [103] PL 71,793B–795A = B. Krusch (Ed.), Gregorii Turonensis Opera (= MGH SRM I), Hannover 1885, p. 555,20–557,5.
223 PLRE II 898 f. (Pompeius 2); Greatrex 1996 (s. Anm. 152) 129 f.
224 Marc. Com. ad ann. 512,5 p. 98 Mommsen.
225 Vgl. Georg. Mon. p. II 620,13–16 de Boor; Zon. 14,3,34 p. 139,1 Pinder.
226 S. PLRE II 898.

auswärtige Raubscharen, ein Ereignis, das – nicht ganz sicher – in das Jahr 517 datiert wird.[227] Im Jahr 528 erscheint er erneut als Truppenkommandeur und Anführer eines Heeres, das als Verstärkung an die Perserfront entsandt wurde.[228]

Pompeios wurde nicht nur in den *Staurotheis*-Aufstand hineingezogen, sondern auch in die Nika-Revolte des Jahres 532; letztere kostete ihn das Leben: Justinian ließ ihn gemeinsam mit seinem Bruder Hypatios, der von den Aufständischen zum Kaiser ausgerufen worden war, hinrichten.[229]

Die Inbrandsetzung des Hauses des Pompeios während des *Staurotheis*-Aufstandes mag auf den ersten Blick erstaunen: Denn bei Pompeios handelte es sich um einen bekennenden und gerade in dieser Hinsicht auch einflußreichen Chalkedonier.[230] Auch er schaltete sich unter Justin I. in die Verhandlungen mit Papst Hormisdas über eine Beendigung des Akakianischen Schismas ein[231] und gehörte sogar (gemeinsam mit Vitalian und Justinian) der Delegation der *sublimes et magnifici viri* an, die im Jahr 519 die päpstlichen Legaten vor Konstantinopel empfingen und in die Stadt geleiteten.[232] Dem exilierten Patriarchen Makedonios gewährte er seine Unterstützung, woraufhin ihn Anastasios gezielt gedemütigt haben soll (ἐταπείνου);[233] schon vor dem *Staurotheis*-Aufstand stattete seine Frau Anastasia – ebenso wie Anicia Iuliana – dem 511/512 in Konstantinopel weilenden Hl. Sabas häufige Besuche ab.[234]

Warum also wurde das Haus des Pompeios dann ebenfalls niedergebrannt? Geoffrey Greatrex, der auschließen möchte, daß es sich dabei schlichtweg um einen Unfall gehandelt haben könnte,[235] schlägt dazu folgende Erklärung vor: Nach der fehlgeschlagenen Proklamation des Areobindos hätten die aufrührerischen Massen vorgehabt, nunmehr Pompeios zum Kaiser auszurufen, ihn aber nicht in seinem Haus vorgefunden und dieses daraufhin wütend niedergebrannt –

---

227 Th. Mommsen (Ed.), Iordanis Romana et Getica, Berlin 1882 (= MGH AA V.1), p. 46 (*Rom.* 356). Die Datierung dieses Ereignisses in das Jahr 517 beruht auf den Überlegungen von Stein (s. Anm. 6) 105 f. Al. Cameron, The Date of Priscian's *De laude Anastasii*, GRBS 15 (1974), 313–316, hier 314, mit Anm. 10, plädiert hingegen für das Jahr 503.

228 Malal. p. 369,73–75 Thurn.

229 Zu diesen Vorgängen s. im einzelnen Cameron (s. Anm. 215) 263 ff.; M. Meier, Der ‚Kaiser der Luppa'. Aspekte der politischen Kommunikation im 6. Jahrhundert n. Chr., Hermes 129 (2001), 410–430.

230 Vgl. etwa Charanis (s. Anm. 6) 39; Greatrex 1996 (s. Anm. 152) 129: „[...] there is no question that Pompey was a supporter of the Council"; vgl. ebd., 136.

231 *Coll. Avell.* 163 p. 614–615; 174 p. 630–631 Guenther.

232 *Coll. Avell.* 167 p. 619; 223 p. 683 Guenther.

233 Theod. Anagn. *fr.* 505 p. 144,9–11 Hansen; Theoph. a. m. 6005 p. 158,4–8 de Boor.

234 Kyrill. Skythop. *V. Sabae* 53 p. 145,7–13 Schwartz.

235 Vgl. Greatrex 1996 (s. Anm. 152) 131, Anm. 25.

ganz so, wie im Jahr 532 während des Nika-Aufstandes das Haus des Probos in
Flammen aufgegangen sei, als dieser zum Kaiser proklamiert wurde und ebenfalls
nicht anzutreffen war.[236] Diese Hypothese überzeugt allerdings nicht: Zum einen
wird in keinem unserer Zeugnisse auch nur angedeutet, daß neben Areobindos
(und Vitalian) auch Pompeios zum Kaiser ausgerufen worden sein soll – daß all
unsere Gewährsmänner ein derart wichtiges Detail unterschlagen haben sollten,
ist aber wohl kaum anzunehmen. Zum anderen bringt Marcellinus die Inbrandsetzung der Häuser des Marinos und des Pompeios sprachlich – und damit auch
inhaltlich – in einen sehr engen Zusammenhang (*domibus Marini et Pompei suc-
censis*) und suggeriert damit, daß dieser Akt bei beiden aus ähnlichen Gründen
geschehen sein muß, die im Fall des Marinos ja auch hinlänglich bekannt sind:
Allgemeine Wut gegen Anastasios und sein Umfeld. Und schließlich wäre zur
Klärung des Sachverhalts noch eine Notiz Kyrills von Skythopolis heranzuziehen: Dieser berichtet nämlich im Kontext seiner *Vita* des Hl. Sabas, daß dessen
Unglücks-Prophezeiung gegenüber Marinos (s. o.) sich dadurch erfüllt habe, daß
das Haus des Finanzfachmannes im *Staurotheis*-Aufstand niedergebrannt worden sei. Als Quelle für diese Information führt er dabei ausgerechnet Anastasia
an, die Frau des Pompeios, die wiederum durch ihren Mann über die Vorgänge
unterrichtet gewesen sei.[237] Pompeios bemühte sich somit ganz offenkundig
darum, die Verwüstung des Hauses des Marinos in einen Kausalzusammenhang
mit dessen Politik zu stellen und über das Schicksal seines eigenen Anwesens
schweigend hinwegzugehen. Offenbar war es seine Intention, gezielt die Unter-
schiede zwischen sich selbst und Marinos zu propagieren, und der Grund dafür
kann nur darin liegen, daß man beide Personen während des *Staurotheis*-Auf-
standes aus ähnlichen Gründen attackiert hat – nämlich aufgrund ihrer großen
Nähe bzw. Verwandtschaft zu Kaiser Anastasios. Dies wiederum wirft ein interessantes Licht auf die Ursachen der Unruhen: Wenn auch ein bekennender
Chalkedonier wie Pompeios nicht vor den tobenden Massen geschützt war, sondern ebenfalls von ihnen angegriffen wurde, dann kann der Aufstand nicht nur
aus rein religiösen Gründen ausgebrochen sein, sondern muß sich mit genuin
politischen Aspekten vermengt haben (die in diesem Fall – trotz der Differenzen
zwischen Anastasios und Pompeios – im Aspekt der Kaisernähe liegen), und
genau dies wäre ja auch aufgrund der Rahmenbedingungen im Konstantinopel
des frühen 6. Jahrhunderts zu erwarten gewesen. Die Inbrandsetzung des Hauses
des Pompeios verweist somit auf die politischen Implikationen des *Staurotheis*-
Aufstandes und zeigt, daß seine Deutung als rein religiös motiviertes Ereignis
deutlich zu kurz greift.

---

236 Greatrex 1996 (s. Anm. 152) 130 f.
237 Kyrill. Skythop. *V. Sabae* 54 p. 147,2–9 Schwartz.

6. Vitalian[238]

Die wechselvolle Karriere dieser schillernden Persönlichkeit in allen Einzelheiten nachzuzeichnen, ist hier nicht der Ort. Im folgenden soll lediglich eine kurze Skizze gegeben werden, die zum Verständnis der Rolle Vitalians beim *Stauro-theis*-Aufstand beitragen soll. Dabei wird es insbesondere darauf ankommen zu zeigen, wie sehr sich in Vitalian politische und religiöse Motivationen zu entschlossenem Handeln verbunden haben. Vitalian, der sich selbst als Vorkämpfer der Orthodoxie im Sinne Chalkedons sah und vielfach auch so wahrgenommen wurde,[239] gelang es nämlich nicht nur, Anastasios mit seiner Rebellion in schwere Verlegenheit zu bringen, sondern er schaltete sich unter Justin I. auch prominent als Wortführer in die Verhandlungen um die Aufhebung des Schismas ein – wie Pompeios gehörte er den *sublimes et magnifici viri* an, die die päpstliche Delegation 519 vor Konstantinopel empfingen[240] – und wurde für das Jahr 520 sogar – offenbar um ihn ruhig zu stellen – mit dem Konsulat bedacht. Anscheinend konnte aber auch dies seine ausgeprägten politischen Ambitionen nicht hinreichend befriedigen, so daß der umtriebige und einflußreiche Unruhestifter schließlich beseitigt wurde (520) – wahrscheinlich auf Betreiben Justinians, der in Vitalian einen gefährlichen Konkurrenten um den Kaiserthron sehen mußte.[241]

Vitalian, der offenbar gotischer Abstammung war,[242] erscheint zunächst im Gefolge seines Vaters Patrikiolos, den er 503 in den Perserkrieg des Anastasios begleitete.[243] Später kommandierte er eigenständig größere Truppenkörper (*foederati*), wohl im Amt eines *comes foederatorum*.[244] Seine erste Revolte gegen Anastasios, der sich augenscheinlich auch reguläre Verbände anschlossen, erfolgte im Jahr 513, nachdem Anastasios die erforderliche Versorgung der Soldaten Vitalians nicht gewährleistet hatte und sich unter den regulären Truppen eine

---

238 PLRE II 1171–1176 (Fl. Vitalianus 2); R. Scharf, Foederati. Von der völkerrechtlichen Kategorie zur byzantinischen Truppengattung, Wien 2001, 129.

239 Vgl. etwa Marc. Com. ad ann. 514,1 p. 98 Mommsen; Vict. Tunn. ad ann. 510 p. 194,33–195,2 = p. 30 Placanica = p. 29 Cardelle de Hartmann; 514 p. 195,24–27 Mommsen = p. 32 Placanica = p. 32 Cardelle de Hartmann; E. Schwartz (Ed.), Concilium Universale Chalcedonense, Vol. V: Collectio Sangermanensis (= ACO II.5), Berlin/Leipzig 1936, p. 133 (= Liberat. *Brev.* 19: *[...] a Vitaliano magistro militum viro religioso et orthodoxo*); Theoph. a.m. 6005 p. 157,12–13 de Boor.

240 *Coll. Avell.* 167 p. 619; 223 p. 683 Guenther.

241 Vgl. dazu auch Meier (s. Anm. 221) 186 f., mit den Belegen (bes. Anm. 401).

242 Marc. Com. ad ann. 514,1 p. 98; 519,3 p. 101 Mommsen (*Vitalianus Scytha*); Ps.-Zach. *HE* 7,13 p. 136,27; 8,2 p. 141,23; 142,5 Ahrens/Krüger.

243 Jos. Styl. 60 p. 74 Luther; Prok. *BP* 1,8,3. Vgl. Charanis (s. Anm. 6) 81.

244 Theoph. a.m. 6005 p. 157,11–12 de Boor. Vgl. PLRE II 1171 f.; Stein (s. Anm. 6) 178; Croke (s. Anm. 11) 117.

starke Unzufriedenheit mit dem *magister militum per Thracias* Hypatios (wohl nicht der gleichnamige Neffe des Kaisers)[245] verbreitete.[246] Rasch erlangte Vitalian gegen Hypatios die Kontrolle über Thrakien, die Moesia Secunda und die Scythia.[247] Sein demonstratives, gezielt gegen Anastasios gerichtetes Bekenntnis zu Chalkedon verschaffte ihm dabei noch zusätzliche Sympathien und offene Unterstützung.[248] Mit einem großen Aufgebot erschien Vitalian schließlich vor Konstantinopel und bezog auf dem Hebdomon Stellung.[249] Zu Verhandlungen mit dem Aufrührer entsandte Anastasios u. a. nunmehr ausgerechnet Patrikios, der als früherer Wohltäter Vitalians galt und offenkundig besondere Beziehungen zu ihm unterhielt.[250] Interessant sind die Forderungen, die Vitalian bei dieser Gelegenheit erhob: Neben einer ausreichenden Anerkennung und Versorgung seiner Truppen verlangte er nämlich Unterstützung für das *Chalcedonense* und für den exilierten Patriarchen Makedonios.[251] Damit kann die Makedonios-Affäre, die ja bereits für den Ausbruch des *Starotheis*-Aufstandes nicht unerheblich ist (s. u.), auch als bedeutsames Element innerhalb der Rebellion Vitalians angesehen werden und verknüpft somit beide Einzelereignisse zu einem durchaus kohärenten Geschehniskomplex. Überdies gewinnt vor diesem Hintergrund auch die in einigen Quellen erwähnte Kaiserproklamation Vitalians während des *Starotheis*-Aufstandes (s. o.) an Wahrscheinlichkeit: Vitalian könnte aus diesem Beweis seines Ansehens bei großen Teilen der hauptstädtischen Bevölkerung die

---

245 PLRE II 577 (Hypatius 5) und 577–581 (Hypatius 6); vgl. Cameron (s. Anm. 227) 313 f.; Greatrex 1996 (s. Anm. 152) 132, mit Anm. 28; 140–142.

246 *Exc. de insid.* 103 p. 143,13–14 de Boor [aus Joh. Ant.]: […] ἀφαιρεθεὶς γὰρ σιτήσεως δημοσίας τῶν καλουμένων φοιδερατικῶν ἀνώνων […].

247 Malal. p. 329,13–14 Thurn; Euagr. *HE* 3,43 p. 145,1–4 Bidez/Parmentier; Joh. Nik. 89,72 p. 130 Charles; Theoph. a. m. 6006 p. 160,13–14 de Boor; Kedren. PG 121 p. 688 [632] D; Zon. 14,3,28 p. 137,14–16 Pinder.

248 Theoph. a.m. 6005 p. 157,12–13 de Boor.

249 Marc. Com. ad ann. 514,1 p. 98 Mommsen; Ps.-Zach. *HE* 7,13 p. 137,1–3 Ahrens/Krüger; *Exc. de insid.* 103 p. 143,27–28 de Boor [aus Joh. Ant.]; Euagr. *HE* 3,43 p. 145,1–4 Bidez/Parmentier. Vgl. Stein (s. Anm. 6) 180; Charanis (s. Anm. 6) 82.

250 *Exc. de insid.* 103 p. 144,4–9 de Boor [aus Joh. Ant.]. Capizzi (s. Anm. 6) 124; Charanis (s. Anm. 6) 82 f.

251 Marc. Com. ad ann. 514,1 p. 98 Mommsen: *scilicet pro orthodoxorum se fide proque Macedonio urbis episcopo incassum ab Anastasio principe exulato Constantinopolim accessisse asserens*; *Exc. de insid.* 103 p. 144,11–14 de Boor [aus Joh. Ant.]: […] καὶ νῦν ἥκειν αὐτοὺς δεομένους ἐπανορθωθῆναι μὲν τῶν ἀδικημάτων τοῦ τῆς Θρακῶν στρατηγοῦ, κυρωθῆναι δὲ καὶ τὴν ὀρθῶς ἔχουσαν τοῦ θείου δόξαν. Vgl. Malal. p. 329,12 Thurn (διὰ τοὺς ἐξορισθέντας ἐπισκόπους); Vict. Tunn. ad ann. 510 p. 194,33–195,2 = p. 30 Placanica = p. 29 Cardelle de Hartmann; 514 p. 195,24–27 Mommsen = p. 32 Placanica = p. 32 Cardelle de Hartmann; Theoph. a.m. 6006 p. 160,18–28 de Boor; Kedren. PG 121 p. 689 [632] A.

Motivation und Bereitschaft zu seinem Vorgehen gegen Anastasios bezogen haben.

Nach einigen Verhandlungen und der angekündigten Bereitschaft des Kaisers zu Konzessionen und Kompromissen zog Vitalian wieder ab, am achten Tag nach seiner Ankunft.[252] Anastasios jedoch ließ ihn durch eine Armee unter dem neuen *magister militum per Thracias* Kyrillos verfolgen; dieses Unternehmen scheiterte, Kyrillos wurde ermordet.[253] Auch die nachfolgenden Truppen des Anastasios unter dem Kommando des neuen *magister militum per Thracias* Alathar und des Kaiserneffen Hypatios als oberstem Feldherrn konnten nichts gegen Vitalian ausrichten – Hypatios geriet sogar in dessen Gefangenschaft, wurde dabei gezielt gedemütigt und erst im folgenden Jahr, nach Zahlung eines Lösegeldes von 1100 Goldpfund, wieder freigelassen.[254]

Das Verhalten des Anastasios blieb nicht ohne Folgen: Im Jahr 514 erschien Vitalian erneut vor Konstantinopel,[255] und wiederum entsandte der Kaiser Senatoren zu Verhandlungen, die zu einem günstigen Ende geführt werden konnten: Gegen eine Goldzahlung (die als ‚Rest' des für Hypatios fälligen Lösegeldes deklariert wurde), gegen weitere Geschenke und Zusagen, die Ernennung des Rebellen zum *magister militum per Thracias* sowie das kaiserliche Versprechen, exilierte chalkedonische Bischöfe zurückzuberufen und mit Blick auf die Beendigung des Schismas ein Konzil für 515 einzuberufen, ließ sich Vitalian beruhigen

---

252 Marc. Com. ad ann. 514,1 p. 98 Mommsen; *Exc. de insid.* 103 p. 144,14–22 de Boor [aus Joh. Ant.]. Stein (s. Anm. 6) 180.

253 Marc. Com. ad ann. 514,3 p. 99 Mommsen; Malal. p. 329,18–330,28 Thurn; Euagr. *HE* 3,43 p. 145,5–16 Bidez/Parmentier (mit konfuser Ereignischronologie, s. Whitby [wie Anm. 69] 194, Anm. 169); Joh. Nik. 89,74–76 p. 130 Charles; *Exc. de insid.* 103 p. 144,23–27 de Boor [aus Joh. Ant.]; vgl. Theoph. a.m. 6006 p. 160,15–16 de Boor; Kedren. PG 121 p. 688–689 [632] D-A. Vgl. PLRE II 335 (Cyrillus 3); daneben Charanis (s. Anm. 6) 83.

254 Iord. *Rom.* 358 p. 46 Mommsen; Vict. Tunn. ad ann. 511 p. 195,4–7 Mommsen = p. 30 Placanica = p. 30 Cardelle de Hartmann; Ps.-Zach. *HE* 7,13 p. 137,3–18; 8,2 p. 141,31–35 Ahrens/Krüger; Kyrill. Skythop. *V. Sabae* 56 p. 151,13–15 Schwartz; Joh. Nik. 89,73 p. 130 Charles; *Exc. de insid.* 103 p. 144,27 ff. de Boor [aus Joh. Ant.]; Theoph. a. m. 6005 p. 157,16–19; a.m. 6006 p. 160,28–31 de Boor. Verwirrend, weil zu stark zusammenfassend und verkürzend, sind die Berichte Malal. p. 329,14–18 Thurn, und Euagr. *HE* 3,43 p. 145,4–16 Bidez/Parmentier. Vgl. auch Stein (s. Anm. 6) 180 f.; Charanis (s. Anm. 6) 83 f.; Greatrex 1996 (s. Anm. 152) 132 f., sowie ausführlich P. Peeters, Hypatius et Vitalien. Autour de la succession de l'empereur Anastase, AIPHO 10 (1950), 5–51. Zu Alathar s. PLRE II 49 f.

255 Marc. Com. ad ann. 515,2 p. 99 Mommsen; Vict. Tunn. ad ann. 514 p. 195,24–27 Mommsen = p. 32 Placanica = p. 32 Cardelle de Hartmann; Malal. p. 330,28–32 Thurn; Joh. Nik. 89,77 p. 130 Charles; Theoph. a. m. 6006 p. 160,13 ff. de Boor; *Exc. de insid.* 103 p. 146,5–8 de Boor [aus Joh. Ant.].

und zog ab.[256] Und tatsächlich wandte sich Anastasios noch 514 brieflich an Papst Hormisdas wegen eines möglichen Konzils in Herakleia;[257] auch Vitalian nahm – und dies bezeugt seinen durchaus ernstzunehmenden religiösen Eifer – Kontakt zum Papst auf.[258]

Die Initiative verlief jedoch im Sande: Anastasios zeigte kein Interesse daran, das Vorhaben weiterhin energisch zu verfolgen, und kümmerte sich nun, da Vitalian als neuer und reichhaltig ausgestatteter *magister militum per Thracias* endgültig beschwichtigt schien,[259] nicht mehr um die Organisation eines allgemeinen Konzils.[260] Die Folge war ein dritter Vorstoß Vitalians gegen Konstantinopel.[261] Dieses Mal wählte der Kaiser jedoch von vornherein eine andere, wesentlich aggressivere Taktik: Marinos von Apameia und dem späteren Kaiser Justin I.[262] war es zu verdanken, daß die Flotte Vitalians vernichtet wurde und auch seine Landtruppen geschlagen wurden; der Rebell mußte nach Thrakien fliehen.[263] Sein Amt als *magister militum per Thracias* ging an Rufinos über.[264] Bis zur Thronbesteigung Justins I. wird es still um Vitalian, der nunmehr offenbar nicht mehr die erforderlichen Ressourcen besaß, um Anastasios noch einmal offen die

---

256 Theod. Anagn. *fr.* 509 p. 145,20–28 Hansen; Marc. Com. ad ann. 515,3–4 p. 99 Mommsen; Vict. Tunn. ad ann. 514 p. 195,24–27 Mommsen = p. 32 Placanica = p. 32 Cardelle de Hartmann; Theoph. a. m. 6006 p. 160,13 ff. de Boor; *Exc. de insid.* 103 p. 146,8–21 de Boor [aus Joh. Ant.]; Kedren. PG 121 p. 689 [632] A. Vgl. Stein (s. Anm. 6) 181; Capizzi (s. Anm. 6) 125; Charanis (s. Anm. 6) 84 f.

257 *Coll. Avell.* 109 p. 501–502 Guenther: *quia igitur dubitationes quaedam de orthodoxa religione in Scythiae partibus videntur esse commota, id specialiter clementiae nostrae placuit, ut venerabilis synodus in Heracleotana civitate provinciae Europae celebretur, quatenus concordantibus animis et omni veritate discussa vera fides nostra orbi terrarum omni manifestius innotescat, ut deinceps nulla possit esse dubitatio vel discordia.* Vgl. dazu Stein (s. Anm. 6) 182; Charanis (s. Anm. 6) 87; Grillmeier (s. Anm. 29) 352.

258 *Coll. Avell.* 116,7 p. 514 Guenther. Vgl. E. Caspar, Geschichte des Papsttums von den Anfängen bis zur Höhe der Weltherrschaft, Bd. 2, Tübingen 1933, 130 ff.

259 Dazu s. PLRE II 1173 f.

260 Vgl. im einzelnen zu den Vorgängen Schwartz (s. Anm. 6) 250–253; Charanis (s. Anm. 6) 87 ff.; zur Haltung des Anastasios s. auch Wirth (s. Anm. 5) hier 116.

261 Vgl. auch Stein (s. Anm. 6) 184; Charanis (s. Anm. 6) 92 ff.; Greatrex 1996 (s. Anm. 152) 133 f.

262 Zu seiner Rolle bei der Abwehr Vitalians s. Greatrex 1996 (s. Anm. 152) 135, der darin einen der Gründe für den späteren Aufstieg Justins zum Kaiser sieht.

263 Malal. p. 330,32–332,85 Thurn; Euagr. *HE* 3,43 p. 145,17–29 Bidez/Parmentier; Joh. Nik. 89,78–86 p. 130–131 Charles; Theoph. a.m. 6007 p. 161,14–17 de Boor; *Exc. de insid.* 103 p. 146,22–147,21 de Boor [aus Joh. Ant.]; Kedren. PG 121 p. 689 [632–633] A–B; Zon. 14,3,28–30 p. 137,18–138,11 Pinder; vgl. auch *Anth. Graec.* 15,50; 16,347–350, mit Cameron (s. Anm. 8) 125–130.

264 Marc. Com. ad ann. 516,1 p. 99 Mommsen; vgl. PLRE II 954–957 (Rufinus 13).

Stirn zu bieten; trotzdem blieb er eine stete Bedrohung, die die letzten Jahre des Anastasios überschattete.[265]

Das neue, von Anastasios und seiner Familie unabhängige und strikt chalkedonisch orientierte Regime in Konstantinopel ermöglichte Vitalian – wie schon angedeutet – noch einmal eine neue Karriere, die seinen Einfluß kurzfristig derart zunehmen ließ, daß seine Beseitigung durch Justinian unumgänglich erschien. Das ordentliche Konsulat (520), ein Honorarkonsulat, der *patricius*-Titel und die Würde eines *comes et magister militum praesentalis* (518–520) stehen für die hohen Ehren, mit denen der umtriebige Truppenführer jetzt ausgezeichnet wurde.[266] In den mit dem Herrschaftsantritt Justins einsetztenden Verhandlungen mit Rom spielte er eine herausragende Rolle,[267] und auch aus seinem Haß gegen Severos von Antiocheia machte er kein Hehl.[268] Immerhin war Vitalian Taufpate des – u. a. aufgrund der Umtriebe des Severos – im Jahr 512 abgesetzten antiochenischen Patriarchen Flavianos (und verfolgte somit in seinen Rebellionen auch ,private' Rachegelüste gegenüber dem Kaiser, der Severos gefördert hatte).[269] Severos seinerseits zelebrierte die Niederlage Vitalians in einer feurigen, gegen den Heerführer gerichteten Homilie.[270]

Bei vordergründiger Betrachtungsweise erscheint Vitalian als ebenso ehrgeiziger wie unberechenbarer Kommandeur föderierter Truppenverbände, der es verstand, sich seine militärische Unabhängigkeit zu bewahren und daraus konkrete politische Forderungen abzuleiten. Aus dieser Perspektive entspräche er dem in jener Zeit vielfach anzutreffenden Typus eines ,Warlords' und würde damit exemplarisch für ein grundsätzliches strukturelles Problem des *Imperium Romanum* seit dem frühen 5. Jahrhundert stehen.[271] Diese Sichtweise scheint mir

---

265 Vgl. Greatrex 1996 (s. Anm. 152) 134. Kyrill von Skythopolis behauptet, Anastasios sei unter dem Druck Vitalians nahezu handlungsunfähig gewesen (und erklärt damit, warum der Kaiser sich in den Auseinandersetzungen zwischen Severos von Antiocheia und Johannes von Jerusalem [dazu s. u.] letztendlich nicht mehr engagiert habe), vgl. Kyrill. Skythop. *V. Sabae* 58 p. 158,4–6 Schwartz.

266 PLRE II 1174f mit den Belegen.

267 Dazu s. PLRE II 1175 mit den Belegen.

268 Liberat. *Brev.* 19 p. 133 Schwartz; Ps.-Zach. *HE* 8,2 p. 142,11–17 Ahrens/Krüger Euagr. *HE* 4,4 p. 155,10–13 Bidez/Parmentier; Joh. Nik. 90,8 p. 133 Charles.

269 Vgl. Schwartz (s. Anm. 6) 250.

270 Sev. Ant. *hom.* 34: M. Brière/F. Graffin/C. J. A. Lash (Edd.), Les *Homiliae Cathedrales* de Sévère d'Antioche, Turnout 1972 (PO 36.3), p. 430–437.

271 S. etwa Duchesne (s. Anm. 6) 37; Charanis (s. Anm. 6) 81: „Hoping to utilize the religious discontent of the western provinces and of the capital, he [...] made himself the champion of orthodoxy. [...] but the real object of his revolt was nothing less than the deposition of Anastasius and his elevation to the imperial throne"; Haacke (s. Anm. 6) 134 f.; Beck (s. Anm. 6) 14: „Um in der Hauptstadt Freunde zu gewinnen, arbeitete er mit prochalkedonischen Parolen"; Tinnefeld (s. Anm. 6) 190; Scharf (s. Anm. 238) 68:

jedoch allzu einseitig zu sein und den Anliegen Vitalians nicht gerecht zu werden. Sicherlich ließ sich der Einsatz für Chalkedon, für vertriebene oder drangsalierte Chalkedonier und insbesondere für den exilierten Makedonios gerade im thrakisch-illyrischen Raum als wirksames Instrument einsetzen, um größere Anhängerschaften zu gewinnen, mit denen dann unmittelbar politische Ambitionen verfolgt werden konnten. Andererseits ist aber auffällig, daß Vitalian spätestens nach seinem zweiten Vorstoß gegen Konstantinopel eigentlich mit dem Verhandlungsergebnis hätte zufrieden sein können: Seine Ernennung zum *magister militum per Thracias* und die gleichzeitig erhaltenen Goldsummen und Geschenke sowie die demonstrative Versöhnung mit dem Kaiser[272] hätten hinreichend prestigeträchtig sein müssen, um einen vagabundierenden Heerführer zumindest für einige Jahre ruhigzustellen. Daß Vitalian dann ausgerechnet die Tatsache, daß Anastasios das versprochene Konzil nicht einberief, zum Anlaß für einen erneuten Angriff nahm und damit all die zuvor erkämpften Vorteile riskierte, zeigt, daß er mit der Sache der Chalkedonier durchaus ein ernstes und persönliches Anliegen verfolgte.[273] Letzteres spiegelt sich auch in seinem intensiven Mitwirken an der Aufhebung des Schismas mit Rom sowie in seiner Vermittlung zwischen den sog. Skythischen Mönchen und den Gesandten des Papstes.[274] Möglicherweise war es sogar weniger der Einfluß, den Vitalian aufgrund seiner hohen Ämter und Würden zwischen 518 und 520 erlangen konnte, als vielmehr sein Ansehen als Vorkämpfer für Chalkedon, die Justinian dazu bewogen, ihn zu beseitigen. Denn diese Rolle beanspruchten die neuen Herrscher ausschließlich für sich, und gerade Justinian dürfte kaum die Bereitschaft gezeigt haben, den entsprechenden Ruhm mit einem Vitalian (und mit einer Anicia Iuliana!) zu teilen.

Vor diesem Hintergrund erscheint es angebracht, die Revolten Vitalians zwar einerseits als Folgen politischen Ehrgeizes, andererseits aber eben auch als Aus-

---

„Damit scheint er genau die gleichen Ziele verfolgt zu haben wie die beiden Theoderiche vor ihm". Vgl. auch etwa Greatrex 1996 (s. Anm. 152) 133, der ebenfalls vor allem die materiellen Forderungen Vitalians als Motivation seines Handelns hervorhebt; daneben Stein (s. Anm. 6) 179; Grillmeier (s. Anm. 29) 352, mit ähnlicher Tendenz.

272 Zu dieser Versöhnungsgeste vgl. *Exc. de insid.* 103 p. 146,19–20 de Boor [aus Joh. Ant.]: ὅρκοι τε περὶ φιλίας παρείχοντο καὶ τὸ τῆς θρησκείας ἀνενεοῦτο κήρυγμα.

273 In diese Richtung argumentiert auch Lee (s. Anm. 6) 56, der ebenfalls die religiösen Forderungen Vitalians als durchaus ernsthaft ansieht: „[…] but the real issue for him […] was Anastasius' stance on Chalcedon. That this was not a mere pretext for Vitalian's personal ambitions is indicated by the way he was prepared, on the first two occasions when he advanced against Constantinople (513 and 514), to withdraw after Anastasius agreed to take steps which offered the hope of resolving the religious issue".

274 *Coll. Avell.* 216,5 p. 675; 217 p. 677–679; 224 p. 685–687 Guenther.

druck ernstzunehmender religiöser bzw. kirchenpolitischer Anliegen zu sehen. Daß seine erste Erhebung dabei ausgerechnet im Jahr 513 erfolgte, dürfte kein Zufall gewesen sein: Der *Staurotheis*-Aufstand im November 512 war zwar nach der kaiserlichen Demutsgeste zusammengebrochen, aber die Wunden, die insbesondere die vorausgegangene Absetzung des Makedonios gerissen hatte, saßen tief. Da genügte ein marginaler äußerer Anlaß wie die Reduktion der Versorgungslieferungen für die föderierten Truppenverbände Vitalians, um dem verbreiteten Unmut offenen Ausdruck zu verleihen. Und so zeigen die Rebellionen Vitalians denn auch erhebliche Parallelen zum *Staurotheis*-Aufstand – zumindest im Hinblick auf die Politik des Anastasios: Ein Bündel politischer und religiöser Motivationen führt in beiden Fällen zum Ausbruch der Unruhen; Anastasios gibt Verhandlungsbereitschaft vor und entsendet klug ausgewählte Personen, um diese Verhandlungen zu führen; der Kaiser macht weitreichende Zusagen (Vitalian) bzw. bekennt öffentlich und voller Demut sein Fehlverhalten (*Staurotheis*-Aufstand); anstatt jedoch die Zusagen einzuhalten, setzt Anastasios nach dem Abflauen der unmittelbaren Gefahr rigoros seinen Kurs durch: Nach dem Ende des *Staurotheis*-Aufstandes wird die Weihe des umstrittenen Severos zum Patriarchen von Antiocheia nicht verhindert (obwohl dies möglich gewesen wäre); unter den Aufständischen erfolgt ein hartes Strafgericht; nach dem ersten Abzug Vitalians sendet ihm der Kaiser heimtückisch Truppen hinterher, um ihn zu beseitigen, nach dessen zweitem Abzug hält er sich nicht an die Zusage, ein allgemeines Konzil einzuberufen. Als unsichere Schaukelpolitik eines gutmütigen alten Herrn läßt sich all dies jedenfalls nicht interpretieren.

Auf eine nähere prosopographische Behandlung der weiteren im Kontext des *Staurotheis*-Aufstandes genannten Akteure – Severos, Makedonios und Timotheos – sei an dieser Stelle verzichtet. Ihre jeweilige Rolle wird im nächsten Abschnitt im einzelnen zu diskutieren sein, wenn es um die Frage nach dem religiösen bzw. kirchenpolitischen Hintergrund der Unruhen im November 512 gehen wird.

Als vorläufiges Ergebnis der Betrachtung der in die Geschehnisse verwickelten Persönlichkeiten läßt sich vorerst folgendes festhalten: Der Aufstand stellte innerhalb eines komplexen Geflechts vielschichtiger Personalbeziehungen einflußreicher Gestalten des ausgehenden 5. bzw. frühen 6. Jahrhunderts offensichtlich einen entscheidenden Einschnitt dar, insofern in seinem Verlauf Personen der oströmischen Führungselite miteinander konfrontiert wurden, die aus unterschiedlichen Gründen in einem vielfach gespannten, zumindest jedoch zumeist emotionsgeladenen Verhältnis zueinander gestanden haben müssen. Innerhalb der komplizierten Gemengelage, die sich dabei ergab, hebt sich der Kaiser als ruhender Pol ab; ihm ist es auch in einer extremen Konfliktsituation offenbar

erstaunlich gut gelungen, eine Eskalation der Unruhen zu vermeiden und dabei
sogar noch entscheidende kirchen- und personalpolitische Weichenstellungen
vorzunehmen. Vor diesem Hintergrund wird man die Beförderung des Marinos,
eines engen Vertrauten des Anastasios, zum *praefectus praetorio Orientis* im
Anschluß an den Aufstand zu sehen haben (gleichsam als Belohnung für seinen
mutigen Einsatz und als Entschädigung für die materiellen Verluste, die Marinos
zu erleiden hatte), ebenso wie die Übertragung der nachfolgenden Säuberungsaktionen (die bezeichnenderweise *trotz* der demütigen Geste des Kaisers erfolgten)
an Platon, der in diesen Dingen offenbar den Ruf eines zuverlässigen Fachman-
nes genoß. Wie der Finanzbeamte Marinos und der Stadtpräfekt Platon wurden
auch der *magister officiorum* Keler sowie der *magister militum praesentalis* Patrikios, der schon früher eng mit Keler zusammengearbeitet hatte, vom Kaiser
offenbar gezielt in die kirchenpolitischen Verwicklungen hineingezogen – dies
bereits im Kontext der Absetzung des Makedonios; einmal mehr zeigt sich somit,
daß gerade für die Ereignisse des Jahres 512 jeder Versuch einer Trennung der
politischen und der religiösen Sphäre und damit auch die Deutung des Aufstandes als rein religiös motiviertes Ereignis vollkommen aussichtslos erscheinen muß.
Mit der Involvierung der beiden letztgenannten Senatoren wiederum scheint
Anastasios gezielt auf die Proklamation des Areobindos zum Kaiser reagiert zu
haben – und dabei werden nicht nur die diplomatischen Qualitäten Kelers und
des Patrikios (der dann wenig später aufgrund seiner Beziehungen zu Vitalian mit
diesem ebenfalls zu verhandeln hatte) den Ausschlag gegeben haben. Denn mit
diesen beiden Personen konnte Anastasios dem Areobindos zwei ehrgeizige und –
wie ihre Karrieren zeigen – auch durchaus opportunistisch agierende Gestalten
entgegenstellen, die die eigene Motivation für ihr Vorgehen aus persönlichen
Spannungen und Konflikten gegenüber Areobindos beziehen konnten, die sie
noch aus dem Perserkrieg (503–506) mitbrachten, und denen sehr daran gelegen
gewesen sein dürfte, eine Beförderung des Areobindos zum Kaiser nach Möglichkeit zu verhindern. Der *Staurotheis*-Aufstand konfrontierte somit – wenn
auch nicht direkt – Teile der oströmischen hauptstädtischen Eliten miteinander,
und Anastasios scheint sich die dort vorhandenen Bruchlinien gezielt zur Sicherung der eigenen Stellung zunutze gemacht zu haben.

Insbesondere die Proklamationen des Areobindos und Vitalians verweisen
nämlich darauf, daß die Position des Kaisers keineswegs gefestigt war, zumal
nach der umstrittenen Absetzung des Makedonios im Jahr 511, auf die noch
näher einzugehen sein wird. Dabei dürften die Figur des Areobindos sowie vor
allem auch seine Frau Anicia Iuliana aufgrund ihrer Herkunft zum einen für tra-
ditionalistisch gesinnte Kreise gestanden haben, die in der nunmehr herrschenden Familie des Anastasios unbeliebte Aufsteiger sahen und sich rückwärts-
gewandt an der oströmischen Militärelite des 5. Jahrhunderts (Areobindos) bzw.
sogar am theodosianischen Kaiserhaus (Anicia Iuliana) orientierten. Daß sich das

insofern bereits prominente und einflußreiche Paar überdies auch noch nachhaltig im Kampf für Chalkedon engagierte, machte es für Anastasios umso gefährlicher und dürfte in der Situation des Jahres 512 mit den Ausschlag gegeben haben dafür, daß die Aufständischen Areobindos zum Kaiser ausriefen. Erstaunlicherweise kam es in dieser brisanten Situation nicht zu noch größeren und vor allem blutigeren Auseinandersetzungen; dies war der politischen Klugheit des Anastasios und des Areobindos zu verdanken. Während Areobindos nach dem *Staurotheis*-Aufstand aus der Überlieferung verschwindet und somit entweder bald gestorben, zumindest aber bedeutungslos geworden ist, ist es <u>Vitalian</u>, dem zweiten Kaiserkandidaten der Aufständischen, hingegen gelungen, die Rolle eines Vorkämpfers für Chalkedon, die ihm aufgrund seiner Ausrufung 512 nunmehr automatisch zukommen mußte, ganz für sich einzunehmen und ab dem folgenden Jahr in konkretes politisches Handeln umzusetzen. Wie oben bereits gezeigt, hat sich dabei persönlicher Ehrgeiz mit durchaus ernsthaften kirchenpolitischen Anliegen verbunden. Daß sich aus diesem Umstand jedoch keineswegs ein Argument für eine rein religiöse Deutung des *Staurotheis*-Aufstandes ableiten läßt, geht wiederum aus dem Schicksal des Kaiserneffen <u>Pompeios</u> hervor, dessen Haus offenbar ebenfalls während der Unruhen in Brand gesetzt wurde, und dies, *obwohl* er ein bekennender Chalkedonier war. In der erhitzten Atmosphäre des Aufstandes genügte offenbar schon seine enge Verwandtschaft mit dem Kaiser, um Pompeios massiv zu attackieren.

III

Aufgrund seines unmittelbaren Anlasses, der Ergänzung des *Trisagion*s durch die als ,monophysitisch' stigmatisierte Formel σταυρωθεὶς δι' ἡμᾶς, läßt sich der Aufstand gegen Anastasios im Jahr 512 vordergründig als zentrale Zäsur innerhalb der kirchenpolitischen Entwicklungen in Konstantinopel interpretieren. Denn die Ereignisse signalisierten dem Kaiser in aller Deutlichkeit, daß die Bevölkerung der Hauptstadt mehrheitlich nicht bereit war, vom *Chalcedonense* abzurücken. Konstantinopel blieb denn auch in der Folgezeit eine vornehmlich chalkedonisch geprägte Stadt, wenngleich etwa ein Erdbeben im Jahr 533 noch einmal kurzfristig antichalkedonisch-miaphysitische Tendenzen an die Oberfläche brachte[275] und unter dem Chalkedonier Justinian miaphysitische Kleriker ausgerechnet in der Kaiserstadt am Bosporus eine wohlorganisierte und sorgsam behütete Zufluchtsstätte vor Verfolgungen in ihrer Heimat finden konnten – und zwar über den Tod ihrer ,Beschützerin' Theodora im Jahr 548 hinaus.[276] Eine

---

275 Vgl. Meier (s. Anm. 221) 357–359.
276 Vgl. etwa Stein (s. Anm. 6) 683.

derartige retrospektive Zuspitzung der Geschehnisse im Jahr 512 auf einen klaren
Antagonismus zwischen Chalkedoniern und Miaphysiten (bzw. korrekter: Chal-
kedon-Gegnern) wird der Komplexität des Sachverhaltes jedoch nicht annähernd
gerecht. Auf die eindeutig vorhandenen ‚reichs‘- bzw. ‚macht‘-politischen Implikationen der Revolte wurde bereits mehrfach hingewiesen; hinzu kommt noch
ein weiterer Aspekt: Die modernen Kategorien ‚Monophysitismus‘ (besser, weil
weniger polemisch und inhaltlich präziser: ‚Miaphysitismus‘), ‚Nestorianismus‘
oder ‚Chalkedonismus‘ sowie insbesondere natürlich Kennzeichnungen wie
‚orthodox‘ oder ‚katholisch‘ suggerieren die Existenz kohärenter, widerspruchs-
freier und eindeutig festgelegter Lehrmeinungen, die sich über einen längeren
Zeitraum hin als Konstanten scharf voneinander abgrenzen lassen und klar
definierte Positionen umschreiben. Diese Vorstellung erweist sich bei näherer
Betrachtung jedoch als modernes Hilfskonstrukt, das die zeitgenössischen Verhältnisse nur sehr partiell zu erfassen vermag und vornehmlich dazu dient, kom-
plizierte Gemengelagen und Prozesse, die für den modernen Betrachter verwirrend und chaotisch erscheinen, nachträglich zu strukturieren und damit als
Untersuchungsgegenstand überhaupt erst einmal zugänglich zu machen. Tatsächlich aber lassen sich die Positionen der einzelnen in die kirchenpolitischen
und christologischen Kontroversen verwickelten Akteure nur sehr selten mit solchen vereinfachenden Schlagworten klar erfassen; vielmehr waren sie ihrerseits
zumeist, wenn nicht gänzlich im Fluß begriffen, so doch steten Diskussionspro-
zessen und damit Modifikationen ausgesetzt, und können daher nur unter
Berücksichtigung der jeweiligen Situation sowie der konkreten Umstände, unter
denen ein Protagonist argumentiert, analysiert werden. Die große Gefahr, die die
Anwendung unserer geläufigen Kategorien mit sich bringt, beruht zum einen in
dem Umstand, daß Elemente, die Teile spezifischer Gemengelagen sind und nur
in deren Zusammenhängen verstanden werden können, isoliert und in vorgegebene ‚Schubladen‘ eingeordnet werden (aber ein Chalkedon-Gegner kann nun
einmal nur in bestimmten Kontexten und unter spezifischen Voraussetzungen als
‚Miaphysit‘ qualifiziert werden); zum anderen wird dabei zumeist unreflektiert
die polemische Terminologie der Quellen übernommen, in denen z. B. jeder, der
nicht im Sinne eines ‚monophysitischen‘ Standpunktes argumentiert, sofort als
‚Nestorianer‘ gebrandmarkt wird, wobei der ‚monophysitische‘ Standpunkt seinerseits wiederum häufig nur in einer ‚nestorianischen‘ Perspektive als solcher
erkennbar ist. Die Übernahme dieser Kampfbegriffe aus den Quellen, ihre Auf-
ladung mit bestimmten, vermeintlich objektivierbaren Kriterien und ihr daraus
abgeleiteter gleichsam überzeitlicher Geltungsanspruch, der es scheinbar erlaubt,
langjährige, wechselvolle und ausgesprochen dynamische Entwicklungen mittels
so gewonnener statischer Konzepte als ‚Miaphysitismus‘, ‚Chalkedonismus‘ oder
‚Nestorianismus‘ zu qualifizieren, verstellt den Blick auf eben diese Dynamik der
Entwicklungen: So ließe sich etwa nach modernen Kategorisierungen der sog.

Neuchalkedonismus Justinians durchaus auch als eine gemäßigte Spielart des Miaphysitismus beschreiben; Justinian selbst, ein strikter Gegner der Miaphysiten, hätte eine derartige Einordnung seiner theologischen Position jedoch entschieden zurückgewiesen und sich selbst den ‚Orthodoxen‘ zugesellt,[277] und in dieser Weise ist seine Haltung denn auch weithin rezipiert worden. Für den frühen Justinian mag diese Qualifizierung denn auch unter heutigen Maßstäben noch gerechtfertigt sein; für den späteren Eiferer im sog. Drei-Kapitel-Streit und abschließenden Sympathisanten mit dem Aphthartodoketismus – dies seinerseits wieder ein problematischer Begriff – bereitet sie dann aber schon erhebliche Probleme.

Mit der Darlegung dieser Schwierigkeiten sollen keineswegs lediglich methodische Quisquilien verhandelt werden, sondern es geht hier um ein grundsätzliches hermeneutisches Problem, das insbesondere im Fall des Anastasios von besonderer Relevanz ist: Bekanntlich ist bei diesem Kaiser ja besonders umstritten, ob er dem ‚Miaphysitismus‘ bzw. ‚Monophysitismus‘ zugeneigt habe oder nicht.[278] Der Streit ist bis heute nicht entschieden, und er läßt sich auch nicht ent-

---

277 Vgl. dazu im einzelnen Meier (s. Anm. 221) 273 ff.

278 Vgl. etwa Stein (s. Anm. 6) 157 ff.; G. Ostrogorsky, Geschichte des Byzantinischen Staates, München ³1963, 57; Capizzi (s. Anm. 6) 130–137; ders., Il monofisismo di Anastasio I e il suo influsso sullo scisma laurenziano, in: G. Mele/N. Spaccapelo (Hgg.), Il papato di San Simmaco (498–514). Atti del Convegno Internazionale di studi Oristano 19–21 novembre 1998, Cagliari 2000, 79–110, bes. 97 („[...] Anastasio I [...] non solo fu personalmente monofisita convinto, ma mise con zelo il potere imperiale al servizio del monofisismo“); Charanis (s. Anm. 6) 40 („Anastasius himself inclined toward Monophysitism“); 41 f. („But if Anastasius inclined toward Monophysitism, he was not a ‚blind devotee‘ of the sect“); D. Feissel, Anastasius I, in: Bowersock/Brown/Grabar (s. Anm. 191) 297 f., bes. 298 („a devoted Monophysite“); Lee Eastern Empire (s. Anm. 6) 53 („heterodox theological views“), die in Anastasios einen Monophysiten erkennen zu können glauben. Anders hingegen etwa Günther (s. Anm. 6) 422: „Man mag darüber streiten, ob jene drastischen kirchenpolitischen Maßnahmen Anastasius wirklich als den feurigen Anhänger des Monophysitismus entlarven, als der er geschmäht wird, desgleichen darüber, inwiefern er erst im Laufe seiner Regierung unter den Einfluß radikaler Kirchenlehrer, etwa des Severus von Sozopolis, geraten war“. Eine allmähliche Hinwendung des Anastasios zum Miaphysitismus seit dem Ende des letzten Jahrzehnts des 5. Jahrhunderts konstatiert Wirth (s. Anm. 5) bes. 113 f. Vorsichtiger hingegen äußert sich Haacke (s. Anm. 6) 125: „Ist es schon schwer, seinen eigenen Standpunkt in den religiösen Angelegenheiten zu bestimmen, so erhöht sich diese Schwierigkeit, wenn es gilt, das Verhältnis seiner persönlichen Überzeugung zu seinem taktischen Vorgehen zu begreifen. Zudem wird man mit der Möglichkeit rechnen müssen, daß er in seinen Auffassungen einen Wandel durchgemacht hat, wie es tatsächlich für die Zeit nach seiner Fühlungnahme mit dem großen Theologen der monophysitischen Partei, Severos, der Fall gewesen sein mag“; vgl. allerdings ebd., 126: „Anastasios scheint tatsächlich von vornherein mit seinen persönlichen Sympathien auf Seiten der Monophysiten gestanden zu haben“.

scheiden, solange weiterhin an den starren Kategorien im skizzierten Sinn festgehalten wird. Denn ein solcher Zugriff blendet – wie angedeutet – dynamische Prozesse und ständige Verschiebungen aus und muß somit geradezu permanent Widersprüche produzieren, die dann in die bekannten Schwierigkeiten münden, Anastasios einer vorgegebenen ‚Schublade' zuzuordnen. Wichtiger als eine solche Kategorisierung wäre aber ohnehin, das politische Handeln dieses Kaisers im Spannungsfeld verschiedener politischer und theologischer Gravitationskräfte zu beschreiben sowie die Reaktionen darauf in der zeitgenössischen kirchenpolitischen (bzw. durch Kirchenpolitik beeinflußten) Publizistik zu analysieren und diese Stellungnahmen nicht nur zur Ausbildung starrer Schematismen heranzuziehen. Die persönliche theologische Position des Kaisers ist uns aufgrund mangelnder sog. Ego-Dokumente ohnehin nicht zugänglich, und es sollte auch nicht mittels fragwürdiger Kategorien suggeriert werden, daß in dieser Frage Lösungen möglich seien.

Unter diesen Voraussetzungen kann es bei der nachfolgenden kurzen Betrachtung, welche kirchenpolitischen Entwicklungen für den Ausbruch des *Staurotheis*-Aufstandes relevant sind, nicht darum gehen, einen möglicherweise stetig zunehmenden, wie auch immer zu definierenden ‚Miaphysitismus' bzw. ‚Monophysitismus' des Anastasios herauszuarbeiten. Vielmehr erscheint es angebracht, nach Möglichkeit lediglich zwischen den – freilich zunächst einmal sehr unspezifischen – Großgruppen der Chalkedonier und der Chalkedon-Gegner zu unterscheiden und Binnendifferenzierungen nur im Kontext besonderer Situationen vorzunehmen, wo sie sich als sinnvoll erweisen. Wenn dabei dann dennoch von ‚Miaphysiten' o. ä. gesprochen wird, dann ist dies nicht im Sinne starrer Kategorisierungen zu verstehen, sondern als Kennzeichnung, die ihre Rechtfertigung jeweils aus spezifischen Kontexten heraus bezieht und vor allem als relative Größe aufzufassen ist. So läßt sich etwa die Religions- und Kirchenpolitik des Anastasios seit ca. 506 in diesem Sinne in Relation zum *Henotikon* oder zum *Chalcedonense* als ‚miaphysitisch' bezeichnen; daraus muß freilich keineswegs folgen, daß sie auch nach modernen Definitionen von ‚Miaphysitismus' ‚miaphysitisch' gewesen sein muß.

Prinzipiell läßt sich die Religionspolitik des Anastasios in drei Phasen unterteilen:[279] Sie erscheint zunächst deutlich von dem Bemühen geprägt, im Streit um Chalkedon einen Kompromißkurs zu wahren, der sehr eng an das sog. *Henotikon*[280] angelehnt war und den Versuch erkennen läßt, dieser Glaubensformel, die

---

279 Ähnlich sieht dies auch Charanis (s. Anm. 6) 85. Anders etwa Haacke (s. Anm. 6) 126, der von vier Phasen ausgeht.

280 CPG 5999. Zum *Henotikon* vgl. etwa Schwartz (s. Anm. 6) 197 ff.; Haacke (s. Anm. 6) 174 ff.; Beck (s. Anm. 6) 8 ff.; Grillmeier (s. Anm. 29) 279 ff.; H. Chr. Brennecke, Chalcedonense und Henotikon. Bemerkungen zum Prozeß der östlichen Rezeption

ja ursprünglich vor allem mit Blick auf Ägypten formuliert worden war,[281] nunmehr eine reichsweite Gültigkeit zu verschaffen, um sie als Grundlage für weitere Verhandlungen und Differenzierungen verwenden zu können. In einer zweiten Phase, die gegen Ende des ersten Jahrzehnts des 6. Jahrhunderts immer deutlichere Konturen gewinnt, zeichnet sich ab, daß Anastasios zu wachsenden Zugeständnissen bereit ist gegenüber Positionen, die das *Henotikon* zwar weiterhin als Diskussionsgrundlage beibehalten, seine Auslegung aber zunehmend in die Richtung einer Einnaturenlehre vorantreiben, die in Philoxenos von Mabbug (Hierapolis) und Severos von Sozopolis bzw. Antiocheia ihre zentralen Vordenker und Protagonisten fand.[282] Diese Phase kulminierte in der Absetzung des konstantinopolitanischen Patriarchen Makedonios (511) und der Einsetzung des Severos zum Bischof von Antiocheia (512) nach der Vertreibung Flavianos' II. (512) und erfuhr massive Gegenreaktionen im *Staurotheis*-Aufstand, den Revolten Vitalians und den Agitationen der Mönchsführer Sabas und Theodosios in Palästina. Die letzte Phase, also die Jahre 515–518, waren von diesen Ereignissen überschattet. Die Forschung ist sich dabei nicht einig, ob die Politik des Anastasios in diesem Zeitraum eher im Sinne eines Festhaltens an den Positionen, wie sie sich bis zum Jahr 512 entwickelt hatten, oder im Sinne einer Rückkehr zu chalkedonischen Haltungen zu deuten ist.[283] Fest steht jedenfalls, daß Anasta-

---

der christologischen Formel von Chalkedon, in: J. van Oort/J. Roldanus (Hgg.), Chalkedon: Geschichte und Aktualität. Studien zur Rezeption der christologischen Formel von Chalkedon, Leuven 1998, 24–53.

281 Brennecke (s. Anm. 280) 42 ff.; vgl. auch Charanis (s. Anm. 6) 43.

282 Zu Philoxenos s. bes. A. de Halleux, Philoxène de Mabbog. Sa vie, ses écrits, sa théologie, Louvain 1963; ferner P. Bruns, Philoxenus von Mabbug, in: Döpp/Geerlings (s. Anm. 6) 577–578, mit neuerer Literatur. Zu Severos s. den kurzen Überblick bei I. R. Torrance, Severus von Antiochien (ca. 456–538), TRE 31 (2000), 184–186, mit weiteren Literaturverweisen; ferner – ebenfalls mit neuerer Literatur – P. Bruns, Severus von Antiochien, in: Döpp/Geerlings (s. Anm. 6) 636–637, sowie Allen/Hayward (s. Anm. 138).

283 Vgl. Charanis (s. Anm. 6) 85 f. („he made an effort to reconcile the disgruntled orthodox element of his empire"); Gray (s. Anm. 6) 40 („The later years of Anastasius' reign [512–518] marked not so much a change in policy as a more restrained and nuanced attempt to put it into effect"); Allen (s. Anm. 30) 167 („[…] the imperial policy veered – unsuccessfully – towards accomodating Chalcedonian claims"); Greatrex 1996 (s. Anm. 152) 134 („[…] between 515 and 518 Anastasius accomplished little for the anti-Chalcedonian cause […]"; „[…] the weakness of Anastasius […]"); ebd., 134, Anm. 31 („He at any rate became more pragmatic and circumspect about enforcing anti-Chalcedonian doctrines"); Wirth (s. Anm. 5) 117: „Altersresignation"; zuletzt P. T. R. Gray, The Legacy of Chalcedon. Christological Problems and Their Significance, in: Maas (s. Anm. 221) 215–238, hier 225: „At the end of his reign […] Anastasius backed away from the anti-Chalcedonians, engaging in futile attempts to win Rome over and to restrain anti-Chalcedonians from outright and divisive domination of the churches in the East".

sios – wie so viele Kaiser vor und nach ihm – versucht hat, durch massive Eingriffe in kirchliche Belange die religiöse Einheit des *Imperium Romanum* zu erreichen, und dabei letztlich gescheitert ist.[284]

Als Anastasios im Jahr 491 die Nachfolge Zenons antrat, war er kirchenpolitisch keine unbekannte Größe – immerhin hatte man ihn bereits nach dem Tod Petros' des Walkers als Kandidat für den antiochenischen Patriarchenstuhl gehandelt.[285] Seine Sympathien gegenüber dem *Henotikon* dürften jedenfalls nicht verborgen geblieben sein. Auch wenn Theodoros Anagnostes die angeblichen Vorbehalte des chalkedonisch gesinnten Euphemios[286] gegen die Wahl des Anastasios ein wenig übertrieben haben mag,[287] so läßt sich doch nicht leugnen, daß das Verhältnis zwischen Kaiser und Patriarch von Beginn an belastet war. Euphemios verlangte von Anastasios sogar ein schriftliches Bekenntnis zu Chalkedon[288] und ließ die Konzilsbeschlüsse auf einer Endemousa im Jahr 492 noch einmal ausdrücklich bestätigen.[289] Wenngleich es dem Patriarchen nie gelang, auch Rom von seiner Chalkedon-Treue zu überzeugen (Papst Gelasius sandte ihm nicht einmal eine Wahl-Anzeige),[290] blieb er seinem Standpunkt dennoch treu und wurde daher im Jahr 496 abgesetzt;[291] Anastasios' *Henotikon*-Politik war mit dem strikt chalkedonischen Kurs des Euphemios nicht vereinbar.

Der Kaiser verfolgte in dieser Phase eine klare und durchaus verständliche kirchenpolitische Linie: Angesichts der politischen Auflösung des Weströmischen Reiches, die trotz aller ideellen Rombeschwörungen unverkennbare Reali-

---

284 Dies hat schon Euagrios gegen Ende des 6. Jh. so gesehen, vgl. Euagr. *HE* 3,30 p. 125,32–127,4 Bidez/Parmentier; dazu s. Allen (s. Anm. 30) 145–147. Vgl. auch Alleny (s. Anm. 6) 818: „This policy caused confusion and polarization".

285 Theod. Anagn. *fr.* 445 p. 125,20–23; *fr.* 38 p. 125,16–19 Hansen; Theoph. a.m. 5983 p. 135,21–25 de Boor.

286 Zu Euphemios s. auch Grillmeier (s. Anm. 29) 299 („[ein] eindeutiger, aber verkannter Anhänger Chalcedons"); 301 („Mit Patriarch Euphemius haben wir einen aufrichtigen Bekenner Chalcedons vor uns"). Vgl. auch Schwartz (s. Anm. 6) 219 („eifriger Chalkedonenser"); Charanis (s. Anm. 6) 54 („active adherent of the Council of Chacedon").

287 Theod. Anagn. *fr.* 441 p. 123,12–17; *fr.* 446 p. 125,25–27 Hansen; vgl. Theoph. a.m. 5982 p. 134,19–24 de Boor.

288 Theod. Anagn. *fr.* 446 p. 125,25–126,15; *fr.* 39 p. 126,1–8 Hansen; Euagr. *HE* 3,32 p. 130,10 Bidez/Parmentier. Dazu vgl. auch Charanis (s. Anm. 6) 38; Grillmeier (s. Anm. 29) 299, mit Anm. 98.

289 Theod. Anagn. *fr.* 451 p. 127,18–19; *fr.* 41 p. 127,1–3 Hansen; Theoph. a.m. 5984 p. 137,11–13 de Boor. Vgl. ferner Kyrill. Skythop. *V. Sabae* 50 p. 140,8–15 Schwartz.

290 Dazu s. Schwartz (s. Anm. 6) 219 ff.; Grillmeier (s. Anm. 29) 299–301.

291 Theod. Anagn. *fr.* 45 p. 128,5–8; *fr.* 455 p. 128,14–20; *fr.* 457 p. 128,22–27 Hansen; Marc. Com. ad ann. 495 p. 94 Mommsen. Vgl. Schwartz (s. Anm. 6) 222; Haacke (s. Anm. 6) 128; Frend (s. Anm. 6) 200; Charanis (s. Anm. 6) 54–56.

tät war, erschien ihm die religiöse Einheit des Ostens – und dabei vor allem ein Einvernehmen mit Ägypten – als vorrangige Aufgabe;[292] diese war jedoch mit einer strikt chalkedonischen Politik nicht zu erzielen, wohl aber – so scheint er zumindest kalkuliert zu haben – mit einer wohlmeinenden Auslegung des *Henotikon*. Es ist daher auch nicht erstaunlich, daß vorsichtige Sondierungen in Richtung einer Aufhebung des Schismas lediglich unter dem Pontifikat Anastasius' II. (496–498) erfolgten, die jedoch aufgrund der kurzen Amtszeit dieses Papstes keine längerfristigen Konsequenzen hatten.[293] Die anderen Päpste während der Herrschaft des Anastasios zeigten sich jedenfalls nicht bereit, dessen *Henotikon*-Politik als Bedingung für die Auflösung des Schismas mitzutragen.[294]

Unter Euphemios' Nachfolger Makedonios spitzte sich die Situation im Osten zu und die Kirchenpolitik des Anastasios trat allmählich über in die zweite Phase. Verschiedene Faktoren – die hier nur ganz grob und unvollständig skizziert werden können – waren dabei ausschlaggebend: Zum einen schien Makedonios zunächst die kaiserliche *Henotikon*-Politik mitzutragen[295] – er soll auf einer Endemousa im Jahr 497 sogar die Anhänger Chalkedons verurteilt haben[296] –, stieß dabei aber auf den energischen Widerstand chalkedonischer Kreise in Konstantinopel (vor allem der Akoimeten-Mönche) und schwenkte schließlich selbst auf deren Chalkedon-Kurs ein,[297] während der Kaiser eine zunehmend antichalkedonische, sich in Richtung des miaphysitischen Spektrums bewegende

---

292 In diesem Sinne vgl. etwa Charanis (s. Anm. 6) 29; Gray (s. Anm. 6) 34 f.; Lee (s. Anm. 6) 56.

293 Zu diesen kurzfristigen Annäherungen s. etwa Schwartz (s. Anm. 6) 226–230; Frend (s. Anm. 6) 197 ff.; Charanis (s. Anm. 6) 52 f.; Grillmeier (s. Anm. 29) 302, mit Anm. 112; 346 ff. Immerhin schien sich für Anastasios hoffnungsvolle Bewegung im Streit um das Schisma abzuzeichnen; es ist sicherlich kein Zufall, daß er ausgerechnet im Jahr 497 die Stellung Theoderichs in Italien anerkannte und ihm die *ornamenta palatii* zurücksandte, die einst Odoaker nach Konstantinopel hatte verbringen lassen.

294 Vgl. Gray (s. Anm. 6) 36: „No pope would agree to accept it"; Grillmeier (s. Anm. 29) 326 ff.

295 Vgl. Theod. Anagn. *fr.* 456 p. 128,21 Hansen (Μακεδόνιος πεισθεὶς βασιλεῖ τῷ ἑνωτικῷ Ζήνωνος καθυπέγραψεν); Theoph. a.m. 5988 p. 140,15–16; a.m. 6004 p. 154,29–155,1 de Boor; Zach. *Vita Sev.* (PO 2.1) p. 113 Kugener; Joh. Nik. 89,46–47 p. 126–127 Charles.

296 Vgl. Theod. Anagn. *fr.* 46 p. 129,1–4 Hansen. Die Nachricht ist jedoch nicht unproblematisch. Möglicherweise handelte es sich bei dieser Äußerung des Makedonios auch lediglich um das, „was schon mehr oder minder im Wortlaut des Henotikons lag" (Grillmeier [wie Anm. 29] 303).

297 Vgl. Theod. Anagn. *fr.* 459 p. 129,15–25 Hansen; Theoph. a. m. 5991 p. 141,19–142,5 de Boor; Charanis (s. Anm. 6) 59; Grillmeier (s. Anm. 29) 303 f. Zur zunehmenden Rigidität, mit der Makedonios die Sache der Chalkedonier betrieb, vgl. Gray (s. Anm. 6) 38.

Politik betrieb. Die Gründe dafür dürfen nicht in der persönlichen Religiosität des Kaisers gesucht werden, die für uns – wie gesagt – nicht faßbar ist. Stattdessen wäre vor allem auf den Perserkrieg der Jahre 502–506 zu verweisen, der den Osten des Reiches deutlich geschwächt zurückgelassen hatte und in dessen Folge weitere religiöse Verwerfungen gerade in den vom Krieg betroffenen Regionen verheerende Konsequenzen gezeitigt hätten.[298] Da die Antichalkedonier in jenen Jahren dort offenbar größeren Zustrom durch christliche Flüchtlinge aus dem Perserreich genossen,[299] ist es nicht verwunderlich, daß auch Anastasios zunächst behutsam auf sie zuzugehen versuchte,[300] zumal es auch nicht gelungen war, das Laurentianische Schisma in Rom zugunsten einer Annäherung zwischen Konstantinopel und dem Westen zu nutzen.[301] In dem Maße wie der Kaiser sich dabei von seinem Patriarchen und von gemäßigten Klerikern wie etwa dem Patriarchen Flavianos II. von Antiocheia entfremdete, näherte er sich dem miaphysitischen Spektrum an und geriet dabei – zumindest suggerieren es so die Quellen, die das unabhängige Kalkül des Kaisers aber möglicherweise unterschätzen – unter den Einfluß miaphysitischer Autoritäten aus dem Osten: Auf Einladung des Kaisers erschien im Jahr 507 Philoxenos von Mabbug in Konstantinopel, überwarf sich aber erwartungsgemäß mit Makedonios, der ihm die Kommunion verweigerte; es drohte offener Aufruhr, und Anastasios mußte Philoxenos schließlich heimlich zurückschicken.[302] Bereits im Jahr 508 erschien jedoch Severos,[303] und sein bis 511 während Aufenthalt zeigte deutliche Wirkungen, wenngleich Anastasios zur Wahrung des Friedens weiterhin jegliche öffentliche Verfluchung Chalkedons streng untersagte.

Mehrere Synoden in jenen Jahren führten vor allem durch die Agitationen des Philoxenos und die Umtriebe des Severos zu einer nochmaligen Zuspitzung

---

298 Vgl. Gray (s. Anm. 6) 37. Wirth (s. Anm. 5) 139: „Es fällt auf, daß die kirchenpolitischen Entscheidungen, die Anastasius traf, in die Jahre unmittelbar nach diesem Frieden [sc. mit den Persern] fallen".

299 Frend (s. Anm. 6) 201; Charanis (s. Anm. 6) 59 f.; Gray (s. Anm. 6) 37.

300 Vgl. Gray (s. Anm. 6) 37: „At a time of uneasy peace, Anastasius needed the strong support of such elements in the shaky border province of Syria".

301 Vgl. Gray (s. Anm. 6) 36: „The anti-*Henoticon* majority in Rome was clearly victorious and Rome was henceforth even more adamantly opposed to the *Henoticon*". Zum Laurentianischen Schisma vgl. bes. die Arbeit von E. Wirbelauer, Zwei Päpste in Rom. Der Konflikt zwischen Laurentius und Symmachus (498–514). Studien und Texte, München 1993.

302 Theod. Anagn. *fr.* 470 p. 134,20–23 Hansen; Theoph. a. m. 5999 p. 150,4–8 de Boor; vgl. Ps.-Zach. *HE* 7,8 p. 128,14–20 Ahrens/Krüger. Charanis (s. Anm. 6) 60; vgl. bes. de Halleux (s. Anm. 282) 59–63.

303 Zu dieser Reise s. Schwartz (s. Anm. 6) 239 f.

des Konfliktes,[304] dessen prominenteste Opfer schließlich Makedonios von Konstantinopel (511) und Flavianos II. von Antiocheia (512) sowie – etwas später, im Jahr 516 – Elias von Jerusalem wurden.[305] Unklar bleibt in diesem Kontext freilich die exakte Datierung und Bedeutung des sog. *Typos* des Anastasios, eines Dokumentes, das wohl um 510 von Severos verfaßt wurde und eine für den Kaiser jedoch nicht tragbare Verfluchung Chalkedons enthielt.[306]

Die eigentliche Bewährungsprobe für eine Politik, die unter Aufgabe des Westens zumindest den Osten unter einem allgemein akzeptablen Bekenntnis zu vereinen intendierte, stellte jedoch Konstantinopel dar.[307] Nur wenn es gelang, auch die Hauptstadt auf einen miaphysitisch ausgerichteten *Henotikon*-Kurs zu bringen, konnte dieses Programm überhaupt irgendwelche Erfolgsaussichten

---

304 Es handelt sich dabei um die Synoden von Konstantinopel (507), Antiocheia (509), Sidon (511) und nochmals Antiocheia (513). Dazu s. im einzelnen Grillmeier (s. Anm. 29) 305 ff.

305 Zur Absetzung Flavians s. etwa Frend (s. Anm. 6) 214–219; Charanis (s. Anm. 6) 63 ff.; 73–76; Gray (s. Anm. 6) 37; Zur Absetzung des Makedonios s. im einzelnen u. Zu Elias s. ebenfalls u.

306 Im einzelnen vgl. zu diesem schwer zu beurteilenden Dokument Gray (s. Anm. 6) 39 f. („The evidence for the authenticity of this text is, however, only circumstantial, and too much should not therefore be predicated upon it“ [40]), sowie insbesondere Grillmeier (s. Anm. 29) 311–314. Der Text wurde auf Anweisung des Kaisers von Severos verfaßt (vgl. Sev. Ant. *epist.* 1,1 p. 3–11 Brooks) und ist nur in zwei Auszügen auf Armenisch erhalten (vgl. Ch. Moeller, Un fragment du Type de l’empereur Anastase I, Studia Patristica 3 [1961], 240–247; dazu Grillmeier [wie Anm. 29] 311, mit Anm. 141 und 142). Grillmeier betont, daß das brisante Schriftstück nicht mit der *Enkyklia* des Basiliskos oder dem *Henotikon* verglichen werden dürfe, da es sich lediglich um ein vom Kaiser erbetenes Gutachten zur Interpretation des *Henotikons* handele und zudem für Anastasios nicht tragbar gewesen sein dürfte, weil es Chalkedon verflucht (so auch Gray [wie Anm. 6] 40). Der Kaiser regte offenbar im Anschluß an die Abfassung des *Typos* Gespräche – u. a. im Haus des Patrikios – an, um Severos zu einer konzilianteren Haltung zu bewegen, was aber scheiterte (Sev. Ant. *epist.* 1,1 p. 3–11 Brooks). Severos schien darauf zu beharren, daß „der *Typos* zur Herstellung der Einheit mehr geeignet war als das *Henotikon*. Ob dies aber vom Wortlaut der uns zugänglichen armenischen Fragmente gelten kann, bleibt fraglich. Sosehr die erhaltene fragmentarische Fassung den persönlichen Wünschen des Mönches entspricht, so wäre sie wohl dem Kaiser zu stark gewesen, wenigstens für die Zeit zwischen 508 und 511“ (Grillmeier [wie Anm. 29] 314). Aus diesem Grund wurde auch eine Datierung der Fragmente auf die Patriarchenzeit des Severos (512–518) erwogen, vgl. etwa de Halleux (s. Anm. 282) 68, Anm. 32; Allen (s. Anm. 6) 819.

307 Vgl. Gray (s. Anm. 6) 38 f.: „In fact, Anastasius had been put in the position of choosing between the pro- and anti-Chalcedonians of the empire. To choose for the former would imply a radical change in his oriental and Egyptian policy; to choose for the latter would necessitate bringing Constantinople into line, and – at this point – giving up all hope of reconciling Rome and the West. Anastasius chose the second course“.

versprechen. Dieser Sachverhalt erklärt zum einen die besondere Bedeutung des Aufenthalts des Severos in Konstantinopel (508–511) als vorbereitende und sondierende Maßnahme: Es wurden Gespräche geführt, und der mögliche Spielraum, innerhalb dessen sich eine ‚miaphysitische Wende' vollziehen konnte, wurde dabei ausgelotet;[308] auch der sog. *Typos* des Anastasios dürfte in diesen Kontext gehören.[309] Zum anderen erklärt sich aus der Bedeutung Konstantinopels die auffallende Intensität, mit der Anastasios den nunmehr eingeschlagenen Kurs durchzusetzen versuchte: Abgesehen von der (vorläufigen?) Rücknahme des *Trisagion*-Zusatzes nach dem *Stauroutheis*-Aufstand blieb es trotz der Unruhen bei der – seitens des Kaisers – maßvollen, aber durchaus konsequenten, miaphysitisch geprägten *Henotikon*-Politik, deren Beendigung auch von Vitalian nicht erzwungen werden konnte, die sich u. a. in der Zulassung der Weihe des Severos, der Absetzung des Elias von Jerusalem und dem endgültigen Bruch mit Rom[310] manifestiert, die aber letztlich durch die extremen Agitationen prominenter Kleriker (Philoxenos, Severos) ihrerseits wiederum konterkariert wurde und Anastasios dadurch in die Defensive zwang.

Um Konstantinopel für die skizzierte Position zu gewinnen, war der Bruch mit Makedonios schließlich unvermeidlich. Im Jahr 510 versuchte Anastasios, die Patriarchen Elias von Jerusalem und Makedonios von Konstantinopel zu einer Distanzierung von Chalkedon zu bewegen. Während Elias lediglich Nestorios, Eutyches, Diodoros von Tarsos und Theodoros von Mopsuestia anathematisierte, Chalkedon hingegen bestätigte (καὶ τὴν ἐν Χαλκηδόνι σύνοδον κρατύνων),[311] bestand Makedonios auf ein neues ökumenisches Konzil unter Vorsitz des Papstes; vorher werde er überhaupt nichts tun (ὁ δὲ χωρὶς οἰκουμενικῆς συνόδου ἐχούσης πρόεδρον τὸν τῆς μεγάλης Ῥώμης ἐπίσκοπον οὐδὲν ποιεῖν ἔλεγεν).[312] Dies, so fügt Theodoros Anagnostes hinzu, habe ihm die Feindschaft

---

308 Vgl. Zach. *Vita Sev.* (PO 2.1) p. 106–110 Kugener; Schwartz (s. Anm. 6) 240.
309 Vgl. Grillmeier (s. Anm. 29) 309–314.
310 Dieser Bruch manifestiert sich in drastischer Weise im letzten Brief des Anastasios an Papst Hormisdas vom 11. Juli 517 (*Coll. Avell.* 138 p. 564–565 Guenther), dem „Ausdruck einer christlichen Tragödie" (Grillmeier [s. Anm. 29] 357), dessen Schluß in dieser Hinsicht besonders charakteristisch ist: „[…] unsere Forderung unterdrücken wir aber von jetzt an schweigend, da wir es für unvernünftig halten, bei jenen das Gut der Bitte heranzuziehen, die sich in ihrer hartnäckigen Zurückweisung nicht bitten lassen wollen. Denn beleidigt und nicht ernstgenommen zu werden – das können wir ertragen; aber wir lassen uns nichts befehlen" (*sed postulationem nostram a praesenti tempore taciturnitate comprimi<mu>s, inrationabile iudicantes illis precum adhibere bonitatem, qui rogari se nolint contumaciter respuentes. iniuriari enim et adnullari sustinere possumus, iuberi non possumus*).
311 Theod. Anagn. *fr.* 473 p. 135,25–29 Hansen.
312 Theod. Anagn. *fr.* 474 p. 135,30–32 Hansen; vgl. Theoph. a. m. 6002 p. 152,21–27 de Boor (mit der unzutreffenden Behauptung, Elias habe der Verfluchung Chalkedons

des Kaisers eingebracht (ὅθεν εἰς ἔχθραν τὸν βασιλέα ἐκίνησεν).[313] Die Ereignisse nahmen nun einen dramatischen Verlauf und kulminierten in Unruhen um das *Trisagion*: Antichalkedonische Kräfte in Konstantinopel versuchten jetzt – im Jahr 510 oder 511 – zunehmend provokativ, das *Trisagion* um die Formel σταυρωθεὶς δι' ἡμᾶς zu erweitern; dies führte zu heftigen Tumulten, an denen Makedonios nicht unbeteiligt war und die mitunter mit dem ‚großen' *Staurotheis*-Aufstand des Jahres 512 vermengt oder verwechselt werden.[314] Dieser ‚erste' *Staurotheis*-Aufstand – aufgrund der Bedrängnis, in die auch der Kaiser dabei geriet, ist die Bezeichnung ‚Aufstand' durchaus gerechtfertigt – schuf aber lediglich die Ausgangslage für die im folgenden inszenierte Intrige zur Absetzung des Makedonios, die im November 512 ja bereits vollzogen war und erheblich zur Heftigkeit der Erregung mit beigetragen haben dürfte.

Über die Vorgänge, die, begonnen mit dem ‚ersten' *Staurotheis*-Aufstand, zur Absetzung des Makedonios geführt haben, sind wir verhältnismäßig gut unterrichtet:[315]

Dem oben bereits kurz diskutierten fragmentarischen Brief des Severos an Soterichos ist zu entnehmen, daß einige Miaphysiten, die in der Hagia Sophia das *Trisagion* mit dem *Staurotheis*-Zusatz sangen, *auf Anweisung des Makedonios* von gewalttätigen Randalierern niedergeprügelt worden seien – ja sogar die Bevölkerung insgesamt sei dabei gegen sie aufgehetzt worden.[316] Auch bei Ps.-Zacharias findet sich eine Andeutung, wonach Makedonios Unruhen gegen den Kaiser inszeniert haben soll.[317] Die chalkedonische Version – repräsentiert durch Theodoros Anagnostes – klingt ein wenig anders:[318] Demzufolge hätten die Chalkedon-Gegner (οἱ ἀποσχισταί) mit gedungenen Gewalttätern einen Gottesdienst der Chalkedonier gestürmt und das dort gesungene *Trisagion* mutwillig um den inkriminierten Zusatz ergänzt; am folgenden Sonntag hätten sie dasselbe, dieses Mal mit Stöcken bewaffnet, sogar in der Hagia Sophia veranstaltet. Tumulte

---

zugestimmt; korrekt hingegen Theoph. a. m. 6001 p. 151,27–31 de Boor). Charanis (s. Anm. 6) 66.

313 Theod. Anagn. *fr.* 474 p. 135,32 Hansen.

314 So bereits von Euagrios, vgl. Euagr. *HE* 3,44 p. 146,3–12 Bidez/Parmentier, der als Quelle für den *Staurotheis*-Aufstand den bereits erwähnten Brief des Severos an Soterichos anführt, welcher sich aber auf die Ereignisse des Jahres 510 bezieht. Eine ausdrückliche Trennung der beiden Aufstände nimmt Allen (s. Anm. 6) 819 vor.

315 Zum ‚ersten' *Staurotheis*-Aufstand s. Charanis (s. Anm. 6) 67; Frend (s. Anm. 6) 218; Gray (s. Anm. 6) 39.

316 Garitte (s. Anm. 68) 191–195.

317 Ps.-Zach. *HE* 7,7 p. 120,24–30 Ahrens/Krüger.

318 In den Fragmenten des Theodoros Anagnostes erscheinen die folgenden Geschehnisse – was signifikant ist – unter der Überschrift: Πολλοὺς ὁ βασιλεὺς κατὰ Μακεδονίου τρόπους ἐπενόει, vgl. Theod. Anagn. *fr.* 483 p. 137,23 Hansen.

seien die Folge gewesen.[319] Nun habe sich das Volk mitsamt Frauen und Kindern unter Führung der Mönche versammelt, sei mit Sprechchören durch die Stadt gezogen und habe dabei sogar Anastasios einen der Herrschaft nicht würdigen Manichäer gescholten (ὕβριζον δὲ τὸν βασιλέα Μανιχαῖον καλοῦντες καὶ τῆς βασιλείας ἀνάξιον). Der Kaiser sei immerhin so sehr eingeschüchtert gewesen, daß er sich in seinem Palast eingeschlossen und Schiffe für eine eventuelle Flucht bereitgestellt habe.[320] Danach sei jedenfalls das Tuch zwischen Kaiser und Patriarch zerschnitten gewesen.[321]

Die Geschehnisse um diesen ‚ersten' *Staurotheis*-Aufstand brauchen hier nicht näherhin analysiert zu werden; in unserem Zusammenhang genügt die Feststellung, daß es bereits ca. 510/11 zu gewaltsamen Ausschreitungen um den *Trisagion*-Zusatz gekommen ist, in deren Kontext Anastasios massiv attackiert wurde; die Situation scheint für den Kaiser nicht ganz ungefährlich gewesen zu sein. In diese Vorgänge war Makedonios offenbar prominent verwickelt.[322] Spätestens jetzt muß Anastasios deutlich gewesen sein, daß er entweder einen radikalen Kurswechsel in seiner Religions- und Kirchenpolitik vollziehen oder den widerborstigen Patriarchen auf irgendeine Art loswerden mußte. In realistischer Einschätzung der Sachlage wählte er die zweite Alternative.

Am 20. Juli 511[323] hatten sich Severos und Makedonios vor einem vom Kaiser eingesetzten Schiedsgericht einer Diskussion über die christologischen Streitpunkte zu stellen. Makedonios unterlag und sah sich zu Zugeständnissen gegenüber der miaphysitischen Richtung gezwungen;[324] dem geschickten Diplomaten Keler gelang es dabei, den so in die Enge getriebenen Patriarchen zur Unterzeichnung eines für ihn verhängnisvollen Dokumentes zu überreden, das letztlich die *Henotikon*-Position bestätigte (der Makedonios bei seinem Amtsantritt

---

319 Theod. Anagn. *fr.* 483 p. 137,23–29 Hansen; vgl. Theoph. a.m. 6003 p. 154,3–7 de Boor.

320 Theod. Anagn. *fr.* 485 p. 138,9–14 Hansen; Theoph. a.m. 6003 p. 154,11–16 de Boor; vgl. auch Ps.-Zach. *HE* 7,7 p. 120,24–26 Ahrens/Krüger: „Als er [sc. Makedonios] nun den Willen des Kaisers sah, sann er nach, um sogar einen Aufruhr gegen ihn zu erregen, pflegte ihn einen Haeretiker und Manichäer zu nennen".

321 Theod. Anagn. *fr.* 486 p. 138,15–20 Hansen; Theoph. a. m. 6003 p. 154,16–22 de Boor.

322 Vorsichtiger hinsichtlich der Person des Makedonios äußert sich Charanis (s. Anm. 6) 68.

323 Zum Folgenden s. auch Charanis (s. Anm. 6) 70f.; W. H. C. Frend, The Fall of Macedonius in 511 – a Suggestion, in: A. M. Ritter (Hg.), Kerygma und Logos. Beiträge zu den geistesgeschichtlichen Beziehungen zwischen Antike und Christentum, Göttingen 1979, 183–195; Grillmeier (s. Anm. 29) 315.

324 Zach. *Vita Sev.* (PO 2.1) p. 109–110 Kugener; Ps.-Zach. *HE* 7,8 p. 122,10–14 Ahrens/Krüger.

ja ebenfalls noch beigeflichtet hatte).[325] Dies wiederum erregte verständlicherweise die chalkedonischen Mönche, und Makedonios mußte sich nunmehr im Dalmatos-Kloster (vor der konstantinischen Mauer, in der Nähe des Xerolophos)[326] beeilen, ihnen gegenüber – im Widerspruch zu den am 20. Juli gemachten Zusagen – seine weiterhin bestehende Chalkedon-Treue zu betonen.[327] Seine Lage wurde nun immer auswegloser: Am 22. Juli zeigten Kaiser und Kaiserin dem Patriarchen in einer entwürdigenden Szene offen ihren Unmut.[328] Am 24. Juli wiederum demonstrierten einige Mönche ihre Unterstützung für Makedonios, was den Kaiser noch weiter erzürnte.[329] Die Reaktion darauf erfolgte nur einen Tag später, am 25. Juli: Dem *magister militum* Patrikios wurde von einigen anderen Mönchen ein Dokument zur Weitergabe an den Kaiser überreicht, in dem der Patriarch angeklagt wurde, das Andenken des Nestorios gefeiert zu haben.[330] Weitere Vorwürfe gegen Makedonios folgten.[331] Am 27. Juli berief Anastasios ein *silentium* ein und präsentierte den Anwesenden sämtliche Beschuldigungen, die gegen den Patriarchen erhoben wurden.

Ps.-Zacharias berichtet dabei von einer erstaunlichen Szene: Denn während dieser Versammlung benannte der Kaiser „mit Betrübnis und Weinen vor seinen Patrikioi die Schmähung, mit der er von Makedon geschmäht war, und schwur ihnen, daß (es) nicht aus Furcht (geschehe), sondern wenn er in Wahrheit ihnen nicht als Kaiser gefiele, oder wenn sie wüßten, daß die Lüge der Haeresie in ihm (wohne), so sollten sie ihm seine Herrschaft nehmen, und er müßte als Ungläubiger vertrieben werden. Da fielen sie weinend vor ihm auf ihr Antlitz, erregt über die Frechheit des Makedon, indem sie (laut) rufend ihn schmähten, dagegen den Kaiser priesen".[332] Dies ist bemerkenswert; denn das Verhalten des Anastasios gemahnt in signifikanter Weise an seine Demutsgeste, mit der er den *Staurotheis*-Aufstand kollabieren ließ: Das bei diesen Unruhen inszenierte Verhalten hatte sich also bereits im Kontext der Vertreibung des Makedonios – freilich in kleinerem Kreise – bewährt. Dies wiederum erlaubt die Vermutung, daß Anastasios

---

325 Vgl. Theod. Anagn. *fr.* 487 p. 138,21–26 Hansen; Theoph. a. m. 6004 p. 154,25–28 de Boor; Grumel, Regestes (s. Anm. 97), p. 141, Nr. 189. Charanis (s. Anm. 6) 68: „[...] it was no more than a reaffirmation of the Henotikon of Zeno".

326 Vgl. Janin (s. Anm. 17) 82–84; Berger (s. Anm. 49) 629–631.

327 Theod. Anagn. *fr.* 488 p. 139,1–5 Hansen; Theoph. a. m. 6004 p. 155,1–5 de Boor; vgl. Mich. Syr. 9,9 p. 163 Chabot. Charanis (s. Anm. 6) 69.

328 Ps.-Zach. *HE* 7,8 p. 122,14–18 Ahrens/Krüger.

329 Ps.-Zach. *HE* 7,8 p. 122,18–20 Ahrens/Krüger.

330 Ps.-Zach. *HE* 7,8 p. 122,20–29 Ahrens/Krüger; Theoph. a. m. 6004 p. 155,9–11 de Boor; vgl. Mich. Syr. 9,9 p. 163–164 Chabot.

331 Ps.-Zach. *HE* 7,8 p. 122,34–123,7 Ahrens/Krüger.

332 Ps.-Zach. *HE* 7,7 p. 120,31–121,7 Ahrens/Krüger. Zu dieser Sitzung s. auch Mich. Syr. 9,9 p. 164–165 Chabot.

demonstrative Demutsgesten bzw. Rücktrittsangebote offenbar ganz gezielt als Instrument zur Stabilisierung seiner Position einzusetzen verstand. Die berühmte und in der Forschung vielfach hervorgehobene Geste im November 512 war jedenfalls kein Einzelfall.

Im Anschluß an das *silentium* erging der Befehl, alle Gewalttäter gegenüber denjenigen, die das *Trisagion* in der erweiterten Form gesungen hatten, zu verhaften. Die Aufgabe wurde in die bewährten Hände des Stadtpräfekten Platon gelegt, der dem Kaiser bereits am folgenden Tag die Aufrührer vorführen konnte.[333]

Nunmehr zeichnete sich ab, daß die Entscheidung im Machtkampf zwischen Kaiser und Patriarch unmittelbar bevorstand. Anastasios agierte geschickt, indem er sich durch Geldgeschenke eidlich die Treue der in der Hauptstadt anwesenden Heerführer, der Palastgarden und der *patricii* versichern ließ (29. Juli)[334] und die Truppen durch ein Donativ ruhigstellte (30. Juli).[335] Den Bericht einiger Presbyter und Diakone, wonach Makedonios ihn einen Manichäer genannt habe,[336] nutzte er klug dazu aus, um noch einmal vor einem u. a. aus Klerikern bestehenden Publikum nachdrücklich seinen ‚orthodoxen‘ Glauben zu bekennen, und provozierte damit einmal mehr eine kollektive, unter Tränen kundgegebene Zustimmungsgeste (31. Juli).[337]

Die folgenden Ereignisse verraten weiterhin große Vorsicht und Behutsamkeit in der Vorgehensweise: Stadttore und Häfen wurden abgeriegelt; es erfolgten erste Verhaftungen.[338] In einem *silentium* am 6. August sprach Anastasios die Absetzung des Patriarchen aus.[339] Am 7. August wurde Makedonios nach Euchaita ins Exil geschickt; der *magister officiorum* Keler, der dem Kaiser nun beweisen durfte, daß er es doch nicht mit Makedonios hielt, kommandierte die Truppen, die ihn abführten.[340]

Anstelle des Makedonios installierte Anastasios in der weisen Einsicht, die Geduld der Bevölkerung Konstantinopels nicht überstrapazieren zu dürfen, nicht Severos, sondern den farblos-loyalen Timotheos,[341] der denn auch bemerkenswerterweise in den Berichten über den anschließenden *Staurotheis*-Aufstand

---

333 Ps.-Zach. *HE* 7,8 p. 123,7–28 Ahrens/Krüger; vgl. 7,7 p. 121,14–19 Ahrens/Krüger.
334 Ps.-Zach. *HE* 7,8 p. 123,29–124,10 Ahrens/Krüger.
335 Ps.-Zach. *HE* 7,8 p. 124,11–12 Ahrens/Krüger; vgl. Mich. Syr. 9,9 p. 164 Chabot.
336 Ps.-Zach. *HE* 7,8 p. 124,13–18 Ahrens/Krüger.
337 Ps.-Zach. *HE* 7,8 p. 124,18–125,15 Ahrens/Krüger.
338 Ps.-Zach. *HE* 7,8 p. 125,27–126,1; vgl. 7,7 p. 121,10–19 Ahrens/Krüger.
339 Ps.-Zach. *HE* 7,8 p. 126,1–30 Ahrens/Krüger.
340 Ps.-Zach. *HE* 7,8 p. 127,22–128,9; ferner 7,7 p. 121,8–10 Ahrens/Krüger. Vgl. Theod. Anagn. *fr.* 489–492 p. 139,6–140,13 Hansen; Theoph. a. m. 6004 p. 155,12–13 de Boor; *Chronik von Zuqnîn* p. 10–11 Witakowski = p. 44 Harrak; Mich. Syr. 9,9 p. 165 Chabot.
341 Vgl. dazu auch Gray (s. Anm. 6) 39.

eher eine marginale Rolle gegenüber den kaiserlichen Beamten spielt. Die Chalkedonier setzten ihre Hoffnungen zunächst wohl vor allem in den Besuch des angesehenen Mönchsführers Sabas, der sich 511/12 in Konstantinopel aufhielt, aber
außer reichlichen Geschenken und vornehmer Ehrerbietung nichts beim Kaiser
erreichen konnte.[342] Anastasios blieb seiner Linie weiterhin treu. Im November
512 ließ er durch Platon und Marinos die Ergänzung des *Trisagion*s verkünden.
Nun brach der *Staurotheis*-Aufstand aus.

Vor diesem Hintergrund erweisen sich die Tumulte des Jahres 512 unter dem
Blickwinkel der kirchenpolitischen Zusammenhänge als Kulminationspunkt
einer prozeßhaften Zuspitzung der Entwicklungen in Konstantinopel: Anastasios hatte seine Politik, die zunächst auf eine Sicherung der Allgemeingültigkeit
des *Henotikons* ausgerichtet war, nach dem Ende des Perserkriegs zunehmend in
die miaphysitische Richtung hin ausgerichtet und benötigte dazu insbesondere
die Zustimmung der hauptstädtischen Bevölkerung. Der Versuch, sich diese zu
sichern, erfolgte in mehreren Schritten: Einem mehrjährigen Diskussionsprozeß,
der sich zwischen 508 und 511 insbesondere in der Person des Severos kristallisierte, folgte ein wachsender Druck auf Makedonios, dessen chalkedonische Haltung damit einhergehend allerdings eher verhärtete, so daß der erneute Konflikt
zwischen Kaiser und Patriarch schließlich unausweichlich war: Nach einem
ersten Test, wie Konstantinopel auf den Zusatz zum *Trisagion* reagieren würde,
und dem von Makedonios mitorganisierten Widerstand dagegen, erfolgte die
Absetzung des Patriarchen und ein erneuter Vorstoß hinsichtlich des *Trisagion*s –
dieses Mal als klare kaiserliche Anordnung, übermittelt nicht durch den Patriarchen, sondern durch kaiserliche Beamte. Die unmittelbare Folge war der *Staurotheis*-Aufstand, der Anastasios zumindest scheinbar erst einmal in die Knie
zwang. Tatsächlich aber ließ der Kaiser lediglich die *Trisagion*-Frage zunächst auf
sich beruhen, nutzte dafür aber die Revolte, um im nachfolgenden Strafgericht
massiv gegen die Unruhestifter vorzugehen, worunter die Chalkedonier besonders gelitten haben dürften. Auch sein Umgang mit den Erhebungen Vitalians,
die sich als Ausweitung der Unruhen über Konstantinopel hinaus nicht nur
durch die Person des Rebellen direkt mit dem *Staurotheis*-Aufstand in Verbindung bringen lassen, deuten auf dieselbe Taktik: Vordergründiges Nachgeben
ohne merkliche Bewegung in den eigentlichen Streitfragen.
  Anastasios änderte in seinen späten Jahren nichts Grundsätzliches an seinem
religionspolitischen Kurs – auch die neuerlichen Bemühungen um einen Ausgleich mit Rom scheiterten ja –, scheint aber seine eigenen Aktivitäten eingeschränkt zu haben: Während die Absetzung des Elias (516) noch einmal Anasta-

---

342 Vgl. Schwartz (s. Anm. 6) 244 f.

sios' ordnende Hand erkennen läßt, deuten die anschließenden chaotischen Verhältnisse in Jerusalem eher auf einen Rückzug des Kaisers aus den Kontroversen – trotz der Anwesenheit seines Neffen Hypatios in Jerusalem.[343] Insbesondere für Konstantinopel erfolgten keine weiteren Initiativen mehr in Richtung einer miaphysitischen Auslegung des *Henotikons*, während sich Philoxenos und Severos im Osten mit ihren zugespitzten Positionen unbehelligt profilieren konnten: Immerhin nutzte Severos bereits die erste Ansprache nach seiner Weihe für einen massiven Angriff auf Chalkedon – ganz gegen die Intention des Kaisers (s. o.).

---

343 Nach seiner Ordination zum Patriarchen von Antiocheia versuchte Severos auch Elias auf seinen Kurs zu bringen. Dieser jedoch, unterstützt von palästinischen Mönchen unter der Führung des Sabas, blieb seiner chalkedonischen Position treu (Kyrill. Skythop. *V. Sabae* 56 p. 148,23–149,6 Schwartz), was letztlich zu seiner Absetzung am 1. September 516 führte. Anastasios machte Johannes III. zu seinem Nachfolger (Kyrill. Skythop. *V. Sabae* 56 p. 149,27–150,11 Schwartz), der zwar versprochen hatte, mit Severos in Kommunion zu treten, dann aber ebenfalls unter dem Druck der palästinischen Mönche seine Treue gegenüber Chalkedon bekräftigte (Kyrill. Skythop. *V. Sabae* 56 p. 150,11–16 Schwartz) und sich auch durch Arrestierung in Kaisareia nicht davon abbringen ließ (Kyrill. Skythop. *V. Sabae* 56 p. 150,16–151,7 Schwartz). Gegen Ende des Jahres 516 veranstalteten angeblich 10.000 Mönche unter Führung des Hl. Theodosios und des Hl. Sabas eine eindrucksvolle Demonstration ihrer Chalkedon-Treue und ihrer Macht über die heilige Stadt Jerusalem. Johannes schloß sich mit einer gegen Severos gerichteten Erklärung der allgemeinen Stimmung an, während der Vertreter des Kaisers, der *dux Palaestinae* Anastasios (PLRE II 80 f. [Anastasius 10]), sogar von Jerusalem nach Kaisareia fliehen mußte (Kyrill. Skythop. *V. Sabae* 56 p. 151,7–152,6 Schwartz). Der Neffe des Kaisers Hypatios, der nach seiner Freilassung aus der Gefangenschaft Vitalians wegen eines Gelübdes (εὐχῆς ἕνεκεν, Kyrill. Skythop. *V. Sabae* 56 p. 151,15 Schwartz) nach Jerusalem gekommen war, geriet offenbar ebenfalls derartig unter Druck, daß er sogar eidlich versicherte (ὅρκοις ἔπεισεν τοὺς πατέρας), er habe mit Severos nichts zu tun (!) (μὴ κοινωνήσας Σευήρωι, Kyrill. Skythop. *V. Sabae* 56 p. 152,6–8 Schwartz; vgl. Greatrex 1996 [wie Anm. 152] 122 f.; 137). Ein neuerlicher Versuch des Kaisers, nun auch Johannes abzusetzen, scheiterte am geschlossenen Widerstand der Mönche, die explizit auf ihre Gewalt- und Martyriumsbereitschaft im Falle einer weiteren Zuspitzung der Lage hinwiesen (Kyrill. Skythop. *V. Sabae* 56–57 p. 152,16–158,11 Schwartz). Eine Zusammenfassung der Vorgänge findet sich auch bei Theoph. a. m. 6005 p. 158,22–159,5 de Boor, basierend auf Theod. Anagn. *fr.* 518 p. 149,20–31 Hansen. – Zu diesen Ereignissen vgl. auch Frend (s. Anm. 6) 228–231; Charanis (s. Anm. 6) 98–102; Gray (s. Anm. 6) 42 f.; Grillmeier (s. Anm. 29) 297; K. Hay, Impact of St Sabas: The Legacy of Palestinian Monasticism, in: P. Allen/E. M. Jeffreys (Hgg.), The Sixth Century – End or Beginning?, Brisbane 1996, 118–125, hier 122 f.; K. Trampedach, Reichsmönchtum? Das politische Selbstverständnis der Mönche Palästinas im 6. Jahrhundert und die historische Methode des Kyrill von Skythopolis, Millennium 2 (2005), 271–296, hier 273 ff.

IV

Euagrios gliedert seine Darstellung der Herrschaft des Anastasios in zwei Teile: Der erste ist *grosso modo* kirchlichen Belangen bzw. der Kirchenpolitik sowie religiösen Fragen gewidmet, während der Fokus des zweiten Abschnitts sich eher auf profanhistorische Ereignisse richtet.[344] Es ist bemerkenswert, daß der Autor den *Staurotheis*-Aufstand ausgerechnet im letztgenannten Kontext verortet, ja daß er mit ihm sogar seinen Bericht über die Herrschaft des Anastasios ganz abschließt.[345] Selbst für einen Kirchenhistoriker des späten 6. Jahrhunderts bedeuteten die Geschehnisse des Jahres 512 also mehr als lediglich einen Einschnitt innerhalb der kaiserlichen *Kirchenpolitik*. Vielmehr lassen sie sich nämlich auch als Kulminationspunkt einer Serie von Aufständen in Konstantinopel – und nicht nur dort[346] – interpretieren, bei denen eine generelle Unzufriedenheit mit dem Kaiser, seiner Politik und seinen engeren Gefolgsleuten ihren blutigen Ausdruck fand und bei denen die Zirkusgruppen eine zunehmend prominente Rolle spielten.

Als Anastasios 491 die Kaiserwürde übernahm, trat er kein leichtes Erbe an. Die Herrschaft Zenons war nicht unumstritten gewesen und hatte u. a. in der Hauptstadt phasenweise zu chaotischen Zuständen geführt.[347] Um die Person des Usurpators Basiliskos (475/76) hatte sich massiver Widerstand gegen den Kaiser gruppiert, der insbesondere auf eine Entmachtung der Isaurier, als deren Anführer Zenon (Tarasikodissa) an die Macht gekommen war, zielte[348] – Basiliskos' Griff nach dem Purpur ging dementsprechend mit einem Massaker an den Isauriern einher.[349] Mit seiner demonstrativ antichalkedonischen Politik hatte Basilis-

---

344 Vgl. Euagr. *HE* 3,30–34 p. 125,32–134,23 Bidez/Parmentier (kirchliche Angelegenheiten); *HE* 3,35–44 p. 134,24–147,3 Bidez/Parmentier (profanhistorische Angelegenheiten); vgl. zu dieser Gliederung auch Allen (s. Anm. 30) 143.

345 Vgl. Euagr. *HE* 3,44 p. 146,3–147,3 Bidez/Parmentier.

346 Malalas berichtet für das Jahr 494/95 von einem Aufstand der Grünen in Antiocheia (Malal. p. 319,13–22 Thurn); die Grünen waren zudem Ausgangspunkt eines weiteren Aufstandes in Antiocheia im Jahr 507 (Malal. p. 324,75–325,25 Thurn; vgl. *Exc. de insid.* 40 p. 168,35–36 de Boor [aus Malal.]); 515/16 kam es zu Unruhen in Alexandreia (Malal. p. 328,4–329,10 Thurn; vgl. Theoph. a.m. 6009 p. 163,9–16 de Boor; Joh. Nik. 89,35 p. 125 Charles; *Exc. de insid.* 41 p. 169,1–7 de Boor [aus Malal.]).

347 Zur Herrschaft Zenons s. etwa Stein (s. Anm. 6) 7 ff.; Demandt (s. Anm. 6) 188–190, bes. 188: „Die Regierungszeit Zenos […] ist charakterisiert durch langjährigen Bürgerkrieg um den Thron von Byzanz"; Lee, (s. Anm. 6) 49 ff., bes. 49: „[…] his reign was overshadowed by a succession of revolts and usurpations".

348 Vgl. Demandt (s. Anm. 6) 188 f.; K. Feld, Barbarische Bürger. Die Isaurier und das Römische Reich, Berlin/New York 2005, 252.

349 R. C. Blockley (Ed.), The Fragmentary Classicising Historians of the Later Roman Empire. Eunapius, Olympiodorus, Priscus and Malchus, Vol. II: Text, Translation and

kos aber auf die falsche Karte gesetzt und konnte sich u. a. aus diesem Grund nicht lange in Konstantinopel halten.[350] Umso entsetzter dürften die Reaktionen auf Zenons *Henotikon* ausgefallen sein, das dem Kaiser die Union mit Ägypten sichern sollte, ohne dabei Rom allzu sehr zu beleidigen, und dem Patriarchen einen entscheidenden Vorteil innerhalb der Konkurrenz der Kirchenführer verschaffen sollte.[351] Folgerichtig forderte das Volk nach Zenons Tod nachdrücklich einen „orthodoxen" Kaiser.[352] Daß dann ausgerechnet Anastasios gekrönt wurde, dessen ‚Orthodoxie' durchaus nicht unumstritten war (s. o.), erzeugte von Beginn an ein spannungsgeladenes Verhältnis zwischen Kaiser und hauptstädtischer Bevölkerung, das sich in der erwähnten Kette von Unruhen niederschlug. Bereits im Kontext seiner ersten Ansprache als Kaiser wurde Anastasios durch Sprechchöre auf das Vorbild Markians und damit implizit, aber noch immer deutlich genug, auf Chalkedon verwiesen.[353] Noch im Jahr 491 erfolgte dann der erste Aufstand gegen den neuen Herrscher (ein *bellum plebeium*, an dessen Inszenierung Patriarch Euphemios möglicherweise nicht ganz unbeteiligt war)[354] – weitere Tumulte erschütterten Konstantinopel in dichter Folge,[355] darunter die bereits erwähnten Ausschreitungen der Grünen im Hippodrom, bei denen Anastasios beinahe durch einen Steinwurf in das Kathisma niedergestreckt worden wäre,[356] sowie der ‚erste' *Staurotheis*-Aufstand, bei dem der Kaiser angeblich sogar eine Flucht aus der Hauptstadt erwogen haben soll.[357]

Historiographical Notes, Liverpool 1983, p. 466,57 (= Kandidos *fr.* 1): περὶ [...] τῆς Ἰσαύρων ἐν Κωνσταντινουπόλει ἀμυθήτου σφαγῆς. Vgl. Jos. Styl. 12 p. 41 Luther.

350 Demandt (s. Anm. 6) 188 f. Zur antichalkedonischen Politik des Basiliskos, die sich insbesondere in seiner *Enkyklia* mit ihrer Anathematisierung der Beschlüsse von Chalkedon und des *Tomus Leonis* manifestiert, s. Haacke (s. Anm. 6) 112–116; Grillmeier (s. Anm. 29) 267 ff.; Brennecke (s. Anm. 280) 34–38.

351 Akakios intendierte, die im 28. Kanon des Konzils von Chalkedon festgelegte kirchliche Gleichrangigkeit Roms und Konstantinopel beizubehalten, den Antichalkedoniern dabei aber theologisch entgegenzukommen; dies führte zu einem ambivalenten Verhältnis gegenüber Chalkedon: „Annahme der Kanones, nicht aber der Lehrdefinition", vgl. Grillmeier (s. Anm. 29) 290.

352 *De caerim.* 1,92 p. 418,19–20 Reiske (ὀρθόδοξον βασιλέα τῇ οἰκουμένῃ); vgl. 1,92 p. 421,12–13 Reiske.

353 *De caerim.* 1,92 p. 425,3–4 Reiske (ὡς Μαρκιανός, οὕτως βασίλευσον).

354 Marc. Com. ad ann. 491,2 p. 94 Mommsen: *Bellum plebeium inter Byzantios ortum parsque urbis plurima atque circi igne combusta.*

355 Eine – unvollständige – Liste gibt Cameron (s. Anm. 8) 233 f. (zu ergänzen um seine Auflistung von Aufständen ohne Beteiligung der Zirkusgruppen, S. 235); vgl. auch die Aufzählung bei Wirth (s. Anm. 5) 111.

356 S. o. Anm. 143.

357 S. o. Anm. 320.

Wie in der Forschung schon seit längerem gesehen worden ist, fügen sich diese Aufstände in eine längerfristige Entwicklung seit etwa Mitte des 5. Jahrhunderts, die durch eine generelle Zunahme von Unruhen in Konstantinopel gekennzeichnet ist.[358] Die Frage nach den Ursachen dieser Entwicklung, die in engem Zusammenhang steht mit der Etablierung des nachtheodosianischen sog. hauptstädtischen Kaisertums und der damit einhergehenden Ausbildung spezifischer Kommunikationsmuster zwischen Kaiser und Bevölkerung[359] – zu denen im weiteren Sinne auch der Aufstand als besondere Form der Auseinandersetzung zu zählen ist –, braucht in unserem Kontext nicht näher diskutiert zu werden. Erklärungsbedürftig ist jedoch die Tatsache, daß diese Entwicklung – insbesondere (aber nicht nur) mit Blick auf die Aktivitäten der Zirkusgruppen – ausgerechnet unter Anastasios ihren Höhepunkt erreichte,[360] für dessen Herrschaft man wohl – gemessen an der Anzahl und Qualität der Aufstände – ein grundsätzlich konfliktgeladenes, man könnte auch sagen: gestörtes Verhältnis zwischen Kaiser und hauptstädtischer Bevölkerung konstatieren darf.

Neben dem bereits erwähnten Stigma einer vermeintlichen Heterodoxie, das Anastasios mit in seine Herrschaft einbrachte und in der Folge nicht mehr losgeworden ist (s. o.), lassen sich noch weitere Faktoren für diese Asymmetrie beibringen:

1.) Anastasios führte während seiner Herrschaft zwei größere Bürgerkriege – zum einen gegen die Isaurier (491–497/98), zum anderen gegen Vitalian (513–515). Aus beiden Konflikten ging er letztendlich erfolgreich hervor, aber in beiden Fällen dürfte er auch die Bevölkerung im Hinblick auf seine Person polarisiert haben. Zwar genossen die Isaurier – zumal nach Zenons Tod – keine besondere Beliebtheit in der Hauptstadt, aber gänzlich ohne Einfluß waren sie nicht.

---

358 Cameron (s. Anm. 8) 233.

359 Zu diesem Fragenkomplex s. vor allem die ausgezeichneten Arbeiten von St. Diefenbach, Frömmigkeit und Kaiserakzeptanz im frühen Byzanz, Saeculum 47 (1996), 35–66; ders., Zwischen Liturgie und *civilitas*. Konstantinopel im 5. Jahrhundert und die Etablierung eines städtischen Kaisertums, in: R. Warland (Hg.), Bildlichkeit und Bildort von Liturgie, Wiesbaden 2002, 21–47.

360 Vgl. Cameron (s. Anm. 8) 232: „[...] there can be little doubt that the reign of Anastasius marked a turning-point in the growth of factional violence. [...] there is nothing on record to compare with the series of bloody riots deliberately provoked by the rivalry of the Blues and Greens from the reign of Anastasius on"; ebd., 233: „The picture changes completely with the accession of Anastasius [...]"; vgl. auch ebd., 239. Daß man diesen Befund nicht lediglich auf eine für die Zeit des Anastasios dichtere Überlieferungslage zurückführen kann, veranschaulicht Cameron (s. Anm. 8) 235. – Cameron betont im übrigen ausdrücklich, daß nicht nur die Unruhen der Zirkusgruppen unter Anastasios zunahmen, sondern Aufstände generell häufiger wurden (239).

Zenons Bruder Longinos etwa wurde durchaus als ernstzunehmender Nachfolgekandidat gehandelt, und dies konnte nur dann zumindest ansatzweise Erfolgsaussichten haben, wenn Longinos auch eine gewisse Unterstützung in der Aristokratie besaß.[361] Die Auseinandersetzungen zwischen Anastasios und Vitalian hingegen verdeutlichten das kirchenpolitische Dilemma, in das ersterer sich mit seiner zunehmend miaphysitisch geleiteten *Henotikon*-Politik hineinmanövriert hatte, und manifestierte die sich radikalisierende Unversöhnlichkeit von Chalkedoniern und Antichalkedoniern in besonderer Schärfe: Der Abbruch der Beziehungen zu Rom (s. o.) und die turbulenten Ereignisse in Jerusalem nach der Absetzung des Patriarchen Elias (516)[362] veranschaulichen dies.

2.) Der Perserkrieg und insbesondere die Geschehnisse in Amida während und nach der Einnahme durch die Perser (Januar 503) sowie während der römischen Belagerung[363] scheinen vielfache Unzufriedenheit hervorgerufen zu haben. Zwar hat Anastasios nach dem Abschluß des Friedensvertrages 506 großzügige Steuererleichterungen für die betroffenen Städte gewährt, was in den Quellen auch vielfach panegyrisch gefeiert wird,[364] aber die vom Krieg heimgesuchten Regionen waren dennoch längerfristig ruiniert, ihre Bevölkerung traumatisiert. Zudem scheint dieser Krieg – wie bereits angedeutet – zu erheblichen Friktionen in der römischen Führungselite geführt zu haben, die nicht ohne Einfluß auf die Situation in Konstantinopel geblieben sein können (s. o.).

3.) In den Jahren vor und nach 500 ist generell eine höhere Sensibilität gegenüber Handlungen und Ereignissen, die zu anderen Zeiten keine größeren Reaktionen hervorgerufen hätten, zu verzeichnen. Ursache dafür ist die akute und weit verbreitete Endzeiterwartung jener Jahre,[365] die nicht nur eine latente angstvolle Unruhe und die entsprechende Disposition zu eruptiven Reaktionen auf bestimmte Geschehnisse bewirkt haben dürfte, sondern die unweigerlich auch den Kaiser in den Kontext einer nachhaltig eschatologisch geprägten Wahrnehmung zeitgenössischer Entwicklungen integriert und somit unter besonders kritische Beobachtung gestellt haben dürfte. Zwar ist die auf eine spezifische

---

361 PLRE II 689 f. (Longinus 6). Theoph. a. m. 5983 p. 135,33–136,5 de Boor, verweist dezidiert auf die einflußreiche Stellung des Longinos im Senat (δὶς μὲν ὑπατεύσαντα καὶ τῆς συγκλήτου βουλῆς πάσης ἡγούμενον), vgl. Euagr. *HE* 3,29 p. 125,6–13 Bidez/Parmentier. Feld (s. Anm. 348) 332 ff.

362 Dazu s. o. Anm. 343.

363 Zu den Ereignissen s. im einzelnen Greatrex 1998 (s. Anm. 156) 83 ff.

364 Vgl. Greatrex 1998 (s. Anm. 156) 115 f.

365 Dazu s. im einzelnen W. Brandes, Anastasios ὁ δίκορος. Endzeiterwartung und Kaiserkritik in Byzanz um 500 n. Chr., BZ 90 (1997), 24–63; Meier (s. Anm. 221) 11 ff.; 64 ff. und *passim*; ders., Eschatologie und Kommunikation im 6. Jahrhundert n. Chr. – oder: Wie Osten und Westen beständig aneinander vorbei redeten, in: W. Brandes/ F. Schmieder (Hgg.), Endzeiten, Berlin/New York 2007 (im Druck).

Rolle im endzeitlichen Prozeß verweisende Bezeichnung des Anastasios als δίκορος, als „Mann mit den verschiedenfarbigen Pupillen", erst seit Malalas, d. h. seit dem fortgeschrittenen 6. Jahrhundert belegt,[366] sie dürfte aber zeitgenössische Diskurse spiegeln, zumal Malalas sich für die Zeit des Anastasios auf eigene Erfahrungen bzw. auf Zeitzeugen gestützt hat;[367] und im übrigen zeichnet das um 503/04 verfaßte *Orakel von Baalbek* Anastasios bereits klar als Endzeit-kaiser.[368]

4.) Trotz der aufwendigen Kriege gegen Isaurier, Perser und Vitalian, trotz der Abschaffung des Chrysargyron[369] und trotz einiger weiterer kostspieliger Maßnahmen gelang es Anastasios bzw. seinen findigen Finanzfachmännern – insbesondere Marinos von Apameia –, im Jahr 518 die gewaltige Finanzreserve von 320.000 Goldpfund zu hinterlassen.[370] Die Anhäufung eines derartigen Schatzes kann nicht ohne erhebliche Belastungen für große Teile der Bevölkerung erfolgt sein. Es ist daher auch nicht erstaunlich, daß Zeitgenossen den Geiz des Kaisers mitunter als dessen herausragende Eigenschaft benannten;[371] daß sich darin eine deutliche Unzufriedenheit spiegelt, steht außer Frage. Einzelne Maßnahmen des Anastasios, die vornehmlich einer effektiveren Verwaltung dienen sollten, stehen in den Quellen daher auch besonders in der Kritik, wie z. B. die bereits kurz erwähnte Einführung der *vindices*, wodurch die Steuererhebung in den Städten neu organisiert werden sollte.[372] Diese Maßnahme wird in den Quellen – wie angedeutet – mit Marinos von Apameia verbunden und zeigt damit deutlich, daß nicht nur der Kaiser selbst, sondern auch seine Umgebung in das Visier der Kritik gerieten – wie etwa auch der Stadtpräfekt Platon, an dessen Händen seit dem ‚Steinwurf'-Aufstand das Blut zahlreicher Konstantinopolitaner klebte.[373]

---

366 Malal. p. 319,3–4 Thurn. Vgl. Brandes (s. Anm. 365) 58.

367 So ist wohl seine Aussage Malal. p. 3,4–14 Thurn, zu verstehen; vgl. dazu Jeffreys (s. Anm. 30) 502.

368 P. J. Alexander (Ed.), The Oracle of Baalbek. The Tiburtine Sibyl in Greek Dress, Washington 1967, p. 19,161–166. Dazu Brandes (s. Anm. 365) 57 ff.; Al. Cameron, Oracles and Earthquakes. A Note on the Theodosian Sibyl, in: C. Sode/S. Takács (Hgg.), Novum Millennium: Studies on Byzantine History and Culture Dedicated to Paul Speck, Aldershot u. a. 2001, 45–52; Meier (s. Anm. 221) 67 ff.

369 Dazu s. Brandes (s. Anm. 32) 22 f.; 34, mit weiterer Literatur.

370 Prok. *HA* 19,7. Dazu s. Brandes (s. Anm. 32) 72, Anm. 60.

371 Etwa *Anth. Graec.* 11,270; 271; vgl. auch Joh. Lyd. *mag.* 3,46 p. 204,15–16; 3,49 p. 208,23–28 Bandy; Joh. Ant. *fr.* 215 FHG IV 621 Müller = *fr.* 312 p. 542–543 Roberto. Justin I. verwies auf die *parca [...] subtilitas* des Anastasios (*Cod. Iust.* 2,7,25 pr.). Zur Finanzpolitik des Anastasios s. auch Stein (s. Anm. 6) 192 ff.; Brandes (s. Anm. 32) Index s. v. Anastasios I.

372 S. o. sowie Stein (s. Anm. 6) 210.

373 S. o. Anm. 143.

5.) Victor von Tunnuna berichtet, daß auch die Zirkusgruppen in den *Staurotheis*-Aufstand involviert waren.[374] Obwohl er mit dieser Nachricht allein steht, ist er dennoch ernstzunehmen.[375] Denn gerade unter Anastasios scheinen die Zirkusgruppen eine besondere Aktivität entfaltet und dabei wiederholt schwere Ausschreitungen provoziert zu haben.[376] In der Forschung wurde die These vertreten, daß die von Anastasios ausgesprochenen Verbote von *venationes* (499) und Pantomimenaufführungen (502) (die ihrerseits wohl bereits gewaltsamen Tumulten vorbeugen sollten)[377] zu einer Kanalisierung öffentlicher, von großem Zulauf gekennzeichneter Unterhaltungsveranstaltungen auf die Wagenrennen im Hippodrom geführt und damit erst die Wagenrennen – und mit ihnen die Anhänger der ‚Rennställe‘, die Zirkusgruppen – zu einem politisch derartig brisanten Faktor ausgeformt hätten, als der sie dann in den folgenden Jahrzehnten immer wieder hervortreten.[378] Auch wenn diese These die Komplexität einer langwierigen Entwicklung möglicherweise allzu sehr reduziert, so ist dennoch offenkundig, daß die Zirkusgruppen sich unter Anastasios zu einem massiven

---

374 Vict. Tunn. ad ann. 513 p. 195,18–20 Mommsen = p. 30–32 Placanica = p. 31 Cardelle de Hartmann.

375 Dies betont zu Recht auch Cameron (s. Anm. 10) 132.

376 Dies konstatiert bereits Prok. *BP* 1,24,2–3. Vgl. Cameron (s. Anm. 8) 232–239; zur Aktivität der Zirkusgruppen in der Spätantike vgl. – in Auseinandersetzung mit Cameron – auch Liebeschuetz (s. Anm. 10) 163 ff.

377 *Venationes*: Jos. Styl. 34 p. 52 Luther; vgl. Theod. Anagn. *fr.* 553 p. 156,15 Hansen; Theoph. a.m. 5993 p. 143,17–18 de Boor (allerdings existieren noch Hinweise auf eine Fortexistenz von *venationes* nach dem Verbot, doch scheinen sie tatsächlich seltener geworden zu sein und sind offenbar allmählich ausgestorben; Anastasios hat diesen Prozeß offenbar mit seinem Verbot ein wenig beschleunigt, vgl. Cameron (s. Anm. 8) 228–230). Chr. Epplett, Anastasius and the *Venationes*, Nikephoros 17 (2004), 221–230, will in der Maßnahme nur ein Verbot der *damnatio ad bestias* sehen. – Pantomimen: Marc. Com. ad ann. 501 p. 95 Mommsen; Theoph. a. m. 5997 p. 147,17–20 de Boor; *Exc. de insid.* 101 p. 142,29–143,4 [aus Joh. Ant.]; 36 p. 167,21–23; 39 p. 168,26–34 de Boor [aus Malal.].
Für das Verbot der Pantomimenaufführungen ist die Intention, mit diesem Schritt Unruhen vorzubeugen, explizit bezeugt (der Maßnahme vorausgegangen waren massive Unruhen beim von Pantomimenaufführungen begleiteten Brytai-Fest, bei denen sogar ein illegitimer Sohn des Anastasios den Tod fand). Im Fall der *venationes* nennen die Panegyriker humanitäre Motive (A. Chauvot [Ed.], Procope de Gaza, Priscien de Césarée. Panégyriques de l'empereur Anastase Ier. Textes traduits et commentés, Bonn 1986, p. 65 [= Prisk. *Pan.* v. 223–228]; p. 17 [= Prok. Gaz. *Pan.* 15]), „but in the context it is hard to resist the suspicion that here too it was the impetus such violent spectacles offered to the already violence-prone factions that moved him [sc. Anastasios] most", vgl. Cameron (s. Anm. 8) 242. Auch im Fall der Pantomimen führte das kaiserliche Verbot freilich nicht sofort zu einem abrupten Abbruch der Tradition.

378 Vgl. Cameron (s. Anm. 8) 228–232; 242; ders. (s. Anm. 10) 226 f.; 275.

Unruhefaktor entwickelten. Der Kaiser selbst reagierte darauf, indem er weder mit den Grünen noch mit den Blauen sympathisierte, sondern sich als Anhänger der völlig unbedeutenden Roten gerierte (und damit letztlich Neutralität demonstrierte), ja sogar besonders scharf gegen Grüne und Blaue vorging, wenn diese unruhig wurden.[379] Dieses Verhalten mag auf den ersten Blick geschickt anmuten. Es nahm dem Kaiser aber die Möglichkeit, über die persönliche Anhängerschaft in brisanten Situationen die eine Partei gegen die andere ausspielen zu können und drohende Gefahren dadurch zu entschärfen – auch der Umstand, daß Anastasios den Demen andererseits großzügig die Errichtung von Siegesmonumenten für ihre Wagenlenker – wie z.B. den berühmten Porphyrios – gestattete,[380] dürfte dieses Problem nicht grundsätzlich entschärft haben. Ein Zusammenschluß der Grünen und der Blauen war somit wesentlich leichter möglich als im Fall einer einseitigen Parteinahme des Kaisers.[381] Die von Victor von Tunnuna geschilderte Vereinigung dieser beiden Zirkusgruppen gegen den Kaiser im Jahr 512 gewinnt vor diesem Hintergrund Plausibilität.

V

Diese knappe Skizze mag ausreichen, um zu zeigen, daß der *Staurotheis*-Aufstand keineswegs als isoliertes, lediglich religiös bzw. kirchenpolitisch motiviertes Ereignis angesehen werden darf. In ihm floß eine Reihe von Faktoren zusammen, die sich zu einer ganz spezifischen, höchst brisanten Gemengelage verbanden: Eine aufgrund verbreiteter Endzeiterwartungen prinzipiell erhitzte Stimmung, eine generelle Unzufriedenheit mit einem Kaiser, der seit Beginn seiner Herrschaft gegen Vorurteile zu kämpfen hatte; ferner eine ohnehin stetige Zunahme gewalttätiger Konflikte in der Hauptstadt, die Unzufriedenheit mit einzelnen Regierungsmaßnahmen (nicht nur in der Finanzpolitik) sowie Konflikte und Verwerfungen innerhalb der aristokratischen Führungsschicht – dies alles kam im Jahr 512 zusammen mit dem Befehl, das *Trisagion* um den *Staurotheis*-

---

379 Malal. p. 320,23–24 Thurn: ἐφίλει δὲ ὁ αὐτὸς βασιλεὺς τὸ ῾Ρούσιον μέρος Κωνσταντινουπόλεως, τοῖς δὲ Πρασίνοις καὶ Βενέτοις πανταχῇ ἐπεξήρχετο στασιάζουσιν. Vgl. Cameron (s. Anm. 8) 236 f.; 241; ders. (s. Anm. 10) 62; 71 f.; 102; 180.

380 Vgl. Cameron (s. Anm. 8) 241; zu Porphyrios ebd., *passim*.

381 Natürlich konnte in besonderen Situationen auch eine eindeutige Parteilichkeit des Kaisers nicht vor einem Zusammenschluß der Zirkusgruppen schützen, wie etwa der Nika-Aufstand unter Justinian belegt; allerdings hatte Justinian seine Sympathien gegenüber den Blauen vor allem vor seiner Herrschaftsübernahme demonstriert, während er danach beiden Parteien gegenüber einen rigorosen Kurs einschlug – was nicht zuletzt der Nika-Aufstand bezeugt, vgl. Meier (s. Anm. 221) 187, mit Anm. 403.

Zusatz zu ergänzen, ein Befehl, der nunmehr als Bestätigung der aufgezeigten
negativen Urteile über den Kaiser und seine Politik – und zwar nicht nur der Kirchenpolitik – angesehen werden konnte, der dem Haß gegen Anastasios und sein
ganzes Umfeld derart deutlichen Ausdruck verlieh, daß sogar das Haus seines
chalkedonisch gesinnten Neffen Pompeios in Flammen aufging; ein Befehl, der
ohnehin unbeliebte Beamte wie Platon und Marinos endgültig zu desavouieren
schien und die seit längerem latent schwelenden Auseinandersetzungen in der
Aristokratie offenlegte. Im November 512 kochte der seit längerem gefährlich
vor sich hinbrodelnde Schmelztiegel endgültig über, und erst die aufgezeigten
komplexen Zusammenhänge, in die der *Staurotheis*-Aufstand eingeordnet werden muß, erklären seine Heftigkeit und verdeutlichen zugleich auch sein Gefah-
renpotential. Daß Anastasios in dieser erregten Situation kühlen Kopf bewahrt
hat und noch einmal eine Beruhigung der Lage herzustellen vermochte, kann als
herausragende Leistung angesehen werden; jetzt zahlte sich seine wohlüberlegte,
gerade in Krisensituationen geschickt dirigierte Personalpolitik (die sich anhand
der Karrieren Kelers, Patrikios', Platons oder Marinos' nachvollziehen läßt) aus.

Das grundsätzliche Dilemma, in dem der ungeliebte Kaiser sich befand, war
aber weder durch seine spektakuläre Demutsgeste noch durch die nachfolgenden
politischen Säuberungen zu lösen. Der *Staurotheis*-Aufstand führte auf keinem
Politikfeld zu einer grundsätzlichen Kurskorrektur, und man wird wohl vermuten dürfen, daß sich die Situation des Kaisers auch nicht entschieden verbessert
hätte, wenn er eine solche Korrektur vorgenommen hätte, da die Gräben zwischen Chalkedoniern und Anti-Chalkedoniern immer tiefer wurden. Der Aufstand veranschaulicht aber, daß das geläufige Anastasios-Bild, das die Züge eines
gutmütigen, alten Herren betont, der von den Tumulten mehr oder weniger
überrascht worden ist, einer gründlichen Korrektur bedarf: Bereits nach dem
,ersten' *Staurotheis*-Aufstand mußte dem Kaiser klar sein, welches Gefahrenpo-
tential eine Modifikation des *Trisagions* barg; daß er den brisanten Schritt dann
dennoch wagte, noch dazu mittels eines klaren kaiserlichen Befehls und in einer
nach der Demission des Makedonios weiterhin extrem angespannten Situation,
verdeutlicht die Konsequenz seiner Vorgehensweise, die im übrigen klar durch-
dachten Aktionsmustern folgte, wie ein Vergleich mit dem Agieren des Anastasios während der Revolten Vitalians zeigt, wo sich erstaunliche Parallelen aufzei-
gen lassen.

Nicht nur die Kirchenpolitik des Anastasios weist damit zumindest bis zur
Erhebung Vitalians klare Konturen und Ziele auf und beginnt erst seit ca. 515 angesichts des zunehmenden Widerstands der Chalkedonier ins Stocken zu geraten.
Bemerkenswert ist vor allem die Hartnäckigkeit, mit der dieser Kaiser Wider-
ständen begegnete: Trotz aller öffentlich bekundeten Demut scheute er nicht vor
massiven Säuberungsaktionen zurück, beförderte gerade in Krisensituationen
Personen, von denen er sich politischen Nutzen versprach, in hohe Ämter (Pla-

ton, Marinos) und hielt konsequent an seinem einmal eingeschlagenen Kurs fest; die Tatsache, daß er die Ordination des Severos zum Bischof von Antiocheia – nur wenige Tage nach dem *Staurotheis*-Aufstand – nicht verhinderte, spricht dabei eine deutliche Sprache. Anderseits war er aber auch darum bemüht, gänzlich unkontrollierbare Eskalationen zu vermeiden: So setzte er nach der politisch höchst brisanten Absetzung des Makedonios mit Timotheos einen Kandidaten durch, der derart farblos war, daß es durch seine Person kaum zu weiteren Polarisierungen kommen konnte, und nahm nach dem *Staurotheis*-Aufstand den Befehl, das *Trisagion* mit dem theopaschitischen Zusatz zu singen, wohlweislich zurück – freilich erst nach dem ,zweiten', großen Aufstand. Sein Abdankungsangebot im *silentium* unmittelbar vor der Absetzung des Makedonios und sein berühmter Auftritt im Hippodrom während des *Staurotheis*-Aufstandes weisen Anastasios schließlich als Politiker mit einem bemerkenswerten Geschick sowie mit einem ausgezeichneten Gespür für das Suggestions-Potential symbolischer Handlungen und Gesten aus.

Mit dem *Staurotheis*-Aufstand findet die zweite, auf eine miaphysitische Interpretation des *Henotikon* ausgerichtete und von immer rigoroseren Maßnahmen gekennzeichnete Phase der Religions- und Kirchenpolitik des Anastasios ihren Kulminationspunkt. Zugleich stehen die Ereignisse aber auch für den Übergang in die dritte und letzte Phase: Die Unruhen, ihr blutiges Nachspiel und die zunächst weiterhin wenig konziliante Haltung des Kaisers müssen erhebliche Verbitterungen ausgelöst bzw. bestärkt haben. Mit der Ausrufung Vitalians zum Kaiser während des Aufstandes 512 betritt der letzte große Antagonist des Kaisers die politische Bühne. Seine Forderungen, die er gegen Anastasios erhob, verweisen deutlich darauf, daß die Intrige gegen Makedonios, die anschließende Absetzung des Patriarchen sowie die Demission des Flavianos II. und schließlich der *Staurotheis*-Aufstand ein Kontinuum einer sich zuspitzenden Dynamik darstellen, das folgerichtig und konsequent in die Rebellion Vitalians mündete.

Der *Staurotheis*-Aufstand gegen Anastasios im Jahr 512 gewinnt vor diesem Hintergrund seine herausragende Bedeutung: Neben dem Nika-Aufstand und zahlreichen weiteren Unruhen des 5. und 6. Jahrhunderts verweist er auf das prekäre Verhältnis zwischen Kaiser und hauptstädtischer Bevölkerung im Oströmischen Reich und präsentiert eine mögliche Variante, wie der Herrscher mit Situationen umgehen konnte, in denen dieses Verhältnis sich zu konkreten Gefahrensituationen kristallisierte; eine weitere, ungleich kaltblütigere Variante sollte im Jahr 532 Justinian erproben.[382] Im Kontext der Regierung des Anastasios eröffnet der *Staurotheis*-Aufstand, sofern er in längerfristige und umfassen-

---

382 Justinian hat den Nika-Aufstand möglicherweise ganz gezielt provoziert und eskalieren lassen, um dadurch Widerstände auszuschalten und seine eigene Position zu festigen; vgl. dazu im einzelnen Meier (s. Anm. 1) 273 ff.

dere Zusammenhänge eingeordnet wird, interessante Einblicke in die religiöse und kirchenpolitische Situation zu Beginn des 6. Jahrhunderts, in die komplizierten Rahmenbedingungen kaiserlichen Handelns jener Jahre und die Strategien, mit denen Anastasios darauf reagierte, sowie schließlich in die Konflikte innerhalb der zeitgenössischen Aristokratie. Und nicht zuletzt sind es quellenkritische Aspekte, unter denen eine Auseinandersetzung mit der Revolte des Jahres 512 lohnt.

Abstract

The *staurotheis* revolt can by no means be regarded as an isolated incident which was merely motivated by religion or church policy. In it, a range of factors merged, and united in a specific and highly explosive mixture: a fundamentally heated atmosphere due to widespread eschatological expectations; a general discontentment with an emperor who had to struggle against prejudices from the beginning of his reign; furthermore an already steady increase in violent conflicts in the capital; the discontentment with certain government measures, as well as conflicts within the arictocratic ruling classes – all of this combined in 512 AD with the order to supplement the Trisagion with the *staurotheis* addendum. In November of 512 AD, the long seething melting pot finally boiled over, and only the complex connections which are highlighted in this essay and in which the *staurotheis* revolt must be integrated explain its ferocity, and underline at the same time its danger potential. The fact that Anastasius kept calm in this turbulent situation and managed to restore peace again can be regarded as an extraordinary achievement.

The fundamental dilemma, in which the unpopular emperor was trapped, could not be solved – neither by his spectacular gesture of humility nor by the subsequent political cleansing. The *staurotheis* revolt did not lead to a fundamental change of direction in any political field, and one can suppose that the situation of the emperor would not have improved decidedly even if he had undertaken such a change, since the rift between Chalcedonians and Anti-Chalcedonians was continuously growing. However, the revolt illustrates that the familiar image of Anastasius, which emphasizes the traits of a benevolent old man who is more or less surprised by the tumults needs to be thoroughly revised.

With the *staurotheis* revolt, the second phase of the religious and ecclesiastical policy of Anastasius, which was directed toward a miaphysitic interpretation of the *Henoticon* and marked by ever more rigorous growing measures, finds its culmination point. At the same time these events also stand for a transition to the third and final phase, which was mainly characterized by the rebellion of Vitalian.

Against this background, the *staurotheis* revolt gains its outstanding significance: Beside the *nika* riots and numerous other unrests in the fifth and sixth century it points to the precarious relationship between the emperor and the population of the capital in the Eastern Roman Empire and presents a possible option of how the ruler could deal with situations in which this relationship crystallized into genuine threats. In the context of Anastasius's reign, the *staurotheis* revolt opens up interesting insights into the state of religious and ecclesiastical policy at the beginning of the sixth century AD, into the complicated framework for imperatorial action during these years and the strategies with which Anastasius reacted, and finally into the conflicts within the contemporary aristocracy. In the end, it is source critical aspects which make the examination of the revolt of the year 512 AD rewarding.

'After his death a great tribulation came to Italy …' Dynastic Politics and Aristocratic Factions After the Death of Louis II, c. 870–c. 890

Simon MacLean

1. Introduction

Near the end of his continuation of Paul the Deacon's *History of the Lombards*, the late-ninth century historian Andrew of Bergamo recorded the death of the emperor Louis II (855–75), in whose funeral he had participated.[1] Louis was in many ways the central figure of Andrew's text, and he regarded the emperor's demise as having grave consequences: 'after his death a great tribulation came to Italy' he lamented in his penultimate extant chapter.[2] Italy had been ruled since 774 by the Carolingians, a Frankish dynasty from north of the Alps. The disintegration of their empire in 888, followed by several decades during which the political landscape was dominated by complex struggles between rival rulers and aristocratic factions, has given Andrew's gloomy statement the ring of eery prophecy.[3] By the time the powerful Saxon king Otto I arrived to assert himself on this fractured landscape in the 950s, he was but the latest in a long line of transalpine rulers who sought to benefit from the internecine divisions which ran through the Italian political community. It is little wonder that Liutprand of Cremona, the kingdom's next major historian, looked back from Otto's reign over the pockmarked history of the previous half century and remarked that 'the Italians always like to have two kings, so that they can use one to terrorise the other.'[4] Accordingly, modern historians have come to agree that 875 was a major turning point in Italian political history, and that the historical era bookended by Louis's death and Otto's arrival (and by the remarks of Andrew and Liutprand) should be regarded as a distinct period, characterised above all by weak kingship and conflict between aristocratic factions.[5]

---

1   Andrew, *Historia*, ed. G. Waitz, MGH SRL (Hanover, 1878), c. 18, p. 229. For help with this article I am grateful to Marios Costambeys, Matthew Innes, Conrad Leyser, Janet Nelson, Geoff West and Chris Wickham.
2   Andrew (cf. fn. 1) c. 19, p. 229: *Post cuius obitum magna tribulatio in Italia advenit.*
3   The classic narrative of the period is still G. Fasoli, *I Re d'Italia (888–962)* (Florence, 1949).
4   Liutprand, *Antapodosis*, ed. P. Chiesa, Corpus Christianorum Continuatio Mediaevalis 156 (Turnhout, 1998), I.37, p. 26.
5   P. Delogu, 'Vescovi, conti e sovrani nella crisi del regno Italico (ricerche sull'aristocra

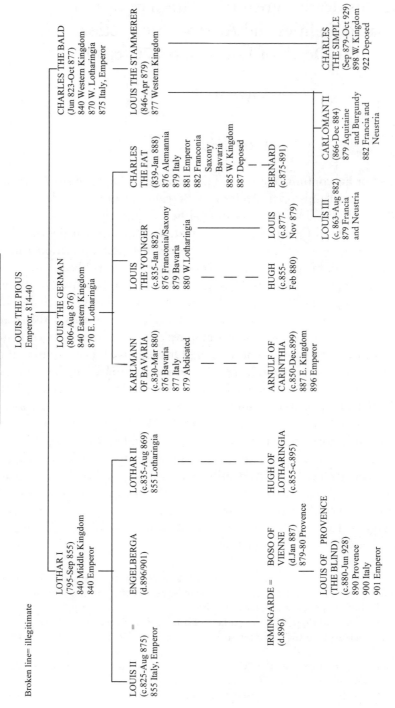

FAMILY TREE (SIMPLIFIED)

Broken line= illegitimate

LOUIS THE PIOUS
Emperor, 814-40

LOTHAR I
(795-Sep 855)
840 Middle Kingdom
840 Emperor

LOUIS THE GERMAN
(806-Aug 876)
840 Eastern Kingdom
870 E. Lotharingia

CHARLES THE BALD
(Jun 823-Oct 877)
840 Western Kingdom
870 W. Lotharingia
875 Italy, Emperor

LOUIS II = ENGELBERGA
(c.825-Aug 875)   (d.896/901)
855 Italy, Emperor

LOTHAR II
(c.835-Aug 869)
855 Lotharingia

KARLMANN
OF BAVARIA
(c.830-Mar 880)
876 Bavaria
877 Italy
879 Abdicated

LOUIS
THE YOUNGER
(c.835-Jan 882)
876 Franconia/Saxony
879 Bavaria
880 W.Lotharingia

CHARLES
THE FAT
(839-Jan 888)
876 Alemannia
879 Italy
881 Emperor
882 Franconia
    Saxony
    Bavaria
885 W. Kingdom
887 Deposed

LOUIS THE STAMMERER
(846-Apr 879)
877 Western Kingdom

CHARLES
THE SIMPLE
(Sep 879-Oct 929)
898 W. Kingdom
922 Deposed

IRMINGARDE = BOSO OF
(d.896)   VIENNE
               (d.Jan 887)
               879-80 Provence

HUGH OF
LOTHARINGIA
(c.855-c.895)

ARNULF OF
CARINTHIA
(c.850-Dec.899)
887 E. Kingdom
896 Emperor

HUGH
(c.855-
Feb 880)

LOUIS
(c.877-
Nov 879)

BERNARD
(c.875-891)

LOUIS III
(c. 863-Aug 882)
879 Francia
and Neustria

CARLOMAN II
(866-Dec 884)
879 Aquitaine
and Burgundy
882 Francia and
    Neustria

LOUIS OF PROVENCE
(THE BLIND)
(c.880-Jun 928)
890 Provence
900 Italy
901 Emperor

This is hard to argue with as a general description of this period, which coincides with an era of uncertainty across the continent between the end of the Carolingian Empire and the rise of its Ottonian successor, but it is more difficult to explain *why* warring aristocratic factions came to dominate the political stage. Historians have tended to avoid this question by using a generalised vocabulary of 'chaos' and 'crisis' derived from two central assumptions: that groups within the Italian nobility harboured 'pro-French' and 'pro-German' sympathies[6]; and that the aristocracy 'rose' in the ninth century at the expense of the kings.[7] In this view, most systematically and influentially expounded in a classic article by Hagen Keller, the weak post-Louis II kings were not only unable to restrain their nobles but were even forced to recognise, empower and institutionalise rising aristocratic power.[8] However, recent scholarship has thrown doubt on the central assumptions underpinning these arguments, which ultimately stem from the grand narratives of European history established in the nineteenth century. Historians are increasingly cautious about both the projection of modern nation-

---

zia Carolingia in Italia III)', in *Annali della scuola speciale per archivisti e bibliotecari dell'Università di Roma* 8 (1968), pp. 3–72, at p. 3. On 875 as a turning point: O. Capitani, *Storia dell'Italia medievale, 410–1216* (Rome and Bari, 1986), p. 126; G. Arnaldi, *Natale 875. Poetica, ecclesiologica, cultura del papato altomedievale* (Rome, 1990), p. 25; G. Albertoni, *L'Italia Carolingia* (Rome, 1997), pp. 55–8; D. Arnold, *Johannes VIII. Päpstliche Herrschaft in den karolingischen Teilreichen am Ende des 9. Jahrhunderts* (Frankfurt, 2005), pp. 64–5.

6   Delogu (cf. fn. 5) 35–58.

7   W. Schlesinger, 'Die Auflösung des Karlsreiches', in W. Braunfels (ed.), *Karl der Grosse* vol. 1 (Düsseldorf, 1965) pp. 792–857 was influential. For critiques of this view see G. Sergi, 'L'Europa Carolingia e la sua dissoluzione', in N. Tranfaglia and M. Firpo (eds.), *La storia. I grandi problemi dal medioevo all'Età contemporanea* (10 vols., Turin, 1986), ii, pp. 231–62; S. MacLean, *Kingship and Politics in the Late Ninth Century: Charles the Fat and the End of the Carolingian Empire* (Cambridge, 2003), pp. 1–22.

8   H. Keller, 'Zur Struktur der Königsherrschaft im karolingischen und nachkarolingischen Italien. Der "consiliarius regis" in den italienischen Königsdiplomen des 9. und 10. Jahrhunderts', *Quellen und Forschungen aus italienischen Archiven und Bibliotheken* 47 (1967) pp. 123–223; P. Delogu, 'Strutture politiche e ideologia nel regno di Lodovico II (recherché sull'aristocrazia Carolingia in Italia II)', in *Bullettino dell'Istituto storico Italiano per il medio evo e archivio Muratoriano* 80 (1968), pp. 137–89, at p. 188; C. Wickham, *Early Medieval Italy. Central Power and Local Society, 400–1000* (London and Basingstoke, 1981), pp. 168–70; Albertoni, *L'Italia Carolingia*, pp. 50–5; P. Cammarosano, *Nobili e re. L'Italia politica dell'alto medioevo* (Rome, 1999), pp. 200–2. For a brief critique of Keller see F. Bougard, 'La cour et le gouvernement de Louis II (840–875)', in R. Le Jan (ed.), *La royauté et les elites dans l'Europe carolingienne (début IXe siècle aux environs de 920)* (Lille, 1998), pp. 249–67, at p. 259.

al identities onto the past and the characterisation of relationships between kings and aristocrats as a zero-sum game in which one became more powerful in direct proportion to the weakness of the other. The fortunes of rulers in this period were determined less by institutional stability than by their ability to create and manipulate patronage networks among the nobility, whose alliance was essential to the effectiveness of royal power.[9]

Due to the regional traditions of Italian historiography and the relative paucity of narrative sources, the implications of all this for the dynastic politics of late-ninth- and tenth-century Italy have not been fully explored, with notable exceptions such as Barbara Rosenwein's important work on the charters of Berengar I (888–924).[10] Taking its cue from Rosenwein's insights, the present article focuses on royal-aristocratic politics between about 870 and 890 and aims to throw some light on the detail of a period whose political history has hitherto received minimal scholarly attention. The central argument is that most descriptions of the immediate post-Louis II era mischaracterise the motivations of both aristocrats and kings, and thus misunderstand the relationship between them. By writing them off as symptomatic of 'chaos', historians have neglected the extent to which the formation of aristocratic factions was conditioned by their ongoing relationship with the political centre, whether or not it was strong. In challenging the simple correlation of royal weakness with aristocratic factionalism, I aim to restore kings to the political history of this period by emphasising the importance of shifts in patterns of dynastic politics and patronage in explaining the behaviour of the nobility.[11] The article is structured chronologically to emphasise change over time, but does not seek to provide a comprehensive political narrative. I will look at the factors shaping royal patronage of the aristocracy in two distinct periods: the immediate aftermath of Louis II's death; and the reign of the last Carolingian king of Italy, Charles the Fat. By way of conclusion, I contrast my findings with the period after the end of the empire in 888.

---

9   For example: W. Davies and P. Fouracre (eds), *Property and Power in the Early Middle Ages* (Cambridge, 1995); M. Innes, *State and Society in the Early Middle Ages: the Middle Rhine Valley, 400–1000* (Cambridge, 2000).

10 B. H. Rosenwein, 'The Family Politics of Berengar I, King of Italy (888–924)', *Speculum* 71 (1996), pp. 247–89; B. H. Rosenwein, *Negotiating Space. Power, Restraint and Privileges of Immunity in Early Medieval Europe* (Manchester, 1999), pp. 137–55.

11 The dynamics here described are quite well-known in general: see S. Gasparri, 'The Aristocracy', in C. La Rocca (ed.), *Italy in the Early Middle Ages* (Oxford, 2002), pp. 59–84, esp. pp. 79–82. My argument is that the role of kings has not properly been documented or taken into account.

2. Aristocratic factions and the death of Louis II (875)

As Andrew lamented, the immediate aftermath of Louis II's death was indeed turbulent. The wealthy Italian realm, with the associated imperial title, was much coveted by various of the late ruler's transalpine relatives who were poised to take advantage of his heirlessness. Louis's uncle, the west Frankish king Charles the Bald, emerged victorious after fighting off the east Frankish bid of his cousin Karlmann of Bavaria. The conflict came perilously close to open warfare, unusual in Frankish politics of the ninth century, and much incidental damage was done to the property of various important Lombard monasteries.[12] The intrigues did not come to an end when Karlmann succeeded Charles as Italian king in 877. The king's ill health (he may have suffered a stroke) kept him in Bavaria most of the time and his relatives began jostling for position to succeed him. Meanwhile, Pope John VIII, indignant at Karlmann's failure to defend Rome from Muslim and aristocratic assailants, travelled to Troyes in 878 and invited Louis the Stammerer, Charles the Bald's son, to take up the imperial dignity.[13]

For present purposes, the intricacies of these events are less important than the deep divisions within the aristocracy that underpinned them. Immediately following Louis II's death the major nobles of northern Italy divided into two factions: one, based in the north east, supported the claim of Karlmann to the throne; the other, focused on Milan in the north west, supported Charles the Bald. It is clear that these groups were regarded by contemporaries as relatively coherent factions. Paolo Delogu's analysis of the charter evidence showed that while Charles the Bald reigned the Milan faction prospered and the north-easterners were deliberately excluded from the circuits of royal patronage; and that the reverse held true once Karlmann came to power.[14] These groups had acknowledged leaders. The north-eastern faction was led by the *marchio* Berengar of Friuli and the widowed Empress Engelberga, and included other influential figures such as Bishop Wibod of Parma. Berengar was the guardian of Louis and Engelberga's daughter, and papal letters imply he was perceived to have the abili-

---

12 Andrew (cf. fn. 1) c. 19–20, pp. 229–30; F. Grat et al (eds.), *Annales de Saint-Bertin* (Paris, 1964), s. a. 877, p. 216; *Registrum Johannes VIII. Papae*, ed. E. Caspar, MGH Epp vol. 7 (Berlin, 1928), no. 43. See also J. L. Nelson, 'Violence in the Carolingian World and the Ritualization of Ninth-Century Warfare', in G. Halsall (ed.), *Violence and Society in the Early Medieval West* (Woodbridge, 1998), pp. 90–107, at pp. 101–3.

13 J. Fried, 'Boso von Vienne oder Ludwig der Stammler? Der Kaiserkandidat Johanns VIII.', *Deutsches Archiv für Erforschung des Mittelalters* 32 (1976), pp. 193–208.

14 Delogu (cf. fn. 5) esp. 21–31. See also P. Delogu, 'Lombard and Carolingian Italy', in R. McKitterick (ed.), *The New Cambridge Medieval History II c.700–c.900* (Cambridge, 1995), pp. 290–319.

ty to control the loyalties of the north-eastern nobility.[15] The other grouping was focused on Archbishop Ansbert of Milan and backed initially by Pope John. The extent of Ansbert's influence is illustrated by a subsequent dispute with the pope. After the archbishop and his subordinate prelates failed to meet John on his return from west Francia in 878, the pope excommunicated him.[16] However, the anathema was not observed in the north-west, where, much to John's disgust, Ansbert managed to consecrate a new bishop to the see of Vercelli with the approval of his subordinates. The precise issue at stake in the dispute is unclear, but may have been connected with the question of the succession: in one letter the pope forbade the archbishop to confer with any would-be king without permission.[17] It is striking that John thought Ansbert was in a position to intervene decisively in the succession to the Italian throne. This suggests his influence extended to the formation of opinion among the secular aristocracy as well as the bishops of the north-west.

How and why did these factions come into being? Our starting point must be the observation that they appeared fully-formed in 875, and were already being played out at Louis's funeral: having been buried in Brescia, a power-base of Engelberga, the king was subsequently disinterred and translated to Milan by Ansbert.[18] Rather than reading the prominence of these factions as a symptom of royal weakness after 875, we must therefore seek reasons for their formation within the pattern of Carolingian politics before Louis's death.

The politics of the Carolingian dynasty during the 860s were defined by the extended divorce case of Lothar II, the king of middle Francia, on whose outcome depended a series of succession issues.[19] It was only towards the end of the decade, and especially after Lothar's death in 869, that the succession to his heirless brother Louis II became an increasingly pressing diplomatic issue. The rise of Italy to the top of the agenda is reflected in the meeting held in 868 by Louis's uncles Charles the Bald and Louis the German, kings of west and east Francia respectively, who agreed that if the opportunity arose they would divide their nephews' realms between them.[20] Meanwhile Pope Hadrian II (867–72) dangled

---

15   Caspar (cf. fn. 12) nos. 74, 109, 241.
16   Caspar (cf. fn. 12) nos. 188, 202, 212, 228.
17   Caspar (cf. fn. 12) no. 203.
18   Andrew (cf. fn. 1) c. 18, p. 229. The monastery of St-Ambrose also housed the bodies of the Italian kings Pippin I and, perhaps, Bernard: C. Brühl, *Fodrum, Gistum, Servitium Regis. Studien zu den wirtschaftlichen Grundlagen des Königtums im Frankenreich und in der fränkischen Nachfolgestaaten Deutschland, Frankreich und Italien vom 6. bis zur Mitte des 14. Jahrhunderts* (Cologne, 1968), pp. 373–4.
19   See S. Airlie, 'Private Bodies and the Body Politic in the Divorce Case of Lothar II', *Past and Present* 161 (1998), pp. 3–38.
20   A. Boretius and V. Krause (eds.), *Capitularia regum Francorum*, vol. 2 (Hanover, 1897), no. 245, pp. 167–8; J. L. Nelson, *Charles the Bald* (London and New York,

the promise of his backing before both rulers.[21] Recognising the mounting importance of the issue, in 872 the Empress Engelberga travelled north for discussions with both Louis the German and Charles the Bald about the succession, hoping in return to acquire influence in Francia. However, only Louis was ready to make such concessions, and received in return guarantees that his eldest son Karlmann would succeed the heirless emperor; Charles refused to negotiate.[22] Shortly before Louis II died, the east Frankish king renewed this deal by making a grant of Italian properties to the emperor's daughter: he must have received these estates, which were normally controlled by female members of the Italian ruling dynasty, from Engelberga during the original negotiations in 872.[23]

Developments in papal-east Frankish relations interacted with these events. As the pontificate of Hadrian II drew to a close, news arrived that the Bulgars, whose ecclesiastical allegiance had been a recent bone of contention between Rome and Constantinople, had succumbed to the insistent overtures of the Byzantine church. Fearing that the influence of the Greek rite might reach even further west, Hadrian approved the request of the Slavic prince Kocel (a Frankish client) to revive the ancient see of Sirmium and appoint the Greek missionary Methodius as archbishop of Pannonia and Moravia, and papal legate to the Slavs.[24] This decision greatly angered the archbishop of Salzburg and his suffragans, who considered the evangelisation of the Slavs as part of their natural remit. A pamphlet was produced to bolster the Salzburg case, and helped the archbishop to draw Louis the German into the dispute.[25] Louis had his own aspirations

---

1992), p. 217; E. J. Goldberg, *Struggle For Empire: Kingship and Conflict Under Louis the German, 817–876* (Ithaca, 2006), p. 294.

21 Nelson (cf. fn. 20) 238.

22 Grat et al (cf. fn. 12) s. a. 872, p. 186. The east Frankish designation is also indicated by Basil I's diplomatic contact with Louis the German, probably initiated to discuss the future of Italy: F. Kurze (ed.), *Annales Fuldenses*, MGH SRG (Hanover, 1891), s.a. 873, p. 81. For a general outline of Louis's dealings with Italy see W. Hartmann, *Ludwig der Deutsche* (Darmstadt, 2002), pp. 120–2.

23 P. Kehr (ed.), *Die Urkunden Ludwigs des Deutschen, Karlmanns und Ludwigs des Jüngeren* (MGH Diplomata regum Germaniae ex stirpe Karolinorum 1) (Berlin, 1932–4), no. 157; P. Darmstädter, *Das Reichsgut in der Lombardei und Piemont (568–1250)* (Strasbourg, 1896), pp. 106–8.

24 J. Shepard, 'Slavs and Bulgars', in McKitterick (ed.), *New Cambridge Medieval History II*, pp. 228–48, at pp. 241–3; B. Bigott, *Ludwig der Deutsche und die Reichskirche im Ostfränkischen Reich (826–876)* (Husum, 2002), pp. 155–6, 167–77; Arnold (cf. fn. 5) 167–72; Goldberg (cf. fn. 20) 309–20.

25 *De conversione Bagoariorum et Carantanorum Libellus*, ed. G. H. Pertz, MGH SS 11 (Hanover, 1854), pp. 1–15; S. Airlie, 'True Teachers and Pious Kings: Salzburg, Louis the German, and Christian Order', in R. Gameson and H. Leyser (eds.), *Belief and Culture in the Middle Ages. Studies Presented to Henry Mayr-Harting* (Oxford, 2001), pp. 89–105.

on the eastern frontier which coincided with the interests of the aggrieved prelates, and following military action Methodius was captured, condemned before
a kangaroo court of Salzburg suffragans and confined to a monastery. On his succession in December 872, John VIII immediately turned up the pressure on Louis
over the Methodius affair, pressing for the missionary's release and attempting to
place Pannonia directly under papal control. John also summoned the bishops
who had tried Methodius to Rome, threatened them with excommunication, and
began to make overtures to Charles the Bald, Louis's rival.[26] At exactly the time
when Louis II and Engelberga were establishing close political links with the east
Frankish royal family, therefore, the pope was adopting a hostile stance towards
them.

The stage was thus set for a dispute. Louis II may well have foreseen the
trouble these dormant tensions would cause after his death, and he seemingly
brokered a reconciliation between the pope and the east Frankish king at Verona
in 874.[27] Yet this last-minute display of solidarity cannot mask the fact that the
succession to Louis II had by this time been a matter of open dispute for some
years. This uncertainty provides a context for the formation of political factions
within Italy: the contrasting relationships being simultaneously formed by the
papacy and the imperial couple with the east and west Frankish rulers must have
had a significant role in shaping Italian aristocratic loyalties. These relationships
legitimised the adoption of mutually exclusive positions on the part of the
nobles.

The pressure on leading aristocrats to declare for one or other side was intensified by active lobbying on the part of both claimants, who doggedly courted
opinion-formers in Italy in the early years of the 870s through the regular
dispatch of embassies.[28] More importantly, both kings were willing to press their
claims with decisive and sometimes violent political manoeuvres. In 871, when a
false rumour spread that Louis II had been killed, Louis the German immediately sent his youngest son Charles the Fat to establish east Frankish influence in the
Italian-controlled area around Lake Geneva which included important Alpine
passes.[29] In response to the same rumour, Charles the Bald imprisoned his rebellious son Carloman, in part to prevent him from trying his luck across the Alps

---

26 Caspar (cf. fn. 12) frg. nos. 21, 23; Nelson (cf. fn. 20) 231–8.
27 Caspar (cf. fn. 12) no. 293; Kurze (cf. fn. 22) s. a. 874, pp. 82–3; Goldberg (cf. fn. 20)
     324–5, 331–2.
28 The scattered references to these legations are collected by: Nelson (cf. fn. 20) 241–2;
     Bigott (cf. fn. 24) 155; Hartmann (cf. fn. 22) 204.
29 S. MacLean, 'The Carolingian Response to the Revolt of Boso, 879–87', *Early Medie-
     val Europe* 10 (2001), pp. 21–48, at pp. 40–3.

and hence to preserve his own opportunity of seizing Italy.[30] Louis II soon reasserted his control of the kingdom. Within a year, however, the succession prompted another bout of political intrigue when a faction of nobles tried to persuade the emperor to divorce Engelberga and marry the daughter of Count Winigis of Siena. It is likely that this attempt was underwritten by the Holy See and reflected the pope's hostility to the east Franks: the pressure was put on Louis while he was in Rome.[31] Moreover, the attempt to undermine Engelberga must have been a reaction to the deal that she had just weeks earlier brokered with Louis the German concerning the succession. The empress herself responded to these events by sending letters of friendship to Charles the Bald. According to the west Frankish annalist Hincmar of Rheims this was done in an attempt to disguise the arrangement already made with Louis the German; but it also makes sense as an attempt to mollify those Italian magnates who were pressuring her husband to repudiate her, and who may thus have preferred the prospect of being ruled by Charles the Bald. The record of an assembly held by Charles at this time makes an obtuse reference to Italy as a land 'that God will grant you hereafter', which shows that he, in response to Engelberga's negotiations with his brother, was girding his loins to pitch a claim to the *regnum*.[32]

All this very physical jostling for position came to a head when Louis died in late summer 875, opening up a short-lived but spectacular bout of hot conflict whose course confirms the idea that the factional lines between the key players had already been drawn. Both Italian factions invited their respective candidates to come and take the throne.[33] Charles the Bald immediately moved across the Alps and his brother reacted by invading west Francia and sending two of his sons into Italy.[34] Both east Frankish armies entered Italy through Berengar's territory. While one son, Karlmann, confronted Charles the Bald, the other, Charles the Fat, was joined by Berengar and 'a multitude of the rest of his people' in an attack on various north-western locations including Milan.[35] Hincmar clearly

---

30 This is my inference from Grat et al (cf. fn. 12) s. a. 871, pp. 183–4. On Carloman's career see J. L. Nelson, 'A Tale of Two Princes: Politics, Text, and Ideology in a Carolingian Annal', *Studies in Medieval and Renaissance History* 10 (1988), pp. 105–41; reprinted in J. L. Nelson, *Rulers and Ruling Families in Early Medieval Europe* (Aldershot, 1999).
31 Grat et al (cf. fn. 12) s. a. 872, p. 188; E. Hlawitschka, *Franken, Alemannen, Bayern und Burgunder in Oberitalien (774–962). Zum Verständnis der fränkischen Königsherrschaft in Italien*, (Freiburg, 1960), p. 68, n. 6.
32 Boretius/Krause (cf. fn. 20) vol. 2, no. 277, pp. 341–2.
33 Andrew (cf. fn. 1) c. 19, p. 229.
34 Kurze (cf. fn. 22) s. a. 875, pp. 84–5; Grat et al (cf. fn. 12) s. a. 875, pp. 198–9; Caspar (cf. fn. 12) no. 43.
35 Andrew (cf. fn. 1) c. 19, p. 230; Kurze (cf. fn. 22) s. a. 875, p. 84.

refers to the north-eastern faction as 'some of the leading men of Italy [who] did not come over to Charles [the Bald].'[36] The other faction was alluded to by the Mainz annalist in his description of Charles 'carving up the kingdom with his followers.'[37] The conflict also had repercussions in Rome, where an aristocratic party allied to Formosus, sometime bishop of Porto and future pontiff, used the arrival of Karlmann and Charles the Fat to bring their opposition to John into the open.[38] Although on this occasion the pope prevailed, the episode shows how the succession dispute resonated with and legitimised conflicts even within Rome itself.[39]

Between 871 and 875, then, the succession to Louis II developed from a relatively abstract issue in diplomatic negotiations into a cause of concrete political action on the part of Carolingian rulers and their supporters. Consequently, a hypothetical debate about the future became a pressing issue in the political present. Members of the Italian aristocracy were forced to choose sides in advance: loyalties were created, reinforced and put into action, not merely projected.

It is more difficult to be sure why individual power-brokers decided which way to jump. Although a long-standing east/west division in Lombard political geography helps us make some sense of the general pattern, we still have to explain why such a division was reactivated at this time. Bribery and threats must have played a part in this process, as they often did in Carolingian politics. Indeed, an annalist writing at Mainz claimed that Charles the Bald's ultimate success was more or less exclusively a result of his superior ability to bribe the pope.[40] However, underlying sympathies were also important. Berengar's support for Karlmann finds a context in the close political links which existed between Friuli and Bavaria during the ninth century.[41] Engelberga, who had con-

---

36   Grat et al (cf. fn. 12) s. a. 875, p. 199.
37   Kurze (cf. fn. 22) s. a. 875, p. 85.
38   Arnaldi (cf. fn. 5) 18–23; Arnold (cf. fn. 5) 63–4, 181–5.
39   This group was later involved in the murder of John: Kurze (cf. fn. 22) s. a. 882, p. 99; Arnaldi (cf. fn. 5) 23–5.
40   Kurze (cf. fn. 22) s. a. 875, p. 85. Gifts to St Peter would have been expected of the emperor-elect, and are noted by various sources; the Mainz annalist spins this as corruption. However, Caspar (cf. fn. 12) frg. no. 59 suggests that John had declared for Charles immediately after Louis II's death.
41   See A. Schmid, 'Bayern und Italien vom 7. bis zum 10. Jahrhundert', in H. Beumann and W. Schröder (eds.), *Die transalpinen Verbindungen der Bayern, Alemannen und Franken bis zum 10. Jahrhundert* (Sigmaringen, 1987), pp. 51–91; U. Ludwig, *Transalpine Beziehungen der Karolingerzeit im Spiegel der Memorialüberlieferung: prosographische und sozialgeschichtliche Studien unter besonderer Berücksichtigung des Liber vitae von San Salvatore in Brescia und des Evangeliars von Cividale* (Hanover, 1999).

sistently supported the east Frankish designation since 872, also provided a focal point for the north-easterners.[42] Berengar was the guardian of the empress's daughter and was related to the empress at two generations: his paternal aunt was married to Engelberga's cousin, while his own wife was her niece.[43] These immediate associations may have played a part in drawing his allegiances away from his maternal uncle Charles the Bald and towards his cousin Karlmann. The north-western faction, on the other hand, must have been shaped in part by the influence of archbishop Ansbert. Behind him stood the pope, who had for the most part favoured Charles since 872.[44] In any case, these antagonistic factions were forged in the heat generated by disputes within the Carolingian dynasty, and between some of its members and the papacy, during the late 860s and early 870s. Existing aristocratic rivalries were given form and legitimacy by wider dynastic conflicts. Tensions at the highest level created and resonated with rivalries among the aristocracy, sending fault lines down through the bedrock of the political community. These factions did not represent 'pro-French' and 'pro-German' interests, but were a product of the interaction between political deals, royal interventions, doubt over the future and fast-moving circumstances.

The significance of these aristocratic groups during the second half of the 870s was not so much a symptom of weak kingship as of a situation in which two strong rulers disputed the crown. That these disputes were still articulated within the Carolingian dynastic system is illustrated by Bishop Anthony of Brescia's letter to his counterpart Salomon II of Constance early in the year 878.[45] Anthony feared that the manoeuvrings of the three healthy kings north of the Alps to position themselves to succeed Karlmann would end in violence: 'we expect with great reluctance the plundering of first one, then the other, until they agree amicably among themselves to whom they want to concede that province.' The anxious bishop added: 'accordingly, it is proper that we submit to one alone, and

---

42 Engelberga's influence was built on her imperial status and her membership of an important aristocratic family: see C. Odegaard, 'The Empress Engelberge', *Speculum* 26 (1951), pp. 77–103; S. MacLean, 'Queenship, Nunneries and Royal Widowhood in Carolingian Europe', *Past and Present* 178 (2003), pp. 3–38 at pp. 26–32; T. Lazzari, 'Una mamma carolingia e una moglie supponide: percorsi femminili di legittimazione e potere nel regno italico', in G. Isabella (ed.), *'C'era una volta un re ...' Aspetti e momenti della regalità* (Bologna, 2005), pp. 41–57.

43 G. Arnaldi, 'Berengario I', in *Dizionario Biografico degli Italiani* vol. 9 (Rome, 1967), pp. 1–26, at pp. 3–4.

44 Caspar (cf. fn. 12) frg. no. 59 suggests John backed Charles in 875. The pope's correspondence on east Frankish affairs confirms his frosty attitude to Louis the German: Arnold (cf. fn. 5) 158–67.

45 K. Zeumer (ed.), *Collectio Sangallensis*, MGH Formulae Merowingici et Karolini Aevi (Hanover, 1886), no. 39.

serve the rest gladly as far as we can.' Salomon, a partisan of Charles the Fat, one of the kings in question, tried to reassure Anthony that the issue was not as confused as he feared, and was being settled by negotiation.[46] The fact that Anthony felt compelled to decide which potential ruler to support vividly illustrates the unenviable pressure placed on nobles who got caught in the middle of royal disputes. At the same time, it is notable that both bishops assumed the matter would be resolved between the ruling Carolingians. Succession disputes such as the one that produced the Italian factions of the 870s were endemic in the Frankish world, and the tribulations which followed Louis II's death did not stand out qualitatively from the normal texture of Carolingian politics: even Anthony, nervous about the future and clearly out of the loop, did not doubt that the dispute would be resolved, like numerous earlier ninth-century conflicts, within the context of the Carolingian dynasty.[47] Such tension was a perennial by-product of Frankish dynastic politics, not a symptom of Carolingian power entering a terminal tailspin after 875.

3. Patterns of patronage, 879–88

The factions that dominated Italian politics in the years 875–9 did not remain absolutely static: John VIII, for instance, was ultimately forced to put his trust in Karlmann as premature death eroded the list of alternatives.[48] Nevertheless, they are usually seen by historians as playing a key role until at least the 890s.[49] This view has been encouraged by a negative view of the reign of Charles 'the Fat', Italy's last male-line Carolingian ruler, whose flaccid grip on power is thought to have handed more power to the aristocracy and hastened the rapid descent in the fortunes of Italian kingship after 875.[50] However, there are reasons to question this interpretation. During his eight years as ruler of the *regnum* (November 879–November 887) Charles, called Carlito (Charlie) by the Italians to distinguish him from his uncle,[51] made no less than six trips across the Alps, each lasting be-

---

46 Zeumer (cf. fn. 45) no. 40.
47 Cf. S. Airlie, '*Semper fideles*? Loyauté envers les carolingiens comme constituant de l'identité aristocratique' in Le Jan (cf. fn. 8) 129–43.
48 Though his claim that he ruled Italy in the king's absence was hardly guaranteed to reconcile him to such as the archbishop of Milan or the *dux* of Spoleto: Caspar (cf. fn. 12) no. 241.
49 To some extent, the supporters of the Berengarian/east Frankish party during the 870s formed the core of Berengar's following after 888: Delogu (cf. fn. 5) 31.
50 Hlawitschka (cf. fn. 31) 71–2; Cammarosano (cf. fn. 8) 200–2. Delogu (cf. fn. 5) 30 noted in passing the easing of factional tensions under Charles.
51 Andrew (cf. fn. 1) c. 19, p. 229.

tween four and ten months. Over this period he spent around 50 % of his time in Italy and issued about half of his charters for cisalpine recipients.[52] Given that Charlemagne himself only visited his southern realm four times in 40 years, and Louis the Pious never, these figures look even more striking. The fact that in 882 Charles was able to command a Lombard contingent on a campaign against the Vikings on the River Meuse strongly suggests that he was not as insignificant a king of Italy as has been assumed.[53]

When Charles came to power the most influential figures in Italian affairs, John VIII, Engelberga, Berengar and Ansbert, were set against each other to a greater or lesser degree, each pursuing their own agendas and carrying significant bodies of opinion with them. However, the new king's charters suggest that he made great efforts to avoid the problems caused by his predecessors' reliance on exclusive factions. This is illustrated by the list of counts present at an assembly in Siena in March 881, who were accompanying him back from his imperial coronation in Rome.[54] They were: Berengar of Friuli; John VIII's kinsman and *comes* of the Holy See Farulf; another count called Berengar; Count Waltfred of Verona; Bertold count of the palace; Winigis count of Siena; Gotfred, count somewhere around Asti; Adalbert, probably the *dux* of Tuscany; Maurinus, active around Ravenna; and Erardus, possibly count in or near Modena.[55] These men represented not only wide geographical origins, but also came from all sides of the political rifts which had opened up in the years before 879. Farulf, therefore, was able to sit as a representative of the pope alongside Adalbert and Maurinus, two of John VIII's most hated opponents during the 870s.[56] Maurinus seems to have been an associate of Engelberga's, as was Gotfred, whom John VIII

---

52   For slightly varying figures see P. Hirsch, *Die Erhebung Berengars I. von Friaul zum König in Italien* (Strasbourg, 1910), pp. 137–8; F. Bougard, *La Justice dans le royaume d'Italie de la fin du VIIIe siècle au début du XIe siècle* (Rome, 1995), pp. 57–8.

53   Regino of Prüm, *Chronicon*, ed. F. Kurze, MGH SRG (Hanover, 1890), s. a. 882, p. 119. See now A. Zettler, 'Der Zusammenhang des Raumes beidseits der Alpen in karolingischer Zeit – Amtsträger, Klöster und die Herrschaft Karls III.,' in H. Maurer et al (eds.), *Schwaben und Italien im Hochmittelalter* (Stuttgart, 2001), pp. 25–42; MacLean (cf. fn. 7) 91–6, 178–85.

54   P. Kehr (ed.), *Die Urkunden Karls III.* (MGH Diplomata regum Germaniae ex stirpe Karolinorum 2) (Berlin, 1936–7), no. 31 = C. Manaresi (ed.), *I Placiti del "Regnum Italiae"*, (vol. 1, Rome, 1955), no. 92.

55   See Hlawitschka (cf. fn. 31) 175–6, 189–90, 237 and *s.v.*

56   E. Hlawitschka, 'Die Widonen im Dukat von Spoleto', *Quellen und Forschungen aus italienischen Archiven und Bibliotheken* 63 (1983), pp. 20–92, at pp. 69–75; on Farulf see also A. Spicciani, 'I Farolfingi: una familia comitale a Chiusi e a Orvieto (secoli XI–XII)', in G. Andenna et al (eds.), *Formazione e strutture dei ceti dominanti nel Medioevo: marchesi, conti e visconti nel regno italico (secoli IX–XII)* (Rome, 1996), pp. 229–95, at pp. 251–2.

commanded, along with two of her brothers, to protect the empress's properties in 879.[57] Meanwhile Winigis, as we have seen, was at the centre of a faction which in 872 had attempted to force Louis II to repudiate Engelberga and marry his daughter instead; and north-western nobles like Gotfred and Suppo sat alongside north-easterners like Berengar and Erardus for the first time in years. Attendance at court was not a matter of course. Presence or absence could be a political statement on the part of king or noble, as was the case when one or other faction was either excluded or absented itself from major assemblies during the period 875–9.[58] Whether or not they had forgotten all their differences, it is significant that Charles's entourage included men and women who had hitherto been political opponents.

The roots of this concord went back to the very beginning of his reign in Italy. Charles initially requested to meet John VIII at Pavia in November 879, suggesting that he preferred this as the venue for his inauguration.[59] John wrote back to say he could not make it, and Charles rescheduled the assembly at Ravenna in early January 880. Pavia, the old centre of the Lombard realm, was not visited often by Carolingian kings, so the selection of this north-western venue hints that Charles envisaged a role in his inauguration for Ansbert of Milan, friendship with whom he now urged on the pope. Their reconciliation was symbolically confirmed at the Ravenna coronation, which was presided over by Ansbert, John VIII, and Patriarch Walpert of Aquileia.[60] The extent to which Charles had managed to effect a formal reconciliation between the pope and the archbishop is highlighted by the fact that, probably at the same assembly, he succeeded in resolving their dispute over the see of Vercelli by having his archchancellor and chief adviser Liutward installed as bishop.[61]

This newly-constructed alliance did not form accidentally: in part, it was the outcome of a deliberate royal strategy. What we know about the significance and

---

57 Caspar (cf. fn. 12) nos. 62, 239; Hlawitschka (cf. fn. 31) 189–90; Arnold (cf. fn. 5) 192–8.

58 Note that Charles the Bald had also been criticised for ruling west Francia with the help of a group of *speciales*: Nelson (cf. fn. 20) 240, 244.

59 Caspar (cf. fn. 12) nos. 233–4.

60 Notker, *Erchanberti Breviarium Continuatio*, ed. G. H. Pertz, MGH SS 2 (Hanover, 1829), pp. 329–30.

61 K. Schmid, 'Liutbert von Mainz und Liutward von Vercelli im Winter 879/80 in Italien. Zur Erschließung bisher unbeachteter Gedenkbucheinträge aus S. Giulia in Brescia', in E. Hassinger, J. H. Müller and H. Ott (eds.), *Geschichte, Wirtschaft, Gesellschaft. Festschrift Clemens Bauer zum 75. Geburtstag* (Berlin, 1974), pp. 41–60, at p. 53; H. Zielinski, *Die Regesten des Kaiserreichs unter den Karolingern 751–918 (926)* vol. 3/1 (Cologne and Vienna, 1991), no. 601; Arnold (cf. fn. 5) 186–92. Caspar (cf. fn. 12) no. 264 shows John and Ansbert on good terms in November 880 (no. 233 shows Charles's role in this).

stage-management of early medieval assemblies suggests that the orchestration of this display of unity would have been carefully negotiated in advance.[62] Charles's part in this negotiation may have left traces in the first two charters he issued as king for Italian recipients in late 879. In one, he confirmed six holdings in the estate of Limonta near Lake Como to the monastery of St-Ambrose in Milan.[63] This intensely exploited property, which among other things provided a rich harvest of olive oil to the monks, was the object of a very long-running dispute between St-Ambrose and the house of Reichenau in Alemannia, with which Charles had extremely close links.[64] The second charter also saw the king intervening in an ancient conflict, this time between the churches of Arezzo and Siena.[65] Bishop John of Arezzo, whose church benefited from the document, was the pope's go-between with Charles the Bald, an arrangement that was undoubtedly connected with Charles's concession in 876 of influence to the papacy in the diocese of Arezzo.[66] The fact that Charles the Fat's first two acts in Italy were peremptory decisions in favour of long-standing claims of the church of Milan and the chief envoy of the pope is significant, and can be seen as part of a strategy for winning over Ansbert and John VIII.[67] By neither act could he have hoped to solve the relevant dispute, and indeed both came back to court within a matter of months. Yet the important point is that he decided to intervene in these matters at all, and in view of the timing we should see them primarily as gestures issued with short-term political considerations in mind and intended for specific audiences.[68] The symbolism of these gestures not only publicised Charles's attitude

---

62   G. Althoff, *Spielregeln der Politik im Mittelalter: Kommunikation in Frieden und Fehde* (Darmastadt, 1997); T. Reuter, 'Assembly Politics from the Eighth Century to the Twelfth', in P. Linehan and J. L. Nelson (eds.), *The Medieval World* (London and New York, 2001), pp. 432–50.

63   Kehr (cf. fn. 23) no. 11a.

64   R. Balzaretti, 'The Monastery of Sant'Ambrogio and Dispute Settlement in Early Medieval Milan', in *Early Medieval Europe* 3 (1994), pp. 1–18 discusses the estate at length.

65   Kehr (cf. fn. 23) no. 12.

66   The arrangement was cemented with royal gifts to the bishop: G. Tessier et al (eds.), *Recueil des actes de Charles II le Chauve* (Paris, 1943–55), nos. 383, 404, 413; J. P. Delumeau, *Arezzo. Espace et sociétés, 715–1230* (Rome, 1996), pp. 228–30, 253.

67   Ansbert's involvement with the affairs of St-Ambrose is suggested by his orchestration of Louis II's funeral there and other evidence: see G. Porro-Lambertenghi et al (eds.), *Codex Diplomaticus Langobardiae* (Historiae Patriae Monumenta 13) (Turin, 1873), no. 291; Kehr (cf. fn. 23) no. 21.

68   Arezzo vs. Siena: Kehr (cf. fn. 23) no. 31 = Manaresi (cf. fn. 54) no. 92; Delumeau (cf. fn. 66) 230, 475–9. Limonta: Kehr (cf. fn. 23) no. 23a; Balzaretti (cf. fn. 64) 5–8. On charters as public documents capable of delivering this sort of political message see T. Reuter, '*Regemque, quem in Francia pene perdidit, in patria magnifice receipt:*

to pope and archbishop, but also advertised his involvement with the broader
political traditions of his new realm: they echoed, for example, the actions of
Charlemagne, whose first act after his imperial coronation in 801 had been to
assert his new position by ruling on the Arezzo – Siena dispute.[69]

Our source for Charles's inauguration at Ravenna, which was based on an
eye-witness report, relates that 'all the bishops and counts and the rest of the
leading men of Italy' were in attendance, and that 'he bound all of them except
the bishop of the apostolic see to the devotion of his service by swearing oaths.'[70]
A survey of more of Charles's early charters confirms that his contacts were
indeed as extensive as this version of events suggests. In addition to further grants
to the church in Milan, he made an early concession to Bishop Wibod of Parma,
on whose shoulders responsibilities were laid by several Italian kings, and who
was also in attendance at Ravenna.[71] Charles further entrusted Wibod with
strategic properties in the Apennines which were crucial for provisioning royal
expeditions to and from Rome.[72] The Empress Engelberga and members of her
entourage also benefited from considerable royal largesse early in the year 880.[73]
At Christmas in the same year the king cemented his relationship with the
empress by confirming properties and privileges of the royal abbey of S. Salvatore / S. Giulia in Brescia at the request of her daughter Irmingarde, its proprie-
tor.[74] Berengar of Friuli's association with the new ruler was advertised when the
pair sat in judgement, together with members of the *marchio*'s extended family,
on a *placitum* at Pavia in November 880.[75] The king also advertised his relationship with some of the kingdom's main power-brokers by making them a series of
interconnected land grants near the royal palace of Corteolona in 880–1.[76]

Ottonian Ruler Representation in Synchronic and Diachronic Comparison', in
   G. Althoff and E. Schubert (eds.), *Herrschaftsrepräsentation im ottonischen Sachsen*
   (Sigmaringen, 1998), pp. 363–80, at pp. 376–8.

69   M. Becher, 'Die Kaiserkrönung im Jahr 800. Eine Streitfrage zwischen Karl dem
   Grossen und Papst Leo III.', *Rheinische Vierteljahrsblätter* 66 (2002), pp. 1–38, at
   pp. 24–6. Arezzo almost always won in rulings on this dispute.

70   Notker (cf. fn. 60) 329–30.

71   Kehr (cf. fn. 23) nos. 21 and 23 for Milan; no. 15 for Wibod, issued at the Ravenna
   assembly.

72   Kehr (cf. fn. 23) nos. 32–3; K. Schrod, *Reichsstrassen und Reichsverwaltung im König-
   reich Italien (765–1197)* (Stuttgart, 1931), pp. 27–31; R. Schumann, *Authority and the
   Commune. Parma, 833–1133* (Parma, 1973), pp. 25–6.

73   Kehr (cf. fn. 23) nos. 18 and 22.

74   Kehr (cf. fn. 23) no. 28. On his first visit in 879–80, Charles left Italy via S. Salvatore
   in Brescia, where his party's names were recorded in the memorial book: see Schmid
   (cf. fn. 61). He had some bridges of his own to rebuild here after having damaged the
   abbey on his previous visit across the Alps in 875: Caspar (cf. fn. 12) no. 43.

75   Kehr (cf. fn. 23) no. 25 = Manaresi (cf. fn. 54) no. 89.

76   MacLean (cf. fn. 7) 93–6.

Charles's many charters, then, do not constitute a checklist of alienated rights and properties which diminished royal power in favour of aristocratic. Rather, they hint at attempts to form, maintain and advertise the political alliances with powerful aristocrats on which early medieval kingship depended. That this endeavour was still working even in the very last years of Carolingian Italy is confirmed by the broad nature of the support that followed Charles the Fat to Rome in 881. Nonetheless, such alliances between kings and aristocrats in this period could never be taken for granted, but had to be constantly maintained. Charles mostly succeeded in this respect, but not without setbacks. A feud between Berengar and the archchancellor, Bishop Liutward of Vercelli, temporarily set two of his chief supporters against each other in 886–7, a result of the parvenu bishop's unwelcome attempts to forcibly marry one of his relatives into the *marchio*'s blue bloodline which may have reactivated north-east/north-west tensions.[77] A clearer failure was in central and southern Italy, where Charles's influence was only as good as his unstable relationship with the rebellious Guy, *dux* of Spoleto; he was never able to intervene there in as direct a fashion as had Louis II.[78] Despite this article's emphasis on coherent aspects of royal strategy, such moments of crisis are an equally important part of the story, and serve to illustrate the contingent and precarious nature of royal power.

Nevertheless, Charles the Fat's reign is striking in its contrast to the period of Italian conflict after the death of Louis II. Why? The king's careful use of patronage is part of the answer, but cannot completely explain why previously antagonistic parties were willing to back him. Other candidates for the kingship were available: Charles's brother Louis the Younger, king of Saxony and Franconia, was also manoeuvring to make a bid for the crown after 876, and both he and Louis the Stammerer were courted by John VIII as possible successors during the illness of Karlmann. However, the lessons taught by the divisions of the years 875–9, which were not confined to Italy, were taken on board by this new generation of Carolingians, and in 879–80 they agreed a new family settlement which brought to an end a number of outstanding political and territorial disputes. These included the destination of the Italian realm, which was acknowledged by all parties as belonging to Charles the Fat.[79] As the anxious letter of Anthony of Brescia showed, divisions in the ruling house caused tensions in the aristocracy. The need, present or foreseen, to choose sides created considerable insecurity which damaged the confidence of nobles in the stability of their future positions and consequently undermined royal authority. The fragile consensus in the con-

77   Kurze (cf. fn. 22) s. a. 886, 887, pp. 105–6, 114; Schmid (cf. fn. 61) 45–7.
78   Kurze (cf. fn. 22) s. a. 883, pp. 100, 109–10.
79   As argued by MacLean (cf. fn. 29).

figuration of the royal house during the early 880s meant that Charles could be acknowledged by all aristocratic factions in Italy as the single source of royal patronage, and provided a fixed reference point around which disputes among the kingdom's ruling elite could revolve.

This situation was not guaranteed to last. To some extent the status quo was perpetuated by the early deaths of the emperor's relatives, which by late 884 left him as the only surviving legitimate male Carolingian. His more frequent sojourns north of the Alps after that date, particularly to west Francia, did not therefore have the same destabilising effect as had Karlmann's absenteeism. Another potential cause of division was the revolt of Boso of Vienne, who had himself proclaimed king in Provence in late 879. Boso was married to Irmingarde, the daughter of Engelberga and Louis II, and had audaciously named his children after his in-laws, marking his closeness to the former empress and his aspiration to appropriate a royal Carolingian identity.[80] The count had further Italian links from the time he spent as Charles the Bald's representative in the *regnum*.[81] Mindful of the potential rift that the revolt could open up between himself and Engelberga, Charles the Fat took the empress with him to Alemannia to prevent her from mobilising her influence in favour of her son-in-law. Although he kept her there for about two years, only releasing her on the final defeat of Boso in autumn 882, the emperor worked hard to maintain his relationship with her. The flow of charters in favour of Engelberga, her followers and her institutions did not abate.[82] She may or may not have colluded in her 'kidnap': either way, she came quietly, thus avoiding the danger of fractures appearing in the network of political alliances established by Charles the Fat in his kingdom of Italy.

4. Conclusion: Factionalism and conflict after 888

Boso's rising was unique in the ninth century in its overt challenge to the Carolingians' monopoly on royal power.[83] His defeat ensured the continuation of this dynastic monopoly. However, when Charles the Fat died in January 888 without a legitimate heir, causing the definitive break-up of the Frankish empire, the situation necessarily changed. Rival bids for the Italian throne from the *marchio-*

---

80 S. Airlie, 'The Nearly Men: Boso of Vienne and Arnulf of Bavaria', in A. Duggan (ed.), *Nobles and Nobility in Medieval Europe* (Woodbridge, 2000), pp. 25–41, esp. pp. 32–5.

81 Nelson (cf. fn. 20) 242–3.

82 Kehr (cf. fn. 23) nos. 22, 28, 29, 56; cf. F. Bougard, 'Engelberga', in *Dizionario Biografico degli Italiani* (vol. 13, Rome, 1993), pp. 668–76, at p. 673.

83 Airlie (cf. fn. 47).

nes Berengar of Friuli and Guy of Spoleto renewed conflict among the aristocracy. However, these events cannot be explained simply by invoking a tipping of the scales from royal to aristocratic power: the factional politics of the 890s were superficially similar to those of the 870s, but were not driven by the same dynamics.[84] To finish this article, a few impressionistic examples will serve to illustrate some of the subtle but significant changes in patterns of royal patronage after 888.

The claims of the post-888 competitors were not only equal but also inter-rather than intra-dynastic. Although Berengar was a female-line descendant of Louis the Pious, unlike Guy, none of the 'kinglets' who rose to power after the death of Charles the Fat could lay claim to the rhetoric of male-line legitimacy which had sustained the Carolingians, except perhaps Arnulf of Carinthia, Karlmann's bastard son.[85] The second new development was that each contender had spent his whole political career in Italy, although Guy's initial bid for a crown in 888 was made in west Francia.[86] As a result, each had well-established entourages and connections among the aristocracy. These were focused primarily in their home bases of Friuli and Spoleto, but both men had connections in the heart of the *regnum* as well. The fight was therefore very even in terms of both practical support and rhetorical justification.

Guy won the first round with victory in the battle of the River Trebbia, forcing Berengar back to his north-eastern stronghold in Verona. However, despite Guy's ascendancy Berengar maintained his claim to control all of Italy, and continued to issue charters as king. This situation actively fomented tension within the aristocracy. A telling example is the case of the county of Piacenza which, in the aftermath of Guy's victory at the Trebbia, was granted to Sigefrid, one of his leading supporters.[87] However, in a charter issued by the would-be ruler Beren-

---

84 Cf. Capitani (cf. fn. 5) 149–52. Rosenwein (cf. fn. 10) esp. pp. 265–76 discusses networks within the aristocracy which helped determine the political behaviour of individual nobles; here I am only dealing with more general patterns of royal-aristocratic interaction.

85 Kurze (cf. fn. 53) s. a. 888, p. 129 is the classic account; Kurze (cf. fn. 22) s. a. 888, p. 116 uses the term 'kinglets'; E. Hlawitschka, 'Waren die Kaiser Wido und Lambert Nachkommen Karls des Großen?', in *Quellen und Forschungen aus italienischen Archiven und Bibliotheken* 49 (1969), pp. 366–86 discusses the contenders' Carolingian credentials.

86 B. Simson (ed.), *Annales Vedastini*, MGH SRG (Hanover, 1909), s. a. 888, p. 64.

87 Manaresi (cf. fn. 54) no. 97; F. Bougard, 'Entre Gandolfingi et Obertenghi: les comtes de Plaisance aux Xe et XIe siècles', in *Mélanges de l'école française de Rome. Moyen age* 101 (1989), pp. 11–66, at p. 17; Hlawitschka (cf. fn. 31) 264–8. This shift of control had implications for the administration of the city: F. Bougard, 'Pierre de Niviano, dit le Spolétin, sculdassius, et le gouvernement du comté de Plaisance à l'époque carolingienne', in *Journal des Savants* (1996), pp. 291–337, at p. 294.

gar at Verona in 890 we meet Adelgisus, the nephew of Engelberga who had been count of the city under Charles the Fat, also bearing the title of 'illuster comes'.[88] Although Berengar did not control the region where Piacenza lay, he evidently backed Adelgisus's claims in the city, which was one of the main centres of his family's power. It is not difficult to see how a situation in which two men as powerful as Sigefrid and Adelgisus claimed the same *honores* (offices), and both with (competing) royal approval, was inherently destabilising. Indeed, there is some evidence that the kings of the 890s actively encouraged this latent tension. In 898 Berengar gave Count Ermenulf, his 'comes militiae', rights in the county of Stazzona, on the western shore of Lake Maggiore, where he had interests before 888.[89] This grant was, however, made after the implementation of a regnal division between Berengar and Lambert, Guy's son, and Stazzona was well into Lambert's territory. The grant thus created an aspiration rather than establishing effective possession, as with Adelgisus's claim to Piacenza. The respective aristocratic followings of Berengar and Guy were thus given vested interests in continuing the struggle between their kings.[90]

The tactic of 'hypothetically' granting the offices of hostile aristocrats to kings' allies was occasionally employed by Carolingian rulers.[91] However, in Italy during the 890s such grants were used by kings to wrest control of the kingdom's heartlands, not just to snap up contested frontier regions, and also played out in the context of a new zero-sum dynastic game: rival Carolingian rulers at least recognised each other as potential kings. Multiple rulers meant multiple sources of patronage, and this helped aristocratic insecurity and conflict become an inbuilt feature of Italian politics, exacerbated by the arrival of transalpine pretenders who had no deep roots in the kingdom. These patterns of patronage had an effect on the status of *honores*, an important basis of aristocratic authority.[92] Institutional rivalries were actively enhanced and perpetuated by successive kings: for example, shortly after Berengar confirmed long-disputed rights in

---

88 L. Schiaparelli (ed.), *I Diplomi di Berengario I* (Fonti per la Storia d'Italia 35) (Rome, 1903), no. 9.
89 Schiaparelli (cf. fn. 88) no. 19. He had been involved in the administration of Engelberga's properties in the region: see Hlawitschka (cf. fn. 31) 177–8; Schiaparelli (cf. fn. 88) no. 13.
90 Although the grant was made after Berengar's advance to Milan, it was before Lambert's death.
91 For an example see Grat et al (cf. fn. 12) s. a. 869, p. 167 (Charles the Bald's grant to Boso of *honores* outside his kingdom). A similar model of conflict is proposed for Stephen's England by E. King, 'The Anarchy of Stephen's Reign', *Transactions of the Royal Historical Society* 34 (1984), pp. 133–53.
92 On *honores* see S. Airlie, 'The Aristocracy', in McKitterick (ed.), *New Cambridge Medieval History II*, pp. 431–50, at pp. 443–7.

Limonta to St-Ambrose in Milan, Arnulf granted them to Reichenau, before Lambert returned them to Milan.[93] Where Charles the Fat had intervened in the Limonta dispute as a way of constructing consensus, the emergence of multiple aspirant dynasties meant that it now became an arena in which dynastic competition was played out. Examples like this suggest a situation in which key estates and *honores* distributed by one king to build aristocratic alliances could be swiftly redistributed by the next, creating a plurality of claims and a general lack of confidence in the security of office- and property-holding. The resulting insecurity made it a small step for losers among the magnates to seek to restore their standing by inviting in 'their own' king.

The post-888 period is desperately in need of renewed historiographical attention. These brief comments are intended only to highlight the complexity of the contemporary political scene and hence to underline this article's central argument: namely, that the factionalism that dominated Italian politics after 875 cannot be explained as a simple manifestation of the progressive decline of royal authority at the expense of disruptive aristocratic power. Rather, fluctuating patterns of royal patronage must be seen as central to understanding aristocratic behaviour. Dynastic politics did not cease to matter after the death of Louis II, as historians have often assumed. On the contrary, dynastic and aristocratic politics remained intimately linked. The turmoil in the years following 875 was played out in a Carolingian framework, and its partial resolution in the reign of Charles the Fat followed from the restoration of concord within the ruling house. The real breach came after 888 when the end of the Carolingian male line sparked off a struggle for kingship fought out by two native competitors who were equal in legitimacy and military strength. Even when dynastic politics helped to perpetuate conflict through the weakness of rulers rather than to create consensus through their strength, in early medieval politics kings always mattered. With this in mind, it is surely time that the political history of Italy after the death of Louis II was re-evaluated.

Abstract

This article deals with the neglected political history of Italy in the last decades of the ninth century. This period is conventionally regarded by historians as a chaotic era of weak kingship and structural decay, dominated by unruly aristocratic power. Drawing on recent studies of royal charters, the article engages with the traditional view and argues that the undeniable turbulence of the period

---

93 Manaresi (cf. fn. 54) no. 101.

needs to be analysed in much more nuanced terms. The appearance of aristocratic factions in Italy should not be seen as a simple consequence of the absence of strong kingship after the death of Louis II in 875, but instead must be understood in connection with wider dynastic politics. The article argues that the succession to the heirless Louis created a drawn-out and often violent crisis that forced leading members of the Italian nobility to choose sides and form into distinct interest groups; that these factions were submerged during the 880s because significant disputes between members of the ruling dynasty had been resolved; and that when they re-emerged after the end of the empire in 888 they did so for very different reasons than those of the 870s. The implication of the article is that the political centre remained important even when it was weak and that kings need to be written back into the political history of this period.

Mönchsorden in Byzanz? – Zur Entstehung und Entwicklung monastischer Verbände in Byzanz (8.–10. Jh.)*

Thomas Pratsch

Bereits die Frage nach Mönchsorden in Byzanz erscheint provokant, äußert sich doch die moderne Forschung recht einhellig zu dieser Thematik. „Etwas einem Orden Vergleichbares gibt es im Orient nicht", schrieb im Jahre 1898 (und nicht als erster) der Kirchenhistoriker Karl Holl in einem Artikel „Über das griechische Mönchtum"[1]. Der Byzantinist Peter Schreiner bemerkte im Jahre 1994 in der zweiten Auflage seines Grundrisses der byzantinischen Geschichte über das orthodoxe Mönchtum: „… ebensowenig existiert eine Gliederung in Orden"[2]. Im Jahre 1998 schrieb Karl Suso Frank für das „Lexikon für Theologie und Kirche" unter dem Stichwort „Orthodoxes Mönchtum" dazu: „Das orthodoxe Mönchtum blieb in der byzantinischen Kirche in seiner spätantiken Form erhalten. Eine Organisation als monastische Orden gab und gibt es nicht, wesentlich ist vielmehr das Einzelkloster."[3] Im Jahre 2003 drückte sich der Theologe Richard Cemus in der deutschen Ausgabe des Sammelbandes „Mönchtum in Ost und West" diesbezüglich folgendermaßen aus: „Anders als im westlichen Mönchtum gibt es im Osten keine religiösen ‚Orden'."[4] Derartige pauschale Feststellungen über das byzantinische Mönchtum lassen sich überall in der Forschungsliteratur – sowohl der Mediävistik und der Kirchengeschichte als auch der Byzantinistik – finden; die Beispiele ließen sich also beliebig mehren.

Wie stets in der historischen Forschung ist bei solch eindeutigen und scheinbar unverrückbar feststehenden Lehrmeinungen Vorsicht geboten. Betrachtet man nämlich die Quellen, ergibt sich ein etwas differenzierteres Bild: Bereits in einer recht frühen Phase des christlichen Mönchtums,[5] insbesondere im und nach

---

* Für wertvolle Hinweise aus Sicht der Mediävistik und Ordensforschung danke ich Wolfram Brandes, Nikolas Jaspert und Olaf Rader.

1   K. Holl, Über das griechische Mönchtum, in: Preußische Jahrbücher 94 (1898) 407–424 = K. Holl, Gesammelte Aufsätze zur Kirchengeschichte, Band II: Der Osten, Tübingen 1928 (Ndr. Darmstadt 1964), 270–282, hier 272.

2   P. Schreiner, Byzanz, 2. überarb. Aufl., München 1994 (Oldenbourg Grundriß der Geschichte), 79.

3   LThK 7 (1998) 403.

4   J. M. Laboa (Hrsg.), Mönchtum in Ost und West. Historischer Atlas, Regensburg 2003, 104.

5   Vgl. dazu immer noch H. Lietzmann, Geschichte der Alten Kirche, Band IV, Berlin

dem 4. Jahrhundert, in der Folge der Anerkennung des Christentums unter Konstantin dem Großen, war es aufgrund des raschen Anstiegs der Zahl der Mönche zur Ausbildung regionaler und organisatorischer Zentren des Mönchtums gekommen. Dies wird in zahlreichen, meist hagiographischen Berichten in etwa folgendermaßen beschrieben: Der weltflüchtige Anachoret zog sich zunächst allein (daher die Bezeichnung als μοναχός) in unwirtliche Gegenden zurück (in Wüsten, unzugängliche Berglandschaften und Wälder, in öde und unfruchtbare Landstriche usw.). Dennoch stießen Schüler zu ihm, um bei ihm zu leben und von ihm zu lernen. Die wachsende Zahl der Schüler machte schließlich die Gründung einer Kirche sowie von Wohn- und Wirtschaftsgebäuden notwendig, so entstand zunächst ein einzelnes Kloster. Der Zustrom weiterer Mönche führte zur Gründung von Tochterklöstern, häufig in der Nähe des Mutterklosters, dem sie administrativ unterstellt und verbunden blieben. Auf diese Art und Weise entstanden Klosterbünde bzw. monastische Kongregationen. Bekannte Klosterbünde bzw. Kongregationen dieser Art sind beispielsweise die des Pachomios in Ägypten (4. Jh.),[6] die des Augustinus von Hippo in Nordafrika (4./5. Jh.),[7] die des Sabas in Palästina (5./6. Jh.)[8] und die des Benedikt von Nursia in Italien (6. Jh.).[9] Das aber bedeutet, daß die Organisation des Mönchtums bereits in recht früher Zeit – und zwar im Orient ebenso wie im Okzident – einen bedeutenden Schritt über das Einzelkloster als wesentliche Form hinausgegangen war![10]

Innerhalb dieser Klosterbünde bzw. monastischen Kongregationen wurden auch Klosterregeln verfaßt, die dann für alle Klöster des Bundes maßgeblich waren. Am bekanntesten ist die Regel des Benedikt (Regula Benedicti), die dieser

---

1944, 116–194 (Ndr. in einem Band Berlin 1999 [de Gruyter Studienbuch], 1108–1186).

6 Vgl. Laboa (s. Anm. 4) 44–47.

7 Vgl. Laboa (s. Anm. 4) 64–67.

8 Vgl. Laboa (s. Anm. 4) 92–95.

9 Vgl. Laboa (s. Anm. 4) 76–79.

10 Zum Mönchtum im Westen vgl. exemplarisch aus einer Flut von Literatur: F. Prinz, Frühes Mönchtum im Frankenreich, Oldenbourg 1965; dens., Askese und Kultur. Vor- und frühbenediktinisches Mönchtum an der Wiege Europas, München 1984; dens., Mönchtum, Kultur und Gesellschaft, München 1989; dens., Das wahre Leben der Heiligen. Zwölf historische Porträts von Kaiserin Helena bis Franz von Assisi, München 2003; G. Jenal, Zum Asketen- und Mönchtum Italiens in der Zeit vor Benedikt. Forschungsstand und Probleme, in: Atti del 7. Congresso internazionale di studi sull'alto medioevo, Spoleto 1982, 137–183, dens., Italia ascetica atque monastica: Das Asketen- und Mönchtum in Italien von den Anfängen bis zur Zeit der Langobarden (ca. 150/250–604) Stuttgart 1995; G. Melville, Ordensstatuten und allgemeines Kirchenrecht. Eine Skizze zum 12./13. Jahrhundert, in: P. Landau – J. Müller (Hgg.), Proceedings of the 9th International Congress of Medieval Canon Law, Vatikanstadt 1997 (Monumenta Iuris Canonici, Series C, Vol. 10), 691–712.

in seinem Klosterbund um das Hauptkloster Monte Cassino in Latium in Italien einführte und die von dort aus im gesamten abendländischen Mönchtum eine weite Verbreitung fand.[11] Aber auch die anderen frühen Klosterbünde verfügten über Klosterregeln, die jedoch nicht in jedem Falle überliefert sind.

Der Bestand der erhaltenen byzantinischen Quellen – der zugegebenermaßen von der Selektion der Überlieferung beeinflußt ist und daher nur vorbehaltliche und näherungsweise Schlüsse erlaubt – vermittelt den Eindruck, daß sich der Trend zur Bildung von Klosterbünden bzw. monastischen Kongregationen im byzantinischen Reich des 8. und besonders des 9. Jahrhunderts fortsetzte und noch erheblich verstärkte. Einige ausgewählte Beispiele sollen dies hier illustrieren:

1. Byzantinische Mönchskongregationen

1.1 Stephanos der Jüngere vom Auxentiosberg (die Auxentiten bzw. Auxentioten)

Die Informationen über das Leben des Stephanos sind uns aus seiner Heiligenvita bekannt, die fast ein halbes Jahrhundert nach seinem Tode von dem Diakon Stephanos verfaßt wurde.[12]

Dort wird über die monastische Karriere des Stephanos folgendes berichtet: Als er fünfzehn Jahre alt war (etwa im Jahre 730), übergaben ihn seine Eltern[13] dem Einsiedler Ioannes[14] auf dem Auxentiosberg in Bithynien. Stephanos wurde Schüler des Ioannes. Nachdem sein Vater gestorben war, brachte Stephanos auch

---

11 Vgl. LexMa 1 (1980) 1870–1902. Dabei kamen die Kollektivbezeichnungen „Benediktiner" und auch „Benediktinerorden" (*fratres qui secundum Deum et beati Benedicti regulam vivunt* bzw. *ordo sancti Benedicti*) für die Gesamtheit aller Mönche, die nach der Regel des Benedikt lebten, in Gebrauch lange bevor der Ordo Sancti Benedicti (OSB) tatsächlich unter einem Abtprimas zusammengeschlossen wurde (1893). Vgl. dazu auch G. Melville, Zur Semantik von ordo im Religiosentum der ersten Hälfte des 12. Jahrhunderts. Lucius II., seine Bulle vom 19. Mai 1144 und der „Orden" der Prämonstratenser, in: I. Crusius – H. Flachenecker (Hgg.), Studien zum Prämonstratenserorden, Göttingen 2003 (Studien zur Germania Sacra 25), 201–224.

12 Vita Stephani iunioris (BHG 1666), ed. M.-F. Auzépy, La Vie d'Étienne le Jeune par Étienne le diacre, Aldershot 1997 (Birmingham Byzantine and Ottoman Monographs 3); dazu dies., L'Hagiographie et L'Iconoclasme Byzantin. Le cas de la Vie d'Étienne le Jeune, Aldershot – Brookfield 1999 (Birmingham Byzantine and Ottoman Monographs 5). Zu Stephanos dem Jüngeren vgl. PmbZ: # 7012, zu Stephanos Diakonos: # 7055.

13 Vgl. PmbZ: # 2389 (Gregorios) und # 442 (Anna).

14 Vgl. PmbZ: # 2970.

seine Mutter und seine Schwester Theodote[15] in ein Frauenkloster auf dem Auxentiosberg (zu diesem Kloster noch im folgenden) und wurde, so wird ausdrücklich gesagt, ihr geistlicher Vater. Als er 30 Jahre alt war, starb sein Lehrer Ioannes, und Stephanos nahm dessen Stelle als Bewohner der Auxentioshöhle und als geistliches Oberhaupt der Mönche des Berges ein. Zum Zeitpunkt von Stephanos' Eintreffen am Auxentiosberg in Bithynien gab es dort also bereits eine monastische Gemeinschaft, die von dem Einsiedler und Abt Ioannes geleitet wurde, dessen Schüler und Nachfolger Stephanos wurde. Dabei handelte es sich um die von dem aus Syrien stammenden Asketen Auxentios im 5. Jahrhundert begründete Gemeinschaft von Einsiedlern, die bei einer Höhle am Auxentiosberg lebten (der Berg ist nach diesem Auxentios benannt, vor dessen Wirken dort hieß er Skopa). Dazu gehörte auch ein Frauenkloster mit dem Namen Trichinaria[16], das sich in einer Meile Entfernung von der Asketenhöhle am Fuße des Auxentiosberges befand und ebenfalls bereits im 5. Jahrhundert gegründet worden war. Nach dem Tode des Ioannes übernahm also Stephanos diese Einrichtungen und ihre Leitung als geistliches Oberhaupt.

Bald fanden sich weitere Schüler bei ihm ein. Als ihre Zahl auf zwölf[17] angewachsen war, begann Stephanos mit dem Bau eines Schlafsaales und anderer Wirtschaftsgebäude und begründete somit ein Koinobion, nämlich das Hagios-Auxentios-Kloster[18]. Nachdem dies vollendet und die Zahl der Mönche inzwischen auf 20 angewachsen war, setzte Stephanos einen von ihnen namens Marinos[19] zum Oikonomos und Proestos, also zum Verwalter und Vorsteher dieses Klosters ein (Μαρῖνον τὸν θεοστήρικτον ἄνδρα εἰς τὰ τῆς οἰκονομίας καὶ πάντα τὰ τῆς μονῆς ὁ παμμάκαρ [sc. Stephanos] προεστήσατο). Er selbst aber blieb der geistliche Führer (ἡγούμενος) der Gemeinschaft von Mönchen und Nonnen, auch wenn er außerhalb des Klosters, nämlich in der erwähnten Höhle sowie in einer Mönchszelle auf dem Gipfel des Berges, lebte.

Nach dem Konzil von Hiereia vom Jahre 754 geriet Stephanos in zunehmenden Konflikt mit Kaiser Konstantin V. (741–775) in der Frage der Rechtmäßigkeit der Ikonenverehrung (dem sogenannten byzantinischen Ikonoklasmus oder „Bilderstreit"),[20] weil er die Beschlüsse dieses Konzils nicht anerkennen wollte.

---

15 Vgl. PmbZ: # 7897.

16 Vgl. R. Janin, Les églises et les monastères des grands centres byzantins (Bithynie, Hellespont, Latros, Galèsios, Trébizonde, Athènes, Thessalonique), Paris 1975, 45 f.

17 Dabei könnte es sich um einen Topos handeln, nach dem Vorbild der Zahl der Jünger Jesu im NT.

18 Vgl. Janin (s. Anm. 16) 43–45, 47.

19 Vgl. PmbZ. # 4803.

20 Vgl. dazu jetzt zusammenfassend und unter Heranziehung der älteren Literatur L. Brubaker – J. Haldon, Byzantium in the Iconoclast Era (ca. 680–850). The Sources, Birmingham 2001 (Birmingham Byzantine and Ottoman Monographs 7).

Er wurde schließlich verhaftet und anschließend auf die Insel Proikonnesos verbannt.

Nachdem er in Proikonnesos angekommen war, fand er an der Südküste der Insel, an einem steil zum Meer hin abfallenden Felsen namens Kissuda eine höhlenartige Behausung (σπηλοειδὲς οἴκημα), in deren Nähe sich auch eine Kirche befand, die der Anna, der Mutter der Theotokos, geweiht war (τῆς τοῦ Θεοῦ προμήτορος ″Αννης πανσεβάσμιος ναός)[21]. Stephanos verbrachte längere Zeit, wohl mehrere Jahre, auf Proikonnesos. Nach einiger Zeit kamen auch die meisten Mönche seines Klosters, also des Hagios-Auxentios-Klosters am Auxentiosberg in Bithynien, die von dort vertrieben worden waren, zu ihm nach Proikonnesos. Zusammen mit diesen gründete er in Kissuda ein neues Kloster. Außerhalb des Klosters errichtete er für sich selbst auf einer Säule oder einem säulenartigen Felsen eine Klause (στυλοειδὲς μικρὸν ἔγκλειστρον), in der er seinen asketischen Lebensstil fortführte. Stephanos ordnete also das monastische Leben seiner Gemeinschaft auf Proikonnesos in auffälliger Analogie zur Ordnung der Gemeinschaft am Auxentiosberg: ein Koinobion für seine Schüler und Mönche und eine Klause außerhalb dieses Klosters für ihn, den Abt und Asketen. Später kamen auch die Mutter und die Schwester des Stephanos, die Nonnen des Trichinariaklosters waren, zu ihm nach Proikonnesos. Es wird nicht ausdrücklich gesagt, ist aber nicht auszuschließen, daß Stephanos nun – wiederum in Analogie zum Auxentiosberg – auch noch ein Frauenkloster auf Proikonnesos gründete.

Wohl gegen Ende des Jahres 765 kam Stephanos auf kaiserliche Veranlassung in Konstantinopel zu Tode und wurde anschließend als Märtyrer für den rechten Glauben gefeiert, nämlich für die Sache der Ikonenverehrung[22].

Stephanos hatte wenigstens drei Klöstern, einer Asketenhöhle und mehreren Mönchszellen vorgestanden. Die monastische Kongregation des Stephanos am Auxentiosberg wurde allem Anschein nach spätestens nach der Wiedereinfüh-

---

21 Vgl. Janin (s. Anm. 16) 210.
22 Vgl. dazu Iconoclasm. Papers given at the Ninth Spring Symposium of Byzantine Studies, University of Birmingham, March 1975, ed. by A. Bryer and J. Herrin, Birmingham 1977; P. Speck, Kaiser Konstantin VI. Die Legitimation einer fremden und der Versuch einer eigenen Herrschaft. Quellenkritische Darstellung von 25 Jahren byzantinischer Geschichte nach dem ersten Ikonoklasmus, I–II, München 1978; dens., Artabasdos, der rechtgläubige Vorkämpfer der göttlichen Lehren. Untersuchungen zur Revolte des Artabasdos und ihrer Darstellung in der byzantinischen Historiographie, Bonn 1981 (ΠΟΙΚΙΛΑ BYZANTINA 2); dens., Ich bin's nicht, Kaiser Konstantin ist es gewesen: die Legenden vom Einfluß des Teufels, des Juden und des Moslem auf den Ikonoklasmus, Bonn 1990 (ΠΟΙΚΙΛΑ BYZANTINA 10); M.-F. Auzépy (s. Anm. 12); Brubaker – Haldon (s. Anm. 20); dies., Byzantium in the Iconoclast Era (ca. 680–850). A History, Cambridge 2005.

rung der Ikonenverehrung im Jahre 843 wiederbelebt. Der Komplex wurde später wohl noch durch zusätzliche Klostergründungen erweitert – so z. B. um das im 11. Jahrhundert belegte Hagios-Stephanos-Kloster, wobei es sich höchstwahrscheinlich um ein Patrozinium des Stephanos des Jüngeren handelte. Die Kongregation am Auxentiosberg ist bis in das ausgehende 13. Jahrhundert hinein belegt.[23]

1.2 Petros von Atroa

Ein weiterer prominenter Vertreter des byzantinischen Mönchtums jener Zeit ist der wohl 773 geborene Petros von Atroa.[24] Die meisten Informationen über die von ihm begründete und geleitete monastische Kongregation beziehen wir wiederum aus seiner Heiligenvita.[25]

Petros war zunächst Schüler des Mönchs Iakobos[26], dann des Asketen Paulos[27] geworden, der ihn auch zum Mönch schor und später zum Priester weihen ließ. Anschließend brach Petros zusammen mit Paulos zu einer Pilgerfahrt ins Heilige Land auf. Am Fluß Halys sei Paulos dann vom Heiligen Geist an der Durchführung seiner Pilgerfahrt gehindert und ihm der Gedanke eingegeben worden, ein Kloster zu gründen. Petros und Paulos reisten zurück zum bithynischen Olymp und gründeten dort, bei der Kapelle des Propheten Zacharias, das Zachariaskloster[28], dessen erster Abt Paulos wurde.

Als Paulos erkrankte und schließlich starb, setzte er Petros zu seinem Nachfolger und Hegumenos des Zachariasklosters ein. Nach dem erneuten Verbot der Ikonenverehrung unter Kaiser Leon V. (813–820) vom April 815 versammelte Petros seine Bruderschaft und ordnete an, daß die Mönche das Kloster verlassen und in kleinen Gruppen von jeweils zwei oder drei Brüdern sich in verlassene Gebiete (πρὸς τὴν ἔρημον) zurückziehen sollten, um ihren Glauben unbefleckt bewahren zu können. Petros selbst ging zusammen mit dem Mönch Ioannes[29] zunächst nach Ephesos in die Ioannes-Theologos-Kirche, dann weiter nach Cho-

---

23 Vgl. Janin (s. Anm. 16) 47.
24 Vgl. PmbZ: # 6022.
25 Σάβα μοναχοῦ εἰς τὸν βίον τοῦ ὁσίου Πατρὸς ἡμῶν καὶ θαυματουργοῦ Πέτρου τοῦ ἐν τῇ ᾿Ατρώᾳ, ed. V. Laurent, La Vie Merveilleuse de Saint Pierre d'Atroa († 837), éditée, traduite et commentée, Bruxelles 1956 (Subsidia hagiographica 29), (Text: 5–225).
26 Vgl. PmbZ: # 2628.
27 Vgl. PmbZ: # 5838.
28 Vgl. Janin (s. Anm. 16) 151.
29 Vgl. PmbZ: # 3240.

nai in die Kirche des Erzengels Michael. Im Anschluß reiste er nach Zypern, wo
er sich zehn Monate aufhielt und zahlreiche Kirchen besuchte, ehe er zum bithynischen Olymp zurückkehrte. Er ließ sich dort in einer Hesychastenzelle an dem
Ort Mesolympon nieder, wo sich auch bald ein Teil seiner Bruderschaft einfand.
Petros und seine Mönche konnten anscheinend gelegentlich in der Zacharias-
kirche ihres Klosters den Gottesdienst abhalten.[30]

Petros hielt sich dann in verschiedenen Hesychastenhöhlen auf und zog mit
seinem Begleiter Ioannes von Ort zu Ort, wobei sie größere Siedlungen mieden.
Schließlich kam er jedoch in seine Geburtsstadt Elaia in Asia und begegnete dort
seinem leiblichen Bruder Christophoros, der sich ihm anschloß. In einer Höhle
in den Bergen bei Hippos schor Petros seinen Bruder Christophoros zum Mönch
und gab ihm den Mönchsnamen Paulos.[31] Kurz darauf schickte ihre kranke Mutter[32] nach ihnen und ließ sie zu sich rufen. Als Petros und Paulos bei der Mutter
eintrafen, äußerte diese den Wunsch, Nonne zu werden. Der Wunsch wurde ihr
erfüllt, und sie starb. Die Brüder bestatteten sie auf dem Berge Hippos und kehr-
ten in ihre Höhle zurück. Petros nahm auch die Angehörigen der Familie seiner
Schwester (nämlich die Schwester selbst, ihren Mann, vier Söhne und zwei Töch-
ter)[33] in die ihm unterstehenden Klöster auf.[34]

In der folgenden Zeit zog Petros weiter umher und wechselte ständig seine
Aufenthaltsorte, genannt werden unter anderem die Örtlichkeiten Daguta, das
Zachariaskloster, eine Höhle bei Dele, Apollonia, Maurusias, Kalon Oros, Plateia
Petra. Es entsteht dabei der Eindruck, daß er an einigen seiner Stationen bereits
vorhandene Gründungen der Kongregation visitierte oder sogar neue Klöster
gründete, ohne daß dies in der Vita näher ausgeführt würde.

Petros hatte mehreren Klöstern vorgestanden, außerdem auch etlichen An-
sammlungen von Hesychastenzellen (ἡσυχαστικὰ κελλία). Nach der Analyse
von Vitalien Laurent, dem Editor der Viten des Petros von Atroa, unterstanden
ihm das Zachariaskloster, das Porphyrioskloster am Rhyndakos und das Balen-
tia- bzw. Baleakloster im nördlichen Lydien sowie die Einsiedeleien Kalon Oros
in Lydien und Hippos in Asia und möglicherweise ein (zusätzliches) Frauenklo-

---

30 Die Entfernung zwischen beiden Örtlichkeiten betrug allerdings 10 km in unweg-
     samem Gelände mit ca. 800 m Höhenunterschied, cf. B. Menthon, Une terre de légen-
     des, l'Olympe de Bithynie: ses saints, ses couvents, ses sites, Paris 1935: Carte du
     Mont Olympe, dies schränkt die Nutzung der Zachariaskirche von Mesolympon aus
     stark ein.
31 Vgl. PmbZ. # 5839.
32 Vgl. PmbZ. # 446 (Anna).
33 Vgl. PmbZ. # 4102 A–D.
34 Zu frommen Familien und ihren Klosterstiftungen im Westen ist manches bei Gregor
     von Tours zu finden.

ster in Lydien.[35] Sein leiblicher Bruder Paulos stand ihm als Oikonomos des Klosterbundes zur Seite.

Im Jahre 836 erkrankte Petros. Er bestimmte seinen eben erwähnten Bruder Paulos zum neuen Hegumenos des Zachariasklosters und der anderen Klöster des Klosterbundes und starb im Kloster Balentia/Balea im Alter von 63 Jahren, am 1. Januar des Jahres 837. Er wurde zunächst in der Kapelle des Heiligen Hierarchen Nikolaos beigesetzt. Später wurde sein Leichnam in seine alte Asketenhöhle (τὸ ἀγωνιστικὸν αὐτοῦ σπήλαιον) überführt und dort in einer Kapelle der Gottesmutter (Παναγίας Θεοτόκου) bestattet.

Die Existenz des Zachariasklosters von Atroa und damit wohl auch der monastischen Kongregation des Petros von Atroa ist bis in die erste Hälfte des 10. Jahrhunderts hinein bezeugt.[36]

1.3 Theodoros Studites (die Studiten)

Im betrachteten Zeitraum vergleichsweise am besten dokumentiert ist die Entstehung und frühe Entwicklung der Mönchskongregation des Theodoros Studites[37], der sogenannten Studiten. Wir haben in diesem Falle nicht nur drei unterschiedliche Versionen der Vita des Theodoros zur Verfügung,[38] sondern auch viele Schriften aus der Feder des Theodoros selbst: nämlich seine zahlreichen Briefe und Katechesen, verschiedene Klosterverordnungen und anderes mehr.[39]

---

35 Vgl. Laurent (s. Anm. 25) 35–44.

36 Vgl. Vita Lucae Stylitae (BHG 2239), ed. H. Delehaye, in: H. Delehaye, Les Saints Stylites, Brüssel 1923 (Ndr. Brüssel 1989; Subsidia hagiographica 14), 195–237, hier cap. 8, p. 203 (ca. 921 a. d.).

37 Vgl. PmbZ. # 7574; ferner Th. Pratsch, Theodoros Studites (759–826) – zwischen Dogma und Pragma, Frankfurt a. M. u. a. 1998 (Berliner Byzantinistische Studien 4) passim.

38 Vita et Conversatio S. P. N. et confessoris Theodori praepositi Studitarum: Βίος καὶ πολιτεία τοῦ ὁσίου Πατρὸς ἡμῶν καὶ ὁμολογητοῦ τοῦ Θεοδώρου τοῦ τῶν Στουδίων ἡγουμένου, in: PG 99, 113–232; Vita et Conversatio S. P. N. et confessoris Theodori abbatis monasterii Studii a Michaele Monacho conscripta: Βίος καὶ πολιτεία τοῦ ὁσίου Πατρὸς ἡμῶν καὶ ὁμολογητοῦ Θεοδώρου ἡγουμένου μονῆς τῶν Στουδίου συγγραφεὶς παρὰ Μιχαὴλ μοναχοῦ, in: PG 99, 233–328; Vita S. Theodori Studitae: Βίος καὶ πολιτεία τοῦ ὁσίου πατρὸς ἡμῶν καὶ ὁμολογητοῦ Θεοδώρου ἡγουμένου τῶν Στουδίου, ed. B. Latyšev, Vita S. Theodori Studitae in codice Mosquensi musei Rumianzoviani no 520, in: VV 21 (1914) 255–304 (Text: 258–304).

39 Vgl. dazu Pratsch (s. Anm. 37) 9 f., ausführlich G. Fatouros, in: Theodori Studitae Epistolae, rec. G. Fatouros, I–II, Berlin – New York 1992 (CFHB vol. XXXI/1–2, Series Berolinensis), 21*–38*.

Theodoros ging etwa im Frühsommer des Jahres 781 unter Führung seines Onkels Platon[40], der bereits Abt des Symbolaklosters[41] in Bithynien war, gemeinsam mit den anderen männlichen Familienmitgliedern (nämlich dem Vater, Brüdern, Onkeln usw.)[42] auf den Landsitz der Familie nach Boskytion in Bithynien und war an dessen Umbau in ein Kloster (das Sakkudionkloster[43], benannt nach einer nahegelegenen Ortschaft) beteiligt. Der erste Abt dieses Klosters wurde Theodoros' Onkel Platon, der seinen Neffen auch zum Mönch weihte und zu seinem engsten Mitarbeiter machte. Platon sorgte ferner dafür, daß Theodoros etwa 789/90 vom Patriarchen von Konstantinopel Tarasios[44] zum Priester geweiht wurde. Im Jahre 794 ließ Platon (wohl unter dem Vorwand einer Krankheit) seinen Neffen von den Mönchen zu seinem Nachfolger im Amt des Hegumenos des Sakkudionklosters wählen. Platon widmete sich anschließend der Askese und übergab die Amtsgeschäfte als Abt seinem Neffen Theodoros[45].

Im Jahre 798 wurde Theodoros zum Abt des Studiosklosters[46] in Konstantinopel erhoben, das nunmehr Mittelpunkt eines Klosterbundes war. Vermutlich hatte die Gründung des familiären Sakkudionklosters in Bithynien bereits zur Bildung eines kleinen Klosterbundes geführt, als Platon, der damalige Abt des Symbolaklosters, auch den Hegumenat des Sakkudionklosters übernahm. Theodoros stieg dann 794 mit seiner Wahl zum Hegumenos und Nachfolger Platons gleichzeitig auch zum Abt des Symbolaklosters auf. Er „erbte" somit den Hegumenat zweier Klöster. Ein Beleg für diese Annahme findet sich in einem Brief des Theodoros aus den Jahren 816–818 an den Oikonomos des Symbolaklosters, wo der Studitenabt das Symbolakloster als „sein Kloster" bezeichnet. Hierzu würde auch passen, daß Platon auf dem zweiten Konzil von Nikaia im Jahre 787 als ἡγούμενος καὶ ἀρχιμανδρίτης Σακκουδεῶν (Σακκουδεῶνος) unterzeichnete.[47] Zusätzlich könnte auch das Studioskloster, als Theodoros es übernahm, bereits

---

40 Vgl. PmbZ: # 6285.

41 Vgl. Janin (s. Anm 16) 181–183.

42 Vgl. dazu Pratsch (s. Anm. 37) 45–76.

43 Vgl. Janin (s. Anm. 16) 177–181; zur Lage und zum archäologischen Befund vgl. jetzt M.-F. Auzépy – O. Delouis – J.-P. Grélois – M. Kaplan, À propos des monastères de Médikion et de Sakkudiôn, in: REB 63 (2005) 183–194.

44 Vgl. PmbZ. # 7235, ferner C. Ludwig – Th. Pratsch, in: Die Patriarchen der ikonoklastischen Zeit. Germanos I. – Methodios I. (715–847), hrsg. von R.-J. Lilie, mit Beiträgen von R.-J. Lilie, C. Ludwig, T. Pratsch, I. Rochow, D. Stein, B. Zielke, Frankfurt a. M. u. a. 1999 (Berliner Byzantinistische Studien 5), 57–108.

45 Vgl. dazu Pratsch (s. Anm. 37) 71–81.

46 Vgl. dazu R. Janin, Constantinople byzantin. Développement urbain et répertoire topographique, 2e éd., Paris 1964 (Archives de l'Orient Chrétien 4A) 430–440.

47 Cf. ODB I, 156: "From the 6th C. onward, according to <J.> Pargoire, *archimandrite* began to be used for the chief of a region or urban federation of monasteries, akin to EXARCH or PROTOS. In this sense *archimandrite* is applied to the *protos* of holy

Mittelpunkt eines kleinen Klosterbundes gewesen sein, da auch dessen Abt Sabas auf dem Konzil 787 als ἀϱχιμανδϱίτης ϰαὶ ἡγούμενος μονῆς τῶν Στουδίων geführt wurde. Somit hatte Theodoros unter Umständen nicht nur einen kleinen Klosterbund von seinem Onkel Platon geerbt, sondern auch einen weiteren zusammen mit dem Studioskloster übernommen.[48]

Die Kongregation war bereits zuvor um ein weiteres Kloster bereichert worden. Wohl noch im Herbst 797 war das Katharakloster[49] in Bithynien der Botmäßigkeit des Theodoros, damals Abt des Sakkudion- und Symbolaklosters, unterstellt worden. Wenigstens zwei weitere Klöster gesellten sich nach dem Umzug in die Hauptstadt hinzu: Das Tripyliana- und das Hagios-Christophoros-Kloster.[50] Wann sie dazukamen, ist nicht ganz klar. Es handelt sich jedoch vermutlich nicht um Übernahmen, sondern um Neugründungen, mit deren Entstehung erst nach dem Erstarken des Studiosklosters zu rechnen ist, als überzählige Mönche des Mutterklosters damit beauftragt werden konnten, weitere Klöster zu gründen. Wir sollten etwa den Zeitraum zwischen 802 und 806 für die Gründung dieser Klöster veranschlagen. Später dürften wenigstens noch zwei weitere Klöster dazugekommen sein, einmal ein Hagios-Georgios-Kloster[51] und zum anderen das Hagios-Tryphon-Kloster am Kap Akritas[52]. Zur Zeit des Patriarchen Methodios I. (843–847)[53] gehörte auch ein Kloster namens Κατὰ Σάβα dem Verbund an.[54] Mit diesem Verbund von wenigstens fünf, möglicherweise bis zu neun Klöstern – in der Hauptstadt und im monastischen Zentrum Bithynien – war Theodoros die Gründung einer beachtlichen Kongregation gelungen.[55]

Ohne Zweifel bestand die studitische Kongregation auch nach dem Tode des Theodoros am 11. November 826 fort, sie ist jedoch nur noch einmal in den erhaltenen Quellen nachzuweisen, nämlich anläßlich der Translation der Gebeine des Theodoros von der Insel Prinkipo in das Studioskloster nach Konstantinopel im Jahre 844.[56] Während die kleinasiatischen Besitzungen der studitischen Kongregation früher verlorengingen, spielte das Studioskloster bis zum Fall Konstan-

---

mountains like Athos, Latros, and Olympos, or to the head of a group of monasteries in one city, as in Athens."
48 Vgl. dazu Pratsch (s. Anm. 37) 115–123.
49 Vgl. Janin (s. Anm. 16) 158–160.
50 Vgl. Janin (s. Anm. 16) 179, 187 f.
51 Dieses Kloster ist weder lokalisiert, noch liegt sonst irgendeine andere Information dazu vor. Zu den zahlreichen Klöstern mit dem Patrozinium des Märtyrers Georg vgl. Janin (s. Anm. 16) 466 (Index).
52 Cf. dazu Janin (s. Anm. 16) 55 f.
53 Zu ihm s. B. Zielke (s. Anm. 44) 183–260.
54 Vgl. dazu Pratsch (s. Anm. 37) 130 Anm. 90.
55 Vgl. dazu Pratsch (s. Anm. 37) 123–134.
56 Vgl. Pratsch (s. Anm. 37) 290 f.

tinopels im Jahre 1453 eine bedeutende Rolle und stellte mehrere Synkelloi und Patriarchen von Konstantinopel.

Die Beispiele dürften zur Darstellung des Phänomens an dieser Stelle genügen. Es sollte aber darauf hingewiesen werden, daß sich im betrachteten Zeitraum weitere Mönchskongregationen dieser Art in Byzanz nachweisen lassen. Genannt seien hier nur Theophanes Homologetes und die Agriniten (benannt nach dem Mutterkloster der Kongregation: Megas Agros) sowie Niketas von Medikion und die Medikioten (benannt nach der Ortschaft Medikion, an der sich das Mutterkloster befand).[57] Auch außerhalb des byzantinischen Reichsgebietes lebten einige „byzantinische" monastische Kongregationen weiter fort, so etwa die Sabbaiten um die Sabaslaura in Palästina und die Basilianer[58] in Unteritalien und Sizilien.[59]

2. Die Organisation der Studitenkongregation

Die im Falle der Studiten außergewöhnlich günstige Quellenlage erlaubt es uns, in die Organisation der Kongregation etwas näheren Einblick zu nehmen und dabei einige nützliche Detailbeobachtungen zu machen:

Die Quellen betonen, daß Theodoros das Studioskloster von Grund auf neu organisierte: Er richtete Werkstätten und Arbeitsräume ein. Es läßt sich dabei jedoch nicht mehr feststellen, welche Werkstätten und Handwerke er bereits vorfand und welche er einführte. Der Einrichtung des Skriptoriums und der Bibliothek schenkte er besonderes Augenmerk, und die Innendekoration der Ioannes-Prodromos-Kirche des Studiosklosters wurde nach seinen Vorstellungen restauriert und erweitert. Beim gesamten Ausbau des Klosters ging er – so sein Biograph – mit größtem Eifer, Sorgfalt und Sinn für Vollständigkeit zu Werke. So verfaßte er etwa kleine jambische Gedichte (die sogenannten „Mön-

---

57 Auf die Herausbildung von Kollektivbezeichnungen für die Angehörigen dieser Kongregationen (meist abgeleitet vom Hauptkloster der Kongregation) soll hier nur kurz hingewiesen werden; so sind etwa die Studiten, die Agriniten, die Medikioten, die Herakleioten und andere in den Quellen belegt. Zur Lage und zum archäologischen Befund des Medikionklosters vgl. jetzt Auzépy – Delouis – Grélois – Kaplan (s. Anm. 43) 183–194.

58 Das ist die westliche Bezeichnung für die griechischen Mönche in Unteritalien und Sizilien. Die Benennung „Ordo sancti Basilii" erscheint im 13. Jh. zunächst in Papsturkunden und ist um 1300 im Westen allgemein gebräuchlich. Im Griechischen wird diese Bezeichnung nicht verwendet.

59 Zu diesen s. H. Enzensberger, in: LexMa 1 (1980) 1523 f.; I. Patrylo, in: LThK 2 (1994) 57 f.

chsgedichte"), in denen er die Obliegenheiten jedes einzelnen Amtes des Studios-klosters genau festlegte und die er an den jeweiligen Arbeitsplätzen der Mönche (sowohl im Studioskloster als auch in den anderen Klöstern der studitischen Kongregation) als Inschriften anbringen ließ.[60]

Nach der Darstellung in seinen Viten führte er dabei auch neue Ämter ein, gab ihnen neue Namen und errichtete so innerhalb des Klosters eine perfekte Hierarchie der verschiedenen Ämter, die es ihm ermöglichte, alles persönlich unter Kontrolle zu haben, obwohl er selbst nicht überall sein konnte. Zu diesem Zweck verfaßte er auch eine Klosterordnung (ὑποτύπωσις)[61] sowie einen Buß-katalog (ἐπιτίμια)[62], in dem Strafen für Verstöße festgelegt sind. Ferner erließ er eine Fastenordnung (διδασκαλία χρονική)[63] und noch eine ganze Reihe weiterer Verordnungen und Regelungen,[64] die heute zwar nicht mehr vollständig über-schaut werden können, die sich jedoch zum Teil aus seinen Viten sowie aus ande-ren Werken erschließen lassen.[65]

Ferner berichten die Viten, daß die vorbildliche Organisation des Klosters eine große Zahl an Mönchen und Laien anzog, so daß das Kloster bald an die 1000 Mönche beherbergte. Auch die Patria Konstantinupoleos aus dem 10. Jahr-hundert berichten in der Gründungslegende des Klosters davon, daß sein Stifter, der Patrikios Studios, bereits zum Zeitpunkt der Einrichtung des Klosters, Mitte des 5. Jahrhunderts, dort 1000 Mönche angesiedelt habe.[66] Die Chronographie des Theophanes nennt für das Jahr 806 die Zahl von ungefähr 700 Mönchen unter Theodoros.[67] Es ist bereits verschiedentlich darauf hingewiesen worden, daß die Zahl der Mönche wohl auf die gesamte studitische Kongregation (das Studios-

---

60 Theodoros Studites, Jamben auf verschiedene Gegenstände, Einleitung, kritischer Text, Übersetzung u. Kommentar besorgt von P. Speck, Berlin 1968 (Supplementa Byzantina 1).

61 Constitutiones Studitanae, in: PG 99, col. 1703–1720. Zu byzantinischen Klosterord-nungen, meist als Typika bezeichnet, vgl. auch Byzantine monastic foundation docu-ments: a complete translation of the surviving founders' typika and testaments, ed. John Thomas – Angela Constantinides Hero (with the assistance of Giles Constable), vols. I–V, Washington 2000.

62 Poenae monasteriales, in: PG 99, col. 1733–1758.

63 Doctrina chronica, in: PG 99, col. 1693–1704.

64 Vgl. De confessione et pro peccatis satisfactione, in: PG 99, col. 1721–1730; Quaestio-nes, in: PG 99, col. 1729–1734; Testamentum, in: PG 99, col. 1813–1823.

65 Vgl. dazu Fatouros (s. Anm. 39) 21*–38*.

66 Πάτρια Κωνσταντονιυπόλεως, in: Scriptores originum Constantinopolitanarum, rec. T. Preger, II, Leipzig 1907 (Ndr. Leipzig 1989), Nr. 87 (64, ξδ`), p. 247. Dabei ist aber nicht klar, ob die Nachricht in den Patria wiederum auf die Viten des Theodoros zurückgeht.

67 Theophanis chronographia, I, rec. C. de Boor, Leipzig 1883, 481, 29.

kloster mit allen bithynischen Dependancen) zu beziehen ist.[68] Jedenfalls steht außer Frage, daß das Studioskloster unter Theodoros so viele Mönche anzog, daß einige von ihnen, nachdem sie im Mutterkloster eine Ausbildung in einem Handwerk erhalten hatten, in die anderen Klöster der Kongregation nach Bithynien geschickt werden konnten.[69]

In die Jahre seines Aufenthalts im Studioskloster zwischen 798 und 809 fiel auch die fruchtbarste Periode des schriftstellerischen Schaffens des Studitenabts. Davon wissen auch seine Viten zu berichten. Neben den Regeln und Verordnungen sowie den „Mönchsgedichten" schrieb er in dieser Zeit einen großen Teil seiner zahlreichen Katechesen und Homilien.[70] Auch andere Schriften – etwa seine Laudatio matris[71] und sein sogenanntes Testament[72] – dürften am Anfang seiner Abtstätigkeit im Studioskloster entstanden sein. Weiterhin wird er auch zahlreiche Briefe in diesen Jahren verfaßt haben, von denen allerdings die meisten verloren sind.[73]

Die Grundlage für die effiziente Verwaltung der Kongregation und den Zusammenhalt der vergleichsweise weit verstreuten Klöster war eine intensive Kommunikation zwischen dem Abt beziehungsweise dem zentralen Kloster in Konstantinopel und seinen Dependancen in der Provinz.[74] Theodoros hatte dieses Problem erkannt und entwickelte ein Kommunikationswesen, das es ihm

---

68 Vgl. A. Berger, Untersuchungen zu den Patria Konstantinupoleos, Bonn 1988 (ΠΟΙ-ΚΙΛΑ ΒΥΖΑΝΤΙΝΑ 8) 363 f.

69 Vgl. Pratsch (s. Anm. 37) 126 f.

70 S. P. N. Theodori Studitae Magna Catechesis, ed. J. Cozza-Luzi, in: Nova Patrum Bibliotheca IX 2 (Rom 1888); X 1 (Rom 1905); Theodoros Studites, Magna Catechesis, ed. A. Papadopoulos-Kerameus, Megale Katechesis, St. Petersburg 1904; S. P. N. et Confessoris Theodori Studitis Praepositi Parva Catechesis, ed. E. Auvray, Paris 1891.

71 S. P. N. et confessoris Theodori Catechesis funebris in matrem suam: Τοῦ ὁσίου Πατρὸς ἡμῶν καὶ ὁμολογητοῦ Θεοδώρου κατήχησις ἐπιτάφιος εἰς τὴν ἑαυτοῦ μητέρα, in: PG 99, 883–902.

72 Sancti ac Deiferi patris nostri et confessoris Theodori Studiensis praepositi Testamentum: Τοῦ ὁσίου καὶ Θεοφόρου Πατρὸς ἡμῶν καὶ ὁμολογητοῦ Θεοδώρου, ἡγουμένου τοῦ Στουδίου διαθήκη, in: PG 99, 1813A–1824D.

73 Theodori Studitae Epistolae, rec. G. Fatouros, I–II, Berlin–New York 1992 (CFHB vol. XXXI/1–2, Series Berolinensis). Die erhaltenen Briefe des Theodoros stammen überwiegend aus den Zeiten seiner Verbannung, also aus den Jahren 796/97, 809–811 und 815–826.

74 Vgl. dazu ausführlicher Th. Pratsch, Dezentrales Netz und Chiffre – zum Kommunikationswesen byzantinischer Mönchsgemeinschaften, in: Mediengesellschaft Antike? Information und Kommunikation vom Alten Ägypten bis Byzanz, hrsg. von der Berlin–Brandenburgischen Akademie der Wissenschaften, Berlin 2006 (Berlin–Brandenburgische Akademie der Wissenschaften – Berichte und Abhandlungen, Sonderband 10), 69–91.

sowohl ermöglichte, die anderen Klöster von der Hauptstadt aus zu verwalten, als auch eine enge Bindung dieser Klöster an das Studioskloster wie auch der Klöster untereinander zu gewährleisten. Voraussetzung und Substanz dieser Kommunikation war seine eigene, enorme schriftstellerische Produktion. Durch seine Briefe und Katechesen, deren auf uns gekommene Zahl erstaunlich ist, hielt er den Kontakt zu seinen Mönchen aufrecht, tauschte Informationen aus und traf Anordnungen. Darüber hinaus versuchte er besonders mit Hilfe seiner Katechesen, aber auch später mit einigen Briefen, in seinen Klöstern während seiner physischen Abwesenheit gleichsam „geistlich" (πνευματικῶς) präsent zu sein, indem er Predigten bzw. Katechesen schrieb, die dann in den Klöstern der Kongregation verlesen wurden. Somit konnte er aus der Ferne predigen und seinen Mönchen verdeutlichen, daß er auch während seiner Abwesenheit ihr Hirte war, der ein teilnahmsvolles, vor allem aber ein wachsames Auge auf sie hatte.[75] Diese Kommunikation war keineswegs einseitig, denn die Mönche, besonders natürlich diejenigen in verantwortungsvollen Positionen, schickten ihm ebenfalls Schreiben oder ließen ihm mündliche Botschaft überbringen.

Dies führt uns schließlich zu den Boten. Die erwähnte serienmäßige Niederschrift von Katechesen und Briefen erfüllte nur dann ihren Zweck, wenn die Schreiben auch ihre jeweiligen Adressaten erreichten. Daher hat Theodoros bereits frühzeitig damit begonnen, den regelmäßigen Austausch von Boten (sowohl von Briefboten als auch von Überbringern mündlicher Botschaft) anzuordnen. Aus den erhaltenen Briefen und Katechesen sind uns 15 Boten namentlich und weitere 25 anonyme Boten bekannt, die als solche zwischen Theodoros und den Klöstern der Kongregation, zwischen Gruppen von Angehörigen der Kongregation oder einzelnen Mönchen unterwegs waren. Dieser Botendienst der studitischen Kongregation war so weit entwickelt, daß man beinahe schon von einem eigenen Post- oder Kurierdienst sprechen könnte. Doch nicht nur untereinander, auch nach außen hin kommunizierte die Kongregation über dieses Botenwesen. In diesem Zusammenhang werden auch tragische Ereignisse überliefert: Im Winter/Frühjahr 815/16 waren die Studitenmönche Gaianos und Zosimas[76] mit einem Brief des Theodoros zum Metropoliten Euthymios von Sardeis[77] unterwegs, der sich zu diesem Zeitpunkt im Exil auf der Insel Thasos aufhielt. Bei der Überfahrt geriet das Schiff in einen Sturm und sank, wobei die beiden zuverlässigen Boten ums Leben kamen. Der Bote Dionysios[78] erkrankte auf der Rückreise von einer Mission nach Palästina, wurde dann im Myelakloster gepflegt, erlag aber dort seiner Krankheit und wurde im Kirchhof dieses Klosters begraben.

---

75 Im Westen Hildegard von Bingen und Burkhard von Clairvant (beide 12. Jh.).
76 Vgl. PmbZ: # 1925 (Gaianos) und # 8663 (Zosimas).
77 Vgl. PmbZ: # 1838.
78 Vgl. PmbZ: # 1346.

Angesichts der Tatsache, daß Theodoros in den byzantinischen Quellen durchweg als herausragend und vorbildhaft dargestellt wird, ist die Annahme berechtigt, daß einzelne Aspekte seiner Klosterorganisation von den anderen byzantinischen Mönchskongregationen seiner und der späteren Zeit übernommen wurden[79].

3. Mönchsorden in Byzanz?

Doch kehren wir nun zu der eingangs aufgeworfenen Frage zurück: Gab es Mönchsorden in Byzanz?

Die moderne Ordensforschung – eingebettet in Mediävistik und Kirchengeschichte und vertreten durch so namhafte Wissenschaftler wie Kaspar Elm, Friedrich Prinz, Georg Jenal, Giles Constable und Gert Melville[80] – hat den Ordensbegriff in jüngerer Zeit wesentlich enger gefaßt als die ältere Forschung. Sie betrachtet nunmehr als den ersten monastischen Orden „im eigentlichen Sinne" die Kongregation um das Mutterkloster von Cîteaux, besser bekannt als die Zisterzienser. Die neue Qualität der Zisterzienser liegt dabei vor allem in ihrer eigenen Ordensverfassung (der sogenannten Charta caritatis, deren endgültige Fassung aus der zweiten Hälfte des 12. Jh.s stammt). Diese Ordensverfassung regelt sowohl die Beziehungen der einzelnen Klöster untereinander als auch die Entscheidungskompetenzen innerhalb des Ordens genau. Da keine der byzantinischen Mönchskongregationen eine solche Ordensverfassung vorweisen kann, gab es im byzantinischen Reich folglich auch keine Orden „im eigentlichen Sinne"!

Klosterbünde und monastische Kongregationen hatte es im Westen freilich bereits vor dem 12. Jh. gegeben, diese werden in der modernen Ordensforschung zur Unterscheidung von den „monastischen Orden" als „monastische Verbandsbildungen" bezeichnet. Solche monastischen Verbände waren etwa verschiedene Klosterbünde der Benediktiner oder etwa der Klosterbund von Cluny im 10. Jahrhundert, der nach einer reformierten benediktinischen Regel lebte und auch als Cluniazenser oder *ecclesia cluniacensis* bezeichnet wurde. Diese monastischen Verbände weisen allerdings bereits eine ganze Reihe von Charakteristika auf, die auch für die späteren Orden als typisch gelten: etwa die Leitung durch einen Oberen, die gemeinsame, einheitliche Regelobservanz, Probezeit und Ablegung feierlicher Gelübde beim Eintritt. Alle diese Charakteristika eignen auch den hier in den Blick genommenen byzantinischen Klosterbünden bzw. Mönchskongregationen dieser Zeit.

---

79 Vgl. dazu Thomas – Hero (s. Anm. 61), bes. G. Constable, Preface, xi–xxxvii.
80 S. dazu exemplarisch oben Anm. 10.

Fassen wir nun zusammen. Zwei Dinge scheinen mir wichtig zu sein:

Erstens: Im 8., 9. und 10. Jahrhundert läßt sich innerhalb des byzantinischen Mönchtums ein starker Trend zur Bildung von Klosterbünden bzw. Mönchskongregationen erkennen, die nach der Terminologie der westlichen Ordensforschung als „monastische Verbände" bezeichnet werden müssen. Dieser Trend setzte sich fort und führte vom 10. Jahrhundert an zur Entstehung „monastischer Verbände" auf dem Athos und vom 14. Jahrhundert an in Meteora in Thessalien. Die historischen Rahmenbedingungen – Gebietsverluste und feindliche Eroberungen, Piraterie an den Küsten, die Eroberung von Konstantinopel durch die Kreuzfahrer im Jahre 1204 und die anschließende Lateinerherrschaft, schließlich die endgültige Eroberung der byzantinischen Hauptstadt im Jahre 1453 durch die Osmanen – waren in der Folge der weiteren Verbreitung und Entwicklung dieser monastischen Verbände insgesamt nicht förderlich, so daß diese einen Endpunkt der organisatorischen Entwicklung des byzantinischen Mönchtums darstellen.

Zweitens: Es gab in Byzanz keine monastischen Orden im eigentlichen bzw. westlichen Sinne. Aber es gab doch in der organisatorischen Entwicklung des Mönchtums (und nicht nur dort) bis zum 10./11. Jahrhundert insgesamt viel größere Übereinstimmungen, Parallelen und Ähnlichkeiten zwischen Okzident und Orient, als dies meines Erachtens bisher genügend deutlich gemacht wurde.

Abstract

Monastic Orders in Byzantium? – On the Foundation and Development of Monastic Communities in Byzantium (8th–10th cc.)

In many a scholarly study on Church History, Medieval and Byzantine Studies one may easily read sentences like this: In the Eastern Church there were no monastic orders and the single, individual cloister remained the prevailing form of monasticism. But does this really hold true in face of the sources? Already the first flourishing of monasticism in the 4th century A.D. saw a relatively strong tendency towards the foundation of monastic centres, i.e. agglomerations of monks and monasteries in certain regions. These are for example the communities of Pachomios in Egypt (4th c.), of Augustine of Hippo in Northern Africa (4th/5th c.), of Sabas in Palestine (5th/6th c.) and of Benedict of Nursia in Italy (6th c.). These communities consisted of a number of monasteries and cells under the rule of one superior. The tendency towards the foundation of monastic centres also continued in Byzantium during the 8th to 10th centuries. There were figures like Stephen the Younger, Peter of Atroa and Theodore the Studite and others who founded and developed congregations of a main monastery and a number of dependent and subordinate monasteries under one rule. These congregations did not develop into monastic orders in the strict sense of the word as they did in the West, mainly due to external factors: the invasions by Seljuk Turks, loss of territory, piracy at the seashores, the fall of Constantinople in 1204 and the following Latin rule, and finally the conquest of Constantinople by the Ottoman Turks in 1453. Nevertheless, before the great schism of 1054 there are much more similarities in the development of monasticism in East and West than have been so far generally acknowledged.

Autoren dieses Bandes

Prof. Dr. Susan E. Alcock, Department of Classics, Brown University, Macfarlane House, 48 College Street, Providence, RI 02912, USA
Susan_Alcock@brown.edu

Dr. Joy Connolly, Assistant Professor of Classics, 120 West Fifteenth Street, #4-J, New York, NY 10011, USA
joyc@nyu.edu

PD Dr. Ulrike Egelhaaf-Gaiser, Institut für Altertumswissenschaften, Justus-Liebig-Universität Gießen, Otto-Behaghel-Str. 10 G, D-35394 Gießen
Ulrike.Egelhaaf-Gaiser@klassphil.uni-giessen.de

Prof. Dr. Stephen Hinds, Department of Classics, 218 Denny Hall, University of Washington, Box 353110, Seattle, WA 98195-3110, USA
shinds@u.washington.edu

Prof. Dr. Helmut Krasser, Institut für Altertumswissenschaften, Justus-Liebig-Universität Gießen, Otto-Behaghel-Str. 10 G, D-35394 Gießen
Helmut.Krasser@klassphil.uni-giessen.de

Dr. Simon MacLean, Department of Mediaeval History, University of St Andrews, 71 South Street, St Andrews, Fife, Scotland, KY16 9AL, United Kingdom
sm89@st-andrews.ac.uk

Prof. Dr. Mischa Meier, Historisches Seminar, Abteilung für Alte Geschichte, Eberhard-Karls-Universität Tübingen, Wilhelmstr. 36, D-72074 Tübingen
mischa.meier@uni-tuebingen.de

Dr. Dennis Pausch, Institut für Altertumswissenschaften, Justus-Liebig-Universität Gießen, Otto-Behaghel-Str. 10 G, D-35394 Gießen
Dennis.Pausch@klassphil.uni-giessen.de

PD Dr. Thomas Pratsch, Berlin-Brandenburgische Akademie der Wissenschaften, Prosopographie der mittelbyzantinischen Zeit, Jägerstr. 22/23, D-10117 Berlin
pratsch@bbaw.de

Prof. Dr. Thomas A. Schmitz, Institut für Griechische und Lateinische Philologie, Romanistik und Altamerikanistik, Abteilung für Griechische und Lateinische Philologie, Am Hof 1 e, D-53117 Bonn
thomas.schmitz@uni-bonn.de

Prof. Dr. Christian Tornau, Juniorprofessor für Klassische Philologie/Spätantike, Friedrich-Schiller-Universität Jena, Fürstengraben 1, D-07737 Jena
christian.tornau@uni-jena.de

Abkürzungen
(Editionen, Zeitschriften, Reihen, Nachschlagewerke)

AA	Archäologischer Anzeiger
AASS	Acta Sanctorum
AB	Analecta Bollandiana
ABSA	Annual of the British School at Athens
ACO	Acta conciliorum oecumenicorum
ACR	American Classical Review
ADSV	Antičnaja drevnost' i srednie veka
AE	L'année épigraphique
AHC	Annuarium historiae conciliorum
AION	Annali del Istituto Orientale di Napoli
AIPHO	Annuaire de l'Institut de Philologie et d'Histoire Orientales et Slaves
AJA	American Journal of Archaeology
AJAH	American Journal of Ancient History
AJPh	American Journal of Philology
AJSLL	American Journal of Semitic Languages and Literatures
AKG	Archiv für Kulturgeschichte
AnatSt	Anatolian Studies
AncSoc	Ancient Society
ANRW	Aufstieg und Niedergang der römischen Welt
AntAfr	Antiquitès africaines
AnTard	Antiquité tardive
AntCl	L'antiquité classique
AOC	Archives de l'Orient chrétien
AP	Ἀρχεῖον Πόντου
APF	Archiv für Papyrusforschung
ArchDelt	Ἀρχαιολογικὸν Δελτίον
ASS	Archivio storico Siracusano
AT	Antiquité tardive
B.	Basilica, edd. H. J. Scheltema/N. van der Wal/D. Holwerda
BAR	British Archaeological Reports
BASOR	Bulletin of the American Schools of Oriental Research
BASP	Bulletin of the American Society of Papyrologists
BBA	Berliner Byzantinistische Arbeiten
BBS	Berliner Byzantinistische Studien
BCH	Bulletin de correspondence héllenique
BF	Byzantinische Forschungen
BGA	Bibliotheca Geographorum Arabicorum

BGU	Berliner griechische Urkunden
BHG	Bibliotheca Hagiographica Graeca
BJ	Bonner Jahrbücher
BK	Bedi Kartlisa
BKV	Bibliothek der Kirchenväter
BM²	J. F. Böhmer, Regesta Imperii I: Die Regesten des Kaiserreiches unter den Karolingern 751–918, neubearbeitet von E. Mühlbacher. Innsbruck ²1908 (Nachdruck Hildesheim 1966).
BMFD	Byzantine Monastic Foundation Documents: A Complete Translation of the Surviving Founder's *Typica* and Testaments edited by J. Thomas and A. Constantinidis Hero with the assistance of G. Constable (DOS 35), Bd. 1–5, Washington, D.C., 2000
BMGS	Byzantine and Modern Greek Studies
BN	Catalogue général des livres imprimés de la bibliothèque nationale
BNF	Beiträge zur Namenforschung
BNJ	Byzantinisch-Neugriechische Jahrbücher
BollGrott	Bollettino della Badia Greca di Grottaferrata
BS	Basilikenscholien
BS/EB	Byzantine Studies/Études byzantines
BSOAS	Bulletin of the School of Oriental and African Studies
BSOS	Bulletin of the School of Oriental Studies
BSl	Byzantinoslavica
BThS	Bibliotheca theologica salesiana
BV	Byzantina Vindobonensia
BWANT	Beiträge zur Wissenschaft vom Alten und Neuen Testament
Byz	Byzantion
ByzBulg	Byzantinobulgarica
BZ	Byzantinische Zeitschrift
BzA	Beiträge zur Altertumskunde
BZNW	Beihefte zur Zeitschrift für die neutestamentliche Wissenschaft
C.	Codex Iustinianus, ed. P. Krueger
CAG	Commentaria in Aristotelem Graeca
CahArch	Cahiers archéologiques
CAH	Cambridge Ancient History
CANT	Clavis apocryphorum Novi Testamenti
CAVT	Clavis apocryphorum Veteris Testamenti
CC	Corpus christianorum
CCAG	Corpus Codicum Astrologorum Graecorum
CC SG	Corpus christianorum, series Graeca

CC SL	Corpus christianorum, series Latina
CCCM	Corpus Christianorum continuatio medievalis
CE	Chronique d'Égypte
CFHB	Corpus fontium historiae byzantinae
CIG	Corpus Inscriptionum Graecarum
CIL	Corpus Inscriptionum Latinarum
CJ	Classical Journal
CLA	E. A. Lowe, Codices Latini antiquiores: A Paleographical Guide to Latin Manuscripts prior to the Ninth Century, I–XI, Suppl. Oxford 1934/1072.
CPG	Clavis patrum Graecorum
CPh	Classical Philology
CPL	Clavis patrum Latinorum
CPPM	Clavis patristica pseudepigraphorum medii aevi
CQ	Classical Quarterly
CR	Classical Review
CRAI	Comptes rendus des séances de l'Académie des inscriptions et belles-lettres
CRI	Compendia rerum Iudaicarum ad Novum Testamentum
CSHB	Corpus scriptorum historiae Byzantinae
CSCO	Corpus scriptorum christianorum Orientalium
CSEL	Corpus scriptorum ecclesiasticorum Latinorum
CTh	Codex Theodosianus
D.	Digesta, ed. Th. Mommsen
DA	Deutsches Archiv für Erforschung des Mittelalters
DACL	Dictionnaire d'archéologie chrétienne et de liturgie
DHGE	Dictionnaire d'histoire et de géographie ecclésiastiques
Dölger, Regesten	F. Dölger, Regesten der Kaiserurkunden des Oströmischen Reiches von 565–1453, I. München 1924.
Dölger/Müller, Regesten	Regesten der Kaiserurkunden des Oströmischen Reiches, bearbeitet von F. Dölger. I/2. zweite Auflage neu bearbeitet von A. E. Müller, München 2003.
DOP	Dumbarton Oaks Papers
DOS	Dumbarton Oaks Studies
DOT	Dumbarton Oaks Texts
DThC	Dictionnaire de théologie catholique
EA	Epigraphica Anatolica
EEBS	Ἐπετηρὶς ἑταιρείας Βυζαντινῶν σπουδῶν
EPhS	Ὁ ἐν Κωνσταντινουπόλει Ἑλληνικὸς Φιλολογικὸς Σύλλογος
EEQu	East European Quarterly
EHR	English Historical Review

EI²	The Encyclopedia of Islam, second edition
EKK	Evangelisch-katholischer Kommentar zum Neuen Testament. Neukirchen
EWNT	Exegetisches Wörterbuch zum Neuen Testament, hrsg. von Horst Balz und Gerhard Schneider, I–III. Stuttgart u. a. 1992.
EO	Échos d'Orient
FDG	Forschungen zur deutschen Geschichte
FHG	Fragmenta historicorum Graecorum, collegit, disposuit, notis et prolegomenis illustravit C. Mullerus, I–VI. Paris 1841/1870.
FM	Fontes Minores
FMSt	Frühmittelalterliche Studien
FR	Felix Ravenna
FRLANT	Forschungen zur Religion und Literatur des Alten und Neuen Testaments
GCS	Die griechischen christlichen Schriftsteller
GRBS	Greek, Roman and Byzantine Studies
Grumel, Regestes	V. Grumel, Les regestes des actes du patriarcat de Constantinople, I/1: Les regestes de 381 à 751. Paris ²1972; V. Grumel, Les regestes des actes du patriarcat de Constantinople, I/1–3: Les regestes de 715 à 1206, 2ᵉ éd. par J. Darrouzès. Paris 1989.
Gym	Gymnasium
Hell	Ἑλληνικά
HBS	Henry Bradshaw society
HdAW	Handbuch der Altertumswissenschaften
HJb	Historisches Jahrbuch
HNT	Handbuch zum Neuen Testament
HSPh	Harvard Studies in Philology
HThK	Herders theologischer Kommentar zum Neuen Testament
HThR	Harvard Theological Review
HZ	Historische Zeitschrift
I.	Institutiones, ed. P. Krueger
İA	İslâm Ansiklopedisi
ICC	International critical commentary
IG	Inscriptiones Graecae
IEJ	Israel Exploration Journal
IGRRP	R. Cagnat/J. Toutain/P. Jougnet (Hgg.), Inscriptiones Graecae ad res Romanas pertinentes, 4 Bde, Paris 1927
IJMES	International Journal of Middle East Studies
ILS	Inscriptiones Latinae Selectae
IstMitt	Istanbuler Mitteilungen
JA	Journal asiatique

JAOS	Journal of the American Oriental Society
JbAC	Jahrbuch für Antike und Christentum
JDAI	Jahrbuch des Deutschen Archäologischen Institutes
JE	Ph. Jaffé, Regesta pontificum Romanorum ab condita ecclesiae ad annum post Christum natum MCXCVIII ..., auspiciis W. Wattenbach curaverunt S. Loewenfeld/F. Kaltenbrunner/ P. Ewald. Leipzig ²1885/1888.
JECS	Journal of Early Christian Studies
JEH	Journal of Ecclesiastical History
JESHO	Journal of the Economic and Social History of the Orient
JHS	Journal of Hellenic Studies
JJP	Journal of Juristic Papyrology
JJS	Journal of Jewish Studies
JNES	Journal of Near Eastern Studies
JÖAI	Jahrbuch des Österreichischen Archäologischen Instituts
JÖB	Jahrbuch der Österreichischen Byzantinistik
JÖBG	Jahrbuch der Österreichischen Byzantinischen Gesellschaft
JQR	Jewish Quarterly Review
JRA	Journal of Roman Archaeology
JRAS	Journal of the Royal Asiatic Society of Great Britain and Ireland
JRGZM	Jahrbuch des Römisch-Germanischen Zentralmuseums
JRS	Journal of Roman Studies
JS	Journal des Savants
JSS	Journal of Semitic Studies
JThS	Journal of Theological Studies
JWarb	Journal of the Warburg and Courtauld Institutes
KAT	Kommentar zum Alten Testament
KEK	Kritisch-exegetischer Kommentar über das Neue Testament. Begr. von Heinrich August Wilhelm Meyer. Göttingen 1832ff.
LAW	Lexikon der Alten Welt
LexMa	Lexikon des Mittelalters
LIMC	Lexicon Iconographicum Mythologiae Classicae
LThK	Lexikon für Theologie und Kirche
MAMA	Monumenta Asiae Minoris Antiqua
Mansi	G.D. Mansi, Sacrorum conciliorum nova et amplissima collectio, I–LIII. Paris/Leipzig 1901/1927.
MBM	Miscellanea Byzantina Monacensia
MDAI(A)	Mitteilungen des Deutschen Archäologischen Instituts, Athenische Abteilung
MDAI(R)	Mitteilungen des Deutschen Archäologischen Instituts, Römische Abteilung
MEFRA	Mélanges de l'École française de Rome: Antiquité

MEFRM	Mélanges de l'École française de Rome: Moyen âge – Temps modernes
MGH	Monumenta Germaniae Historica
AA	= Auctores antiquissimi
Capit.	= Capitularia
Conc.	= Concilia
Epp.	= Epistolae
Poet.	= Poetae Latini aevi Carolini
SRG	= Scriptores rerum Germanicarum in usum scholarum separatim editi
SRL	= Scriptores rerum Langobardicarum et Italicarum
SRM	= Scriptores rerum Merovingicarum
SS	= Scriptores
MH	Museum Helveticum
MIÖG	Mitteilungen des Instituts für Österreichische Geschichtsforschung
Mus	Le Muséon
N.	Novellae, edd. R. Schöll/W. Kroll
NA	Neues Archiv der Gesellschaft für ältere deutsche Geschichtskunde
NC	Numismatic Chronicle
NE	Νέος Ἑλληνομνήμων
NP	Der Neue Pauly. Enzyklopädie der Antike
NTS	New Testament Studies
OC	Oriens Christianus
OCA	Orientalia Christiana Analecta
OCP	Orientalia Christiana Periodica
ODB	The Oxford Dictionary of Byzantium, ed. by A. Kazhdan. Oxford 1991.
OGIS	Wilhelm Dittenberger (Hg.), Orientis Graeci Inscriptiones Selectae. Supplementum Sylloges Inscriptionum Graecarum, 2 Bde, Leipzig 1903–1905
ÖTK	Ökumenischer Taschenbuchkommentar zum Neuen Testament
PBB	Beiträge zur Geschichte der deutschen Sprache und Literatur (Pauls und Braunes Beiträge)
PBE	Prosopography of the Byzantine Empire
PBSR	Papers of the British School at Rome
PCPhS	Proceedings of the Cambridge Philological Society
PG	Patrologia Graeca
PIR	Prosopographia Imperii Romani
PL	Patrologia Latina
PLRE	Prosopography of the Later Roman Empire

PmbZ	Prosopographie der mittelbyzantinischen Zeit. Erste Abteilung (641–867). Nach Vorarbeiten F. Winkelmanns erstellt von Ralph-Johannes Lilie, Claudia Ludwig, Thomas Pratsch, Ilse Rochow, Beate Zielke u.a., 7 Bde. Berlin – New York 1998–2002
PO	Patrologia Orientalis
P&P	Past and Present
QFIAB	Quellen und Forschungen aus italienischen Archiven und Bibliotheken
RA	Revue archéologique
RAC	Reallexikon für Antike und Christentum
RB	Revue bénédictine
RbK	Reallexikon zur byzantinischen Kunst
RE	Pauly's Real-Encyclopaedie der classischen Altertumswissenschaft
REA	Revue des études anciennes
REArm	Revue des études arméniennes
REB	Revue des études byzantines
REG	Revue des études grecques
REI	Revue des études islamiques
REJ	Revue des études juives
REL	Revue des études latines
RESEE	Revue des études sud-est européennes
RevPhil	Revuc de philologie
RBPhH	Revue belge de philologie et d'histoire
RGA	Reallexikon der germanischen Altertumskunde
RGG	Religion in Geschichte und Gegenwart
RGVV	Religionsgeschichtliche Versuche und Vorarbeiten
RH	Revue historique
RHE	Revue d'histoire ecclésiastique
RHM	Römische Historische Mitteilungen
RhM	Rheinisches Museum für Philologie
RHR	Revue de l'histoire des religions
RIDA	Revue international des droits de l'antiquité
RIS	Rerum Italicarum Scriptores
RN	Revue numismatique
RNT	Regensburger Neues Testament
ROC	Revue de l'Orient chrétien
RPh	Revue philologique
RQ	Römische Quartalschrift für christliche Altertumskunde und Kirchengeschichte
RSBN	Rivista di studi bizantini e neoellenici
RSI	Rivista Storica Italiana

RSLR	Rivista di storia e letteratura religiosa
RSO	Rivista degli studi orientali
SBB	Stuttgarter biblische Beiträge
SBN	Studi Bizantini e Neoellenici
SBS	Studies in Byzantine Sigillography
SC	Sources chrétiennes
SE	Sacris erudiri
Script	Scriptorium
SEG	Supplementum epigraphicum Graecum
Set	Settimane di studio del centro italiano di studi sull'alto medioevo
SI	Studia Islamica
SM	Studi medievali
SNTS.MS	Society for New Testament Studies. Monograph Series
SO	Symbolae Osloenses
Spec	Speculum
StT	Studi e testi
SubHag	Subsidia Hagiographica
TAM	Tituli Asiae Minoris
TAVO	Tübinger Atlas des Vorderen Orients
TAPA	Transactions and Proceedings of the American Philological Association
ThLL	Thesaurus Linguae Latinae
ThLZ	Theologische Literaturzeitung
ThR	Theologische Rundschau
TIB	Tabula Imperii Byzantini
TM	Collège de France. Centre de recherche d'histoire et civilisation de Byzance. Traveaux et Mémoires
TRE	Theologische Realenzyklopädie
TU	Texte und Untersuchungen zur Geschichte der altchristlichen Literatur
UaLG	Untersuchungen zur antiken Literatur und Geschichte
VChr	Vigiliae Christianae
VSWG	Vierteljahrschrift für Sozial- und Wirtschaftsgeschichte
VTIB	Veröffentlichungen der Kommission für die Tabula Imperii Byzantini
VuF	Vorträge und Forschungen
VV	Vizantijskij Vremennik
WBC	Word Biblical Commentary
WBS	Wiener Byzantinistische Studien
WdF	Wege der Forschung
WI	Die Welt des Islam

WSt	Wiener Studien
WZKM	Wiener Zeitschrift für die Kunde des Morgenlandes
ZA	Zeitschrift für Assyrologie
ZBK.AT	Züricher Bibelkommentare. Altes Testament
ZBLG	Zeitschrift für bayerische Landesgeschichte
ZDA	Zeitschrift für deutsches Altertum und deutsche Literatur
ZDMG	Zeitschrift der Deutschen Morgenländischen Gesellschaft
ZDPV	Zeitschrift des Deutschen Palästina-Vereins
ZKG	Zeitschrift für Kirchengeschichte
ZMR	Zeitschrift für Missionskunde und Religionswissenschaft
ZNW	Zeitschrift für die neutestamentliche Wissenschaft
ZPE	Zeitschrift für Papyrologie und Epigraphik
ZRVI	Zbornik radova vizantološkog instituta
ZRG germ. Abt.	Zeitschrift der Savigny-Stiftung für Rechtsgeschichte, germanistische Abteilung
ZRG kan. Abt.	Zeitschrift der Savigny-Stiftung für Rechtsgeschichte, kanonistische Abteilung
ZRG rom. Abt.	Zeitschrift der Savigny-Stiftung für Rechtsgeschichte, romanistische Abteilung
ZThK	Zeitschrift für Theologie und Kirche